*This encyclopedia is dedicated to the memory of Rick Snyder—friend,
colleague, and leading scholar in the field of positive psychology.
Rick always gave far more than he took and made this world a better place.*

ENCYCLOPEDIA OF
MEASUREMENT
AND
STATISTICS

*This encyclopedia is dedicated to the memory of Rick Snyder—friend,
colleague, and leading scholar in the field of positive psychology.
Rick always gave far more than he took and made this world a better place.*

ENCYCLOPEDIA OF
MEASUREMENT

AND

STATISTICS

VOLUME 1

EDITOR
NEIL J. SALKIND
UNIVERSITY OF KANSAS

MANAGING EDITOR
KRISTIN RASMUSSEN
UNIVERSITY OF KANSAS

A SAGE Reference Publication

SAGE Publications
Thousand Oaks ▪ London ▪ New Delhi

For information:

SAGE Publications, Inc.
2455 Teller Road
Thousand Oaks, California 91320
E-mail: order@sagepub.com

SAGE Publications Ltd.
1 Oliver's Yard
55 City Road
London EC1Y 1SP
United Kingdom

SAGE Publications India Pvt. Ltd.
B-42, Panchsheel Enclave
Post Box 4109
New Delhi 110 017 India

Printed in the United States of America.

Library of Congress Cataloging-in-Publication Data

Encyclopedia of measurement and statistics / editor Neil J. Salkind.
        p. cm.
A SAGE Reference Publication.
Includes bibliographical references and index.
ISBN 1-4129-1611-9 or 978-1-4129-1611-0 (cloth)

  1. Social sciences–Statistical methods–Encyclopedias. 2. Social sciences–Research—Methodology–Encyclopedias.
I. Salkind, Neil J.
HA29.S2363 2007
001.403—dc22

                                    2006011888

This book is printed on acid-free paper.

06 07 08 09 10 10 9 8 7 6 5 4 3 2 1

Publisher:	Rolf Janke
Acquisitions Editor:	Lisa Cuevas Shaw
Reference Systems Coordinator:	Leticia Gutierrez
Project Editor:	Tracy Alpern
Copy Editors:	Bonnie Freeman
	Liann Lech
	Carla Freeman
Typesetter:	C&M Digitals (P) Ltd.
Indexer:	David Luljak
Cover Designer:	Michelle Kenny

Contents

Editorial Board

List of Entries

Reader's Guide

The purpose of the Reader's Guide is to provide you with a tool you can use to locate specific entries in the encyclopedia, as well as to find out what other related entries might be of interest to you. For example, if you are interested in the visual display of information and want to learn how to create a bar chart (under the general heading of Charts, Graphs, and Visual Displays in the Reader's Guide), you can also find reference to such entries as Histogram, Line Chart, and Mosaic Plots, all related to the same general topic.

The Reader's Guide is also a very direct and simple way to get an overview of which items are contained in the encyclopedia. Although each of the categories lists items in alphabetic order (as the encyclopedia is organized), you can glance through the main headings of the guide and then focus more on a particular area of interest. Then, just turn to any particular entry you want to locate. These are easily found because they appear in alphabetical order.

Biographies

Babbage, Charles
Bernoulli, Jakob
Bonferroni, Carlo Emilio
Bruno, James Edward
Comrey, Andrew L.
Cronbach, Lee J.
Darwin, Charles
Deming, William Edwards
Fisher, Ronald Aylmer
Galton, Sir Francis
Gauss, Carl Friedrich
Gresham, Frank M.
Jackson, Douglas N.
Malthus, Thomas
Markov, Andrei Andreevich
Pascal, Blaise
Pearson, Karl
Poisson, Siméon Denis
Reynolds, Cecil R.
Torrance, E. Paul
Wilcoxon, Frank

Charts, Graphs, and Visual Displays

Area Chart
Bar Chart
Box Plot (Box and Whisker Plot)
Contour Plot
Eyeball Estimation
Frequency Distribution
Histogram
Line Chart
Mosaic Plots
Ogive
Parallel Coordinate Plots
Pie Chart
Q-Q Plot
Scattergram
Scree Plot
Smoothing

Evaluation

Experimental Methods

Inferential Statistics

Binomial Test
Bonferroni, Carlo Emilio
Complete Independence Hypothesis
Data Analysis ToolPak
Exploratory Factor Analysis
Factorial Design
Fisher, Ronald Aylmer
Hierarchical Linear Modeling
Hypothesis and Hypothesis Testing
Inferential Statistics
Logistic Regression Analysis
Markov, Andrei Andreevich
Null Hypothesis Significance Testing
Pairwise Comparisons
Part and Partial Correlations
Repeated Measures Analysis of Variance
Type I Error
Type II Error
Wilcoxon, Frank

Organizations and Publications

Abstracts
American Doctoral Dissertations
American Psychological Association
American Statistical Association
Association for Psychological Science
Buros Institute of Mental Measurements
Centers for Disease Control and Prevention
Educational Testing Service
Journal of the American Statistical Association
Journal of Modern Applied Statistical Methods
Journal of Statistics Education
National Science Foundation
Psychological Abstracts
Psychometrics
PsycINFO
Society for Research in Child Development
Sociological Abstracts

Prediction and Estimation

Attributable Risk
Bernoulli, Jakob
Chance
Conditional Probability
Confidence Intervals

Continuous Variable
Curse of Dimensionality
Decision Boundary
Decision Theory
File Drawer Problem
Gambler's Fallacy
Generalized Estimating Equations
Law of Large Numbers
Maximum Likelihood Method
Nonprobability Sampling
Pascal, Blaise
Probability Sampling
Random Numbers
Relative Risk
Signal Detection Theory
Significance Level
Three-Card Method

Probability

Alternate Assessment
Audit Trail
Authenticity
Categorical Variable
Essay Items
Grounded Theory
Observational Studies
Portfolio Assessment
Self-Report
Text Analysis

Qualitative Methods

Active Life Expectancy
Assessment of Interactions in Multiple Regression
Eyeball Estimation
Orthogonal Predictors in Regression
Regression Analysis
Survival Analysis

Samples, Sampling, and Distributions

Acceptance Sampling
Adaptive Sampling Design
Age Norms
Attrition Bias
Career Maturity Inventory

Statistical Techniques

About the Editor

Neil J. Salkind (PhD, University of Maryland, 1973) is a Professor of Psychology and Research in Education at the University of Kansas in Lawrence, Kansas. He completed postdoctoral training as a member of the Bush Child and Family Policy Institute at the University of North Carolina and has authored and coauthored more than 125 scholarly papers and books. Most recently, he is the author of *Statistics for People Who (Think They) Hate Statistics: The Excel Edition* (2007), *Tests & Measurement for People Who (Think They) Hate Tests & Measurement* (2006), the *Encyclopedia of Human Development* (2006), *Theories of Human Development* (2004), and *Statistics for People Who (Think They) Hate Statistics* (2004), all published by Sage. He was the editor of *Child Development Abstracts and Bibliography*, published by the Society for Research in Child Development (SRCD), from 1988 through 2001, and he is the treasurer-elect of Division 7 of the American Psychological Association.

Contributors

Francisco J. Abad
Universidad Autonoma de Madrid

Inmaculada Aban
University of Alabama at Birmingham

Hervé Abdi
University of Texas at Dallas

Phillip L. Ackerman
Georgia Institute of Technology

Demetrios S. Alexopoulos
University of Patras, Greece

Audrey Amrein-Beardsley
Arizona State University

Lauren E. Auld
DePauw University

Carrie R. Ball
University of Wisconsin–Madison

Kimberly A. Barchard
University of Nevada, Las Vegas

Jonathan Barzilai
Dalhousie University

Edward J. Bedrick
University of New Mexico

Mark L. Berenson
Montclair State University

Dongsheng Bi
University of Nebraska Lincoln

Damian P. Birney
University of Sydney

David M. Boynton
Saint Michael's College

Bruce A. Bracken
College of William & Mary

Jennifer Bragger
Montclair State University

Gary G. Brannigan
State University of New York–Plattsburgh

Ernest W. Brewer
University of Tennessee

Carolyn Brodbeck
Chapman University

Sarah Brookhart
American Psychological Society

Duane Brown
University of North Carolina, Chapel Hill

Jennifer Ann Brown
University of Canterbury

Shawn T. Bubany
University of Minnesota

Michael J. Burke
Tulane University

Mary Margaret Capraro
Texas A&M University

Robert M. Capraro
Texas A&M University

Joseph E. Cavanaugh
University of Iowa

Hua-Hua Chang
University of Illinois

Elaine Chapman
University of Western Australia

Bernard C. K. Choi
Public Health Agency of Canada

Siu L. Chow
University of Regina

Michelle D. Chudleigh
Alberta Hospital Edmonton

Moo K. Chung
University of Wisconsin

M. H. Clark
Southern Illinois University

Murray Clayton
University of Wisconsin–Madison

A. Jill Clemence
Austen Riggs Center

Roberto Colom
Universidad Autonoma de Madrid

John Colombo
University of Kansas

Andrew L. Comrey
University of California, Los Angeles

Dianne Cook
Iowa State University

R. Kelly Crace
College of William & Mary

Bonnie Cramond
University of Georgia

William L. Curlette
Georgia State University

Larry Daniel
University of North Florida

Craig Darch
University of Auburn

Duncan Day
Queen's University

E. Jacquelin Dietz
Meredith College

Bryan J. Dik
Colorado State University

Heather Doescher
University of Wisconsin–Madison

Romilia Domínguez de Ramírez
University of Houston

Joseph A. Doster
University of North Texas

Donald M. Dougherty
Wake Forest University Baptist Medical Center

Ronald C. Eaves
Auburn University

Anna Ebel-Lam
Queen's University

Maeghan N. Edwards
Pennsylvania State University

Stephen N. Elliott
Vanderbilt University

Susan Embretson
Georgia Institute of Technology

Craig K. Enders
Arizona State University

Marie Joelle Estrada
University of North Carolina, Chapel Hill

Martin G. Evans
University of Toronto

Leandre R. Fabrigar
Queen's University

Gail F. Fahoome
Wayne State University

Andy P. Field
University of Sussex

Barry Forer
University of British Columbia

Robert A. Forsyth
University of Iowa

Brian F. French
Purdue University

Kathryn H. Ganske
Georgia State University

Travis L. Gee
University of Queensland, Australia

Carole E. Gelfer
William Paterson University

James E. Gentle
George Mason University

Morton A. Gernsbacher
University of Wisconsin–Madison

Maribeth Gettinger
University of Wisconsin–Madison

Marjan Ghahramanlou-Holloway
Uniformed Services University of the Health Sciences

Lisa M. Given
University of Alberta

Kevin W. Glavin
Kent State University

Charles Golden
Nova Southeastern University

Adele Eskeles Gottfried
California State University, Northridge

Naomi Grant
Queen's University

James W. Grice
Oklahoma State University

Erik J. Groessl
VA San Diego / University of California, San Diego

Lyndsi M. Grover
University of North Texas

Suzanne M. Grundy
California State University, San Bernardino

Anthony J. Guarino
University of Auburn

Mads Haahr
Trinity College Dublin

John W. Hagen
Society of Research in Child Development

Brian Haig
University of Canterbury

Thomas Haladyna
Arizona State University

Young-Hoon Ham
University of Tennessee

Ronald K. Hambleton
University of Massachusetts

Chirok Han
Victoria University of Wellington

David Hann
University of Kansas

Jo-Ida C. Hansen
University of Minnesota

James W. Hardin
University of South Carolina

Clay Helberg
SPSS Inc.

Susanne Hempel
University of York

Ryan G. Henry
Brigham Young University

Kristin Heron
Syracuse University

Matthew J. Hertenstein
DePauw University

Christine L. Himes
Syracuse University

Nathaniel R. Hirtz
Murray State University

David B. Hitchcock
University of South Carolina

James S. Ho
Alberta Hospital Edmonton

Heike Hofmann
Iowa State University

Cody S. Hollist
University of Nebraska–Lincoln

Johnny Holloway
American University

Robert Hopkins
Queens University

Jennifer R. Hsu
William Paterson University

Louis M. Hsu
Fairleigh Dickinson University

Allison Huck
University of Kentucky

Schuyler W. Huck
University of Tennessee

Bradley E. Huitema
Western Michigan University

Russell T. Hurlburt
University of Nevada, Las Vegas

Jennifer Ivie
University of Kansas

Robert A. Jacobs
University of Rochester

John Jamieson
Lakehead University

Galin L. Jones
University of Minnesota

Samuel Juni
New York University

Sema A. Kalaian
Eastern Michigan University

Matthew E. Kaler
University of Minnesota

Kristen M. Kalymon
University of Wisconsin–Madison

Robert M. Kaplan
University of California, Los Angeles

Michael A. Karchmer
Gallaudet Research Institute

Michael Karson
University of Denver

Rafa M. Kasim
Kent State University

Allison B. Kaufman
University of California, Riverside

James C. Kaufman
California State University, San Bernardino

Lisa Keller
University of Massachusetts, Amherst

Lindy Kilik
Queen's University

Kyung Hee Kim
Eastern Michigan University

Roger E. Kirk
Baylor University

Steve Kirkland
University of Regina

Theresa Kline
University of Calgary

James Randolph Knaub, Jr.
U.S. Government, Energy Information Administration

John C. Kolar
Medical City Children's Hospital, Dallas

Nicole B. Koppel
Montclair State University

Richard M. Kreminski
Texas A&M University–Commerce

Joachim I. Krueger
Brown University

Thomas Kubiszyn
University of Houston

Jouni Kuha
London School of Economics

Jonna M. Kulikowich
Pennsylvania State University

Wilda Laija-Rodriguez
California State University, Northridge

David M. Lane
Rice University

Sean Laraway
San Jose State University

Michael D. Larsen
Iowa State University

Nicole Lazar
University of Georgia

Howard B. Lee
University of California, Riverside

W. Vanessa Lee
University of Minnesota

Nancy L. Leech
Colorado University, Denver

Lawrence Leemis
College of William & Mary

Pui-Wa Lei
Pennsylvania State University

Russell V. Lenth
University of Iowa

Ming-Ying Leung
University of Texas at El Paso

Melanie Leuty
University of Minnesota

Ronald F. Levant
University of Akron

Robert W. Levenson
University of California, Berkeley

Jacob J. Levy
University of Tennessee

Bruce Lindsay
Pennsylvania State University

Brian R. Little
Carleton University and Harvard University

David F. Lohman
University of Iowa

Jeffrey D. Long
University of Minnesota

Sarah A. Lopienski
Kent State University

Kathryn Lou
University of Pennsylvania

Gerard H. Maassen
Utrecht University

Karen MacGregor
Queens University

Effie Maclellan
University of Strathclyde

W. Todd Maddox
University of Texas at Austin

Silvia A. Madrid
University of Arizona

Susan J. Maller
Purdue University

Dawn M. Marsh
Wake Forest University Baptist Medical Center

Luci A. Martin
University of North Texas

Kenneth B. Matheny
Georgia State University

Charles W. Mathias
Wake Forest University Health Sciences

Sonia Matwin
University of Utah

Mary Ann McCabe
American Psychological Association

Geoffrey McLachlan
University of Queensland

Adam W. Meade
North Carolina State University

Christopher J. Mecklin
Murray State University

Franklin Mendivil
Acadia University

Jorge L. Mendoza
University of Oklahoma

George Michailidis
University of Michigan

Jeremy Miles
University of York

Richard B. Miller
Brigham Young University

Ross E. Mitchell
Gallaudet University

Amitava Mitra
Auburn University

Geert Molenberghs
University Hasselt

Paul Molin
University of Bourgogne

Dirk F. Moore
University of Medicine and Dentistry of New Jersey

Kevin E. Moore
DePaul University

Bernice S. Moos
Stanford University

Rudolf H. Moos
Stanford University

Mark Mostert
Regent University

Ronald Neath
University of Minnesota

Liqiang Ni
University of Central Florida

Adelheid A. M. Nicol
Royal Military College

Meghan E. Norris
Queen's University

Anthony J. Onwuegbuzie
University of South Florida

J. Shelly Paik
Queen's University

Anita W. P. Pak
University of Ottawa

Paul E. Panek
Ohio State University–Newark

Hans Anand Pant
Humboldt University of Berlin

Dong-Ho Park
University of Tennessee

Scott Parker
American University

Sandrine Pavoine
Muséum National d'Histoire Naturelle, Paris

Manohar Pawar
Charles Sturt University

Edsel Pena
University of South Carolina

Sarah Peterson
University of Kansas

Andrew M. Pomerantz
Southern Illinois University Edwardsville

Jennifer L. Porter
DePauw University

Ronald D. Porter
Queen's University

Patricia Ramsey
Fordham University

Philip H. Ramsey
Queens College of City University of New York

John Randal
Victoria University of Wellington

Kristin Rasmussen
University of Kansas

Marco Reale
University of Canterbury

John R. Reddon
Alberta Hospital Edmonton

Malcolm James Ree
Our Lady of the Lake University

Jerome Reiter
Duke University

Bixiang Ren
University of Tennessee

Alberto Restori
California State University, Northridge

James C. Rhoads
Westminster College

Andrew T. Roach
Vanderbilt University

Beth Rodgers
University of Wisconsin–Milwaukee

Michael C. Rodriguez
University of Minnesota

Ward Rodriguez
California State University, East Bay

Javier Rojo
Rice University

Patrick J. Rosopa
University of Central Florida

Thomas E. Rudy
University of Pittsburgh

André A. Rupp
Humboldt University

Charles J. Russo
University of Dayton

Thomas Rutledge
UC San Diego

Steve Saladin
University of Idaho

Neil J. Salkind
University of Kansas

Elizabeth M. Salter
University of Texas at Dallas

Mark L. Savickas
Northeast Ohio Universities College of Medicine

Shlomo S. Sawilowsky
Wayne State University

Khalid Sayood
University of Nebraska–Lincoln

Carl J. Scarrott
University of Canterbury

Stanley L. Sclove
University of Illinois at Chicago

Kyoungah See
Miami University

William R. Shadish
University of California, Merced

Ramalingam Shanmugam
Texas State University

Boris Shulkin
Wayne State University

Dean Keith Simonton
University of California, Davis

Gary N. Siperstein
University of Massachusetts, Boston

Stephen G. Sireci
University of Massachusetts, Amherst

William P. Skorupski
University of Kansas

Joshua Smyth
Syracuse University

Robert A. Spies
University of Nebraska–Lincoln

Christopher J. Sroka
Ohio State University

Douglas Steinley
University of Missouri–Columbia

Steven E. Stemler
Wesleyan University

Michael Stewart
University of Sydney

David W. Stockburger
United States Air Force Academy

Eugene F. Stone-Romero
University of Texas, San Antonio

Bryce F. Sullivan
Southern Illinois University Edwardsville

Jun Sun
Texas A&M University

Martin A. Tanner
Northwestern University

Christopher P. Terry
Syracuse University

Robert M. Thorndike
Western Washington University

Davood Tofighi
Arizona State University

Larry Toothaker
University of Oklahoma

Marietta J. Tretter
Texas A&M University

George C. Tseng
University of Pittsburgh

Ping-Lun Tu
University of Tennessee

Jung-Ying Tzeng
North Carolina State University

Graham Upton
University of Essex

Dominique Valentin
University of Bourgogne

Nicholas G. Velissaris
Society for Research in Child Development

Geert Verbeke
Katholieke Universiteit Leuven

Fran Vertue
Child and Family Psychology Centre

Abdus S. Wahed
University of Pittsburgh

Harald Walach
University College Northampton

Russell F. Waugh
Edith Cowan University

Ann M. Weber
University of Wisconsin–Madison

Gail Weems
University of Arkansas Little Rock

Kimberly Weems
North Carolina State University

Kirsten Wells
Kansas University

Shane M. Whippler
Alberta Hospital Edmonton

Rand R. Wilcox
University of Southern California

Todd J. Wilkinson
University of Minnesota

Siân E. Williams
Canterbury Christ Church University

Thomas O. Williams, Jr.
Virginia Polytechnic Institute

Jay K. Wood
Queens University

Suzanne Woods-Groves
Auburn University

Daniel B. Wright
University of Sussex

Karl L. Wuensch
East Carolina University

Hongwei Yang
University of Tennessee–Knoxville

Keming Yang
University of Reading

Zhiliang Ying
Columbia University

Vincent R. Zalcik
Alberta Hospital Edmonton

April L. Zenisky
University of Massachusetts, Amherst

Jin Zhang
University of Manitoba

Zhigang Zhang
Oklahoma State University

Shuangmei (Christine) Zhou
University of Minnesota

Marvin Zuckerman
University of Delaware

Bruno D. Zumbo
University of British Columbia

Preface

It's an interesting paradox when an important subject, which can help us make sense of our busy, everyday world, is considered very difficult to approach. Such is the case with measurement and statistics. However, this does not necessarily have to be the case, and we believe that the *Encyclopedia of Measurement and Statistics* will show you why.

These two areas of study encompass a very wide range of topics, and a knowledge of even the basic concepts and ideas allows us to be much better prepared as intelligent consumers of information.

Whether we are interested in knowing if there is a difference between two groups in their preference for a particular brand of cereal or how the Americans with Disabilities Act works, we need to know how to analyze and interpret information. And often, when that information is in the form of numbers, that's where statistics and measurement come into play. That basic stat course in college might have been a nightmare, but the material is no more difficult to grasp and apply than is any other discipline in the social and behavioral sciences.

Although hundreds of books have been written about the different topics that are contained in the *Encyclopedia of Measurement and Statistics,* and there are thousands upon thousands of studies that have been conducted in this area, what we offer here is something quite different—a comprehensive overview of important topics. What we hope we have accomplished are entries that comprise a comprehensive overview of the most important topics in the areas of measurement and statistics—entries that share this important information in a way that is informative; not too technical; and even, in some cases, entertaining.

Through almost 500 contributions and some special elements that will be described later in this preface, experts in each of the entries contained in these pages contribute an overview and an explanation of the major topics in these two fields.

The underlying rationale for the selection of particular topics and their presentation in this encyclopedia comes from the need to share with the educated reader topics that are rich, diverse, and deserving of closer inspection. Within these pages, we provide the overview and the detail that we feel is necessary to become well acquainted with these topics.

As in many other encyclopedias, the *Encyclopedia of Measurement and Statistics* is organized in alphabetical order, from A through Z. However, particular themes were identified early on that could be used to organize conceptually the information and the entries. These themes or major topic areas constitute the Reader's Guide, which appears on page xiii. Categories such as Experimental Methods, Qualitative Methods, and Organizations and Publications are only a few of the many that help organize the entire set of contributions.

The Process

The first task in the creation of a multivolume encyclopedia such as this is the development of a complete and thorough listing of the important topics in the disciplines of measurement and statistics. This process started with the identification of entries that the editor and advisory board thought were important to include. We tried to make sure that these entries included topics that would be of interest to a general readership, but we wanted to exclude terms and ideas that were too highly technical or too far removed from the interests of the everyday reader. This list was reviewed several times until we felt that it was a comprehensive set of topics that best fit the vision for the encyclopedia.

Like many other disciplines, there is a great deal of overlap between different important concepts and ideas in measurement and statistics. For example, although there is an entry titled Descriptive Statistics (which is a general overview), there is much greater detail in the entries titled Mean and Median. That overlap is fine because it provides two different, and compatible, views of the same topic and can only help reinforce one's knowledge. We hope that the cross-references we provide will help the user understand this and get the most out of learning about any one idea, term, or procedure.

As expected, this list was edited and revised as we worked and as authors were recruited to write particular entries. Enthusiastic authors suggested new topics that might have been overlooked as well as removing topics that might have no appeal. All of these changes were taken into consideration as the final list was assembled.

The next step was to assign a length to a particular entry, which ranged from 500 words for simple definitions or biographies (such as the one for the Arithmetic Mean or Charles Babbage, respectively) to almost 4,000 words for longer, more in-depth exploration for topics (such as the entry on Aptitude Tests). In between were articles that were 1,500 and 2,000 words in length. (At times, authors asked that the length be extended because they had so much information they wanted to share and they felt that the limitation on space was unwarranted. In most cases, it was not a problem to allow such an extension.)

The final step was the identification of authors. This took place through a variety of mechanisms, including the identification of individuals based on the advisory board recommendations and/or the editor's professional and personal experiences, authors of journal articles and books who focused on a particular area directly related to the entry, and referrals from other individuals who were well known in the field.

Once authors were identified and invited, and once they confirmed that they could participate, they were sent detailed instructions and given a deadline for the submission of their entry. The results, as you well know by now, after editing, layout, and other production steps, are in your hands.

How to Use This Reference

We know the study of measurement and statistics can be less than inviting. But, as we mentioned at the beginning of this preface, and want to emphasize once again here, the ideas and tools contained in these pages are approachable and can be invaluable for understanding our very technical world and an increasing flow of information.

Although many of the ideas you read about in these pages are relatively recent, some are centuries old. Yet both kinds hold promise for your being able to better navigate the increasingly complex world of information we each face every day.

So, although many of us believe that this encyclopedia should only be consulted when a term or idea needs some clarification, why not take some time and just browse through the material and see what types of entries are offered and how useful you might find them?

As we wrote earlier, a primary goal of creating this set of volumes was to open up the broad discipline of measurement and statistics to a wider and more general audience than usual.

Take these books and find a comfortable seat in the library, browse through the topics, and read the ones that catch your eye. We're confident that you'll continue reading and looking for additional related entries, such as "Applying Ideas on Statistics and Measurement," where you can find examples of how these ideas are applied and, in doing so, learn more about whatever interests you.

Should you want to find a topic within a particular area, consult the Reader's Guide, which organizes entries within this two-volume set into one general category. Using this tool, you can quickly move to an area or a specific topic that you find valuable and of interest.

Finally, there other elements that should be of interest.

Appendix A is a guide to basic statistics for those readers who might like a more instructional, step-by-step presentation of basic concepts in statistics and measurement. It also includes a table of critical values used in hypothesis testing and an important part of any reference in this area. These materials are taken from *Statistics for People Who (Think They) Hate Statistics,* written by the editor and also published by Sage.

Appendix B represents a collection of some important and useful sites on the Internet that have additional information about measurement and statistics. Although such sites tend to remain stable, there may be some changes in the Internet address. If you cannot find the Web page using the address that is provided, then search for the name of the Web site using Google or another search engine.

Finally, Appendix C is a glossary of terms and concepts you will frequently come across in these volumes.

Acknowledgments

This has been a challenging and rewarding project. It was ambitious in scope because it tried to corral a wide and diverse set of topics within measurement and statistics into a coherent set of volumes.

First, thanks to the Advisory Board, a group of scholars in many different areas that took the time to review the list of entries and make invaluable suggestions as to what the reader might find valuable and how that topic should be approached. The Advisory Board members are very busy people who took the time to help the editor develop a list that is broad in scope and represents the most important topics in human development. You can see a complete list of who these fine people are on page vi.

My editor and my publisher at Sage Publications, Lisa Cuevas Shaw and Rolf Janke, respectively,

deserve a great deal of thanks for bringing this project to me and providing the chance to make it work. They are terrific people who provide support and ideas and are always there to listen. And perhaps best of all, they get things done.

Other people also helped make this task enjoyable and helped create the useful, informative, and approachable set of volumes you hold in your hands. Among these people are Tracy Alpern, Sage senior project editor, and Bonnie Freeman, Liann Lech, and Carla Freeman, copy editors.

I'll save one of the biggest thank-yous for Kristin Rasmussen, the managing editor, who managed this project in every sense of the word, including the formidable tasks of tracking entries, submissions, reviews, and resubmissions. All of this was easily accomplished with enthusiasm, initiative, and perseverance when answering endless questions through thousands of e-mails to hundreds of authors. She is currently a doctoral student at the University of Kansas and has an exceptionally bright future. Thank you sincerely.

And, of course, how could anything of this magnitude ever have been done without the timely execution and accurate scholarship of the contributing authors? They understood that the task at hand was to introduce educated readers (such as you) to new areas of interest in a very broad field, and without exception, they did a wonderful job. You will see throughout that their writing is clear and informative—just what material like this should be for the intelligent reader. To them, a sincere thank you and a job well done.

Finally, as always, none of this would have happened or been worth undertaking without my comrade in (almost all) ups and down and ins and outs, and my truest and best friend, Leni. Sara and Micah, versions 1.1 and 1.2, didn't hurt either.

—Neil J. Salkind
University of Kansas

Sometimes it is useful to know how large your zero is.

—Author unknown

ABILITY TESTS

Ability tests are assessment instruments designed to measure the capacity of individuals to perform particular physical or mental tasks. Ability tests were developed in the individual differences tradition of psychology and evolved from early tests of general intelligence. Most major ability tests assess a range of broad ability factors that are conceptually and empirically related to general intelligence (or *g*, also referred to as general cognitive ability). Ability tests are frequently used in settings such as schools, military organizations, business and industry, hospitals and rehabilitation centers, and private practice. Several ability tests with strong evidence of reliability and validity are currently available and are commonly used for purposes such as educational screening or diagnosis, personnel selection and classification, neuropsychological assessment, and career guidance and counseling.

Historical Overview

The first successful "mental test," predecessor to all subsequent tests of characteristics of individual differences characteristics (including ability), is generally considered to be the intelligence test developed by French psychologist Alfred Binet and his associate, Théodore Simon. First published in 1905, the Binet-Simon Intelligence Scale was designed to identify children presumably unable to benefit from regular classroom instruction by measuring their ability to judge, understand, and reason. The test was found to be an effective predictor of scholastic achievement. The success of the Binet-Simon scales and of later measures, such as Lewis M. Terman's Stanford-Binet Intelligence Scale (published in 1916), led the emerging testing industry to focus on the further development of intelligence measures. Many of these early intelligence tests actually measured a range of different abilities.

At the outset of World War I, leading psychologists in the intelligence testing movement began attending to the problem of selecting and classifying recruits for the United States military. These efforts resulted in the development of group-administered intelligence tests such as the Army Alpha and Beta. The practical usefulness of these assessments and the efficiency with which they could be administered to large numbers of people led to the widespread use of tests and also to intensified research on specific areas of ability relevant to success in a variety of contexts. During the 1920s and 1930s, this shift from measures of general intelligence to measures of specific abilities was accompanied by the development of a statistical technique called factor analysis. By identifying underlying factors on the basis of patterns of intercorrelations among a large number of variables, factor analysis made it possible to demonstrate that specific abilities (e.g., reading speed, reaction time) are indicators of broad areas of ability (e.g., broad visual perception, broad cognitive speediness) and that these broad abilities are somewhat independent of g.

Largely on the basis of evidence obtained from early factor analytic studies, two opposing theoretical approaches to understanding the ability domain emerged. The London school, led by Charles Spearman, emphasized g as the single most important ability. In contrast, a group of American scientists, led by Truman Kelley and Louis L. Thurstone, identified several relatively independent, broad ability factors. A classic study of mechanical ability, led by D. G. Paterson, provided early empirical evidence to support the claim that general areas of ability other than g accounted for significant variance in practical outcomes, such as job performance.

With World War II came the demand for follow-up efforts to the work conducted in the 1920s and 1930s. During the 1940s and 1950s, general multiple-ability test batteries, such as the Differential Aptitude Tests (DAT) and General Aptitude Test Battery (GATB), among many others, were developed and used frequently in subsequent decades. During the 1980s, controversy erupted over the question of fair use of the GATB, which was developed by the United States Employment Service, with prospective employees from racial and ethnic minorities. This controversy led to its suspension from use pending further study. A variety of alternative test batteries (three of which are reviewed below) measuring multiple areas of ability are available and in use today.

Definition and Dimensions of Ability

The construct of ability, as defined above, refers to the power of an individual to perform a specified act or task. Abilities are generally assumed to be fairly stable, to have a biological basis, and to be both learned and innate. Ability may be differentiated from related constructs, such as *achievement*, which is defined as the level of knowledge or skill that has already been attained in an endeavor; *aptitude*, which is defined as the capacity to develop particular knowledge or skills in the future; and *intelligence*, which is typically defined as a general, higher-order ability relevant to tasks that have cognitive demands. These constructs clearly are related, and in practice the terms are sometimes used interchangeably. To further complicate the matter, tests of abilities or intelligence technically measure achievement and usually are used to infer aptitude. In the context of assessment, a general rule of thumb is as follows: achievement tests typically are designed to measure knowledge of a specified content area that has been explicitly taught; ability tests typically are designed to measure current performance in a particular content area or, when composed of a battery of subtests, across multiple content areas; and intelligence tests typically are designed to measure general cognitive ability. All three are used to infer aptitude, although the terms *aptitude tests* and *multiaptitude tests* usually refer to tests of ability.

There are a variety of theoretical approaches to understanding human ability, but the view most commonly held by scholars is that the domain of abilities can be represented using a hierarchical structure. For example, the Cattell-Horn-Carroll (CHC) theory of cognitive abilities, supported by one of the most comprehensive factor-analytic investigations of abilities in history, posits a three-level hierarchy. Like many hierarchical theories of abilities, CHC theory places g at the highest level, followed by several broad factors at the intermediate level of specificity and, in turn, by a large number of more narrowly defined, specific abilities at the lowest level (in the CHC model, these are approximately 70 in number). The 10 broad ability factors in the second level of the CHC model are similar to those posited by other hierarchical ability models and are as follows:

- *Fluid intelligence*: The ability to reason and solve problems involving novel information or procedures using processes that are not learned or culture bound

- *Crystallized intelligence*: The ability to communicate and reason using previously learned information and procedures
- *Quantitative knowledge*: The ability to manipulate numerical symbols and reason procedurally with quantitative information; includes mathematics achievement and knowledge
- *Short-term memory*: The ability to hold information in immediate awareness and effectively use it within seconds
- *Visual processing*: The ability to perceive, manipulate, analyze, and synthesize visual stimuli; includes visual memory and spatial relations
- *Auditory processing*: The ability to perceive, discriminate, analyze, and synthesize patterns in auditory stimuli; includes phonetic coding, memory for sound patterns, and ability to discriminate tones
- *Processing speed*: The speed with which information is attended to and processed; involves rapid, automatic cognitive processing
- *Long-term retrieval*: The ability to store information in long-term memory and accurately retrieve it later
- *Reading/writing*: The ability to read and understand written material accurately and efficiently and to write in a clear and organized manner with proper grammar, punctuation, and spelling
- *Decision/reaction time or speed*: The quickness with which problems of moderate difficulty are accurately encoded and mentally manipulated; includes simple reaction time and semantic processing speed

The preceding list of broad abilities in the CHC model is generally representative of the ability factors traditionally targeted for measurement by multiaptitude test batteries, although some differences exist across competing models of ability and measures of the domain. For example, because the CHC model targets cognitive ability, some abilities that are not traditionally considered cognitive in nature (e.g., psychomotor dexterity) and that are integral parts of other models of ability are excluded from the list. Also, some scholars have called for an expanded view of abilities that may include, for example, emotional intelligence, social intelligence, situational judgment, and other areas of human performance not typically included in traditional theoretical models of the ability domain.

Assumptions of Ability Tests

Although the specific features of various theoretical models underlying particular ability tests may differ, most major ability tests assume the following: (a) There are multiple abilities that can be reliably and validly measured using a single, wide-range test or battery; (b) there are differences between people in terms of level of performance in each area of ability; (c) there are differences within people in terms of level of performance across different areas of ability; (d) differences between a person's level of abilities relative to a normative group, and differences within a person's pattern of ability scores, predict real-world outcomes (e.g., academic and occupational performance); and thus (e) scores from ability tests offer useful information in settings where decisions related to education, employment, and rehabilitation are made. It should also be noted that ability tests measure *maximal* performance; some have proposed that *typical* performance may better predict some real-world outcomes.

Examples of Ability Tests

Several multiaptitude test batteries are currently available. Users are encouraged to select an instrument according to such criteria as the evidence for reliability and validity; the appropriateness of the normative samples used to standardize the test; the ease with which the test can be obtained, administered, and scored; the extent to which scale scores provide clear, unambiguous results; and the extent to which proposed applications of the test coincide with the needs of the user. The following are brief descriptions of three commonly used multiaptitude test batteries.

Armed Services Vocational Aptitude Battery

The Armed Services Vocational Aptitude Battery (ASVAB; U.S. Department of Defense) is best known for its use in military selection and classification and for its inclusion as part of a comprehensive career exploration program for high school and college students. The ASVAB consists of the following subtests, each separately timed: General Science, Arithmetic Reasoning, Word Knowledge, Paragraph

Comprehension, Numerical Operations, Coding Speed, Auto and Shop Information, Mathematical Knowledge, Mechanical Comprehension, and Electronics Information. Factor analytic evidence suggests that the ASVAB measures general cognitive ability, verbal-math ability, clerical speed, and technical knowledge. The ASVAB was developed using impressive norms, but its usefulness for differential prediction has been questioned.

Occupational Information Network Ability Profiler

The Occupational Information Network (O∗NET) Ability Profiler (published by the U.S. Department of Labor) is a component of the O∗NET Career Exploration Tools system. The O∗NET Ability Profiler is an updated version of the GATB and is available in paper-and-pencil format with optional apparatus subtests. The O∗NET Ability Profiler consists of 11 subtests that measure nine job-related abilities: verbal ability, arithmetic reasoning, computation, spatial ability, form perception, clerical perception, motor coordination, manual dexterity, and finger dexterity. A major strength of the battery is that it generates a computer-generated score report that can be linked to a wealth of occupational data in the O∗NET database, allowing individuals to, for example, compare their pattern of abilities to those required by different occupations.

Differential Aptitude Tests

The DAT, published by the Psychological Corporation, was designed primarily for educational and career guidance of individuals in middle school, high school, and adulthood. The DAT provides scores for the following eight areas of ability: verbal reasoning, numerical ability, abstract reasoning, perceptual speed and accuracy, mechanical reasoning, space relations, spelling, and language usage. The DAT scores are computed using very good norm groups, and efforts to address test fairness have been thorough. Evidence supporting the reliability of the DAT scores is strong, although relatively little evidence is available to assess the validity of the scale scores for predicting outcomes other than academic achievement.

Each of the preceding test batteries has garnered evidence of reliability and validity, and this evidence is reviewed in the user's manuals. As indicated in their descriptions, the ASVAB, O∗NET Ability Profiler, and DAT typically are used for educational and vocational counseling and personnel selection. Other purposes for testing abilities, such as neuropsychological evaluation or educational diagnosis, naturally require tests with validity evidence supporting their use for those purposes.

Gender and Ethnicity in Ability Testing

As is the case with any test, users must be sensitive to the ways in which personal or group characteristics such as age, gender, ethnicity, linguistic background, disability status, and educational and work history may influence performance on ability tests. Although the weight of evidence suggests no difference between females and males in general cognitive ability, consistent differences have been found favoring females on tests of some verbal abilities and males on tests of some visual-spatial tasks. Evidence also suggests that scores on quantitative abilities tend to favor females in the early years of school and males from adolescence onward. Most scholars suggest that biological and social factors work in tandem to produce such differences.

Some differences between ethnic groups have been found in scores on tests of ability. This finding contributed to the previously noted controversy over the GATB, for example. The crux of the controversy was that some minority groups tended to score lower than the majority on some GATB subscales and, since the U.S. Department of Labor had suggested that states use the test as part of a new employment selection system, members of these groups were adversely impacted. However, scores on the GATB (and other tests of ability) tended to predict educational and occupational outcomes equally well, regardless of ethnicity. Eventually the use of within-group norms in employee selection was proposed, but this suggestion was also controversial, and as mentioned earlier, the GATB was eventually suspended from use. Because many tests measure abilities that are influenced by education and training, users must take into account the quality of the respondent's educational background. This is particularly important when interpreting scores of ethnically diverse respondents because minority groups are more likely than members of the majority to be socioeconomically disadvantaged, which in turn is related to poorer school systems and fewer educational opportunities that might improve test performance. Of course, it bears remembering that within-group differences are larger than between-group differences and that meaningful generalizations from the group to the individual can never be made responsibly without additional information.

Conclusion

Ability tests allow users to identify current and potential performance strengths for individuals, information that is useful for a wide range of purposes in a variety of contexts. Many ability tests are laden with positive features that likely contribute to their widespread use, such as ease of administration and scoring, strong psychometric evidence, and the provision of a large amount of meaningful information in a relatively brief period of time. With recent advances in technology, ability testing has become increasingly automated, and in the future, computer-administered testing will continue to improve convenience of use and also will allow users to customize their batteries to better suit their specific needs. When combined with other sources of information, the potential benefits of ability tests to individuals and society are substantial.

—*Bryan J. Dik*

See also Iowa Tests of Basic Skills; Reliability Theory; Validity Theory

Further Reading

American Educational Research Association. (1999). *Standards for educational and psychological testing.* Washington, DC: Author.

Carroll, J. B. (1993). *Human cognitive abilities: A survey of factor-analytic studies.* New York: Cambridge University Press.

Spearman, C. (1927). *The abilities of man.* New York: Macmillan.

Thurstone, L. L. (1938). *Primary mental abilities* (Psychometric Monograph No. 1). Chicago: University of Chicago Press.

U.S. Department of Labor. (2002). *Ability Profiler: Administration manual.* Washington, DC: U.S. Government Printing Office.

Armed Services Vocational Aptitude Battery: http://www.asvabprogram.com/

Cattel-Horn-Carroll Human Cognitive Abilities Project: www.iapsych.com/chchca.htm

Differential Aptitudes Tests: www.psychcorpcenter.com

O*NET Ability Profiler: www.onetcenter.org

ABSTRACTS

An abstract is a brief, concise, accurate, and generally nonevaluative summary of a work such as a journal article, a presentation, or a book. The length of an abstract varies but is typically a paragraph and never more than a page. An abstract for a periodical source often appears at the top of the article, underneath the title. For prepared manuscripts, an abstract is presented by itself on a single page that follows the title page. Abstracts are often collected in volumes and presented in either print or electronic format to provide potential readers of scholarly work with a quick and time-saving overview of the main document.

There are two common forms of abstracts. A *descriptive* abstract is often written prior to the completion of a specific work. Therefore, it may not provide results, conclusions, or recommendations. This type of abstract may be submitted to a local or a national conference, for instance, as a summary of one's planned presentation. A descriptive abstract may simply contain the problem and methods with a brief section on expected outcome. In contrast, an *informative* abstract is written following the completion of a specific work and summarizes the entire content of the original document. It commonly consists of an overview of the following four sections: (a) problem, (b) methodology, (c) results, and (d) conclusion. This type of abstract provides a condensed version of the original work so that a reader can choose whether to review the entire piece.

Abstract writing is an acquired skill that may be strengthened with continued practice. To present an effective abstract, the writer should follow the organization of the original article closely. In abstracts of scientific papers, the reader is first presented with information about the topic or central issue(s) in the main document. A statement about the study's objectives or the tested hypotheses may be provided. Second, the reader is educated about the methods used to approach the main topic. For example, the abstract may provide information relevant to the number of participants enrolled in a given study or the assessment strategies used to examine the stated hypotheses. Third, there is a brief description of the study's findings and conclusions. The reader is presented with an explanation of the significance and possible implications of the obtained results. Fourth, there is some reference to the recommendations. In summary, a well-written, self-contained abstract presents a capsule description of the original article, without adding new information, in language that is understandable to a wide audience.

—*Marjan Ghahramanlou-Holloway*

See also American Doctoral Dissertations; American Psychological Association

Further Reading

Hartley, J. (1998). *An evaluation of structured abstracts in journals published by the British Psychological Society.* Retrieved from http://cogprints.org/587/00/199801001.html

Kamler, B., & Thomson, P. (2004). Driven to abstraction: Doctoral supervision and writing pedagogies. *Teaching in Higher Education*, 9(2), 195–209.

Ono, H., Phillips, K. A., & Leneman, M. (1996). Content of an abstract: De jure and de facto. *American Psychologist*, 51(12), 1338–1340.

Pierson, D. J. (2004). How to write an abstract that will be accepted for presentation at a national meeting. *Respiratory Care*, 49(10), 1206–1212.

ACCEPTANCE SAMPLING

Acceptance sampling is a procedure used for product acceptance or rejection and is based on inspecting only a sampled number of units from the total number produced. In many situations in which the inspection is destructive, such as testing flashbulbs, it is not feasible to inspect all the bulbs produced. Acceptance sampling can be performed during incoming inspection of raw materials or components, in various phases of in-process operations, or during final inspection. Such a procedure may be applied to cases in which inspection is by attributes or by variables.

Acceptance sampling is a scheme that determines whether a batch or lot of product items should be accepted or rejected. It does not control or improve the quality level of the process. Although acceptance sampling offers some advantages associated with its feasibility in destructive testing, its economies in inspection cost, and its usefulness in improving quality, it also poses some risks because an entire batch may be rejected based on inspection of a few items.

Risks in Acceptance Sampling

Two types of risks are inherent in acceptance sampling plans: *producer's risk* and *consumer's risk*.

Producer's Risk

This is the risk (denoted by α) associated with rejecting a lot that is of "good" quality, and a numerical definition of a "good" lot is prescribed by the *acceptable quality level* (AQL). The AQL may be viewed as the maximum proportion of nonconforming items in a batch that can be considered satisfactory as a process average. Thus, the interpretation of the statement that the producer's risk is 5% for an AQL of 0.03 is as follows: Batches that are 3% nonconforming are considered satisfactory, and it is desirable that such batches, or those that are better, not be rejected more than 5% of the time.

Consumer's Risk

This is the risk (denoted by β) associated with accepting a "poor" lot. A numerical definition of a poor lot is indicated by the limiting quality level (LQL), also referred to as the lot tolerance percent defective. The statement that the consumer's risk is

10% for an LQL of 0.09 means that batches that are 9% or more nonconforming are considered poor. Consequently, such batches should be accepted no more than 10% of the time by the selected acceptance sampling plan.

Acceptance Sampling by Attributes and Variables

In attribute acceptance sampling, a product is classified as nonconforming or unacceptable if it contains one or more nonconformities or defects. For example, a hair dryer may be nonconforming if the speed control switch does not operate at each of the settings.

Alternatively, acceptance sampling may be used in the context of product-related variables, which can be measured and on the basis of which a decision about the product can be made. An example is the monitoring of the weight of cereal boxes. Suppose a minimum acceptable weight of 12 ounces is specified. By the selection of reasonable protection levels associated with errors that could be made in decision making using acceptance sampling, an *acceptance limit* is found. For sampled cereal boxes, sample statistics such as the mean and the standard deviation may be calculated. Using these measures, if the calculated sample mean is less than the acceptance limit, the batch of boxes could be rejected.

Parameters of an Attribute Sampling Plan

In the simplest of the attribute sampling plans, namely, a single sampling plan, a decision is made on a batch or lot on the basis of information from a single sample. There are two parameters for such a plan, the *sample size* (n) and the *acceptance number* (c). These parameters are chosen on the basis of acceptable levels of the producer's (α) and consumer's (β) risks and values of AQL and LQL. Standardized procedures exist whereby, on the basis of on chosen levels of the above-mentioned parameters, the values of n and c may be determined.

Suppose, for example, the batch size (N) for a product is 2,000. On the basis of a producer's risk (α) of 5%, AQL of 2%, a consumer's risk (β) of 10%, and

an LQL of 8%, the sample size (n) and acceptance number (c) are determined to be, say, 50 and 3, respectively, for the single sampling acceptance plan. The plan operates as follows. A sample of 50 units is randomly selected from the batch of 2,000 units, and the number of nonconforming units is found. If the number of nonconforming units is less than or equal to the acceptance number, which in this example is 3, the batch is accepted. Otherwise, the batch is rejected.

—Amitava Mitra

See also Hypergeometric Distribution; Sample; Sampling Error

Further Reading

American National Standards Institute (ANSI)/American Society for Quality (ASQ). (2003). *Sampling procedures and tables for inspection by attributes*, ANSI/ASQ Z1.4. Milwaukee, WI: ASQ Quality Press.

American National Standards Institute (ANSI)/American Society for Quality (ASQ). (2003). *Sampling procedures and tables for inspection by variables for percent nonconforming*, ANSI/ASQ Z1.9. Milwaukee, WI: ASQ Quality Press.

Mitra, A. (2005). *Fundamentals of quality control and improvement* (2nd ed.). Mason, OH: Brooks/Cole.

ACHIEVEMENT TESTS

Any test that is designed to measure student learning in the context of an educational or training program can be called an achievement test. An achievement test comprises one to many test items. Each test item can be scored dichotomously (right or wrong) or with a rating scale, on which degrees of performance are determined by a judge, called a rater. Achievement test items are usually distinguished by the kind of response they generate: selected or constructed. The selected response item is often referred to as multiple choice because the test respondent chooses among the choices offered. The constructed response item requires that the respondent generate a written or oral response or a response in the form of a product or process. There is considerable variety in selected and constructed response test items.

The publication *Standards for Educational and Psychological Testing* provides definitions relevant to achievement tests. This publication also offers many guidelines for the development and validation of achievement tests. Another useful, comprehensive reference about the development and validation of achievement tests is the *Handbook of Test Development*.

The length of an achievement test varies according to many factors, all of which relate to validity and the intended purpose of the test. One of the most important factors is reliability. Longer tests tend to yield more reliable scores. If an achievement test represents a domain of identifiable knowledge and skills, then it should be a representative sample from this domain. Reliability and adequate sampling of content are two major types of evidence that support the validity of an achievement test score interpretation or use.

Another useful distinction is the difference between a *test* and a *quiz*. A quiz is shorter than a test and measures only several student learning objectives, whereas a test is longer than a quiz and measures many student learning objectives. Both test and quiz, as distinguished here, constitute a measure of student achievement, but the distinction is in the amount of coverage of the domain or content to be learned. Thus, any quiz is also an achievement test in this broader sense.

The term *assessment* is often used synonymously with the term *achievement test*. Strictly speaking, the two are not the same. Assessment is a judgment, usually by a teacher, about how well a student has learned and what a student needs to learn. An assessment should be based on valid information, which includes results of achievement tests and other information collected during a semester or school year or in a training program. Thus, an achievement test that is used for an assessment purpose may be given the name *assessment* because the test information is used for an assessment of student learning.

What Is Achievement?

Achievement is generally considered change in cognitive behavior that we attribute to learning, which can occur both within and outside a planned learning experience, such as a course, class, or training. What students learn can be thought of as existing in one of two related domains. Each domain has a large collection of test items that represent it.

The first domain, which is more familiar to educators, consists of knowledge and skills. We have many examples, including reading, mathematics, and social studies. Generally, states and school districts have content standards that explicitly define each domain. One type of achievement test is intended to be a representative sample from a domain of knowledge and skills. This kind of achievement test is generally created in a selected-response format because of the great efficiency of this format when compared to a constructed-response format. One of the major shortcomings of the latter format is that it does not yield an adequate sample from the intended domain of tasks that represent achievement.

The second domain, which is less familiar to educators, consists of many complex tasks that represent an ability. For example, writing is an ability. The domain of tasks that represent this ability may include making a report based on some experience; writing a creative story; writing a memorandum, e-mail, or letter; writing an invitation to a social event; and writing a critique, among many others. Many educators and psychologists have suggested that each ability is complex in nature. Each ability is learned slowly and unevenly over a lifetime. Each ability requires the application of knowledge and skills in unique ways to situations that we commonly encounter. The abilities that we learn in school are reading, writing, speaking, listening, mathematical and scientific problem solving, critical thinking, and creative thinking. Most states have adopted content standards that contain learning objectives that describe the kinds of student behaviors that can be tested. The testing format that seems most appropriate for this type of content is performance based. The scoring of these performance-based tests can be done subjectively, using trained, experienced raters and rating scales, which are referred to as *rubrics*, or the scoring can be done objectively, as we often see in mathematics, where there is likely to be a correct answer or a step-by-step algorithm to apply to reach a correct answer.

The scores from these achievement tests can be reported as the number of correct answers (raw score); as a percentage of the total number of items on the test; as a percentile rank or stanine; or in some derived scale, such as grade equivalent, standard score, or normal-curve equivalent. The choice of a scale to report a person's score depends on many factors related to the purpose of the test. *Norm-referenced* interpretations of test scores value the rank of scores in a set of test scores. Knowing how students rank in achievement is useful for some test purposes. *Criterion-referenced* interpretations are more concerned with how much a student has learned, usually relative to a standard, called a *cut score*. Another term for criterion-referenced is *domain-referenced* because the score a student obtains (e.g., 75% correct) refers to the degree of learning that has occurred relative to a domain of knowledge and skills. The terms *criterion-referenced test* and *norm-referenced test* are commonly used, but like the term *assessment*, they are not used accurately. Any test can yield a norm-referenced interpretation by using a norm-referenced test score scale. Many achievement tests lend themselves to criterion-referenced or domain-referenced interpretations due to the way they were designed. Thus, we use the terms *norm-referenced test* and *criterion-referenced test* to refer to the type of interpretation we desire from the test, but strictly speaking, these are not types of tests.

The Distinction Between Achievement Tests and Intelligence Tests

Psychologists and others have spent more than a hundred years studying human intelligence. Depending on one's experiences and background, this field has been controversial, but some ideas have survived this controversy. Intelligence and achievement are often considered as being on a continuum in the cognitive domain. Achievement is generally viewed as something that changes with experience and instruction. Achievement tests can detect these changes, which we know as student learning. Intelligence is generally viewed as a group of complex abilities that are less resistant to change. These abilities are verbal, quantitative, and analytical. Some standardized tests are indicators of intelligence, and other tests are indicators of achievement. Sometimes the distinction is not clear. Validation is a process whereby the truth of what a test measures is studied and the claim for what it measures is supported by reasoning and evidence.

Purpose

An achievement test can also be distinguished by its purpose. A major difference in purpose distinguishes a classroom achievement test and the standardized achievement test. The design of each type of achievement test and the uses of its test scores will vary according to its purpose.

Classroom Achievement Tests

A classroom achievement test is a category that seems focused on two central purposes: *formative* and *summative*. During instruction, formatively used achievement tests inform both student and teacher about the extent of learning. These achievement tests do not count toward a student grade. Instead, formatively used achievement tests guide the student to improve learning. Summatively used tests are used for some important purpose, such as grading. During a grading period, usually 9 weeks, a test can be used as part of the criteria for a student grade. A test score, by itself, is never recommended by evaluation specialists as the sole indicator of a grade. A test result is only one important piece of information about the extent and quality of student learning.

The validity of formative and summative tests depends on several factors. First, the content must be clearly stated to students. Second, factors that prevent learning should be removed or minimized. Third, instruction should be aligned to this content. Fourth, the achievement test should also be aligned to this content. Fifth, test design and administration can be modified to remove factors that may invalidate test performance. Finally, students should have additional opportunities to learn what they have not learned.

Standardized Achievement Tests

Standardized achievement tests are numerous. Two comprehensive references on standardized achievement testing are the *Sixteenth Mental Measurement Yearbook* and *Tests in Print*. A useful Web address for these and similar publications is http://www.unl.edu/buros/.

A major distinction among standardized tests is whether they are intended to help assess student learning in an educational program or to help determine who passes or fails for a promotion, graduation, certification, or licensing decision. Achievement tests that have significant consequences for the test taker or the public are considered *high-stakes* achievement tests.

Standardized achievement tests have common characteristics. The population that is to take this test is well described. The content of the test is clearly specified. Items are systematically developed and validated. The test is designed to maximize information that will be validly interpreted and used by its recipients. The conditions for administration and scoring are uniform. If multiple test forms exist, these test forms are usually equated so that interpretations are consistent from test form to test form. Standards are set validly using procedures that are widely known and accepted as producing valid results. The interpretation of test scores is consistent with the intended purpose of the test. Thus, the term *standardized* refers to these aspects of test design, test development, administration, scoring, and reporting.

To ensure that the test scores are validly interpreted and used, all standardized achievement tests are subject to validation. The process of validation is a responsibility of the test developer and the sponsor of the testing program. The *Standards for Educational and Psychological Testing* are very clear about the conditions and evidence needed for validation. A technical report or test manual contains the argument and evidence supporting each intended test score interpretation or use. If subscores are used, each subscore should also be validated. Test scores should never be used for purposes that have not been validated.

A major distinction among standardized achievement tests is whether a test has been aligned to a set of content standards *specifically* or *generally*.

Specifically aligned tests provide the public with assurance that what content is mandated in a state or a school district is represented on the aligned test. An alignment ensures that curriculum, instruction, and test all correspond to each another. A good example of a set of national content standards is the one developed in 1991 by the National Council of Teachers of Mathematics. It is reasonable to expect that a state's or school district's aligned test scores will also be based on national standards and that test scores from a state- or district-aligned test will correlate highly with scores from one of several generally aligned achievement tests, such as the Stanford Achievement Test, the Iowa Tests of Basic Skills, or the TerraNova.

All standardized achievement tests can be used for various purposes. However, each purpose should be validated. For instance, some standardized achievement tests can be used diagnostically to identify a student's strengths and weaknesses. The same tests can also be used to identify strengths and weaknesses in a curriculum or instructional program for a school or a school district. This kind of analysis can even be done at the state, national, or international level. In some instances, a standardized achievement test can be used for making pass-fail decisions for promotion to a higher grade or for graduation. Validation should focus on the legitimacy of using any test score for any purpose.

Summary

Any test that is intended by its developer to reflect the amount of learning that has occurred in the past can be considered an achievement test. Assessment is a term often mistakenly used for a test. Assessment involves the use of information about student learning to reach a conclusion about what a student knows and can do and what the student needs to learn. The content of achievement tests can be considered in two ways: as a domain of knowledge and skills and as a domain of complex tasks. To complete a complex task, a student has to have knowledge and skills and be able to apply each in a complex way to perform the task. Achievement tests are of two major types: (a) tests used in the classroom for formative or summative assessment and (b) standardized tests, which serve many purposes, including assessment. Any use of a test should be validated.

—*Thomas Haladyna*

See also Iowa Tests of Basic Skills; Iowa Tests of Educational Development

Further Reading

American Educational Research Association. (1999). *Standards for educational and psychological testing.* Washington, DC: Author.

Downing, S. M., & Haladyna, T. M. (Eds.). (2006). *Handbook of test development*. Mahwah, NJ: Erlbaum.

Haladyna, T. M. (2004). *Developing and validating multiple-choice test items* (3rd ed.). Mahwah, NJ: Erlbaum.

Kane, M. T. (2006). Content-related validity evidence in test development. In S. M. Downing & T. M. Haladyna (Eds.). *Handbook of test development*. Mahwah, NJ: Erlbaum.

Lohman, D. F. (1993). Teaching and testing to develop fluid abilities. *Educational Researcher, 22,* 12–23.

Murphy, L. L., Plake, B. S., Impara, J. C., & Spies, R. A. (2002). *Tests in print VI*. Lincoln: University of Nebraska Press.

National Council of Teachers of Mathematics. (1989). *Curriculum and evaluation standards for school mathematics*. Reston, VA: Author.

Spies, R. A., & Plake, B. S. (Eds.). (2005). *The sixteenth mental measurement yearbook*. Lincoln: University of Nebraska Press.

Buros Center for Testing: http://www.unl.edu/buros/

ACTIVE LIFE EXPECTANCY

Active life expectancy (ALE) refers to the number of years of life one can be expected to live without a disability. ALE answers the question, Of the remaining years of life for this cohort of persons, what proportion is expected to be spent disability-free? As such, it is used to evaluate the quality of life rather than just the quantity. The term was first introduced by Katz and colleagues in 1983, although others had described similar concepts in the mid-1960s and early 1970s. ALE is a summary measure of population health, is based on aggregate statistics, and is used in demography and epidemiology to measure and compare the health and functional status of national populations.

ALE is usually expressed as a component of total life expectancy at a certain age. In the measurement of ALE, disability is usually defined as difficulty in performing one or more activities of daily living (ADLs), which include eating, dressing, bathing, toileting, walking, and transferring to a bed or chair. There are two closely related concepts, disability-free life expectancy (DFLE) and healthy, or health-adjusted, life expectancy (HALE). While ALE uses the presence of a limitation in any one of the activities of daily living as an endpoint, disability-free life expectancy uses the presence of limitations in either ADLs or instrumental activities of daily living (IADLs), and HALE uses a measure of general health status, or good health versus poor health.

ALE can be computed in one of two ways, by using multistate life tables or by the Sullivan method. The Sullivan method requires a period life table for the population and observed age-specific prevalence of disability in the population (π_i). Using standard life table notation, at each age i, the number of person years lived in that age interval (L_i) is multiplied by the proportion of people at that age who are not disabled ($1 - \pi_i$). ALE is the total of all person years lived above an age i divided by the number of survivors to age i, l_i. In contrast, the multistate life table method requires age-specific transition probabilities. These transition probabilities, usually derived from longitudinal survey data, give the rates of moving from health to disability (and back), as well as the risk of death for both the healthy and disabled states at each age. Survival models incorporate these transition probabilities to estimate the time expected to be spent in the two states, active and disabled. The advantages of the multistate method include the ability to model recovery and the ability to include covariates in the models.

This method was used in 2005 by Reynolds and colleagues to examine the effect of obesity on ALE. They found that being obese at age 70 has virtually no effect on the total number of years of life remaining but reduces ALE by 2.4 years for women and 1.5 years for men.

—*Christine L. Himes*

See also Longitudinal/Repeated Measures Data; Survival Analysis

Further Reading

Katz, S., Branch, L. G., Branson, M. H., Papsidero, J. A., Beck, J. C., & Greer D. S. (1983). Active life expectancy. *New England Journal of Medicine, 309,* 1218–1224.

Reynolds, S. L., Saito, Y., & Crimmins, E. M. (2005). The impact of obesity on active life expectancy in older American men and women. *Gerontologist, 45,* 438–444.

Sanders, B. (1964). Measuring community health level. *American Journal of Public Health, 54,* 1063–1070.

Schoen, R. (1988). *Modeling multigroup populations.* New York: Plenum.

Sullivan, D. F. (1971). A single index of mortality and morbidity. *HSMHA Health Reports, 86,* 347–354.

ADAPTIVE SAMPLING DESIGN

In adaptive sampling, information gained during the sampling process is used to modify, or adapt, how the subsequent sample units are selected. Traditionally, the selection procedure is defined prior to sampling. For example, a sample scheme may be to select *n* units at random from the population, as in simple random sampling. In adaptive sampling, the select procedure may change during the survey.

In biology, plant or animal populations are often spatially aggregated, and when the population is rare, sampling can be challenging. Adaptive sampling can be used in this situation. An initial sample of plants may be undertaken within quadrats placed randomly in the area. Additional sampling is undertaken around the quadrats where plants were found. The final sample combines information from the initial sample and from the additional sampling. In this adaptive design, survey effort was concentrated in the localities where plants were found. The information from the initial sample was used to "adapt" the sample because additional sampling was directed to the localities where plants were known to be. In this regard, adaptive sampling is considered more informative than traditional sampling.

There are many forms of adaptive sampling; the one described above could be called adaptive cluster sampling. Another adaptive design is to adaptively allocate extra survey effort in stratified sampling. In traditional stratified sampling, the population is divided into homogeneous groups or regions, called strata. Survey effort is allocated among strata according to some criterion, usually estimates of the within-stratum variance or mean. If there is no information on these strata statistics or if the information is poor, adaptive stratified sampling can be used. After an initial survey of the strata, estimates of stratum variance or mean are used to decide on allocation of additional survey effort. Usually this additional survey effort is allocated to the strata with the highest variances. Information on the strata gained during the survey is used to adapt the final allocation of survey effort.

—*Jennifer Ann Brown*

See also Sample; Sampling Error

Further Reading

Smith, D. R., Brown, J. A., & Lo, N. C. H. (2004). Applications of adaptive sampling to biological populations. In W. L. Thompson (Ed.), *Sampling rare or elusive species* (pp. 77–122). Washington, DC: Island Press.

Thompson, S. K. (1990). Adaptive cluster sampling. *Journal of the American Statistical Association, 85,* 1050–1059.

Thompson, S. K., & Seber, G. A. F. (1996). *Adaptive sampling.* New York: Wiley.

ADJECTIVE CHECKLIST

The Adjective Checklist (ACL) is a measure of children's attitudes that utilizes a checklist format first employed by Harrison Gough. The ACL has been employed in more than 30 studies to assess children's attitudes toward persons from potentially stigmatized groups, with a focus on peers with mental retardation. Other studies have examined attitudes toward children with visual impairments, autism, obesity, cancer, and physical disabilities, as well as toward tobacco users.

The ACL was developed to assess the *cognitive* component of children's attitudes (opinions and beliefs about a person), one of three components that make up attitudes (together with the *affective* component, i.e., emotions and feelings about a person, and the *behavioral intentions* component, i.e., intentions to interact with a person). It uses an open-ended format that allows children to select from a provided list as many positive and negative adjectives as they wish to select to describe a specific person (known as a *target*). The open-ended approach of the ACL does not restrict children to making judgments that they may not ordinarily make, the way a forced choice format might. That is, the ACL mirrors the behavior of children in classroom settings where children express their opinions or beliefs about a peer by using common descriptors such as "smart," "mean," "friendly," and so on.

The ACL was developed by asking large samples of children in Grades 1 through 6 to identify terms they would use to describe a person they liked and a person they did not like. Those terms that were mentioned most often were compiled into a list, and new samples of children were asked to judge each term as a "good" thing or a "bad" thing to say about someone. As a result, 34 adjectives were identified that describe a person's affective feelings, physical appearance, academic behavior, and social behavior. Within these broad categories, the ACL includes equal numbers of positive and negative descriptors. Factor analysis of ACL responses from more than 2,000 elementary school children revealed three distinct factors: positive (P factor, e.g., "proud," "happy"), negative (N factor, e.g., "careless," "ugly"), and negative affect (NA factor, e.g., "lonely," "ashamed").

The ACL can be administered to children individually or in groups by asking the children to use the checklist to describe a particular target. The target may be either a hypothetical student depicted in a videotaped vignette, a photograph, a verbal description, or a real individual. In each instance, the target is presented, and then the children are asked to describe the target using as few or as many words from the list as they would like. There are two methods for scoring the ACL. The first method involves summing up a child's selection of adjectives on each of the three factors noted above. The second method results in a composite score in which the number of negative adjectives chosen by a child is subtracted from the number of positive adjectives chosen, and a constant of 20 is added. In this method, the negative adjectives would include all adjectives in the N factor and the NA factor (i.e, Total Score = P − N − NA + 20). A resulting score below 20 represents a negative attitude toward the target, and a score above 20 represents a positive attitude.

The ACL has good construct validity: Correlations with measures of behavioral intentions include Pearson *r* values of .76 with the Foley Scale and .67 with the Siperstein Activity Preference Scale, .35 with Selman's Friendship Activity Scale, and .46 with the Shared Activities Questionnaire. Cronbach's alpha has been reported to range from .67 to .91, with values of .83, .76, and .73 reported for the P, N, and NA factors, respectively.

—Gary N. Siperstein

See also Attitude Tests

Further Reading

Bak, J. J., & Siperstein, G. N. (1987). Similarity as a factor effecting change in children's attitudes toward mentally retarded peers. *American Journal of Mental Deficiency*, *91*(5), 524–531.

Bell, S. K., & Morgan, S. B. (2000). Children's attitudes and behavioral intentions toward a peer presented as obese: Does a medical explanation for the obesity make a difference? *Journal of Pediatric Psychology*, *25*(3), 137–145.

Campbell, J. M., Ferguson, J. E., Herzinger, C. V., Jackson, J. N., & Marino, C. A. (2004). Combined descriptive and explanatory information improves peers' perceptions of autism. *Research in Developmental Disabilities*, *25*(4), 321–339.

Castagano, K. S. (2001). Special Olympics unified sports: Changes in male athletes during a basketball season. *Adapted Physical Activity Quarterly*, *18*(2), 193–206.

Gough, H. G. (1952). *The Adjective Check List*. Palo Alto, CA: Consulting Psychologist Press.

Graffi, S., & Minnes, P. M. (1988). Attitudes of primary school children toward the physical appearance and labels associated with Down syndrome. *American Journal of Mental Retardation*, *93*(1), 28–35.

Kury, S. P., Rodrigue, J. R., & Peri, M. G. (1998). Smokeless tobacco and cigarettes: Differential attitudes and behavioral intentions of young adolescents toward a hypothetical new peer. *Journal of Clinical Child Psychology*, *27*(4), 415–422.

Manetti, M., Schneider, B. H., & Siperstein, G. N. (2001). Social acceptance of children with mental retardation:

Testing the contact hypothesis with an Italian sample. *International Journal of Behavioral Development, 25,* 279–286.

Siperstein, G. N. (1980). *Instruments for measuring children's attitudes toward the handicapped.* Boston: University of Massachusetts.

Siperstein, G. N., & Gottlieb, J. (1997). Physical stigma and academic performance as factors affecting children's first impressions of handicapped peers. *American Journal of Mental Deficiency, 81,* 455–462.

Swaim, K. F., & Morgan, S. B. (2001). Children's attitudes and behavioral intentions toward a peer with autistic behaviors: Does a brief educational intervention have an effect? *Journal of Autism & Developmental Disorders, 31*(2), 195–205.

AGE NORMS

Age norms are used to represent typical performance or some aspect of development for children within a particular age group. Used as an indication of the average age at which certain behaviors are expected to occur, they provide a metric against which same-aged peers can be compared. Alternatively, they provide guidelines to determine where along a developmental continuum an individual's skill or behavior may fall. Depending on the measure of interest, these norms may be expressed in various ways.

The use of age norms assumes homogeneity of a group with respect to particular skills or behaviors. Because these can be expected to be normally distributed within a population, age norms can be computed on the basis of the average performance of the individuals within that population. For example, a vocabulary of 50 words is considered to be the norm for typically developing children between the ages of 12 and 18 months. Children whose vocabulary size falls within, above, or below this range may therefore be considered typical, precocious, or delayed, respectively. Age norms exist as well for certain physiological measures (e.g., the pitch of the voice) as well as developmental milestones (e.g., crawling or walking).

Age norms are also employed in characterizing the acquisition or emergence of certain skills. These norms assume an ordering of developmental stages and are often used to characterize motor functions, aspects of speech and language acquisition, social behaviors, and so forth. Often, the emergence of behaviors is considered to be predicated on the acquisition of prerequisite skills, thus implying a fixed and orderly developmental sequence. This pattern would be typical of sensorimotor phenomena such as locomotion and manual dexterity. For example, the ability to stabilize the trunk using large muscle groups typically occurs at a certain age and precedes the development of movements necessary for more precise distal movements. By extension, failure to develop earlier skills would predict the delay, impairment, or absence of later-emerging skills.

Other behaviors may also appear along a developmental continuum. For example, starting as early as 1 year of age, norms exist for the production of classes of speech sounds (e.g., stop consonants vs. fricatives), individual sounds within those classes, the ways those sounds are used in words, syllable structure, and so on. Although motorically complex sounds often appear later than simpler ones, a fixed order does not necessarily apply. Age norms exist as well for the acquisition of grammatical structures and various parts of speech. Failure to acquire speech and language according to these norms is considered grounds for further evaluation or intervention.

Age norms are typically easy to understand, with respect to performance both at a particular age and over time. However, their usefulness is limited to certain types of developmental behaviors or skills. Moreover, although skills or milestones that fall at or within age norms may be considered to be normal or typical, interpretation is more problematic when performance lies outside those norms. As a result, measures are typically standardized so that (a) a child's performance can be characterized with respect to other children of the same age or grade and (b) a comparison of performance across different assessment instruments can be made for the same child.

—*Carole E. Gelfer*

See also Data Collection; Longitudinal/Repeated Measures Data

Further Reading

Anastasi, A. (1988). *Psychological testing* (6th ed.). New York: Macmillan.

Applying Ideas on Statistics and Measurement

The following abstract is adapted from Sherry, A., Henson, R. K., & Lewis, J. G. (2003). Evaluating the appropriateness of college-age norms for use with adolescents on the NEO Personality Inventory—Revised. *Assessment, 10*(1), 71–78.

The NEO Personality Inventory measures normal personality characteristics and has demonstrated appropriate score reliability and validity. **Age norms** are available for two groups of individuals, college-age individuals 17 to 20 years old and adults 21 and older. Often, personality instruments normed on older individuals have been used with adolescent populations. To examine the appropriateness of this decision, the current study explored the differences between an adolescent sample and a college-age sample on the 30 facets and the five domains of the NEO. Group differences on the facet and domain scales were analyzed using discriminant analysis. Results indicated that the adolescent and college groups differed on each of the five domains. As expected, the groups also scored differently when the aggregated domain-level variables were used as the outcome measures.

AKAIKE INFORMATION CRITERION

In statistical modeling, one of the main challenges is to select a suitable model from a candidate family to characterize the underlying data. Model selection criteria provide a useful tool in this regard. A selection criterion assesses whether a fitted model offers an optimal balance between goodness-of-fit and parsimony. Ideally, a criterion will identify candidate models that are either too simplistic to accommodate the data or unnecessarily complex.

The Akaike information criterion (AIC) was the first model selection criterion to gain widespread acceptance. AIC was introduced in 1973 by Hirotogu Akaike as an extension to the maximum likelihood principle. Conventionally, maximum likelihood is applied to estimate the parameters of a model once the structure of the model has been specified. Akaike's seminal idea was to combine estimation and structural determination into a single procedure.

The minimum AIC procedure is employed as follows. Given a family of candidate models of various structures, each model is fit to the data via maximum likelihood. An AIC is computed based on each model fit. The fitted candidate model corresponding to the minimum value of AIC is then selected.

AIC serves as an estimator of Kullback's directed divergence between the generating, or "true," model (i.e., the model that presumably gave rise to the data) and a fitted candidate model. The directed divergence assesses the disparity or separation between two statistical models. Thus, when entertaining a family of fitted candidate models, by selecting the fitted model corresponding to the minimum value of AIC, one is hoping to identify the fitted model that is "closest" to the generating model.

Definition of AIC

Consider a candidate family of models denoted as M_1, $M_2, \ldots, M_L$. Let θ_k ($k = 1, 2, \ldots, L$) denote the parameter vector for model M_k, and let d_k denote the dimension of model M_k, that is, the number of functionally independent parameters in θ_k. Let $L(\theta_k \mid y)$ denote the likelihood for θ_k based on the data y, and let $\hat{\theta}_k$ denote the maximum likelihood estimate of θ_k. The AIC for model M_k is defined as

$$\mathrm{AIC}_k = -2\log L\left(\hat{\theta}_k \mid y\right) + 2d_k.$$

The first term in AIC_k, $-2\log L(\hat{\theta}_k \mid y)$, is based on the empirical likelihood $L(\hat{\theta}_k \mid y)$. This term, called the goodness-of-fit term, will decrease as the conformity of the fitted model M_k to the data improves. The second term in AIC_k, called the penalty term, will increase in accordance with the complexity of the model M_k. Models that are too simplistic to accommodate the data are associated with large values of the goodness-of-fit term, whereas models that are unnecessarily complex are associated with large values of the penalty term. In principle, the fitted candidate model corresponding to the minimum value of AIC should provide an optimal tradeoff between fidelity to the data and parsimony.

The Assumptions Underlying the Use of AIC

AIC is applicable in a broad array of modeling frameworks because its justification requires only conventional large-sample properties of maximum likelihood estimators. However, if the sample size n is small in relation to the model dimension d_k (e.g., $d_k \approx n/2$), AIC_k will be characterized by a large negative bias. As a result, AIC_k will tend to underestimate the directed divergence between the generating model and the fitted candidate model M_k. This underestimation is potentially problematic in applications in which the sample size is small relative to the dimensions of the larger models in the candidate family. In such settings, AIC may often select a larger model even though the model may be unnecessarily complex and provide a poor description of the underlying phenomenon. Small-sample variants of AIC have been developed to adjust for the negative bias of AIC. The most popular is the "corrected" AIC (AICc), which was first proposed in 1978 for the framework of normal linear regression by Nariaki Sugiura. A decade later, AICc was generalized, advanced, and popularized in a series of papers by Clifford M. Hurvich and Chih-Ling Tsai.

AIC can be used to compare nonnested models. AIC can also be used to compare models based on different probability distributions, such as normal versus Poisson. However, if the models in the candidate family are based on different distributions, all terms in each empirical likelihood must be retained when the values of AIC are evaluated. (If the models in the candidate family are based on the same distribution, terms in the empirical likelihood that do not depend on the data may be discarded in the AIC computations.) AIC cannot be used to compare models

based on different transformations of the response variable.

An Application

The following data set appears in Annette J. Dobson's text *An Introduction to Generalized Linear Models* (2nd ed.), 2002, pp. 51–53. The response variable y_i consists of the number of deaths from coronary heart disease in a 5-year age group for men in the Hunter region of New South Wales, Australia, in 1991. Table 1 features the values of y_i, the age groups and the group indices i, the population sizes n_i, and the mortality rates per 100,000 men (i.e., $y_i / n_i \times 100,000$).

Figure 1 features a plot of the log of the mortality rate (per 100,000 men) versus the age group index i. Dobson notes that the plot is approximately linear. Thus, if $\mu_i = E[y_i]$, the plot might suggest that $\log(\mu_i/n_i)$ could be modeled as a linear function of the group index i. If the response y_i is regarded as a Poisson random variable, then a generalized linear model (GLM) of the following form might be postulated for the data:

$$M_1: \log\mu_i = \log n_i + \alpha + \beta_1 i, \ y_i \sim \text{Poisson }(\mu_i).$$

However, one could also argue that the plot exhibits slight curvature for the older age groups and that the

Table 1   Number of Deaths From Coronary Heart Disease and Population Sizes by 5-Year Age Groups for Men in the Hunter Region of New South Wales, Australia, 1991

Group index, i	Age group (years)	Number of deaths, y_i	Population size, n_i	Mortality rate per 100,000 men, $y_i/n_i \times 100,000$
1	30–34	1	17,742	5.6
2	35–39	5	16,554	30.2
3	40–44	5	16,059	31.1
4	45–49	12	13,083	91.7
5	50–54	25	10,784	231.8
6	55–59	38	9,645	394.0
7	60–64	54	10,706	504.4
8	65–69	65	9,933	654.4

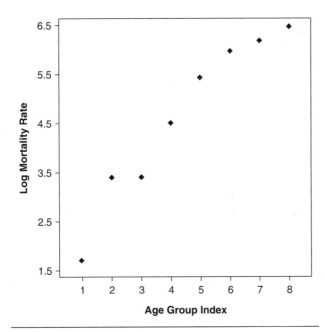

Figure 1   Log Mortality Rate (per 100,000 Men) Versus Age Index

mean structure of the model should account for this curvature. Following this reasoning, an alternative GLM might be postulated that describes $\log(\mu_i/n_i)$ as a quadratic function of i:

$$M_2: \log\mu_i = \log n_i + \alpha + \beta_1 i + \beta_2 i^2, \; y_i \sim \text{Poisson}\,(\mu_i).$$

AIC provides a tool for determining which model is more appropriate, M_1 or M_2. If the GLM's M_1 and M_2 are fit to the data using PROC GENMOD in SAS (version 9.1), the empirical log-likelihood $\log L(\hat{\theta}_1 \,|\, y)$ is produced as part of the standard output. For model M_1, we have $\theta_1 = (\alpha, \beta)'$, $d_1 = 2$, $\log L(\hat{\theta}_1 \,|\, y) = 539.0088$, and $\text{AIC}_1 = -1074.02$. For model M_2, we have $\theta_2 = (\alpha, \beta_1, \beta_2)'$, $d_2 = 3$, $\log L(\hat{\theta}_2 \,|\, y) = 544.8068$, and $\text{AIC}_2 = -1083.61$. Thus, the minimum AIC procedure favors the quadratic model, M_2.

For model M_2, the Wald test based on the null hypothesis $\beta_2 = 0$ yields a p value of .0016. Thus, the Wald test further supports the inclusion of the quadratic term. (The statistics for marginal Wald tests are also produced as standard output for PROC GENMOD in SAS.)

We include the Wald p value for the test of $\beta_2 = 0$ merely for the sake of illustration. In general, the use of AIC should not be combined with hypothesis testing, because each tool is formulated according to a different paradigm.

—*Joseph E. Cavanaugh*

See also Probability Sampling

Further Reading

Akaike, H. (1973). Information theory and an extension of the maximum likelihood principle. In B. N. Petrov and F. Csáki (Eds.), *2nd International Symposium on Information Theory* (pp. 267–281). Budapest, Hungary: Akadémia Kiadó.

Burnham, K. P., & Anderson, D. R. (2002). *Model selection and multimodel inference: A practical information-theoretic approach* (2nd ed.). New York: Springer.

Hurvich, C. M., & Tsai, C.-L. (1989). Regression and time series model selection in small samples. *Biometrika, 76,* 297–307.

McQuarrie, A. D. R., & Tsai, C.-L. (1998). *Regression and time series model selection.* River Edge, NJ: World Scientific.

Model selection criteria PDF presentations, with an emphasis on AIC and its corrected variants, by Joseph Cavanaugh: http://www.myweb.uiowa.edu/cavaaugh/ms_seminar.html

Applying Ideas on Statistics and Measurement

The following abstract is adapted from Weakliem, D. L. (2004). Introduction to the special issue on model selection sociological methods research. *Sociological Methods & Research, 33*(2), 167–187.

The model selection literature has been generally poor at reflecting the deep foundations of the **Akaike information criterion** (AIC) and at making appropriate comparisons to the Bayesian information criterion (BIC). There is a clear philosophy, a sound criterion based in information theory, and a rigorous statistical foundation for AIC. AIC can be justified as Bayesian using a "savvy" prior on models that is a function of sample size and the number of model parameters. Furthermore, BIC can be derived as a non-Bayesian result. Therefore, arguments about using AIC versus BIC for model selection cannot be made from a Bayes versus frequentist perspective. The philosophical context of what is assumed about reality, approximating models, and the intent of model-based inference should determine whether AIC or BIC is used. Various facets of such multimodel inference are presented here, particularly methods of model averaging.

Alcohol Use Inventory

The Alcohol Use Inventory (AUI; Pearson Assessments, www.pearsonassessments.com/tests/aui.htm) was designed to assess the nature of and problems associated with alcohol use. The AUI is a 228-item self-report inventory that comprises 24 scales, including 17 primary scales, 6 second-order factor skills, and 1 general alcohol involvement scale. These scales provide a basis for describing the multiple dimensions of alcohol use in individuals 16 years of age or older who drink to some extent. It describes the different ways in which individuals use alcohol, such as the benefits they derive from their alcohol use, their style of alcohol use, consequences associated with their use of alcohol, and their degree of concern and acknowledgment of alcohol use.

The AUI is appropriate for individuals who can read at a sixth-grade level or higher. Although the AUI was designed as a self-report inventory, the inventory items can be read to an individual if the respondent cannot read at that level. When taking the AUI, the respondent should be sober and preferably should have been sober for the 8 hours prior to the test. The approximate time for administration is 35–60 minutes. Administration can take longer if the inventory items need to be read to the respondent or if the respondent ponders over items. The AUI can be administered by pencil and paper or by computer. A variety of scoring options are available. The AUI can be scored through computer software, by hand, or through a mail-in scoring service.

Combinations of the previously mentioned scale scores can be used to derive scores and develop typologies and profiles that indicate ways to relate to a client and help with treatment planning. There are some exceptions, however, to the use of the AUI for alcohol-related problems and treatment programs. Even though the AUI was designed to assess the drinking styles of problem drinkers, caution is suggested in using the AUI with individuals convicted of driving under the influence (DUI). It was found that individuals convicted of DUI tended to have lower profiles and that their results should be interpreted with caution.

The AUI was also reported as not appropriate for pre- and posttreatment administration because of the historical nature of the test items. However, the AUI would be appropriate as a baseline measure for a program based on outcomes measurement.

The AUI has a sound basis in research and theory. It was normed on 1,200 individuals who had been admitted to a public in-patient alcohol treatment program. The AUI also demonstrated good reliability and presented evidence of validity. Suggested users of the AUI include psychologists, social workers, chemical dependency counselors, and physicians who work with individuals with alcohol problems. They may find the AUI a useful assessment tool for obtaining information concerning multiple dimensions of problem drinking in their clients.

—*Thomas O. Williams, Jr.*

See also Reliability Theory; Validity Theory

Further Reading

Horn, J. L., Wanberg, K. W., & Foster, F. M. (1990). *Guide to the Alcohol Use Inventory (AUI)*. Minneapolis, MN, National Computer Systems.

Impara, J. C., & Murphy, L. L. (Eds.) (1996). *Buros desk reference: Assessment of substance abuse*. Lincoln, NE: Buros Institute of Mental Measurements.

Wanberg, K. W., Horn, J. L., & Foster, F. M. (1977). A differential assessment model for alcoholism. *Journal of Studies on Alcohol, 38*, 512–543.

John Leonard Horn: http://www.usc.edu/projects/nexus/faculty/dept-ldsg/hornjohn/horn.shtml

Alternate Assessment

Alternate assessment is a generic term for a family of methods used to assess the academic performance of students with significant disabilities or limited proficiency with English. A small but meaningful number of students have disabilities or limited proficiency with English that make their participation in general state- and district-wide tests impractical, if not impossible, and likely to result in inaccurate measures of their academic achievement. According to the U.S. Department of Education (USDOE), "An alternate assessment must be aligned with the State's content standards, must yield results separately in both reading/language arts and mathematics, and must be designed and implemented in a manner that supports use of the results as an indicator of AYP (adequate yearly progress)."

Alternate assessments are an important component of each state's assessment system and, as such, are required to meet the federal regulations outlined in Title I of the Elementary and Secondary Education Act. Specifically, Title I mandates that "State assessment shall be aligned with the State's challenging content and student performance standards and provide coherent information about student attainment of such standards" (§1111[b][3][B]). In 2002, the No Child Left Behind (NCLB) legislation increased the federal government's emphasis on assessment and accountability systems. Specifically, NCLB requires annual statewide assessments for all students in Grades 3–8 and once in high school in reading and language arts, mathematics, and (by 2007) science. Moreover, NCLB requires a disaggregated annual reporting of students' performance to ensure that all groups (including students with disabilities and English language learners) are making adequate progress toward the goal of all students' being "proficient" on statewide assessments within the next 12 years.

As noted by Ken Warlick, "The purpose of an alternate assessment should reasonably match, at a minimum, the purpose of the assessment for which it is an alternate. One might ask, 'If an alternate assessment is based on totally different or alternate standards, or a totally separate curriculum, what is the alternate assessment an alternate to?'"

Alternate Assessments for Students With Disabilities

In 2003, the USDOE reinterpreted the NCLB requirements to allow up to 1% of students in states, school districts, and schools to demonstrate "proficient" performance through participation in statewide alternate assessment for students with significant cognitive disabilities. However, this interpretation also requires that states' alternate assessments be reliable and valid measures of students' achievement of the same rigorous academic content expected of all students. Many states have struggled to meet these requirements because (a) the skills and concepts in the state academic standards were deemed inappropriate or irrelevant for students with significant disabilities, resulting in alternate assessments that focus primarily on functional domains; and (b) the development of the alternate assessment was considered a special education function and therefore only nominally connected to the state's overall assessment system.

In 2005, the USDOE announced a new policy with respect to students with disabilities as part of the NCLB education reform law. According to this new policy, states may develop modified academic achievement standards and use alternate assessments based on those modified achievement standards for students with disabilities who are served under the Individuals with Disabilities Education Act. States may include proficient scores from such assessments in making AYP decisions, but those scores will be capped at 2% of the total tested population. This provision does not limit how many students may be assessed against modified achievement standards. Individualized education program teams will decide which individual students should take such an assessment.

Like the regulations regarding alternate assessments for students with the most significant cognitive disabilities, the USDOE believes this provision regarding students served under the Individuals with Disabilities Education Act will meet the needs of individual students while ensuring the goals of NCLB are achieved. The provision is intended to allow the success of a student who takes an alternate assessment based on modified achievement standards to be included in calculating school and district performance under AYP. This policy is for those students with disabilities who are expected to make significant academic progress but, because of their disability, are not likely to reach grade-level achievement in the same time frame as all other students.

In order to take advantage of the flexibility provided by the "2% rule," states are required to develop modified achievement standards and new alternate assessment instruments, provide training and support for individualized education program team members and teachers, and demonstrate that students with disabilities have access to the general curriculum and effective, research-based instruction and intervention. If states meet these requirements, the combination of alternate assessments based on modified achievement standards and alternate assessments for students with significant cognitive disabilities will allow up to 3% of students to demonstrate their proficiency without taking their state's general large-scale assessment.

Alternate Assessment for English Language Learners

Title I regulations require that English language learners be included in large-scale assessments and accountability "to the extent practicable in the language and form most likely to yield accurate and reliable information on what such students know and can do, to determine such students' mastery of skills in subjects other than English" [§1111(b)(3); 34.C.F.R. 200.4(b)(7)]. Prior to the passage of NCLB, many states and districts exempted from participation in large-scale testing those students who had not been in the United States and in an English language development or bilingual program for at least 3 years. When English language learners are exempted from a general large-scale assessment, however, both NCLB and Title VI mandate that districts and "schools gather information about the academic progress of the exempted students that is comparable to the information from the large-scale assessment."

Required Characteristics

According to the 2005 USDOE nonregulatory document *Alternate Achievement Standards for Students with the Most Significant Cognitive Disabilities*, alternate assessments must meet standards of high technical quality—validity, reliability, accessibility, objectivity, and consistency—expected of other educational tests (i.e., *The Standards for Educational and Psychological Testing*, by the American Educational Research Association, 1999). In addition, alternate assessments must have an explicit structure, guidelines for determining which students may participate, clearly defined scoring criteria and procedures, and a report format that communicates student performance in terms of academic achievement standards.

Approaches to Alternate Assessment

Currently, there is no consensus approach to alternate assessment. Three approaches are commonly used and are characterized as (a) portfolios, (b) performance tasks or events, and (c) rating scales. In a review of states' alternate assessment practices completed by the National Center of Education Outcomes (NCEO), 46% of states indicated they were using some form of portfolio assessments. Performance and portfolio assessments are appealing because of their potential to provide rich descriptions of students' real-life knowledge and skills. Researchers Browder, Fallin, Davis, and Karvonen, however, have expressed concerns with performance-based approaches and have suggested that the technical characteristics of these alternate assessments may negatively influence students' and schools' outcome scores. Initial data from Kentucky's efforts suggest that reliability of scores may be a source of challenge for states' portfolio-based alternate assessments. Challenges to the reliability of ratings were also observed by states (e.g., Vermont and Arizona) attempting to use portfolios and performance assessments as part of their general large-scale assessment systems. These difficulties resulted in states' inability to publicly report assessment results. Moreover, to demonstrate adequate alignment to state standards, performance assessments may need to include numerous tasks and work samples, resulting in an extensive and time-consuming assessment process. Browder and colleagues' review also identifies student risk factors (e.g., instability of student behavior or health status) as potential influences on students' alternate assessment results. In the case of on-demand performance tasks, fluctuations in student behavior or physical well-being could potentially result in inaccurate and invalid assessment results.

Extended Reading and Math Tasks, developed by Tindal and colleagues in 2003, represents a performance task or event approach. Based on curriculum-based measurement technology, this approach consists of a continuum of tasks that measure students' basic skills in reading and mathematics. An extensive literature on the validity and utility of curriculum-based measurement for monitoring students' academic progress provides support for this approach. By including assessment tasks at a range of skill levels, this alternate assessment strategy allows test users to individualize the assessment by administering only those tasks that are considered appropriate to the student's current skills and instructional experiences.

The most recent review of state alternate assessment practices indicates that 30% of states are using a teacher-completed rating scale for their alternate assessment for students with disabilities. A substantial body of evidence on the validity of teachers' judgments of student behavior and academic performance provides support for this approach. In addition, alternate assessments in states using rating scales (e.g., Idaho and Wisconsin) have been judged as adequately aligned to state content standards using the nationally recognized Webb approach to alignment analysis.

Underlying all the approaches to alternate assessment are (a) the collection of classroom-based evidence as indicators of knowledge and skills representative of academic content standards, (b) a scoring rubric for evaluating the knowledge and skills, and (c) a framework for summarizing the level of proficiency exhibited by the collected evidence.

The collection of evidence is a function that consistently is a teacher responsibility. In some cases, evidence is organized in a structured portfolio system that is submitted to a third party for scoring, whereas in others it is loosely organized and remains in the possession of the student's teacher, who is directly involved in scoring. The scoring of the knowledge and skills reflected in the evidence always involves at least two raters, who use an objective rubric to yield item-level and total test scores. The persons involved in the ratings vary across states; in some cases, educators within the student's school do the scoring; in some cases, scoring is completed in a centralized scoring center; and in still other cases, a combination of local and centralized scoring of evidence is involved. In all cases, significant attention is given to the interrater reliability of scores. In cases in which all the scoring is done within a student's school, states have implemented both preassessment scorer training sessions and postassessment monitoring of evidence collection and scoring practices.

The federal requirements for using the results of an alternate assessment for determining AYP resulted in the need to set proficiency standards for these assessments. Thus, states have had to conduct *standard settings* to generate cut scores for reading and mathematics ratings that correspond to a 3- or 4-level proficiency framework (e.g., minimal performance, basic performance, proficient performance, and advanced performance) commonly used for traditional achievement tests. Perhaps the most important outcome of a standard setting is not the cut scores associated with proficiency levels in each content area but the descriptors of what students who achieve the various performance levels typically know and are able to do. By examining the description of typical student performance in a given performance level, one can gain an understanding of the knowledge, skills, and abilities typically held by students in that performance level and identify things that a given student is not yet able to perform consistently. This type of information helps teachers communicate with others about a student's progress, next year's instructional goals for the student, and the status of the student relative to the state's learning standards.

One area of difficulty is the validity and utility of currently available educational assessments, including alternate assessments. For example, serious questions have been raised about using the results of statewide assessments for (a) monitoring educational performance at the levels of student, classroom, school, and system and (b) making decisions about curriculum and instruction. In the case of English language learners or students with disabilities, narrowing the enacted curriculum and de-emphasizing other important educational outcomes (e.g., self-determination, social skills, or conversational English) may be unintended consequences of the "new accountability." Additional research needs to be conducted to determine the curricular validity, instructional utility, and effects of participation in alternate assessments for students with disabilities and for English language learners.

Concluding Points

The development and use of alternate assessments are evolving in a variety of ways across the country. Recent surveys indicate that states are aligning their alternate assessment to varying degrees with the general education curriculum and content standards. The surveys also indicated that a variety of assessment approaches (i.e., direct observation, personal interview, behavioral rating scales, analysis and review of progress, and student portfolios) are being used to evaluate students with severe disabilities. As indicated by the NCEO survey and the authors' experiences, it appears that a majority of states are borrowing heavily from technology used in the development of behavior rating scales, portfolios, or performance assessments. These technologies are based on teacher observations and the collection of student work samples. These methods, if used appropriately, have the potential to offer statistically sound results. Although relatively little research has been published under the name of alternate assessment, one should not conclude that there is not a research base for alternate assessments. In fact, the conceptual and measurement foundations for alternate assessment are well developed and are based on years of research, in both education and psychology, covering performance assessment, behavioral assessment, developmental assessment, structured observations, and clinical assessment. Although these assessment methods differ somewhat, they all (a) are based on some direct or indirect observation of students, (b) are criterion referenced or domain referenced in nature, and (c) require summary judgments about the synthesis of data and the meaning of the scores or results.

This last quality, the use of judgments by knowledgeable assessors, is the empirical foundation for alternate assessment in many states. A sound research literature exists that supports the fact that teachers can be highly reliable judges of students' academic functioning.

In summary, information collected through alternate assessments is likely to be different from that collected for students who take large-scale standardized tests, but if it is well aligned with the same academic standards, performance on an alternate assessment can serve as a meaningful index of student progress toward achieving the essential skills and knowledge expected of all students.

—*Stephen N. Elliott and Andrew T. Roach*

See also Ability Tests; Text Analysis

Further Reading

Baker, E. L., & Linn, R. L. (2002). *Validity issues for accountability systems.* Los Angeles: University of California, Los Angeles, National Center for Research on Evaluation, Standards, and Student Testing.

Browder, D. M., Fallin, K., Davis, S., & Karvonen, M. (2003). Consideration of what may influence student outcomes on alternate assessment. *Education and Training in Developmental Disabilities, 38,* 255–270.

Elementary and Secondary Education Act, 20 U.S.C. 6311(b)(3)(C)(ii) (2002).

Elliott, S. N., & Fuchs, L. S. (1997). The utility of curriculum-based measurement and performance assessment as alternatives to traditional intelligence and achievement tests. *School Psychology Review, 26,* 224–233.

Individuals with Disabilities Education Act Amendments of 1997, Pub. L. No. 105–17, 111 Stat. 37 (codified as amended at 20 U.S.C. § 1400 *et seq.*).

Korpiva, R. (2000). *Ensuring accuracy in testing for English language learners.* Washington, DC: Council of Chief State School Officers.

Roach, A. T., & Elliott, S. N. (2004, April). *Alignment analysis and standard setting procedures for alternate assessments.* Paper presented at the annual meeting of the American Educational Research Association, San Diego, CA.

Tindal, G., McDonald, M., Tedesco, M., Glasgow, A., Almond, P., Crawford, L., et al. (2003). Alternate assessments in reading and math: Development and validation for students with significant disabilities. *Exceptional Children, 69,* 481–494.

U.S. Department of Education. (2005, August). *Alternate achievement standards for students with the most significant cognitive disabilities: Nonregulatory guidance.* Washington, DC: Author. Retrieved from http://www.ed.gov/policy/ elsec/guid/altguidance.pdf

ALTERNATIVE HYPOTHESIS

The term *alternative hypothesis* describes a critical element of hypothesis testing, a popular statistical procedure used by researchers in a wide array of disciplines to evaluate null hypotheses. Although hypothesis testing involves other important elements (such as the level of significance and power), the alternative hypothesis is needed so that the probability associated with the sample data can be computed. If this probability is quite low, the null hypothesis— which initially is presumed to be true—is rejected. Without an alternative hypothesis, there would be no way to compute the sample's probability of occurring, and thus the hypothesis testing procedure would not work.

The Alternative and Null Hypotheses: Similarities and Differences

Both the alternative hypothesis (symbolized as H_1 or as H_a) and the null hypothesis (symbolized as H_0) are statements as to the possible state of affairs in the population(s) of interest. These statements are similar in two other respects: In any given study, both the null and alternative hypotheses must deal with the same statistical concept. Thus, if the null hypothesis deals with the difference between two population means (μ_1 and μ_2), then the alternative hypothesis must also deal with the difference between μ_1 and μ_2. Moreover, in the usual applied situation, neither H_1 nor H_0 can be proven true on the basis of the study's data.

Although the alternative hypothesis and the null hypothesis are alike in certain ways, they differ in three important ways. First, H_1 and H_0 are "opposites" in the sense that they say different things about a study's population(s). Second, the hypothesis testing procedure is focused more on the null hypothesis than on the alternative hypothesis. The null hypothesis is always stated first, and it is H_0 that will or will not be rejected after the sample data are analyzed. Finally, it is the alternative hypothesis (and not H_0) that causes a statistical test to be either one-tailed or two-tailed.

Directional and Nondirectional Alternative Hypotheses

The directionality of the alternative hypothesis determines whether a statistical test is conducted in a one-tailed or a two-tailed manner. The alternative hypothesis is said to be directional if it stipulates that the population parameter is positioned on one particular side of the number specified in H_0. For example, the alternative hypothesis would be directional if it said that a population mean is greater than 20 while the null hypothesis said that 20 is the value of the population mean. Stated symbolically, this situation could be summarized as follows:

$$H_0: \mu = 20$$

$$H_1: \mu > 20.$$

Of course, the alternative hypothesis in this example would also be directional if it were set up to say $H_1: \mu < 20$. Regardless of which way the directional H_1 points, such alternative hypotheses lead to one-tailed tests. This is because the critical region is positioned entirely in one tail of the test statistic's sampling distribution.

The alternative hypothesis is said to be nondirectional if it stipulates that the population parameter is positioned on either side of the number specified in H_0. For example, the alternative hypothesis would be nondirectional if it says that a population correlation, ρ, has either a positive or negative value while the null hypothesis says that ρ is equal to zero. Stated symbolically, this situation could be summarized as follows:

$$H_0: \rho = 0$$

$$H_1: \rho \neq 0$$

Nondirectional alternative hypotheses lead to two-tailed tests. This is because the critical region is positioned in both tails of the test statistic's sampling distribution.

It should be noted that two-tailed tests require a larger difference between sample statistics and the hypothesized population parameter in order for the null hypothesis to be rejected. This is the case because the threshold for the critical region will be positioned closer to the center of the test statistic's sampling distribution if that critical region is located entirely in one tail. Because the edges of the critical region are located farther away from the middle of the sampling distribution, some people consider nondirectional alternative hypotheses to be more "conservative" than directional ones.

When H_1 Should Be Specified

For the hypothesis testing procedure to operate properly, the alternative hypothesis must be specified prior to the time any sample data are collected and examined. Unfortunately, some applied researchers violate this rule by switching to a one-tailed test after finding out that they are unable to reject H_0 with H_1 set up in a nondirectional fashion. Such a switch is considered to be a breach of statistical ethics, for the computed probability that is used to decide whether or not H_0 should be rejected is not accurate if H_1 is changed in midstream. (It would be just as "illegal," of course, for a researcher to change H_0 so as to get a desirable result—usually a reject decision—after initially analyzing the data and finding out that a fail-to-reject decision is in the offing.)

—*Dong-Ho Park*

See also Null Hypothesis Significance Testing; Type I Error

Further Reading

Gold, M. S., Byars, J. A., & Frost-Pineda, K. (2004). Occupational exposure and addictions for physicians: Case

studies and theoretical implications. *Psychiatric Clinics of North America, 27*(4), 745–753.

Shanteau, J. (2001). *What does it mean when experts disagree?* Mahwah, NJ: Erlbaum.

Applying Ideas on Statistics and Measurement

The following abstract is adapted from Romero, D. W. (2003). Divisive primaries and the House district vote: A pooled analysis. *American Politics Research, 31*(2), 178–190.

The **alternative hypothesis** in a research study is the one that presents the "foil" or the "educated guess" the researcher makes regarding the exact nature of an absence of a relationship between variables. In this example, the authors point out how the political concept of the divisive primary has fluctuated as investigators have pursued a variety of theoretical and methodological debates. Although most recent studies find that divisive primaries harm general election outcomes, some claim that this effect is spurious, an artifact of uncontrolled electoral prospects phenomena. David Romero argues that this claim is debatable because it rests on questionable conceptual and model constructs and evidence inconsistent with an investigation that controls for the phenomena central to the spurious effect claim. He shows that null and alternative hypothesis findings turn on an unfeatured design characteristic, pooling election years.

AMERICAN DOCTORAL DISSERTATIONS

American Doctoral Dissertations (ADD) is an annual hardcover publication by University Microfilms International (UMI; Ann Arbor, Michigan) for the Association of Research Libraries. As a reference tool, the ADD provides citations to nearly all dissertations written in a given academic year within the United States. In addition to an author index, it provides full bibliographic citations for each dissertation, grouped by subject and by institution. Citations include title of the dissertation, name of the author, degree awarded, awarding institution, year of completion, and UMI order number.

Systematic listing of doctoral dissertations in the United States was begun by the Library of Congress in 1912 in an annual publication titled *List of American Doctoral Dissertations Printed*, which was discontinued in 1938. *Doctoral Dissertations Accepted by American Universities* (1933/34–1955/56) and the *Index to American Doctoral Dissertations* (1955/56–1963/64) were two subsequent annual publications generated by the H. W. Wilson Company. The ADD was introduced in 1934 by Xerox University Microfilms.

The ADD is compiled from the ProQuest Information and Learning database as well as information obtained directly from American universities. The ADD differs from *Dissertation Abstracts International* (DAI) in that it does not include abstracts for each dissertation and does not cover international dissertations. However, the ADD is more comprehensive than the DAI because the ADD includes titles of unpublished dissertations from the ProQuest database.

Currently, the most enhanced version of the ADD and the DAI is ProQuest Digital Dissertations, which is a database of more than 2 million entries for doctoral dissertations and master's theses submitted from more than 1,000 universities and covering the years 1861 to date. ProQuest Digital Dissertations provides the citation, abstract, and first 24 pages of dissertations submitted to UMI within the preceding 2 years. Full versions of these manuscripts and older dissertations may be obtained from UMI in a variety of formats for a fee. Many academic institutions in the United States provide free access to this database for their faculty, staff, and students.

—*Marjan Ghahramanlou-Holloway*

See also American Psychological Association; Association for Psychological Science

Further Reading

Glatthorn, A. A. (1998). *Writing the winning dissertation: A step-by-step guide.* Thousand Oaks, CA: Corwin Press.

UMI Dissertation Services. (1997). *Publishing your dissertation: How to prepare your manuscript for publication.* Ann Arbor, MI: UMI.

Kirschenbaum, M. G. Electronic theses and dissertations in the humanities: A directory of online references and resources: http://etext.virginia.edu/ETD/

UMI ProQuest Digital Dissertations: http://wwwlib.umi.com/dissertations/

AMERICAN PSYCHOLOGICAL ASSOCIATION

The American Psychological Association (APA) is the world's largest association of psychologists and is the largest scientific and professional association that represents psychology in the United States. The membership of the APA includes more than 150,000 researchers, educators, clinicians, consultants, and students. The APA's organizational structure includes 55 divisions representing various subfields in psychology and 60 state, provincial, and territorial psychological associations. The association maintains its headquarters in Washington, DC.

Mission

The mission of the APA is to advance psychology as a science and profession and as a means of promoting health, education, and human welfare through the application of science to practice and policy. To achieve this goal, the APA (a) promotes research in psychology and the improvement of research methods and conditions, (b) encourages and advocates for psychology in all its branches and forums, (c) establishes the highest standards of professional conduct and ethics for members of the APA, (d) promotes ongoing improvement of the qualifications and usefulness of psychologists through education and recognition of achievement, and (e) promotes the dissemination of scientific knowledge through meetings, professional contacts, reports, papers, discussions, and publications.

Organizational Structure

The APA governance structure employs a complex system of checks and balances that can be difficult to comprehend. The APA is chartered in the District of Columbia, and because the charter trumps the association's bylaws, the charter limits what the organization can do in the public policy and advocacy realm to promoting psychology in the public interest. A constitution and bylaws were ratified by the membership more than 50 years ago and remain virtually unchanged today. The primary structural components of the APA include the council of representatives, the board of directors, officers, standing boards and committees, and the central office staff, including a chief executive officer. The members of the APA exercise their power through direct vote and through the election of members to serve on the council of representatives. The primary constituencies from which the representatives are elected are the divisions, which are an integral part of the association, and the state and provincial psychological associations, which are affiliates. The APA divisions include a Division of Evaluation, Measurement and Statistics (Division 5). Much of the work of the Association is done on a volunteer basis by the members of the boards, committees, and ad hoc task forces and working groups. The committees carry out a wide variety of tasks, as indicated by some of their titles: ethics, psychological tests and assessments, membership, and accreditation, to name a few.

The chief executive officer is responsible for the management and staffing of the central office and for running the business aspects of the APA. With nearly 500 employees, the central office provides staff support for all boards and committees; runs one of the largest scientific publishing houses in the world; invests in stocks; manages real estate; and interacts with private, state, and federal agencies and organizations. Member dues represent only 16% of the revenues needed to run the APA.

—*Thomas Kubiszyn*

See also Association for Psychological Science

Further Reading

APA Web site: www.apa.org

Applying Ideas on Statistics and Measurement

The following abstract is adapted from Finch, S., Thomason, N., and Cumming, G. (2002). Past and future American Psychological Association guidelines for statistical practice. *Theory & Psychology, 12*(6), 825–853.

The publication guidelines of the **American Psychological Association** (APA) have been the discipline's de facto standards since 1929, and this article documents their advice for authors about statistical practice. Although the advice has been extended with each revision of the guidelines, it has largely focused on null hypothesis significance testing (NHST) to the exclusion of other statistical methods. In parallel, Sue Finch and her colleagues review more than 40 years of critiques of NHST in psychology. Until now, the critiques have had little impact on the APA guidelines. The guidelines are influential in broadly shaping statistical practice although in some cases, recommended reporting practices are not closely followed. The guidelines have an important role to play in reform of statistical practice in psychology. Following the report of the APA's Task Force on Statistical Inference, we propose that future revisions of the guidelines reflect a broader philosophy of analysis and inference, provide detailed statistical requirements for reporting research, and directly address concerns about NHST. In addition, the APA needs to develop ways to ensure that its editors succeed in their leadership role in achieving essential reform.

AMERICAN PSYCHOLOGICAL SOCIETY

See ASSOCIATION FOR PSYCHOLOGICAL SCIENCE

AMERICAN STATISTICAL ASSOCIATION

The American Statistical Association (ASA) is a nonprofit organization devoted to the promotion of statistical practice, applications, and research. Its mission includes improving statistical education, fostering excellence in the statistics profession, and enhancing human welfare. Established in 1839, the ASA currently has 19,000 members in the United States, Canada, and worldwide, and more than 75 chapters and 20 specialized sections. ASA members in government, academia, and the private sector work in diverse areas, including environmental risk assessment, medicine, computing, and social programs.

Formation

The ASA was founded on a commitment to statistical science in service to the public interest, particularly in areas related to public health. The inaugural meeting was held in Boston, Massachusetts, with five founding members: William Cogswell (teacher and genealogist), Richard Fletcher (lawyer and U.S. congressman), John Dix Fisher (physician), Oliver Peabody (lawyer, clergyman, and editor), and Lemuel Shattuck (statistician, genealogist, and publisher). By 1841, the ASA had more than 100 members, primarily in the Boston area; its early membership included Andrew Carnegie, Alexander Graham Bell, and Florence Nightingale. By 1898, the ASA was recognized as a national organization, and membership swelled to more than 500. It is now the largest professional statistical association in the world.

Publications

The ASA publishes refereed journals, books, and newsletters devoted to issues relevant to statistical research and practice. The *Journal of the American Statistical Association* (founded in 1888 as *Publications of the American Statistical Association*) is one of the leading journals in the statistical sciences. *Biometrics Bulletin* was introduced in 1945 to promote the use of statistics in the biological sciences. *Technometrics*, with a focus on statistics applications in the physical, chemical, and engineering sciences, was launched in 1959. In 1976, with the American Educational Research Association, the ASA launched the *Journal of Educational & Behavioral Statistics*. Other ASA publications include the *Journal of Business & Economic Statistics* (1983), the *Journal of Computational & Graphical Statistics* (1992), the *Journal of Agricultural, Biological & Environmental Statistics* (1996), and the *Journal of Statistical Education* (1999). An annual *Current Index for Statistics* was introduced in 1975.

Annual Meetings

The ASA hosts annual meetings, symposia, and research conferences. Joint Statistical Meetings are held in conjunction with International Biometric Society, the Institute of Mathematical Statistics, and the Statistical Society of Canada and attract more than 5,000 delegates. Activities of the Joint Statistical Meetings include oral presentations, panel sessions, poster presentations, career placement services, committee meetings, and networking opportunities.

Awards and Educational Programs

The ASA offers research grant programs (cosponsored by the National Science Foundation) and numerous scholarships and awards, including the Statistics in Chemistry Award, the Outstanding Statistical Application Award, and the Gertrude Cox Scholarship, awarded annually to encourage women to enter the statistics professions. Through the Center for Statistics Education, the ASA offers workshops, short courses, and internships, including support for graduate and professional education for teachers of kindergarten through Grade 12.

—Lisa M. Given

See also American Psychological Association; Association for Psychological Science; *Journal of the American Statistical Association*

Further Reading

American Statistical Association Web site: www.amstat.org

AMERICANS WITH DISABILITIES ACT

Patterned largely after Section 504 of the Rehabilitation Act, the Americans with Disabilities Act

(ADA; 42 U.S.C. §§ 12101 et seq.) protects the disabled by imposing far-reaching obligations on private-sector employers, public services and accommodations, and transportation. The ADA provides a comprehensive federal mandate to eliminate discrimination against people with disabilities and provides "clear, strong, consistent and enforceable standards" (§ 12101(b)(2)) for doing so. The ADA's broad definition of a disability is comparable to the one in Section 504: "(a) a physical or mental impairment that substantially limits one or more of the major life activities; (b) a record of such an impairment; or (c) being regarded as having such an impairment (§ 12102(2)). Further, like Section 504, "[M]ajor life activities" include caring for oneself, hearing, walking, speaking, seeing, breathing, and learning. As with Section 504, the ADA does not require one to have a certificate from a doctor or a psychologist in order to be covered.

The ADA specifically excludes a variety of individuals, most notably those who use illegal drugs (§ 12210). The ADA also specifically excludes transvestites (§ 12208); homosexuals and bisexuals (§ 12211(a)); transsexuals, pedophiles, exhibitionists, voyeurs, and those with sexual behavior disorders (§ 12211(b)); and those with conditions such as psychoactive substance use disorders stemming from current illegal use of drugs (§ 12211(c)). However, the ADA amends Section 504 in that individuals who have successfully completed drug treatment or have otherwise been rehabilitated and are no longer engaged in illegal drug use and who have been "erroneously" regarded as being drug users are covered if they are no longer using illegal drugs (§ 12110). The ADA permits drug testing by employers to ensure that workers are in compliance with the Drug-Free Workplace Act of 1988 (41 U.S.C. Sec. 701). Although it permits employers to prohibit the use of illegal drugs or alcohol in the workplace, the ADA is less clear about the status of alcoholics; it appears that the protections afforded rehabilitated drug users extend to recovering alcoholics.

The ADA addresses three major areas: First, it addresses employment in the private sector and is directly applicable to private schools and colleges. Second, it addresses state and local governments both as employers and as providers of public services, including transportation, and part of the law applies to public educational institutions. Insofar as the reasonable accommodations requirements in these provisions imply academic program accommodations, qualified students with disabilities can participate in educational institutions at all levels. Third, it deals with private sector public accommodations in buildings and transportation services, and so it may apply to schools and colleges that provide public accommodations. Under its miscellaneous provisions, the ADA stipulates that it cannot be construed as applying a lesser standard than that under Section 504 and its regulations.

—Charles J. Russo

Further Reading

Americans with Disabilities Act of 1990, 42 U.S.C. §§ 12101 et seq.

Drug-Free Workplace Act of 1988, 41 U.S.C. Sec. 701 et seq.

Miles, A. S., Russo, C. J., & Gordon, W. M. (1991). The reasonable accommodations provisions of the Americans with Disabilities Act. *Education Law Reporter, 69*(1), 1–8.

Osborne, A. G., & Russo, C. J. (2006). *Special education and the law: A guide for practitioners* (2nd ed.). Thousand Oaks, CA: Corwin Press.

Council for Exceptional Children: http://www.cec.sped.org

U.S. Department of Education (updates on regulations, articles, and other general information on the Individuals with Disabilities Education Act and special education): http://www.ed.gov/offices/OSERS/IDEA/

U.S. Department of Education, (information from the federal Office of Special Education Programs): http://www.ed.gov/about/offices/list/oscrs/osep/index.html?src=mr

Applying Ideas on Statistics and Measurement

The following abstract is adapted from Harrison, T. C. (2002). Has the Americans With Disabilities Act made a difference? A policy analysis of quality of life in the post-Americans With Disabilities Act era. *Policy, Politics, & Nursing Practice, 3*(4), 333–347.

A major challenge in any policy program is to evaluate its effectiveness. One such policy, the

Americans with Disabilities Act (ADA), was signed more than 10 years ago. Policymakers hoped to enable persons with disabilities to combat social barriers such as unemployment by preventing discrimination. It has been the most comprehensive piece of legislation for persons with disabilities in the United States, but the effects of the ADA have been debatable. This article evaluates the effect of the ADA on quality of life for persons with disabilities and offers suggestions for health care policy.

ANALYSIS OF COVARIANCE (ANCOVA)

The analysis of covariance (ANCOVA) can be used to test the null hypothesis of the equality of two or more population means. Alternatively, it can be used in the construction of confidence intervals on differences between means. Although the analysis of variance (ANOVA) is also used for these purposes, ANCOVA has two major advantages over ANOVA in randomized group experiments. First, it generally has higher power. Second, it reduces bias associated with chance differences between groups that exist before the experiment is carried out. These advantages are realized because measurements on one or more nuisance variables are incorporated into the analysis in such a way that (a) the ANCOVA error term is usually smaller (often dramatically so) than the corresponding ANOVA error term and (b) the dependent variable means are adjusted to partially account for chance pretreatment differences between the groups. Hence, nuisance variables play a role in both inferential and descriptive aspects of ANCOVA.

A nuisance variable is defined as a variable that is known to be related to the dependent variable but is of no experimental interest. Suppose, for example, that there is interest in comparing two methods of training workers to perform complex repairs on electronic components; the dependent variable (Y) measures repair proficiency. Two groups are formed using random assignment, and reading skill measurements (X) are obtained. Each group is then exposed to one of two methods of training. It is known that reading skill is related to performance on the dependent variable, but this relationship is not the focus of the study. Rather, the major focus is whether the two training methods have a differential effect. If some of the within-group variation on the dependent variable is related to reading skill, it is of interest to control for this nuisance variable because it contributes to the error (i.e., within-group) variance. Power is increased whenever a source of nuisance variation is removed from the error variance estimate. This can be accomplished using ANCOVA.

Nuisance variables are usually called *covariates* in the context of ANCOVA. Covariates may be variables that measure constructs that differ from the construct measured by the dependent variable, or they may measure the same construct as the dependent variable does (as in the case of a multiple group pretest-posttest design). In either case, they should be measured before the treatments are applied.

Although ANCOVA is used with several types of research design, it (or the equivalent regression model) is generally most successful with randomized experiments and regression-discontinuity quasi-experiments. Although ANCOVA continues to be widely used in the analysis of observational studies, these designs present special problems that are frequently better handled using other approaches. A strong case can be made for analyzing observational studies using propensity score methods instead of or in combination with modified versions of ANCOVA.

Comparison of ANOVA and ANCOVA

The data presented in Table 1 were collected in a randomized groups pretest-posttest experiment that contained three groups ($n_1 = 10$, $n_2 = 12$, $n_3 = 12$). The purpose of the experiment was to evaluate whether there are differential effects of three training conditions (designated I, II, and III in Table 1) applied to children diagnosed with Down syndrome. Pretest and posttest scores were obtained on a measure known as the Doman-Delacato Profile. The pretest measure was used as the covariate (X), and the posttest was used as the dependent variable (Y). Key differences between

Table 1 Comparison of ANOVA and ANCOVA Summary Tables and Descriptive Statistics Example Data

Treatment

I		II		III	
X	*Y*	*X*	*Y*	*X*	*Y*
35	39.5	52	60	35	39.5
32	35	12	12	48	54
15	18	48	56	44	52
46	54	48	50	18	18
38	42.5	13	15	33.5	36.5
6	10.5	39.5	42	23	23
38	38	17	17	29	33
16	17	38	39.5	9	9
29	32	40	42	32	33
32	35	50	60	37	41
		29	33	32	33

ANOVA summary						ANCOVA summary				
Source	SS	df	MS	F		Source	SS	df	MS	F
Among	253.16	2	126.6	.56		Adj. among	4.64	2	2.32	.47
Within	6536.34	29	225.4			Resid. within	137.25	28	4.90	
Total	6789.50	31				Resid. total	141.89	30		

Sample means

$$\overline{Y}_1 = 32.15$$
$$\overline{Y}_2 = 38.77$$
$$\overline{Y}_3 = 33.82$$

Sample adjusted means

$$\overline{Y}_{1\ adj.} = 35.6$$
$$\overline{Y}_{2\ adj.} = 34.8$$
$$\overline{Y}_{3\ adj.} = 34.7$$

Notes: I, II, and III represent the training conditions tested; X = pretest scores on Doman-Delacato Profile (covariate); Y = posttest scores on Doman-Delacato Profile (dependent variable); SS = sum of squares; df = degree of freedom; MS = mean square; F = Fisher's F ratio; adj. = adjusted; Resid. = residual.

ANOVA and ANCOVA applied to these data are described below.

One-Factor ANOVA

Essential descriptive statistics relevant to ANOVA include the sample means on the dependent variable. These means are $\overline{Y}_1 = 32.15$, $\overline{Y}_2 = 38.77$, and $\overline{Y}_3 = 33.82$. An informal inspection of these means (without the aid of inferential methods) might lead one to conclude that the second treatment is the most effective. After all, the mean for this group is almost seven points higher than is the mean for the first group. But, if one were to also inspect the means for the three groups on the pretest variable X, the picture would not seem so clear. These means are $\overline{X}_1 = 28.70$, $\overline{X}_2 = 35.14$, $\overline{X}_3 = 30.95$. Notice that the rank order of the three means on X is the same as the order of the three means on Y. Further, the sizes of the mean differences are about the same on both X and Y. The interpretation of the descriptive results on the dependent variable is clouded by the annoyingly large differences between the means on the pretest variable. The pattern of the pretest differences strongly suggests that the posttest results are simply a reflection of differences that existed before the treatments were carried out. In this example, random assignment resulted in groups that have substantial pretest differences. Because the differences do not appear to be trivial, it is likely that the researcher would like to know the answer to the following question: "What would the means on the posttest have been if the pretest means had been exactly equal?" ANCOVA provides an answer to this question.

One-Factor ANCOVA

Just as the ANOVA F test applies to the means associated with the different treatment conditions, the ANCOVA F test applies to the "adjusted" treatment means. The adjusted means are estimates of what the means on Y would be if all the group means on X were equal to the grand covariate mean. The grand covariate mean is simply the average X score obtained by summing all X scores in the whole experiment and dividing by the total number of X scores. (It is sometimes denoted as $\bar{X}\ldots$) In the case of the example data, $\bar{X}.. = 31.69$. Hence, ANCOVA attempts to answer the following question: "What would the means on Y have been if each group had a mean score on X of 31.69?" ANCOVA provides the following adjusted mean estimates:

$$\bar{Y}_{1adj} = 35.56, \bar{Y}_{2adj} = 34.84, \text{ and } \bar{Y}_{3adj} = 34.65.$$

A comparison of the unadjusted means with the adjusted means indicates that the adjustment process has substantially changed the means. The adjusted means remove most of the descriptive ambiguity caused by the pretest differences.

Adjustment to the means in this example is substantial, but this is not always the case. The amount of adjustment depends on the size of the mean differences on the covariate and the degree of relationship between the covariate and the dependent variable. There will be no adjustment whatsoever if either (a) there are no differences among the covariate means or (b) there is no linear relationship between the covariate and the dependent variable. Large differences among covariate means are likely in randomized experiments only if the sample sizes are small (as in the example). Consequently, there is likely to be very little (if any) adjustment of means in large clinical trials or other large randomized groups experiments. But this does not mean that there is no reason to use ANCOVA in place of ANOVA with large experiments. Indeed, the major justification for using ANCOVA rather than ANOVA in randomized experiments is not mean adjustment.

The major reason to prefer ANCOVA over ANOVA is that it is likely to provide a smaller error term. This is important with respect to both the power of hypothesis tests and the width of confidence intervals. These advantages will be large when the within-group linear relationship between X and Y is substantial.

Consider the example data. The error mean square associated with ANOVA on Y is 225, whereas the error mean square associated with ANCOVA is only 4.9. If the power for detecting the maximum difference between the three population means is set at 5 points, the power estimate for ANOVA is only .09; the corresponding power estimate for ANCOVA is more than .99. These data can also be analyzed using other methods of analysis (including the split-plot ANOVA and the one-factor ANOVA applied to change scores), but ANCOVA is usually the method of choice because it generally has higher power. The power advantage of ANCOVA in this experiment is rather dramatic because the pretest (covariate) is very highly correlated with the posttest (dependent variable). Pretests are almost always excellent covariates. There is no requirement, however, that the covariate be a pretest measure. In most randomized groups designs, some easily measured variable that is correlated with but different from the dependent variable is used as the covariate. Sometimes scores on multiple nuisance variables are available. In this case, all nuisance variables can be employed simultaneously as covariates in what is known as a multiple analysis of covariance.

Assumptions and Design Issues

Several assumptions and design aspects are at the foundation of ANCOVA. Strong inferences from

ANCOVA are most easily justified when (a) random assignment is used to form the comparison groups, (b) the covariate(s) is measured before treatments are applied, (c) the individual regression slopes within the groups are homogeneous, (d) the relationship between the covariate and the dependent variable is linear, and (e) the conventional assumptions associated with parametric tests (i.e., independence of errors, homogeneous error distributions, and normally distributed error distributions) are approximately met.

The first two items in this list are easily confirmed design issues. The third issue (homogeneity of regression slopes assumption) should be evaluated whenever ANCOVA is applied. The homogeneity of slopes assumption states that the slope of Y on X is the same within each individual treatment population. When the individual slopes are not the same, both the descriptive and the inferential aspects of the analysis are suspect. If the slopes are not the same, the size of the treatment effect is a function of the value of the covariate, but the results of ANCOVA will not acknowledge this important fact.

When any of the design aspects or assumptions are incompatible with the nature of the study, remedial solutions are available. These include modifications of ANCOVA and alternative methods of analysis that either correct for the problems or are less sensitive to them.

—*Bradley E. Huitema*

See also Analysis of Variance (ANOVA)

Further Reading

Huitema, B. E. (in preparation). *The analysis of covariance and alternatives: Statistical methods for experiments, quasi-experiments, and observational studies* (2nd ed.). Hoboken, NJ: Wiley.

Maxwell, S. E., & Delaney, H. D. (2004). *Designing experiments and analyzing data: A model comparison perspective* (2nd ed.). Mahwah, NJ: Erlbaum.

McKean, J. W., & Vidmar, T. J. (1994). A comparison of two rank-based methods for the analysis of linear models. *American Statistician, 48,* 220–229.

Rubin, D. B. (1997). Estimating causal effects from large data sets using propensity scores. *Annals of Internal Medicine, 127,* 757–763.

Visual Statistics with Multimedia, an online tutorial that covers ANCOVA: http://pages.infinit.net/rlevesqu/spss.htm

Web-based software that performs both traditional ANCOVA and a more recently developed, robust ANCOVA (based on the work of McKean & Vidmar, 1994): www.stat.wmich.edu/slab/RGLM/. Click the Online Resources button under the Site Guide, and then click on RGLM.

ANALYSIS OF VARIANCE (ANOVA)

Analysis of variance (ANOVA) was developed by Ronald A. Fisher in the 1930s (although the name "analysis of variance" came later from John W. Tukey). ANOVA refers to a family of statistical procedures that use the F test to test the overall fit of a linear model to the observed data. Although typically associated with the analysis of experimental research designs in which categorical independent variables are manipulated to see the effect (if any) on a continuous dependent variable, these designs are merely special cases of a general linear model in which the categorical independent variables are expressed as dummy variables. As such, ANOVA embodies a family of tests that are special cases of linear regression in which the linear model is defined in terms of group means. The resulting F test is, therefore, an overall test of whether group means differ across levels of the categorical independent variable or variables.

Different Types of ANOVA

ANOVA can be applied to a variety of research designs and takes specific names that reflect the design to which it has been applied. The computational details of the analysis become more complex with the design, but the essence of the test remains the same. The first distinction that is made is in the number of independent variables in the research design. If there is simply one independent variable, then the ANOVA is called a one-way ANOVA. If two independent variables have been manipulated in the research, then a two-way ANOVA can be used to analyze the data; likewise if three independent variables have been manipulated, a three-way ANOVA is appropriate. The logic of the test extends to any number of independent variables; however, for ease of interpretation, researchers rarely go beyond a three-way ANOVA.

The second distinction that needs to be made is whether data in different conditions are independent or related. If data representing different levels of an independent variable are independent (i.e., collected from different entities), then an independent ANOVA can be used (also known as a between-groups ANOVA). If two independent variables have been used and all levels of all variables contain data from different entities, then a two-way independent ANOVA could be employed, and so on. When data are related—for example, when different entities have provided data for all levels of an independent variable or all levels of several independent variables—then a repeated measures ANOVA (also known as within-subjects ANOVA) can be employed. As with independent designs, it is possible to have one-way, two-way, three-way, n-way repeated measures ANOVAs. A final type of ANOVA is used when a mixture of independent and related data have been collected. These mixed designs require at least two independent variables, one of which has been manipulated using different entities (and so data are independent) and the other of which has been manipulated using the same entities (data are related). In these situations, a mixed ANOVA is used. It is possible to combine different numbers of independent variables measured using different entities or the same entities to come up with three-way, four-way, or n-way mixed ANOVAs. ANOVAs involving more than one independent variable are known as factorial ANOVAs.

Similarities Among Different ANOVAs

All the ANOVAs above have some common features. All of them produce F tests that are the ratio of the variance explained or accounted for by a particular effect compared to the variance that cannot be explained by that effect (i.e., error variance). The computational details of a simple ANOVA are described in the entry titled "One-Way Analysis of Variance." In experimental scenarios, the F test can be thought of as the ratio of the experimental effect to the individual differences in performance. The observed value of F is compared with critical values of F from a special distribution known as the F distribution, which represents the values of F that can be expected at certain levels of probability. If the observed value exceeds the critical value for a small probability (typically 0.05), we tend to infer that the model is a significant fit of the observed data or, in the case of experiments, that the experimental manipulation has had a significant effect on performance.

Differences Among ANOVAs

The main difference among ANOVAs is the effects that they produce. In an ANOVA with one independent variable, a single value of F is produced that tests the effect of that variable. In factorial ANOVAs, multiple Fs are produced: one for each effect and one for every combination of effects. The entry "One-Way Analysis of Variance" describes an example about the effect of mood induction on the number of items people would generate when asked to list as many items as they could that needed checking before the people left on holiday. This experiment involved groups reflecting different levels of the independent variable: negative mood, positive mood, and no mood induction. In the study proper, a second independent variable related to whether participants were instructed to generate as many items as they could or to generate items until they felt like stopping. This second independent variable could be called the *stop rule* and had two levels: "as many as can" and "feel like stopping." This experiment requires a factorial ANOVA, and the result would be an F ratio for the effect of mood (this is known as a *main effect*), a different F ratio for the main effect of the stop rule, and a third F ratio representing the combined effect of mood and the stop rule, known as the mood-by-stop-rule interaction.

Regardless of whether the factorial ANOVA is independent, repeated measures, or mixed design, the result is the same: F associated with each main effect, and Fs associated with each interaction term. Sticking with the example above, if we added a third variable, such as gender, into the design, we would end up with three main effects: (a) mood, (b) stop rule, and (c) gender.

Three interaction terms involving two variables (known as two-way interactions) would result in the following main effects:

1. Mood × Stop rule

2. Mood × Gender

3. Stop rule × Gender

One interaction of all three variables (known as a three-way interaction) would result in one main effect:

Mood × Stop rule × Gender

Each of these effects would have an associated F ratio that tested whether the effect had an influence on the group means. The derivation of these Fs is affected by whether the design is repeated measures, independent, or mixed, but the interpretation of these Fs is unaffected by the design.

Follow-Up Tests

Unless a main effect represents a difference between two groups (such as the main effect of the stop rule, above), the F tells us only that the groups' means differ in some way (across one or more variables, depending on whether it is a main effect or an interaction). Main effects are usually followed up either with planned comparisons, which compare specific sets of means, or with post hoc tests, which compare all combinations of pairs of means (see, for example, the entries on Bonferroni Test and Newman-Keuls Test). In factorial designs, the interactions are typically more interesting than the main effects. Interactions are usually broken down using simple effects analysis or specific contrasts designed by the researcher.

ANOVA as a General Linear Model

When ANOVA is used to analyze data from groups, it is a special case of a linear model. Specifically, the linear model can be expressed in terms of dummy variables. Any categorical variable can be expressed as a series of 0s and 1s; there will always be one less variable than there are groups, and each variable compares each group against a base category (e.g., a control group). The example from the entry "One-Way Analysis of Variance," described above (ignoring the second independent variable of the stop rule, to keep things simple), can provide an illustration. Remember that this experiment involved groups reflecting different levels of the independent variable: negative mood, positive mood, and no mood induction. This scenario can be represented by a standard regression equation:

$$\text{Items Generated}_i = b_0 + b_1\text{Negative Mood}_i + b_2\text{Positive Mood}_i + \varepsilon_i$$

in which Negative Mood is a binary variable coded 1 for people undergoing a negative mood induction and 0 for all other groups, and Positive Mood is a binary variable coded 1 for the positive mood induction group and 0 for all other groups. The control group (no mood induction) is coded zero for both variables. It turns out that b_0 represents the mean of the control group (i.e., the mean number of items generated when no mood induction is performed); b_1 is the difference between the mean number of items generated when a negative mood induction is done and the mean number of items generated when no mood induction is done; and b_2 is the difference between the mean number of items generated when a positive mood induction is done and the mean number of items generated when no mood induction is done. More complex designs such as factorial ANOVA can be conceptualized in a similar way.

Assumptions

For the F ratio to be accurate, the following assumptions must be met: (a) observations should be statistically independent, (b) data should be randomly sampled from the population of interest and measured at an interval level, (c) the outcome variable should be sampled from a normal distribution, and (d) there must be homogeneity of variance.

Differences With Repeated Measures

When data are related (i.e., when the independent variable has been manipulated using the same entities), the basic logic described above still holds true. The resulting *F* can be interpreted in the same way, although the partitioning of variance differs somewhat. However, when a repeated measures design is used, the assumption of independence is violated, giving rise to an additional assumption of *sphericity*. This assumption requires that the variances of difference scores between conditions be roughly equal. When this assumption is not met, the degrees of freedom associated with the *F* value must be corrected using one of two estimates of sphericity: the Greenhouse-Geisser estimate or the Huynh-Feldt estimate.

—*Andy P. Field*

See also Analysis of Covariance (ANCOVA); Bonferroni Test; Dependent Variable; Factorial Design; Fisher, Ronald Aylmer; Homogeneity of Variance; Independent Variable; Linear Regression; Newman-Keuls Test; One-Way Analysis of Variance; Tukey-Kramer Procedure; Variance

Further Reading

Cohen, J. (1968). Multiple regression as a general data-analytic system. *Psychological Bulletin, 70*(6), 426–443.

Davey, G. C. L., Startup, H. M., Zara, A., MacDonald, C. B., & Field, A. P. (2003). Perseveration of checking thoughts and mood-as-input hypothesis. *Journal of Behavior Therapy & Experimental Psychiatry, 34,* 141–160.

Field, A. P. (2005). *Discovering statistics using SPSS* (2nd ed.). London: Sage.

Howell, D. C. (2002). *Statistical methods for psychology* (5th ed.). Belmont, CA: Duxbury.

Applying Ideas on Statistics and Measurement

The following abstract is adapted from Castaiieda, M. B., Levin, J. R., & Dunham, R. B. (1993). Using planned comparisons in management research: A case for the Bonferroni procedure. *Journal of Management, 19*(3), 707–724.

This article describes the Bonferroni multiple-comparison procedure (used in conjunction with the robust *F* test) and makes a case for researchers' more frequent and appropriate use of it. The procedure is discussed as a test that facilitates investigation of precise and powerful a priori multiple comparisons. Characteristics of the Bonferroni procedure are described in relation to the more familiar Scheffe post hoc multiple-comparison method, and a step-by-step guide for comparing and choosing between the two is provided. The Bonferroni procedure is discussed in detail in the context of one-factor **analysis of variance (ANOVA)** designs. Application of the technique is then considered in the context of factorial designs, analyses of covariance, univariate repeated measures analyses, multivariate ANOVAs, and recent sequential hypothesis-testing extensions.

ANTHROPOMETRY

Anthropometry is the measurement of the human body. It is distinct from osteometry, which is the measurement of skeletal material. Anthropometry is sometimes subdivided into craniofacial anthropometry (measurement of the head and face) and somatometry (measurement of the body). Two-dimensional measurement of the head from x-ray cephalograms is known in the United States as cephalometry. In Europe, on the other hand, cephalometry refers to measurement of the head and face, while measurement of x-ray tracings is known as roentgen-cephalometry.

Canons, or simple rules of proportionality based on multiples of specific body parts, were used by classical Greek, Roman, and Renaissance artists to describe the shape of the human body and were based on aesthetic ideals rather than measurement. Anthropometry, which uses actual body measurements, did not develop until 1654, when a German anatomist at the University of Padua, Johann Sigismund Elsholtz, developed a standardized measuring tool for his doctoral dissertation on the symmetry of the human body. He created a vertical rod divided into six equal parts, which he called *pedis* (feet). He then subdivided each foot into twelve equal parts, which he called *uncias* (inches). This "anthropometron" is virtually identical to the modern anthropometer, used in most doctors' offices for measuring height.

After graduation, Elsholtz abandoned anthropometry for research in botany, herbal medicine, distillation, and intravenous infusion. However, his technique was adopted widely in the 18th century in early studies of human growth and development. In the early 19th century, the applications of anthropometry expanded to include measurements used to classify human populations on the basis of quantitative morphology. This research grew out of an interest in Linnaean systematics and taxonomy, with its emphasis on typology and "ideal" types to define contemporary populations.

More sophisticated measuring instruments, including spreading and sliding calipers, were devised to measure the human body, especially the skull, in greater detail than was possible with Elsholtz's anthropometron. Numerous landmarks on the head and body were identified for measuring an ever-increasing number of linear and contour dimensions. These early techniques were highly idiosyncratic, with researchers using their own measurement system. Ambiguity in the names and descriptions of the landmarks and confusion as to the actual measurements being taken made interobserver error a serious problem when comparing anthropometric measurements taken by different researchers. For example, one of the most basic measurements, maximum cranial length, is also known as head length, maximum glabello-occipital length, maximum head length, *diamètre antero-posterior maximum ou glabellaire*, or *grösste Kopflange*. This measurement usually is taken between the landmarks of the glabella, which is defined as the most prominent point in the median sagittal plane between the supraorbital ridges, and the *opisthocranion*, the most prominent posterior point in the median plane of the occiput, or back of the skull. Both landmarks have numerous synonyms. Glabella also is known as the nasal eminence or *bosse moyen*, while *point occipital maximum* and *extremum occiput* are synonyms for opisthocranion.

Much of the early anthropometric research focused on the Cephalic Index, the ratio of cranial width to length, developed by Swedish anatomist Anders Retzius to classify living populations according to head shape. Variations in measurement technique, plus disparities in classification systems, resulted in a bewildering variety of categories in this index. These differences produced so much confusion about this simple ratio that French anthropologist Paul Topinard devoted an entire chapter of his textbook on anthropology to the Cephalic Index.

By 1870, a consensus had developed around the work of French anatomist Paul Broca. However, the emergence of the modern German state following the Franco-Prussian War of 1870 led to the establishment of a separate, distinctly German school of anthropometry, which was formalized by the Frankfurt Convention of 1882. The Convention had one long-term scientific result, the establishment of the Frankfurt horizontal plane, a standard reference line connecting the upper edge of the ear canal and the inferior rim of the orbit. This plane is still used in anthropometric and cephalometric studies to ensure standardization of head position while measurements are taken.

Following the Convention, several international attempts were made to standardize anthropometry, but these collapsed by the beginning of World War I. Two textbooks developed out off these efforts. The first was Rudolf Martin's *Lehrbuch der Anthropologie*, the standard reference for the German school. In 1920, Aleš Hrdlička, one of the founders of American anthropology, wrote *Anthropometry*, based on his studies in France, to set the North American standards in the field. Hrdlička also was the first to propose the use of anthropometry in medicine.

As anthropometry developed during the 19th century, anthropometric data often were misapplied by scientists of the day to substantiate racial, class, and gender stereotypes. For example, during the period 1820 to 1851, an American scientist, Samuel George Morton, collected more than 1,000 human skulls to measure their cranial capacity as a way to rank races. (At the time, it was mistakenly assumed that a large cranial capacity equated with increased intelligence.) Morton would scientifically measure the skulls but would bias his sample by omitting individuals or groups that would not prove the superior cranial capacity of the white race. Cesare Lombroso (1835–1909), an Italian physician and criminologist, claimed that he could identify criminals using anthropometric features that reflected what he considered to be "atavistic" traits (or traits that demonstrate a reappearance of ape-like characteristics). Some of the "criminal characteristics" he used were shape and size deviations in the head; large jaws, teeth, and cheekbones; long arms; and protruding lips. The measurements themselves were not faulty. Instead, the anthropometric traits used in these pseudoscientific studies were carefully chosen to reinforce the prejudices of the day.

Anthropometry as a technique for studying human populations fell out of favor at the beginning of the 20th century. One reason was a reaction against the misuse of anthropometric data in racial studies. Other causes were the discovery of blood group genetics, which provided a much more precise way to study populations, and the recognition that the Linnaean "types" anthropologists studied were not fixed but were subject to environmental influences. This was based in part on Hrdlička's research on growth in immigrant families, which demonstrated that the children of first-generation immigrants were nearly always taller than their parents. The genetics of the immigrant children had not changed, but their nutritional status had improved. Also, the development of x-ray technology permitted more detailed two-dimensional measurements to be taken of skeletal features than could be obtained through direct measurement.

Although racial typology lost favor as a subject of anthropometric research, the study of human growth and development has continued, with anthropometry the primary means of evaluation. Much of the emphasis has shifted from academic studies to applied research. Following the advice of Hrdlička, anthropometry now is used widely in the medical field. Measurements of height and weight provide data for the calculation of body composition, which assists in the assessment of nutrition, physiology, growth, and development, as well as adding to the understanding of human obesity. Craniofacial measurements are used to analyze the patterns of dysmorphology associated with a wide range of congenital craniofacial anomalies, calculate the quantitative surgical changes needed to improve the deformities, and evaluate postoperative growth and outcomes.

Detailed measurement of the human body and its segments is used in the field of kinanthropometry to analyze the relationship between anatomy and movement, an application of particular importance in sports medicine. Anthropometry is used extensively in human engineering, or ergonomics, to study the fit between human morphology and the physical environment in which humans function. This field ranges from the fit of clothing, especially personal protective equipment, to the design of furniture, living and working spaces, and transportation.

Both somatometry and craniometry are employed in forensic science as tools for human identification. Body measurements are correlated with skeletal dimensions to create regression equations that estimate body height, determine sex, determine age in subadults, and identify possible racial affinities. Craniofacial measurements aid in reconstructing the facial features of skeletal remains and in age enhancement of photographs of missing children.

Psychologists use anthropometry to study the mechanisms of facial recognition, increasingly important in security issues. Other research attempts to quantify facial attractiveness. Some researchers, like Elsholtz some 350 years ago, have focused on the influence of facial symmetry, and others have identified the importance of statistical averages in defining attractiveness, updating the research of Sir Francis Galton on composite photographs.

The increasing use of anthropometry has led to further expansion of measurement instruments. Measurements of the body can be taken directly through spreading and sliding calipers, skin fold calipers, tape measures, and weight scales and can also be obtained from radiographs, dual energy x-ray absorptiometry scans, CAT scans, and other radiographic techniques. With direct measurement of the body, there is an inherent problem with body contours. In contrast to a dry skull that has many observable landmarks, such as sutures, which reflect where the bones unite, the living body is covered with skin and therefore has fewer easily discernable landmarks for measurement. On the body of someone who has anomalies due to disease or illness, the difficulty in locating landmarks is further exacerbated.

The lack of standardization in anthropometry remains a major problem. In even the most basic anthropometric texts, the definition of the landmarks used for measurement, the instruments to use, and the best methodology to take a given measurement often remain unclear. It is difficult to improve on an accuracy of better than 5 mm in most body measurements. In an application such as craniofacial reconstructive surgery, a measurement error this large would jeopardize the surgical outcome, so the cranial landmarks, synonyms, instruments, and techniques are more elaborately described, along with a discussion of variables to consider when taking the measurements, to minimize measurement error.

Care must be taken with measurement techniques. For example, individual height decreases by 1–3 mm during the day, so to track the growth of a child accurately, height should be measured at the same time of day. Height also should be consistently measured with an individual in stocking feet. Adult height decreases with age as a result of compression of intervertebral discs and bone thinning and cracking due to diseases such as osteoporosis. Other factors that affect measurement accuracy are well-calibrated instruments; replacement of instruments such as tape measures, which stretch with repeated use; standardized positioning of the body, such as the Frankfurt horizontal plane in cranial measurements, to eliminate error; a good source of natural light for ease of reading the instruments; a sequence for ease of taking the measurements; and finally, a good recording system to track the measurements.

With thousands of anthropometric measures available, proper scientific study using these measurements depends on the careful selection of the most meaningful measures to eliminate wasted research time collecting irrelevant data. With small samples, the data may have to be standardized before any analysis can begin to ensure that the results are meaningful. In studies based on larger groups of individuals, results can be broken down easily by sex, age, population of origin, health status, and other categories to provide reliable data for subsequent applications.

With improved techniques, anthropometry has been resurrected from its earlier confusion and misapplication to become an integral component in fields as diverse as forensic identification, growth and development studies, reconstructive surgery, ergonomics, and nutritional evaluation.

—*Elizabeth M. Salter and John C. Kolar*

See also Measurement; Measurement Error

Further Reading

Elsholtz, J. S. (1654). *Anthropometria*. Padua: M. Cadorini.

Galton, F. (1878). Composite portraits. *J Anthropol Inst Gr Brit & Ireland, 8*, 132.

Garson, J. G. (1884). The Frankfort Craniometric Convention, with critical remarks thereon. *J Anthropol Inst Gr Brit & Ireland, 14*, 64–83.

Gould, S. J. (1996). *The mismeasure of man* (rev. & exp. ed.). New York: Norton.

Kolar, J. C., & Salter, E. M. (1997). *Craniofacial anthropometry. Practical measurement of the head and face for clinical, surgical and research use*. Springfield, IL: Charles C Thomas.

Lombroso, C. (1876). *L'uomo delinquente*. Milan, Italy: Hoepli.

Applying Ideas on Statistics and Measurement

The following abstract is adapted from Yin, Z., Hanes, J., Jr., Moore, J. B., Humbles, P., Barbeau, P., & Gutin, B. (2005). An after-school physical activity program for obesity prevention in children. *Evaluation & the Health Professions, 28*(1), 67–89.

This article describes the process of setting up a 3-year, school-based afterschool physical activity intervention in elementary schools. The primary aim of the study is to determine whether adiposity and fitness will improve in children who are exposed to a "fitogenic" versus an "obesogenic" environment. Eighteen schools were randomized to the control (obesogenic) or intervention (fitogenic) group. The intervention consisted of (a) academic enrichment, (b) a healthy snack, and (c) physical activity in a mastery-oriented environment, and outcome measures were **anthropometry**, body composition, blood samples, psychological tests, and other measures. Successful implementation would show the feasibility of schools' being able to provide a fitogenic environment, and significant differences between the groups would provide evidence that a fitogenic environment after school has positive health benefits. If feasibility and efficacy are demonstrated, implementing an afterschool program like this one in elementary schools could play a major role in preventing and reducing childhood obesity.

APPLIED RESEARCH

Whereas basic research is the study of fundamental principles and processes, the defining characteristic of applied research is that its research findings have immediate application to the general topic under consideration.

Another characteristic of applied research is that its goal is to solve practical questions, and in contrast to basic research, applied research is aimed not at understanding or accumulating more knowledge about some phenomenon but at describing the phenomenon. While applied research has a more pragmatic element than basic research does, basic research forms the foundation for applied research.

For example, reading is a skill that involves many different processes, including visual and intellectual skills. The basics of how the eyes focus on letters and words and how that message is transmitted to the brain and then translated into meaningful symbols may very well constitute a set of basic research questions. In contrast, an example of an applied research endeavor is taking those findings and using them to understand why some children read better than others or creating an intervention and providing it for a group of children who are poor readers.

—*Neil J. Salkind*

See also Basic Research

Further Reading

Cochran, E. L. (1994). Basic versus applied research in cognitive science: A view from industry. *Ecological Psychology, 6,* 131–135.

Basic vs. applied research (discussion from the Ethical, Legal, and Social Issues in Science site at the University of California): http://www.lbl.gov/Education/ELSI/research-main.html

APTITUDE TESTS

The term *aptitude*, according to most dictionaries, is derived from the Latin term *aptitudo*, meaning fitness. The psychological use of the term is similar in that it has traditionally referred to a potential for acquiring knowledge or skill. Traditionally, aptitudes are described as sets of characteristics that relate to an individual's ability to acquire knowledge or skills in the context of some training or educational program. There are two important aspects of aptitude to keep in mind. First, aptitudes are present conditions (i.e., existing at the time they are measured). Second, there is nothing inherent in the concept of aptitudes that says whether they are inherited or acquired or represent some combination of heredity and environmental influences. Also, aptitude tests do not directly assess an individual's future success; they are meant to assess aspects of the individual that are indicators of future success. That is, these measures are used to provide a probability estimate of an individual's success in a particular training or educational program. While the meaning of *aptitude* is well delineated, there is much controversy over how to distinguish aptitude tests from other kinds of psychometric measures, specifically intelligence and achievement tests, partly because the major salient difference between intelligence, aptitude, and achievement tests has to do with the purpose of testing rather than with the content of the tests. What makes an assessment instrument an aptitude test rather than an intelligence or achievement test is mainly the future orientation of the predictions to be made from the test scores.

Historians generally date the movement of modern psychological testing from the 1905 work by Alfred Binet and Théodore Simon in developing a set of measures to assess intelligence. The Binet-Simon measures, and especially the English translation and refinement made by Lewis Terman in 1916, called the Stanford-Binet, are in widespread use even today. Few adults living in industrialized countries today have avoided taking at least one test of intelligence during their school years. Intelligence tests were designed with the goal of predicting school success.

Thus, in terms of the definition of aptitude provided above, when the purpose of an intelligence test is prediction, then the intelligence test is essentially an aptitude test—although an aptitude test of general academic content (e.g., memory, reasoning, math, and verbal domains). Aptitude tests, however, sample a wider array of talents than those included in most general intelligence measures, especially in the occupational domain. By the late 1910s and early 1920s, dozens of different aptitude tests had been created for prediction of success in a variety of different occupations (e.g., auto mechanic, retail salesmen, waitress, telegrapher, clerk, Hollerith operator, musician, registered nurse).

It is important to distinguish between so-called trade tests and aptitude tests. The distinction rests more on the characteristics of the examinee population than on the content of the tests. That is, when all the examinees can be expected to have similar prior exposure to the knowledge and skills needed to perform well on the test, the test is essentially one of ability or aptitude. But when prior knowledge and skills have an important impact on the examinees' success on the test, it is essentially an achievement test, or a measure of learned knowledge or skills, rather than an assessment of potential for acquiring such knowledge or skills. For psychologists who design aptitude tests, this is a critical concern. For example, the psychologist must be able to determine whether reading skills are an important determinant of test performance in order to present the test material in a paper-and-pencil format. Intelligence test developers assumed that individual differences in reading skills in young children were possible confounding influences, and so the developers created intelligence tests that did not require a child to know how to read or write. For assessing the aptitude of adults for an office clerk job, however, being able to read would be a prerequisite skill, so a paper-and-pencil aptitude test would certainly be appropriate.

Utility of Aptitude Tests

Aptitude tests are useful for the purpose of aiding educational or occupational selection when there are marked individual differences in the likelihood of success that are, in turn, determined by cognitive, perceptual, or physical abilities. The degree of utility of an aptitude test is determined by three major factors: (a) the cost of training or education, (b) the correlation between the aptitude test scores and success on the educational or occupational criterion, and (c) the ratio of the number of applicants to the number of places to be filled. When training is expensive, the cost to the organization of having trainees fail can be an important factor in adopting an aptitude testing program for screening applicants. When training is brief or inexpensive, such as for retail sales or other entry-level positions, the value of aptitude testing is diminished because the cost of accepting applicants who fail is not as burdensome for the organization. The correlation between aptitude test scores and success measures will determine how accurate the prediction of success or failure is. The larger the correlation, the more accurate the prediction. Finally, when there are many more applicants than spaces to be filled, the aptitude test will be more effective in maximizing the overall success rate. In contrast, when there are few applicants for each position, and thus nearly all applicants are accepted, the ranking of applicants by aptitude becomes largely irrelevant.

Two Types of Aptitude Tests

The aptitude tests developed over the past century have generally bifurcated into two different types: job-specific tests and multiaptitude batteries. Similar to the early aptitude tests described above, job-specific aptitude tests are typically designed to determine which candidates are best suited to particular occupations. In theory, there can be as many different occupational aptitude tests as there are differentiable occupations. In practice, however, there are common aptitudes underlying many occupations. For example, different kinds of mechanical jobs (e.g., auto mechanic, electronics service repair, assembly worker) may all involve aptitudes for dexterity, fine motor coordination, visual perception, and so on. An organization that wishes to select employees for a particular occupational placement might attempt to identify (through job analysis) what particular aptitudes are needed for successful job performance. The organization, in order to select the applicants who are most likely to succeed in a training program, can then create an aptitude measure that samples these specific aptitudes. Alternatively, among the dozens of commercially available tests, the organization may find an off-the-shelf aptitude measure that covers the most important aptitudes for training success for the particular job.

The other kind of aptitude measure is the multiaptitude battery. These tests are used frequently in educational contexts, and some are used in large-scale employment testing situations. In the educational context, multiaptitude tests may be very general, such as the Scholastic Aptitude Test, which was created in 1926 for selecting high school students for college and university placement. Today, the Scholastic Aptitude Test is one of the most widely used aptitude test batteries in the United States and is administered to more than 1 million students each year. The original Scholastic Aptitude Test assessed only two broad academic aptitudes: verbal and math. The most recent modification of the Scholastic Aptitude Test also includes a writing component. Multiaptitude test batteries can also be designed to provide assessments across several different aptitudes. The first large-scale multiaptitude batteries for use in educational contexts were developed by Thurstone and Thurstone in the early 1940s and became known as the Primary Mental Abilities battery. Another battery, the Differential Aptitude Tests (DAT), was introduced in 1947 and is still in use today. The DAT provides scores on eight different aptitudes (verbal, numerical, abstract reasoning, clerical speed and accuracy, mechanical reasoning, spatial relations, spelling, and language use).

There are many more such multiaptitude batteries that are administered in schools throughout the United States each year. Many of these tests do not have the term *aptitude* in their titles, but they are similar in content coverage and in the general purposes of testing. Such educational aptitude batteries are primarily used for counseling purposes. That is, the underlying premise for the utility of these tests is that they allow a parent or counselor to identify an individual

student's aptitude strengths and weaknesses. Usually, the test information is presented as a profile, a set of bar graphs that show where the student stands in respect to some norming group on each of the different aptitudes. Counselors may use this information to help guide the student in a way that either builds on the student's strengths or attempts to remediate the student's weaknesses. In practice, however, many of the different aptitudes assessed with these measures are themselves substantially positively correlated because of shared variance with general intelligence. When that happens, it is more difficult to provide a reliable differentiation among the individual's strengths and weaknesses. This is one of the most intractable problems associated with the counseling use of multiaptitude test batteries.

Multiaptitude batteries for occupational selection tend to be somewhat more useful for selection and classification purposes. (Classification is the process of assigning particular individuals to specific jobs by matching the individual's profile of aptitude strengths and weaknesses to the job requirements.) The two largest occupational multiaptitude test batteries used in the United States are the Armed Services Vocational Aptitude Battery (ASVAB) and the General Aptitude Test Battery (GATB). The ASVAB is used by the U.S. armed forces, and until recently, the GATB was used by federal and state employment agencies. In contrast to the multiaptitude batteries described above for educational contexts, these two tests are explicitly linked to a wide variety of specific occupations. For example, when individuals complete the ASVAB, they are each provided with a set of scores that determines the their suitability for all the different entry-level occupations within the military. With that information, they can be classified into the occupation in which they are most likely to succeed.

Concerns About Aptitude Tests

Although aptitude tests have been shown to be quite effective predictors of future academic and occupational performance, they have been somewhat controversial because of the meaning inherent in the assessment of *potential* and because of a wide variety of group differences in performance on standardized aptitude tests. Experience with the Scholastic Aptitude Test, for example, has indicated marked mean score differences between male and female test takers; between black, white, Hispanic, and Asian-American test takers; and between socioeconomic status groups. Because the Scholastic Aptitude Test is not traditionally considered to be taken by a representative or random sample of 16–18 year olds (since those students taking the test essentially are self-selected college-bound individuals), group differences on the Scholastic Aptitude Test do not provide direct evidence for overall group differences in academic potential. However, the differences between group means are significant and sometimes substantial, which has led many commentators to question whether and how much the test is associated with prior educational background and other demographic variables. Much of the difficulty centers around the term "potential" associated with aptitude tests, in contrast with achievement measures. That is, if these different groups differ only in terms of academic achievement, there would be perhaps less controversy than there is if the groups are determined to differ in terms of academic potential. Many testing organizations have in fact revised the names of their aptitude tests to remove the term that is associated with potential (e.g., the Scholastic Aptitude Test became the Scholastic Assessment Test in the 1990s). At one level, such a change may be cosmetic, but at another level, it does show that testing organizations have come to recognize that one does not need to imbue a test with the notion of potential in order to make predictions about future academic or occupational performance. That is, there is nothing inherently problematic in using an intelligence or achievement test for the same purpose as an aptitude test as long is it taps the same underlying knowledge and skills that are critical for performance on the predicted criterion measure. Given that intelligence, aptitude, and achievement tests assess only current performance, it is ultimately the prediction aspect of a test that makes it an aptitude test. Furthermore, it is fundamentally impossible to know what an individual's actual potential is for academic or occupational knowledge or skills, because it is not possible to know what the universe of instructional or training programs may be. Should methods of instruction or training be improved at some time in the future, even those individuals with relatively lower aptitudes may show marked increases in performance. In that sense, the operational conceptualization of aptitude has to be in terms of whatever instructional or training methods are actually in use at any one time.

Over- and Underachievement

One aspect of aptitude tests that has been very much misunderstood is the notion of over- and underachievement. Typically, the term *overachiever* is given to individuals who have relatively higher scores on achievement tests than they do on aptitude tests, and the term *underachiever* is given to individuals who have relatively lower scores on achievement tests than on aptitude tests. However, given that both aptitude and achievement tests often assess the same underlying knowledge and skills, the choice of labeling one test or another an aptitude or achievement test is generally arbitrary. That means that one could just as easily assert that individuals have higher or lower aptitude in association with their achievement test performance, which makes little conceptual sense but is entirely consistent with the underlying properties of the tests. In fact, given the nature of statistical regression-to-the-mean phenomena, which are associated with taking the difference between any two measures, it is common for individuals with low scores on one test (e.g., aptitude) to have relatively higher scores on the other test (e.g., achievement), and similarly, individuals with higher-than-average scores on one test will have somewhat lower scores on the other test. The attribution that low-aptitude individuals are often overachievers and high-aptitude individuals are often underachievers is most often an artifact of this regression-to-the-mean phenomenon and thus does not provide any useful diagnostic information. Only extremely large differences between such scores (i.e., differences that significantly exceed the difference attributable to regression-to-the-mean effects) can provide any potential diagnostic information.

—Phillip L. Ackerman

See also Ability Tests; Armed Services Vocational Aptitude Battery; Differential Aptitude Test; Multidimensional Aptitude Battery

Further Reading

Anastasi, A., & Urbina, S. (1997). *Psychological testing* (7th ed.). New York: Prentice Hall.

Cronbach, L. J. (1990). *Essentials of psychological testing* (5th ed.). New York: Harper & Row.

Thorndike, R. L. (1963). *The concepts of over- and under-achievement*. New York: Bureau of Publications, Teachers College, Columbia University.

Scholastic Aptitude Test information: http://www.college-board.com

Test reviews: http://www.unl.edu/buros/

Testing standards and procedures information: http://www.apa.org/science/testing.html

AREA CHART

Area charts are used to simultaneously display visual information in multiple categories. The categories are stacked so that individual as well as cumulative values are shown.

Area charts, like other charts, such as bar and column charts, are most often used for categorical data that are, by definition, not dynamic in nature. For example, if one were interested in illustrating money spent across the first quarter of the year in certain categories, an area chart would be a useful way to do so, as in the following example. First, here are the data:

	Food	Car	Fun	Miscellaneous
January	$165	$56	$56	$54
February	$210	$121	$87	$34
March	$227	$76	$77	$65

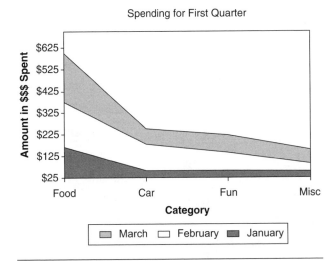

Figure 1 Area Chart Created in Excel

These data represent the amount of money spent in four categories, food, car, fun, and miscellaneous, in each of the first three months of the year. The value for each category by month is shown in the area chart below, with each month containing a series of data points.

An area chart is not an easy chart to create manually; Figure 1 was created using Excel.

—Neil J. Salkind

See also Bar Chart; Line Chart; Pie Chart

Further Reading

Tufte, E. (2001). *The visual display of quantitative information* (2nd ed.). Cheshire, CT: Graphics Press.

ARITHMETIC MEAN

The most widely used measure of central tendency is the arithmetic mean. Most commonly, *mean* refers to the arithmetic mean. The arithmetic mean is defined as all the scores for a variable added together and then divided by the number of observations. Therefore, the formula to compute the arithmetic mean is as follows:

$$\bar{X} = \frac{\sum X}{n},$$

where

X represents the data points,

Σ is the summation of all the *X*s,

n is the number of data points or observations, and

$\bar{X}$ is the computed mean.

Descriptive Statistics

	N	Minimum	Maximum	Mean	Std. Deviation
Data points	10	1	10	5.00	2.539
Valid N (listwise)	10				

Figure 1   SPSS Output for the Descriptives Mean

For example, take the data presented in Table 1.

The sum of the observations (Σ*X*) is 1 + 5 + 7 + 2 + 10 + 4 + 6 + 5 + 4 + 6 = 50. Then, we divide this value by *n*, which in this example is 10 because we have 10 observations. Thus, 50/10 = 5. The arithmetic mean for this set of observations is 5.

The SPSS statistical software package provides several ways to compute a mean for a variable. The Mean command can be found under Descriptives, then Frequencies, Explore, and finally Means. Furthermore, the mean can be added to output for more advanced calculations, such as multiple regression. The output for the Descriptives mean is presented in Figure 1.

As seen in the output, the variable "data points" has a total of 10 observations (seen under the column headed *N*), the lowest value in the data set is 1, the highest value is 10, the mean is 5, and the standard deviation is 2.539.

There are two major issues you should be aware of when using the arithmetic mean. The first is that the arithmetic mean can be influenced by outliers, or data values that are outside the range of the majority of the data points. Outliers can pull the mean toward themselves. For example, if the data set in Figure 1 included a data point (which would be observation 11) of 40, the mean would be 8.2. Thus, when the data set is extremely skewed, it can be more meaningful to use other measures of central tendency (e.g., the median or the mode).

The second issue is that the arithmetic mean is difficult to interpret when the variable of interest is nominal with two levels (e.g., gender) and not meaningful when there are more than two levels or groups for a given variable (e.g., ethnicity). The mean has been found to be consistent across time. With repeated measures of the same variable, the arithmetic mean tends not to change radically (as long as there are no extreme outliers in the data set). Furthermore, the arithmetic mean is the most commonly used measure of central tendency in more advanced statistical formulas.

—*Nancy L. Leech,*
Anthony J. Onwuegbuzie, and Larry Daniel

See also Average; Median

Further Reading

Glass, G. V., & Hopkins, K. D. (1995). *Statistical methods in education and psychology* (3rd ed.). Boston: Allyn & Bacon.

Leech, N. L., Barrett, K. C., & Morgan, G. A. (2005). *SPSS for intermediate statistics: Use and interpretation* (2nd ed.). Mahwah, NJ: Erlbaum.

Table 1   Data for Arithmetic Mean Computation

Observation	Data Points
1	1
2	5
3	7
4	2
5	10
6	4
7	6
8	5
9	4
10	6

Armed Forces Qualification Test

The Armed Forces Qualification Test (AFQT) is the name given to a series of tests constantly in use from 1950 to the present. The current AFQT is a composite of subtests from the Armed Services Vocational Aptitude Battery (ASVAB). Constituent members of the composite are verbal and quantitative components, weighted to be of equal variance contribution. The AFQT is used by the U.S. military as a measure of quality and trainability. Although AFQT scores are reported in percentiles, it also has five categories that are used for legal and classification purposes. By law, the American military is not permitted to enlist individuals who score in the lowest category, that is, at the 10th percentile or less, except by direction or legal exception.

The AFQT is the successor to the World War II Army General Classification Test and the Navy General Classification Test. Although these two tests had similar names, their content was not identical. The first AFQT (1950) was equated to a mixed Army-Navy sample based on percentile equivalent scores from these two tests. The American military calls this procedure "calibrating" and used it for many years. All forms of the AFQT were scored on the basis of a normative sample of men in uniform as of 1944.

The 1950 AFQT had four content areas; verbal, arithmetic, spatial, and spatial visualization. In 1953, the content areas of the AFQT were changed to verbal, arithmetic, spatial, mechanical ability, and tool knowledge. The content remained more or less unchanged through the first seven versions of the test. When the ASVAB was adopted (1976), the AFQT became a part of it. In ASVAB versions 5, 6, and 7, the AFQT strongly resembled the numbered AFQT forms. Scores were reported on the 1944 normative sample.

With the implementation of ASVAB forms 8, 9, and 10, the AFQT portion was reworked to add a timed subtest, Numerical Operations. With the implementation of the 1980 nationally representative normative sample in 1984, a problem was encountered with the timed subtests of the ASVAB. A small mistiming of these subtests could and did have large impacts on the resultant scores. The AFQT composite was then changed to be equally verbal and arithmetic in importance. Scores were still reported on the metric of the 1980 normative sample.

In 1997, another nationally representative normative sample was collected, and the ASVAB subtests,

including those contributing to the AFQT, were placed on this new metric as of July 1, 2004. The current AFQT still consists of verbal and arithmetic components. It is basically a measure of general cognitive ability.

Although the AFQT is not available for commercial use, it has been used in nonmilitary research, most notably in Herrnstein and Murray's *The Bell Curve* (1994) and in numerous econometric and occupational studies. It has been offered as an ability measure and related to training and job performance, earnings, educational attainment, and interregional migration.

—*Malcolm James Ree*

See also Ability Tests

Further Reading

Orme, D. R., Brehm, W., & Ree, M. J. (2001). Armed Forces Qualification Test as a measure of premorbid intelligence. *Military Psychology, 13*(4), 187–197.

ARMED SERVICES VOCATIONAL APTITUDE BATTERY

The Armed Services Vocational Aptitude Battery (ASVAB) is a multiple aptitude battery used for two purposes. The first is proprietary: enlistment qualification and job classification for all the branches of the American military and the Coast Guard. The second purpose is to provide vocational guidance for high school and vocational students. These two uses are called the Enlisted Testing Program (ETP) and the Student Testing Program (STP), respectively.

The ASVAB consists of nine subtests. In the past, it had contained some purely timed subtests and some subtests well characterized as mixed speed and power. Subtest content is verbal ability, quantitative ability, spatial ability, and job knowledge. The subtests are General Science, Arithmetic Reasoning, Mathematics Knowledge, Word Knowledge, Paragraph Comprehension, Electronics Information, Auto and Shop Information, Mechanical Comprehension, and

Assembling Objects. Paragraph Comprehension is a short subtest and is never used alone but always combined with Word Knowledge to increase reliability. All subtest raw scores are converted to normative population standard scores and then combined to make composites for use.

For use in the ETP, the ASVAB is administered in both paper-and-pencil and computer-adapted forms. In the ETP, all armed service members are required to pass a composite called the Armed Forces Qualification Test (AFQT) for minimal enlistment qualification. In addition to the AFQT, each service computes unit or simple weighted composites for classification of enlistees into specific occupations or clusters of occupations. The scores are reported either in normative percentiles or in service-specific normative standard scores. In the normative sample, the composites reflect the high loading of general cognitive ability in all the subtests. This loading also makes the composites valid for predicting occupational criteria.

The STP uses only paper-and-pencil administration and is aimed at career exploration. The ASVAB and its supporting interpretive materials are offered free of charge. In this program, the scores are reported by grade norms in the form of percentiles with error bands. Grades are reported for each of eight subtests and three content composites. The STP does not use the Assembling Objects subtest. Included in the program are copious materials to aid the student in exploring potential occupational goals. In the STP, an associated interest inventory is offered, and the relationships between interests and test scores are clearly explained in a guide titled *Exploring Careers*.

—*Malcolm James Ree*

See also Armed Forces Qualification Test

Further Reading

Exploring Careers: The ASVAB career exploration guide. (2005). DD Form 1304-5WB, July 2005. U.S. Government Printing Office.

Ree, M. J., & Carretta, T. R. (1994). Factor analysis of ASVAB: Confirming a Vernon-like structure. *Educational and Psychological Measurement, 54,* 457–461.

Ree, M. J., & Earles, J. A. (1991). Predicting training success: Not much more than g. *Personnel Psychology, 44,* 321–332.

Ree, M. J., Earles, J. A., & Teachout, M. S. (1994). Predicting job performance; Not much more than g. *Journal of Applied Psychology, 79,* 518–524.

ARTIFICIAL NEURAL NETWORK

An artificial neural network (ANN) is a class of models, inspired by the central nervous system, used in machine learning and pattern recognition and classification. These models are nonlinear parametric regression models with either automatic, unsupervised training (setting of the model parameters) or supervised training from some training set of known input-output relations, depending on the type of network.

An ANN consists of a collection of *neurons* (processing units) and connections between these neurons. Usually these neurons accumulate "information" from neighboring neurons and either fire or not, depending on some local threshold level.

The simplest type of ANN is the *feed-forward net*, in which all the information flows in a single direction. Figure 1 shows a four-layer feed-forward net, with an *input* layer, followed by two *hidden* layers, followed in turn by an *output* layer.

Many neurons are modeled (and constructed or simulated) to have binary outputs (and often binary inputs as well). Each neuron has some rule (called a

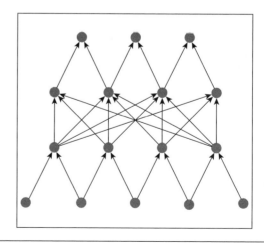

Figure 1   A Simple Four-Layer Feed-Forward Net

firing rule) for deciding which combination of inputs results in which output. One particularly simple rule would be to sum all the inputs (multiplied perhaps by weights) and check to see if the sum was more than some threshold value; if so, then fire, and if not, then do not fire (a binary output). Notice that this firing rule is discontinuous in that it has a sudden jump at the threshold. This rule is sometimes called the *hardlimit* firing rule.

As a simple example (for the neuron illustrated in Figure 2), let $w1 = 0.3$, $w2 = 0.5$, $w3 = 0.3$, and the threshold $q = 1.5$. Then for the inputs 1.2, 2.1, and 0.7, we get accumulated sum $(.3)(1.2) + (.5)(2.1) + (.3)(0.7) = 1.62 > 1.5$, so the neuron would fire.

The parameters of a feed-forward net include the weights and thresholds for each neuron. These parameters must be set during the *training phase* of the network. During training (a *supervised learning* situation), one uses a set of known input-output relationships to set the parameters of the network. One common technique for training is the *backpropagation* algorithm. This algorithm basically computes a gradient of the error with respect to the weights in order to adjust the weights. The computation proceeds by propagating influences backwards in the network (and hence the name).

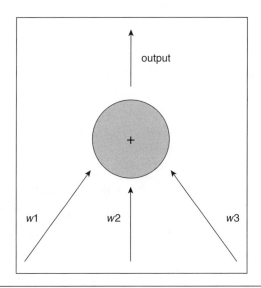

Figure 2 A Single Neuron

Many other kinds of firing rules are possible, including a sigmoid (a continuous version of the hardlimit rule), Gaussian rules, and others. The sigmoid firing rule has the functional form

$$output = \frac{1}{1 + exp(- \text{ sum of weighted inputs}/T)}.$$

Many other kinds of connection *topologies* are possible. A *Hopfield* net, for example, is a neural network with bidirectional connections (and with the same weight in each direction). These networks act as associative memories in the sense that the network can store a set of patterns and fire if a similar pattern is presented to it.

The presence of loops in a network allows for feedback, so these types of networks are sometimes called *recurrent* networks.

Many popular software systems, including Matlab, SPSS, SAS, and R (a open source version of S), have neural network toolboxes. It is also fairly easy to get software packages (as either executables or source) from the Internet to simulate various neural networks; one such place is http://www.neural-networks-at-your-fingertips.com/.

—*Franklin Mendivil*

Further Reading

Hertz, J., Krogh, A., & Palmer, R. G. (1991). *Introduction to the theory of neural computation*. Reading, MA: Addison-Wesley.

Artificial neural networks technology: http://www.dacs.dtic.mil/techs/neural/neural_ToC.html

Assessment of Interactions in Multiple Regression

With theories growing ever more complex, analytic tools for their analysis and testing need to be developed. In exploring moderator variables that are found in theory tests in both experimental and nonexperimental research, we need to be careful to assess the interactions between the moderator variable and the predictor variable(s) in an appropriate way. Prior to the early 1990s, many nonexperimentalists using a correlational paradigm often used it inappropriately by (a) correctly creating a product term for the moderator and independent variable and then (b) inappropriately correlating it with the dependent variable. This paradigm is inappropriate for both theoretical and empirical reasons.

Theoretically, as Jacob Cohen has argued, while the interaction is carried by the product term, it is not the product term. The product term alone also carries variance due to the main effects of the independent variable and the moderator variable. The appropriate analysis is to partial out the main effects in a multiple regression analysis, as pointed out by Saunders as long ago as 1956.

Empirically, as Schmidt has shown, the correlation between a product term and the dependent variable is sensitive to the scale numbers used in the analysis. Changing from a scale of 1 to 5 to a scale of -2 to $+2$ will change the correlation dramatically. The proper analysis, as Arnold and Evans have shown, results in the incremental R^2 between an equation containing just main effects and one containing the main effects plus the product term being invariant under linear transformations of the data (unlike the simple correlation between the product term and the dependent variable, which changes dramatically). This invariance translates to a proper test of theory only if the measurement scales and the underlying psychological constructs are linearly related. More recent developments involving structural equation modeling do not have this limitation.

—*Martin G. Evans*

See also Analysis of Variance (ANOVA); Correlation Coefficient

Further Reading

Arnold, H. J., & Evans, M. G. (1979). Testing multiplicative models does *not* require ration scales. *Organizational Behavior and Human Performance, 24,* 214–224.

Bollen, K. A., & Paxton, P. (1998). Interactions of latent variables in structural equations models. *Structural Equation Modeling, 5,* 267–293.

Busemeyer, J., & Jones, L. R. (1983). Analysis of multiplicative causal rules when the causal variables are measured with error. *Psychological Bulletin, 93,* 549–562.

Cohen, J. (1978). Partialed products *are* interactions; partialed powers *are* curve components. *Psychological Bulletin, 85,* 858–866.

Evans, M. G. (1985). A Monte-Carlo study of correlated error in moderated multiple regression analysis. *Organizational Behavior and Human Decision Processes, 36,* 305–323.

Evans, M. G. (1991). The problem of analyzing multiplicative composites: Interactions revisited. *American Psychologist, 46,* 6–15.

Ping, R. A. (1996). Latent variable interaction and quadratic effect estimation: A two-step technique using structural equation analysis. *Psychological Bulletin, 119,* 166–175.

Saunders, D. R. (1956). Moderator variables in prediction. *Educational and Psychological Measurement, 16,* 209–222.

Schmidt, F. L. (1973). Implications of a measurement problem for expectancy theory research. *Organizational Behavior and Human Decision Processes, 10,* 243–251.

ASSOCIATION FOR PSYCHOLOGICAL SCIENCE

The Association for Psychological Science (APS) is the leading national organization devoted solely to scientific psychology. Its mission is to promote, protect, and advance the interests of scientifically oriented psychology in research, application, and improvement of human welfare.

Established in 1988, APS was instantly embraced by psychology's scientific community, and its membership grew rapidly. By the end of its first year, APS opened an office in Washington, D.C., and now has approximately 15,000 members from around the world. Members are engaged in scientific research or the application of scientifically grounded research spanning all areas of psychology. There are also student affiliates and institutional members. Distinguished contributions are recognized by Fellow status.

Formation

APS was created out of recognition that (a) the needs and interests of scientific and academic psychologists are distinct from those of members of the professional community primarily engaged in clinical practice and (b) there was a strong need for a society that would advance the interests of the discipline in ways that more specialized organizations were not intended to do. An interim group, the Assembly for Scientific and Applied Psychology, had sought to reform the American Psychological Association from within, but its efforts were rejected by a membership-wide vote of the APA. APS then became the official embodiment of the reform effort, and the new organization was launched on August 12, 1988.

Publications

APS publishes four journals:

1. *Psychological Science* publishes authoritative articles of interest across all of scientific psychology's subdisciplines.

2. *Current Directions in Psychological Science* offers concise invited reviews spanning all of scientific psychology and its applications.

3. *Psychological Science in the Public Interest* provides definitive assessments by panels of distinguished researchers on topics for which psychological science has the potential to inform and improve the well-being of society.

4. APS's newest journal, *Perspectives on Psychological Science*, features longer integrative reviews and a variety of eclectic articles.

APS also publishes the monthly *Observer*, featuring news and opinion pieces; a Current Directions Readers series in conjunction with Prentice Hall; a Festschrift series in conjunction with LEA Press; and self-published books on the teaching of psychology.

Annual Convention

APS holds a meeting in late spring each year to showcase the best of scientific psychology. The program features presentations by the field's most distinguished researchers and educators in a variety of formats, including invited addresses and symposia, submitted symposia, "hot topic" talks, and posters. The convention also includes workshops on specialized topics.

APS Fund for the Teaching and Public Understanding of Psychological Science

In 2004, the David and Carol Myers Foundation pledged $1 million to APS for the creation of an endowed fund that aims "to enhance the teaching and public understanding of psychological science for students and the lay public, in the United States, Canada, and worldwide."

Achievement Awards

APS recognizes exceptional contributions to scientific psychology with two annual awards: the APS William James Fellow Award (for significant intellectual contributions to the basic science of psychology) and the James McKeen Cattell Fellow Award (for outstanding contributions to the area of applied psychological research).

APS Student Caucus

Students are an important and active component of APS. The APS Student Caucus is the representative body of the society's student affiliates. The Student Caucus organizes research competitions, convention programs, and a variety of membership activities aimed at professional development and enhanced education in psychological science.

Advocacy

APS is widely recognized as an active and effective leader in advancing the interests of basic and applied psychological, behavioral, and social science research in the legislative arena and in the federal agencies that support these areas of research.

—*Morton A. Gernsbacher,*
Robert W. Levenson, and Sarah Brookhart

See American Psychological Association

Further Reading

Association for Psychological Science Web site: www.psychologicalscience.org

ASYMMETRY OF *g*

Is the strength of the general factor of intelligence uniform? That is, do the various indicators of crystallized intelligence correlate similarly at all levels of intelligence? This question was first explored in 1927, by Spearman, who, on the basis of his data, suggested a law of diminishing returns (also known as the divergence hypothesis, or in my terms, the asymmetry of *g*). This observation states that at low levels of intelligence, the various facets of intelligence are very highly correlated, but at higher levels of intelligence, the correlations between the various facets are less strong.

Between 1927 and 1990, this work disappeared from sight, and as late as 1989, Detterman and Daniel could argue that "it was thought that the positive manifold [the loading of ability tests onto a single factor] was uniformly distributed over the whole range of ability." This finding has been supported in a number of other studies.

The best estimate is for a linear decline in average correlations between IQ measures from $r = 0.46$ for the least gifted group to average correlations of about $r = 0.30$ for the more highly gifted. If this picture is sustained through additional research, then perhaps much of the conflict between those arguing for a pervasive *g* factor and those arguing for specific abilities can be reconciled by considering that both may be true, with *g* dominating at the lower levels of intelligence and specific factors dominating at higher levels of intelligence.

In practice, this means that we will have to reconsider our use of intelligence as a selection tool in job performance. It is fine to use *g* at low levels of intelligence, but at high levels, the specific abilities needed for a task will come into play, so predictive studies will have to explore the interaction between *g* and specific abilities to understand who the high performers will be.

—*Martin G. Evans*

See also Ability Tests; Intelligence Tests

Further Reading

Deary, I. J., Egan, V., Gibson, G. J., Austin, E. J., Brand, C. R., & Kellaghan, T. (1996). Intelligence and the differentiation hypothesis. *Intelligence, 23,* 105–132.

Detterman, D. K., & Daniel, M. H. (1989). Correlates of mental tests with each other and with cognitive variables are highest for low IQ groups. *Intelligence, 13,* 349–359.

Evans, M. G. (1999). On the asymmetry of g. *Psychological Reports, 85,* 1059–1069.

Evans, M. G. (2002). The implications of the asymmetry of g for predictive validity. In W. Auer-Rizzi, E. Szabo, & C. Innreiter-Moser (Eds.), *Management in einer Welt der Globalisierung und Diversitaet: Europaeische und nordamerikanische Sichtweisen* (pp. 433–441). Stuttgart, Germany: Schaeffer-Poeschel Verlag.

Jensen, A. R. (2003). Regularities in Spearman's law of diminishing returns. *Intelligence, 31,* 95–105.

Spearman, C. E. (1927). *The abilities of man.* London: Macmillan.

ATTENUATION, CORRECTION FOR

Attenuation is a term used to describe the reduction in the magnitude of the correlation between the scores of two measurement instruments that is caused by their unreliabilities. Charles Spearman first recognized the value of correcting for attenuation by noting that we are interested in determining the true relationship between the constructs we study, not the relationship between flawed empirical measures of these constructs. His solution was to estimate the correlation between two variables using perfectly reliable empirical measures. He developed the following formula:

$$r_{x'y'} = \frac{r_{xy}}{\sqrt{r_{xx}r_{yy}}}, \qquad (1)$$

where r_{xx} and r_{yy} equal the reliability coefficients of the two instruments, and r_{xy} equals the obtained correlation between the scores of the two instruments. It is assumed that X and Y are imperfect measures of underlying constructs X' and Y', containing independent, random errors, and $r_{x'y'}$ equals the true correlation between X' and Y'. If r_{xx} equals .61, r_{yy} equals .55, and r_{xy} equals .43, then

$$r_{x'y'} = \frac{.43}{\sqrt{(.61)(.55)}} = .74. \qquad (2)$$

The use of the formula allows the researcher to answer the question, What would the correlation (i.e., $r_{x'y'}$) be if both of the empirical measures were error free? The example illustrates the considerable reduction in the size of r_{xy} caused by the unreliabilities of the scores for the two instruments.

Although correcting for the attenuation of both empirically measured constructs is useful for investigating theoretical problems, it is more difficult to justify for practical applications. For instance, when predicting who will succeed in higher-education programs or who will benefit from special education services, we are limited by the fallible instruments at hand; after all, the application of the correction for attenuation does not make the empirical scores more reliable than they really are! Although it may not be appropriate to correct for attenuation of a predictor variable, it may well be justifiable to adjust for the inaccuracy of criterion measures. For instance, why should inaccurate graduate grade point averages be allowed to make Graduate Record Examinations scores appear less valid than they really are? For this single correction problem, the formula is as follows:

$$r_{x'y'} = \frac{r_{xy}}{\sqrt{r_{yy}}}. \qquad (3)$$

Confirmatory factor analysis (CFA) provides a second way to correct for attenuation. In CFA, the measurement error of each latent variable is explicitly modeled. In research comparing the results of correcting for attenuation via the two approaches, Fan found highly comparable results for the same data. That is, both approaches provided nearly identical point estimates and confidence intervals for the relationship between the true scores of his variables. Nevertheless, it should be mentioned that the CFA approach might be less applicable, given the constraints of modeling item-level data (e.g., extreme item skewness and kurtosis, different item distributions, and item unreliability).

History

Over the years, various writers have debated whether attenuation should be corrected at all. Although he supported the use of correction for attenuation, Nunnally called it a "bandy fiction" the results of which are always hypothetical. However, given its use in adjusting effect sizes in substantive research and meta-analysis, it appears that correction for attenuation is here to stay. One reason is the alarm expressed by some scholars that doctoral programs in the United States are giving short shrift to the measurement curriculum. Some suggest that the lack of attention given measurement issues in higher education has led to the finding that as many as 50% of contemporary published research articles fail to report the reliability and validity of the independent and dependent variables employed. This fact takes on added importance when one realizes that some variables used in published research are so unreliable as to make it virtually impossible to obtain statistically significant results. Furthermore, an increasing number of professional journals have begun to suggest strongly, and even demand, that appropriate corrections be provided readers in order to better inform their judgments regarding the practical importance of statistically significant p values.

Which Type of Reliability Should Be Used?

One pertinent issue concerns the selection of the type of reliability coefficient that should be used: test-retest, internal consistency, or alternative-form reliability. Obviously, the selection of the type of reliability influences the corrected true-score correlation. For instance, the long-term stability of an instrument (e.g., using a 1-year test-retest interval) is expected to be much lower than an internal consistency estimate of reliability. Consider the case in which the 1-year test-retest reliability coefficient for a criterion test equals .65, coefficient alpha (an estimate of internal consistency reliability) equals .80 for the same test, and the validity coefficient between the predictor variable and the criterion test is .49. If we apply

Equation 2 to correct for the attenuation of the criterion variable on the validity coefficient, we obtain $r_{x'y'}$ equal to .61 for the test-retest estimate and .55 for the coefficient alpha estimate. Without knowing the specific interest of the researcher, we have no basis for identifying the better estimate of the true validity coefficient. Over the-years, different writers have suggested aggregating corrections for attenuation across several data sets and using the average value as the best estimate of the true relationship between the sets of scores. Cronbach and others have pointed out that, should the average value be based on corrections using different sorts of reliability coefficients, a basic requirement of classic measurement theory would be violated: Different types of reliability estimates may not be used interchangeably.

In the literature, each of the three forms of reliability has been recommended for use in correction for attenuation. Most recently, researchers are advised to choose on the basis of the intent and context of their research objectives. Although such advice is easy to follow in some contexts, it is murky in others. For instance, if one is interested in determining the ability of a first-grade readiness test to predict student academic achievement 1 year later, then the test-retest reliability (i.e., 1-year stability) of the readiness test would be of greater interest to the researcher than would other forms of reliability. Should the researcher be interested in increasing the number of items in a test (and thus improving the sampling of the item domain and increasing reliability) in order to increase the validity of the instrument, then internal consistency reliability estimates offer more informative results.

What Is Done When Appropriate Reliability Estimates Are Unavailable

Although it is less problematical in individual research reports, in meta-analyses it often happens that reliability estimates of the appropriate types are unavailable to the analyst. There are no elegant solutions to this dilemma; the following are some of the common practices in calculating the correction for attenuation:

1. When appropriate reliability coefficients are presented in the published report, they are used to correct for attenuation.

2. When only inappropriate reliability coefficients are presented in the published report, they are used to correct for attenuation.

3. When no reliability coefficients are presented in the published report, published values from technical manuals and other sources are used to correct for attenuation.

4. When no published reliability coefficients are available for use, then average reliability coefficients from other, similar instruments are used to correct for attenuation.

Clearly, this is not an enviable state of affairs. However, until such time as researchers and professional publications rectify the omissions that remain commonplace in published reports, the correction for attenuation will remain a stepchild in research practice.

—*Ronald C. Eaves*

See also Correlation Coefficient

Further Reading

American Psychological Association. (2001). *Publication manual of the American Psychological Association* (5th ed.). Washington, DC: Author.

Baugh, F. (2002). Correcting effect sizes for score reliability: A reminder that measurement and substantive issues are linked inextricably. *Educational and Psychological Measurement, 62*, 254–263.

Fan, X. (2003). Two approaches for correcting correlation attenuation caused by measurement error: Implications for research practice. *Educational and Psychological Measurement, 63*, 915–930.

Kuncel, N. R., Hezlett, S. A., & Ones, D. S. (2001). A comprehensive meta-analysis of the predictive validity of the Graduate Record Examinations: Implications for graduate student selection and performance. *Psychological Bulletin, 127*, 162–181.

Muchinsky, P. M. (1996). The correction for attenuation. *Educational and Psychological Measurement, 56*, 63–75.

Nunnally, J. C. (1978). *Psychometric theory* (2nd ed.). New York: McGraw-Hill.

Schmidt, F. L., & Hunter, J. E. (1996). Measurement error in psychological research: Lessons from 26 research scenarios. *Psychological Methods, 1*, 199–223.

Wilkinson, L., & American Psychological Association Task Force on Statistical Inference. (1999). Statistical methods in psychology journals: Guidelines and explanations. *American Psychologist, 54*, 594–604. (Available for purchase at http://www.psycinfo.com/psycarticles/1999–03403–008.html)

Yin, P., & Fan, X. (2000). Assessing the reliability of Beck Depression Inventory scores: A meta-analytic generalization across studies. *Educational and Psychological Measurement, 60*, 201–223.

ATTITUDE TESTS

Although definitions have varied, the most common contemporary definition is that an attitude is a relatively general and enduring evaluation of a person, object, or concept along a dimension ranging from positive to negative. Because attitudes have played a central role in psychological theory and application, numerous and diverse attitude tests have been developed to assess this construct.

Direct Measures of Attitudes

The most common way to assess attitudes is simply to directly ask people to report them. Traditionally, this approach has been accomplished using formal scaling procedures to construct multiple-item tests of attitudes.

Multiple-Item Direct Attitude Measures

Formal attitude measurement began with the work of Louis L. Thurstone. Although he proposed several procedures, his most popular approach was the equally appearing interval scale. This procedure requires development of a series of opinion statements that represent varying levels of positivity or negativity toward the attitude object. Judges then sort these statements into equal-interval categories of favorability toward the attitude object (e.g., 11 intervals, where 1 = *extremely unfavorable* and 11 = *extremely favorable*). Next, a scale value is computed for each statement that corresponds to the median (or mean) score of judges' ratings, eliminating items with highly variable ratings. From the remaining items, the researcher selects a final set of statements representing equal intervals on the evaluative dimension. The final scale consists of these items in random order, with instructions for respondents to check the items with which they personally agree. The mean scale values of marked items are computed to obtain individual attitude scores.

Although Thurstone scales generally work well, the procedure is time consuming because it requires items to initially be rated by judges. In response to this and other concerns, in 1932 Rensis Likert developed the method of summated ratings. This procedure requires a set of opinion items that are clearly positive or negative in relation to the attitude object. The items are then administered to the sample of interest, whose members are instructed to indicate their level of agreement on a 5-point continuum (where *strongly agree* is assigned a value of 5 and *strongly disagree* is represented by 1). When the sample has completed the items, negative items are reverse coded, and each respondent's item scores are summed to create an overall attitude score. Item-total correlations are computed to identify poorly performing items (i.e., items with low item-total correlations). These items are discarded, and the final attitude scale scores are computed. Research has suggested this procedure tends to produce highly reliable scales.

In response to concerns that prior procedures did not guarantee unidimensional attitude tests, Louis Guttman proposed scalogram analysis. This approach involves constructing a set of opinion statements that are ranked in order, from least extreme to most extreme (i.e., a set of statements ranging from mildly positive to extremely positive or a set of items ranging from mildly negative to extremely negative). Scalogram analysis assumes that agreeing with a more extreme position implies agreement with less extreme positions. The pattern of responses to the set of items is examined to assess the extent to which items satisfy this assumption. Items are discarded if they frequently fail to meet this criterion. Although Guttman scales have the advantage of producing scales that are likely to be unidimensional, the difficulty of constructing scales that satisfy its stringent requirements has prevented it from becoming a widely used method of attitude measurement.

One of the most popular measures of attitudes is Charles Osgood's semantic differential. The semantic differential consists of a set of bipolar adjective pairs (e.g., good-bad, wise-foolish) that represents the evaluative continuum. Because these bipolar adjective pairs tend to be very general, they can typically be applied to any attitude object. Usually the attitude object is placed at the top of the page and participants are asked to rate this object by marking a category on each of the bipolar pairs (reserving the middle category for neutral responses). Attitudes are calculated by summing or averaging the scores for each bipolar scale. Semantic differential scales have generally been found to have adequate psychometric properties and are easy to use. However, because of their generality, they may provide somewhat less precise and comprehensive measurement of specific attitudes than Thurstone or Likert scales do.

Single-Item Direct Attitude Measures

Attitude measures are traditionally composed of multiple items. However, in some cases, attitudes are measured with a single semantic differential item or opinion statement. This practice is common in situations such as telephone surveys in which attitudes toward a wide range of topics must be assessed in a short time. Unfortunately, any single item may have biases or ambiguities and may lack the breadth to fully capture an attitude. Thus, single-item measures can have inadequate reliability and validity. A large literature has developed regarding the optimal way to construct such items and organize them within a questionnaire.

Alternatives to Direct Measures of Attitudes

Direct measures of attitudes presume people are willing and able to discuss their attitudes openly. This may not always be the case, and researchers have developed numerous alternatives to direct methods of attitude measurement.

Indirect Measures of Attitudes

One of the earliest and best known indirect measures is the information-error test, developed by Kenneth Hammond. This procedure begins with generating a large number of objective knowledge questions about the target issue. The goal is to create questions that in principle have objective answers but to which respondents are unlikely to know the answers. These questions are presented in a multiple-choice format, with answers implying various levels of negativity or positivity toward the target position (e.g., a question on capital punishment might ask respondents to guess the percentage of executed criminals who were later found to have been falsely convicted). The assumption underlying this method is that when individuals are faced with questions for which they do not know the answer, they will tend to guess in an attitude-consistent manner. Attitude scores can be calculated by assigning scale values to increasingly positive or negative answers and then summing or averaging the responses across items.

More recently, indirect attitude measures have received renewed attention stemming largely from the increasing literature on unconscious (or implicit) attitudes and the suggestion that indirect measures may be more effective than direct measures in capturing unconscious attitudes, As a result, new indirect measures (called implicit measures of attitudes) are being introduced with increasing frequency. Two implicit measures have received particular attention.

Russell Fazio's evaluative priming technique (also called the bona fide pipeline or affective priming) is based on the notion that even if we are not specifically asked to report our attitudes, they will automatically come to mind when we encounter the attitude object. Interestingly, automatically activated attitudes influence our judgments of other objects. It has been shown that if a negative attitude is activated, people can make quick judgments about other objects that are negatively evaluated but are slower in making judgments about objects that are positively evaluated. The opposite is true if the initial attitude activated is positive. This effect is central to the evaluative priming technique.

The evaluative priming procedure involves presenting respondents with a dual judgment task. They are told that first they will be briefly presented on computer with a word prime that they should try to remember and then they will be presented with a second word, for which they will need to make an evaluative judgment (i.e., judge if the word is positive or negative). Respondents are presented with numerous word pairs, and the time it takes them to make judgments about the second word in the pair is recorded. Attitudes are measured by including the target attitude object among the primes. The speed of judgments using the attitude object are then examined when it serves as a prime for words that are almost universally liked (e.g., *love*) and as a prime for some words that are almost universally disliked (e.g., *death*). If a person's attitude is positive, that person should be faster in making judgments about the second words when the attitude object is a prime for positive words than when it is a prime for negative words. The reverse is true for negative attitudes.

Another recently developed indirect test is the Implicit Association Test (IAT). This measure is designed to tap the (automatic) associations between two concepts (e.g., homosexual, heterosexual) with positive and negative evaluations. In this procedure, respondents are told that they will be given a list of words on computer that will fall into one of four categories: the target attitude object (e.g., *homosexuals*), a comparison attitude object (e.g., *heterosexuals*), positive words, and negative words. Respondents assign each word to one of the four categories by pressing one of two response keys. In one set of trials, respondents are told to hit one key if the word is a word related to the target object *or* a positive word and to hit a different key if the word is related to the comparison object *or* a negative word. In a second set of trials, the task is reversed so that target object words and negative words share the same response key, and comparison object words and positive words share the same response key. The computer records the time it takes for respondents to make their categorizations.

The logic underlying the IAT is that if a person's attitude toward the target attitude object is positive, that person will be able to perform the task more quickly when target object words share the same response key with positive words than they will when target object words share the same response key with negative words. In contrast, if the person's attitude is negative, the reverse will be true. Attitude scores are created by computing a numerical index that reflects the difference between the average speed with which people perform the two versions of the task.

Both the evaluative priming procedure and the IAT are new measures of attitudes, and research is still being conducted to assess their reliability and validity.

Physiological Measures of Attitudes

Another alternative to direct measures of attitudes is the use of physiological measures. Although some early physiological measures of attitudes were problematic, more recent measures have proved promising. For example, the use of event related brain potentials (ERP) has proven effective in assessing attitudes. The ERP is measured by attaching electrodes to certain areas of the scalp and monitoring the pattern of electrocortical activity that occurs when people are categorizing objects. Specifically, a sequence of stimuli that is evaluatively consistent (i.e., all positive or all negative) is presented to the participant, with the target attitude object at the end of this sequence. If the attitude object differs in categorization from the previous stimuli (e.g., it is evaluated negatively and the previous sequence is positive), a large ERP will occur. If the attitude object's categorization is consistent with the previous objects (e.g., all positive), a small ERP will occur. By presenting the attitude object at the end of both a sequence of positive objects and a sequence of negative objects, the overall attitude score can be computed by comparing the size of the ERP for the two sequences.

Recently, brain-imaging techniques have been applied to the measurement of attitudes. For example, functional magnetic resonance imaging (fMRI), a procedure for measuring changes in brain activity through increases in blood flow and oxygen consumption, can be used to assess attitudes. By placing participants in the fMRI scanner and presenting them with an image of the attitudinal object, researchers can see what parts of the brain are activated in response to the target stimuli. Such activation can then be examined in relation to distinct patterns of brain activity associated with particular emotional and cognitive responses. Use of this technique enables researchers to assess attitude valence and possibly even attitude structure (e.g., emotional or cognitive).

—*Sonia Matwin and Leandre R. Fabrigar*

See also Guttman Scaling; Likert Scaling; Questionnaires; Thurstone Scales

Further Reading

Edwards, A. L. (1957). *Techniques of attitude scale construction*. New York: Appleton-Century-Crofts.

Fabrigar, L. R., Krosnick, J. A., & MacDougall, B. L. (2005). Attitude measurement: Techniques for measuring the unobservable. In C. T. Brock & M. C. Green (Eds.), *Persuasion: Psychological insights and perspectives* (pp. 17–40). Thousand Oaks, CA: Sage.

Guttman, L. (1944). A basis for scaling qualitative data. *American Sociological Review, 9,* 139–150.

Himmelfarb, S. (1993). The measurement of attitudes. In A. H. Eagly & S. Chaiken, *The psychology of attitudes* (pp. 23–87). Orlando, FL: Harcourt Brace Jovanovich.

Likert, R. (1932). A technique for the measurement of attitudes. *Archives of Psychology, 140,* 44–53.

Thurstone, L. L., & Chave, E. J. (1929). *The measurement of attitude.* Chicago: University of Chicago Press.

Project Implicit: https://implicit.harvard.edu/implicit/

Applying Ideas on Statistics and Measurement

The following abstract is adapted from Shlaes, J. L., Jason, L. A., & Ferrari, J. R. (1999). The development of the Chronic Fatigue Syndrome Attitudes Test: A psychometric analysis. *Evaluation & the Health Professions, 22*(4), 442–465.

Chronic Fatigue Syndrome (CFS) is characterized by debilitating symptoms including persistent or relapsing fatigue, and as a result of CFS, some individuals experience significant stigma. Many medical professionals are skeptical of the validity of the illness, and employers often fail to appreciate its seriousness. There is presently no tool to measure attitudes toward this illness or toward people who have CFS. The purpose of these studies was to create a scale that measures attitudes toward individuals with CFS—the Chronic Fatigue **Attitudes Test** (CAT)—and to assess the scale's reliability and validity. The 13-item scale was created using several constructs outlined in the literature regarding negative attitudes toward people with CFS, disabilities, and AIDS.

ATTRIBUTABLE RISK

The attributable risk statistic provides an estimate of the proportion or number of events that can be explained by a particular risk factor. Epidemiologists frequently use attributable risk calculations to determine the population impact associated with a disease,

Table 1 Attributable Risk Hypothetical Sample

	Event	No event			Lung cancer at follow-up		
					Yes	No	
Exposed	A	B	A + B	Smoker	3,000	7,000	10,000
Unexposed	C	D	C + D	Nonsmoker	1,000	9,000	10,000
	A + C	B + D			4,000	16,000	

Notes: Attributable risk = (A/A + B) − (C/C + D); (3,000/[3,000 + 7,000]) − (1,000/[1,000 + 9,000]) = .30 − .10 = .20; Attributable risk = C/(C + D) × [(A/A + B) / (C/C + D) − 1]; Attributable risk = .10 × (3 − 1) = .20

behavior, or condition. The U.S. Surgeon General's estimate that smoking accounts for up to 400,000 deaths annually in the United States is an example of an attributable risk inference.

In the context of cohort studies, attributable risk is also referred to as risk difference, in this case quantifying the excess risk in exposed versus unexposed groups. Attributable risk can be calculated in several ways. When accompanied by a relative risk statistic, the attributable risk is equal to the rate of events in the unexposed group × (relative risk −1). A more widely applicable formula requires the creation of a 2 × 2 contingency table, as illustrated in Table 1 with a hypothetical sample of smokers and nonsmokers.

In Table 1, A through D represent the number of cases in each study cell. The event rate among smokers (3,000/10,000) is three times higher than among nonsmokers (1,000/10,000). Half the sample is composed of smokers, and 20% develop cancer over the course of the study. Attributable risk uses both the group event rates and the prevalence of the exposure (smoking) for calculation purposes. The attributable risk value of .20 tells us that if smokers in the study became nonsmokers, the incidence of lung cancer would decrease by 20 per 100 individuals. This represents a potential 66% decrease in lung cancer cases.

Important facts about attributable risk:

- The attributable risk statistic alone does not imply that a causal relationship exists between the exposure factor and the event.
- Because attributable risk uses information about exposure prevalence, the attributable risk values between two exposure factors that each double the risk of an event such as cancer can differ dramatically if one exposure (e.g., working in coal mines) is much more rare than a more common exposure (e.g., smoking).
- Attributable risk can be used to calculate the population attributable risk by use of the following formula: attributable risk × rate of exposure in the population.
- The proportion of events potentially eliminated in a population by changing the exposure rate to that of the unexposed group is often referred to as the attributable proportion.
- By combining attributable risk with the financial costs of a health event, researchers can estimate the health care expenses associated with an exposure factor and calculate the health care savings achievable by modifying a risk factor in a population.

—*Thomas Rutledge*

See also Probability Sampling

Further Reading

Centers for Disease Control and Prevention. (2003, September 5). Cigarette smoking-attributable morbidity—United States, 2000. *MMWR, 52*(35), 842–844. Available from http://www.cdc.gov/mmwr/preview/mmwrhtml/mm5235a4.htm

Sedgwick, J. E. C. (2001). Absolute, attributable, and relative risk in the management of coronary heart disease. *Heart, 85,* 491–492.

Thun, M. J., Apicella, L. F., & Henley, S. J. (2000). Smoking vs other risk factors as the cause of smoking-attributable deaths. *JAMA, 284,* 706–712.

Disease rates comparison: http://bmj.bmjjournals.com/epidem/epid.3.html

ATTRITION BIAS

When data are collected over two or more points in time, it is common for some participants to drop out of the study prematurely. The attrition of the original sample can occur in longitudinal research as well as in experimental designs that include pretest, posttest, and follow-up data collection. In longitudinal research, which often lasts many years, some participants move between data points and cannot be located. Others, especially older persons, may die or become too incapacitated to continue participation in the study. In clinical treatment studies, there may be barriers to continued participation in the treatment program, such as drug relapse or lack of transportation.

Attrition of the original sample represents a potential threat of bias if those who drop out of the study are systematically different from those who remain in the study. The result is that the remaining sample becomes different from the original sample, resulting in what is known as attrition bias. However, if sample attrition over time is not systematic, meaning that there are no unique characteristics among those who drop out, then there is no attrition bias, even though the sample has decreased in size between waves of data collection. It is important, then, for researchers who collect multiple waves of data to check for attrition bias.

Attrition bias is one of the major threats to multi-wave studies, and it can bias the sample in two ways. First, attrition bias can affect the external validity of the study. If some groups of people drop out of the study more frequently than others, the subsequent longitudinal sample no longer resembles the original sample in the study. As a result, the remaining sample is not generalizable to the original population that was sampled. For example, a longitudinal sample examining the grieving process of women following the death of a spouse may fail to retain those participants who have become too distraught to fill out the questionnaire. The nonparticipation of this group may bias the findings of the study toward a minimization of depressive symptomatology as a component of the grieving process. In other words, the composition of the sample changes to the point that the results are no longer generalizable to the original population of widows.

Second, systematic, as opposed to random, attrition can negatively affect the internal validity of the study by altering the correlations among the variables in the study. This problem occurs in longitudinal research because the subsamples that are dropping out of the study at a higher rate are underrepresented in the longitudinal sample, which may lead to correlations between variables that are different from the true correlations in the original sample. For example, the underrepresentation of widows with depressive symptomatology in the second or third wave of a study may alter the correlation between insomnia and length of time since the death of the spouse.

Selective attrition affects the internal validity of experimental research when there are differential dropout rates between the treatment and control groups. In a clinical trial of a depression treatment, if the participants in the treatment group drop out at a higher rate than do the participants of the control group, the results of the study will be biased toward showing artificially successful treatment effects, thus compromising the internal validity of the study. However, if the dropout rates are comparable, the threats to internal validity due to attrition are minimal.

Preventing Attrition

Because of the threat of attrition bias to the external and internal validity of studies, it is important to minimize sample attrition when conducting multiwave research. Researchers who have conducted experimental and longitudinal research have made a number of recommendations and suggestions to reduce sample attrition. Mason emphasized the importance of creating a project identity, offering cash and other incentives, developing a strong tracking system to constantly identify the location and status of participants, and keeping follow-up interviews brief. Others recommend collecting detailed contact information about participants to increase the likelihood of locating them for the second and subsequent interviews. Follow-up postcards and telephone reminders also help retain participants in the sample.

Detecting Attrition Bias

Differences in characteristics between those who prematurely drop out a study ("droppers") and those who remain in the sample ("stayers") can be assessed by conducting a logistical regression analysis. Because both groups participated in the first wave of the study, data are available on which to compare the two groups. A dichotomous dependent variable is created with 1 representing the stayers and 0 representing the droppers. Variables from the first wave of data are used as independent variables in the analysis. These variables should include key demographic variables, such as race, income, age, and education, as well as substantive variables that are salient in the study, such as depression, drug abuse, or marital quality. A statistically significant coefficient for any of the variables means that there is a difference between the stayers and the droppers, indicating attrition bias.

Threats to internal validity due to attrition bias can be tested by comparing the first-wave correlation matrices of the overall sample and the longitudinal sample, which includes only the stayers. This can be done in two ways:

1. Each of the correlation coefficients (for example, the correlation between age and level of depression) is compared using Fisher's z statistical test. A significant z score means that the two coefficients are statistically significantly different, indicating attrition bias.

2. A structural equation modeling program, such as LISREL or AMOS, can be used to test whether the two correlation matrices are invariant, that is, the same. If the test for invariance is nonsignificant, then the two matrices are assumed to be equivalent, with no apparent attrition bias.

Correcting Attrition Bias

Although the strategies used to detect attrition bias are straightforward, there is substantial debate about appropriate strategies to correct attrition bias. Despite the lack of consensus, though, the need for correcting the problem of attrition bias is crucial and continues to motivate statisticians to pursue solutions.

Correction of nonrandom attrition can be broken into two categories. The first category is correction of data when the mechanism of dropping out is known, or in other words, when the researcher knows which characteristics are related to dropping out of the study. The second category is attrition whose causes the researcher does not know.

Known Cause of Attrition

When the cause of attrition is known, the researcher can take steps to control the data analysis procedure to account for the missing data. A model has been developed that simultaneously calculates the research question and the mechanism for missing data. This model is a sample selection model in which two simultaneous regression models are calculated. The first model is a regression model that addresses the research question, with the hypotheses of the study being examined by the regression of the dependent variable on the key independent variables in the study. The second model includes the variables that

are causing attrition, with the dependent variable being a dichotomous variable indicating either continued participation or nonparticipation in the study. The error terms of the substantive dependent variable in the first regression model and the participation dependent variable in the second regression model are correlated. A significant correlation between the two error terms indicates attrition bias. If the correlation is significant, the inclusion of the second model provides corrected regression coefficients for the first, substantive regression model. Thus, the inclusion of the second model that examines attrition bias serves as a correction mechanism for the first, substantive model and enables the calculation of unbiased regression coefficients.

Unknown Cause of Attrition

Heckman proposed a two-step procedure to correct for attrition bias when the cause of the attrition is not readily apparent. He conceptualized the issue of attrition bias as a specification error, in which the variable that accounts for systematic attrition in the study is not included in the regression equation. This specification error results in biased regression coefficients in the analysis. His solution is to first create a proxy of the variable that explains attrition. This is done by conducting a logit regression analysis, similar to the one described in the section on detecting attrition bias. The dependent variable is whether or not each participant participated in the second wave of data collection, and the independent variables are possible variables that may explain or predict dropout. This first step not only tests for attrition bias but also creates an outcome variable, which Heckman calls λ (lambda). Thus, a λ value is computed for all cases in the study, and it represents the proxy variable that explains the causation of attrition in the study.

The second step of Heckman's procedure is to merge the λ value of each participant into the larger data set and then include it in the substantive analysis. In other words, the λ variable is included in the regression equation that is used to test the hypotheses in the study. Including λ in the equation solves the problem of specification error and leads to more accurate regression coefficients.

While Heckman's model has been used by longitudinal researchers for many years, some concerns have arisen regarding its trustworthiness. Stolzenberg and Relles argue that Heckman's model has been shown to compute inaccurate estimates, and they suggest several cautions when using his model. Nevertheless, Heckman's model offers a possible solution when systematic attrition threatens to bias the results of a study.

—*Richard B. Miller and Cody S. Hollist*

See also Longitudinal/Repeated Measures Data

Further Reading

Boys, A., Marsden, J., Stillwell, G., Hatchings, K., Griffiths, P., & Farrell, M. (2003). Minimizing respondent attrition in longitudinal research: Practical implications from a cohort study of adolescent drinking. *Journal of Adolescence, 26,* 363–373.

Cuddeback, G., Wilson, E., Orme, J. G., & Combs-Orme, T. (2004). Detecting and statistically correcting sample selection bias. *Journal of Social Service Research, 30,* 19–33.

Goodman, J. S., & Blum, T. C. (1996). Assessing the nonrandom sampling effects of subject attrition in longitudinal research. *Journal of Management, 22,* 627–652.

Graham, J. W., & Donaldson, S. I. (1993). Evaluating interventions with differential attrition: The importance of nonresponse mechanisms and use of follow up data. *Journal of Applied Psychology, 78,* 119–128.

Heckman, J. J. (1976). The common structure of statistical models of truncation, sample selection and limited dependent variables and a simple estimator for such models. *Annals of Economic and Social Measurement, 5,* 475–492.

Heckman, J. J. (1979). Sample selection bias as a specification error. *Econometrica, 47,* 153–161.

Jacobson, J. O. (2004). Place and attrition from substance abuse treatment. *Journal of Drug Issues, 34,* 23–50.

Mason, M. (1999). A review of procedural and statistical methods for handling attrition and missing data in clinical research. *Measurement and Evaluation in Counseling and Development, 32,* 111–118.

Miller, R. B., & Wright, D. (1995). Correction for attrition bias in longitudinal analyses. *Journal of Marriage and the Family, 57,* 921–929.

Stolzenberg, R. M., & Relles, D. A. (1997). Tools for intuition about sample selection bias and its correction. *American Sociological Review, 73,* 142–167.

Audit Trail

An audit trail is a collection of documentation that enables tracing the steps of any process or procedure. The term *audit* is commonly applied in accounting situations. In such a context, an audit involves reviewing records of accounting procedures and transactions to assess the validity of financial reports. The assortment of documentation and the pathways available for reviewing that documentation constitute the audit trail. Information technology contexts use audit trails for computer security, to trace, for instance, the path of a system intruder and, ideally, identify the source of any intrusion. Audit trails also are used in food distribution to ascertain the actual nature of food described as organic, for example; to trace the presence or absence of additives; and to locate the origin and pathways of items distributed across various settings. This latter function can be invaluable in public health situations; for example, a food-borne illness can be traced to an infected animal, processing plant, or food service handler.

The audit trail serves a comparable purpose in research applications. In research, the audit trail is used to evaluate decisions and analytic procedures throughout a study to demonstrate the soundness, appropriateness, and in essence the validity of conclusions. One of the original uses of an audit trail in relation to research was in association with large-scale program evaluation projects, and a specific audit process may be included as part of such a study. For example, evaluation of a statewide program to increase graduation rates from high school may involve a review of expenditures, test scores, student progress, graduation rates, and other outcome data. The researchers also might choose to conduct interviews or focus groups with teachers and students involved in the program. To confront questions that the results could be biased by political or personal aims, auditors can be employed to review the procedures of the researchers, ensuring that appropriate data were collected, that conclusions were consistent with the data, and that the results present a valid evaluation of the program under review.

In qualitative studies, because the entire parameters of a study cannot be anticipated in advance, changes often are implemented during a study. The researcher must maintain documentation of decisions and the rationale for any changes as a way to recall and substantiate that such actions were appropriate. In addition to documenting procedures for credibility purposes, an audit trail in qualitative research may include field notes, or notes regarding the behaviors and actions of people and other events happening in the situation where data are collected; methodological documentation; analytic documentation reflecting the researcher's thought processes during data analysis; and documentation of personal responses to capture the investigator's role and reactions as the study progresses. Ongoing developments in software for qualitative data analysis help to consolidate some of these processes by making the creation of field notes and methodological journals a part of the electronic data set.

—*Beth Rodgers*

See also Authenticity; Text Analysis

Further Reading

Creswell, J.W., & Miller, D. L. (2000). Determining validity in qualitative inquiry. *Theory Into Practice*, *39*(3), 124–130.

Petterson, M. (2005). The keys to effective IT auditing. *Journal of Corporate Accounting and Finance*, *16*(5), 41–46.

Rodgers, B. L., & Cowles, K. V. (1993). The qualitative research audit trail: A complex collection of documentation. *Research in Nursing and Health*, *16*, 219–226.

AUTHENTICITY

Authenticity in education is the fidelity of the intellectual learning environment to the real-world ways in which knowledge is used in the field of study into which the student is being inducted. In other words, the learning that is engendered in formal education and the mechanisms through which such learning is judged are authentic to the extent that there is congruence between the institutionally derived tasks and reality. In reality, significant accomplishment requires the production, rather than the reproduction, of knowledge. Production of knowledge is a particular type of cognitive work that constructs new knowledge in a meaningful way and has a personal, utilitarian, or aesthetic value beyond the demonstration of competence. Therefore, formal learning tasks are authentic when they meet one or more of criteria for significant accomplishment. Within education, authenticity connotes the quality of intellectual engagement required in reading; writing; speaking; coping with challenges that do not have single solutions; and producing tangible artifacts such as a research report, a musical score, an exhibition of artwork, or a demonstration of an invention. There are three standards by which intellectual engagement can be judged authentic:

1. *Analysis*: The task requires higher-order thinking with content by organizing, synthesizing, interpreting, evaluating, and hypothesizing to produce comparisons, contrasts, arguments, new applications of information, and appraisals of competing perspectives.

2. *Disciplinary concepts*: The task requires an understanding of ideas, concepts, theories, and principles that are central to the academic or professional disciplines into which the student is being inducted.

3. *Elaborated written communication*: The task requires production of detail, qualification, argument, and conclusions that are clear, coherent, and rich.

This interpretation of authenticity is entirely consistent with contemporary theories of learning and knowing, which emphasize how knowledge is represented, organized, and processed in the mind. Because these theories imply that instruction and assessment should be integrated, authenticity can refer to both achievement (the correspondence between classroom instruction and reality) and assessment (the correspondence between instruction and assessment).

Educational practices often assert authenticity through using interactive video environments to engage students in simulated real-life problems. These have produced gains in problem solving, communication skills, and more positive attitudes to domain knowledge. However, it is not simulations per se but the extent to which they replicate the conditions in which people are challenged in context that determines authenticity. No matter how authentic a task seems, the institutional constraints and policy variables in formal education contexts mean that authenticity in education is an approximation that need not necessarily capture the totality or urgency of all the real-life variables. Currently, the lack of systematic investigation into the effects of the learning context, the learning task, and the learners' interpretations of context and task in the simulated experiences means that the validity and reliability of the simulations are not yet well understood.

—Effie Maclellan

See also Audit Trail

Further Reading

Petraglia, J. (1998). *Reality by design: The rhetoric and technology of authenticity in education*. Mahwah, NJ: Erlbaum.

For information on the Internet, key the term *Authentic Education* into any search engine.

AUTOCORRELATION

Many parametric statistical procedures (e.g., ANOVA, linear regression) assume that the errors of the models used in the analysis are independent of one another (i.e., the errors are not correlated). When this assumption is not met in the context of time-series research designs, the errors are said to be *autocorrelated* or *dependent*. Because time-series designs involve the collection of data from a single participant at many points in time rather than from many participants at one point in time, the assumption of independent errors inherent in many parametric statistical analyses may not be met. When this occurs, the outcome of these analyses and the conclusions drawn from them are likely to be misleading unless some corrective action is taken.

The error in a time-series linear model usually refers to an observed value Y_t (i.e., a dependent variable score observed in a theoretical process at time t) minus the predicted value $\hat{Y}_t$ (based on parameters in the model). When actual sample data are involved (instead of theoretical process data), the predicted values are based on the estimates of the parameters in the model, and the difference $Y_t - \hat{Y}_t$ is called a residual. Hence, a residual is an estimate of an error. For example, if a researcher proposes an ANOVA model for a two-phase interrupted time-series design, the residual is defined as an observed value in a realization (i.e., a sample) of the process minus the mean of the relevant phase. If the sign and size of the residuals are unrelated to the sign and size of the residuals that follow them, there will be no autocorrelation, and this implies that the errors of the model are independent. If, however, positive residuals tend to be followed in time by positive residuals and negative residuals tend to be followed by negative residuals, the autocorrelation will be positive; this is evidence that the independence assumption is violated. Similarly, if positive residuals tend to be followed by negative residuals and negative residuals tend to be followed by positive residuals, the autocorrelation will be negative, and once again, this is evidence that the independence assumption is violated. Autocorrelated errors are especially likely to occur when (a) the time between observations is very short, (b) the outcome behavior changes very slowly, (c) important predictor variables are left out of the model, or (d) the functional form (e.g., linear) of the relationship between the predictors and the outcome is incorrectly specified.

Why Autocorrelation Is Important

Autocorrelation is important because (a) it can affect the validity of inferential statements associated with conventional hypothesis tests and confidence intervals (e.g., positive autocorrelation leads to underestimated p values and confidence intervals that are too narrow), (b) knowledge of its presence can lead a researcher to select a more appropriate statistical analysis, and (c) the precision of predictions made using regression equations can be improved using information regarding autocorrelation.

How Autocorrelation Is Measured

Although one can measure autocorrelation in many different ways, the most frequently encountered method involves the computation of a single coefficient called the *lag-1 autocorrelation coefficient*. This autocorrelation coefficient represents the correlation between the residuals at their associated time t and those same residuals shifted ahead by one unit of time. The sample coefficient computed on actual data is denoted as r_1 whereas the population (or process) parameter is denoted as ρ_1. Like most two-variable correlation coefficients, the autocorrelation coefficient must fall between -1.0 and $+1.0$. The conventional formula for computing the sample coefficient is

$$r_1 = \frac{\sum_{t=2}^{N}(e_t)(e_{t-1})}{\sum_{t=1}^{N}e_t^2},$$

where

e_t is the residual (i.e., the estimate of the error of the model), measured at time t, and

N is the number of residuals in the observed time series.

Consider the data presented in Table 1. The first column lists the time points at which performance measures on a complex job task were obtained. Observations 1 through 10 were obtained during the first (baseline) phase of a two-phase experiment, and observations 11 through 20 were obtained during the second (intervention) phase. The third column contains the residuals, which were computed by subtracting the mean for phase 1 from each observation in phase 1. Similarly, the residuals for phase 2 were computed by subtracting the mean for phase 2 from each observation in phase 2. This approach for computing residuals was used because the investigator chose a simple ANOVA model for the data analysis. This model defines the error as $(Y_t - \mu_t) = \varepsilon_t$ and the estimate of the error (i.e., the residual) as $(Y_t - \bar{Y}_j) = e_t$, where j indicates the phase. The fourth column contains the same residuals shown in column three, except they have been shifted

forward by one time unit. No observation appears in the first row because there is no observation at time point zero. The sum of the values shown in column 5 is 26.3 and the sum of the squared residuals (not shown in the table) is 123.15. The lag-1 autocorrelation coefficient is the ratio of 26.3 over 123.15, which is .21.

Often researchers apply a formal inferential procedure (such as the Durbin-Watson test) to test the hypothesis $\rho_1 = 0$. Using the Durbin-Watson test, we obtain a p value associated with the example autocorrelation coefficient ($r_1 = .21$) that falls above .10, so we have insufficient evidence to conclude that the residuals are autocorrelated. Consequently, the ANOVA model appears acceptable with respect to meeting the independence assumption. Two-phase designs often require more complex models, but regardless of the

Table 1 Values Used in Computing the Lag-1 Autocorrelation Coefficient on the Residuals

Time t	Y_t	e_t	e_{t-1}	$(e_t)(e_{t-1})$
1	5	−1.28	—	—
2	6	−.26	−1.28	.34
3	6	−.25	−.26	.06
4	7	.77	−.25	−.19
5	7	.79	.77	.61
6	8	1.81	.79	1.43
7	4	−2.17	1.81	−3.93
8	7	.85	−2.17	−1.84
9	7	.86	.85	.73
10	5	−1.12	.86	−.97
11	16	1.12	−1.12	−1.25
12	19	4.14	1.12	4.63
13	14	−.85	4.14	−3.50
14	16	1.17	−.85	−.99
15	11	−3.81	1.17	−4.47
16	10	−4.79	−3.81	18.25
17	10	−4.77	−4.79	22.87
18	19	4.25	−4.77	−20.26
19	18	3.26	4.25	13.86
20	15	.28	3.26	.92

Notes: Y_t = observed values (values at $t = 1$–10 are from Phase 1, and values at $t = 11$–20 are from Phase 2); e_t = residuals, computed by subtracting the mean for Phase 1 from each observation in Phase 1 and the mean for Phase 2 from each observation in Phase 2; e_{t-1} = residuals shifted forward by one time unit.

complexity of the design or the model, researchers should attempt to determine whether the errors of the model are independent by evaluating the residuals.

More Complete Evaluations of Dependency

The lag-1 autocorrelation coefficient measures the degree of relationship between residuals measured one time period apart. That is, it measures the relationship between residuals of adjacent scores. Although dependency in a time series usually appears in the lag-1 coefficient, this is not always true. Adjacent values may possibly show little or no relationship, while values separated by more than one time unit may show a substantial relationship. One can measure relationships of this type by computing autocorrelation coefficients at lags greater than lag-1. If the autocorrelation is computed between the original series and the original series lagged by two time units, the resulting coefficient is called the lag-2 autocorrelation, denoted r^2. We can extend this idea to many lags. It is possible to compute K coefficients from N observations, where K is equal to $N - 1$. The whole collection of autocorrelation coefficients (i.e., r_1, r_2, . . . , r_K) is called the *autocorrelation function*.

Most time-series computer programs compute autocorrelations for a fraction (usually one sixth to one quarter) of the possible lags. These programs usually represent the coefficients graphically in a correlogram. The vertical dimension of the correlogram indicates the size of the autocorrelation coefficient, and the horizontal dimension indicates the lag. The information displayed in the correlogram is very useful in characterizing the dependency structure in a time series. If all the lagged autocorrelation coefficients in the correlogram hover around zero, this implies that the values in the series are independent. But if large coefficients appear at one or more lags, we have reason to suspect dependency in the series. Most time-series software packages provide formal tests of independence that consider the whole set of coefficients in the correlogram. The most popular of these tests are known as *Box-Pierce* and *Ljung-Box* tests.

Relevant Autocorrelations for Various Time-Series Models

Sometimes investigators estimate autocorrelation on dependent variable scores rather than on errors. It is important to distinguish between autocorrelations estimated on these two types of scores to understand the difference between two popular approaches to time-series analysis. In the approach known as autoregressive, integrated, moving averages (ARIMA) modeling, autocorrelation among *dependent variable scores* is relevant. In the approach known as time-series regression modeling, autocorrelation among *errors of a regression model* is relevant. Although both approaches require the computation of autocorrelation measures, they use information regarding autocorrelation for somewhat different purposes. ARIMA models use autocorrelation measures to identify the type of time-series parameters necessary for modeling the dependent variable scores. In contrast, time-series regression models most often use measures of autocorrelation to determine whether the errors of the regression model show independence. In these regression models, significant autocorrelation should warn researchers that they have misspecified the model (i.e., chosen a substantially wrong model) and that alternative models should be considered. The alternative model may contain parameters that either (a) eliminate autocorrelation among the errors or (b) accommodate that autocorrelation.

—*Bradley E. Huitema and Sean Laraway*

See also Correlation Coefficient; Time Series Analysis

Further Reading

Enders, W. (2004). *Applied econometric time series* (2nd ed.). Hoboken, NJ: Wiley.

Huitema, B. E. (1988). Autocorrelation: 10 years of confusion. *Behavioral Assessment, 10*, 253–294.

Huitema, B. E., & McKean, J. W. (1998). Irrelevant autocorrelation in least-squares intervention models. *Psychological Methods, 3*, 104–116.

Judd, C. M., & Kenny, D. A. (1981). *Estimating the effects of social interventions.* New York: Cambridge University Press.

McKnight, S., McKean, J. W., & Huitema, B. E. (2000). A double bootstrap method to analyze an intervention time series model with autoregressive error terms. *Psychological Methods*, 5, 87–101.

Software for estimating time series regression models with autoregressive errors (output includes regression coefficients, associated bootstrap tests, and a reduced bias autocorrelation estimate): http://www.stat.wmich.edu/, click on Stat Lab → Software → Timeseries. A design matrix and outcome data must be entered.

AVERAGE

To describe a group of values, it is useful to have a typical value or an average value. An average is a summary, so the average value should be representative of a group of values. An average can be used primarily to describe a sample and can also be used to estimate a population value. For example, researchers might want to find an average value in their sample that lets them predict what the average value in the population might be.

There are various measures of central tendency, or average, of a data set, and all have different statistical properties, which makes them sometimes more and sometimes less useful descriptors. Specific problems associated with the distribution the group of values represents are the shape of the distribution (symmetrically distributed or skewed, for example) and the presence or absence of outliers in the data set. Either the average value can be computed, taking all or only some values in the group into account, or it can be a chosen value from the group, seen fit to represent the group.

Most commonly, people refer to the *arithmetic mean* as the average (and vice versa), although this language is ambiguous and should be avoided. The arithmetic mean is the sum of all the values divided by the number of values in the group. There are many variations of the mean, two of the most common ones being the *geometric mean* and the *harmonic mean*. A *trimmed mean* excludes a specific percentage of the upper and the lower end of a distribution, commonly 5% in either direction. A *midmean* is a special case of a trimmed mean in which the mean is calculated for the data between the 25th and 75th percentiles.

The *mode*, the most frequently occurring value, can also be a descriptor of a group of values. The *median* is also a frequently used term for expressing an average value. Especially in skewed data, the mean would be less informative than the median.

It is important to remember that an average value should be presented together with a measure of dispersion.

More about average:

- The mean as the most commonly used average measure is sensitive to extreme scores.
- The median is a suitable average for nonsymmetric distributions and is not affected by outliers.
- The mode is an average value actually represented in the group of values, whereas the mean, as a derivative, can take a value that is not actually represented in the group of values (e.g., the average number of children is 1.2).

—*Susanne Hempel*

See also Arithmetic Mean; Mean; Measures of Central Tendency; Median; Mode

Further Reading

Molden, D. C., & Dweck, C.-S. (2006). Finding "meaning" in psychology: A lay theories approach to self-regulation, social perception, and social development. *American Psychologist*, 61(3), 192–203.

Descriptive Statistics: http://www.physics.csbsju.edu/stats/descriptive2.html (application that computes the mean once data are entered)

Applying Ideas on Statistics and Measurement

The following abstract is adapted from See, W. Y., Wagner, T. H., Shuo, C., & Barnett, P. G. (2003). Average cost of VA rehabilitation, mental health, and long-term hospital stays. *Medical Care Research and Review*, 60(3 suppl), 40S–53S.

One of the most common methods used to better understand a collection of data points is through the calculation of an **average** (which includes such descriptive statistics as the mean, the mode, and the median). In this article, researchers Wei You See and his colleagues at

Stanford University describe the development of a database for the cost of inpatient rehabilitation, mental health, and long-term care stays in the Department of Veterans Affairs from fiscal year 1998. As a unit of analysis, they used bedsection, which is similar to a hospital ward, and they classified inpatient services into nine categories, including rehabilitation, blind rehabilitation, spinal cord injury, psychiatry, substance abuse, intermediate medicine, domiciliary, psychosocial residential rehabilitation, and nursing home. For each of these nine categories, they estimated a national and a local average per diem cost. The next step was to calculate what they call encounter-level costs, which was done by multiplying the average per diem cost by the number of days of stay in the fiscal year. Their conclusion? The national cost estimates for hospitalization are more reliable than the local cost estimates for the same.

AVERAGE DEVIATION

The *average deviation* (AD) is used as a measure of dispersion or within-group interrater agreement and may be referred to as the *average absolute deviation* or *mean deviation*. The average deviation is often defined in one of two ways: by deviations from the mean (AD_M) or by deviations from the median (AD_{Md}). The average deviation is calculated by taking the difference between each score and the mean (or median), summing the absolute values of these deviations, and then dividing the sum by the number of deviations. As a measure of dispersion, the larger the AD, the greater is the variability in a distribution of scores. As a measure of within-group interrater agreement, the larger the AD, the greater is the disagreement among raters evaluating a single target on a categorical rating scale.

The formula for the computation of the average deviation using the mean is

$$AD_M = \frac{\sum |X - \bar{X}|}{n}$$

where

Σ directs you to add together what follows it,

X is each individual score in the distribution of scores,

$\bar{X}$ is the mean,

the vertical lines are the absolute value symbols and direct you to disregard the fact that some deviations are positive and some negative, and

n is the number of cases or number of raters.

The formula for the computation of average deviation using the median (AD_{Md}) would substitute the median for the mean in the above equation.

More about the average deviation as a measure of dispersion:

- It gives equal weight to the deviation of every value from the mean or median.
- The average deviation from the median has the property of being the point at which the sum of the absolute deviations is minimal compared with any other point in the distribution of scores.
- Given that the AD is based on every value in the distribution of scores, it provides a better description of the dispersion than does the range or quartile deviation.
- In comparison with the standard deviation, the AD is less affected by extreme values and easier to understand.

More about the average deviation as a measure of within-group interrater agreement:

- The AD provides an index of interrater agreement in the metric (measurement units) of the original rating scale.
- A statistically derived cutoff for an acceptable level of disagreement in raters' evaluations of a single target is c/6values, where c is the number of response options or rating categories. Values of AD exceeding this cutoff value (e.g., values of AD exceeding a cutoff value of 1.2 on a 7-point rating scale) would indicate disagreement among raters, and values of AD below the cutoff would indicate agreement in raters' scores of the single target.
- In comparison with other measures of within-group interrater agreement, including the standard

deviation, the AD index is easiest to understand and interpret.

—Michael J. Burke

See also Standard Deviation; Variance

Further Reading

Dunlap, W. P., Burke, M. J., & Smith Crowe, K. (2003). Accurate tests of statistical significance for r sub(WG) and average deviation interrater agreement indexes. *Journal of Applied Psychology, 88*(2), 356–362.

Averages and deviations: http://www.sciencebyjones.com/average_deviation.htm

B

Although he may not always recognize his bondage, modern man lives under a tyranny of numbers.

—Nicholas Eberstadt

BABBAGE, CHARLES (1791–1871)

Charles Babbage is best known as the Father of Computing, having formulated the idea of a mechanical calculator during his student days.

Babbage was born in London on Boxing Day, December 26, 1791. His father was a banker from Devon, and Babbage was educated in Totnes, with the family moving to Teignmouth in 1808. Babbage was a sickly child who therefore received much of his education from private tutors at home. One consequence was that, on arriving at Cambridge University in 1810, he was somewhat disappointed with the standards expected. In 1812, with fellow undergraduates, he established the Analytical Society with the aim of promoting the use of our modern notation for differential calculus over the Newtonian presentation then in vogue.

He graduated in 1814, the year of his marriage to Georgiana Whitmore (who died in 1827 following the birth of their eighth child—only three survived to adulthood). In 1816, following the publication of two major papers, and as a consequence of his work with the Analytical Society, Babbage was elected a Fellow of the Royal Society. In 1820, he was elected a Fellow of the Royal Society of Edinburgh and was a founding member of what is now the Royal Astronomical Society. In 1828, he was appointed Lucasian Professor of Mathematics at Cambridge University (a post he held until 1839). In 1834, the decision to found a statistics society (now the Royal Statistical Society) was made at his house.

Babbage conceived the notion of constructing a machine for automated calculations while at Cambridge, but it was not until 1822 that he completed a working model. This machine was able to calculate the values of $n^2 + n + 1$ for successive values of n at the rate of 12 a minute. The machine worked by using differences: thus the successive values of $n^2 + n + 1$ are 3, 7, 13, 17, . . . , with constant differences of 4. The machine that Babbage conceived is therefore known as a *difference engine*. The initial model was well received, and Babbage received a grant to build a bigger, more powerful engine. However, as is so often the case with construction projects, the costs escalated enormously, and the project was finally abandoned in 1834.

Babbage then turned his attention to the construction of a more versatile *analytical engine*, which used punched cards adapted from a Jacquard loom (which enabled intricate woven patterns in cloth). The initial, 1835 design was for a machine five meters (16.4 feet) tall. For the next 10 years, the plans were refined, and it was at this time that Babbage corresponded with Ada, Countess of Lovelace, in the construction of algorithms for the embryonic machine—in other words, the world's first computer programs. Babbage died in London on October 18, 1871.

—*Graham Upton*

See also Probability Sampling

Further Reading

Swade, D. (2002). *The difference engine: Charles Babbage and the quest to build the first computer.* New York: Penguin.

Babbage's machines: http://www.sciencemuseum.org.uk/on-line/babbage/index.asp

BAR CHART

A bar chart is a specific type of chart that visually represents data as a series of horizontal bars, with the Y axis representing the categories contained in the data and the X axis representing the frequency. It is different from a column chart in that column charts display the data vertically.

Bar charts are most often used for categorical data that is, by definition, not dynamic in nature. For example, if one were interested in an examination of sales figures by brand before and after a marketing campaign, a bar chart would be the appropriate way to illustrate such information, as shown in the following example. First, here are the data.

	Brand X	*Brand Y*
Before	56.3	76.8
After	97.4	87.5

Note: Figures represent sales in millions of dollars.

A bar chart is relatively simple to construct manually. Following these steps and using graph paper is the easiest way to be accurate.

1. Group the data as shown in the above example.
2. Define the Y axis as "Brand."
3. Indicate on the X axis the scale that is to be used, which in this case is millions of dollars, ranging from 55 to 100.
4. Draw each bar for each brand to correspond with the data, making sure that the bars are appropriately colored or patterned so they are easily distinguishable from one another.

Using Excel, the process is much simpler.

1. Create the data on a new worksheet and save it.
2. Using the mouse, select all the data, including the column and row headings.
3. Click on the Chart Wizard icon on the Excel toolbar.
4. Click Finish in the dialog box.

While the finished bar chart may not appear as attractive as you might like, modifications are relatively easy to make, as shown in Figure 1.

The following changes were made:

- Major gridlines were removed.
- All coloring was deleted except for the gray added to one of each pair of bars to help distinguish it from the other.
- Value labels were added at the end of each bar.
- A title was added, as were labels for each axis.

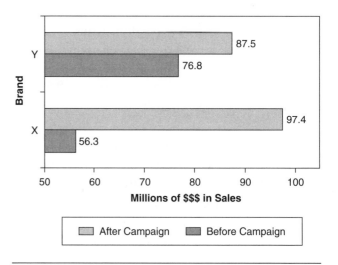

Figure 1   Sales by Brand

- The X axis minimum and maximum were changed from Excel's default values to 50 and 105.
- The border was removed from the legend.

—Neil J. Salkind

See also Area Chart; Line Chart; Pie Chart

Further Reading

Tufte, E. R. (2001). *The visual display of quantitative information* (2nd ed.). Cheshire, CT: Graphics Press.

BASAL AGE

Basal age represents the highest level, on a test standardized in units corresponding to mental age or age-equivalents, below which it can be assumed that all items would be answered correctly. For example, a child who correctly answers the required number of items at a certain age level would be given credit for all preceding items on the test even though the child has not actually been tested on those items. The term *basal age* is often used interchangeably with *basal score* or *basal*.

The point at which to begin the calculation of basal age is usually estimated from a child's chronological age or, for children with learning or language disabilities, from a functional estimate of age. For children who demonstrate considerable scatter in their performance or who perform at significantly different levels from their age-matched peers, the calculation of a basal age makes it easier to determine a meaningful starting point on a test.

Although tests vary somewhat in how basal scores are calculated, the procedure is usually very similar. The Stanford-Binet Intelligence Scales (fifth edition), for example, uses basal levels in all its 11 testing blocks. Testing is begun at a block that is believed to represent a child's general ability level. If a basal is not obtained, testing moves back to successively lower blocks until a basal is established. On the Peabody Picture Vocabulary Test (third edition), a basal is established when a respondent makes no or only one error within a set of items. On the Woodcock Language Proficiency Battery-Revised, the number of correct responses required to establish a basal age varies between four and six, depending on the particular subtest.

On almost all tests, the examiner administers test items in reverse order from the estimated starting point until a basal is obtained in the manner specified. In the event that no basal level is achieved, the first item on the test is usually considered to represent the basal age.

Tests that employ basal scores typically also use *ceiling scores*, or previously defined accuracy levels that determine the point at which a test is terminated. Thus, the basal and ceiling essentially define an examinee's functional range. Moreover, they serve to limit the number of test items that are administered. Usually, age-equivalent scores are calculated based on the raw score derived from the ceiling item and the number of correct responses below it.

—Carole E. Gelfer

Further Reading

Anastasi, A. (1988). *Psychological testing* (6th ed.). New York: Macmillan.

BASIC PERSONALITY INVENTORY

The Basic Personality Inventory (published by Sigma Assessment Systems, www.sigmaassessmentsystems.com) was developed by Douglas N. Jackson and is currently in its second edition (BPI-II). The Basic Personality Inventory was derived through factor analysis of the 28 scales of the Differential Personality Inventory, and the resulting 11 dimensions identified were augmented with the critical item scale deviation to form the basis for a multiscale inventory of psychopathology and psychosocial adjustment. Once the 12 dimensions to be measured had been defined as constructs, new items were written and selected for the scales. The result was 20 items per scale, balanced in terms of true and false keying for 11 of the 12 scales (all 20 deviation items are true keyed). There is no item overlap between scales. Items selected correlated more highly with their own scale than with any other scale. In order to foster local independence, the items are ordered such that one item is presented from each of the 12 scales in succession, and then this block of 12 items repeats in the same sequence with alternative keying.

The 12 scales are grouped according to three primary factors: internalizing psychopathology (hypochondriasis, anxiety, thinking disorder, persecutory ideas, and deviation), affective psychopathology (depression, social introversion, and self-deprecation), and externalizing psychopathology (deviation, interpersonal problems, alienation, and impulse expression). The denial scale is not included in these factors because it is used for validity purposes as a measure of the dimension representing the Differential Personality Inventory scales of repression, shallow affect, and defensiveness. Deviation is also used as a critical item index of deviant behaviors requiring further exploration, such as suicidal ideation or substance abuse. In addition to the 12 standard scales, a 20-item supplementary social desirability scale was formed by taking the most desirable item and most undesirable item from 10 of the 12 scales (validity scales denial and deviation excluded). Additional indices that can be scored for validity assessment are number of true responses, perseveration, person reliability, fake good, and fake bad.

The BPI-II is available in English, French, and Spanish and can be administered in paper-and-pencil format with a reusable question booklet and answer sheet to individuals or to groups in about 35 minutes. Computerized administration with automated scoring and reporting is also available. Reports generated by the software are either clinical with some limited interpretation or ASCII (text) data file reports for research. Mail-in and Internet scoring and report generation are available. The reading level is estimated to be between Grades 5 and 6. Normative data stratified by gender are available separately for juveniles and adults.

—*John R. Reddon*

See also Comrey Personality Scales; Jackson, Douglas N.; Minnesota Multiphasic Personality Inventory; NEO Personality Inventory; Personality Tests

Further Reading

Holden, R. R., & Jackson, D. N. (1992). Assessing psychopathology using the Basic Personality Inventory: Rationale and applications. In J. Rosen & P. McReynolds (Eds.), *Advances in psychological assessment* (Vol. 8, pp. 165–199). New York: Plenum.

Kroner, D. G., Black, E. R., & Reddon, J. R. (1996). Item content of the Basic Personality Inventory. *Multivariate Experimental Clinical Research, 11*, 61–73.

Basic Personality Inventory: http://www.sigmaassessmentsystems.com/assessments/bpi.asp

BASIC RESEARCH

Basic research consists of empirical studies that "answer fundamental questions about the nature of behavior" (Cozby, 1985, p. 8). Its main goal is the understanding of a phenomenon. Basic research is less concerned with understanding and solving practical problems, which are the primary foci of applied research. Instead, basic research strives to develop a body of knowledge that has no obvious or immediate practical application. However, this knowledge can lead to interventions that alleviate human problems and distress. For example, Skinner's research with pigeons in the 1930s eventually led to the development of theoretical principles that had a profound impact on clinical and educational practices.

Basic research is most effective and influential when its explicit goal is the development of theory. Although research that is conducted solely for the sake of knowledge represents valid and worthy basic research, research that tests hypotheses that are deductively derived from a theory offers much greater promise of advancing science. Indeed, the primary purpose of basic research is the testing of hypotheses that are generated by a particular theory. As theory-based hypotheses are rejected and supported, theories are validated, rejected, and refined.

The interaction among research, theory, and application is represented in Figure 1, which is a model adopted from Olson. Theories are developed to explain human behavior and interaction. These theories are then applied to practical situations, such as childhood behavioral problems or distressed marriages. For example, the theoretical principles of childhood attachment have been extended to adult attachment, and Emotionally Focused Therapy has been developed from these principles to assess and treat conflicted romantic relationships. Within this therapy model, relationship difficulties are conceptualized from an attachment perspective, and treatments have been developed that seek to repair attachment injuries and promote secure attachment in relationships.

As illustrated in Figure 1, the purpose of basic research is to test the validity of particular theories. In the case of attachment theory, a large body of empirical research has accumulated that provides robust evidence for the general principles of the theory. This empirical support has validated attachment theory, providing important credibility to the techniques that were derived from the theory to assess and treat couples.

In some cases, research has rejected significant theoretical propositions. For example, for many years the dominant theoretical conceptualization of autism was that it was caused by poor parenting. Based on this theory of autism, treatment focused on providing adequate care outside the realm of the family. Subsequent research has consistently failed to support this theory, and more recent research has supported theories that link autistic symptoms to neurological impairment. With the conceptualization of autism as a neurological disorder, parents are included as essential partners in the treatment of their child because they provide consistency between behavioral treatments at school and at home.

Thus, basic research serves as a scientific watchdog by providing vital empirical evidence in the process of developing and validating theories. Without this validation role, science stagnates because theory development is curtailed. The system of checks and balances between theoretical generation and basic research enables the continual refinement of valid theories. These theories can then be deductively applied to a variety of human and social problems.

Figure 1 also illustrates the role of applied research, which has a primary aim of directly testing the effectiveness of applications and interventions. Multiple clinical outcome studies have demonstrated that Emotionally Focused Therapy, which is based on attachment theory, is effective in improving relationship functioning among couples. Thus, basic and applied research are complementary, with basic research examining the validity of theories and applied research testing the effectiveness of applications and interventions that are derived from validated theories.

—*Richard B. Miller and Ryan G. Henry*

See also Applied Research

Further Reading

Bettelheim, B. (1967). *The empty fortress*. New York: Free Press.

Cozby, P. C. (1985). *Methods in behavioral research* (3rd ed.). Palo Alto, CA: Mayfield.

Evans, J. D. (1985). *Invitation to psychological research*. New York: Holt, Rinehart, & Winston.

Handleman, J. S., & Harris, S. L. (1986). Educating the developmentally disabled: Meeting the needs of children and families. San Diego, CA: College-Hill Press.

Johnson, S. M. (1996). The practice of emotionally focused marital therapy: Creating connections. New York: Brunner/Mazel.

Johnson, S. M., Hunsley, J., Greenberg, L., & Schindler, D. (1999). Emotionally focused couples therapy: Status and challenges. *Clinical Psychology: Science & Practice, 6,* 67–79.

Olson, D. H. (1976). *Treating relationships*. Lake Mills, IA: Graphic.

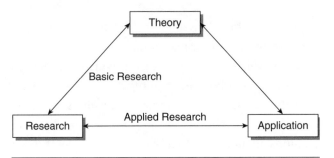

Figure 1   The Relationship Between Theory, Research, and Application

Source: Adapted from Olson, 1976 (p. 565).

Shaughnessy, J. J., & Zechmeister, E. B. (1994). *Research methods in psychology* (3rd ed.). New York: McGraw-Hill.

Spata, A. V. (2003). *Research methods: Science and diversity.* New York: Wiley.

Bayes Factors

The problem of comparing multiple competing models is a difficult one and has been the focus of much research over the years. For statisticians of a Bayesian inclination, the *Bayes factor* offers an easy way of comparing two models. Simply defined, the Bayes factor is the ratio of the posterior and the prior odds. More specifically, denote the data as $x = x_1, x_2, \ldots, x_n$ and the two models as M_1 and M_2, respectively. The Bayes factor in favor of model M_1, and thus against model M_2, is

$$B_{12}(x) = \frac{p(M_1|x)}{p(M_2|x)} \bigg/ \frac{p(M_1)}{p(M_2)},$$

where $p(M_i)$ is the prior probability assigned to model i and $p(M_i \mid x)$ is the posterior probability of model i after observing the data.

Since the posterior probability of model i can be expressed as $p(M_i \mid x) = p(x \mid M_i) \, p(M_i)$, the Bayes factor is also sometimes given as $B_{12}(x) = p(x \mid M_1)/p(x \mid M_2)$. It follows that the posterior odds are equal to the Bayes factor times the prior odds.

The first representation provides an intuitive explanation of what the Bayes factor measures, namely, how the data have affected the odds in favor of model M_1. If $B_{12}(x) > 1$, then the posterior odds in favor of the first model are higher than the prior odds in favor of the first model. In other words, the data have increased our relative amount of belief in the first model. If, on the other hand, $B_{12}(x) < 1$, the posterior odds in favor of model M_1 have decreased on observing the data.

In practice, values of $B_{12}(x)$ smaller than 3 are often taken as providing no evidence in favor of M_1 over M_2, values of $B_{12}(x)$ between 3 and 20 give positive evidence, values between 20 and 150 are indicative of strong evidence, and any value of the Bayes factor over 150 is taken to be very strong evidence. Although these values are only guidelines, they are useful for the calibration of results.

One advantage of Bayes factors over traditional approaches to model comparison is that the models do not have to be nested, as this simple example demonstrates. Suppose we have data $x_1, \ldots, x_n$, independent, identically distributed, coming from either a negative binomial distribution with probability p of success (this is model M_1) or from a Poisson distribution with mean λ (this is model M_2). We use different notation for the parameters of these two models to emphasize that there is no need for the models under consideration to be related to each other in any way. Both these models are completely specified, and so the Bayes factor for comparing the two models is simply the likelihood ratio, that is

$$B_{12}(x) = \frac{p^n(1-p)^{n\bar{x}}}{\lambda^{n\bar{x}} e^{-n\lambda}(\prod x_i!)^{-1}}.$$

Now, suppose that p and λ are not known. To carry out a Bayesian analysis, it is necessary to assign prior distributions to the unknown parameters of the two models. For simplicity, suppose that $p \sim Beta(\alpha_1, \beta_1)$ and $\lambda \sim Gamma(\alpha_2, \beta_2)$. Then it can be shown that

$$p(x|M_1) = \frac{\Gamma(\alpha_1 + \beta_1)}{\Gamma(\alpha_1)\Gamma(\beta_1)} \frac{\Gamma(n + \alpha_1)\Gamma(n\bar{x} + \beta_1)}{\Gamma(n + n\bar{x} + \alpha_1 + \beta_1)}$$

and

$$p(x|M_2) = \frac{\Gamma(n\bar{x} + \alpha_2)\beta_2^{\alpha_2}}{\Gamma(\alpha_2)(n + \beta_2)^{n\bar{x}+\alpha_2}} \frac{1}{\prod x_i!};$$

the Bayes factor is the ratio of these two. In this case, we need to have information on α_1, β_1, α_2, and β_2 in order to evaluate the Bayes factor, which will always depend on the prior specification. As we assign different values to these four parameters, resulting in different prior distributions (representing our different opinions about p and λ and how sure we are of those opinions), the Bayes factor will in turn vary.

A simple numerical example demonstrates this. Table 1 shows values of the Bayes factor for three different sample configurations and three choices of

Table 1 Values of the Bayes Factor for Comparing the Negative Binomial and Poisson Models, With Different Data and Prior Configurations

	$\alpha_1 = 3, \beta_1 = 6$ $\alpha_2 = 6, \beta_2 = 3$	$\alpha_1 = 30, \beta_1 = 60$ $\alpha_2 = 60, \beta_2 = 30$	$\alpha_1 = 1, \beta_1 = 4$ $\alpha_2 = 8, \beta_2 = 2$
$\sum_{i=1}^{4} x_i = 0$	4.89	25.59	93.73
$\sum_{i=1}^{4} x_i = 8$	0.09	0.09	0.12
$\sum_{i=1}^{4} x_i = 16$	0.08	0.22	0.02

parameters for the prior distributions. For ease of calculation, the size of the sample is only 4, and in each of the three cases, $x_1 = x_2 = x_3 = x_4$. The priors are chosen so that $\alpha_1 \alpha_2 = \beta_1 \beta_2$. As can be seen, the Bayes factor can change quite dramatically as the nature of the data or of the prior is changed.

The effect of the sample is seen in particular by comparing the first and second lines of the table. The Bayes factor is dramatically reduced, no matter what the choice of priors. Indeed, looking at the second and third lines, the practical effect of the prior is minimal—the same conclusion would be reached in all these cases, that the data do not speak in favor of the negative binomial model. The top line of the table tells a very different story. There, the negative binomial model is preferred to the Poisson model, with moderately positive to strongly positive evidence in favor of the former. The value of the Bayes factor and the conclusions we would draw from the analysis depend quite heavily for this sample configuration on the prior distribution. Even though for all three priors the same model would be indicated, the strength of our belief in that model would vary greatly.

In spite of the convenience of the Bayes factors for comparing the strength of evidence in favor of different, possibly non-nested, models, they are not without drawbacks. Among the major criticisms leveled at the Bayes factor is that it never loses its dependence on the prior specification, in contrast to Bayesian inferential procedures, in which the influence of the prior distribution weakens as more data are collected. Another critique of the Bayes factor is that it corresponds to a zero-one loss on the decision "Which of these two models pertains?" What this means is that if the wrong choice is made, that is, the wrong model is chosen, it

doesn't matter how far off the choice is. This does not correspond to the way in which statisticians usually think about model selection problems. Furthermore, Bayes factors are hard to calculate and to interpret if improper priors are used.

Because of these various difficulties with the ordinary Bayes factor, researchers have developed a range of alternatives, most of which aim at some form of automatic model selection, particularly to avoid the problems associated with the dependence on priors. These include intrinsic Bayes factors (arithmetic and geometric), fractional Bayes factors, posterior Bayes factors, and others. However, these have also been criticized on the grounds of being arbitrary, of lacking any real Bayesian justification, and of avoiding the difficult issue of prior choice altogether.

The *Bayesian information criterion* (BIC) is related to the Bayes factor and is useful for model comparison in its own right. The BIC of a model is defined as −2 (log maximized likelihood) + (log n)(number of parameters). BIC penalizes more-complex models (those with many parameters) relative to simpler models. This definition permits multiple models to be compared at once; the model with the highest posterior probability is the one that minimizes BIC. The BIC can also be derived by an approximation to the logarithm of the Bayes factor, given by the *Schwarz criterion* for comparing two models,

$$S = \log p(x|\hat{\theta}_1, M_1) - \log p(x|\hat{\theta}_2, M_2)$$
$$- \frac{1}{2}(d_1 - d_2) \log n,$$

where

$\hat{\theta}_i$ is the maximum likelihood estimator for the parameter q_1 under model M_1,

d_i is the dimension of θ_i, and

n is the sample size.

One computational advantage of this approximation is that there is no need to introduce a prior into the calculation at all. However, it is only a rough approximation, and if a detailed analysis is required, it will generally not be suitable. The Schwarz criterion multiplied by −2 is the BIC for the comparison of two models.

In summary, the Bayes factor inherits the strengths of the Bayesian paradigm, namely, a logical foundation that transfers easily to new situations. In addition, Bayes factors allow researchers to compare nonnested models and to incorporate prior information or beliefs about a theory into the testing situation. On the other hand, Bayes factors are heavily dependent on the prior specifications, even for large sample sizes, correspond to an "all or nothing" approach to model comparison, and can be difficult to calculate.

—Nicole Lazar

See also Bayesian Information Criterion; Bayesian Statistics

Further Reading

Bernardo, J. M., & Smith, A. F. M. (1994). *Bayesian theory.* Chichester, UK: Wiley.

Gelfand, A. E. (1996). Model determination using sampling-based methods. In W. R. Gilks, S. Richardson, & D. J. Spiegelhalter (Eds.), *Markov chain Monte Carlo in practice.* Boca Raton, FL: Chapman & Hall/CRC.

Gelman, A., Carlin, J. B., Stern, H. S., & Rubin, D. B. (2004). *Bayesian data analysis* (2nd ed.). Boca Raton, FL: Chapman & Hall/CRC.

Kass, R. E., & Raftery, A. E. (1995). Bayes factors and model uncertainty. *Journal of the American Statistical Association, 90,* 773–795.

BAYESIAN INFORMATION CRITERION

The Bayesian information criterion (BIC) is a statistic used for comparison and selection of statistical models. BIC is given by a simple formula that uses only elements of standard output for fitted models. It is calculated for each model under consideration, and models with small values of BIC are then preferred for selection. The BIC formula and the sense in which the model with the smallest BIC is the "best" one are motivated by one approach to model selection in Bayesian statistical inference.

Definition

Suppose that we are analyzing a set of data D of size n. Here is the sample size if D consists of statistically independent observations and the "effective sample size" in some appropriate sense when the observations are not independent. Suppose that alternative models M_k are considered for D, and that each model is fully specified by a parameter vector θ_k with p_k parameters. Let $p(D \mid \theta_k; M_k)$ denote the likelihood function for model M_k, $l(\theta_k) = \log p(D \mid \theta_k; M_k)$ the corresponding log-likelihood, and $\hat{\theta}_k$ the maximum likelihood estimate of θ_k.

Let M_s denote a saturated model that fits the data exactly. One form of the BIC statistic for a model M_k is

$$\begin{aligned} \mathrm{BIC}_k &= -2[l(\hat{\theta}_k) - l(\hat{\theta}_s)] - df_k \, \log n \\ &= G_k^2 - df_k \log n, \end{aligned} \tag{1}$$

where

$l(\hat{\theta}_s)$ is the log-likelihood for the saturated model,

G_k^2 is the deviance statistic for model M_k, and

df_k is its degrees of freedom.

This version of BIC is most appropriate when the idea of a saturated model is natural, such as for models for contingency tables and structural equation models for covariance structures. The deviance and its degrees of freedom are then typically included in standard output for the fitted model. In other cases, other forms of BIC may be more convenient. These variants, all of which are equivalent for purposes of model comparison, are described at the end of this entry.

Motivation as an Approximate Bayes Factor

The theoretical motivation of BIC is based on the idea of a Bayes factor, which is a statistic used for comparison of models in Bayesian statistical analysis. First, define for model M_k the integrated likelihood

$$p(D|M_k) = \int p(D|\theta_k, M_k) \, p(\theta_k|M_k) \, d\theta_k, \tag{2}$$

where $p(\theta_k | M_k)$ is the density function of a prior distribution specified for the parameters θ_k, and the integral is over the range of possible values for θ_k. Defining $p(\theta_k | M_s)$ similarly for the saturated model, the Bayes factor between models M_s and M_k is the ratio $BF_k = p(D | M_s)/p(D | M_k)$. It is a measure of the evidence provided by the data in favor of M_s over M_k. The evidence favors M_s if BF_k is greater than 1 and M_k if BF_k is less than 1.

BIC_k is an approximation of $2\log BF_k$. The approximation is particularly accurate when each of the prior distributions $p(\theta_k | M_k)$ and $p(\theta_s | M_s)$ is a multivariate normal distribution with a variance matrix comparable to that of the sampling distribution of the maximum likelihood estimate of the parameters based on a hypothetical sample of size $n = 1$. An assumption of such prior distributions, which are known as *unit information priors*, thus implicitly underlies BIC Equation 1. Their motivation and the derivation of BIC are discussed in detail in the Further Reading list below.

A positive value of BIC_k indicates that the saturated model M_s is preferred to M_k (i.e., that $BF_k > 1$), and a negative BIC_k indicates that M_k is preferred. Values of BIC can also be compared between different nonsaturated models, and the model with the smaller BIC is then preferred. The model with the smallest value of BIC overall is regarded as the best model in the Bayes factor sense of being supported most strongly given the data D and the prior distributions of the parameters of all the models.

Example

For an illustration of the use of BIC, consider the data in Table 1. This shows the cross-tabulation of the passengers of RMS *Titanic*, classified according to sex (men vs. women or children), the class they traveled in (first, second, or third), and whether they survived

Table 1 Passengers of the *Titanic*, Classified According to Passenger Class, Sex, and Survival Status

Class	Group	Survivor Yes	Survivor No	Total
First	Man	57	118	175
		(0.326)	(0.674)	(1.000)
	Woman or child	146	4	150
		(0.973)	(0.027)	(1.000)
	Total	203	122	325
		(0.625)	(0.375)	(1.000)
Second	Man	14	154	168
		(0.083)	(0.917)	(1.000)
	Woman or child	104	13	117
		(0.889)	(0.111)	(1.000)
	Total	118	167	285
		(0.414)	(0.586)	(1.000)
Third	Man	75	387	462
		(0.162)	(0.838)	(1.000)
	Woman or child	103	141	244
		(0.422)	(0.578)	(1.000)
	Total	178	528	706
		(0.252)	(0.748)	(1.000)
Total		499	817	1316
		(0.379)	(0.621)	(1.000)

Note: Numbers in parentheses are proportions within the rows.

the sinking of the ship. Table 2 shows results for some models fitted to these data. These are standard loglinear models, identified in the second column of Table 2 using conventional concise notation for such models. For example, the expression (CY, SY) for model 5 indicates that it includes the two-way interactions between class (C) and survival (Y) and between sex (S) and survival, but no interaction between class and sex. The saturated model here is model 10.

The model with the smallest BIC is model 9, for which BIC = −7.1. This is also the only model with a negative BIC, i.e., the only one preferred to the saturated model. Model 9 includes all one-way and

Table 2 Results for Loglinear Models Fitted to the Data in Table 1

Model	Terms	G^2	df	BIC
1	(C, S, Y)	582.1	7	531.8
2	(C, SY)	229.7	6	186.6
3	(S, CY)	449.4	5	413.5
4	(CS, Y)	568.8	5	532.9
5	(CY, SY)	97.0	4	68.3
6	(CS, SY)	216.4	4	187.7
7	(CS, CY)	436.2	3	414.7
8	(CS, CY, SY)	89.1	2	74.7
9	8 + (Class 3)*S*Y	0.051	1	−7.1
10	(CSY)	0	0	0

Notes: C = class; S = sex; Y = survival status; G^2 = goodness of fit; df = degree of freedom; BIC = Bayesian information criterion.

two-way interactions, and the three-way interaction between sex, survival, and traveling in third class. In other words, the model specifies two patterns of association between sex and survival, one for third-class passengers and one jointly for first- and second-class passengers. Considering Table 1, it appears that the main difference between these groups was that there was a smaller disparity between men's chances of survival and those for women and children in the third class than there was in the other two classes.

Relations to Other Methods of Model Selection

In BIC Equation 1, the deviance G_k^2 is a measure of the goodness of fit of a model, with well-fitting models having small values of G_k^2. In the second term, df_k is a decreasing function of the number of parameters p_k, which can be regarded as a measure of the complexity of the model. The term $-df_k \log n$ is known as the penalty term of BIC because it is an increasing function of p_k and thus "penalizes" a model for its complexity. Considering increasingly complex models will generally lead to a decrease in the deviance but an increase in the penalty term. The terms thus pull in different directions, apparently expressing a trade-off between fit and complexity. Small values of BIC are

obtained for models that achieve a good balance between these two, or in other words, a good fit with relatively little complexity.

Other choices of the penalty term give different penalized model selection criteria of the same general form. The most common of these is the Akaike information criterion, where the $-df_k \log n$ in Equation 1 is replaced by $-2df_k$. The Akaike information criterion is used for model selection in broadly the same way as BIC even though the two statistics have very different theoretical motivations.

BIC and other penalized criteria are often used as complements to standard significance tests in model selection. For example, for the models in Table 2, both the deviances G_k^2 and their differences between nested models can be used as test statistics for this purpose. In this example, both BIC and significance tests identify model 9 as the preferred model, but in general they will not always be in agreement. In particular, conclusions often differ in large samples, where significance tests are sensitive to even small observed discrepancies and may reject most models as having significant lack of fit. The penalty term of BIC offsets some of this tendency, so BIC will often favor less-complex models more than goodness-of-fit tests do.

Alternative Formulas for BIC

Forms of BIC other than Equation 1 may be more convenient when the deviance G_k^2 is not immediately available. For many regression models, it is easier to replace the saturated model as the baseline for comparisons with a null model M_0, which includes no explanatory variables. This gives the statistic

$$BIC'_k = -2[l(\hat{\theta}_k) - l(\hat{\theta}_0)] + df'_k \log n$$
$$= -LR_k + df'_k \log n,$$

(3)

where

$l(\hat{\theta}_0)$ is the log-likelihood for the null model,

LR_k is the likelihood ratio test statistic for testing M_0 against M_k, and

df'_k is its degrees of freedom.

For example, for linear regression models, $BIC'_k = n\log(1 - R^2_k) + p'_k \log n$, where R^2_k is the standard R^2 statistic for model M_k and p'_k denotes the number of explanatory variables (excluding the intercept term) in M_k. In terms of the Bayesian motivation, BIC'_k is an approximation of $2\log[p(D \mid M_0)/p(D \mid M_k)]$.

When standard computer output includes only the log-likelihood $l(\hat{\theta}_k)$ instead of G^2_k or LR_k, the most convenient BIC-type statistic is simply $-2l(\hat{\theta}_k) + p_k \log n$. This is an approximation of $2\log p(D \mid M_k)$ under the unit information prior for θ_k discussed above. Models with small values of this statistic are again preferred, as they are for Equations 1 and 3. All these three variants of BIC will always lead to the same conclusions about preferences among models and the selection of the best model.

—Jouni Kuha

See also Akaike Information Criterion; Bayes Factors

Further Reading

Kass, R. E., & Raftery, A. E. (1995). Bayes factors. *Journal of the American Statistical Association, 90*, 773–795.

Kass, R. E., & Wasserman, L. (1995). A reference Bayesian test for nested hypotheses and its relationship to the Schwarz criterion. *Journal of the American Statistical Association, 90*, 928–934.

Kuha, J. (2004). AIC and BIC: Comparisons of assumptions and performance. *Sociological Methods & Research, 33*, 188–229.

Raftery, A. E. (1995). Bayesian model selection in social research (with discussion). In P. V. Marsden (Ed.), *Sociological methodology* (pp. 111–163). Cambridge, MA: Blackwell.

Weakliem, D. L. (1999). A critique of the Bayesian information criterion for model selection. *Sociological Methods & Research, 27*, 359–397.

BAYESIAN STATISTICS

The term *Bayesian statistics* refers to the field of statistical analysis that deals with the estimation of probability distributions for unobserved or "latent" variables based on observed data. When a researcher collects data from an educational assessment, for example, the test score itself is not typically of interest, but rather the "trait" or "ability" that is thought to underlie and influence an examinee's responses to the test questions. Indeed, most measurements in the social sciences are collected as substitutes for some latent variable or variables that cannot be observed directly. That is, the data (denoted x) are not of as much interest to the researcher as the true parameter values (denoted θ) that gave rise to the data. Under the framework of a Bayesian data analysis, statistical inferences are therefore based on a quantity that is of direct interest to the analyst (i.e., θ), not some proxy for that quantity of interest (i.e., the data, x).

Bayesian statistical analysis is named after its founder, Thomas Bayes (1702–1761), an 18th-century minister and mathematician who first introduced what is now known as Bayes' theorem or Bayes' rule. Bayes' theorem posits that the conditional probability of an event, A, occurring, given that another event, B, has occurred, is a function of the joint probability of A and B (the probability of events A and B co-occurring) divided by the marginal probability of B. Given this result, the conditional probability of A given B can be stated as the conditional probability of B given A, multiplied by the marginal probability of A, divided by the marginal probability of B:

$$P(A|B) = \frac{P(A,B)}{P(B)} = \frac{P(B|A)P(A)}{P(B)}.$$

This probability statement can be used in a variety of situations for determining the conditional probability of a given event. Applications of Bayes' theorem are especially useful to statisticians when the theorem is phrased in terms of distributions of observed and unobserved variables:

$$f(\theta|x) = \frac{f(x|\theta)f(\theta)}{f(x)}.$$

By using this formulation of Bayes' theorem, statisticians are able to make inferences about some parameter of interest, θ, given the observed data, x. This density function, $f(\theta|x)$, is referred to as the *posterior distribution* of θ, and it represents a probability density function for the latent variable, θ, the primary quantity of interest, based on the observed data, x. In order to estimate the posterior distribution and make inferences about it, three pieces of information are required: (a) estimation of the function, $f(x|\theta)$, often termed the *likelihood function*, which represents a statistical model that has been fit to the distribution of observed data, x, given the underlying parameter, θ; (b) estimation of $f(\theta)$, referred to as the *prior distribution*, which represents either the empirical or the expected distribution of the parameter, θ, in the population; and (c) estimation of $f(x)$, which represents the empirical distribution of the observed data, x.

In most practical applications, the use of Bayes' theorem for estimating the posterior distribution is simplified because, for any given data analysis, the empirical distribution of observed data, $f(x)$, will be a constant for any given value of the parameter, θ, and therefore does not need to be included. That is, the observed distribution of data will not affect estimation of θ because $f(x)$ is fixed and does not change. As a result, it is typically dropped from the formula for estimating the posterior distribution:

$$f(\theta|x) \propto f(x|\theta)f(\theta).$$

The preceding formula is read, "the posterior distribution of θ given x, $f(\theta|x)$, is proportional to the likelihood function, $f(x|\theta)$, multiplied by the prior distribution of θ, $f(\theta)$." Bayesian statisticians typically rely on estimating a function that is proportional to $f(\theta|x)$ because estimation of $f(x)$ is unnecessary to estimating the parameters from the posterior distribution. Leaving $f(x)$ out of the formula for the posterior distribution will not affect any of the resulting parameter estimates.

For any analytical application that involves fitting a parametric statistical model to observed data (e.g., an item response model fit to test data, a linear regression model fit to a matrix of continuous variables, or any other analysis that involves the estimation of parameters thought to model the behavior of observed data), analysis proceeds by estimating the likelihood

function, $f(x|\theta)$, and multiplying it by the prior distribution, $f(\theta)$. This produces an estimate that is proportional to the posterior distribution of θ given x, and this distribution is used to make inferences about the parameter, θ.

Inferences from the posterior distribution are typically made by determining point estimates for θ, either by finding the mean of the posterior distribution (referred to as an *expected a posteriori* estimate) or by determining the mode of the posterior distribution (referred to as a *modal a posteriori* estimate). The standard error of θ is determined by estimating the standard deviation of the posterior distribution.

Bayesian statistical methods are distinguished from the more traditional approach (referred to as *Frequentist* methods) in that inferences are made based on the posterior distribution, which cannot be directly observed. Frequentist statisticians typically rely solely on the likelihood function, $f(x|\theta)$, as a basis for making inferences because it represents the model that was actually fit to the observed data. Both methodologies estimate the likelihood function based on observed data, but Bayesian procedures also incorporate information from the prior distribution in order to make inferences. Because of this difference, there exists a philosophical schism between Bayesian and Frequentist statisticians, and it occurs because, generally speaking, the prior distribution for θ is an unobserved probability density function that must be somehow estimated by the analyst. This can often be done by making some reasonable assumptions about the distribution of θ in the population or by collecting data and empirically estimating this function. However, the fact remains that the statistician can never be sure that the particular choice of a prior distribution is accurate and therefore cannot be sure how well the posterior distribution represents the distribution of θ given x. The impact of the prior distribution on the final results of the analysis (i.e., the posterior distribution) will vary depending on the statistician's choice for the distribution. Prior distributions that have significant influence on the posterior distribution are referred to as relatively *informative*, and prior distributions with relatively little influence are called *noninformative* priors.

One cannot know how well suited a particular prior distribution is for estimating a posterior distribution, and so the choice of whether to conduct a Frequentist or a Bayesian data analysis often comes down to philosophical concerns. The perspective of the Bayesian statistician is that by making some reasonable assumptions about the underlying distribution of θ in the population, one can make inferences about the quantities that are of direct interest to the analyst. The perspective of the Frequentist statistician is that one can never appropriately make inferences that go beyond what the data alone suggest. Many statisticians subscribe to the Bayesian school of thought, not only for its intuitive appeal, but also because situations exist in which Bayesian methodologies may be employed where Frequentist analyses are either intractable or impossible. These situations may occur when (a) the likelihood function from a Frequentist analysis is irregular, possibly indicating relatively poor model-data fit, which results in difficulties when determining point estimates and standard errors for θ, or (b) the statistical model is being fit to a relatively sparse data matrix (i.e., there are very few observed data points), making estimation of parameters difficult with Frequentist methods. In both of these situations, Bayesian methods may be employed to produce reasonable parameter estimates.

—*William P. Skorupski*

See also Posterior Distribution; Prior Distribution

Further Reading

Gelman, A., Carlin, J. B., Stern, H. S., & Rubin, D. B. (1995). *Bayesian data analysis.* Boca Raton, FL: Chapman & Hall.

Bayley Scales of Infant Development

The Bayley Scales of Infant Development (BSID-II, published by Psychological Corporation) are a set of scales that take approximately 45 minutes to administer to infants and young children (ages 1 month to 42 months) in order to assess mental, physical, emotional, and social development. The BSID has four main uses: to identify developmental delays (diagnostic tool), to monitor progress after intervention (intervention tool), to teach parents about their child's development (teaching tool), and to compare individual and group differences (research tool).

The BSID is composed of three scales: the Mental Scale, the Motor Scale, and the Behavior Rating Scale. The Mental Scale assesses sensory and perceptual ability, acquisition of object constancy, memory, problem solving, learning, the beginning of verbal communication, and mental mapping. Sample items include discriminating between a bell and a rattle and tracking a moving person with the eyes. The Motor Scale assesses degree of body control, large muscle coordination (sitting and walking), finer manipulation skills of the hands and fingers (picking up small objects), dynamic movement and praxis, and postural imitation. Both the mental and motor scales produce a standardized score. The Behavior Rating Scale assesses attention and arousal, orientation and engagement, and emotional regulation. The Behavior Rating Scale is a 5-point scale (formerly called the Infant Behavior Record) and assesses the developmental level for the status of emotional and social development. The Behavior Rating Scale scores are based on caregivers' reports as well as an examiner's judgments and is completed after the administration of the Mental and Motor scales. This process produces a percentile score for comparison to a nonclinical population.

The test was updated and released in October 2005 by Harcourt Assessment (www.harcourt.com) as the Bayley Scales of Infant and Toddler Development, third edition (Bayley-III). The Bayley-III additions include a Social-Emotional subtest, Adaptive Behavior subtest, Screening Test, Caregiver Report, Scoring Assistant, Growth Scores, and Growth Chart. The Bayley-III uses a current normative sample representing 1,700 children stratified according to age, based on the 2000 U.S. Census. The Bayley-III also has nonnormative data available for children with specific clinical diagnoses, such as autism and Down syndrome. The BSID is widely used in research settings and has excellent psychometric characteristics.

—Heather Doescher

See also Fagan Test of Infant Intelligence; Intelligence Tests

Further Reading

Black, M. (1999). *Essentials of Bayley Scales of Infant Development II assessment.* New York: Wiley.

Schaefer, E. S., & Bayley, N. (1963). Maternal behavior, child behavior, and their intercorrelations from infancy through adolescence. *Monographs of the Society for Research in Child Development, 28*(3).

Nancy Bayley biography: http://www.webster.edu/~woolflm/bayley.html

BECK DEPRESSION INVENTORY

The Beck Depression Inventory (BDI) and the second edition, the Beck Depression Inventory-II (BDI-II), are depression screening instruments published by the Psychological Corporation (www.harcourtassessment.com). The BDI-II is a 21-item self-report instrument (approximate administration time: 5–10 minutes) used to detect and estimate the overall severity of depression in adolescents and adults aged 13 years and older. The instrument can be administered orally as well as in group settings to clinical and normal patient populations. Symptoms of depression are evaluated according to criteria set forth in the American Psychiatric Association's *Diagnostic and Statistical Manual of Mental Disorders* (4th ed.).

The original BDI, developed in 1961, was based on the clinical observations of Dr. Aaron T. Beck and his associates and the typical verbal descriptions reported by depressed psychiatric patients. Representative depressive attitudes and symptoms were consolidated into 21 items read aloud to patients by trained interviewers. The inventory underwent revisions in 1971 at the Center for Cognitive Therapy, University of Pennsylvania, and the amended version, the BDI-IA, was copyrighted in 1978 and published in 1979. In the original version, respondents were instructed to rate various domains relating to their mood "right now," whereas in the revised version, instructions asked for mood ratings for the "past week, including today." The most significant revision of the BDI took place in 1996. This edition, the BDI-II, instructs respondents to provide ratings for the past two weeks. Recently, the BDI-FastScreen, a 7-item self-report measure, has been introduced for use with medical patients.

Each BDI-II item represents a particular symptom of depression: sadness, pessimism, past failure, loss of pleasure, guilty feelings, punishment feelings, self-dislike, self-criticalness, suicidal thoughts or wishes, crying, agitation, loss of interest, indecisiveness, worthlessness, loss of energy, changes in sleeping pattern, irritability, changes in appetite, concentration difficulty, tiredness or fatigue, and loss of interest in sex. Four statements in order of severity are presented to the patient for each item and rated on a 4-point scale ranging from 0 to 3. A total depression score is obtained by summing the ratings for the responses to all 21 items. The suggested cutoff scores are 0–13, minimal depression; 14–19, mild; 20–28, moderate; and 29–63, severe.

During the past four decades, the BDI has been used extensively for clinical as well as research purposes and translated into more than 25 languages. In clinical settings, the BDI is often an important component of a comprehensive psychiatric evaluation, and it is used to monitor treatment progress. In empirical studies, the instrument is commonly selected as an outcome measure to demonstrate treatment efficacy. The psychometric characteristics of the BDI-II have been established in groups of college students and psychiatric outpatients.

—Marjan Ghahramanlou-Holloway
and Kathryn Lou

See also Carroll Depression Scale; Clinical Assessment of Depression

Further Reading

Kendall, P. C., Hollon, S. D., Beck, A. T., Hammen, C. L., & Ingram, R. E. (1987). Issues and recommendations regarding use of the Beck Depression Inventory. *Cognitive Therapy & Research, 11,* 289–299.

Aaron T. Beck Web page: http://mail.med.upenn.edu/~abeck/

Applying Ideas on Statistics and Measurement

The following abstract is adapted from Boothby, J. L., & Durham, T. W. (1999). Screening for depression in prisoners using the Beck Depression Inventory. *Criminal Justice and Behavior, 26*(1), 107–124.

Especially when it comes to working in the field of mental health, using screening tools that are accurate is extremely important. In this study, 1,494 prisoners completed the **Beck Depression Inventory** as part of the admission process to the North Carolina state prison system. The mean score for this population corresponds to the "mild depression" range on the instrument. While overall scores for prisoners were elevated relative to general population norms for the test, female inmates, younger prisoners, close custody inmates, and those serving their first period of incarceration produced even higher Beck scores. Results suggest that a score of 20 might serve as an appropriate cutting score to determine the need for further assessment and mental health intervention in this group. Other analysis of the inmates' responses yielded four distinct, interpretable factors or groups of variables, labeled (a) cognitive symptoms, (b) vegetative symptoms, (c) emotional symptoms, and (d) feelings of punishment.

BEHAVIOR ASSESSMENT SYSTEM FOR CHILDREN

The *Behavior Assessment System for Children, Second Edition* (BASC-2), published by AGS Publishing (www.agsnet.com), is a set of rating scales and forms that gather information about a child's behavior, including ratings from parents and teachers as well as children's self-reports. It is designed to assess and identify children and young adults 2 to 25 years of age with emotional and behavioral disorders. There are five components, which may be used separately or in combination with one another: (a) a parent rating scale, (b) a teacher rating scale, (c) a self-report scale for the child to describe his or her own emotions and self-perceptions, (d) a structured developmental history form, and (e) a form for recording and classifying classroom behavior. By looking at both positive and negative features, the BASC not only evaluates personality, behavioral problems, and emotional disturbances; it also identifies positive attributes that may help in intervention. Analyzing the child's behavior from three perspectives—self, teacher, and parent—fosters a comprehensive picture that helps with educational classifications and clinical diagnoses.

The teacher and parent scales gather age-appropriate information on descriptions of observable behavior. The forms describe specific behaviors that are rated on a 4-point scale of frequency, ranging from *never* to *almost always*. Respondents are asked to read the statements and mark the response that best describes how the child has acted over the past 6 months. Teacher and parent forms include statements such as "Adjusts well to changes in routine" and "Annoys others on purpose." The child's self-report form consists of 139 statements. For the first 51 items, children choose whether each statement is true or false for them. For the rest of the items, children rate behaviors on the same 4-point scale that the parents and teachers use. The child's self-report scale includes items such as "I never seem to get anything right" and "I get into trouble for not paying attention."

The BASC-2 assesses both positive (adaptive) and negative (clinical) dimensions of behavior. When the questionnaire is scored, it provides information about 14 specific areas of a child's life, which are called scales. Five composite scales provide information about broader aspects of the child's life by combining the scores from 2 or more of the original 14 scales. Composite scales on the child report include School Problems, Internalizing Problems, Inattention/Hyperactivity, an Emotional Symptoms Index, and Personal Adjustment. High scores indicate higher risk on 10 of the clinical scales and 4 of the composite scales. Low scores indicate higher risk on the remaining 4 adaptive scales and 1 composite scale (Personal Adjustment).

Norms are based on a sample of 13,000 students, ages 2 to 18, from throughout the United States. The BASC-2 is used in both schools and clinics. The test was updated in 2004 by the addition of new scales and the extension of the age range to include college students. The new scales include Functional Communication, Activities of Daily Living, Attention Problems, and Hyperactivity.

—Kristen M. Kalymon

See also Vineland Adaptive Behavior Scales

Further Reading

Reynolds, C. R., & Randy, K. W. (2002). *The clinician's guide to the Behavior Assessment System for Children (BASC).* New York: Guilford.

BASC-2 information: http://www.agsnet.com/Group.asp?nGroupInfoID=a30000

BEHRENS-FISHER TEST

A common question in statistics involves testing for the equality of two population means, μ_1 and μ_2, based on independent samples. In many applications, it is reasonable to assume that the population variances, σ_1^2 and σ_2^2, are equal. In this case, the question will be addressed by a two-sample t test. The problem of testing for equality of means when the population variances are not assumed to be the same is harder, and is known as the *Behrens-Fisher problem*.

Suppose we have two samples, $x_{11}, x_{12}, \ldots, x_{1,n_1}$ and $x_{21}, x_{22}, \ldots, x_{2,n_2}$, where the x_{1i} are normally distributed with mean μ_1 and variance σ_1^2 and the x_{2i} are normally distributed with mean μ_2 and variance σ_2^2, all observations are independent, and it is not assumed that $\sigma_1^2 = \sigma_2^2$. Let $\bar{x}_i$ and s_i^2 denote respectively the mean and variance of sample $i = 1, 2$. Now, $\bar{x}_1 - \bar{x}_2 \sim N(\mu_1 - \mu_2, \sigma_1^2/n_1 + \sigma_2^2/n_2)$ exactly if the original samples are from a normal distribution, and asymptotically if they are not. So, the assumption of normality is not in fact needed.

If we define a pooled variance by

$$s^2 = \frac{n_1 - 1}{n_1 + n_2 - 2}s_1^2 + \frac{n_2 - 1}{n_1 + n_2 - 2}s_2^2,$$

then, with or without the assumption of normality, s^2 converges to the same quantity, namely a weighted average of σ_1^2 and σ_2^2,

$$\sigma_w^2 = \frac{w}{1 + w}\sigma_1^2 + \frac{1}{1 + w}\sigma_2^2,$$

where w is the limit of the ratio n_1/n_2 and $n_1/n_2 \rightarrow w$ as $n_1, n_2 \rightarrow \infty$.

It can be shown that the usual t statistic,

$$t = \frac{(\bar{x}_1 - \bar{x}_2) - (\mu_1 - \mu_2)}{s\sqrt{1/n_1 + 1/n_2}},$$

instead of converging to $N(0,1)$ under the null hypothesis of no difference in the population means, converges to a normal distribution with mean 0 and variance $(\delta + w)/(\delta w + 1)$, where δ is the ratio between σ_1^2 and σ_2^2.

In order to understand the effect of the assumption that δ is not necessarily equal to 1 on inference in this setting, it helps to examine how the expression for the asymptotic variance changes as w and δ vary. It is important to realize that if $w = 1$, that is, the two sample sizes are equal, either exactly or in the limit, then the asymptotic variance is 1, no matter the value of δ. Thus, with equal sample sizes, inference, at least asymptotically, is not affected by unequal variances. Having nearly equal samples from the two populations thus mitigates the Behrens-Fisher testing problem. Similarly, if the discrepancies in the population variances are not large, such that $\delta = 1$ or nearly so, then we are back in the standard situation, and again asymptotic inference will proceed as before.

The most worrisome situation is when w is small and δ is large. This corresponds to having a much smaller sample from the first population than from the second, when the variance in the first population is much larger than the variance in the second. In this situation, it is necessary to confront the Behrens-Fisher problem directly. A convenient solution, which is only approximate, is to use Welch's t' statistic, defined as

$$t' = \frac{\bar{x}_1 - \bar{x}_2}{\sqrt{\frac{s_1^2}{n_1} + \frac{s_2^2}{n_2}}},$$

which acknowledges the fact that the two sample variances cannot be assumed equal. The difference in the procedure derives from the degrees of freedom associated with this test, since it can be shown that, approximately,

$$\frac{\frac{s_1^2}{n_1} + \frac{s_2^2}{n_2}}{\frac{\sigma_1^2}{n_1} + \frac{\sigma_2^2}{n_2}} \sim \frac{\chi_v^2}{v},$$

where χ_v^2 is a chi-square distribution with v degrees of freedom. The degrees of freedom, v, can be estimated, using *Satterthwaite's approximation*, as

$$\hat{v} = \frac{(\frac{s_1^2}{n_1} + \frac{s_2^2}{n_2})^2}{\frac{1}{n_1-1}(\frac{s_1^2}{n_1})^2 + \frac{1}{n_2-1}(\frac{s_2^2}{n_2})^2}.$$

To demonstrate that Welch's t' statistic, together with the Satterthwaite approximation for the degrees of freedom, can have an impact on inference, consider the following example, taken from Casella and Berger. Data were collected on wood from a Byzantine church. The samples were from either the core of the church ($n_1 = 14$ measurements) or the periphery ($n_2 = 9$ measurements), and for each, the date of the wood was determined. Is there a difference in the mean age of wood in the core and in the periphery? The data are as follows: core—1294, 1251, 1279, 1248, 1274, 1240, 1264, 1232, 1263, 1220, 1254, 1218, 1251, 1210; periphery—1284, 1274, 1272, 1264, 1256, 1256, 1254, 1250, 1242.

Summary statistics on the two samples are as follows: $\bar{x}_1 = 1249.857$, $s_1^2 = 591.363$, $\bar{x}_2 = 1261.333$, $s_2^2 = 176$. Applying the usual two-sample t test gives $t = -1.29$ on 21 degrees of freedom, which has a p value of 0.21. There is no reason to reject the null hypothesis, and we conclude that there is no significant difference in the age of the wood in the two locations.

Applying Welch's test with the Satterthwaite approximation yields $t' = -1.43$ on 22.3 degrees of freedom, which has a p value of 0.08. Now the result is borderline significant, by traditional standards, and we might conclude that there is evidence for some difference in age.

Other solutions besides Welch's test have been suggested, including the use of nonparametric statistical tests, resampling (bootstrap), and a Bayesian approach using uniform priors on (μ_1, μ_2, log σ_1, log σ_2).

—*Nicole Lazar*

See also Significance Level; Statistical Significance

Further Reading

Casella, G., & Berger, R. L. (2002). *Statistical inference* (2nd ed.). Pacific Grove, CA: Duxbury.

Miller, R. G. (1986). *Beyond ANOVA: Basics of applied statistics.* New York: Wiley.

Scheffé, H. (1970). Practical solutions to the Behrens-Fisher problem. *Journal of the American Statistical Association, 65,* 1501–1508.

BENDER VISUAL MOTOR GESTALT TEST

Lauretta Bender's Visual Motor Gestalt Test was developed in 1938 and is commonly referred to as the Bender-Gestalt Test (published by Riverside Publishing Company, www.riversidepublishing.com). It consists of a series of designs printed on individual cards, to be copied by the examinee with pencil and paper. Bender's scoring system evaluated the overall quality of each design and provided an assessment of visual-motor functioning. For comparative purposes, Bender provided graphs and a summary chart of the types of drawings made by children from 3 to 11 years of age. Over the next 65 years, a number of variations in administering and scoring the test emerged to assess visual-motor functioning, psychopathology, and organic brain dysfunction in children and adults. Some of the more prominent variations included scoring systems that examined specific errors (e.g., failure to integrate parts of designs, rotation of designs, simplification of parts of designs), the use of a background interference procedure during administration of the test (paper containing random lines provided), and a reduction of the number of designs for administration to preschool and early-primary-school children. The test enjoyed considerable success among practitioners and became one of the most widely used tests in psychology.

The revision of the test in 2003 included the addition of several new designs; a memory test; separate tests to assess motor skill and visual perception; a new, easy-to-use scoring system; and a large, nationally representative sample covering the ages 4 to 85+ years. Administration involves the copy phase, followed immediately by the memory phase. In the copy phase, the examinee is instructed to copy each design as it is presented. The memory phase requires the examinee to redraw as many of the designs as possible from memory. Scoring is based on a 5-point scale that assesses the overall quality of each drawing. Standard scores and percentile scores are available for both the copy and the memory phases. If an examinee's scores are low, the supplemental motor and perception tests can be administered to help determine whether the examinee's difficulty is motoric, perceptual, or the integrated visual-motor process.

Research on nonclinical samples as well as a variety of clinical samples, such as individuals with learning disabilities, mental retardation, attention deficit/hyperactivity disorder, autism, and Alzheimer's disease, indicates that the test is a reliable, valid measure of visual-motor functioning and a useful addition to educational, psychological, and neuropsychological test batteries.

—*Gary G. Brannigan*

Further Reading

Tolor, A., & Brannigan, G. G. (1980). *Research and clinical applications of the Bender-Gestalt Test.* Springfield, IL: Charles C Thomas.

Tolor, A., & Schulberg, H. C. (1963). *An evaluation of the Bender-Gestalt Test.* Springfield, IL: Charles C Thomas.

BERNOULLI, JAKOB (1654–1705)

Jakob (James, Jacques) Bernoulli, from Switzerland, was the first of eight members of the mathematically talented Bernoulli family. As directed by his parents, he was trained as a philosopher (master's degree, 1671) and theologian (licentiate, 1676) at the University of Basel.

His career interests, however, were in mathematics and, at least initially, in its application to astronomy. He studied mathematics during his extensive travels, subsequent to graduation, with such luminaries as Nicolas Malebranche (1638–1715) for two years in France, Johann van Waveren Hudde (1628–1704) in the Netherlands, and briefly with Robert Boyle (1627–1691) and Robert Hooke (1635–1703) in England. He then resettled in Basel, and while awaiting a more lucrative offer (and publishing a flawed theory pertaining to comets), he opened a private school of mathematics in 1682. The following year, he was appointed to a teaching post in mechanics at his alma mater, and in 1687, he obtained a professorship and chair in mathematics, which he held until his death.

In 1682, he became a correspondent disciple of Gottfried Wilhelm Leibniz (1646–1716), who coinvented the calculus along with Sir Isaac Newton (1642–1727). This primarily distance-learning arrangement led to Bernoulli's instrumental role in the development of elementary differential and integral calculus and ordinary differential equations.

Among his many discoveries were the system of polar coordinates, the isochrone (the path that an object falls with uniform velocity), and the logarithmic spiral ($r = ae^{b\theta}$). He extended trigonometric functions to complex variables, which led analysis (the study of infinite series) into the study of algebra. Although the $\int$ symbol was invented by his younger brother and student, Johann (1667–1748), the term *integral* was coined by Jakob in an article published in *Acta Eruditorum* in 1690.

His magnum opus, *Ars Conjectandi*, was published posthumously in 1713. Bernoulli spent 20 years writing the book but never brought it to fruition. It was one of the earliest rigorous treatises on probability theory. In the second of four parts, he proves by induction the binomial theorem. The fourth part contains the *theorem of Bernoulli*. Siméon-Denis Poisson (1781–1840), a descendent in Bernoulli's academic genealogy, renamed the theorem the *law of large numbers*. The modern Monte Carlo method, a technique of repeated sampling, is also known as *Bernoulli trials*.

—Shlomo S. Sawilowsky

See also Pascal, Blaise; Probability Sampling

Further Reading

Burton, D. M. (1997). *The history of mathematics.* (3rd ed.). New York: McGraw-Hill.

Sawilowsky, S. S. (2004). A conversation with R. Clifford Blair on the occasion of his retirement. *Journal of Modern Applied Statistical Methods*, 3(2), 518–566.

Strunk, D. J. (1987). *A concise history of mathematics* (4th rev. ed.). New York: Dover.

Binomial Distribution/ Binomial and Sign Tests

The binomial distribution models repeated choices between two alternatives. For example, it will give the probability of obtaining 5 tails when tossing 10 coins or the probability of a rat's choosing 10 times out of 20 the correct branch of a three-branch maze. The binomial test uses the binomial distribution to decide whether the outcome of an experiment using a binary variable (also called a *dichotomy*) can be attributed to a systematic effect. The sign test is applied to before-after designs and uses the binomial test to evaluate whether the direction of change between before and after the treatment is systematic.

Binomial Distribution

The binomial distribution models experiments in which a repeated binary outcome is counted. Each binary outcome is called a *Bernoulli* trial, or simply a

trial. For example, if we toss five coins, each binary outcome corresponds to H or T, and the outcome of the experiment could count the number of T out of these five trials.

Notations and Definitions

We call Y the random variable counting the number of outcomes of interest, N the total number of trials, P the probability of obtaining the outcome of interest on each trial, and C a given number of outcomes. For example, if we toss four coins and count the number of heads, Y counts the number of heads, $N = 4$, and $P = \frac{1}{2}$. If we want to find the probability of getting two heads out of four, then $C = 2$.

With these notations, the probability of obtaining C outcomes out of N trials is given by the formula

$$\Pr(Y = C) = \binom{N}{C} \times P^C \times (1 - P)^{N-C}. \quad (1)$$

The term $\binom{N}{C}$ gives the number of combinations of C elements from an ensemble of N; it is called the *binomial of N and C* and is computed as

$$\binom{N}{C} = \frac{N!}{C!(N-C)!} \text{ where } N! = 1 \times 2 \ldots \times N. \quad (2)$$

For example, if the probability of obtaining two heads when tossing four coins is computed as

$$\begin{aligned} \Pr(Y = 2) &= \binom{N}{C} \times P^C \times (1 - P)^{N-C} \\ &= \binom{4}{2} P^2 (1 - P)^{4-2} \quad (3) \\ &= 6 \times .5^2 \times (1 - .5)^2 \\ &= 6 \times .5^4 = .3750, \end{aligned}$$

the mean and standard deviation of the binomial distribution are equal to

$$\mu_Y = N \times P \text{ and } \sigma_Y = \sqrt{N \times P \times (1 - P)}. \quad (4)$$

The binomial distribution converges toward the normal distribution for large values of N (practically, for $P = \frac{1}{2}$ and $N = 20$, the convergence is achieved).

Binomial Test

The binomial test uses the binomial distribution to decide whether the outcome of an experiment in which we count the number of times one of two alternatives has occurred is significant. For example, suppose we ask 10 children to attribute the name "keewee" or "koowoo" to a pair of dolls identical except for their size and that we predict that children will choose keewee for the smaller doll. We found that 9 children out of 10 chose keewee. Can we conclude that children choose systematically? To answer this question, we need to evaluate the probability of obtaining 9 keewees or more than 9 keewees if the children were choosing randomly. If we denoted this probability by p, we find (from Equation 1) that

$$
\begin{aligned}
p &= \Pr(9 \text{ out of } 10) + \Pr(10 \text{ out of } 10) \\
&= \binom{10}{9} \times P^9 \times (1 - P)^{10-9} + \binom{10}{10} \\
&\quad \times P^{10} \times (1 - P)^0 \\
&= (10 \times .5^9 \times .5^1) + (1 \times .5^{10} \times .5^0) \\
&= .009766 + .000977 \\
&\approx .01074.
\end{aligned}
\quad (5)
$$

Assuming an alpha level of $\alpha = .05$, we can conclude that the children did not answer randomly.

$$P \neq \frac{1}{2}$$

The binomial test can be used with values of P different from $\frac{1}{2}$. For example, the probability p of having five out of six rats choosing the correct door out of four possible doors in a maze uses a value of $P = \frac{1}{4}$ and is equal to

$$
\begin{aligned}
p &= \Pr(6 \text{ out of } 6) + \Pr(5 \text{ out of } 6) \\
&= \binom{6}{6} \times P^6 \times (1 - P)^{6-6} + \binom{6}{5} \\
&\quad \times P^5 \times (1 - P)^{6-5} \\
&= \frac{1}{4^6} + 6 \times \frac{1}{4^5} \times \frac{3}{4} = \frac{1}{4^6} + \frac{18}{4^6} \\
&\approx .0046.
\end{aligned}
\quad (6)
$$

And we will conclude that the rats are showing a significant preference for the correct door.

Large : Normal Approximation

For large values of N, a normal approximation can be used for the binomial distribution. In this case, p is obtained by first computing a z score. For example, suppose that we had asked the doll question to 86 children and that 76 of them chose keewee. Using Equation 4, we can compute the associated z score as

$$Z_Y = \frac{Y - \mu_Y}{\sigma_Y} = \frac{76 - 43}{4.64} \approx 7.12. \quad (7)$$

Because the probability associated with such a value of Z is smaller than $\alpha = .001$, we can conclude that the children did not answer randomly.

Sign Test

The sign test is used in repeated measures designs that measure a dependent variable on the same observations before and after some treatment. It tests whether the direction of change is random or not. The change is expressed as a binary variable taking the value + if the dependent variable is larger for a given observation after the treatment or − if it is smaller. When there is no change, the change is coded 0 and is ignored in the analysis. For example, suppose that we measure the number of candies eaten on two different days by 15 children and that between these two days, we expose the children to a film showing the danger of eating too much sugar. On the second day, of these

15 children, 5 eat the same number of candies, 9 eat less, and eats more. Can we conclude that the film diminished candy consumption? This problem is equivalent to comparing 9 positive outcomes against 1 negative with $P = \frac{1}{2}$. From Equation 5, we find that such a result has a p value smaller that $\alpha = .05$, and we conclude that the film did change the behavior of the children.

—*Hervé Abdi*

Further Reading

Siegel, S. (1956). *Nonparametric statistics for the behavioral sciences.* New York: McGraw-Hill.

BINOMIAL TEST

A binomial experiment is one with two outcomes. If one of the outcomes is identified as a success with probability on each trial of π, then the probability of r successes in N trials of the experiment is given by $P(r)$ where

$$P(r) = \frac{N!}{r!(N-r)!} \pi^r (1-\pi)^{N-r}.$$

To test the null hypothesis, H_0: $\pi = \pi_0$, for some constant, $0 < \pi_0 < 1$, against a one-sided alternative requires the summation of all $P(r)$ for all values from r to the desired end point (0 or N). For example, testing the alternative, H_1: $\pi > \pi_0$, we add $P(X)$ for all $X = r, \ldots, N$ and define the sum as $p = \Sigma P(X)$. The result, p, is known as the p value, or exact probability. If $p \leq \alpha$, then the null hypothesis can be rejected at level α. For directional tests in the opposite direction, we take $p = \Sigma P(X)$, $X = 0, \ldots, r$.

For nondirectional tests, the value of p can be calculated in a variety of ways. The definition used here is $p = \Sigma P(X)$, for all X such that $P(X) \leq P(r)$. If $p \leq \alpha$, the test is significant. The observed success rate, $\pi = r/N$, is significantly different from π_0 at level α.

Suppose a six-sided die is rolled seven times, and the side numbered 5 is defined as a success. Suppose further that in the seven rolls, there is one roll resulting in a 5. That is, $N = 7$ and $r = 1$. The null hypothesis for a fair die would be H_0: $\pi = 1/6$. For the one-sided alternative, we take H_1: $\pi < 1/6$. Alternatively, we could say the expected number of successes is $\mu = N\pi = 7(1/6) = 1.1667$. In that case, we could express the null hypothesis as H_0: $\mu = 1.1667$.

To test the null hypothesis against the alternative that $\pi < 1/6$, we calculate

$$P(0) = \frac{7!}{0!(7-0)!} \left(\frac{1}{6}\right)^0 \left(1 - \frac{1}{6}\right)^{7-0}$$

$$P(0) = \left(\frac{5}{6}\right)^7$$

$$P(0) = 0.279082.$$

We also calculate

$$P(1) = \frac{7!}{1!(7-1)!} \left(\frac{1}{6}\right)^1 \left(1 - \frac{1}{6}\right)^{7-1}$$

$$P(1) = 7\left(\frac{1}{6}\right)\left(\frac{5}{6}\right)^6$$

$$P(1) = 0.390714.$$

The one-sided p value becomes $p = 0.279082 + 0.390714 = 0.669796$. Testing at $\alpha = .05$, we do not reject the null hypothesis because $.67 > .05$. That is, the observed rate of side 5 in the rolls is $\hat{\pi} = 1/7 = .143$ and is not significantly less than $1/6 = .167$.

Now suppose on the seven rolls, we obtain side 5 on four of the seven rolls. That is, $N = 7$ and $r = 4$. If we want to test the one-sided hypothesis that the observed rate of $\hat{\pi} = 4/7 = 0.571$ is significantly greater than $1/6 = 0.167$, we need

$$P(4) = 0.015629$$

$$P(5) = 0.001875$$

$$P(6) = 0.000125$$

$$P(7) = 0.000004.$$

In this case we have

$$p = 0.015629 + 0.001875 + 0.000125 + 0.000004$$
$$p = 0.017633.$$

Again testing at $\alpha = .05$, we reject H_0 because $.0176 < .05$.

In the two-sided test of H_0: $\pi = 1/6$ with $r = 1$ and $N = 7$, we will have $p = 1.0$ because $P(X) < P(1)$ for all other $0 \leq X \leq 7$. Of course, that test is not significant at $\alpha = .05$.

In the two-sided test of H_0: $\pi = 1/6$ with $r = 4$ and $N = 7$, we will have $p = 0.017633$ just as in the one-sided test because $P(X) > P(4)$ for all $0 \leq X \leq 4$. Of course, that test is significant at $\alpha = .05$. In general, we would expect to find that the one-sided and two-sided tests produce different values of p.

There is a normal approximation to the binomial test, and it can be applied with and without a correction for continuity. It has been known for many years that even the continuity corrected version fails to limit the true Type I error rate to the nominal level unless N is extremely large. It is also well known that the binomial test is more powerful than the normal approximation. Therefore, it is somewhat strange that textbooks published as late as 2005 continue to recommend the normal approximations.

With the wide availability of computer analysis and handheld calculators, there is little excuse for the use of the normal approximations. Anyone who anticipates testing binomial hypotheses should probably obtain a suitable calculator and resort to normal approximations only for data sets too large for the calculator.

—*Philip H. Ramsey and Patricia Ramsey*

See also Binomial Distribution

Further Reading

Ramsey, P. H., & Ramsey, P. P. (1988). Evaluating the normal approximation to the binomial test. *Journal of Educational Statistics, 13,* 173–182.

BIOINFORMATICS

A single remarkable breakthrough of the 21st century is likely to be biotechnology based on bioinformatics principles and algorithms. Bioinformatics is advanced by different disciplines. Much scientific, industrial, social, political, economic, and religious activity in upcoming years will be influenced by looming advancements in genetic research. Biostatisticians and computational biologists engaged in bioinformatics are working to clearly comprehend how molecular machinery works, fails, and can be repaired. One needs an excellent command of and expertise in biology, calculus, probability, mathematical statistics, and computer science to follow and make contributions in bioinformatics, an emerging discipline that analyzes large genetic data sets using statistical and information techniques. The discipline is growing quickly as a result of the rapid availability of DNA or protein sequence data on the World Wide Web. Because the biological machine is chance oriented, both probability and statistics are fundamental to understanding DNA or protein sequences.

Bioinformatics is one of three branches in a new discipline. The other two branches are medical informatics and health informatics. Medical informatics concentrates on computational algorithms to improve communication and understanding in order to manage medical knowledge and application. Microarray technology is the driving engine of this discipline. Health informatics studies the dynamics among (a) computers, communications, and other information sciences; (b) engineering, technology, and other sciences; and (c) medical research, education, and practice. Bioinformatics is a collection of tools and ideas for deciphering the complexity of molecular machinery. According to bioinformatics, biology is informational science, and this complex and diversified field is increasingly becoming a cross-disciplinary science. It is in its infancy but evolving rapidly. Biostatisticians, computer scientists, operations researchers, and molecular biologists work hard to enrich bioinformatics.

Since the discovery of the helix structure of DNA by James D. Watson and Francis H. C. Crick, several array-based biotechnologies have been constructed to determine and exploit gene expression levels and their interactions. Gene expression is a basic link between genotype and phenotype. Gene expression data are generated on a massive scale. New statistical principles and computing techniques are necessary to meet the demand for quick and correct interpretations of so much data.

As the territory of bioinformatics is changing dramatically, statisticians have to learn the language and jargon of bioinformatics. For example, much of the so-called simple random sampling, stratifications, randomization, replication, and so on, of the 20th century has become obsolete in the genetic research arena of the 21st century. DNA-oriented research ideas are geared to statistics' being an exact science.

John Naisbitt states in *Megatrends* that "we are drowning in information but starved of knowledge." Fast-improving computing facilities change the way knowledge, discovery, and application in all scientific and day-to-day life are done. Before, genetic data were analyzed using a hypothesis-driven-reductions approach, but now, it is all done by a data-driven approach. Consequently, bioinformatics ideas play a significant role in genetic research.

Bioinformatics is all about identifying genes in genome sequences, figuring out closeness of one sequence to another, and answering questions such as the following: How similar are two different organisms? Where in DNA is a particular gene? What proteins are produced by a particular gene? What are the interrelations between genes and proteins? How are one person's genes different from those of another individual? And how can we design a way to store, process, and analyze this knowledge? Molecular human biology can be summarized as follows: There are 22 chromosomes in paired style. Every human female has two X chromosomes whereas a human male has one X and one Y chromosome. Each chromosome has a single double stranded DNA molecule with complementary nucleotides (A-T, G-C) forming pairs in the strands. The nucleotides are A for adenine, T for thymine, G for guanine, and C for cytosine. There may be redundant information in each strand. Organisms need to produce proteins for a variety of functions in life. There is a code for the start and end of the proteins. Major terms in bioinformatics include *exon* (segment of DNA that supplies information to make proteins), *intron* (a noncoding segment that interrupts exons to produce a proper copy of RNA), and *splice site* (the boundary of an exon and an intron). This site allows the uninterrupted gene or

amino acid sequence of proteins. *Promoter sites* are segments of DNA that start the transcription of genes, enhancing controls of the transcription.

Why should one study bioinformatics? This emerging field seeks to understand the secrets of life's machinery and therefore should be useful in discovering new drugs, custom suited for each patient, to treat illnesses now considered incurable. The complex process of life can perhaps be explained by simple principles of genes!

The Human Genome Project is closely involved with the development of bioinformatics. The project started in 1980 to determine, for medical purposes, patterns in the entire sequence of the 3 million human nucleotides. The draft sequence was completed on October 7, 2000, and was published on February 15, 2001. The sequences of 908 species, including 557 viruses, 112 bacteria, and 172 eukaryotes, have been completed. The human sequence is the largest and was completed on April 25, 2003, the 50th anniversary of the discovery of chromosomes.

The methodologies that are used in bioinformatics may be grouped as follows: The symbolic computations, hidden Markov models, and PERL programming are computer intensive. Another group, consisting of artificial intelligence (using the human paradigm), statistical inference (inductive or deductive), knowledge representation, expert systems, rule-based neural networks, natural languages, pattern discovery, matching machine learning, and hierarchical clustering, is statistical. The probabilistic group consists of decision trees and operations research methods including dynamic programming, probability ideas, information and entropy ideas.

Computer programs such as BAMBE, BLAST, BLAT, FASTA, MEGA, PSI BLAST, VISTA, and VAST do microarray analysis, describe chromosomes, try contig mapping, and explore DNA-RNA databases like EMBL and GENBANK. The hidden Markov models, knowledge discovery, mutations, machine learning methods, neural networks, protein databases, x-y chromosomes, and Zipf's law, among others, are heavy but powerful tools of bioinformatics.

Genetic and molecular epidemiology is evolving into the mainstream of clinical health research. The proliferation of genetic data highlights the importance of analytical and graphical tools. Through an understanding of the genetic architecture of complex diseases, new modern medicines can be developed. Bioinformaticians are expected to play a critical role in the process of discovering new genetics-based medicines.

Several Monte Carlo techniques are used in bioinformatics. Being interdisciplinary, Monte Carlo techniques attract attention from bioinformaticians, DNA researchers, computer scientists, probabilists, and statisticians. Monte Carlo is a computer-assisted problem-solving technique in a complex system. Its methodologies were used first in physics but are now used widely in bioinformatics. Probabilists and statisticians might trace its history all the way back to the Buffon Needle problem in 1777. It is easy to compute that the chances of a needle of length l intersecting one of the parallel lines separated by a distance of D units is $2l/\pi D$. After throwing the needle a sufficiently large number of n times and letting $p_n = \#$ times intersected $/ n$, the value of π can be accurately approximated, and that is a Monte Carlo technique. That is,

$$\hat{\pi} = \lim_{n \to \infty} \frac{2l}{p_n D}.$$

In this genomic age, investigations of complex diseases require genetic concepts for understanding and discussing susceptibility, severity, drug efficacy, and drug side effects. In this process, researchers end up analyzing huge amounts of data. Concepts and tools such as multiple testing and data dredging are valuable in the pursuit of such huge data analyses.

The subtopics of bioinformatics are population genetics, evolutionary genetics, genetic epidemiology, animal and plant genetics, probability theory, several discrete and continuous distributions, moment/probability generating functions, Chebychev's inequality, entropy, correlation, distribution of maximum and

minimum in a set of random quantities, Bayesian and classical inference procedures, stochastic processes, Markov chains, hidden Markov models, computationally intensive methods in statistics, shotgun sequencing, DNA models, r-scans, nucleotide probabilities, alignments, dynamic programming, linear gap models, protein sequences, substitution matrices, edge effects in unaligned sequences, both discrete and continuous time evolutionary Jukes-Cantor models, Kimura neutral models, Felsenstein models, and phylogenetic tree estimations in biology, among others.

BLAST (Basic Local Alignment Search Tool), one of the bioinformatics software programs mentioned above, comes in several versions, BLASTP, BLASTN, and BLASTX, for comparing protein sequences, for nucleotide sequences, and for translated sequences, respectively. All BLAST programs produce similar output, consisting of a program introduction, a schematic distribution of alignments of the

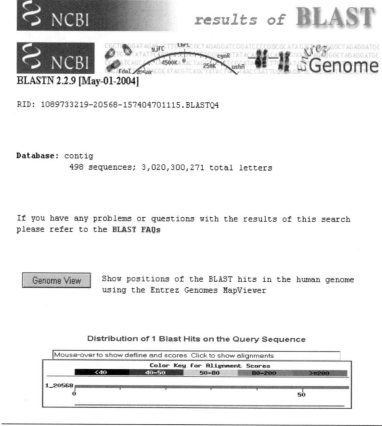

Figure 1   BLAST

Source: www.ncbi.nlm.nih.gov/BLAST/tutorial/Altschul-1.html.

query sequence to those in the databases, a series of one-line descriptions of the database sequences that have significantly aligned to the query sequence, the actual sequence alignments, and a list of statistics specific to the BLAST search method and version number. (See Figure 1.)

The top 100 significant alignments of the query sequence to database sequences are displayed schematically against the query sequence. Colored bars are distributed to reflect the region of alignment onto the query sequence. The color legend represents alignment scores, the higher scores being most significant. Selecting a bar will cause a description of that specific database sequence to be displayed in the window and allow the browser to jump down to that particular alignment for viewing (Figure 2).

FASTA (abbreviation of *fast algorithms*) performs a fast alignment of all protein/nucleotides sequences. This computer program is based on ideas found in Pearson and Lipman (1988). FASTA searches for similarity between a query sequence and a group of sequences of the same type (nucleic acid or protein).

DAMBE (Data Analysis in Molecular Biology and Evolution) can be used for analyzing molecular sequence data. Although science has unlocked several secrets of life, mysteries remain. For example, how do chromosomes organize themselves in meiosis and mitosis? What are the properties of protein value? How do DNA strands wind up? How do genes transmit instructions to make a specific protein? Why do shorter chromosomal arms have higher rates of recombination? Why is recombination less frequent near the centromeres? Why do more recombinations occur during meiosis? Why do chromosomes 13, 18, and 21 have the fewest genes per kilobase? Why is genome size not correlated with an organism's complexity? Why is only 5% of RNA coding while more than 50% of the repeat sequences are not coding? Why do more A-T than G-C pairings occur in general but not in chromosome 19? Why does the genetic material on the Y chromosome remain relatively young? Why is the mutation rate of the Y chromosome 1.57 times greater than that of the X chromosome? Why do thousands of genes produce noncoding RNA, tRNA, and rRNA? Why do more than 25% of tRNA genes exist on chromosome 6? And what are the functions of many proteins?

There are unresolved cloning and ethical issues. People are divided into those who argue in favor and those who are against cloning and stem cell research. Those in favor of doing research work cite forensic issues, finding cures for certain human diseases, advantages of DNA repair in diabetes and other illnesses, and advantages of understanding heritability. Those who are opposed cite security, privacy, ethics, and the fear of making "Frankenstein's monster."

—*Ramalingam Shanmugam*

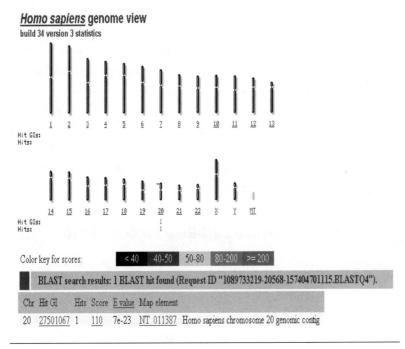

Figure 2   Human Chromosomes

Source: http://www.ensembl.org/Homo_sapiens/mapview.

Further Reading

Pearson, W. R., & Lipman, D. J. (1988). Improved tools for biological sequence comparison. *Proceedings of USA National Academy of Sciences, 85*(8), 2444–2448. Retrieved from http://srs.ebi.ac.uk/srsbin/cgi-bin/wgetz?-e+[MEDLINE-pmid:'3162770']

Xia, X. (2000). *Data analysis in molecular biology and evolution.* Boston: Kluwer Academic.

Xia, X., & Xie, Z. (2001). DAMBE: Data analysis in molecular biology and evolution. *Journal of Heredity, 92,* 371–373.

BLAST resources: http://www.ncbi.nlm.nih.gov/Education/BLASTinfo/tut1.html, http://www.ncbi.nlm.nih.gov/

DAMBE Windows95/98/NT executables: http://aix1.uottawa.ca/~xxia/software/software.htm

National Center for Biotechnology Information Human Genome Resources: http://www.ncbi.nlm.nih.gov/projects/genome/guide/human/

National Center for Biotechnology Information Social Analysis of Gene Expression Tag to Gene Mapping: www.ncbi.nlm.nih.gov/SAGE/

National Center for Biotechnology Information Statistics of Sequence Similarity Scores: www.ncbi.nlm.nih.gov/BLAST/tutorial/Altschul-1.html

Applying Ideas on Statistics and Measurement

The following abstract is adapted from Humphreys, K., Demetriou, G., & Gaizauskas, R. (2000). Bioinformatics applications of information extraction from scientific journal articles. *Journal of Information Science, 26*(2), 75–85.

Information extraction technology developed through the U.S. Defense Advanced Research Projects Agency (DARPA) Message Understanding Conferences (MUCs) has proved successful at extracting information from newswire texts and in domains concerned with human activity. This paper considers the application of this technology to the extraction of information from scientific journal papers in the area of molecular biology. In particular, it describes how an information extraction designed to participate in the MUC exercises has been modified for two **bioinformatics** applications, one concerned with enzyme and metabolic pathways, the other with protein structure. Progress to date provides convincing grounds for believing that information extraction techniques will deliver novel and effective ways for scientists to make use of the core literature that defines their disciplines.

BISERIAL CORRELATION COEFFICIENTS

Biserial correlation coefficients are measures of association that apply when one of the observed variables takes on two numerical values (a binary variable) and the other variable is a measurement or a score. There are several biserial coefficients, with the appropriate choice depending on the underlying statistical model for the data. The point biserial correlation and Pearson's biserial correlation are arguably the most well known and most commonly used coefficients in practice. We will focus on these two coefficients but will discuss other approaches.

Karl Pearson developed the sample biserial correlation coefficient in the early 1900s to estimate the correlation ρ_{YZ} between two measurements Z and Y when Z is not directly observed. Instead of Z, data are collected on a binary variable X with $X = 0$ if Z falls below a threshold level and $X = 1$ otherwise. The numerical values assigned to X do not matter provided the smaller value identifies when Z is below the threshold. In many settings, the latent variable Z is a conceptual construct and not measurable. The sample point biserial correlation estimates the correlation ρ_{YX} between Y and a binary variable X without reference to an underlying latent variable Z.

We will use S. Karelitz and colleagues' data on 38 infants to illustrate these ideas. A listing of the data is given in Table 1. The response Y is a child's IQ score at age 3, whereas $X = 1$ if the child's speech developmental level at age 3 is high, and $X = 0$ otherwise. The (population) biserial correlation ρ_{YZ} is a reasonable measure of association when X is a surrogate for a latent continuum Z of speech levels. The (population) point biserial correlation ρ_{YX} is more relevant when the relationship between IQ and the underlying Z scale is not of interest, or the latent scale could not be justified.

The Point Biserial Correlation

Assume that a random sample (y_1, x_1), (y_2, x_2), ..., (y_n, x_n) of n observations is selected from the (Y, X) population, where Y is continuous and X is binary. Let s_{YX} be the sample covariance between all y_i and all x_i, and let s_y^2 and s_x^2 be the sample variances of all y_i and all x_i, respectively. The population correlation ρ_{YX} between Y and X is estimated by the sample point biserial correlation coefficient, which is just the

Table 1   Data for a Sample of 38 Children

X = 0	Y:	87	90	94	94	97	103	103	104	106	108	109
		109	109	112	119	132						
X = 1	Y:	100	103	103	106	112	113	114	114	118	119	120
		120	124	133	135	135	136	141	155	157	159	162

Note: X = speech developmental level (0 = low; 1 = high), and Y = IQ score.

product-moment correlation between the Y and X samples:

$$r_{YX} = \frac{s_{YX}}{s_Y s_X}.$$

The sample point biserial estimator r_{YX} can also be expressed as

$$r_{YX} = \frac{(\bar{y}_1 - \bar{y}_0)}{s_Y}\{\hat{p}(1 - \hat{p})\}^{1/2},$$

where

$\bar{y}_1$ and $\bar{y}_0$ are the average y values from sampled pairs with $x_i = 1$ and $x_i = 0$, respectively, and

$\hat{p}$ is the proportion of observations that have $x_i = 1$.

The equivalence between the two expressions for r_{YX} requires that the sample variances and covariances be computed using a divisor of n and not the usual divisor of $n - 1$.

The first careful analysis of the properties of r_{YX} was provided by Robert Tate in the middle 1950s. He derived the large-sample distribution of r_{YX} assuming that the conditional distributions of Y given X = 1 and given X = 0 are normal with potentially different means but the same variances. Tate showed that $T = (n - 2)^{1/2}r_{YX}/(1 - r_{YX}^2)^{1/2}$ is equal to the usual two-sample Student t statistic for comparing $\bar{y}_1$ to $\bar{y}_0$ and that the hypothesis $\rho_{YX} = 0$ can be tested using the p value from the two-sample t test. For $\rho_{YX} \neq 0$, large-sample hypothesis tests and confidence intervals can be based on a normal approximation to r_{YX}, with estimated variance

$$\widehat{\text{var}}(r_{YX}) = \frac{(1 - r_{YX}^2)^2}{n}\left\{1 - 1.5r_{YX}^2 + \frac{.25r_{YX}^2}{\hat{p}(1 - \hat{p})}\right\}.$$

The biserial estimate r_{YX} is robust in the sense that the bias in r_{YX} approaches 0 as the sample size increases,

even if the distributional assumptions are not satisfied. However, the estimated variance of r_{YX} is sensitive to the assumption of equal variances for the two subpopulations (X = 0 and X = 1). Somesh Das Gupta generalized Tate's distributional results to allow unequal variances and nonnormal distributions.

Figure 1 gives side-by-side box plots of the IQ data generated by the S-PLUS statistics package. Although the distributions of the IQ scores for the samples with X = 0 and X = 1 are slightly skewed, the assumptions for Tate's analysis seem plausible. The mean IQ scores in the two samples are $\bar{y}_1 = 2779/22 = 126.32$ and $\bar{y}_0 = 1676/16 = 104.75$. Also, $\hat{p} = 22/38 = 0.579$ and $s_Y = 19.126$, which gives $r_{YX} = 0.557$ and $\widehat{\text{sd}}(r_{YX}) = 0.013$. The large difference between the means of the two groups relative to the within-group spreads is consistent with the observed correlations being significantly different from 0 (T = 4.024 on 38 − 2 = 36 df; p value < .001).

A shortcoming of the population point biserial correlation as a measure of association is that ρ_{YX} cannot assume all values between −1 and 1. The limits on ρ_{YX} depend on the distribution of Y and the Pr(X = 1). For example, if Y is normally distributed, then $-.798 \leq \rho_{YX} \leq .798$ regardless of Pr(X = 1). The maximum value can be achieved only when Pr (X = 1) = .50. If Y is normal and Pr(X = 1) = .85, then $-.653 \leq \rho_{YX} \leq .653$. Such restrictions can lead to a misinterpretation of the strength of the sample point biserial correlation. W. Joe Shih and W. H. Huang examined this issue and

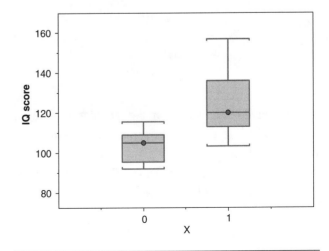

Figure 1   Box plots of IQ Score by X

proposed a way to calibrate the point biserial coefficient.

Pearson's Biserial Correlation

Suppose X is a binary variable that results from categorizing a continuous latent variable Z. Set $X = 1$ when $Z > \theta$ and $X = 0$ otherwise, where θ is a fixed but unknown threshold. Without loss of generality, we can assume that Z is standardized to have mean 0 and variance 1. Let $f(t)$ be the probability density function of Z and note that θ is the upper pth percentile of the distribution of Z; that is,

$$p = \Pr(X = 1) = \Pr(Z > \theta) = \int_\theta^\infty f(t)dt.$$

If the conditional expectation of Y given Z is a linear function of Z, then the population biserial correlation and the point biserial correlation are related by

$$\rho_{YZ} = \rho_{YX} \frac{\{p(1-p)\}^{1/2}}{\lambda(\theta, f)},$$

where $\lambda(\theta, f) = \int_\theta^\infty tf(t)dt$. The linearity assumption is satisfied when (Y, Z) has a bivariate normal distribution, a common assumption, but it holds for other elliptically symmetrical bivariate distributions as well. Under normality,

$$f(t) = \phi(t) \equiv \frac{1}{\sqrt{2\pi}} exp(-.5t^2),$$

$$\lambda(\theta, f) = \phi(\theta), \text{ and}$$

$$\rho_{YZ} = \rho_{YX} \frac{\{p(1-p)\}^{1/2}}{\phi(\theta)}.$$

The relationship between the population biserial correlation ρ_{YZ} and ρ_{YX} can be exploited to estimate ρ_{YZ} from a random sample $(y_1, x_1), (y_2, x_2), \ldots, (y_n, x_n)$ when the distribution of Z is known. Edward J. Bedrick suggested the simple method-of-moments estimator

$$\tilde{r}_{YZ} = r_{YX} \frac{\{\hat{p}(1-\hat{p})\}^{1/2}}{\lambda(\hat{\theta}, f)},$$

where $\hat{\theta}$ is the estimated threshold based on the proportion $\hat{p}$ of sampled pairs with $x_i = 1$ (i.e., $\hat{\theta}$ satisfies $\hat{p} = \Pr(Z > \hat{\theta})$). If Z has a normal distribution, $\tilde{r}_{YZ}$ is Pearson's sample biserial estimator, and

$$r_{Pb} = \frac{r_{YX}}{\phi(\hat{\theta})} \{\hat{p}(1 - \hat{p})\}^{1/2}$$

$$= \frac{(\bar{y}_1 - \bar{y}_0)}{s_Y \phi(\hat{\theta})} \hat{p}(1 - \hat{p}).$$

Bedrick's derivation of $\tilde{r}_{YZ}$ parallels Pearson's original treatment of the biserial correlation coefficient, so $\tilde{r}_{YZ}$ and r_{Pb} have similar distributional properties. Bedrick showed that the large-sample distribution of $\tilde{r}_{YZ}$ is normal with mean ρ_{YZ} and gave an expression for the large-sample variance of $\tilde{r}_{YZ}$. In the early 1900s, H. E. Soper gave an estimator for var (r_{Pb}) when (Y, Z) is normal:

$$\widehat{var}(r_{Pb}) = \frac{1}{n} \left[r_{Pb}^4 + \frac{r_{Pb}^2}{\phi^2(\hat{\theta})} \{\hat{p}(1 - \hat{p})\hat{\theta}^2 \right.$$

$$+ (2\hat{p} - 1)\hat{\theta}\phi(\hat{\theta}) - 2.5\phi^2(\hat{\theta})\}$$

$$\left. + \frac{\hat{p}(1 - \hat{p})}{\phi^2(\hat{\theta})} \right].$$

Tate showed that $r_{Pb} \geq \sqrt{.5\pi} r_{YX}$ (approximately $1.25 r_{YX}$). For the IQ data, $r_{Pb} = .703$ and $\widehat{sd}(r_{Pb}) = .133$.

The derivations of r_{Pb} and $\tilde{r}_{YZ}$ rely heavily on distributional assumptions. Neither estimate is consistent if either the conditional expectation of Y given Z is not linear in Z or the distribution of Z is incorrectly specified. This lack of robustness is problematic because neither assumption can be checked empirically. Another undesirable property of r_{Pb} and $\tilde{r}_{YZ}$ is that the magnitude of these estimates can exceed 1. This anomaly is common in small samples when the population correlation is large but becomes less likely as n increases.

Alternative Estimators

Several researchers developed estimators that eliminate one or more limitations of r_{Pb}. Hubert Brogden,

William Clemans, and Frederic Lord generalized Pearson's biserial estimator by relaxing the assumption that the distribution of Z is known. The Clemans-Lord estimator has the attractive property of being bounded between −1 and +1 and thus is much less variable than r_{Pb} when the population correlation is large. Edward Cureton and Eugene Glass proposed rank-based versions of the biserial estimator.

Tate proposed a maximum likelihood estimator of ρ_{YZ} assuming that (Y, Z) has a bivariate normal distribution. The maximum likelihood estimator is efficient when the model holds, but the estimate is not robust to misspecification of the model and requires specialized software to compute. The maximum likelihood approach could be considered with other probability models. However, Bedrick showed that the large-sample variances of the (noniterative) Clemans-Lord estimator and the maximum likelihood estimator are often close in a variety of normal and nonnormal populations.

—*Edward J. Bedrick*

Further Reading

Bedrick, E. J. (1992). A comparison of modified and generalized sample biserial correlation estimators. *Psychometrika*, *57*, 183–201.

Brogden, H. E. (1949). A new coefficient: Application to biserial correlation and to estimation of selective inefficiency. *Psychometrika*, *14*, 169–182.

Cureton, E. E. (1956). Rank-biserial correlation. *Psychometrika*, *21*, 287–290.

Das Gupta, S. (1960). Point biserial correlation and its generalization. *Psychometrika*, *25*, 393–408.

Karelitz, S., Fisichelli, V. R., Costa, J., Karelitz, R., & Rosenfeld, L. (1964). Relation of crying activity in early infancy to speech and intellectual development at age three years. *Child Development*, *35*, 769–777.

Lord, F. M. (1963). Biserial estimates of correlation. *Psychometrika*, *28*, 81–85.

Pearson, K. (1909). On a new method of determining the correlation between a measured character A and a character B. *Biometrika*, *7*, 96–105.

Shih, W. J., & Huang, W.-H. (1992). Evaluating correlation with proper bounds. *Biometrics*, *48*, 1207–1213.

Tate, R. F. (1954). Correlation between a discrete and a continuous variable: Point-biserial correlation. *Annals of Mathematical Statistics*, *25*, 603–607.

Tate, R. F. (1955). The theory of correlation between two continuous variables when one is dichotomized. *Biometrika*, *42*, 205–216.

SAS macro for computing the point, Pearson, and rank biserial coefficients: http://ftp.sas.com/techsup/download/stat/biserial.html

BIVARIATE DISTRIBUTIONS

Cause and effect between two phenomena in a real-life setting cannot be judged or resolved without configuring their patterns of occurrence, correlation, and uncertainties. Item response theory has been well developed by psychologists to explain the personal ability level of the examinees who answer a series of questions varying in toughness level. The ability and toughness levels are correlated random variables with a degree of dependence between them. Another revealing example is that the safety of a building cannot be ascertained without knowledge of both stress and strength of the materials used in the building. When the strength, Y, exceeds stress level, X, safety is guaranteed. Another serious life-and-death example is the distance of a populous city from the geological epicenter of an earthquake and the severity of damage in the city, as experienced in the tsunami of December 26, 2004, in south Asia. In a health application, X and Y are "susceptibility" and "immunity" levels of a person in the outbreak of a disease epidemic, respectively, and a person is healthy only so long as Y exceeds X. Identification of underlying bivariate probability distribution in these and other applications reveals a volume of related knowledge.

Such two stochastic aspects x and y in experimental or randomly observed studies are well explained by employing an appropriate underlying joint (probability) distribution $f(x, y)$. Their patterns of occurrence, correlation, and the prediction of one aspect using the occurrence level of another aspect are feasible from randomly collected bivariate data. Though the domain for the data could be a shrunken version depending on the cases, it is in general from minus infinity to positive infinity. A truncated or censored version of the bivariate (probability) distributions might be employed in such scenarios. A bivariate distribution could be a count of continuous or mixed type. However, their conditional $f(x \mid Y = y)$ and $f(y \mid X = x)$ distributions reveal interinfluence by one on another, but their marginal distribution $f(x)$ or $f(y)$ does not. For example, the predicted value of Y for a given level $X = x$ is called a regression function of x. The conditional and marginal dispersions obey an inequality $Var(Y \mid X = x) \leq Var(Y)$, which means that the conditional prediction of Y with knowledge of X is more precise than unconditional prediction of Y. The inverse of variance is called precision. Also, the so-called product moment is built in a hierarchical manner in accordance with the result $E(YX) = E[E(Y \mid X)]$, where the outer expectation is with respect to the random variable, X. Their covariance is defined to be $cov(Y, X) = E[E(Y \mid X = x] - E(Y) E(X)$. The covariance is scale oriented, and it could be misleading unless caution is exercised. Furthermore, the variance can also be hierarchically constructed according to a result $Var[Y] = E[Var(Y \mid X = x] + Var[EY \mid X = x)]$.

As done in univariate cases, the moment, cumulant, and probability generating functions are derived and used to identify central and noncentral moments and cumulants, along with their properties in bivariate distributions. The correlation coefficient ρ_{YX} between designated dependent variable Y and chosen independent (more often called *predictor*) variable X is $cov(Y, X)/\sigma_Y\sigma_X$, where $\sigma_Y = \sqrt{var(Y)}$ and $\sigma_X = \sqrt{var(X)}$ are standard deviations. The correlation coefficient is scale free. A simple linear regression function is $Y = \beta_0 + \beta_1 x + \varepsilon$ for predicting Y at a selected level $X = x$, and the so-called regression parameter (slope) is $\beta = \frac{\rho\sigma_Y}{\sigma_X}$. See a variety of popular bivariate distributions in Tables 1 and 2.

The uncorrelated variables Y and X are clearly independent in the case of bivariate Gaussian random variables but not necessarily in other cases. Two variates are uncorrelated if the joint probability distribution is the product of their marginal probability distributions. Equivalently, the conditional probability distribution is equal to the marginal probability distribution. In a collection of bivariate random samples, if Y_i and X_i in an ith pair are independent, then Y_{max} and X_{max} are also independent. The converse is not always true. So Geoffroy proved that if the ratio

$$\frac{1 - F_X(x) - F_Y(y) + F_{X,Y}(x, y)}{1 - F_{X,Y}(x, y)}$$

asymptotically joins the horizontal axis, then the independence of Y_{max} and X_{max} is sufficient for the independence of the random observations on Y and X where $F(.)$ is a cumulative distribution. However, bivariate Gaussian, logistic, Gumbel, and several other distributions of the type

$$F_{X,Y}(x, y) = F_X(x)F_Y(y) \left[1 + \alpha \left(1 - F_X[x]\right) \left(1 - F_Y[y]\right)\right]$$

validate the above ratio condition, independence between Y_{max} and X_{max}. Popularly employed bivariate distributions for continuous data analysis are displayed in Table 1.

Bayesians view nonobservable *latent* parameter θ as a random variable. Its marginal distribution $p(\theta)$ in its admissible domain $-\infty < \theta < \infty$ is called prior distribution. The conditional distribution

$$p(\theta \mid y) = \frac{f(y, \theta)}{m(y)} = \frac{p(\theta)l(y \mid \theta)}{\int_{-\infty}^{\infty} f(y, \theta)d\theta}$$

is called *posterior* (an update of the term *prior*) distribution, where $m(y)$ and $l(y \mid \theta)$ are called marginal distribution and likelihood function, respectively. The posterior distribution is an update of knowledge on parameter θ based on evidence in data, y. For an example, with known data variance σ_y^2, the univariate Gaussian distribution $f(y, \theta / \mid \sigma_y^2) = [2\pi\sigma_y^2]^{-\frac{1}{2}} \exp[-(y - \theta)^2/2\sigma_y^2]$ is considered as a bivariate distribution of random variables Y and Θ. Note the marginal mean $E(Y) = \theta$ is stochastic and follows independently a prior Gaussian distribution:

$$f(\theta \mid m, \sigma_0^2) = [2\pi\sigma_0^2]^{-\frac{1}{2}} \exp[-(y - m)^2/2\sigma_0^2], -\infty < \theta < \infty,$$
$$\sigma_0^2 > 0, -\infty < m < \infty.$$

Then, the posterior distribution $f(\theta / y)$ follows a Gaussian distribution with a weighted mean

$$E(\theta \mid y) = \frac{\frac{1}{\sigma_o^2}y + \frac{1}{\sigma_y^2}m}{\frac{1}{\sigma_o^2} + \frac{1}{\sigma_y^2}}$$

and variance $var(\theta \mid y)$.

$$var(\theta \mid y) = \left(\frac{1}{\sigma_o^2} + \frac{1}{\sigma_y^2}\right)^{-1}.$$

Note that the posterior mean is the weighted average of prior mean m and new data y, where the weights are prior precision and data precision. The precisions moderate prior mean and current data. The importance of the Bayesian style of thinking could not be better advocated by anything other than the concept of bivariate distribution.

Other distributions commonly employed for count data are bivariate versions of binomial, Poisson, inverse binomial, Neyman, Hermite, and logarithmic series distributions.

Consider that a bivariate distribution for the random number of traffic accidents and number of fatalities needs to be selected. The number of accidents Y and number of fatalities X in a specified location during a day can be modeled successfully using a quasi-binomial-Poisson bivariate distribution, as cited in Table 2. The marginal probability distribution of Y is

$$p(Y = y) = \sum_{x=0}^{y} p(y,x) = \lambda_1(\lambda_1+\lambda_2 y)^{y-1} \exp[-(\lambda_1+\lambda_2 y)]/y!,$$

a quasi-Poisson distribution, where $y = 0,1,2,\ldots\infty$, plus the parameters $\lambda_1 > 0$ and $-1 < \lambda_2 < 1$, denote, respectively, the observation space, accident rate, and hazard level. The marginal mean and variance of Y are

$$\frac{\lambda_1}{1-\lambda_2} \quad \text{and} \quad \frac{\lambda_1}{(1-\lambda_2)^3},$$

respectively. When there is no accident proneness (that is, $\lambda_2 = 0$), the above marginal probability mass function reduces to the popular Poisson distribution $p(y) = e^{-\lambda_1}\lambda_1^y / y!$. Not all accidents turn out to be fatal. An accident turns out to be a fatal accident with a probability $0 < p < 1$ due to some uncertain causes. The total number of fatal accidents $X = X_1 + X_2 + \ldots + X_Y$ for a given $Y = y$ follows conditionally a quasi-binomial distribution

$$p(X = x | Y = y)$$

$$= \binom{y}{x} \left(\frac{\lambda_1 p[1-p]}{\lambda_1 + \lambda_2 y}\right) \left(\frac{\lambda_1 p + \lambda_2 x}{\lambda_1 p + \lambda_2 y}\right)^{x-1}$$

$$\left(\frac{\lambda_1[1-p] + \lambda_2[y-x]}{\lambda_1 p + \lambda_2 y}\right)^{y-x-1},$$

where $x = 0,1,2\ldots,y$ and $0 < p < 1$ denote, respectively, the observation space for the random number of fatal accidents and the fatality parameter. In this scenario, the number of accidents splits into fatal and nonfatal types. This kind of branching process is called *damage modeling* in bivariate distribution literature. Marginally, the total number of fatal accidents follows a quasi-Poisson distribution

$$p(x) = \sum_{x=0}^{\infty} p(y,x) = \lambda_1 p(\lambda_1 p + \lambda_2 x)^{x-1} \exp[-(\lambda_1 p + \lambda_2 x)]/x!,$$

where the observation $x = 0,1,2\ldots,\infty$ and $(\lambda_1 p + \lambda_2 x) > 0$. The marginal mean of X is

$$E(X) = \frac{\lambda_1 p}{1-\lambda_2},$$

and the variance is

$$\text{var}(X) = \frac{\lambda_1 p}{(1-\lambda_2)^3}.$$

In the absence of accident proneness, (that is, $\lambda_2 = 0$), the marginal mean and variance of X are $\lambda_1 p$, a unique Poisson property to be watched. Intuitively, the random observations on Y and X must be correlated and not independent. Such an intuition is backed up by the difference between marginal and conditional probability distributions. That is, $p(Y = y | X = x) \neq p(X = x | Y = y)$ and $p(X = x | Y = y) \neq p(X = x)$ where

$$p(Y = y | X = x) = \lambda_1[1-p](\lambda_1[1-p] + \lambda_2[y-x])^{y-x-1}$$
$$\exp[-(\lambda_1[1-p] + \lambda_2[y-x])]/(y-x)!$$

with $y = x, x+1, \ldots,$. This conditional distribution is also quasi-Poisson but shifted x units on the right. It is easy to notice that $E(X | Y = y) = yp$, a regression line with slope p passing through the origin. But the reversed regression curve of Y given $X = x$ is

$$E(Y | X = x) = x + \frac{\lambda_1[1-p]}{[1-\lambda_2]},$$

with an intercept equal to $\dfrac{\lambda_1[1-p]}{[1-\lambda_2]}$

and unit slope. For random observations Y and X to be independent, a rule of thumb is $E(Y | X = x) = E(Y)$ and

Table 1 Selective Bivariate Continuous (Cumulative) Probability Distributions

Name	*Probability density f(x, y) or cumulative distribution function, $F(x, y) = \Pr[Y \le y, X \le x]$*
Gaussian	$f(y, x) = [2\pi\sigma_1\sigma_2(1 - \rho^2)]^{1/2} \exp[-(y - \mu_1)^2/\sigma_1^2$ $\qquad - (x - \mu_2)^2/\sigma_2^2 + 2\rho(x - \mu_1)(x - \mu_1)/\sigma_1\sigma_2]$
Marshall-Olkin exponential	$F(y, x) = \exp[-\lambda_1 y - \lambda_2 x - \lambda_3 \max(y, x)]$
Bivariate logistic	$F(y, x) = [1 + \exp(-[y - \mu_1]/\sigma_1) + \exp(-[x - \mu_2]/\sigma_2)$ $\qquad + (1 - \rho)\exp(-[y - \mu_1]/\sigma_1 - [x - \mu_2]/\sigma_2)]^{-1}$
Pareto first kind	$f(y, x) = \lambda(\lambda + 1)/\theta_1\theta_2 \left(\dfrac{y}{\theta_1} + \dfrac{x}{\theta_2} - 1 \right)^{(\lambda+2)},$ $y > \theta_1, x > \theta_2, \lambda > 0$
Pareto second kind	$F(y, x) = 1 - \left(1 + \dfrac{y - \mu_1}{\theta_1} + \dfrac{x - \mu_2}{\theta_2} \right)^{\lambda},$ $y > \mu_1, x > \mu_2, \lambda > 0$
Pareto third kind	$F(y, x) = 1 - 1/\left[\left(\dfrac{y - \mu_1}{\theta_1} \right)^{1/\delta_1} + \left(\dfrac{x - \mu_2}{\theta_2} \right)^{1/\delta_2} \right],$ $y > \mu_1, x > \mu_2, \delta_1 > 0, \delta_2 > 0$
Dirichlet	$f(y, x) = \dfrac{\Gamma(\theta_o + \theta_1 + \theta_2)}{\Gamma(\theta_0)\Gamma(\theta_1)\Gamma(\theta_2)} y^{\theta_1-1} x^{\theta_2-1} (1 - [y + x])^{\theta_0-1}$
Gumbel	$f(y, x) = e^{-(y+x+\theta yx)}[(1+\theta y)(1+\theta x)-\theta]$ $y, x > 0; 0 \le \theta \le 1$
Freund	$f(y, x) = \begin{cases} \alpha\beta' e^{-\beta' y-(\alpha+\beta-\beta')x} \\ \alpha'\beta e^{-\alpha' x-(\alpha+\beta-\alpha')y} \end{cases} if \begin{cases} 0 \le x \le y \\ 0 \le y \le x \end{cases}$
Block-Basu	$f(y, x) = \begin{cases} \dfrac{\lambda\lambda_1(\lambda_2+\lambda_{12})}{\lambda_1+\lambda_2} e^{-\lambda_1 x-(\lambda_2+\lambda_{12})y} \\ \dfrac{\lambda\lambda_2(\lambda_1+\lambda_{12})}{\lambda_1+\lambda_2} e^{-\lambda_2 y-(\lambda_2+\lambda_{12})x} \end{cases}, if \begin{cases} 0 < x < y < \infty \\ 0 < x < y < \infty \end{cases}$
Bivariate extreme value	$H(x, y) = \exp(-\exp([-(y - \mu_1)/\sigma_1] + \exp[-(x - \mu_2)/\sigma_2])^{-1/\rho})$

Table 2 Selective Bivariate Count Distributions

Name	Probability mass function, $f(x, y)$
Binomial	$p(y, x, n - y - x) = \left(\dfrac{n!}{y!x!(n - y - x)!} \right) \theta_1^y \theta_2^x (1 - \theta_1 - \theta_2)^{n-y-x}$ $0 < \theta_1, \theta_2 < 1; y = 0, 1, 2, \dots, n; x = 0, 1, 2, \dots, n; y + x \leq n$
Inverse binomial	$p(y, x, n - y - x) = \dfrac{\Gamma(r + y + x)}{\Gamma(r)y!x!} \theta_1^y \theta_2^x (1 - \theta_1 - \theta_2)^r$ $0 < \theta_1, \theta_2 < 1; y = 0, 1, 2, \dots, ; x = 0, 1, 2, \dots,$
Poisson	$p(y, x) = e^{-(\theta_1 + \theta_2 + \theta_{12})} \displaystyle\sum_{i=0}^{max(y,x)} \theta_1^{y-i} \theta_2^{x-i} \theta_{12}^i / (y - i)!(x - i)!i!$
Hypergeometric	$p(y, x) = \dfrac{\dbinom{Np_1}{y} \dbinom{Np_2}{x} \dbinom{N - Np_1 - Np_2}{n - y - x}}{\dbinom{N}{n}};$ $y = 0, 1, \dots, \min(N_1, n - x); x = 0, 1, \dots, \min(N_2, n - y);$ $\dbinom{a}{b} = \dfrac{\Gamma(a + 1)}{\Gamma(b + 1)\Gamma(a + b + 1)}$
Bivariate geometric	$p(y, x) = \dbinom{y + x}{y} \theta_1^y \theta_2^x (1 - \theta_1 - \theta_2)$ $y, x = 0, 1, 2, \dots; 0 < \theta_1, \theta_2 < 1$
Sarmonov-Lee family	$p(y, x) = \dbinom{m}{y} \dbinom{n}{x} \theta_1^y (1 - \theta_1)^{m-y} \theta_2^x (1 - \theta_2)^{n-x} [1 + \varpi \phi_1(y)\phi_2(x)];$ $y = 0, 1, 2, \dots, m; x = 0, 1, 2, \dots, n; 0 < \theta_1, \theta_2 < 1$
Quasi-binomial-Poisson	$p(y, x) = \lambda_1^2 p(1 - p)(\lambda_1 p + \lambda_2 x)^{x-1}(\lambda_1[1 - p] + ([y - x]\lambda_2)^{y-x-1}$ $\exp[-(\lambda_1 + \lambda_2 y)]/x!(y - x)!$ $y = 0, 1, 2 \dots, \infty;$ $x = 0, 1, 2 \dots, y; (\lambda_1 + \lambda_2 y) > 0;$ $\lambda_1 > 0; -1 < \lambda_2 < 1; 0 < p < 1$

$E(X | Y = y) = E(X)$. This rule is clearly not validated in this example. So the number of accidents and the number of fatal accidents must be not independent but correlated. Their correlation is

$$\rho_{Y,X} = \frac{cov(Y, X)}{\sqrt{var(Y)var(X)}} = +\sqrt{p}.$$

Also,

$$var(Y) = \frac{\lambda_1}{(1 - \lambda_2)^3},$$

$$var(X) = \frac{\lambda_1 p}{(1 - \lambda_2)^3},$$

$$var(Y | X = x) = \frac{\lambda_1 [1 - p]}{(1 - \lambda_2)^3},$$

and

$$var(X | Y = y) = y^2 p[1 - p]$$
$$- \frac{y(y - 1)\lambda_1 p(1 - p)}{(\lambda_1 + \lambda_2 y)} \sum_{s=0}^{y-2} \frac{(y - 2)s\lambda_2^s}{(\lambda_1 + \lambda_2 y)^s}.$$

These results validate a universal result in bivariate distribution that

$$var(Y) = var(E[Y | X = x]) + E(var[Y | X = x]).$$

The correlation coefficient is a dependence measure. The importance of dependence measures in bivariate distributions cannot be overstated. Of course, all dependent measures are model based, and hence, selecting an appropriate bivariate distribution for a given set of data is vitally important. The concept of *copula* (meaning bond) eases the burden of selecting a bivariate distribution. The copula is a scale-invariant way of dealing with dependency. Only the uniform distribution over a unit square for the copula can detect the independence between bivariates. A departure from uniformity indicates the existence of dependency. What kind of dependencies can a copula detect in bivariate distributions? For a discussion of this wonderful idea, consider the cumulative distribution functions of Y, X, and their joint random variables, which are indicated respectively by $u = G(x) = \Pr[X \leq x]$, $v = F(y) = \Pr[Y \leq y]$, and $H(x, y) = \Pr[X \leq x, Y \leq y]$. The copula is then a mapping of each (x, y) in a two-dimensional domain to a unique value $H(x, y)$ in the unit square. There is a unique copula $C(u, v)$ in the sense $H(G^{-1}[u], F^{-1}[v]) = C(u, v)$. Bivariate random variables Y and X are considered independent if and only if there is a copula validating $B(u, v) = uv$. In general, $\max(u + v - 1, 0) \leq C(u, v) \leq \min(u, v)$.

For the sake of understanding continuous bivariate distributions, consider bivariate logistic distribution (as in Table 1). Bivariate logistic distribution is employed to explain random failing of paired organs such as kidneys in diabetic patients. When their correlation coefficient $\rho = 0$, the random lifetimes Y and X are independent since

$$H(x, y) = \exp(-[y - \mu_1]/\sigma_1)\exp(-[x - \mu_2]/\sigma_2)$$
$$= F(y)G(x) \text{ and } B(u, v) = uv.$$

Consider the bivariate extreme value distribution (as in Table 1) with $\sigma = 1/\rho = \sigma_2$, $\mu_1 = 0 = \mu_2$. This bivariate extreme value distribution illustrates unusual rainfall and farm damage. Its copula is $C(u, v) = \exp(-[(-1nu)^\rho + (-1nv)^\rho]^{1/\rho})$. When the parameter $\rho = 1$, the amount of rainfall and the amount of farm damage are stochastically independent.

In the case of bivariate distributions, copula is related to Spearman's correlation coefficient ρ and Kendall's rank correlation coefficient τ. Bivariate random variables Y and X are *concordant* if large values of one variate tend to be associated with large values of the other variate and smaller values of one variate are associated with small values of the other. Otherwise, the bivariates are *discordant*. Kendall's τ is simply the probability of concordance minus the probability of discordance. The copula is related to Kendall's τ as $C(u, v) = (1 + \tau)/4$. For a given set of data, both ρ and τ could come out differently but should validate an inequality $-1 \leq 3\tau 2\rho \leq 1$.

—*Ramalingam Shanmugam*

Further Reading

Basu, A. P., & Dhar, S. K. (1995). Bivariate geometric distribution. *Journal of Applied Statistical Science, 2*, 33–44.

Geoffroy, J. (1958, 1959). Contribution a la theorie des valeurs extremes. *Publications de l'Institut de Statistique de l'Universite de Paris, 7*, 37–121; 8, 123–184.

Lee, M. L. T. (1966). Properties and applications of the Sarmonov family of bivariate distributions. *Communications in Statistics, 25,* 1207–1222.

Sarmonov, O. V. (1966). Generalized normal correlation and two dimensional Frechet classes. *Soviet Doklady, 168,* 596–599.

Shanmugam, R. (2002). A critique of dependence concepts. *Journal of Mathematical Psychology, 46,* 110–114.

Shanmugam, R., & Singh, J. (1981). Some bivariate probability models applicable to traffic accidents and fatalities. In C. Tallie, G. P. Patil, & B. A. Baldessari (Eds.), *Statistical distributions in scientific work: Vol. 6* (pp. 95–103). Hingham, MA: Reidel.

BONFERRONI, CARLO EMILIO (1892–1960)

Bonferroni was born in Bergamo (near Milan), Italy, on January 28, 1892. Educated at Turin University, his first post was assistant professor in financial mathematics, mechanics, and geometry at the Turin Polytechnic. In 1923, he was appointed professor of financial mathematics at the Economics Institute in Bari, where he served 7 years as rector.

In 1933 he moved to Firenze (Florence), where he remained until his death. During his time in Firenze, he filled a variety of administrative posts. For example, in the immediate postwar years, he acted both as head of the statistics faculty at Bocconi University, Milan, and as head of the Faculty of Architecture in Florence.

His work on inequalities, published in 1935 and 1936, represented only a small part of his interests. For example, his inaugural lecture was concerned with the foundations of probability (which he viewed as the limit of relative frequency when the entire population is sampled).

The handwritten notes he produced for his students reveal his deep insights into mathematics—often revealed through neat and idiosyncratic solutions. By all accounts, he was a sensitive and kind-hearted man and a gentleman. He was a talented pianist and also composed music. In his younger days, he was a keen glacier walker. His garden was described as enchanting.

Bonferroni died on August 18, 1960, in Firenze.

—Graham Upton

Further Reading

Galambos, J., & Simonelli, I. (1996). *Bonferroni-type inequalities with applications.* New York: Springer.

Carlo Emilio Bonferroni biography and readings: http://www.aghmed.fsnet.co.uk/bonf/bonf.html

BONFERRONI TEST

The more tests we perform on a set of data, the more likely we are to reject the null hypothesis when it is true (a Type I error). This is a consequence of the logic of hypothesis testing: We reject the null hypothesis if we witness a rare event. But the larger the number of tests, the easier it is to find rare events, and therefore, the easier it is to make the mistake of thinking that there is an effect when there is none. This problem is called the *inflation* of the alpha level. One strategy for preventing it is to correct the alpha level when performing multiple tests. Making the alpha level more stringent (i.e., smaller) will create fewer errors, but it may also make real effects harder to detect.

The Different Meanings of Alpha

Maybe researchers perform more and more statistical tests on one set of data because computers make statistical analyses easy to run. For example, brain imaging researchers will routinely run millions of tests to analyze an experiment. Running so many tests increases the risk of false alarms. To illustrate, imagine the following "pseudoexperiment":

I toss 20 coins, and I try to force the coins to fall heads up. I know that, from the binomial test, the null hypothesis is rejected at the $\alpha = .05$ level if the number of heads is greater than 14. I repeat this experiment 10 times.

Suppose that one trial gives the "significant" result of 16 heads versus 4 tails. Did I influence the coins on that occasion? Of course not, because the larger the number of experiments, the greater the probability of encountering a low-probability event (like 16 versus 4). In fact, waiting long enough is a sure way of detecting rare events!

Probability in the Family

A *family of tests* is the technical term for a series of tests performed on a set of data. In this section, we show how to compute the probability of rejecting the null hypothesis at least once in a family of tests when the null hypothesis is true.

For convenience, suppose that we set the significance level at $\alpha = .05$. For each test (i.e., one trial in the example of the coins), the probability of making a Type I error is equal to $\alpha = .05$. The events "making a Type I error" and "not making a Type I error" are *complementary events* (they cannot occur simultaneously). Therefore the probability of not making a Type I error on one trial is equal to

$$1 - \alpha = 1 - .05 = .95.$$

Recall that when two events are independent, the probability of observing these two events together is the product of their probabilities. Thus, if the tests are independent, the probability of not making a Type I error on the first *and* the second tests is

$$.95 \times .95 = (1 - .05)^2 = (1 - \alpha)^2.$$

With three tests, we find that the probability of not making a Type I error on all tests is

$$.95 \times .95 \times .95 = (1 - .05)^3 = (1 - \alpha)^3.$$

For a family of C tests, the probability of not making a Type I error for the *whole family* is

$$(1 - \alpha)^C.$$

For our example, the probability of not making a Type I error on the family is

$$(1 - \alpha)^C = (1 - .05)^{10} = .599.$$

Now, what we are looking for is the probability of making one or more Type I errors on the family of tests. This event is the complement of the event of *not making a Type I error on the family*, and therefore it is equal to

$$1 - (1 - \alpha)^C.$$

For our example, we find

$$1 - (1 - .05)^{10} = .401.$$

So, with an α level of .05 for *each* of the tests, the probability of wrongly rejecting the null hypothesis is .401.

This example makes clear the need to distinguish between two meanings of α when performing multiple tests:

- The probability of making a Type I error when dealing only with a specific test. This probability is denoted $\alpha[PT]$ (pronounced "alpha per test"). It is also called the *testwise* alpha.
- The probability of making at least one Type I error for the whole family of tests. This probability is denoted $\alpha[PF]$ (pronounced "alpha per family of tests"). It is also called the *familywise* or the *experimentwise* alpha.

A Monte Carlo Illustration

A Monte Carlo simulation can illustrate the difference between $\alpha[PT]$ and $\alpha[PF]$. The Monte Carlo technique consists of running a simulated experiment many times using random data. This gives the pattern of results that happens on the basis of chance.

Here six groups with 100 observations per group were created with data randomly sampled from the same normal population. By construction, H_0 is true (i.e., all population means are equal). Call that procedure an experiment. We performed five independent tests from these six groups. For each test, we computed an F test. If its probability was smaller than $\alpha = .05$, the test was declared significant (i.e., $\alpha[PT]$ is used). We performed this experiment 10,000 times. Therefore, there were 10,000 experiments, 10,000 families, and $5 \times 10,000 = 50,000$ tests. The results of this simulation are given in Table 1.

Table 1 shows that H_0 is rejected for 2,403 tests of more than 50,000 tests performed. From these data, an estimation of $\alpha[PT]$ is computed as

Table 1 Results of a Monte Carlo Simulation: Numbers of Type I Errors When Performing $C = 5$ Tests for 10,000 Families When H_0 Is True*

Number of Families With X Type I Errors	X: Number of Type I Errors per Family	Number of Type I Errors
7,868	0	0
1,907	1	1,907
192	2	384
20	3	60
13	4	52
0	5	0
10,000		2,403

Note: *For example, 192 families out of 10,000 have two Type I errors; this gives $2 \times 192 = 384$ Type I errors.

$$\alpha[PT] = \frac{\text{number of significant tests}}{\text{total}}$$

$$\text{number of tests} = \frac{2,403}{50,000} = .0479. \quad (1)$$

This value falls close to the theoretical value of $\alpha = .05$.

For 7,868 families, no test reaches significance. Equivalently, for 2,132 families (10,000 − 7,868), at least one Type I error is made. From these data, $\alpha[PF]$ can be estimated as

$$\alpha[PF] = \frac{\substack{\text{number of families with} \\ \text{at least 1 Type I error}}}{\text{total number of families}}$$

$$= \frac{2,132}{10,000} = .2132. \quad (2)$$

This value falls close to the theoretical value of

$$\alpha[PF] = 1 - (1 - \alpha[PT])^C = 1 - (1 - .05)^5 = .226$$

How to Correct for Multiple Tests: Šidàk, Bonferroni, Boole, Dunn

Recall that the probability of making at least one Type I error for a family of C tests is

$$\alpha[PF] = 1 - (1 - \alpha[PT])^C$$

This equation can be rewritten as

$$\alpha[PF] = 1 - (1 - \alpha[PT])^{1/C}$$

This formula—derived assuming independence of the tests—is sometimes called the Šidàk equation. It shows that in order to reach a given $\alpha[PF]$ level, we need to adapt the $\alpha[PT]$ values used for each test.

Because the Šidàk equation involves a fractional power, it is difficult to compute by hand, and therefore several authors derived a simpler approximation, which is known as the Bonferroni (the most popular name), or Boole, or even Dunn approximation. Technically, it is the first (linear) term of a Taylor expansion of the Šidàk equation. This approximation gives

$$\alpha[PT] \approx \frac{\alpha[PF]}{C}.$$

Šidàk and Bonferroni are linked to each other by the inequality

$$\alpha[PT] = 1 - (1 - \alpha[PF])^{1/C} \geq \frac{\alpha[PF]}{C}.$$

They are, in general, very close to each other, but the Bonferroni approximation is pessimistic (it always does worse than the Šidàk equation). Probably because it is easier to compute, the Bonferroni approximation is better known (and cited more often) than the exact Šidàk equation.

The Šidàk-Bonferroni equations can be used to find the value of $\alpha[PT]$ when $\alpha[PF]$ is fixed. For example, suppose that you want to perform four independent tests, and because you want to limit the risk of making at least one Type I error to an overall value of $\alpha[PF] = .05$, you will consider a test significant if its associated probability is smaller than

$$\alpha[PF] = 1 - (1 - \alpha[PT])^{1/C} = 1 - (1 - .05)^{1/4} = .0127.$$

With the Bonferroni approximation, a test reaches significance if its associated probability is smaller than

$$\alpha[PT] = \frac{\alpha[PF]}{C} = \frac{.05}{4} = .0125,$$

which is very close to the exact value of .0127.

Correction for Nonindependent Tests

The Šidàk equation is derived assuming independence of the tests. When they are not independent, it gives a lower bound, and then

$$\alpha[PF] \leq 1 - (1 - \alpha[PT])^C.$$

As previously, we can use a *Bonferroni* approximation because

$$\alpha[PF] < C\alpha[PT].$$

Šidàk and Bonferroni are related by the inequality

$$\alpha[PF] \leq 1 - (1 - \alpha[PT])^C < C\alpha[PT].$$

The Šidàk and Bonferroni inequalities can also be used to find a correction on $\alpha[PT]$ in order to keep $\alpha[PF]$ fixed. The Šidàk inequality gives

$$\alpha[PT] \approx 1 - (1 - \alpha[PF])^{1/C}$$

This is a conservative approximation because the following inequality holds:

$$\alpha[PT] \geq 1 - (1 - \alpha[PF])^{1/C}$$

The Bonferroni approximation gives

$$\alpha[PT] \approx \frac{\alpha[PF]}{C}.$$

Splitting Up $\alpha[PF]$ With Unequal Slices

With the Bonferroni approximation, we can make an unequal allocation of $\alpha[PF]$. This works because with the Bonferroni approximation, $\alpha[PF]$ is the sum of the individual $\alpha[PT]$:

$$\alpha[PF] \approx C\alpha[PT] = \underbrace{\frac{\alpha[PT] + \alpha[PT] + \ldots + \alpha[PT]}{C_{\text{times}}}}.$$

If some tests are judged more important a priori than some others, it is possible to allocate $\alpha[PF]$ unequally. For example, suppose we have three tests that we want to test with an overall $\alpha[PF] = .05$, and we think that the first test is the most important of the set. Then we can decide to test it with $\alpha[PT] = .04$ and share the remaining value, $.01 = .05 - .04$, between the last two tests, which will be evaluated each with a value of $\alpha[PT] = .005$. The overall Type I error for the family is equal to $\alpha[PF] = .04 + .005 + .005 = .05$, which was indeed the value we set beforehand. It should be emphasized, however, that the (subjective) importance of the tests and the unequal allocation of the individual $\alpha[PT]$ should be decided a priori for this approach to be statistically valid. An unequal allocation of the $\alpha[PT]$ can also be achieved using the Šidàk inequality, but it is more computationally involved.

Alternatives to Bonferroni

The Šidàk-Bonferroni approach becomes very conservative when the number of comparisons becomes large and when the tests are not independent (e.g., as in brain imaging). Recently, some alternative approaches have been proposed to make the correction less stringent. A more recent approach redefines the problem by replacing the notion of $\alpha[PF]$ with the false discovery rate, which is defined as the ratio of the number of Type I errors to the number of significant tests.

—*Hervé Abdi*

Further Reading

Benjamini, Y., & Hochberg, Y. (1995). Controlling the false discovery rate: A practical and powerful approach to multiple testing. *Journal of the Royal Statistical Society, Series B, 57*, 289–300.

Games, P. A. (1977). An improved *t* table for simultaneous control on *g* contrasts. *Journal of the American Statistical Association, 72*, 531–534.

Hochberg, Y. (1988). A sharper Bonferroni procedure for multiple tests of significance. *Biometrika, 75*, 800–803.

Holm, S. (1979). A simple sequentially rejective multiple test procedure. *Scandinavian Journal of Statistics, 6*, 65–70.

Rosenthal, R., & Rosnow, R. L. (1985). *Contrast analysis: Focused comparisons.* New York: Cambridge University Press.

Shaffer, J. P. (1995). Multiple hypothesis testing. *Annual Review of Psychology, 46,* 561–584.

Šidàk, Z. (1967). Rectangular confidence region for the means of multivariate normal distributions. *Journal of the American Statistical Association, 62,* 626–633.

BOWKER PROCEDURE

It is often of interest to examine changes in the categorical responses taken from participants before and then after some treatment condition is imposed (i.e., to evaluate repeated measurements of the same participants, using them as their own controls). In 1947, the psychologist Quinn McNemar developed a simple procedure for comparing differences between the proportions in the before and after responses for two categories. In 1948, the statistician Albert Bowker expanded on McNemar's work and developed a test for symmetry that evaluates the changes in before and after responses in contingency tables when there are multiple categories.

Bowker's procedure has been used broadly both in the social and behavioral sciences and in medical research, and some attention has been given to applications in advertising, public relations, and marketing research, wherein it may be desirable to evaluate the significance of changes in attitudes, opinions, and beliefs.

Development

The responses from a sample of n' individuals over two periods of time may be tallied into an $r \times c$ table (where r, the number of rows, equals c, the number of columns) of cross-classifications, as shown in Table 1.

With respect to the population from which the aforementioned sample was taken, let p_{ij} be the probability of responses to the ith category before the treatment condition was imposed and the jth category after. The marginal probabilities before and after treatment sum to unity. That is, $p_{1.} + p_{2.} + \ldots + p_{r.} = 1$ and $p_{.1} + p_{.2} + \ldots + p_{.c} = 1$.

Testing for Significance of Changes in Related Proportions

In order to investigate changes in repeated measurements, the null hypothesis is that of symmetry:

$$H_0: p_{ij} = p_{ji} \text{ for all } i > j.$$

The alternative is that at least one pair of symmetric probabilities is unequal:

$$H_1: p_{ij} \neq p_{ji} \text{ for any } i > j.$$

That is, the null hypothesis tested is conditioned on those

$$n = \sum_{\forall i \neq j} x_{ij}$$

individuals whose responses change, where the probability (p_{ij}) of a switch from response i to response j is equal to the probability (p_{ji}) of a switch from response j to response i, and this probability is 0.5.

The Bowker test statistic B, written as

$$B = \sum_{i=j+1}^{r} \sum_{j=1}^{c} \frac{(x_{ij} - x_{ji})^2}{x_{ij} + x_{ji}},$$

has a chi-square distribution with u degrees of freedom where $u = r(r-1)/2 = c(c-1)/2$ since $r = c$. The

Table 1 $r \times c$ Table of Cross-Classifications for a Sample of n' Subjects

I \ II	1	2	...	$c = r$	Totals
1	x_{11}	x_{12}	...	x_{1c}	$x_{1.}$
2	x_{21}	x_{22}	...	x_{2c}	$x_{2.}$
...	...	...	...	...	...
$r = c$	x_{r1}	x_{r2}	...	x_{rc}	$x_{r.}$
Totals	$x_{.1}$	$x_{.2}$	...	$x_{.c}$	n'

Notes: I = Time period I (before treatment) in a repeated measurements experiment; II = Time period II (after treatment) in a repeated measurements experiment; r = number of rows (number of categories); c = number of columns (number of categories); n' = sample size.

null hypothesis can be rejected at the α level of significance if

$$B > \chi^2_{v,1-\alpha}.$$

A Posteriori Comparisons

If the null hypothesis is rejected, the researcher Alan Stuart suggested a multiple comparison procedure that permits the development of a post hoc evaluation of changes in the correlated proportions (i.e., marginal probabilities) for each response category versus the $c - 1$ other categories combined. Thus, regardless of the size of the initial $c \times c$ table of cross-classifications, this process allows for the formation of a set of c 2×2 tables, one for each of the c categories versus all the other $c - 1$ categories combined. These 2×2 tables take the form

After Before	i	Not i	Totals
i	x_{ii}	$x_{ii'}$	$x_{i.}$
Not i	$x_{i'i}$	$x_{i'i'}$	$x_{i'.}$
Totals	$x_{.i}$	$x_{.i'}$	n'

for all $i = 1, \ldots, c$.

The critical ranges for each of these c a posteriori comparisons arise from the standard error of the differences in two related proportions as used in McNemar-type confidence intervals.

With an experimentwise error rate α, each of the possible c pairwise comparisons is made, and the decision rule is to declare column classification i different from row classification i if

$$|\hat{p}_{.i} - \hat{p}_{i.}| > \sqrt{\chi^2_{\alpha,(c-1)}}$$

$$\bullet \sqrt{\frac{\hat{p}_{.i}\hat{p}_{.i'}}{n'} + \frac{\hat{p}_{i.}\hat{p}_{i'.}}{n'} - \frac{2(\hat{p}_{ii} - \hat{p}_{.i}\hat{p}_{i.})}{n'}}$$

where $\hat{p}_{.i} = \dfrac{x_{.i}}{n'}$ and $\hat{p}_{i.} = \dfrac{x_{i.}}{n'}$ and

where i' is the complement of i, the combined responses from all $c - 1$ other classifications. That is,

the classification in column i and classification in row i are declared significantly different if $|\hat{p}_{.i} - \hat{p}_{i.}|$, the absolute difference in the sample proportions of "success" before and after a treatment intervention, exceeds a critical range given by the product

of $\sqrt{\chi^2_{\alpha,(c-1)}}$ and

$$\sqrt{\frac{\hat{p}_{.i}\hat{p}_{.i'}}{n'} + \frac{\hat{p}_{i.}\hat{p}_{i'.}}{n'} - \frac{2(\hat{p}_{ii} - \hat{p}_{.i}\hat{p}_{i.})}{n'}}.$$

Applying the Bowker Procedure

Consider the following hypothetical example: Suppose a consumer panel consists of $n' = 150$ individuals who have stated their preference for Toyota Camry, Honda Accord, and Nissan Maxima vehicles. The participants were each asked which of these vehicles they were most likely to choose for their next car purchase. Of the 150 participants, 45 stated they were most likely to purchase a Toyota Camry, 66 were most likely to purchase a Honda Accord, and 39 were most likely to purchase a Nissan Maxima.

Suppose the panelists are then presented with a consumer-based rating of customer satisfaction, product quality, and buyer behavior for these vehicles, such as would be found in a J. D. Power automobile report. The ratings provide detailed information about these three vehicles and rank the vehicles overall from best to worst as follows: Toyota Camry, Nissan Maxima, and Honda Accord.

Following this exposure to the research literature, the individuals are asked once again to answer the above question. Of the 45 panelists who initially stated they were most likely to purchase a Toyota Camry, 40 remained consistent in their response, 3 stated they were now more likely to purchase a Honda Accord, and 2 were now more likely to purchase a Nissan Maxima. Of the 66 panelists who initially stated they were most likely to purchase a Honda Accord, 41 remained consistent in their response, 14 stated they were now more likely to purchase a Toyota Camry, and 11 were now more likely to purchase a

Nissan Maxima. Of the 39 panelists who initially stated they were most likely to purchase a Nissan Maxima, 29 remained consistent in their response, 6 stated they were now more likely to purchase a Toyota Camry, and 4 were now more likely to purchase a Honda Accord.

The results are displayed in Table 2.

Bowker's test seeks to measure the ability of the automobile ratings to affect consumer preferences. The null hypothesis for the test of symmetry is

$$H_0: p_{ij} = p_{ji} \text{ for all } i > j.$$

That is, a panelist's car preference is not affected by the information in the automobile ratings. For example, having read the report, a panelist who initially was leaning toward purchasing a Toyota Camry is now just as likely to feel more inclined to purchase a Nissan Maxima as a panelist would be to switch from most likely to purchase a Nissan Maxima to more likely to purchase a Toyota Camry. This null hypothesis of symmetry may be tested against the alternative:

$$H_1: p_{ij} \neq p_{ji} \text{ for any } i > j.$$

That is, exposure to the automobile ratings does influence one's preference for a particular vehicle.

For these data, the Bowker test for symmetry enables an exact test of the null hypothesis with the chi-square probability distribution, where $r = c = 3$ and $\upsilon = 3(3-1)/2 = 3$ degrees of freedom with a "stated" level of significance α. The Bowker test statistic B is calculated as follows, based on the response tallies in symmetric positions off the main diagonal of the 3×3 contingency table (i.e., cells x_{12} versus x_{21}, x_{13} versus x_{31}, and x_{23} versus x_{32} from Table 2:

$$B = \frac{(14-3)^2}{17} + \frac{(6-2)^2}{8} + \frac{(4-11)^2}{15}$$

$$= 12.384.$$

Since $B > \chi^2_{05;3} = 7.815$, the null hypothesis is rejected at the $\alpha = 0.05$ level of significance. The p value is 0.0062. Thus, exposure to the automobile ratings does influence one's preference for a particular vehicle. At least one of the three pairs of symmetric probabilities off the main diagonal of the 3×3 contingency table is unequal, or preference for at least one of the three automobiles has changed significantly.

Given that the null hypothesis is rejected, to determine which of the three automobiles displayed significant change in preferences as a result of the automobile ratings, post hoc evaluations for the $c = 3$ pairwise differences in related proportions (i.e., marginal probabilities) are made. The data, collapsed into three 2×2 contingency tables, are presented in Table 3.

The critical ranges for these pairwise comparisons of preferences for the particular automobiles before and then after the automobile ratings were examined are obtained in Table 4, and the pairwise comparisons of differences in proportions of preference are evaluated in Table 5.

From Table 5 it is clear that preference for the Toyota Camry significantly increased as a result of the automobile ratings while preference for the Honda Accord significantly decreased. However, the observed decline in preference for the Nissan Maxima is not statistically significant.

Discussion

For the special case where $r = c = 2$, the Bowker statistic is identical to the McNemar test for the significance of changes. Unlike McNemar's procedure for a 2×2 contingency table, Bowker's test of the null hypothesis of symmetry in a $c \times c$ contingency table is not equivalent to a test of the null hypothesis of equality of correlated proportions (i.e., marginal probability

Table 2 Hypothetical Results of a Marketing Campaign

Before \ After	Toyota	Honda	Nissan	Totals
Toyota	$X_{11} = 40$	$x_{12} = 3$	$x_{13} = 2$	$x_{1.} = 45$
Honda	$X_{21} = 14$	$x_{22} = 41$	$x_{23} = 11$	$x_{2.} = 66$
Nissan	$X_{31} = 6$	$x_{32} = 4$	$x_{33} = 29$	$x_{3.} = 39$
Totals	$X_{.1} = 60$	$x_{.2} = 48$	$x_{.3} = 42$	$n' = 150$

Table 3   A Posteriori Analysis: Collapsing for Pairwise Comparisons

Before \ After	Toyota	Not Toyota	Totals
Toyota	$X_{11} = 40$	$x_{12} = 5$	$x_{1.} = 45$
Not Toyota	$X_{21} = 20$	$x_{22} = 85$	$x_{2.} = 105$
Totals	$x_{.1} = 60$	$x_{.2} = 90$	$n' = 150$

Before \ After	Honda	Not Honda	Totals
Honda	$X_{11} = 41$	$x_{12} = 25$	$x_{1.} = 66$
Not Honda	$X_{21} = 7$	$x_{22} = 77$	$x_{2.} = 84$
Totals	$x_{.1} = 48$	$x_{.2} = 102$	$n' = 150$

Before \ After	Nissan	Not Nissan	Totals
Nissan	$X_{11} = 29$	$x_{12} = 10$	$x_{1.} = 39$
Not Nissan	$X_{21} = 13$	$x_{22} = 98$	$x_{2.} = 111$
Totals	$x_{.1} = 42$	$x_{.2} = 108$	$n' = 150$

distributions). In 1955, Stuart proposed a test for the latter and, on rejection of the null hypothesis, proposed a set of McNemar-type simultaneous confidence intervals for a posteriori evaluation of differences in the c pairs of correlated proportions.

Taking advantage of the fact that testing a null hypothesis of symmetry is equivalent to testing a null hypothesis of correlated proportions in the 2×2 contingency table, the a posteriori McNemar-type simultaneous confidence intervals proposed by Stuart can be adapted to the Bowker procedure by collapsing the $c \times c$ contingency table on the main diagonal into a set of c 2×2 contingency tables so that one may test globally, for each category, for the significance of change in the proportion of respondents switching from one category to all others combined versus switching to a category from any other. In the hypothetical example presented here, the intervention through exposure to the automobile ratings caused a significant shift in preference to the Toyota Camry and a significant shift away from the Honda Accord.

As a result of the treatment intervention, if the gains are transitive, a rejection of the null hypothesis

Table 4   Computation of Critical Ranges for Post Hoc Pairwise Comparisons

Automobiles	$\sqrt{\chi^2_{\alpha,(c-1)}} \cdot \sqrt{\dfrac{\hat{p}_{.i}\hat{p}_{.i'}}{n'} + \dfrac{\hat{p}_{i.}\hat{p}_{i'.}}{n'} - \dfrac{2(\hat{p}_{ii} - \hat{p}_{.i}\hat{p}_{i.})}{n'}}$
Toyota vs. not Toyota	$\sqrt{5.991} \cdot$ $\sqrt{\dfrac{(0.40)(0.60)}{150} + \dfrac{(0.30)(0.70)}{150} - \dfrac{2[(0.2667) - (0.40)(0.30)]}{150}} = 0.0791$
Honda vs. not Honda	$\sqrt{5.991} \cdot$ $\sqrt{\dfrac{(0.32)(0.68)}{150} + \dfrac{(0.44)(0.56)}{150} - \dfrac{2[(0.2733) - (0.32)(0.44)]}{150}} = 0.0892$
Nissan vs. not Nissan	$\sqrt{5.991} \cdot$ $\sqrt{\dfrac{(0.28)(0.72)}{150} + \dfrac{(0.26)(0.74)}{150} - \dfrac{2[(0.1933) - (0.28)(0.26)]}{150}} = 0.0782$

Table 5 Post Hoc Pairwise Comparisons of Changes in Perceptions for the Automobiles

Automobiles	$|\hat{p}_{.i} - \hat{p}_{i.}|$	Critical range	Decision rule
Toyota vs. not Toyota	$|\hat{p}_{.1} - \hat{p}_{1.}| = 0.1000$	0.0791	Significant
Honda vs. not Honda	$|\hat{p}_{.2} - \hat{p}_{2.}| = 0.1200$	0.0892	Significant
Nissan vs. not Nissan	$|\hat{p}_{.3} - \hat{p}_{3.}| = 0.0200$	0.0782	Not Significant

by the Bowker test should lead to global findings, as shown here.

In recent years, the biostatisticians Warren L. May and William D. Johnson have thoroughly researched the issue of symmetry among several proportions and proposed an alternative approach to the Bowker procedure, along with simultaneous confidence intervals for a posteriori analysis.

Conclusions

It is essential to a good data analysis that the appropriate statistical procedure be applied to a specific situation. The Bowker test may be used when studying symmetry among several proportions based on related samples. A researcher unaware of the procedure may employ an inappropriate chi-square test for the $c \times c$ contingency table and draw incorrect conclusions.

The Bowker test is quick and easy to perform. The only assumption is that the before and after responses of each participant are categorized into a $c \times c$ table.

The pedagogical advantage of the a posteriori multiple comparisons based on McNemar-type confidence intervals is that they demonstrate that all n' participants are being evaluated. The initial B test statistic itself is conditioned on a reduced set of participants, the "brand switching" panelists off the main diagonal of the cross-classification table.

—*Nicole B. Koppel and Mark L. Berenson*

Further Reading

Bowker, A. H. (1948). A test for symmetry in contingency tables. *Journal of the American Statistical Association, 43*, 572–574.

Marascuilo, L. A., & McSweeney, M. (1977). *Nonparametric and distribution-free methods for the social sciences* (167–171). Monterey, CA: Brooks/Cole.

May, W. L., & Johnson, W. D. (1997). Confidence intervals for differences in correlated binary proportions. *Statistics in Medicine, 16*, 2127–2136.

May, W. L., & Johnson, W. D. (2001). Symmetry in square contingency tables: Tests of hypotheses and confidence interval construction. *Journal of Biopharmaceutical Statistics, 11*(1–2), 23–33.

McNemar, Q. (1947). Note on the sampling error of the difference between correlated proportions or percentages. *Psychometrika, 12*, 153–157.

Stuart, A. (1955). A test of homogeneity of the marginal distributions in a two-way classification. *Biometrika, 42*, 412–416.

Stuart, A. (1957). The comparison of frequencies in matched samples. *British Journal of Statistical Psychology, 10*, 29–32.

BOX PLOT (BOX AND WHISKER PLOT)

The box and whisker plot was developed by John Tukey to summarize visually the important characteristics of a distribution of scores. The five descriptive statistics included on a box plot are the minimum and the maximum scores (i.e., the extremes of the distribution), the median (i.e., the middle score), and the 1st (Q_1) and 3rd (Q_3) quartiles. Together these statistics are useful in visually summarizing, understanding, and comparing many types of distributions.

In a box plot, the crossbar indicates the median, and the length (i.e., height) of the box indicates the interquartile range (IQR) (i.e., the central 50% of the data values). The length of the whiskers indicates the range of scores that are included within 1.5 IQRs below and above the 1st and 3rd quartiles, respectively.

Box plots are particularly useful for investigating the symmetry of a distribution and for detecting inconsistent values and outliers. Outliers, which are scores that are more than 1.5 IQRs below Q_1 or above Q_3, are plotted individually on a box plot. In a normal distribution, about 1% of the scores will fall outside the box and whiskers. The symmetry of a distribution is indicated by where the median bifurcates the box (in a symmetrical distribution, the median is close to the center of the box) and by the length of the whiskers (in a distribution with symmetrical tails, the whiskers are of similar length).

Figure 1 summarizes the descriptive statistics and displays the box plots for 100 randomly selected IQ scores and for the subset of all scores that are greater than 99. Figure 1 shows that variable "Random" is roughly symmetrical, with three low IQ-score outliers. Variable ">99" is slightly positively skewed (the median is closer to Q_1 than to Q_3, the upper whisker is longer than the lower whisker, and there are no outliers).

The box plot is a classic exploratory data analysis tool that is easy to construct and interpret. It is resistant to small changes in the data (up to 25% of the scores can change with little effect on the plot) because its major components are the median and the quartiles. When one is interpreting a box plot, the following limitations should be noted:

1. Quartiles (also called "hinges") are defined differently in various computer programs, and these differences can produce very different-looking plots when sample sizes are small.

2. Although the 1.5 IQR value is used in most computer programs to draw the whiskers and define outliers, this value is not universal.

3. Using the box plot to detect outliers is a conservative procedure. It identifies an excessive number of outlying values.

4. Box plots may not have asymmetrical whiskers when there are gaps in the data.

5. Because the length of the box indicates only the spread of the distribution, multimodality and other fine features in the center of the distribution are not conveyed readily by the plot.

In order to address some of these limitations, other forms of the box plot have been developed. For example, the *variable-width box plot* is used to indicate relative sample size, the *notched box plot* is used to indicate the confidence interval of the median to

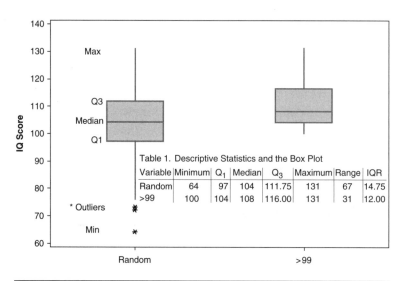

Figure 1   Box Plots of 100 Normally Distributed IQ Scores and a Subset of All IQ Scores Greater Than 99

Table 1. Descriptive Statistics and the Box Plot

Variable	Minimum	Q_1	Median	Q_3	Maximum	Range	IQR
Random	64	97	104	111.75	131	67	14.75
>99	100	104	108	116.00	131	31	12.00

enable comparisons between centers of distributions, and the *violin plot* combines the box plot with density traces to show multimodality and other fine-grain features of the distribution.

—Ward Rodriguez

See also Exploratory Data Analysis; Median; Range

Further Reading

Benjamini, Y. (1988). Opening the box of a boxplot. *American Statistician, 42*, 257–262.

Cleveland, W. S. (1985). *The elements of graphing data.* Monterey, CA: Wadsworth.

Frigge, M., Hoaglin, D. C., & Iglewicz, B. (1989). Some implementations of the boxplot. *American Statistician, 43*, 50–54.

Hintze, J. L., & Nelson, R. D. (1998). Violin plots: A box plot-density trace synergism. *American Statistician, 52*, 181–184.

McGill, R., Tukey, J. W., & Larsen, W. A. (1978). Variations of box plots. *American Statistician, 32*, 12–16.

Applying Ideas on Statistics and Measurement

The following abstract is adapted from Cefai, C. (2004). Pupil resilience in the classroom: A teacher's framework. *Emotional & Behavioural Difficulties, 9*(3), 149–170.

This article describes the development of a teacher's framework for identifying a number of primary school classes in Malta characterized by high levels of pupil resilience, namely socioemotional competence and educational engagement. The article defines resilience as a proactive, contextual, and relational phenomenon concerning all pupils, irrespective of individual characteristics or background. The author, from the University of Malta, outlines and discusses the construction, administration, and scoring of a seven-item framework, followed by an analysis of responses from 22 teachers who rated 465 pupils in their classes, on the basis of which three classes in each school were selected for further study. **Box plots** are used to present the frequency of behavior and the level of variability for both total resilience and individual component scores. The conclusion suggests how schools and teachers may use the framework as a descriptive tool in their efforts to promote socioemotional and cognitive competence.

Bracken Basic Concept Scale—Revised

The Bracken Basic Concept Scale—Revised (BBCS-R) is an instrument designed to assess the basic concept development of children in the age range of 2 years 6 months through 7 years 11 months. The BBCS-R measures children's comprehension of 308 foundational and functionally relevant educational concepts in 11 subtests or concept categories. Of the 11 subtests on the BBCS-R, the first 6 are combined into one score and compose the BBCS-R School Readiness Composite (SRC). The SRC can be used to assess children's knowledge of those readiness concepts that parents and preschool and kindergarten teachers traditionally teach children in preparation for their formal educations (e.g., colors, shapes, sizes). The remaining subtests (7–11) each produce separate scaled scores and assess important concepts that parents and teachers often fail to teach in any systematic manner (e.g., textures/materials, time/sequence). These latter subtests and the SRC

Table 1   BBCS-R Subtests, Composites, and Average Coefficient Alpha Across Age Levels

Subtests/Composites	Alpha
1. Colors	*
2. Letters	*
3. Numbers/counting	*
4. Sizes	*
5. Comparisons	*
6. Shapes	*
School Readiness Composite	**.91**
7. Direction/position	.97
8. Self-/social awareness	.93
9. Texture/material	.93
10. Quantity	.95
11. Time/sequence	.93
Total test score	**.98**

Note: *The first six subtests do not produce individual scores but contribute to the School Readiness Composite; hence, only School Readiness Composite reliability was calculated and presented.

combine and form the BBCS-R Total Test Score. Table 1 presents the BBCS subtests, the test composites, and average cross-sample coefficient alpha estimates of internal consistency.

Historically, concepts have been identified as fundamental agents or building blocks of intelligence, and acquisition of basic concepts has been shown to be strongly related to children's overall intellectual development. Importantly, the BBCS-R is a developmentally sensitive measure of cognitive and linguistic concept attainment across cultures. Thus, the concepts assessed on the BBCS-R are more universal and fundamental in importance than are the graded vocabulary words found typically on measures of receptive vocabulary that are not conceptually oriented. Ironically, researchers have demonstrated that the administration directions of many preschool and primary tests of intelligence also are replete with basic concepts, which may render intelligence test directions the first conceptual challenge children face on tests of intelligence.

Although intelligence is not a construct that is easily improved or sustained through remedial efforts, basic concepts can be directly targeted for instruction, and students can achieve significant and sustainable growth in concept acquisition when direct instruction is linked to BBCS-R assessment results. The *Bracken Concept Development Program* was developed to create a direct assessment–instruction linkage with the BBCS-R.

—*Bruce A. Bracken*

Further Reading

Bracken, B. A. (1986). Incidence of basic concepts in five commonly used American tests of intelligence. *School Psychology International, 7*, 1–10.

Bracken, B. A. (1998). *Bracken Basic Concept Scale—Revised*. San Antonio, TX: Psychological Corporation.

Bracken, B. A., Barona, A., Bauermeister, J. J., Howell, K. K., Poggioli, L., & Puente, A. (1990). Multinational validation of the Bracken Basic Concept Scale. *Journal of School Psychology, 28*, 325–341.

Bracken, B. A., Howell, K. K., Harrison, T. E., Stanford, L. D., & Zahn, B. H. (1991). Ipsative subtest pattern stability of the Bracken Basic Concept Scale and the Kaufman Assessment Battery for Children in a preschool sample. *School Psychology Review, 20*, 309–324.

Howell, K. K., & Bracken, B. A. (1992). Clinical utility of the Bracken Basic Concept Scale as a preschool intellectual screener: Comparison with the Stanford-Binet for Black children. *Journal of Clinical Child Psychology, 21*, 255–261.

Kaufman, A. S. (1978). The importance of basic concepts in the individual assessment of preschool children. *Journal of School Psychology, 16*, 208–211.

Laughlin, T. (1995). The school readiness composite of the Bracken Basic Concept Scale as an intellectual screening instrument. *Journal of Psychoeducational Assessment, 13*, 294–302.

Wilson, P. (2004). A preliminary investigation of an early intervention program: Examining the intervention effectiveness of the Bracken Concept Development Program and the Bracken Basic Concept Scale—Revised with Head Start students. *Psychology in the Schools, 41*, 301–311.

BRUNO, JAMES EDWARD (1940–)

James Edward Bruno was born to Mr. and Mrs. John Bruno in Brooklyn, New York, on December 12, 1940, as part of a set of twins.

Jim grew up in Brooklyn and Long Island before his parents relocated to Pomona, California. Young Jim was always an excellent athlete and scholar. After high school, he attended the University of California, Los Angeles (UCLA). Jim's devotion to UCLA was so strong that he would complete his B.S., M.S., and Ph.D. degrees there. An outstanding educational researcher, he was hired by UCLA as a faculty member in educational policy.

Bruno's early publications applied a balanced blend of engineering, statistics, and economics to education problems. He successfully demonstrated the use of Monte Carlo methods and linear programming in helping school districts develop their substitute teachers pool and states develop school finance programs. His mathematical skills and astute observations of human behavior led him to develop a mathematical model of voter preferences that helped John Tunney get elected to the U.S. Senate. While at the RAND Corporation, Bruno met Dr. Emir Shuford and became interested in Shuford's research on admissible probability measurement and two-dimensional, confidence weighted testing. With his skills as a scientific programmer, Bruno built the first working programs for scoring and reporting tests using a modification of this system and based on an optical scanning format. Bruno would later call this procedure for assessment *information reference testing*. Organizations such as the Federal Aviation Administration and the North Atlantic Treaty Organization used this method to examine the information quality of workers who held important and critical positions. Bruno received a patent for this system of information quality assessment. Knowledge Factor, of Denver, Colorado, is applying the technology to areas of corporate training.

Later Bruno's research turned to the measurement, perception, and differential use of time and its impact on human behavior and demonstrated that at-risk children had an entirely different concept of time with regard to past, present, and future than those children not at risk and that these differences result in antisocial behaviors. Bruno's latest research interest involves the systematic examination of policy issues as they relate to negative geographical space, social well-being, and access to equal education opportunity. This research involves the ways geographical space shapes adolescents' behavior and impacts their attitudes toward schooling and society.

Bruno has nearly 200 publications. He is married to Ann and has two daughters: Jenny and Julia.

—*Howard B. Lee*

Further Reading

Bruno, J. E. (1996). Time perceptions and time allocation preferences among adolescent boys and girls. *Journal of Adolescence, 31*(121), 109–126.

James E. Bruno Research Activities page: http://www.gseis.ucla .edu/faculty/bruno/brunor.htm

Knowledge Factor Web site: http://www.knowledgefactor.com/

Buros Institute of Mental Measurements

During the first quarter of the 20th century, testing became a big business in much of the developed world. Large numbers of authors and publishers started creating tests in fields such as education, psychology, and business to cater to an increasingly strong demand. Within about 25 years, more than 4,000 English-language tests were written and published. Many of these tests promised more than could be practically delivered and were formulated with only a vague understanding of the basic principles of measurement and statistics.

As a young professor of measurement and statistics at Rutgers University, Oscar K. Buros (1905–1978) became acutely aware of the insufficient technical merits of many commercial tests. In the early 1930s, alarmed by the state of testing and seeking to improve the overall quality of tests, Buros began editing a series of books that featured descriptive test bibliographies and critical reviews written by recognized experts in the field. The results of these endeavors became the *Tests in Print* (TIP) and the *Mental Measurements Yearbook* (MMY) publication series. Buros used the term *mental measurements* to describe tests published in the broad areas of "aptitude, educational, intelligence, personality and psychological tests, questionnaires, and rating scales" (Buros, 1938, p. xiii). The Buros Institute of Mental Measurements was subsequently created as the organizational component to continue these publications.

Despite the pressing need for independent test evaluation, Buros initially found little financial support. By locating small grants, borrowing, and using his own funds, he was able to continue publication through the difficult years of the 1930s and 1940s. Financial pressures eased during the 1950s, when the TIP and MMY series became a recognized part of many university and public library collections.

After the death of Oscar Buros, his widow and long-time collaborator, Luella Gubrud Buros, moved the Institute to the University of Nebraska-Lincoln. Publication quickly resumed with *The Ninth Mental Measurements Yearbook* and *Tests in Print III*. At the present time, the Buros Institute is completing *The Seventeenth Mental Measurements Yearbook* (produced every 2 years) and *Tests in Print VIII* (produced every 3 years). In 2001, the Buros Institute introduced Test Reviews Online, a service providing ready access to a wide variety of information about and reviews of commercial testing instruments.

In order to fulfill the long-standing dream of Oscar Buros for an independent testing organization working to improve contemporary testing practices, the Buros Center for Testing was created in 1992. This new testing center brought together the products (MMY and TIP series) of the Buros Institute of Mental Measurements with the services (test oversight, evaluation, and independent psychometric research) of the newly created Buros Institute for Assessment Consultation and

Outreach. Together, these institutes continue the work of improving both the science and the practice of testing that were the primary focus of Oscar Buros's life.

—*Robert A. Spies*

Further Reading

Buros, O. K. (Ed.). (1938). *The nineteen thirty eight mental measurements yearbook*. New Brunswick, NJ: Rutgers University Press.

Buros Institute Test Reviews Online: http://www.unl.edu/buros/

Applying Ideas on Statistics and Measurement

The following abstract is adapted from de la Rosa, I. A., Perry, J., Dalton, L. E., & Johnson, V. (2005). Strengthening families with first-born children: Exploratory story of the outcomes of a home visiting intervention. *Research on Social Work Practice, 15*(5), 323–338.

The **Buros Institute** is very well known for its collection of test reviews. Its online resources are the perfect place to begin looking for the appropriate measure. This study used the Buros Institute in its discussion of the Brigance Diagnostic Inventory of Early Development as a tool to evaluate the effectiveness of intervention, along with other measures. Using a theory-of-change framework, Iván A. de la Rosa and his colleagues examined outcome measures of a home visitation program that provided services to first-born children and their parents living in southwestern New Mexico. Home visitation workers conducted pretest and posttest assessments for prenatal and postpartum periods for 109 families receiving services in the First-Born Program. The results showed that clients participating in the First-Born Program displayed significantly higher posttest scores on measures of family resiliency. Specifically, clients demonstrated improved scores in operationalized measures of resilience: social support, caregiver characteristics, family interaction measures, and a reduction in personal problems affecting parenting.

An experiment is a question which science poses to Nature, and a measurement is the recording of Nature's answer.

—Max Planck

CALIFORNIA PSYCHOLOGICAL INVENTORY

The California Psychological Inventory (CPI; publisher: Consulting Psychologists Press) is a measure of normal personality and behavior. Originally developed in 1956 by Harrison Gough, the CPI provides a useful and accurate picture of people taking the instrument and a means for estimating their behavior across situations. The measure often is used in conjunction with assessing nonclinical populations and is appropriate for individuals age 13 years and older. The inventory takes approximately 45–60 minutes to complete.

Individual profiles are generated from the instrument based on its 20 folk concept scales. These scales are organized into four sectors: interpersonal style, intrapersonal style, achievement style and intellectual efficiency, and stylistic modes of thinking and behavior. The interpersonal style sector represents how individuals may be typed with regard to social interaction and includes the scales of dominance, capacity for status, sociability, social presence, self-acceptance, independence, and empathy. The intrapersonal style sector relates to an individual's values and self-regulation and includes the responsibility, socialization, self-control, good impression, communality, well-being, and tolerance scales. The achievement style sector includes the achievement via conformance, achievement via independence, and intellectual efficiency scales. The stylistic modes sector includes psychological-mindedness, flexibility, and femininity/masculinity.

In addition to the 20 folk scales, the CPI includes 13 research and special purpose scales. These special purpose scales include managerial potential, work orientation, masculinity, femininity, anxiety, social desirability, acquiescence, creative temperament, leadership potential, amicability, law enforcement orientation, tough-mindedness, and narcissism. In addition to research, these scales are often used to explore occupational issues and are used frequently by organizations for such purposes as identifying leadership potential and managerial selection.

Underlying the scores on the folk concepts and special purpose scales are three structural scales that provide a measure of an individual's tendency toward or away from involvement with others, tendency to favor or doubt societal values, and perceived level of fulfillment or realization of abilities. The CPI also provides individual test takers with a description of how they would be described according to the

California Q-sort instrument. Further, the CPI provides a measure of the overall reliability and validity of each individual profile.

The CPI was last updated in 1996. The current (third) edition includes 434 items, 28 fewer than the preceding version. Items related to physical or psychological disabilities were removed for consistency with the 1990 Americans with Disabilities Act. Evidence of validity for the CPI is being collected continuously, and the instrument is used widely in counseling, organizational, and research settings.

—Todd J. Wilkinson and Jo-Ida C. Hansen

See also Minnesota Multiphasic Personality Inventory; NEO Personality Inventory; Sixteen Personality Factor Questionnaire

Further Reading

Gough, H. G. (1996). *The California Psychological Inventory manual*. Palo Alto, CA: Consulting Psychologists Press.

McAllister, L. W. (1996). *A practical guide to CPI interpretation* (3rd ed.). Palo Alto, CA: Consulting Psychologists Press.

Meyer, P., & Davis, S. (1992). *The CPI applications guide*. Palo Alto, CA: Consulting Psychologists Press.

Consulting Psychologists Press, Inc.: www.cpp-db.com

CAREER ASSESSMENT INVENTORY

The Career Assessment Inventory (CAI) is an interest inventory designed to survey an individual's interest in a variety of areas and then provide information on how those interests match up with the interests of people in a variety of occupations. Intended to assist individuals in career planning and decision making, it was authored by Charles B. Johansson and originally published in 1975. The CAI has undergone several revisions and is currently available in two versions: The Enhanced Version, for both college-bound and non-college-bound individuals, and the Vocational Version, for those who want to enter the workforce with little of no postsecondary training.

Both versions of the CAI use the widely accepted Holland model to organize information about general interest patterns into six general theme areas (realistic, investigative, artistic, social, conventional, and enterprising). Individuals are encouraged to develop a better understanding of their interest patterns so that they can use the information from the test when exploring occupations or other areas that are not specifically covered in the inventory. Two to eight Basic Interest Area Scales under each of the theme areas help individuals better understand their interest patterns; for instance, writing, creative arts, and performing and entertaining are under the artistic theme. While these patterns represent interests in specific areas, they are areas that could cover a wide variety of occupations. The greatest degree of specificity is found on the Specific Occupational Scales (111 for the Enhanced and 91 for the Vocational), which are each also organized into the general theme under which it best fits. These scales compare the responses of the individual taking the test with those of people in various occupations and indicate how similar they are.

Four scales are considered nonoccupational and measure one's orientation to learning by doing versus learning through traditional classroom work, introversion versus extroversion in the workplace, fine arts versus mechanical orientation, and the degree of variability of interests. These scales can be very useful in determining the validity of the test as well as in future planning.

The CAI takes 35–40 minutes to complete. Its 370 items are rated on a 5-point scale from *like* to *dislike*. It requires an eighth-grade reading level and is ideally suited for use with high school students who are in the process of career exploration, particularly if they are attempting to choose between attending college and entering the workforce directly. However, a number of other interest inventories are much more widely used (e.g., Strong Interest Inventory, Campbell Interest and Skill Survey, Self-Directed Search).

—Steve Saladin

See also Career Development Inventory; Career Maturity Inventory

Further Reading

Johansson, C. B. (1986). *Manual for the Career Assessment Inventory: The enhanced version.* Minneapolis, MN: National Computer Systems.

Career Assessment Inventory—The Enhanced Version: http://www.pearsonassessments.com/tests/cai_e.htm

CAREER DEVELOPMENT INVENTORY

Career inventories can be separated into two categories, those that measure career choice content and those that measure career choice process. Inventories that deal with career choice content measure an individual's occupational abilities, vocational interests, and work values and then match these characteristics to the requirements, routines, and rewards that characterize a variety of occupations. Inventories that deal with career choice process measure an individual's attitudes toward, beliefs about, and competencies for making educational and vocational decisions as well as coping with vocational development tasks such as securing a job and establishing oneself in an organization. Process-oriented inventories provide a picture illustrating an individual's readiness and resources for career decision making. This picture portrays information regarding attitudes toward planning and exploration as well as knowledge about occupations and competence at decision making.

One popular instrument for measuring readiness and resources for educational and vocational decision making during adolescence is the Career Development Inventory (CDI). The CDI School Form is used with Grades 8 through 12, and the CDI College Form is used with college students.

The CDI is composed of two parts. Part I contains 80 items, takes approximately 40 minutes to complete, and reports scores for four scales: Career Planning (CP), Career Exploration (CE), Decision Making (DM), and Knowledge of the World of Work (WW). CP measures an individual's future orientation with regard to the world of work. Responses indicate the amount of thought an individual has given to future occupational choices and the extent to which an individual has engaged in career planning activities. CE represents the degree to which an individual has made use of quality resources in career planning activities.

DM measures one's ability to apply the principles of rational decision making to educational and vocational choices. Brief scenarios describe individuals in the process of making career decisions. Based on the information given, the respondent must choose the most appropriate solution from a list of possible answers. It is proposed that individuals who can solve the career problems in these scenarios are likely to make wise decisions regarding their own careers. WW assesses one's knowledge regarding specific occupations and ways to attain, establish, and prosper in a job of one's own choosing.

Part II measures Knowledge of Preferred Occupation (PO). It contains 40 items and takes approximately 30 minutes to complete. Individuals are prompted to select their preferred occupational group from a list of 20 groups. The questions that follow address the type of work one should expect, educational requirements, values, and interests that are characteristic of individuals employed in that line of work.

The CDI reports three additional scores: Career Development Attitudes, which combines CP and CE; Career Decision Knowledge, which combines DM and WW; and Career Orientation Total, which combines CP, CE, DM, and WW. An online version of the CDI is available free to qualified professionals at http://www.vocopher.com.

—Kevin W. Glavin and Mark L. Savickas

See also Career Assessment Inventory; Career Maturity Inventory

Further Reading

Savickas, M. L. (1984). Career maturity: The construct and its measurement. *Vocational Guidance Quarterly, 32,* 222–231.

Savickas, M. L. (2000). Assessing career decision making. In E. Watkins & V. Campbell (Eds.), *Testing and assessment in counseling practice* (2nd ed.; pp. 429–477). Hillsdale, NJ: Erlbaum.

CAREER MATURITY INVENTORY

Comprehensive models of vocational development during adolescence address the content of occupational choices and the process of career decision making. Choice content matches an individual's abilities and interests to occupational requirements and rewards. A good match leads to success and satisfaction, a poor match to failure and frustration. Career choice process deals with how individuals make decisions, not which occupation they choose. Individuals who apply a more highly developed and mature decisional process usually make more realistic and suitable choices. Because career maturity is central to adolescent vocational development, several inventories have been designed to measure *career choice readiness*. The Career Maturity Inventory, created by John O. Crites in 1978, was the first such measure to be published, and it subsequently became one of the most popular readiness inventories for students in Grades 6 through 12.

The Career Maturity Inventory measures the process dimension of vocational development during adolescence. The process dimension consists of two group factors: career choice attitudes and career choice competencies. Decision-making attitudes are viewed as dispositional response tendencies that mediate both choice behaviors and the use of the competencies. The decision-making competencies are viewed as comprehension and problem-solving abilities that pertain to making occupational choices. The attitudes are considered affective variables, and the competencies are considered cognitive variables.

The 1978 version of the Attitude Scale of the Career Maturity Inventory remains available in two forms: a screening form and a counseling form. The screening form consists of 50 items that yield a general score to indicate overall degree of career choice readiness. It is best used for performing needs analyses, evaluating career education interventions, and conducting research. The counseling form uses the same 50 items and adds 25 more. It yields the same general score as the screening form and also provides scores for five subscales: decisiveness, involvement, independence, orientation, and compromise. As its name implies, it is best used during individual counseling sessions aimed as fostering vocational development and increasing career choice readiness. The 1978 version of the CMI also included five separate 25-item cognitive tests to measure the five decision-making competencies of self-appraisal, occupational information, goal selection, planning, and problem solving. Because of the 2.5 hours required to complete the five competency tests, few counselors or researchers ever used them.

Attempting to provide a briefer test, Crites and Mark L. Savickas constructed a 1995 version of the CMI that measures both the attitudes and the competencies. The CMI-R includes content appropriate for use with high school students as well as postsecondary adults. The CMI-R yields separate scores for its Attitude Scale, Competence Test, and Career Maturity Inventory. Five items from each of the 1978 counseling form subscales constitute the CMI-R Attitude Scale. The CMI-R Competence Test also consists of 25 items, five for each of the five competencies. The CMI-R total score merely sums the scores for the Attitude Scale and the Competency Test. The CMI screening form is available to qualified professionals free of charge at http://www.vocopher.com. The CMI-R is available from Western Educational Assessment, in Boulder, Colorado.

—*Sarah A. Lopienski*
and Mark L. Savickas

See also Career Assessment Inventory; Career Development Inventory

Further Reading

Crites, J. O. (1978). *Theory and research handbook for the Career Maturity Inventory* (2nd ed.). Monterey, CA: CTB/McGraw-Hill.

Crites, J. O., & Savickas, M. L. (1996). Revision of the Career Maturity Inventory. *Journal of Career Assessment, 4*, 131–138.

Savickas, M. L. (1984). Career maturity: The construct and its measurement. *Vocational Guidance Quarterly, 32*, 222–231.

Savickas, M. L. (2000). Assessing career decision making. In E. Watkins & V. Campbell (Eds.), *Testing and assessment in counseling practice* (2nd ed., pp. 429–477). Hillsdale, NJ: Erlbaum.

Applying Ideas on Statistics and Measurement

The following abstract is adapted from Hardin, E. E., & Leong, F. T. L. (2004). Decision-making theories and career assessment: A psychometric evaluation of the Decision Making Inventory. *Journal of Career Assessment, 12*(1), 51–64.

To address criticism that the empirical literature on assessment of career decision making lacks a theoretical base, the present study explored the relevance of a general theory of decision making to career decision making by assessing the psychometric properties of the Decision Making Inventory (DMI), designed to measure J. Johnson's decision-making styles, and by exploring the usefulness of the DMI as a predictor of career maturity. The DMI, the Attitudes Scale of the **Career Maturity Inventory** (CMI), and the Self-Construal Scale were administered to European American college students. The DMI demonstrated adequate reliability, the expected factor structure, and good convergent validity. Relationships with certain subscales of the CMI suggest the DMI has useful predictive validity. Similarities and differences between genders in the relationships between the DMI and CMI were found.

CARROLL DEPRESSION SCALE

The Carroll Depression Scale is one of three measures of depression developed by Bernard Carroll. The Carroll Depression Scales include the Carroll Depression Scale (CDS), the Carroll Depression Scale Revised, and the Brief Carroll Depression Scale. The CDS is published by Multi-Health Systems (www.mhs.com).

The CDS is a self-report inventory that takes 10–20 minutes to complete. It is used to measure depression symptomatology and symptom severity. The CDS is appropriate for adults age 18 years and older. There is no upper age limit for the CDS. The publishers suggest it is particularly useful for older adults and severely depressed people because of the cognitive simplicity of the yes-no response format.

The self-report items were designed to match the content of the Hamilton Depression Rating Scales. The CDS includes 52 items. The Revised CDS adds 9 items that assess subtypes of depression defined in the fourth edition of the American Psychiatric Association's *Diagnostic and Statistical Manual of Mental Disorders*. The Brief CDS consists of 12 of the 52 CDS items. Items assess central features of depression, such as appetite, energy, crying, and sexual interest.

Field trials for the CDS were conducted at the University of Michigan, Ann Arbor, in the 1970s; the CDS has also been used in trials at Duke University Medical Center. The participant pool from these two settings includes 959 depressed patients and 248 non-depressed people and has been used in a variety of reliability and validity studies. The participant pool is 100% White; other information about it is very limited. Given the test's norm group, it may have limited utility with non-White populations.

Validity data suggest good face, convergent, and discriminant validity. Face validity is demonstrated by a .80 correlation between scores from the CDS and scores from the Hamilton Depression Rating Scales. Convergent validity is demonstrated by moderate to high correlations with the Clinical Global Rating of Depression (.63), the Montgomery-Asberg Depression Rating Scale (.71), the Beck Depression Inventory (.86), and the Center for Epidemiological Studies of Depression Scale (.67). Discriminant validity is shown by the CDS's ability to differentiate depressed from anxious patients. The State-Trait Anxiety Inventory and the CDS correlate at a rate of .26.

Reliability data suggest strong split-half and test-retest reliability. Cronbach's alpha for the CDS is .95. Split-half reliability between odd and even items is .87. The Pearson correlation coefficient is .96. However, test-retest reliability was measured only on those patients whose Hamilton Depression Rating Scales scores did not vary more than two points between administrations. This restriction may have inflated reliability estimates. The authors state they chose to restrict the data in this way in their belief that the CDS is a state rather than a trait measure.

—*Kathryn H. Ganske*

See also Beck Depression Inventory; Clinical Assessment of Depression

Further Reading

Carroll, B. J. (1981). The Carroll Rating Scale for Depression: I. Development, reliability, and validation. *British Journal of Psychiatry, 138,* 194–200.

Feinberg, M., Carroll, B. J., & Smouse, P. E. (1981). The Carroll Rating Scale for Depression: III. Comparison with other rating instruments. *British Journal of Psychiatry, 138,* 205–209.

Smouse, P. E. (1981). The Carroll Rating Scale for Depression: II. Factor analyses of the feature profiles. *British Journal of Psychiatry, 138,* 201–204.

Rating scales for mood disorders: http://www.mhsource.com/disorders/diagdepress.html

CATEGORICAL VARIABLES

A categorical variable is one that takes on values in a set of categories, as opposed to a continuous variable, which takes on a range of values along a continuum. The simplest examples of categorical variables are binary variables with only two possible responses, for instance "yes" and "no." Categorical variables are most common in the social, biological, and behavioral sciences, although they can be found in almost any area of application. For example, the variable of marital status can be described as "single," "married," "divorced," or "widowed": four categories. The variable sex can be described as "male" or "female": two categories. Education level can be classified as "grammar school only," "some high school," "completed high school," "some university," "completed university," or "advanced or professional degree."

When the categories ascribed to the variable are labels only, with no intrinsic ordering, then the variable is *nominal*. For example, it is generally meaningless to say that an individual who is divorced has higher or lower marital status than an individual who is widowed. Hence marital status is a nominal categorical variable. On the other hand, when the categories are naturally ordered, as with education level, socioeconomic status, or evaluation on a scale ranging from *strongly disagree* to *strongly agree*, then the variable is an *ordinal* categorical variable. In this case,

qualitative comparisons of individuals in different categories are meaningful. It is sensible to state that a person who has completed university has attained a higher level of education than a person who has completed only high school.

Categorical variables can be used as either the explanatory or the response variable in a statistical analysis. When the response is a categorical variable, appropriate analyses may include generalized linear models (for dichotomous or polytomous responses, with suitable link functions), log linear models, chi-square goodness-of-fit analysis, and the like, depending on the nature of the explanatory variables and the sampling mechanism. Categorical variables also fill a useful role as explanatory variables in standard regression, analysis of variance, and analysis of covariance models, as well as in generalized linear models. When the data are cross-classified according to several categorical variables (that is, when they come in the form of a table of counts), analyses for contingency tables, including log linear models, are appropriate. It is important to heed the distinction between nominal and ordinal variables in data analysis. When there are ordinal variables in a data set, the ordering needs to be entered explicitly into the model; this is usually achieved by incorporating constraints on parameters, which makes the analysis more complex.

In sum, categorical variables arise in a wide variety of scientific contexts. They require specialized statistical techniques, and these have been developed both theoretically and in terms of practical implementation.

—*Nicole Lazar*

See also Interval Level of Measurement; Nominal Level of Measurement; Ordinal Level of Measurement; Ratio Level of Measurement

Further Reading

Agresti, A. (1990). *Categorical data analysis.* New York: Wiley.

Fienberg, S. E. (1994). *The analysis of cross-classified categorical data* (2nd ed.). Cambridge: MIT Press.

CAUSAL ANALYSIS

Whether causal relationship can be established between two phenomena is highly controversial as a philosophical issue. According to David Hume, causal connections among real events cannot be perceived. Bertrand Russell even suggested that the term *causality* be banned in scientific discourse. Academic researchers, however, simply cannot help asking why and searching for causal explanations. Then Herbert Simon proposed that discussions of causality be restricted to our model of the reality rather than to the reality per se.

The desire to find causality is motivated by at least three potential benefits. First, causal explanation is believed to transcend time and space and therefore has a much wider scope of applications. Second, causal connections constitute the foundation of good control of the interested phenomena, which is especially important for policy making. Third, most causal statements are subject to the laws of logic and therefore more rigorous than they would be if no logic were involved.

It is unjustified, however, to think that causal analysis is always desirable and superior to other types of analysis. Sometimes, it is perhaps more important to know what has happened than why something has happened, because it is either less important or extremely difficult to ascertain the causal mechanism. Carefully produced and interpreted, descriptive statistics are sufficient in many situations. Furthermore, causality is not a prerequisite of precise prediction. For example, in demography and econometrics, making an accurate prediction is more important than identifying a causal chain or measuring a causal effect.

Finally, to *discover* that A causes B is beyond the capacity of statistical analysis. Causal mechanisms are either found through heuristic methods, such as experiment and observation, or simply derived from current theories and knowledge. It is only after the causal relationship is proposed that statistical techniques can be applied to measure the size of the causal effect.

Basic Concepts

Causality implies a force of production. When we say A causes B, we mean the connection is a directed one, going from A to B. A causal relationship is thus asymmetric. Sometimes, the term *reciprocal causality* is used, meaning A causes B and B causes A as well. Although that relationship is possible, very often it indicates that a temporary order or an underlying causal mechanism has not been clearly identified.

In theory, causal relationships are best established when two conditions are satisfied. Call the causal variable X and the outcome variable Y, and suppose there are only two possible values for each of them: for the cause, "exists" or "not exists," and for the outcome, "has happened" or "has not happened." Then four scenarios are possible.

For example, consider whether taking a personal tutorial would improve a student's exam results (Table 1). The tutorial does not help if the student takes it but no improvement follows (scenario 2) or if the student does not take it but improvement is made (scenario 3). We can say the tutorial is a causal factor of improvement only when scenarios 1 and 4 are *both* true, that is, if the student takes the tutorial and improvement follows *and* if not, no improvement. Researchers, however, are often tempted to make a causal connection when only scenario 1 is true, without seriously considering scenario 4. This is not only because it is straightforward to make the casual link from scenario 1 but also because information for scenario 4 is usually not available. A student either has taken the tutorial or has not taken it; it is impossible to have taken and have not

Table 1 Scenarios of Cause and Outcome

		Outcome (Y)	
		Has happened	*Has not happened*
Cause (X)	*Exists*	Scenario 1	Scenario 2
	Does not exist	Scenario 3	Scenario 4

taken a tutorial at the same time. Unless repeated measures are made at different times, either scenario 1 or scenario 4 is counterfactual. (Since the mid-1970s, statisticians and econometricians have developed a series of methods for estimating causal effects in counterfactual situations. The reader is referred to the second item in "Further Reading" below for details.)

Causal relationship in these analyses is probabilistic rather than deterministic. Deterministic causality applies to all cases under study without any exception. In the sciences of human beings, however, researchers can hope to measure only the probability of a causal connection for a particular case, or they have to work at an aggregate level. Exceptional deviant cases should not be taken as evidence of disproof.

The Commonly Used Three Criteria of Causality

Following John Stuart Mill, statisticians have identified three criteria for inferring a causal relationship: (a) covariation between the presumed cause and outcome; (b) temporal precedence of the cause; and (c) exclusion of alternative explanations for cause-outcome connections. All three have to be satisfied at the same time in order for causality to be derived.

The first is the easiest to establish—statistics such as the Pearson correlation coefficient, the score of chi-square, and the odds ratio are readily available for testing and measuring the covariation between two variables. As widely acknowledged, however, covariation alone cannot lead to causal statements.

The second criterion is more complicated and difficult to satisfy. The main problem lies in the uncertain relationship between temporal order and logical order. A cause must both temporally and logically precede an outcome, but a precedent event may or may not be a logical cause. Temporal connection is a special type of covariation and, therefore, does not necessarily lead to causal connection. For example, people acquire several fixed attributes at birth, such as sex, age, ethnicity, order among siblings, and so forth, but it makes little sense to take them as direct causes of other attributes that are developed at later stages of life, such as political affiliation.

The last criterion is said to be the most difficult—researchers can never be completely certain that all alternative explanations have been considered and excluded. The exclusion may be best handled in experiments because all the known possible causes have been kept "constant" so that their effects will not intervene in the causal relationship under study. But experiments are not immune to limitations: There is no way to ensure that *all* possible causes have been or can be taken into account; some variables, especially the fixed variables, or even a variable like education, cannot be manipulated; some participants comply with the experiment rules, but others do not; it may be unethical to conduct experiments on a certain group of participants; and finally, it may be difficult to prevent the participants from influencing one another.

In short, it is very difficult to establish causal relationships firmly, and the problem cannot be solved easily with experimental or longitudinal designs. This does not mean, however, that we should stop doing causal analysis. The logic holds for all statistical analyses—although we cannot prove that something is true, we can measure the *likelihood* that something is *not* true by analyzing the available information. If currently no information casts a serious doubt on the proposed causal relationship, we keep it. Further consistent results will increase the level of our confidence, while new inconsistent evidence will help us modify or even abandon the previous findings.

Causal Analysis in Nonexperimental Research: The Structural Equation Modeling Approach

Due to its aforementioned limitations, the experimental method is often infeasible for most social and behavioral studies. Causal analysis of nonexperimental (or observed) data (surveys, administrative records, etc.) does not aim to confirm causal relationships by manipulating the causal factors. Rather, the objective is to measure the causal effect and to disprove a hypothetical causal connection without any commitment to completely accepting a causal relationship.

The counterfactual approach, although statistically established, has not been widely applied in the social sciences. A more widely followed approach is *structural equation modeling* (SEM). It has two main advantages. First, it combines *path analysis* and *factor analysis*. Path analysis enables us to statistically test causal relations among a set of observed variables, but it does not deal with variables that are not directly measurable (latent variables), such as socioeconomic status, social capital, intelligence, and so on. Factor analysis enables us to link some observed variables to a latent variable, but it is not designed to test causal relations among these variables. SEM is a powerful method that measures causal relations among both observed and latent variables. Second, measurement errors are assumed marginal and thus ignorable in many statistical techniques. In contrast, SEM explicitly incorporates the error terms into a statistical model, generating a more reliable measurement of causal relationship with the measurement errors corrected. The reader who would like to learn more can start with the first reference under "Further Reading."

—*Keming Yang*

See also Structural Equation Modeling

Further Reading

Saris, W. E., & Stronkhorst, H. (1984). *Causal modelling in nonexperimental research: An introduction to the LISREL approach*. Amsterdam: Sociometric Research Foundation.
Winship, C., & Sobel, M. (2004). Causal inference in sociological studies. In M. Hardy and A. Bryman (Eds.), *Handbook of data analysis* (pp. 481–503). London: Sage.

LISREL student version (8.7) for downloading: http://www .ssicentral.com/index.html (Note that there are limitations on the size of the model and no technical support.)

Applying Ideas on Statistics and Measurement

The following abstract is adapted from Henry, S. (2000). What is school violence? An integrated definition. *Annals of the American Academy of Political and Social Science, 567*(1), 16–29.

In this study, **causal analysis** is used to address the wider context of school violence, the wider forms of violence in schools, and the important interactive and causal effects arising from the confluence of these forces. Usually, such studies focus on interpersonal violence between students or by students toward their teachers. Stuart Henry argues that not only does the complexity of this issue defy such a simplistic framing but dealing with the problem at that level does not go far enough. What is needed is an integrated, multi-level definition of the problem that will lead to a multilevel causal analysis and a comprehensive policy response that takes account of the full range of constitutive elements. Here, the first stage of such an approach is outlined with regard to defining the nature and scope of the problem.

CENSORED DATA

Suppose that in an experiment or study, a group of individuals (objects, patients, or devices) is followed over time with the goal of observing an event such as failure or death. Individuals who do not experience the event of interest in the observation period are said to be censored, and the data obtained from such individuals are known as censored data.

In most cases, experiments or studies have a finite observation period, so for some individuals, the observation period may not be long enough to observe the event of interest. Also, individuals may cease to be at risk before the observation period. For example, in a clinical trial setting, patients might drop out of the study, or in the case of testing the reliability of a device, the device may fail for reasons other than the one the experimenter is interested in. Such individuals known not to experience the event within or before the observation period are said to be right censored.

Censored data may demonstrate left censoring and interval censoring, as well. In the former, the event of interest occurs before the observation period. For example, suppose a group of women is selected to be followed for the development of breast cancer. If some of these women had already developed breast cancer, then the time to the development of breast cancer is left censored for them. In the case of interval censoring, one observes an interval within which the event of interest occurred, but the actual time of occurrence remains unknown. Interval censoring occurs when devices are tested only at specific times, say $t_1, t_2, \ldots t_k$, and failures occur between two consecutive times. Right and left censoring are special cases of interval censoring with the intervals (T, ∞) and $(0, S)$, respectively, where S is the starting time and T is the ending time of the study.

When data contain censored observations, special care has to be taken in the analysis. Common statistical methods used to analyze censored data include the Kaplan-Meier estimator, the log-rank test, the Cox proportional hazard model, and the accelerated failure time model.

—*Abdus S. Wahed*

See also Observational Studies

Further Reading

Kalbfleisch, J. D., & Prentice, R. L. (2002). *Statistical analysis of failure time data* (2nd ed.). Hoboken, NJ: Wiley.

Walpole, R. E., Myers, R. H., & Myers, S. L. (1998). *Probability and statistics for engineers and scientists* (6th ed.). Upper Saddle River, NJ: Prentice Hall.

CENTERS FOR DISEASE CONTROL AND PREVENTION

The Centers for Disease Control and Prevention (CDC), a unit of the Department of Health and Human Services, is a U.S. government public health agency with a workforce of almost 6,000 persons currently under the direction of Dr. Julie Louise Gerberding. Headquartered in Atlanta, Georgia, CDC has 10 other locations in the United States and Puerto Rico. CDC's mission encompasses several goals: (a) to protect the public's health and safety; (b) to educate the public through dissemination of reliable scientific health information; (c) to prevent and control disease, injury, and disability; and (d) to establish strong partnerships with numerous public and private entities such as local and state health departments, academic institutions, and international health organizations.

Following World War II, Dr. Joseph W. Mountin formed the Communicable Disease Center on July 1, 1946, in Atlanta as a peacetime infectious disease prevention agency based on the work of an earlier agency, the Malaria Control in War Areas. CDC's original focus was the problems of malaria and typhus, later broadening to diseases such as polio (1951) and smallpox (1966). In 1970, the agency became known as the Center for Disease Control to reflect its broader mission. In 1992, it added the term *prevention* to its name but remained known as CDC.

CDC is now organized into six coordinating offices for Global Health, Terrorism Preparedness and Emergency Response, Environmental Health and Injury Prevention, Health Information and Services, Health Promotion, and Infectious Diseases. These coordinating offices are further divided into 12 centers, each of which has its own areas of expertise and public health concerns. For instance, the National Center for Injury Prevention and Control aims to reduce mortality, disability, and costs related to injuries resulting from events such as motor vehicle accidents, youth violence, child maltreatment, and suicide. The National Center for Health Statistics documents the health status of the United States population, monitors trends in health care delivery and utilization, and evaluates the impact of health policies and programs through statistical computations. The Office of the Director is responsible for the management, oversight, and coordination of the scientific endeavors of all centers.

CDC's working budget for the fiscal year 2005 was estimated at $7.7 billion, with the highest appropriation assigned to efforts to combat HIV and AIDS. From its beginnings in 1946, with a budget of less than $10 million, CDC has become the nation's premiere public health agency with the stated vision for the 21st century of healthy people in a healthy world through prevention.

—*Marjan Ghahramanlou-Holloway*

Further Reading

Etheridge, E. W. (1992). *Sentinel for health: A history of the Centers for Disease Control.* Berkeley: University of California Press.

Snider, D. E., & Satcher, D. (1997). Behavioral and social sciences at the Centers for Disease Control and Prevention: Critical disciplines for public health. *American Psychologist, 52*(2), 140–142.

Department of Health and Human Services—Centers for Disease Control and Prevention: www.cdc.gov

---

Applying Ideas on Statistics and Measurement

The following abstract is adapted from Whitaker, D. J., Lutzker, J. R., & Shelley, G. A. (2005). Child maltreatment prevention priorities at the Centers for Disease Control and Prevention. *Child Maltreatment, 10*(3), 245–259.

The **Centers for Disease Control and Prevention** (CDC) is the United States' public health agency and deals with many different types of public health issues. The Division of Violence Prevention at CDC's National Center for Injury Prevention and Control has had a long-standing interest in the prevention of child maltreatment. As the nation's public health agency, CDC seeks to focus the public health perspective on the problem of child maltreatment and to promote science-based practice in the field. Since 1999, CDC has developed research priorities to address the prevention of child maltreatment. This article provides a brief rationale for applying a public health approach to child maltreatment and a discussion of the priority-setting process, priorities in each of four areas of the public health model, and some of CDC's current child maltreatment prevention activities.

CENTRAL LIMIT THEOREM

The central limit theorem states that, under conditions of repeated sampling from a population, the sample means of random measurements tend to possess an approximately normal distribution. This is true for population distributions that are normal and decidedly not normal.

The central limit theorem is important for two reasons. The first can be understood by examining the *fuzzy central limit theorem*, which avers that whenever an attribute is influenced by a large number of relatively independently occurring variables, the attribute will be normally distributed. Such attributes are ordinarily complex variables that require considerable time in their development. For instance, a multitude of relatively independently occurring variables influence adult reading achievement, each of which may be influential in large or small ways:

1. Quality of teachers in the early grades

2. Variety of reading matter available (books, magazines, newspapers)

3. Parental encouragement to read

4. Genetic endowment

5. Diet during developmental years

6. Socioeconomic level of the child's family

7. Number of competing activities available (e.g., arcade games, sports, television)

8. Interests and activities of friends

9. Initial success (or failure) in reading activities

10. Physical athleticism of the child

It is easy to imagine many other such variables. To the extent that the variables produce small, relatively random effects on adult reading achievement over time, the distribution of adult reading achievement will be normally distributed. Because the variables that influence such attributes produce unrelated effects, one's position in the distribution of scores in the population is largely a matter of luck. Some individuals are very lucky (e.g., they may have parents who encourage reading, access to reading materials, excellent early teachers) and enjoy high adult reading achievement. Some are very unlucky (e.g., they may have impoverished parents who do not support reading, poor diet, frequent illnesses) and remain illiterate. But about two thirds are neither very lucky nor very unlucky and become average adult readers. The fuzzy central limit theorem then, provides an explanation for the relatively common occurrence of normal distributions in nature.

The second reason the central limit theorem is important concerns its use in statistical inference. Because in a normal distribution we know the percentage of cases falling between any two points along the baseline *and* the percentage of cases above and below any single point along the baseline, many useful inferences can be made. Consider an investigation comparing two treatment approaches designed to enhance math achievement. Following the treatment, the dependent variable, a test of math achievement, is administered. By comparing the two treatment group means, the researchers determine the probability that the difference between the means could have occurred by chance if the two treatment groups were drawn from the same population distribution. If the probability were, say, 0.0094, the investigators could have a high degree of confidence in rejecting the null hypothesis of no difference between the treatments. If the central limit theorem did not commonly apply in nature, such inferences could not be made.

—*Ronald C. Eaves*

See also Sampling Distribution of a Statistic

Further Reading

Wolfram, S. (2002). *A new kind of science*. Champaign, IL: Author.

Sampling distributions and the central limit theorem: http://people.hofstra.edu/faculty/Stefan_Waner/RealWorld/finitetopic1/sampldistr.html

Applying Ideas on Statistics and Measurement

The following abstract is adapted from Essex, C., & Smythe, W. E. (1999). Between numbers and notions: A critique of psychological measurement theory & psychology. *Theory & Psychology, 9*(6), 739–767.

The **central limit theorem** plays a critical role in statistics. This article discusses the applications of mathematical machinery to psychological ideas and how that machinery imposes certain requirements on the relationship between numbers and notions. These imposed choices are driven by the mathematics and not the psychology. Attempting a theory-neutral approach to research in psychology, where commitments in response to the options are made unknowingly, becomes instead a theory-by-default psychology. The article begins to catalog some of these mathematical choices to make them explicit in order to allow psychologists the opportunity to make explicit theoretical commitments.

CENTROID

The notion of centroid generalizes the notion of a mean to multivariate analysis and multidimensional spaces. It applies to vectors instead of scalars, and it is computed by associating to each vector a mass that is a positive number taking values between 0 and 1 such that the sum of all the masses is equal to 1. The centroid of a set of vectors is also called the *center of gravity*, the *center of mass*, or the *barycenter* of this set.

Notations and Definition

Let $\mathcal{V}$ be a set of I vectors, with each vector being composed of J elements:

$$\mathcal{V} = \{\mathbf{v}_1, \ldots, \mathbf{v}_i, \ldots, \mathbf{v}_I\} \text{ with } \mathbf{v}_i = [v_{i,1}, \ldots, v_{i,j}, \ldots, v_{i,J}]^{\mathrm{T}}.$$

To each vector is associated a mass denoted m_i for vector i. These masses take values between 0 and 1, and the sum of these masses is equal to 1. The set of masses is a vector denoted $\mathbf{m}$. The centroid of the set of vectors is denoted $\mathbf{c}$, defined as

$$\mathbf{c} = \sum_i^I m_i \mathbf{v}_i.$$

Examples

The mean of a set of numbers is the centroid of this set of observations. Here, the mass of each number is equal to the inverse of the number of observations: $m_i = \frac{1}{I}$.

For multivariate data, the notion of centroid generalizes the mean. For example, with the following three vectors,

$$\mathbf{v}_1 = \begin{bmatrix} 10 \\ 20 \end{bmatrix}, \mathbf{v}_2 = \begin{bmatrix} 8 \\ 24 \end{bmatrix}, \text{ and } \mathbf{v}_3 = \begin{bmatrix} 16 \\ 32 \end{bmatrix},$$

and the following set of masses,

$$m_1 = \frac{1}{2}, \quad m_2 = \frac{1}{8}, \quad \text{and} \quad m_3 = \frac{3}{8},$$

we obtain the following centroid:

$$\mathbf{c} = \sum_i^I m_i \mathbf{v}_i = \frac{1}{2} \begin{bmatrix} 10 \\ 20 \end{bmatrix} + \frac{1}{8} \begin{bmatrix} 8 \\ 24 \end{bmatrix} + \frac{3}{8} \begin{bmatrix} 16 \\ 32 \end{bmatrix}$$

$$= \begin{bmatrix} 12 \\ 25 \end{bmatrix}.$$

In this example, if we plot the vectors in a two-dimensional space, the centroid would be the center of gravity of the triangle made by these three vectors with masses assigned proportionally to their vector of mass. The notion of centroid can be used with spaces of any dimensionality.

Properties of the Centroid

The properties of the centroid of a set of vectors closely parallel the more familiar properties of the mean of a set of numbers. Recall that a set of vectors defines a multidimensional space, and that to each multidimensional space is assigned a generalized Euclidean distance. The core property of the centroid is that the centroid of a set of vectors minimizes the weighted sum of the generalized squared Euclidean distances from the vectors to any point in the space. This quantity that generalizes the notion of variance is called the *inertia* of the set of vectors relative to their centroid.

Of additional interest for multivariate analysis, the *theorem of Huyghens* indicates that the weighted sum of the squared distances from a set of vectors to any vector in the space can be decomposed as a weighted sum of the squared distances from the vectors to their centroid plus the (weighted) squared distance from the centroid to this point. In term of inertia, Huyghens's theorem states that the inertia of a set of vectors to any point is equal to the inertia of the set of vectors to their centroid plus the inertia of their centroid to this point. As an obvious consequence of this theorem, the inertia of a set of vectors to their centroid is minimal.

—*Hervé Abdi*

See also Correspondence Analysis; Discriminant Correspondence Analysis; Distance; DISTATIS; Multiple Correspondence Analysis; Multiple Factor Analysis; STATIS

CHANCE

The word *chance* originated in the Latin word for "to fall." Chance occurs the way things just happen to fall. Like a coin toss, chance events occur unpredictably, without any apparent or knowable causes, or by accident—the latter word deriving from the same Latin root. Although *chance* is a very useful word in everyday language, its status as a term in measurement and statistics is much more ambivalent. On the one hand, the word is almost never treated as a technical term. Thus, it is seldom given a precise definition, or even an intuitive one. Indeed, it is rare to see *chance* as an entry in an index to any book on measurement and statistics.

On the other hand, both the concept and the word permeate articles and books on these subjects. It is especially hard to imagine writing a statistics textbook without having recourse to the word on numerous occasions. Furthermore, the word *chance* is used in a wide variety of ways. In particular, we may distinguish chance as probability, as unknown determinants, as technique, and as artifact.

Chance as Probability

What is now called *probability theory* had its origins in a famous exchange of letters between the mathematicians Pierre de Fermat and Blaise Pascal concerning games of chance. As a consequence, early mathematical treatments would be identified as the "logic of chance" (John Venn) or the "doctrine of chance" (Abraham de Moivre). But by the time Pierre-Simon Laplace published his classic *Analytical*

Theory of Probabilities, the word *chance* had seemingly ceased to have scientific content, thereby returning to the status of a mundane word. It had been replaced by the word *probability*.

Despite this shift in significance, *chance* is still used to refer to the probability of an event or set of events—whether or not they concern outcomes in games of chance. When used in this manner, *chance* is often treated as something tantamount to a rough measure of how much we should anticipate an event's occurring. Some events may have a good chance of happening, others a very poor chance, yet others a middling chance. Two events can also be said to have an equal chance of happening (e.g., the balls in urn models all have an equal chance of being chosen). Here, chance functions as a generic term that encompasses more specialized and precise concepts, including an event's probability (the number of times an event happens divided by the total number of times it could have happened) and an event's odds (the probability of an event occurring divided by the probability of an event not occurring).

One could argue that it is no longer proper to use such a vague word when more-precise terms are readily available. Yet the very imprecision of *chance* can prove to be an asset in certain contexts. In particular, *chance* becomes serviceable when a more precise term is unnecessary to convey a statistical idea. For example, a simple random sample can be defined as a sample in which each case in the entire population has an equal chance of being selected for inclusion. Substituting "probability" for "chance" may not necessarily improve this definition, especially given that the actual probability may not be known or even calculable.

Chance as Unmeasured Determinants

Chance is often assumed to operate as an active agent that helps account for a particular pattern of events. More specifically, chance is frequently invoked as an unknown force or set of forces that explains why certain expectations may be violated. A simple example can be given from classical test theory. A research participant's response on a particular test item may not accurately reflect the participant's actual ability, attitude, or disposition. Instead of the *true score*, we obtain a *fallible score*. According to classical theory, the fallible score is the sum of the true score plus error. The error may encompass a large number of extraneous factors, such as momentary inattentiveness, a careless recording mistake, a misunderstanding of the question, a classically conditioned emotional response, and so forth. Significantly, these causes are assumed to be so numerous and mutually independent that the error can be considered pure chance. Hence, the fallible score is the sum of the true score and unmeasured chance determinants. This assumption is absolutely crucial in the classical theory of measurement. It means that the error is uncorrelated with the true score for that item or any other item, and that the error is equally uncorrelated with the errors of other items. As a consequence, a composite score defined as the sum of fallible scores on a large number of items will contain much less error than the individual items because the separate errors will cancel each other out rather than accumulate. In other words, if errors are determined by chance, then a multi-item test will be much more reliable than any of the items that make it up.

Various statistical techniques also introduce a chance component, but with a different purpose in mind. For example, the dependent variable (or criterion) in a multiple regression equation can be expressed as a function of an intercept (or constant term), the weighted sum of the independent variables (or predictors), and an error term that represents the discrepancies between predicted and observed scores (i.e., the residuals). When regression is applied to correlational data, unbiased least-squares estimators of the weights for the independent variables (i.e., the unstandardized regression coefficients) can be obtained only if this error (or disturbance) term essentially constitutes a "random shock" consisting of pure chance. Here chance consists of a conglomerate of all those unspecified determinants of the dependent variable that are uncorrelated with independent variables specified in the regression equation.

This chance disturbance plays an even bigger role in time series analysis. In particular, this term is essential to the very definitions of autoregressive and moving-average processes. In a first-order autoregressive process, for example, the value of a variable at time t is specified as a function of the value of the variable at time $t-1$ plus a random shock. Even more striking, in a first-order moving-average process, the value of a variable at time t is specified as a function of the value of a random shock at t minus a portion of the random shock at $t-1$ (i.e., the variable consists entirely of concurrent and lagged chance inputs).

Chance as Technique

Many common methodological procedures use chance to obtain certain desirable outcomes. An example was given earlier, namely, the use of random sampling to ensure that the sample is representative of the larger population. Moreover, knowing that each case has an equal chance of entering the sample permits the calculation of statistics that would not be available otherwise, such as the standard error of the mean. Other sampling strategies, such as stratified random sampling and probability sampling, also use chance to attain specific methodological ends. In probability sampling, for instance, each case in the population has a "known chance" (rather than an equal chance) of being selected for inclusion in the sample, a stipulation that still permits the inference of population attributes from sample characteristics.

Another technical use of *chance* is illustrated by experimental research in which the participants are randomly assigned to the various conditions. Such randomization plays an extremely important role in causal inference and has direct consequences for the statistical analyses. Previously it was noted that multiple regression assumes that all unmeasured causes of variation in the dependent variable are contained in an error term. Because the latter term must be uncorrelated with the independent variables in the equation, the error is assumed to be random. Whereas in correlational studies this randomness can only be assumed, in experimental studies the random assignment itself guarantees that the error or residual term represents pure chance. As a result, the estimated effects of the experimental manipulations are far more likely to be unbiased than would be the situation if the conditions were chosen by the participants themselves.

A final example of chance as technique may be found in Monte Carlo methods. Named after the famed casino of Monaco, this approach is specifically inspired by games of chance. A roulette wheel will generate a series of random numbers, and Monte Carlo methods rely on random numbers to simulate processes that are assumed to possess a substantial chance component. Widely used in the natural sciences, Monte Carlo methods also have a significant place in measurement and statistics. When the properties of measures, techniques, or estimators cannot be determined analytically, suitable data can be simulated to test the properties empirically. For example, in studies of exploratory factor analysis, Monte Carlo methods have frequently been used to address such issues as the best factor extraction algorithms, the optimal decision criteria for determining the number of factors, and the most effective rotational schemes. Often these simulations take advantage of programs that generate random numbers with a specified distribution, most commonly a normal distribution (i.e., normal random deviates).

Chance as Artifact

With rare exceptions, such as researchers working with census data, empirical inquiries are most frequently carried out using relatively small samples from a larger population of cases. The characteristics of those samples will necessarily depart from the characteristics of the greater population. Hence, even if the means for two groups (e.g., men and women) are absolutely identical in the population, the means will differ in the sample. Similarly, even if the correlation between two variables was exactly zero in the population, the correlation may be substantially greater or less than zero in the sample. The smaller the sample size, or N, the more extensive the probable error. In fact, when N is very small, say less than a dozen cases, seemingly substantial mean differences or correlations can appear—statistical outcomes that still should be attributed to chance rather than to bona fide effects.

The most common solution to this problem is to implement null hypothesis significance testing. Typically, the null hypothesis is that mean difference, correlation, or another statistic is absolutely zero in the greater population. Using some statistical test, the researcher determines whether the sample values exceed what could reasonably be expected from chance fluctuations alone. So when we conclude that a result is significant at the .05 probability level, we are asserting that the chances are only 5 out of 100 that we could obtain an effect of that magnitude by sampling error. By rejecting the null hypothesis, we are saying that the observed mean difference or correlation is likely not a mere fluke of our little sample and that there is a very high probability that these statistics are nonzero in the larger population.

Unfortunately, this procedure cannot completely solve the problem. Sometimes researchers will adopt measurement strategies or statistical techniques that cause them to "exploit chance," to take advantage of sampling error rather than reduce its impact. For instance, when item analysis is used to select the best items for inclusion in a multi-item test, the investigator naturally picks those items that correlate most highly with the overall score. Yet unless the sample size is large, the relative sizes of the item-composite correlations will be contaminated by considerable sampling error. As a result, the final test may be more representative of the sample than of the population. Some items will be incorrectly included while others are just as incorrectly excluded.

A similar problem arises in a particular form of multiple regression, namely, analyses employing a stepwise procedure for variable inclusion. In forward stepwise regression, for example, predictors are added to the equation one by one. At each step, that variable is inserted which makes the greatest improvement in the equation's predictive power. Potential predictors that make no contribution to the explained variance are then omitted. Regression equations constructed in this way are taking inappropriate advantage of chance fluctuations in sample characteristics. Accordingly, the predictors included in the final equation may not completely replicate in other samples drawn from the same population. Indeed, in small samples, the equation can contain predictors that are almost arbitrary, and the chances of complete replication become virtually zero.

It should be made explicit that the emergence of these chance artifacts is not simply a matter of sample size. Opportunities for exploiting chance also increase as we increase the number of parameters to be estimated (e.g., mean differences, correlations, regression coefficients). For instance, the more correlations computed from the data, the higher is the probability that a coefficient will emerge that is significant at the .05 level, even when all coefficients are zero in the population. Thus, increasing the number of correlations to be estimated increases the chance of rejecting the null hypothesis when the null hypothesis is in fact true (i.e., Type I error). Avoiding this unfortunate repercussion requires that the investigator implement procedures to correct the probability levels (e.g., the Bonferroni correction).

Another example also comes from multiple regression analysis. The more independent variables there are in the equation, the more parameters that must be estimated (viz. regression coefficients). Therefore, for a given sample size, equations with many predictors will have more opportunities to exploit chance than will equations with few predictors. This difference will manifest itself in the "squared multiple correlation" (R^2, where R is the correlation between predicted and observed scores). This statistic will be biased upward by the opportunistic assignment of large regression weights to those independent variables that have their effects inflated by sampling error. To handle this adverse consequence, most statistical software publishes an "adjusted R^2" along with the regular squared multiple correlation. The adjustment makes allowance for the number of regression coefficients estimated relative to the sample size.

Clearly "chance as artifact" has a very different status from chance as probability, as unmeasured determinants, and as technique. The latter three usages take chance as a "good thing." *Chance* provides a generic term for probability, odds, or likelihood, makes measurement and prediction errors less problematic, and offers useful tools for designing research and evaluating statistical methods. Yet the intrusion of sampling error, along with the implementation of methods that accentuate rather than reduce that error, shows that chance can also be a "bad thing" that complicates analyses. Nonetheless, it should be evident that *chance* remains a very useful word despite its varied applications and vague definitions. It provides a catch-all term that can encompass a diversity of issues that are crucial to measurement and statistics.

—*Dean Keith Simonton*

See also Bonferroni Correction; Classical Test Theory; Exploratory Factor Analysis; Least Squares, Method of; Markov Chain Monte Carlo Methods; Null Hypothesis Significance Testing; Pascal, Blaise; Probability Sampling; Random Numbers; Random Sampling; Regression Analysis; Residuals; Sampling Error; Significance Level; Statistical Significance; Type I Error

Further Reading

Everitt, B. (1999). *Chance rules: An informal guide to probability, risk, and statistics.* New York: Springer.

Chance magazine: http://www.amstat.org/publications/chance/
Chance Web site devoted to the teaching of courses dealing with chance: http://www.dartmouth.edu/~chance/

Applying Ideas on Statistics and Measurement

The following abstract is adapted from Oldman, D. (1974). Chance and skill: A study of roulette. *Sociology, 8*(3), 407–426.

If scientists have any job, it is trying to reduce the role that chance, or random variation, plays in scientific research. **Chance** is a ubiquitous factor in all our daily activities, and trying to explain how chance is addressed and dealt with is a central point in the study of measurement and statistics. This article takes an applied approach to the topic and focuses on how people handle random events. Many accounts of the chance element in games and many attempts at general explanations of gambling assume that an individual accepts the events as unpredictable and passively awaits the outcome, but a study of people playing roulette in a gaming club suggests that this is far from the case. Playing roulette can be seen as an exercise in "skill" that depends on the construction and maintenance of predictive theories. One form of theorizing attributes causal efficacy to the croupier, and the game becomes a contest between croupier and player. This behavior is reinforced as players attempt to manipulate their working conditions and status. Players may then adopt a nonarithmetic calculus of win and loss that confirms their theorizing.

CHI-SQUARE TEST FOR GOODNESS OF FIT

The chi-square (pronounced "kai square" and often written as χ^2) family of statistical tests comprises inferential tests that deal with categorical data. In many situations, the researcher may not have data in the form of scores or measurements (ordinal, interval, or ratio level of measurement) for the cases in their sample but instead will have information concerning some classification (categorical level of measurement). For instance, if we were interested in smoking behavior, we may want to know how many cigarettes the average person smokes per day (interval data); alternatively, we may want to look more simply at whether people smoke or not (categorical data).

Typically, when we have scores or interval measurements, we are interested in the mean or the median score (the mean number of cigarettes smoked). With categorical data, however, it would be fairly pointless to calculate the mean (the average of the sample is a semismoker?). Instead, we are interested in the frequency of cases that come up in each classification of the variable we are interested in (how many people smoke and how many do not?). Chi-square tests can look at situations like this, in which cases are categorized on one factor (the chi-square goodness of fit), and also at cases categorized on two factors (sometimes referred to as being *cross categorized*), such as a smoker and an undergraduate (the chi-square measure of association). This entry focuses on the goodness-of-fit test.

Karl Pearson developed the goodness-of-fit test to determine whether observed distributions of frequency data matched, or "fitted," a theoretical distribution. By estimating the cell frequencies one would expect to observe under some theoretical distribution, one could compare the actual frequencies and calculate the difference. The smaller the difference, the better the fit.

The most common use of the chi-square is to compare the observed distribution with the distribution expected under the null hypothesis. The null hypothesis states that categorization will be random, and thus the expected cell frequencies will be based on chance. We can calculate the expected cell frequencies by dividing the number of cases in the sample by the number of possible classifications. If these expected frequencies are very similar to the observed frequencies, then the fit between the observed distribution and the null hypothesis distribution will be good. If they are quite different, then the fit will not be good, and we may reject the null hypothesis.

Using the test statistic and the degrees of freedom, we can estimate the significance value. Degrees of freedom for a goodness-of-fit test are calculated as the number of classifications minus 1.

The following assumptions underlie the test:

1. The data must be treated as categorical.

2. The categories must be mutually exclusive. This means that it must be impossible for a case to be in more than one category. For instance, a person is either a smoker or not.

3. None of the expected values may be less than 1.

4. No more than 20% of the expected values may be less than 5.

An Example

Suppose we asked 100 people to name their favorite season. The null hypothesis would state that there would be a chance distribution of responses, meaning that there would be a fairly even number of people selecting each season. So the expected frequencies under the null hypothesis would be calculated as the number of cases (100) divided by the number of possible classifications (4). Therefore, we would expect, under the null hypothesis, to observe 25 people choosing spring as their favorite season, 25 choosing summer, 25 choosing autumn, and 25 choosing winter. Now we compare this to the frequencies we actually observe, shown in Table 1.

In Table 1, we see that the distribution does not look like a chance distribution. More people chose summer as their favorite season than chose any other season. To see if the null hypothesis model fits the observed data, we look at the difference between the expected cell frequencies and the observed cell frequencies (these differences are called the *residuals*). The sum of these residuals represents the goodness of fit. Before they can be summed, however, the residuals must be squared to avoid positive residuals cancelling out negative residuals. Chi-square is calculated using this equation:

$$\chi^2 = \Sigma([o - e]^2/e)$$

where e is an expected cell frequency and o is an observed cell frequency.

So for our example,

$$\chi^2 = (-4^2/25) + (23^2/25) + (-9^2/25) + (-10^2/25)$$

$$\chi^2 = 29.04.$$

Now we have to compare this value to the distribution of chi-square to assess significance. In this case, there are 3 degrees of freedom (because we have four observed residuals and have to subtract one degree of freedom for the model). Looking at a table of critical values for chi-square, we see that if the observed value is greater than 11.34, then it is significant ($p < .01$); because our observed value of chi-square (29.04) is greater than 11.34, we reject the null hypothesis.

Table 1 Hypothetical Data to Show the Frequency of People Choosing Each Season as Their Favorite

	Spring	Summer	Autumn	Winter
Expected	25	25	25	25
Observed	21	48	16	15
Residual	−4	23	−9	−10

Calculating Chi-Square Goodness of Fit Using SPSS

The chi-square statistic may be calculated in several ways using SPSS. The procedure described here is fairly straightforward for data inputted as per the screenshot in Figure 1.

1. Tell SPSS that the "count" variable is a frequency and not a score: Go to Data → weight cases and click next to "Weight cases by" and then put "count" into the "Frequency variable" box.

2. Go to Analyze → Nonparametric tests → Chi-square . . .

3. Put "count" into the "Test variable list" and click on "OK."

The output will be a table of the descriptive statistics as well as a table that contains the chi-square value, the degrees of freedom, and the *p* value.

—*Siân E. Williams*

See also Chi-Square Test for Independence

Further Reading

Chi-square calculator: http://faculty.vassar.edu/lowry/csfit.html

Figure 1   Screenshot of Data Inputted for a Chi-Square Goodness-of-Fit Test

CHI-SQUARE TEST FOR INDEPENDENCE

The chi-square test for independence is a significance test of the relationship between categorical variables. This test is sometimes known as the "Pearson's chi-square" in honor of its developer, Karl Pearson. As an example of this test, consider an experiment by David M. Lane, S. Camille Peres, Aniko Sándor, and H. Al Napier that evaluated the effectiveness of a new method for initiating computer commands. One group of participants was tested using a mouse; a second group was tested using a track pad. Although for both groups, the new method led to faster performance than did the standard method, the question addressed here is whether there was any relationship between preference for the new method and the type of pointing device (mouse or track pad).

Table 1 is a *contingency table* showing whether preference is contingent on the device used. As can be seen in Table 1, 4 of the 12 participants in the mouse group (33%), compared with 9 of the 10 participants (90%) in the track pad group, preferred the new method. Therefore, in this sample, there is an association between the pointing device used and the method preferred. A key question is whether this association in the sample justifies the conclusion that there is an association in the population.

The chi-square test for independence, as applied to this experiment, tests the null hypothesis that the preferred method (standard or new) is independent of the pointing device used (mouse or track pad). Another way of stating this null hypothesis is that there is no association between the categorical variables of preferred method and pointing device. If the null hypothesis is rejected, then one can conclude that there is an association in the population.

Calculations

The first step in the calculation is to find the expected frequencies in each cell

Table 1   Data From the Example Experiment

	Preferred Method		
Device	*Standard*	*New*	*Total*
Mouse	8	4	12
Track pad	1	9	10
Total	9	13	22

under the assumption that there is no association between the variables. Since 9 of the 22 participants (0.409) preferred the standard method, then if there were no association between pointing device and preferred method, one would expect 0.409 of the participants in the both the mouse condition and track pad condition to prefer the standard method. Of the 12 participants in the mouse condition, one would therefore expect $(0.409)(12) = 4.91$ participants to prefer the standard method. Similarly, in the track pad condition, one would expect $(0.409)(10) = 4.09$ participants to prefer the standard method. Note that this expected frequency is a mathematical concept; the number of participants in a sample with a specific preference would be a whole number.

An easy way to compute the expected frequency for a cell is to multiply the row total for the cell by the column total and then divide by the grand total. For the cell representing preference for the standard method when using the mouse, the expected frequency is $(12)(9)/22 = 4.91$. Table 2 shows the expected frequencies in parentheses.

The next step is to subtract, for each cell, the observed frequency from the expected frequency, square the difference, and then divide by the expected

Table 2   Data From the Example Experiment With Expected Frequencies

	Preferred Method		
Device	*Standard*	*New*	*Total*
Mouse	8 (4.91)	4 (7.09)	12
Track pad	1 (4.09)	9 (5.91)	10
Total	9	13	22

frequency. For the first cell, this is equal to $(4.91 - 8.00)^2/4.91 = 1.94$. The chi-square statistic is then computed by summing the values for all the cells. The formula can be written as

$$\chi^2 = \sum \frac{(E - O)^2}{E},$$

where E is an expected cell frequency and O is an observed cell frequency. For this example,

$$\chi^2 = \frac{(4.91 - 8)^2}{4.91} + \frac{(7.09 - 4)^2}{7.09}$$
$$+ \frac{(4.09 - 1)^2}{4.09} + \frac{(5.91 - 9)^2}{5.91},$$

which is equal to 7.25. The chi-square statistic has a degrees of freedom parameter associated with it that is calculated as $(r - 1)(c - 1)$, where r is the number of rows in the data table and c is the number of columns. For this example, both r and c are equal to 2, so the degrees of freedom is $(2 - 1)(2 - 1) = 1$. The probability associated with a chi-square of 7.25 with one degree of freedom is 0.007. Since this is lower than conventional levels of significance, the null hypothesis of no association between preference and pointing device can be rejected, justifying the conclusion that there is an association in the population.

Assumptions and Accuracy of the Chi-Square Test

A key assumption of the test is that each observation is independent of each other observation. In general, this assumption is met if each participant in the experiment adds 1 to the frequency count of only one cell of the experiment. If this is the case, then the total frequency count will equal the total number of participants. However, even this safeguard does not ensure independence. For example, if 2 participants discussed their possible responses before making them, their responses would not be independent.

Suppose the example experiment had been a little different, with each participant making two preference judgments, one when using the mouse and once when using the track pad. Since judgments from the same participant are not independent, the chi-square test of independence would not be appropriate for this design.

The statistic computed in the chi-square test of independence is only approximately distributed as chi-square, and therefore, the test is only an approximate test. Fortunately, under most circumstances, the approximation is quite good. Generally speaking, if there are at least 20 observations, the approximation will be satisfactory. However, accuracy is reduced if the proportions in the population are extreme. Suppose that the population proportion preferring the new method were 0.95 in both the mouse and track pad conditions. Since there is no association in the population, the null hypothesis is true. If the 0.05 significance level were used, the probability of making a Type I error should be 0.05. However, in this situation (with 12 and 10 participants, as in the experiment), the probability of a Type I error is 0.008. Thus, in this situation, the test is conservative: The true Type I error rate is lower than the nominal rate. In some situations, the actual Type I error rate is slightly higher than the nominal rate. For example, if the population proportions were both 0.60, then the probability of a Type I error would be 0.059 when the 0.05 significance level is used. Interestingly, for the same proportions, the probability of a Type I error using the 0.01 level is very close to 0.01. A simulation that allows one to estimate the probabilities of a Type I error in these designs is available at http://www.ruf.rice.edu/~lane/stat_sim/contingency/index.html.

Some writers have claimed that the chi-square test of independence assumes that all expected frequencies are greater than 5 and that a correction should be done otherwise. The correction is not recommended since, in general, it makes an already conservative test even more conservative.

Comparison to the Fisher Exact Probability Test

Since the chi-square test for independence is an approximate test, it would seem that the Fisher exact probability test, which, as its name implies, results in exact probabilities, would be preferable. However, this is not generally the case. The Fisher exact probability test is based on the assumption that the row and column totals are known before the experiment is conducted. For example, consider a hypothetical experiment designed to determine whether caffeine decreases response time. Suppose 10 participants are given caffeine and an additional 10 participants are given a placebo. After response times are measured, every participant below the median is classified as a fast responder, and every participant above the median is classified as a slow responder. Therefore, even before the data are collected, it is known that the column totals will be as shown in Table 3.

By contrast, in the example experiment, it was not known until the data were collected that 9 participants would prefer the standard method and 13 would prefer the new method. When the Fisher exact probability test is used with designs in which the row and column totals are not known in advance, it is very conservative, resulting in Type I error rates below the nominal significance level.

Using the Computer

For this example, the statistical package SAS JMP was used to compute the test. The output in Figure 1 shows the proportion preferring the new and the standard methods as a function of device. JMP automatically reports the results of two methods of testing for significance. The Pearson chi-square is the method discussed here. As can be seen in Table 4, the chi-square of 7.246 and probability of 0.0071 match the results computed previously.

Table 3 Row and Column Totals in Caffeine Study

Speed	Condition		
	Drug	Placebo	Total
Fast			10
Slow			10
Total	10	10	22

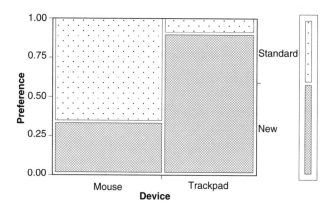

Figure 1   Proportion Preferring the New and the Standard Methods as a Function of Device

Table 4   Text Output From JMP

Test	Chi-square	Prob > chi sq
Likelihood ratio	7.989	0.0047
Pearson	7.246	0.0071

Note: Prob = probability; chi sq = chi-square.

Larger Designs

The example experiment is a 2 × 2 design since the two variables (device and method) each have two levels. The chi-square test for independence can also be used for larger designs. For instance, the example experiment might have used three devices and four methods, resulting in a 3 × 4 design. The calculations for doing the test are the same except that there are more cells over which the values of $(E − O)^2/E$ are summed. The degrees of freedom would be $(3 − 1)(4 − 1) = 6$.

—*David M. Lane*

Further Reading

Bradley, D. R., Bradley, T. D., McGrath, S. G., & Cutcomb, S. D. (1979). Type I error rate of the chi square test of independence in r × c tables that have small expected frequencies. *Psychological Bulletin, 86,* 1290–1297.

Lane, D. M., Peres, S. C., Sándor, A., & Napier, H. A. (2005). A process for anticipating and executing icon selection in graphical user interfaces. *International Journal of Human Computer Interaction, 19,* 241–252.

Java applet to compute probability values for chi-square: http://psych.rice.edu/online_stat/analysis_lab/chi_square_prob.html

Java applet simulation of the chi-square test of association: http://www.ruf.rice.edu/~lane/stat_sim/contingency/index.html

Children's Academic Intrinsic Motivation Inventory

The Children's Academic Intrinsic Motivation Inventory (CAIMI), published by Psychological Assessment Resources (www.parinc.com), measures intrinsic motivation for school learning. CAIMI items are based on theories of intrinsic motivation measuring enjoyment of learning; an orientation toward mastery; curiosity; persistence; and the learning of challenging, difficult, and novel tasks. It is a self-report instrument consisting of 44 items, to which children rate their agreement or disagreement. There are five subscales, four being subject-area specific (reading, math, social studies, and science) and one addressing school in general. The CAIMI was originally developed (in 1985) for students in Grades 4 through 9 and in 2001 was extended through the end of high school. A modified downward extension (YCAIMI) for Grades 1 through 3 was developed in 1990.

The CAIMI may be administered to a group or to individuals and in a classroom or an office setting. Children with sufficient reading ability may complete the CAIMI on their own after instructions and practice items are read aloud. Individual, oral administration is recommended for those with learning, reading, or perceptual difficulties. Individual administration takes approximately 20–30 minutes, and for administration to a group, sufficient time must be allocated for distribution and collection of materials, bringing total time to about an hour. Percentiles and *T* scores are available. Advantages of the CAIMI are that it allows for distinguishing motivation from ability and achievement, provides a motivational profile across the four subject areas and for school in general, is easily administered and scored, and may be applied to a variety of settings. For example, the CAIMI can be used by psychologists and practitioners; teachers and school administrators in regular and special education, including programs for gifted students; program evaluators; and researchers. It has been used by school districts to help identify children for inclusion in programs for the gifted.

The CAIMI has excellent psychometric properties and has been used nationally and internationally. It has been translated into several languages, including Spanish, Japanese, Chinese, and Slovene. Major research findings made with the CAIMI include the following: (a) Motivation is uniquely related to achievement above and beyond IQ; (b) the CAIMI provides stable measurement of children's motivation from upper elementary school through the end of high school; (c) children with higher academic intrinsic motivation function more effectively in school (higher achievement, more positive self-perception of performance, lower academic anxiety, lower extrinsic motivation) from the elementary school years through the end of high school; (d) children whose parents encourage intrinsic motivation and provide a stimulating environment have greater academic intrinsic motivation; (e) intellectually and motivationally gifted children have significantly higher academic intrinsic motivation; and (f) children with exceptionally low motivation (motivationally disadvantaged children) can be identified as early as Grade 4, and such children evidence a variety of associated poor school functioning from that time though the end of high school. Research has been conducted using the CAIMI in the Fullerton Longitudinal Study, in school settings, and with a variety of children, including students in regular and special education populations. Thus, the validity of the CAIMI has been generalized across a variety of populations and settings.

—Adele Eskeles Gottfried

See also Achievement Tests

Further Reading

Gottfried, A. E. (1985). Academic intrinsic motivation in elementary and junior high school students. *Journal of Educational Psychology, 77,* 631–635.

Gottfried, A. E. (1990). Academic intrinsic motivation in young elementary school children. *Journal of Educational Psychology, 82,* 525–538.

Gottfried, A. E., Fleming, J. S., & Gottfried, A. W. (1994). Role of parental motivational practices in children's academic intrinsic motivation and achievement. *Journal of Educational Psychology, 86,* 104–113.

Gottfried, A. E., Fleming, J. S., & Gottfried, A. W. (1998). Role of cognitively stimulating home environment in children's academic intrinsic motivation: A longitudinal study. *Child Development, 69,* 1448–1460.

Gottfried, A. E., Fleming, J. S., & Gottfried, A. W. (2001). Continuity of academic intrinsic motivation from childhood through late adolescence: A longitudinal study. *Journal of Educational Psychology, 93,* 3–13.

Gottfried, A. W., Gottfried, A. E., Cook, C., & Morris, P. (2005). Educational characteristics of adolescents with gifted academic intrinsic motivation: A longitudinal study from school entry through early adulthood. *Gifted Child Quarterly, 49,* 172–186.

CLASS INTERVAL

A fundamental skill in measurement and statistics (and all of science, for that matter) is being able to communicate the greatest amount of information about a data set using as little effort as possible. Such is the case when it comes to consolidating a data set to represent it by a frequency distribution. The first part in the creation of a frequency distribution is the establishment of a class interval, or the range of values that constitutes a category. A class interval is a range of numbers. Class intervals are also called *bins* (something you put data in), *class boundaries,* and *class limits.*

The first step in establishing a class interval is defining how large each class interval will be. In the frequency distribution in Figure 1 (based on the data set that is also shown), each interval spans five possible scores, such as 5–9 (which includes scores 5, 6, 7, 8, and 9) and 40–44 (which includes scores 40, 41, 42, 43, and 44).

The raw data . . .

47	10	31	25	20
2	11	31	25	21
44	14	15	26	21
41	14	16	26	21
7	30	17	27	24
6	30	16	29	24
35	32	15	29	23
38	33	19	28	20
35	34	18	29	21
36	32	16	27	20

The frequency distribution . . .

Class Interval	Frequency
45–49	1
40–44	2
35–39	4
30–34	8
25–29	10
20–24	10
15–19	8
10–14	4
5–9	2
0–4	1

Figure 1   Frequency Distribution

Here are some general rules to follow in the creation of a class interval, regardless of the size of values in the data set you are dealing with.

1. Select a class interval that has a range of 2, 5, 10, or 20 data points. In the example in Figure 1, a class interval of 5 was used.

2. Select a class interval so that 10 to 20 such intervals cover the entire range of data. A convenient way to do this is to compute the range, then divide by a number that represents the number of intervals you want to use (between 10 and 20). In this example, there are 50 scores, and 10 intervals are being used, so 50/10 = 5, which is the size of each class interval. For example, if scores ranged from 100 to 400, 300/20 = 15, so 15 would be the class interval.

3. Begin listing the class interval with a multiple of that interval. In the sample frequency distribution, the class interval is 5 and it started with the lowest class interval of 0.

4. Finally, place the largest interval at the top of the frequency distribution.

Once class intervals are created, the frequency part of the frequency distribution can be completed. That includes counting the number of times a score occurs in the raw data and entering that number in each of the class intervals represented by the count.

—*Neil J. Salkind*

See also Frequency Distribution

Further Reading

Pfeiffer, C., Windzio, M., & Kleimann, M. (2005). Media use and its impacts on crime perception, sentencing attitudes and crime policy. *European Journal of Criminology, 2*(3), 259–285.

Class interval discussion: Scale and impression: http://www.shodor.org/interactivate/discussions/sd2.html

CLASSICAL TEST THEORY

The first theory of measurement has been named classical test theory (CTT) because it was formulated from simple assumptions made by test theorists at the start of testing. It is also called the *theory of true and error scores*, because it is thought to comprise both true scores and error, and *classical reliability theory*, since its major function is to evaluate the reliability of the observed scores on a test; that is, it calculates the strength of the relationship between the observed score and the true score.

CTT makes use of a number of models considered as a group and various procedures with which the test developer tries to provide solutions to complicated problems in order to measure psychological variables. Psychologists are not interested in the score itself but in the conclusions they can draw and the explanations they can make on the basis of the measured behavior of an individual.

Assumptions of CTT

CTT views a test score as having two components, the *true score* and a *random error*. The true score is considered the average of identical values taken from repeated measurements without limit. The error is regarded as unrelated either to the true score or to the error that can occur in another measurement of the same attribute. Although the theory is an oversimplification and does not represent the results, it brings out relationships that are informative and useful in test design and construction as well as in evaluation of test scores. The first basic assumption of CTT is that the obtained score is the sum of true score plus error; that is, the true score and the error score are inextricably mixed. This concept can be expressed as a simple equation:

$$X = T + E,$$

where

X is the obtained score,

T is the true score, and

E represents errors of measurement.

It must be pointed out that the true score is never known. It remains within a certain interval, however, and a best estimate of it can be obtained.

Measurement error is all things except the true score. Errors of measurement can arise from numerous sources, such as item selection, test administration, test scoring, and systematic errors of measurement. The first three sources of error are jointly called *unsystematic measurement error*, meaning that their impact is unexpected and inconsistent. A systematic measurement error occurs when a test consistently measures something different from the trait it was designed to measure.

Measurement error reduces reliability or repeatability of test results. The assumption that the obtained score is made up of the true score and the error score reveals several additional assumptions. An assumption derived from true scores is that unsystematic measurement error affects test scores randomly. The randomness of measurement error is a fundamental assumption of CTT. Since there are random events,

unsystematic measurement errors have some probability of being positive or negative, and consequently they amount to an average of zero across a large group of subjects. It follows that the mean error of measurement is zero. Another assumption of CTT is that measurement errors are not correlated with true scores. A final assumption is that measurement errors are not correlated with errors on other tests. All these assumptions can be summarized as follows: (a) Measurement errors are random, (b) the mean error of measurement is zero, (c) true scores and error are uncorrelated, and (d) errors on different tests are uncorrelated.

From the aforementioned assumptions, we can arrive at some significant conclusions about the reliability of measurement; for example, when we administer a test to a large number of persons, we find variability of scores that can be expressed as a variance, σ^2. According to CTT, the variance of obtained scores has two separate sources, the variance of the true score and the variance of errors of measurement, or

$$\sigma_X^2 = \sigma_T^2 + \sigma_E^2,$$

where

σ_X^2 is the variance of obtained scores,

σ_T^2 is the variance of true scores, and

σ_E^2 is the variance errors of measurement.

The second basic assumption of CTT is that of parallel tests. The term *parallel tests* comes from the fact that each individual item can be viewed as a test; that is, each item coincides with the value of the latent variable. The assumption of the parallel tests model is satisfactory because it leads to useful conclusions about the relationships of the individual items to the latent variable that are grounded in observations of the relations of the items to one another. Thus, the parallel tests model adds two assumptions to CTT:

1. The amount that the latent variable affects each item is regarded as the same for all items.

2. Each item is considered to have the same amount of error as any other item. This means that the factors affect all items equally.

These assumptions imply that the correlation of each item with the true score is identical, and this conclusion leads to quantifying reliability.

In summary, the parallel tests model presupposes: (a) random error, (b) errors that are uncorrelated with each other, (c) errors that are uncorrelated with the true score, (d) the latent variable's influencing all items equally, and (e) an equal amount of error for every item. Thus the model allows us to make inferences about the latent variable that are grounded in the correlation between the items. However, the model achieves this by proposing strict assumptions.

Alternative Models to the Parallel Model

Apart from the strict assumptions referred to above, useful inferences can be made with less-rigid assumptions. Another model is based on what is called *essentially tau-equivalent tests* and makes a more tolerant assumption, namely, that each item requires the same amount of error variance that other items have. This means that the items are parallel with regard to the latent variable but are not essentially affected to the same degree by extraneous factors that are called *error*. Thus, since error can vary, item means and item variances can also vary. This model allows us to reach the same conclusion as the parallel tests model does, but with more lenient assumptions.

However, some theorists think that even the essentially tau-equivalent model is too rigid. For this reason, they put forward what is called the *congeneric model*, with even more liberal assumptions. The model assumes only that all items have a common latent variable. The items do not have equally strong relationships to the latent variable, and their error variances are not required to be equal. The only thing that we must assume is that each item exhibits the true score to some degree.

A Brief History of CTT

In 1904, Charles Spearman put forward CTT, and it is still flourishing. Spearman developed CTT by combining the concept of error with the concept of correlation. He argued that test scores have an error when we measure a human trait, and thus the observed correlation between test scores is lower than the correlation between true scores. Later, other authors restated and worked out the theory. Guilford, for example, tried to synthesize the developments that had taken place in CTT through 1936, Gulliksen gave a detailed account of all the progress through 1950 in his classic work, *Theory of Mental Tests*, and Lord and Novick reanalyzed CTT and combined it with new psychometric theories in 1968. However, the early days of the theory were rather difficult because of the quantitative atmosphere prevalent at that time, and its acceptance was lukewarm at first. However, before long, tests were constructed based on CTT, psychometric technology grew at a rapid rate, significant progress was achieved in psychological assessment, and thus the theory was extended and stabilized.

Controversies Surrounding CTT and Its Impact

CTT is criticized because of its simplicity and because the concept of true score is only a notion. However, new theories, such as item response theory (IRT) and generalizability theory supplement CTT and can never replace it. Most psychological tests currently available are constructed according to CTT. This means that new theories have to be combined with CTT in order to surmount the problems associated with it.

CTT is characterized by its simplicity and flexibility and for this reason can be used in many different circumstances. These qualities guarantee that CTT will be used over and over again in the future. Moreover, the new psychometric models that comprise item response theory, although they have developed rapidly in the past 35 years, have also demonstrated unfulfilled assumptions and uninterpretable parameters, as well as estimation difficulties. For these reasons, the two- and three-parameter models may become less popular in the future. This may lead to revival of interest in CTT, and its use and practice may extend further. Furthermore, the availability and development of computers will make calculating true score, establishing norms, and equating tests easier, no doubt increasing the use of CTT even further.

—Demetrios S. Alexopoulos

See also Item Response Theory; Reliability Theory; Validity Theory

Further Reading

Crocker, L., & Algina, J. (1986). *Introduction to classical and modern test theory*. New York: Holt, Rinehart & Winston.

Guilford, J. P. (1954). *Psychometric methods* (2nd ed.). New York: McGraw-Hill.

Gulliksen, H. (1950). *Theory of mental tests*. New York: Wiley.

Lord, F. M., & Novick, M. R. (1968). *Statistical theories of mental test scores*. Reading, MA: Addison-Wesley.

Nunnally, J. C., & Bernstein, I. H. (1994). *Psychometric theory* (3rd. ed.). New York: McGraw-Hill.

Spearman, C. E. (1904). General intelligence objectively determined and measured. *American Journal of Psychology*, *15*, 205–293.

CLASSIFICATION AND REGRESSION TREE

Classification and regression tree (CART) is a machine learning (or classification) algorithm that constructs a tree-structured classifier to assign group labels to each case based on its attributes. The resulting tree-structured classifier is usually ideal for interpretation and decision making. The algorithm requires that for each case in the data, there be two variables. The first is the group variable to be classified and predicted (such as disease status or treatment), and the second is the variable of attributes that can be multi-dimensional numerical or categorical data (such as smoking status, sex, or abundance of various enzymes in blood). Normally, the method is implemented in a set of training cases to learn a classifier. The classifier is then applied to an independent test set to evaluate the generalized classification accuracy.

CART analysis is performed as a binary recursive partition tree. An impurity measure is defined to describe the purity (concentration in a single group) of cases in a node. The algorithm recursively searches for the attribute criterion that partitions data into two parts with the largest decrease of impurity measure. Normally, the Gini impurity index is used in CART analysis:

$$I(T) = 1 - \sum_{i=1}^{m} p_i^2,$$

where

T is the data set in the node,

m the number of groups, and

p_i the proportion of group i in the node.

When all cases in the node belong to the same group (the purest case), $I(T)$ is minimized at 0, and when each group has the same proportion (the most impure case), $I(T)$ is maximized. The partition of the hierarchical tree continues until either the number of cases in the node is too small or the decrease of the impurity index is not statistically significant. Additional pruning rules may be applied to decide termination of tree growth to prevent a problem of overfitting.

CART has a number of merits compared with other classification algorithms. The method is inherently nonparametric without a distribution assumption of the data (in contrast to methods like linear discriminant analysis). It is thus more robust against skewed or ill-behaved distributed data. Learning in CART is a "white" box, and the learned classification criteria are easy to interpret. Thus CART is most applicable in situations when interpretation and learning of important attributes contributing to classification are the major goals in the application. CART by its nature can easily handle categorical and ordinal data in addition to numerical data. Finally, computation of an exhaustive search for the best partition is very fast, making the method feasible for large data sets.

Software Package

Since CART is a relatively modern statistical technique, it is not implemented in most major statistical software (e.g., SAS and S-PLUS). SPSS contains an add-on module, "SPSS Classification Trees." A commercial software, "Classification and Regression Tree," specifically for CART analysis, is also available. In the following discussion, an extension package "tree" of the free software R is used to implement CART.

Table 1   MPG for a Select Group of Cars

Car	Efficiency	Cylinders	Displacement	Horsepower	Weight	Acceleration
1	Inefficient	4	151	85	2855	17.6
2	Economic	4	98	76	2144	14.7
3	Economic	5	121	67	2950	19.9
4	Inefficient	6	250	105	3353	14.5
5	Inefficient	4	151	88	2740	16
6	Inefficient	6	250	88	3021	16.5
7	Economic	4	71	65	1836	21
8	Economic	4	112	88	2395	18
9	Economic	4	141	71	3190	24.8
10	Inefficient	8	350	155	4360	14.9
11	Inefficient	4	98	60	2164	22.1
12	Economic	6	262	85	3015	17
13	Inefficient	6	200	85	3070	16.7
14	Inefficient	6	258	110	2962	13.5
15	Inefficient	4	116	75	2158	15.5
16	Inefficient	4	140	72	2401	19.5
17	Inefficient	8	350	180	4499	12.5
18	Inefficient	8	307	200	4376	15
19	Inefficient	8	318	140	3735	13.2
20	Economic	4	78	52	1985	19.4
21	Economic	4	89	71	1990	14.9
22	Economic	4	97	75	2265	18.2
23	Inefficient	6	250	98	3525	19
24	Economic	4	83	61	2003	19
25	Inefficient	8	302	140	3449	10.5

An Example

An example of classification of car fuel efficiency is demonstrated as follows. The data shown in Table 1 are a random subsample of 25 cars from the "auto-mpg" data set from the UCI Machine Learning Repository (http://www.ics.uci.edu/~mlearn/MLRepository.html). The group variable for classification is "efficiency," which has two possible values: inefficient (mpg < 25) and economic (mpg ≥ 25). Five attributes for classifying and predicting fuel efficiency are available for prediction: cylinders, displacement, horsepower, weight, and acceleration.

The CART output of this example is shown in Figure 1. The top node represents the whole data set, containing 10 economic and 15 inefficient cars. The algorithm finds that the best way to classify car fuel efficiency is "whether the displacement is larger than

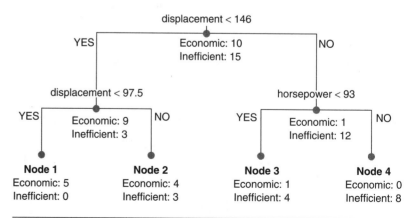

Figure 1   CART Output of Classification of Car Fuel Efficiency

146 or not." This will split the data into two groups. The first ("YES") group (displacement < 146) contains 9 economic and 3 inefficient cars, and the second ("NO") group (displacement > 146) contains 1 economic and 12 inefficient cars. Similarly, the "displacement < 146" group is best split into Node 1 (displacement < 97.5) and Node 2 (97.5 < displacement < 146). The "displacement > 146" group is split by horsepower to generate Node 3 (displacement > 146 & horsepower < 93) and Node 4 (displacement > 146 & horsepower > 93). All nodes except for Node 2 have high classification accuracy in this training data. It should be noted that attributes used for classification may appear repeatedly in different branches (e.g., displacement in this example). Figure 2 demonstrates a scatter plot of the 25 cars. The solid lines represent the splitting rules in the branches of the CART output.

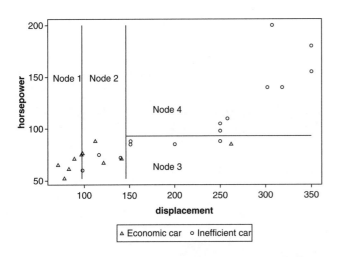

Figure 2   Scatter Plot of Subsample of 25 Cars

—George C. Tseng

Further Reading

Breiman, L. (1984). *Classification and regression trees*. Boca Raton, FL: Chapman & Hall/CRC.

Classification and regression tree downloads: http://cran.au
.r-project.org/src/contrib/Descriptions/tree.html

Clinical Assessment of Attention Deficit

The Clinical Assessment of Attention Deficit (CAT) consists of two comprehensive assessment tools for the objective evaluation of attention deficit disorder and attention deficit/hyperactivity disorder (ADD/ADHD) symptoms in children, adolescents, and adults between 8 and 79 years of age. The CAT is especially useful in clinical, educational, and research settings because it is theoretically conceived and psychometrically sound. Although the CAT is very comprehensive in the context-related behaviors and experiences it assesses, it is brief (10–20 minutes) and easily administered. The CAT can be (a) administered individually or in groups, (b) mailed to respondents' homes to be completed and returned, or (c) completed in its paper-and-pencil format in a professional's office. The CAT Scoring Program performs all scoring and profiling of the assessment and provides a very thorough interpretative report.

The CAT includes a 108-item instrument for adults (CAT-A) and a 42-item instrument for children and adolescents (CAT-C). These instruments are very similar in structure, format, and item content. Each instrument assesses important clinical behaviors related to ADD with and without hyperactivity (as outlined in the American Psychiatric Association's *Diagnostic and Statistical Manual of Mental Disorders*, 4th ed., text rev.) via three clinical scales (inattention, impulsivity, and hyperactivity). Both instruments consider these important clinical behaviors within multiple contexts (as suggested by the American Academy of Pediatrics) by means of the CAT context scales (personal, academic/occupational, and social) and within an individual's personal experiences through the CAT locus scales (internal and external). Figure 1 depicts the CAT theoretical model and shows the clinical, context, and locus scales. The CAT-C and CAT-A assess the same clinical behaviors within the same contexts and consider the same internal feelings and external behaviors.

Context Scales Locus Scales	Clinical Subscales		
Personal	*Inattention*	*Impulsivity*	*Hyperactivity*
Internal	I was bored easily.	I was impatient.	I often felt nervous.
External	It seems I was always spilling something.	I acted without thinking.	I was extremely active.
Academic Occupational			
Internal	I daydreamed a lot in school.	I often regretted my actions in school.	I felt very restless in school.
External	I was frequently tardy for class.	I blurted out answers to questions in class.	I talked too much in school.
Social			
Internal	I often could not recall the names of people I met.	I made quick judgments about other people.	I always had more energy than my friends.
External	When playing games, I often played out of turn.	I took more risks than my friends.	I rarely played quietly with my friends.

Figure 1   CAT-A Conceptual Blueprint (Sample Items From the Childhood Memories Scale)

The minor differences between the two instruments are primarily age-related considerations. Because adult diagnosis of ADD/ADHD requires evidence of both childhood onset and current symptoms, the CAT-A is composed of two subparts: Part I, Current Symptoms, and Part II, Childhood Memories. In contrast, CAT-C assesses only current ADD/ADHD symptoms and therefore is not divided into age-related subparts. Also, CAT-A includes only a self-report form due to the limited availability of raters who could accurately recall an adult client's childhood behaviors. CAT-C includes forms for self, parent, and teacher because of readily available respondents who can reliably report on a child's current behaviors across multiple settings.

CAT normative samples and total scale (Clinical Index) coefficient alpha reliabilities are quite consistent across instruments and forms. The CAT-C self form was normed on 800 children and adolescents 8 to 18 years old; the CAT-C parent form was normed using the ratings from the parents of the 800 children and adolescents who completed the self form. The CAT-C teacher form also was normed on 550 teachers of the same children and adolescents who completed

the self form. CAT-A was normed on 800 adults ranging from 19 to 79 years old. CAT-C Clinical Index internal consistency coefficients range from .92 on the self form to .98 on the teacher form. The CAT-A Clinical Index is .94 for Childhood Memories and .91 for Current Symptoms, with an overall CAT-A Clinical Index (i.e., combining Childhood Memories and Current Symptoms) of .96.

—*Bruce A. Bracken*

Further Reading

American Academy of Pediatrics. (2000). Clinical practice guideline: Diagnosis and evaluation of the child with attention-deficit/hyperactivity disorder. *Pediatrics, 105I,* 1158–1170.

American Psychiatric Association. (2000). *Diagnostic and statistical manual of mental disorders* (4th ed., text rev.). Washington, DC: Author.

Bracken, B. A., & Boatwright, B. S. (2005). *Clinical assessment of attention deficit—adult.* Lutz, FL: Psychological Assessment Resources.

Bracken, B. A., & Boatwright, B. S. (2005). *Clinical assessment of attention deficit—child.* Lutz, FL: Psychological Assessment Resources.

CLINICAL ASSESSMENT OF BEHAVIOR

The Clinical Assessment of Behavior (CAB) is a comprehensive, third-party rating scale for the behavioral assessment of children and adolescents ages 2 to 18 years. The two parent forms (a 170-item CAB—Parent Extended form and a 70-item CAB—Parent form) and the 70-item teacher form (CAB—Teacher) allow for a balanced assessment of both adaptive and clinical (i.e., maladaptive) behaviors across various settings, contexts, and raters. With a single set of items spanning the age range of 2 to 18 years, the CAB permits a longitudinal evaluation of symptoms throughout the course of an individual's treatment, without the introduction of potentially incompatible instruments into the evaluation process as the individual ages.

The CAB structural content includes 3 adaptive and 3 clinical scales and 2 adaptive and 10 clinical clusters. Whereas the CAB scales were designed to reflect "broad brush" psychosocial adjustment domains, CAB clusters reflect specific areas of exceptionality or disorder. Table 1 illustrates the exceptionalities, disorders, and conditions assessed by the CAB scales and clusters across the three forms. Table 1 also presents coefficient alpha reliability indices for each scale and cluster for the standardization sample. With its close alignment to the diagnostic criteria of the American Psychiatric Association's *Diagnostic and Statistical Manual of Mental Disorders* (4th ed., text rev.), legislative mandates of the Individuals with Disabilities Education Act, and a context-dependent model of psychosocial adjustment, the CAB augments the diagnosis of childhood and adolescent psychiatric disorders with comprehensive behavioral content.

The CAB forms require an eighth-grade reading level of respondents and 5–10 minutes to complete the CAB-P and CAB-T forms (the CAB-PX requires 10–20 minutes). Because it is brief and easy to read, the CAB can be completed by raters without the aid of psychologists, thus rendering the evaluation process more efficient than if parents and teachers were to be interviewed. Furthermore, the CAB is computer scored and interpreted, and the resulting data are profiled and reported for professional interpretation and use.

A relatively unique application of the CAB is the ability for professionals to use its data to identify specific behaviors associated with educationally relevant exceptionalities (e.g., mental retardation, learning disabilities, giftedness and talent, attention deficit disorder, and attention deficit/hyperactivity disorder).

Table 1   CAB Scales, Clusters, and Coefficient Alpha Reliabilities for the CAB-PX, CAB-P, and CAB-T

Scale/Cluster	CAB-PX	CAB-P	CAB-T
Clinical scales			
Internalizing behaviors	.95	.89	.92
Externalizing behaviors	.97	.95	.98
Critical behaviors	.91	—	—
Adaptive scales			
Social skills	.95	.92	.96
Competence	.94	.92	.96
Adaptive behaviors	.92	—	—
Clinical clusters			
Anxiety	.93	.88	.92
Depression	.95	.90	.93
Anger	.93	.90	.94
Aggression	.95	.92	.97
Bullying	.97	.94	.97
Conduct problems	.92	.90	.96
Attention deficit/hyperactivity	.94	.94	.97
Autistic spectrum disorders	.92	.89	.93
Learning disability	.92	.90	.95
Mental retardation	.91	.90	.95
Adaptive clusters			
Executive function	.91	.91	.95
Gifted and talented	.94	.92	.96
CAB Behavioral Index	**.98**	**.97**	**.99**

Notes: CAB = Clinical Assessment of Behavior; PX = Parent Extended form; P = Parent form; T = Teacher form.

Too often, educational exceptionalities are diagnosed with only ability measures (e.g., intelligence tests, achievement tests, perceptual/motor tests) and without questioning whether a student's behaviors are consistent with the considered diagnosis. The CAB allows third-party respondents to indicate the frequency with which they observe the child or adolescent demonstrating behavioral characteristics associated with specific educational exceptionalities. Such information provides a multisource, multicontext way to corroborate referral information and ability test data with behavioral indices.

Standardized on more than 2,100 parents and 1,600 teachers, the CAB normative sample is highly representative of the U.S. population. An examination of the extent to which students' behavioral functioning is associated with their demographic characteristics (age, gender, race/ethnicity, parents' educational levels) revealed that generally 3% or less of the variance in the CAB parent-generated ratings was associated with the demographic attributes evaluated. Approximately 9% or less of the variance in teachers' ratings was associated with demographic attributes. These empirical findings, along with comparable reliability coefficients for all age, gender, and ethnic/racial groups, suggest that the CAB may provide the basis for an equitable behavioral assessment regardless of a student's age, gender, race/ethnicity, or socioeconomic status.

—*Bruce A. Bracken*

Further Reading

American Psychiatric Association. (2000). *Diagnostic and statistical manual of mental disorders* (4th ed., text rev.). Washington, DC: Author.

Bracken, B. A. (1992). *Multidimensional self concept scale.* Austin, TX: PRO-ED.

Bracken, B. A. (1996). Clinical applications of a multidimensional, context-dependent model of self-concept. In B. A. Bracken (Ed.), *Handbook of self concept: Developmental, social, and clinical considerations* (pp. 463–505). New York: Wiley.

Bracken, B. A., & Keith, L. K. (2004). *Clinical assessment of behavior.* Lutz, FL: Psychological Assessment Resources.

Individuals with Disabilities Education Act Amendments of 1997, Pub. L. No. 103-218 (GPO 1997).

CLINICAL ASSESSMENT OF DEPRESSION

The Clinical Assessment of Depression (CAD) is a comprehensive assessment of children's, adolescents', and adults' depressive symptoms. CAD content was developed from a review of the literature pertaining to child, adolescent, and adult development and depression and was closely aligned with current diagnostic criteria of the American Psychiatric Association's *Diagnostic and Statistical Manual of Mental Disorders* (4th ed., text rev.).

Notably, the CAD employs a single 50-item form as an overall measure of general affectivity. This comprehensive set of depressive symptoms was employed in part to test previous assumptions that the nature of depression varies across the age span. Multidimensionality was added to the instrument through the inclusion of symptom scales and critical item clusters sensitive to specific dimensions of depression. The CAD produces a total scale score and standard scores for each of four symptom scales and six clusters. The CAD critical item clusters (e.g., Hopelessness, Self-Devaluation) include item content that is especially sensitive to individuals who may be at risk for harming themselves. Table 1 shows the full range of affective symptoms assessed on the CAD and its symptom scales.

The CAD was normed on a sample of 1,900 children, adolescents, and adults aged 8 through 79 years. The normative sample included individuals from a wide range of racial and ethnic backgrounds, geographical

Table 1   Coefficient Alpha Reliabilities for the CAD Symptom Scales by Age

	Age in Years			
	8–11	*12–17*	*18–25*	*26–79*
Depressed mood	.95	.96	.96	.95
Anxiety/worry	.83	.85	.83	.86
Diminished interest	.78	.85	.85	.86
Cognitive and physical fatigue	.82	.83	.85	.87
CAD total scale	*.96*	*.97*	*.96*	*.97*

regions of the United States, and residential communities (urban, suburban, and rural). Table 1 also presents the instrument's total sample symptom scale and total scale internal consistency estimates; CAD total scale reliabilities range from .96 to .97 across the entire age range. Less than 1% of the total scale variability is associated with examinees' age, gender, race/ethnicity, or socioeconomic status. Overall, data from CAD reliability and validity studies suggest that depressive symptoms are common and behave similarly, regardless of the demographic characteristics of the examinee.

The CAD has multiple applications, with broad uses in clinical, educational, and research settings. Although it is very comprehensive as a measure of depressive symptomatology, the CAD is appropriately brief (10 minutes) for use with depressed clients and is easily administered. Because the CAD is a self-report instrument requiring only a fourth-grade reading level, it can be completed by most clients, regardless of age, without help from an examiner. Maximizing scoring and interpretation efficiency, the CAD can be scored either by hand or by computer by individuals with little psychometric training, and resulting data can be collated, profiled, and reported for professional interpretation and use.

—*Bruce A. Bracken*

Further Reading

American Psychiatric Association. (2000). *Diagnostic and statistical manual of mental disorders* (4th ed., text rev.). Washington, DC: Author.

Bracken, B. A., & Howell, K. K. (2005). *Clinical assessment of depression*. Lutz, FL: Psychological Assessment Resources.

Finch, S. M. (1960). *Fundamentals of child psychiatry*. New York: Norton.

Rie, F. H. (1966). Depression in childhood: A survey of some pertinent contributions. *Journal of Child Psychology and Psychiatry and Applied Disciplines, 35*(7), 1289–1308.

CLUSTER ANALYSIS

The objective of cluster analysis is to construct a natural grouping of the objects in a multivariate data set. The grouping captures "similarities" between the objects according to some criterion. An ideal outcome is one in which the objects belonging to the same group are as similar as possible, whereas objects belonging to different groups are as dissimilar as possible. Cluster analysis has proved to be a successful data reduction technique in many scientific fields.

The main steps in cluster analysis are (a) the choice of algorithms for constructing groups (clusters) and (b) the choice of a similarity-dissimilarity measure. Popular choices of dissimilarity measures are various distances, such as Euclidean or Manhattan. An interesting, robust distance measure is discussed in Kaufman and Rousseeuw.

Clustering Algorithms

Clustering algorithms can be classified into two groups: (a) *partition* methods and (b) *hierarchical* methods. Partition methods create a family of clusters in which each object belongs to just a single member of the partition. The requirement to generate such partitions is that distances between pairs of objects belonging to the same cluster are smaller than distances between pairs of objects in different clusters. Formally, suppose that objects i and j belong to cluster A, while object k belongs to cluster B. It is then required that $d_{ij} < d_{ik}$ and $d_{ij} < d_{jk}$, where d_{ij} denotes a dissimilarity measure for objects i and j. The most prominent partition algorithm is k-means. A more robust alternative (partitioning around medoids) is discussed in Kaufman and Rousseeuw, while a model-based version is presented in Banfield and Raftery.

Agglomerative hierarchical algorithms construct a clustering solution that is represented by a tree (dendrogram). Their characteristic feature is that either any two clusters are disjoint or one cluster is a superset of the other. It is usually required for the dissimilarity measure to be an ultrametric; in other words, for every triple set of objects (i, j, k) we have, the two largest values in the set $\{d_{ij}, d_{jk}, d_{ik}\}$ are equal. An agglomerative algorithm starts with as many clusters as objects in the data set and progressively merges them, based on the shortest distance between them, until each object has been assigned to a single cluster.

The mechanism used for merging clusters is based on a distance measure between groups. Some common possibilities include the shortest distance between members of the two groups (single linkage), the largest one (complete linkage), the average distance (average linkage), and the Euclidean distance between the averages of the clusters (centroid method). Some other choices are discussed in Gordon.

An important practical consideration is that since cluster analysis is driven by the distance between objects, variables need to be scaled appropriately so as not to exert excessive influence on the distance measure.

—*George Michailidis*

See also Factor Analysis

Further Reading

Banfield, J. D., & Raftery, A. E. (1993). Model-based Gaussian and non-Gaussian clustering. *Biometrics*, *49*, 803–821.

Everitt, B. S., Landau, S., & Leese, M. (2001). *Cluster analysis*. London: Hodder Arnold.

Gordon, A. D. (1999). *Classification*. London: Chapman & Hall.

Kaufman, L., & Rousseeuw, P. J. (1990). *Finding groups in data*. New York: Wiley.

Mirkin, B. (2005). Clustering for data mining: A data recovery approach. London: Chapman & Hall.

CLUSTER SAMPLING

A cluster sample is a type of sample generated for the purposes of describing a population in which the units, or elements, of the population are organized into groups, called clusters. The goal of a survey is to gather data in order to describe the characteristics of a population. A population can consist of individuals, school districts, plots of land, or a company's invoices. A survey collects information on a sample, or subset, of the population. In cluster sampling, instead of choosing individuals to interview or units on which to record data directly, the survey researcher first chooses clusters of elements. Once

clusters are selected, one often then samples elements from within the selected clusters and collects data on them. A survey following this procedure with two stages of random selection of units is called a *two-stage cluster sample*. A survey that selects units using three or more stages of random selection is called a three-stage or a multistage cluster sample. The groups of units selected at the first stage of sampling are called *primary sampling units* (PSUs). The groups selected at the second stage are called *secondary sampling units* (SSUs). The elements selected at the final stage can be referred to as the *ultimate sampling units*.

Cluster sampling is used widely in large-scale official surveys. The U.S. Department of Agriculture's National Resources Inventory study selects land areas, called segments, as PSUs. It then selects points, defined by latitude and longitude, as SSUs. The U.S. Bureau of Labor's Current Population Survey, which is conducted by the U.S. Bureau of the Census, selects counties as PSUs and then households within counties. Surveys of school students organized by the National Center for Education Statistics and surveys focused on health and nutrition designed by the National Center for Health Statistics rely on sampling designs that involve clustering.

Cluster sampling can be a type of probability sampling, which means that it is possible to compute the probability of selecting any particular sample. The main benefit of probability sampling is that one can estimate means, proportions, and variances without the problem of selection bias. In comparison with *simple random sampling* (SRS), in which units are selected directly from the population list or frame, estimates from a cluster sample design usually have greater variability or random uncertainty. The increase in variance of estimators occurs because each initial selection of a cluster means that multiple units ultimately will be in the sample. Units clustered together typically are more alike than randomly selected units from across the entire population. As a result, each initial selection under cluster sampling has more impact on resulting estimates than it does under SRS. If clusters are small and if two or more stages of random selection are used, the impact of cluster sampling on variances is not too large. The main advantage of cluster sampling is convenience and reduced cost. If one wanted to interview high school students or look at their transcripts in the state of Iowa, an SRS would require sending data collectors all over the state and negotiating permissions with numerous school districts to interview students and look at confidential data. A cluster sample could first select school districts and then schools within districts before selecting students. Fewer schools would need to be visited, thereby reducing travel and setup costs and time. Although cluster sampling is convenient, it is not the same thing as *convenience sampling*, which is a type of nonprobability sampling.

Cluster sampling can be combined with stratification to reduce the variance of estimators. Stratification is the process of dividing the units, or clusters, in a population into strata, or groups. Although similar to cluster sampling, in which several clusters are selected to be in the sample, stratified sampling entails selecting independent samples within every stratum. Stratified sampling typically reduces variance of estimators by forcing the sample to include representatives of all strata. In a survey of high school students in Iowa, the school districts could be stratified into the twelve Area Education Agencies within the state, and then a multistage sample of students could be selected within each Area Education Agency. Stratified cluster samples aim to combine the convenience of cluster sampling with precise estimation produced by stratification.

—*Michael D. Larsen*

See also Probability Sampling

Further Reading

Cochran, W.G. (1977). *Sampling techniques*. New York: Wiley.
Henry, G. T. (1990). *Practical sampling*. Newbury Park, CA: Sage.
Kish, L. (1965). *Survey sampling*. New York: Wiley.
Lohr, S. (1999). *Sampling: Design and analysis*. Pacific Grove, CA: Brooks/Cole.
Scheaffer, R. L., Mendenhall, W., III, & Ott, L. R. (1995). *Elementary survey sampling* (6th ed.). Belmont, CA: Duxbury Press.

Applying Ideas on Statistics and Measurement

The following abstract is adapted from Burnham, K. P., & Anderson, D. R. (2004). Multimodel inference: Understanding AIC and BIC in model selection. *Sociological Methods & Research, 33*(2), 261–304.

This article demonstrates the use of stratified and **cluster sampling** to draw a sample from the U.S. Census Archives for California in 1880. This is a useful exercise for courses in research design and also provides an efficient method for taking samples for historical research. With relatively little effort spent on data collection and data entry, useful knowledge about California in 1880 was acquired pertaining to marriage patterns, migration patterns, occupational status, and categories of race and ethnicity.

COCHRAN *Q* TEST

In a randomized complete block design, it is often of interest to examine a set of *c* binary responses pertaining to the levels of some treatment condition provided either by a sample of participants used as their own controls to make these assessments or by a sample of *c* matched participants randomly assigned to each treatment level as members of a block. In 1950, the statistician William G. Cochran developed a test for the differences in the proportions of "success" among the treatment levels in *c* related groups in which the repeated measurements provided by each participant under *c* different conditions or the measurements provided by the *c* homogeneous participants in each block are binary responses, with success coded 1 and "failure" coded 0.

The Cochran *Q* test is a dichotomous data counterpart of another nonparametric procedure, the Friedman rank test, in which the responses to the *c* treatment levels within each block are ranked. Both these procedures are competitors of the classic two-way ANOVA randomized block *F* test, in which the responses to each treatment are measured on an interval or ratio scale and the assumption of underlying normality of the different treatment groups is made.

Motivation

Cochran's Q test has enjoyed widespread use in behavioral, business, educational, medical, and social science research when it may be desirable to evaluate possible significance of differences in the proportion of successes over several treatment groups.

As an example of a study in which each participant offers repeated measurements, one each for the c levels of the treatment or condition under evaluation, the efficacy of c different drugs prescribed for providing relief from some chronic condition may be investigated. Other examples of this type could involve taste testing wines or other consumer preference studies in which each of c items is classified as "acceptable" or "not acceptable." As an example of a randomized complete block experiment in which the c homogeneous members of a block are randomly assigned, one each, to the c levels of the treatment, an educator may wish to form sets of homogeneous blocks of students and randomly assign the members of the block to each of c learning methods with the goal of assessing whether there are significant differences among the learning methods based on the proportions of successes observed.

Development

The layout for the dichotomous responses from a sample of either r participants or r blocks of matched participants over c levels of a treatment condition is shown in Table 1.

Cochran's Q test statistic is given by

$$Q = \frac{(c-1)(c\sum_{j=1}^{c}x_{.j}^2 - N^2)}{cN - \sum_{i=1}^{r}x_{i.}^2},$$

Table 1   Data Layout for the Cochran Q Test

Block	Treatments 1	2	...	c	Totals
1	x_{11}	x_{12}	...	x_{1c}	$x_{1.}$
2	x_{21}	x_{22}	...	x_{2c}	$x_{2.}$
$\vdots$	$\vdots$	$\vdots$	$\vdots$	$\vdots$	$\vdots$
r	x_{r1}	x_{r2}	...	x_{rc}	x_{r}
Totals	$x_{.1}$	$x_{.2}$	...	$x_{.c}$	N
Proportion of "Success"	$\hat{p}_{.1} = \dfrac{x_{.1}}{r}$	$\hat{p}_{.2} = \dfrac{x_{.2}}{r}$	...	$\hat{p}_{.c} = \dfrac{x_{.c}}{r}$	

Notes: c = the number of treatment groups (i.e., columns); r = the number of blocks (i.e., rows of subjects); x_{ij} = the binary response ("success" = 1, "failure" = 0) for the jth treatment in the ith block; $x_{.j}$ = the total number of successes for treatment j; $x_{i.}$ the total number of successes for block i;

$N = \sum_{j=1}^{c}x_{.j} = \sum_{i=1}^{r}x_{i.}$ the total number of successes.

where

c is the number of treatment groups (i.e., columns),

r is the number of blocks (i.e., rows of subjects),

x_{ij} is the binary response (success = 1, failure = 0) for the jth treatment in the ith block,

$x_{.j}$ is the total number of successes for treatment j,

$x_{i.}$ is the total number of successes for block i, and

$N = \sum_{j=1}^{c}x_{.j} = \sum_{i=1}^{r}x_{i.}$ = the total number of successes.

As the number of "discriminating" blocks (i.e., those in which outcomes for the c treatments are not either all 1s or all 0s) gets large, the Cochran Q test statistic is approximated by a chi-square distribution with $c - 1$ degrees of freedom. The decision rule is to reject the null hypothesis of no differences (i.e., no treatment effect), H_0: $p_{.1} = p_{.2} = \cdots = p_{.c}$, if at the α level of significance, $Q > \chi^2_{\alpha,(c-1)}$.

The researchers M. W. Tate and S. W. Brown recommended that there be at least seven such discriminating blocks in studies for which four treatment levels are involved in order to use the chi-square distribution as an approximation to Q, and both they and the statistician K. D. Patil provided tables of critical values for an exact test of Q that are particularly useful when the numbers of discriminating blocks and treatment levels are small.

A Posteriori Comparisons

If the null hypothesis is rejected, the researchers L. A. Marascuilo and M. McSweeney suggested a multiple comparison procedure that permits a post hoc evaluation of all pairwise differences among the c treatment groups. With an experimentwise error rate alpha, each of the possible $c(c-1)/2$ pairwise comparisons is made, and the decision rule is to declare treatment j different from treatment j' if

$$\left| \frac{x_{.j}}{r} - \frac{x_{.j'}}{r} \right| > \sqrt{\chi^2_{\alpha,(c-1)}} \cdot \sqrt{\frac{2(cN - \sum_{i=1}^{r} x_{i.}^2)}{r^2 c(c-1)}} .$$

That is, treatment j and treatment j' are declared significantly different if $\left| \hat{p}_{.j} - \hat{p}_{.j'} \right|$, the absolute difference in the sample proportions of success, exceeds a critical range given by the product of

$$\sqrt{\chi^2_{\alpha,(c-1)}} \text{ and } \sqrt{\frac{2(cN - \sum_{i=1}^{r} x_{i.}^2)}{r^2 c(c-1)}} .$$

Applying Cochran's Q Test

Consider the following hypothetical example: Suppose a group of 16 faculty members is asked to evaluate the resumes of each of four candidates who have interviewed at the college for the position of dean. Each of the 16 faculty is to assign scores of 1 (would recommend) or 0 (would not recommend) to each of the four candidates. The results are displayed in Table 2. Note that one of the professors (JL) did not recommend any of the four candidates as

qualified for the position of dean while one of the professors (AO) recommended all the candidates. The other 14 faculty were able to discriminate among the applicants and provide favorable recommendations to one or more of these candidates.

For these data, the Cochran Q test is used to test the null hypothesis of no treatment effect (that is, each of the four candidates is preferred equally, and any differences in the observed proportions are due to chance),

$$H_0: p_{.1} = p_{.2} = \cdots = p_{.c},$$

against the general alternative that a treatment effect is present (that is, there are real differences in the proportions; at least one of the candidates is preferred differently from the others):

$$H_1: \text{Not all } p_j \text{ are equal (where } j = 1, 2, \ldots, c).$$

From Table 2, it is observed that $c = 4$, $r = 16$, $N = 31$, and the x_j and x_i are summarized in the column

Table 2   Hypothetical Results of Evaluating Job Candidates

Raters	1 = IC	2 = PE	3 = NP	4 = PS	Totals
			Candidates		
1 = HB	0	0	1	0	1
2 = RB	0	1	1	1	3
3 = KC	1	0	1	1	3
4 = MD	0	0	1	1	2
5 = EF	0	0	1	1	2
6 = KH	0	0	1	0	1
7 = BK	0	0	0	1	1
8 = JK	0	0	1	1	2
9 = JL	0	0	0	0	0
10 = RM	0	0	0	1	1
11 = AO	1	1	1	1	4
12 = RP	0	0	1	1	2
13 = JT	0	0	1	1	2
14 = JW	1	0	1	1	3
15 = JY	0	0	1	1	2
16 = RZ	1	0	1	0	2
Totals	4	2	13	12	31
Proportions	$\hat{p}_{.1} = 0.2500$	$\hat{p}_{.2} = 0.1250$	$\hat{p}_{.3} = 0.8125$	$\hat{p}_{.4} = 0.7500$	

and row totals. Cochran's Q test statistic is then computed as follows:

$$Q = \frac{(c-1)\left(c\sum_{j=1}^{c} x_{.j}^2 - N^2\right)}{cN - \sum_{i=1}^{r} x_{i.}^2}$$

$$= \frac{(3)[(4)(4^2 + 2^2 + 13^2 + 12^2) - 31^2]}{(4)(31) - (1^2 + 3^2 + 3^2 + \cdots + 2^2)}$$

$$= \frac{1113}{49} = 22.714.$$

Since the Cochran Q test statistic is approximated by a chi-square distribution with $c - 1$ degrees of freedom, using an $\alpha = 0.05$ level of significance, the decision rule is to reject the null hypothesis of no differences ($H_0 : p_{.1} = p_{.2} = \cdots = p_{.c}$) if $Q > \chi^2_{0.05,(c-1=3)} = 7.815$, the upper-tailed critical value under the chi-square distribution with 3 degrees of freedom. The null hypothesis is rejected, and it is concluded that significant differences in preferences for the candidates exist.

Given that the null hypothesis is rejected, to determine which candidate(s) significantly stand out, post hoc evaluations of all $(4)(3)/2 = 6$ pairwise differences among the 4 candidates are made. The critical range for these pairwise comparisons is

$$\sqrt{\chi^2_{\alpha,(c-1)}} \cdot \sqrt{\frac{2\left(cN - \sum_{i=1}^{r} x_{i.}^2\right)}{r^2 c(c-1)}} = \sqrt{7.815}$$

$$\cdot \sqrt{\frac{(2)[(4)(31) - (1^2 + 3^2 + 3^2 + \cdots + 2)]}{(16^2)(4)(3)}}$$

$$= 0.499.$$

From the sample proportions of success summarized at the bottom of Table 2, the pairwise comparisons are evaluated in Table 3.

From Table 3 it is clear that candidates 3 and 4 are each significantly preferred to candidates 1 and 2. Nevertheless, the difference in preference between

Table 3   Post Hoc Pairwise Comparisons of Four Candidates

Candidates	$\|\hat{p}_{.j} - \hat{p}_{.j'}\|$	Critical Range	Decision Rule
1 vs. 2	$\|\hat{p}_{.1} - \hat{p}_{.2}\| = 0.1250$	0.499	Not significant
1 vs. 3	$\|\hat{p}_{.1} - \hat{p}_{.3}\| = 0.5625$	0.499	Significant
1 vs. 4	$\|\hat{p}_{.1} - \hat{p}_{.4}\| = 0.5000$	0.499	Significant
2 vs. 3	$\|\hat{p}_{.2} - \hat{p}_{.3}\| = 0.6875$	0.499	Significant
2 vs. 4	$\|\hat{p}_{.2} - \hat{p}_{.4}\| = 0.6250$	0.499	Significant
3 vs. 4	$\|\hat{p}_{.3} - \hat{p}_{.4}\| = 0.0625$	0.499	Not significant

candidates 1 and 2 is not significant, and more important here, the difference in preference between candidates 3 and 4 is not significant. The recommendation from the faculty regarding the appointment of the dean would be for candidate 3 or 4. Other criteria would be needed to finalize the decision process.

Discussion

The Cochran Q test can also be viewed as a c sample generalization of McNemar's test for significance of change in two proportions based on related samples.

It is essential to a good data analysis that the appropriate statistical procedure be applied to a specific situation. When comparing differences in c proportions based on related samples, where the responses in each of the blocks are simply binary rather than ranked or measured on some interval or ratio scale, Cochran's Q test should be selected.

Statisticians P. P. Ramsey and P. H. Ramsey investigated the minimum block sizes or sample sizes needed to apply Cochran's Q test, and biostatisticians S. Wallenstein and A. Berger studied the power properties of the test.

Conclusions

The Cochran Q test is quick and easy to perform. The only assumptions are that the outcomes for each response are binary and that either the participants providing these c binary responses are randomly selected or the blocks of homogeneous participants examining the c treatment levels are randomly selected.

When evaluating the worth of a statistical procedure, statistician John Tukey defined *practical power* as the product of statistical power and the utility of the statistical technique. Based on this, the Cochran Q test enjoys a high level of practical power under many useful circumstances.

—Mark L. Berenson

See also Repeated Measures Analysis of Variance

Further Reading

Cochran, W. G. (1950). The comparison of percentages in matched samples. *Biometrika, 37,* 256–266.

Marascuilo, L. A., & McSweeney, M. (1977). *Nonparametric and distribution-free methods for the social sciences.* Monterey, CA: Brooks/Cole.

Patil, K. D. (1975). Cochran's Q test: Exact distribution. *Journal of the American Statistical Association, 70,* 186–189.

Ramsey, P. P., & Ramsey, P. H. (1981). Minimum sample sizes for Cochran's test. Retrieved May 9, 2006, from http://www.amstat.org/sections/srms/Proceedings/papers/1981_146.pdf

Tate, M. W., & Brown, S. M. (1970). Note on Cochran's Q test. *Journal of the American Statistical Association, 65,* 155–160.

Tukey, J. W. (1959). A quick, compact two-sample test to Duckworth's specifications. *Technometrics, 1,* 31–48.

Wallenstein, S., & Berger, A. (1981). On the asymptotic power of tests for comparing k correlated proportions. *Journal of the American Statistical Association, 76,* 114–118.

COEFFICIENT ALPHA

Two criteria are usually used to assess the quality of a test: reliability and validity. There are several different types of reliability, including test-retest, interrater, alternate form, and internal consistency. These tell us how much of the variance in the test scores is due to true differences between people and how much is due to time, rater, form, and items, respectively. The first three types of reliability can be assessed by calculating a simple correlation. Test-retest reliability can be assessed by correlating total scores from two different testing times. Interrater reliability can be assessed by correlating the scores given by two different raters. Alternate form reliability can be assessed by correlating total scores from different forms of the test. Each of these correlations tells us the reliability of a single measurement: when we use one test, one rater, or one form. However, when it comes to internal consistency, we cannot simply use a correlation, because we very rarely use just a single item. To assess internal consistency, we therefore need to use a formula that tells us the reliability of the sum of several different measurements. The formula we use most often is coefficient alpha.

Other Names for Coefficient Alpha

Coefficient alpha, developed by Lee J. Cronbach in 1951, is mathematically identical to several other formulas developed to assess the reliability of total scores. These include Cyril J. Hoyt's estimate of reliability from 1941 and, if items are dichotomous, G. Frederik Kuder and M. W. Richardson's Formula 20. If all items on a test have the same variance, coefficient alpha is also equal to Kuder and Richardson's Formula 21 and the Spearman-Brown prophecy formula. Coefficient alpha is the most general of the formulas, which probably explains why it is the most commonly used version of the formula. Not surprisingly, it is also known as Cronbach's alpha.

Uses

Coefficient alpha is usually used to assess the reliability of total test scores when a test is made up of many items. It is therefore usually thought of as a measure of internal consistency. However, coefficient alpha can also be used to assess the reliability of other types of total scores. For example, if three letters of reference are solicited when evaluating applicants, coefficient alpha can be used to assess the reliability of total scores from those three letters. Alternatively, in a diary study, respondents may answer the same question every day for a month. The reliability of the total of those scores can be estimated with coefficient alpha. This formula works equally well whether the researcher calculates the sum of the measurements or the average of the measurements: The formula will result in the exact same number.

Formula

The population value of coefficient alpha is calculated as follows:

$$\alpha = \frac{k}{k-1}\left(1 - \frac{\sum_{i=1}^{k}\sigma_i^2}{\sigma_{Total}^2}\right),$$

where

k is the number of measurements,

σ_i^2 is the population variance of the ith measurement, and

σ_{Total}^2 is the population variance of total scores on the k measurements.

However, we rarely have population data. Instead, we estimate the population value of coefficient alpha from the sample data of people we actually measured in our study. The sample value of coefficient alpha is calculated by substituting sample variances for population variances, as follows:

$$\hat{\alpha} = \frac{k}{k-1}\left(1 - \frac{\sum_{i=1}^{k}s_i^2}{s_{Total}^2}\right),$$

where

k is the number of measurements,

s_i^2 is the sample variance of the ith measurement, and

s_{Total}^2 is the sample variance of total scores on the k measurements.

Example of the Hand Calculation

Consider the following example, in which four students completed three items on a test. Scores for each item appear in the columns marked *Item*.

Student	Item 1	Item 2	Item 3	Total
1	3	4	1	8
2	2	2	1	5
3	9	8	4	21
4	6	2	0	8

To calculate coefficient alpha by hand, you must first calculate the variances of each measurement and of the total scores. These are as follows.

	Item 1	Item 2	Item 3	Total
Sample variance	10	8	3	51

Now we can calculate coefficient alpha:

$$\hat{\alpha} = \frac{3}{3-1}\left(1 - \frac{10+8+3}{51}\right)$$

$$= \frac{3}{2}\left(1 - \frac{21}{51}\right) = .88.$$

Hand calculation of coefficient alpha can be quite tedious, especially if there are a large number of respondents and a large number of items. Fortunately, statistical packages like SPSS make these calculations easy.

Example of the Calculation Using SPSS

In SPSS, calculation of coefficient alpha is easy. Enter your data into the Data Editor, with one respondent per row. Then click on the Analyze menu, select Scale from the drop-down menu, and select Reliability Analysis from the side menu. This will bring you to the Reliability Analysis dialogue box. Select your measurements and move them across to the Items box. Click OK. From the same data as in the hand calculation above, Figure 1 was produced.

Reliability

Case Processing Summary

		N	%
Cases	Valid	4	100.0
	Exclude[a]	0	.0
	Total	4	100.0

a. Listwise deletion based on all variables in the procedure

Reliability Statistics

Cronbach's Alpha	N of items
.882	3

Figure 1   SPSS Output for Coefficient Alpha

The first table in Figure 1 shows that there were four respondents. The second table shows that coefficient alpha is .882 and that there were three items on the test.

Interpretation

Like other reliability coefficients, coefficient alpha tells you the proportion of total score variance that is due to true differences among respondents. It also tells you the expected correlation between total scores on your k measurements and total scores on a hypothetical set of k other measurements that were designed to measure the same construct. In 1963, Lee Cronbach, Nageswari Rajaratnam, and Goldine C. Glesser showed that coefficient alpha provides an unbiased estimate of the true reliability of a test if the test user assumes that the items were randomly sampled from a set of other items that could have been used to measure the same construct.

The most common misinterpretation of coefficient alpha is to assume that the level of internal consistency tells the test user something about the other types of reliability. Four types of reliability have been mentioned already: test-retest reliability, interrater reliability, alternate form reliability, and internal consistency reliability. It is possible for a test to have high

internal consistency but low test-retest reliability. Consider, for example, a test of mood. It is also possible for a test to have high test-retest reliability but low internal consistency. Consider, for example, a test that consists of three items: hat size, the last four digits of your phone number, and number of children. Over a two-week period, total scores on this test are likely to be very stable, but these items will have very low internal consistency. Internal consistency is easy to estimate, but it does not substitute for estimates of other types of reliability. Research on other types of reliability is still needed.

Inferential Procedures for Coefficient Alpha

Several inferential procedures for coefficient alpha have been developed. These include confidence intervals, comparisons between independent alpha coefficients, and comparisons between dependent alpha coefficients. Leonard S. Feldt, David J. Woodruff, and Fathi A. Salih wrote a summary of these procedures in 1987. Unfortunately, these inferential tests have fairly restrictive assumptions—that all measurements have equal variances and equal covariances—and Kimberly A. Barchard and A. Ralph Hakstian in two papers in 1997 showed that these procedures are not robust to violation of these assumptions. Hakstian and Barchard's initial attempts to develop a correction for violation of this assumption were only partially successful, and therefore the results of these inferential procedures should be considered tentative.

—*Kimberly A. Barchard*

See also Classical Test Theory; Reliability Theory

Further Reading

Barchard, K. A., & Hakstian, A. R. (1997). The effects of sampling model on inference with coefficient alpha. *Educational & Psychological Measurement, 57*, 893–905.

Barchard, K. A., & Hakstian, A. R. (1997). The robustness of confidence intervals for coefficient alpha under violation of the assumption of essential parallelism. *Multivariate Behavioral Research, 32*, 169–191.

Cortina, J. M. (1993). What is coefficient alpha? An examination of theory and applications. *Journal of Applied Psychology, 78*, 98–104.

Crocker, L. M., & Algina, J. (1986). *Introduction to classical and modern test theory*. New York: Holt, Rinehart & Winston.

Cronbach, L. J. (1951). Coefficient alpha and the internal structure of tests. *Psychometrika, 16*, 297–334.

Feldt, L. S., Woodruff, D. J., & Salih, F. A. (1987). Statistical inference for coefficient alpha. *Applied Psychological Measurement, 11*, 93–103.

Kuder, G. F., & Richardson, M. W. (1937). The theory of the estimation of test reliability. *Psychometrika, 2*, 151–160.

Lord, F. M. (1955). Sampling fluctuations resulting from the sampling of test items. *Psychometrika, 20*, 1–22.

Streiner, D. L. (2003). Starting at the beginning: An introduction to coefficient alpha and internal consistency. *Journal of Personality Assessment, 80*(1), 99–103.

Applying Ideas on Statistics and Measurement

The following abstract is adapted from Lopez, M. N., Lazar, M. D., & Oh, S. (2003). Psychometric properties of the Hooper Visual Organization Test. *Assessment, 10*(1), 66–70.

Coefficient alpha is one of many measures to assess the internal consistency or reliability of a test. In this study, the authors present internal consistency and interrater reliability coefficients and an item analysis using data from a sample (N = 281) of "cognitively impaired" and "cognitively intact" patients and patients with undetermined cognitive status. Coefficient alpha for the Visual Organization Test (VOT) total sample was .882. Of the 30 items, 26 were good at discriminating among patients. Also, the interrater reliabilities for three raters (.992), two raters (.988), and one rater (.977) were excellent. The authors' conclusion is that the judgmental scoring of the VOT does not interfere significantly with its clinical utility and that the VOT is a psychometrically sound test.

COEFFICIENTS OF CORRELATION, ALIENATION, AND DETERMINATION

The coefficient of correlation evaluates the similarity of two sets of measurements (i.e., two dependent variables) obtained on the same observations. The coefficient of correlation indicates the amount of information common to two variables. This coefficient takes values between −1 and +1 (inclusive).

A value of 0 indicates that the two series of measurement have nothing in common. A value of +1 says that the two series of measurements are measuring the same thing. A value of −1 says that the two measurements are measuring the same thing, but one measurement varies inversely with the other.

The squared correlation gives the proportion of common variance between two variables and is also called the *coefficient of determination*. Subtracting the coefficient of determination from the unity gives the proportion of variance not shared between two variables, a quantity also called the *coefficient of alienation*.

The coefficient of correlation measures only the *linear* relationship between two variables, and its value is very sensitive to outliers. Its significance can be tested with an *F* or a *t* test. The coefficient of correlation always overestimates the intensity of the correlation in the population and needs to be "corrected" in order to provide a better estimation. The corrected value is called "shrunken" or "adjusted."

Notations and Definition

We have S observations, and for each observation, we have two measurements, denoted W and Y, with respective means M_W and M_Y. For each observation, we define the cross product as the product of the deviations of each variable to its mean. The sum of these cross products, denoted SCP_{WY}, is computed as

$$SCP_{WY} = \sum_s^s (W_s - M_W)(Y_s - M_Y). \quad (1)$$

The sum of the cross products reflects the association between the variables. When the deviations tend to have the same sign, they indicate a positive relationship, and when they tend to have different signs, they indicate a negative relationship. The average value of the SCP_{WY} is called the covariance (*cov*), and just like the variance, the covariance can be computed by dividing by S or $(S - 1)$:

$$cov_{WY} = \frac{SCP}{\text{Number of Observations}} = \frac{SCP}{S}. \quad (2)$$

The covariance reflects the association between the variables, but it is expressed in the original units of measurement. In order to eliminate them, the covariance is normalized by division by the standard deviation of each variable (σ). This defines the coefficient of correlation, denoted $r_{W.Y}$, which is equal to

$$r_{W.Y} = \frac{cov_{WY}}{\sigma_W \sigma_Y}. \tag{3}$$

Rewriting the previous formula gives a more practical formula:

$$r_{W.Y} = \frac{SCP_{WY}}{\sqrt{SS_W SS_Y}}. \tag{4}$$

An Example: Correlation Computation

We illustrate the computation for the coefficient of correlation with the following data, describing the values of W and Y for $S = 6$ subjects:

$$W_1 = 1 \quad W_2 = 3 \quad W_3 = 4 \quad W_4 = 4 \quad W_5 = 5 \quad W_6 = 7,$$
$$Y_1 = 16 \quad Y_2 = 10 \quad Y_3 = 12 \quad Y_4 = 4 \quad Y_5 = 8 \quad Y_6 = 10.$$

Step 1: Computing the sum of the cross products
First compute the means of W and Y:

$$M_W = \frac{1}{S} \sum_{s=1}^{S} W_s = \frac{24}{6} = 4$$

and

$$M_Y = \frac{1}{S} \sum_{s=1}^{S} Y_s = \frac{60}{6} = 10.$$

The sum of the cross products is then equal to

$$SCP_{YW} = \sum_s (Y_s - M_Y)(W_s - M_W)$$

$$\begin{aligned}
&= (16 - 10)(1 - 4) + (10 - 10)(3 - 4) \\
&\quad + (12 - 10)(4 - 4) \\
&\quad + (4 - 10)(4 - 4) + (8 - 10)(5 - 4) \\
&\quad + (10 - 10)(7 - 4) \\
&= (6 \times -3) + (0 \times -1) + (2 \times 0) + (-6 \times 0) \\
&\quad + (-2 \times 1) + (0 \times 3) \\
&= -18 + 0 + 0 + 0 - 2 + 0 \\
&= -20.
\end{aligned} \tag{5}$$

The sum of squares of W_s is obtained as

$$\begin{aligned}
SS_W &= \sum_{s=1}^{S} (W_s - M_W)^2 \\
&= (1 - 4)^2 + (3 - 4)^2 + (4 - 4)^2 + (4 - 4)^2 \\
&\quad + (5 - 4)^2 + (7 - 4)^2 \\
&= (-3)^2 + (-1)^2 + 0^2 + 0^2 + 1^2 + 3^2 \\
&= 9 + 1 + 0 + 0 + 1 + 9 \\
&= 20.
\end{aligned} \tag{6}$$

The sum of squares of Y_s is

$$\begin{aligned}
SS_Y &= \sum_{s=1}^{S} (Y_s - M_Y)^2 \\
&= (16 - 10)^2 + (10 - 10)^2 + (12 - 10)^2 \\
&\quad + (4 - 10)^2 + (8 - 10)^2 + (10 - 10)^2 \\
&= 6^2 + 0^2 + 2^2 + (-6)^2 + (-2)^2 + 0^2 \\
&= 36 + 0 + 4 + 36 + 4 + 0 \\
&= 80.
\end{aligned} \tag{7}$$

Step 2: Computing $r_{W.Y}$
The coefficient of correlation between W and Y is equal to

$$\begin{aligned}
r_{W.Y} &= \frac{\sum_s (Y_s - M_Y)(W_s - M_W)}{\sqrt{SS_Y \times SS_W}} \\
&= \frac{-20}{\sqrt{80 \times 20}} = \frac{-20}{\sqrt{1600}} = \frac{-20}{40} \\
&= -.5.
\end{aligned} \tag{8}$$

We can interpret this value of $r = -.5$ as an indication of a negative linear relationship between W and Y.

Some Properties of the Coefficient of Correlation

The coefficient of correlation is a number without a unit. This occurs because of dividing the units of the numerator by the same units in the denominator. Hence, the coefficient of correlation can be used to compare outcomes across different variables. The magnitude of the coefficient of correlation is always smaller than or equal to 1. This happens because the numerator of the coefficient of correlation (see Equation 4) is always smaller than or equal to its denominator (this property follows from the Cauchy-Schwartz inequity). A coefficient of correlation equal to +1 or −1 indicates that a plot of the observations will show that they are positioned on a line.

The squared coefficient of correlation gives the *proportion of common variance* between two variables, also called the coefficient of determination. In our example, the coefficient of determination is equal to $r^2_{W.Y} = .25$. The proportion of variance not shared between the variables, or the coefficient of alienation, is, for our example, equal to $1 - r^2_{W.Y} = .75$.

Interpreting Correlation

Linear and Nonlinear Relationship

The coefficient of correlation measures only linear relationships between two variables and will miss nonlinear relationships. For example, Figure 1 displays a perfect nonlinear relationship between two variables (i.e., the data show a *U*-shaped relationship,

with *Y* being proportional to the square of *W*), but the coefficient of correlation is equal to 0.

The Effect of Outliers

Observations far from the center of the distribution contribute a lot to the sum of the cross products. At the extreme, in fact, as illustrated in Figure 2, one extremely deviant observation (often called an *outlier*) can dramatically influence the value of *r*.

Geometric Interpretation: The Coefficient of Correlation Is a Cosine

Each set of observations can also be seen as a vector in an *S* dimensional space (one dimension per observation). Within this framework, the correlation is equal to the cosine of the angle between the two vectors after they have been centered by subtracting their respective means. For example, a coefficient of correlation of *r* = −.50 corresponds to a 150-degree angle.

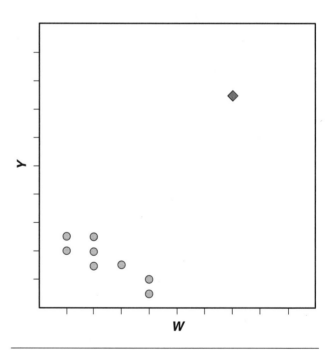

Figure 2   The Dangerous Effect of Outliers on the Value of the Coefficient of Correlation

Note: The correlation of the set of points represented by the circles is equal to −.87, but when the point represented by the diamond is added to the set, the correlation is equal to +.61. This shows that an outlier can completely determine the value of the coefficient of correlation.

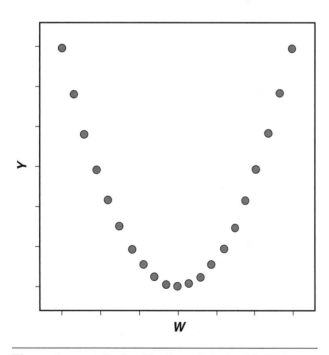

Figure 1   A Perfect Nonlinear Relationship With Coefficient of Correlation = 0

A coefficient of correlation of 0 corresponds to a right angle, and therefore two uncorrelated variables are called *orthogonal* (which is derived from the Greek word for a right angle).

Correlation and Causation

The fact that two variables are correlated does not mean that one variable causes the other one: Correlation is not causation. For example, in France, the number of Catholic churches, as well as the number of schools, in a city is highly correlated with the number of people with cirrhosis of the liver, the number of teenage pregnancies, and the number of violent deaths. Does that mean that churches and schools are sources of vice and that newborns are murderers? Here, in fact, the observed correlation is due to a third variable, namely, the size of the cities: The larger a city, the larger the number of churches, schools, alcoholics, and so on. In this example, the correlation between number of churches or schools and alcoholics is called a spurious correlation because it reflects only their mutual correlation with a third variable (i.e., size of the city).

Testing the Significance of r

A null hypothesis test for r can be performed using an F statistic obtained as follows:

$$F = \frac{r^2}{1 - r^2} \times (S - 2). \qquad (9)$$

When the null hypothesis is true (and when the normality assumption holds), this statistic is distributed as a Fisher's F with $v_1 = 1$ and $v_2 = S - 2$ degrees of freedom. An equivalent test can be performed using $t = \sqrt{F}$, which is distributed under H_0 as a Student's distribution with $v = S - 2$ degrees of freedom.

For our example, we find that

$$F = \frac{.25}{1 - .25} \times (6 - 2) = \frac{.25}{.75} \times 4$$

$$= \frac{1}{3} \times 4 = \frac{4}{3} = 1.33.$$

The probability of finding such a value under H_0 is found using an F distribution with $v_1 = 1$ and $v_2 = 3$ and is equal to $p \approx .31$ Such a value does not lead to rejecting H_0.

Estimating the Population Correlation: Shrunken and Adjusted r

The coefficient of correlation is a *descriptive* statistic that always overestimates the population correlation. This problem is similar to the problem of the estimation of the variance of a population from a sample. In order to obtain a better estimate of the population, the value r needs to be corrected. As suggested earlier, the corrected value of r goes under various names: corrected r, shrunken r, or adjusted r (there are some subtle differences between these terms, but we will ignore them here), and we denote it by $\tilde{r}^2$. Several correction formulas are available; the one used most often estimates the value of the population correlation as

$$\tilde{r}^2 = 1 - \left[(1 - r^2) \left(\frac{S - 1}{S - 2} \right) \right]. \qquad (10)$$

For our example, this gives

$$\tilde{r}^2 = 1 - \left[(1 - r^2) \left(\frac{S - 1}{S - 2} \right) \right]$$

$$= 1 - \left[(1 - .25) \times \frac{5}{4} \right]$$

$$= 1 - \left[.75 \times \frac{5}{4} \right] = 0.06.$$

With this formula, we find that the estimation of the population correlation drops from $r = .{-}50$ to
$\tilde{r} = -\sqrt{\tilde{r}^2} = -\sqrt{.06} = -.24.$

—Hervé Abdi

See also Correlation Coefficient; Multiple Correlation Coefficient; Spurious Correlation

Further Reading

Cohen, J., & Cohen, P. (1983). *Applied multiple regression/ correlation analysis for the social sciences.* Hillsdale, NJ: Erlbaum.

Darlington, R. B. (1990). *Regression and linear models.* New York: McGraw-Hill.

Pedhazur, E. J. (1997). *Multiple regression in behavioral research.* New York: Harcourt-Brace.

COGNITIVE ABILITIES TEST

The Cognitive Abilities Test (CogAT), published by Riverside Publishing (www.riverpub.com), is a group-administered test appraising developed reasoning abilities. Its 11 test levels span Kindergarten through Grade 12. CogAT is the contemporary successor to the Lorge-Thorndike Intelligence Tests. In the spring of 2000, the sixth edition of the test was conormed with the Iowa Tests of Basic Skills (Grades K–8) and the Iowa Tests of Educational Development (Grades 9–12). The standardization sample consisted of more than 180,000 students in public, Catholic, and private non-Catholic schools. When administered with either of the Iowa tests, CogAT discrepancies between observed and predicted achievement scores may be obtained for each examinee.

CogAT measures abstract reasoning abilities in the three major symbol systems used to communicate knowledge in schools: verbal, quantitative, and figural/spatial. It reports both age- and grade-normed scores for all three reasoning abilities, plus a composite score. Verbal, quantitative, and nonverbal reasoning scores are estimated by two subtests in the Primary Edition (Grades K–2) and by three subtests in the Multilevel Edition (Grades 3–12). Items in the Primary Edition are paced by the teacher and require no reading. Tests in the Multilevel Edition require some reading and are administered with time limits. Testing time for the Multilevel Edition is 90 minutes.

The test authors suggest that the most important uses of CogAT scores are (a) to guide efforts to adapt instruction to the needs and abilities of students, (b) to provide a measure of cognitive development that usefully supplements achievement test scores and teacher grades, and (c) to identify for further study those students whose predicted levels of achievement differ markedly from their observed levels of achievement. The first use is supported through several teacher guides and a Web-based system for matching the level and pattern of a student's CogAT scores to specific instructional recommendations (see www.cogat.com). Recommendations are based on recent summaries of the aptitude-by-treatment interaction literature. That literature shows that reasoning abilities in the symbol systems used to communicate new knowledge are among the most important aptitudes for success in school and thus interact with variations in instructional methods.

CogAT manuals provide considerable assistance in avoiding common mistakes when interpreting test scores. In addition to the *Research Handbook* (104 pages) and *Norms Booklet* (128 pages), there are an extensive *Interpretive Guide for Teachers and Counselors* (166 pages) and an *Interpretive Guide for School Administrators* (134 pages). *A Short Guide for Teachers* is available at no charge on the CogAT Web site (www.cogat.com). Scores on Form 6 are flagged if they appear unsound in any of nine different ways. One of the innovative features of CogAT6 is the introduction of confidence intervals for each score. The confidence intervals are based both on the conditional standard error of measurement and an estimate of fit. In this way, users are warned if the response pattern on a battery is aberrant for a particular examinee.

—*David F. Lohman*

See also Cognitive Psychometric Assessment; Kingston Standardized Cognitive Assessment

Further Reading

Corno, L., Cronbach, L. J., Lohman, D. F., Kupermintz, H., Mandinach, E. B., Porteus, A., et al. (2002). *Remaking the concept of aptitude: Extending the legacy of Richard E. Snow.* Hillsdale, NJ: Erlbaum.

Lohman, D. F. (2005). The role of non-verbal ability tests in identifying academically gifted students: An aptitude perspective. *Gifted Child Quarterly, 49,* 111–138.

Lohman, D. F. (in press). Beliefs about differences between ability and accomplishment: From folk theories to cognitive science. *Roeper Review.*

Lorge, I., & Thorndike, R. L. (1954). *The Lorge-Thorndike Intelligence Tests.* Boston: Houghton Mifflin.

CogAT recent research links: www.cogat.com, http://faculty .education.uiowa.edu/dlohman

COGNITIVE PSYCHOMETRIC ASSESSMENT

Cognitive psychometric assessment (CPA) is the assessment of psychological traits such as abilities, interests, and dispositions based on data from instruments such as questionnaires and tests that are analyzed with extensions of psychometric models. The models used for CPA are *cognitive psychometric models* (CPM) that contain discrete or continuous latent variables; their theoretical foundations are in the areas of item response theory and structural equation modeling.

Specifically, CPMs include parameters that operationalize components of mental processes or faculties whose existence can be justified through theories that draw on cognitive psychology. The parameters are provided by specialists and are typically collected in so-called Q-matrices, whose entries may be binary (i.e., indicating the absence or presence of a component) or ordinal (i.e., indicating the degree to which a component is present). In many models, such as the *Linear Logistic Test Model*, the *DINA* and *NIDA Models*, or the *Rule-Space Methodology*, these parameters are fixed whereas in some models, such as the *Reparametrized Unified Model* or *Fusion Model*, they are subject to empirical updating.

Alternatively, the structure of CPMs can reflect a specific combination of components. In this case, the number of components is provided by the specialists, and the model structure is chosen to match the way in which examinees engage in mental processes to respond to items. For example, in the *Multidimensional Rasch Model for Learning and Change*, deficiencies in one component can be compensated for by strengths in another component, which is also known as a compensatory or disjunctive model. In contrast, in the *Multidimensional Logistic Trait Model*, deficiencies in one component cannot be compensated for by strengths in another component; therefore, such a model is known as a noncompensatory or conjunctive model.

In order to conduct CPA successfully in practice, a well-developed theory about the cognitive processes underlying item responses is necessary. Experience has shown that this is much easier to accomplish for tasks that can be easily decomposed into constituent elements such as mathematical addition and subtraction but is much harder for complex reasoning and problem-solving tasks such as reading comprehension. Such a theory entails a detailed description of how the tasks that are utilized provide the kinds of empirical evidence that are needed to make the kinds of inferences that are desired. Moreover, the successful application of CPMs in practice requires that sufficiently large sample sizes be available for model calibration to achieve convergence for parameter estimation routines and to achieve reliable classifications. The process of understanding how response patterns influence the estimation of CPMs is just beginning, however, and more empirical investigation to develop practical recommendations for their use is needed.

—André A. Rupp

See also Cognitive Abilities Test; Kingston Standardized Cognitive Assessment

Further Reading

de la Torre, J., & Douglas, J. (2004). Higher order latent trait models for cognitive diagnosis. *Psychometrika, 69,* 333–353.

Embretson, S. E. (1995). A measurement model for linking individual learning to processes and knowledge: Application to mathematical reasoning. *Journal of Educational Measurement, 32,* 277–294.

Fischer, G. H. (1973). Linear logistic test model as an instrument in educational research. *Acta Psychologica, 37,* 359–374.

Hartz, S. M. (2002). *A Bayesian guide for the Unified Model for assessing cognitive abilities: Blending theory with practicality.* Unpublished doctoral dissertation, University of Illinois, Urbana-Champaign, Department of Statistics.

Junker, B., & Sijtsma, K. (2001). Cognitive assessment models with few assumptions, and connections with non-parametric item response theory. *Applied Psychological Measurement, 25,* 258–272.

Maris, E. (1995). Psychometric latent response models. *Psychometrika, 60,* 523–547.

Mislevy, R. J., Steinberg, L. S., & Almond, R. G. (2003). On the structure of educational assessments. *Measurement: Interdisciplinary Research and perspectives, 1,* 3–62.

Rupp, A. A. (2006). *The answer is in the question: A guide for describing and investigating the conceptual foundations and statistical properties of cognitive psychometric models.* Manuscript submitted for publication.

Tatsuoka, K. K. (1995). Architecture of knowledge structures and cognitive diagnosis: A statistical pattern recognition and classification approach. In P. D. Nichols, S. F. Chipman, & R. L. Brennan (Eds.), *Cognitively diagnostic assessment* (pp. 327–360). Hillsdale, NJ: Erlbaum.

COHEN'S KAPPA

Cohen's kappa statistic was developed to correct for the problem of inflated percent agreement statistics that occur when marginal values on the variables being compared are unevenly distributed. Kappa is typically used with nominal level variables and is often seen in situations in which two independent raters have the task of classifying an object as belonging to a single level of a nominal variable.

For example, consider the following data set in which two raters, Steve and Damian, are asked to read 100 school mission statements. For each mission statement, they are to make a judgment as to the dominant purpose of schooling set forth in the mission statement. Each school may have only one dominant theme, and the theme should fit into one of the following categories: (a) social, (b) cognitive, (c) civic, or (d) emotional. The results of the rater classifications are shown in Table 1, where the values are reported in terms of percentages (e.g., the value of .05 in the social box indicates that 5 out of 100 schools were classified as having a social purpose as their dominant theme).

The marginal totals indicate the percentage of ratings assigned to each category for each rater. In this example, Steve classified 61% of the 100 mission statements as belonging to the civic category, whereas Damian placed 70% of the mission statements in that category. The diagonal values of Table 1 represent ratings on which the two raters agreed exactly. Thus, the raters agreed on their assignment of 5% percent of the mission statements to the social category, 3% percent to the emotional category, 9% to the cognitive category, and 54% to the civic category. Thus, from a simple percentage agreement perspective, the two raters agreed on 71% of the ratings they assigned. The percent agreement calculation can be derived by summing the values found in the diagonals (i.e., the proportion of times that the two raters agreed). Note that the resultant value of 71% generally represents good agreement:

$$P_A = .05 + .03 + .09 + .54 = .71.$$

Yet the high percentage agreement statistic is somewhat artificially inflated given that more than half of the school mission statements were rated as having a civic theme. Consequently, a rater with no knowledge or training could actually simply assign a mission statement to the civic category when in doubt, and the raters would end up with percentage agreement statistics that look very good simply because most schools had a civic purpose as their dominant

Table 1   Example Data Matrix: Rater Classifications of 100 School Mission Statements

| | | Steve | | | | |
		Social	Emotional	Cognitive	Civic	Marginal Total
Damian	Social	.05 (.01)	0 (0)	0 (.01)	0 (.03)	.05
	Emotional	.01 (.01)	.03 (0)	0 (.01)	.01 (.03)	.05
	Cognitive	.04 (.04)	.01 (.02)	.09 (.02)	.06 (.12)	.20
	Civic	.10 (.14)	.03 (.05)	.03 (.08)	.54 (.43)	.70
	Marginal total	.20	.07	.12	.61	1.00

Note: Values in parentheses represent the expected proportions on the basis of chance associations, i.e., the joint probabilities of the marginal proportions.

theme. Unfortunately, such an artificially inflated agreement statistic deceives us into believing that the two raters are perhaps more adept at coding the statements than they actually are. The raters actually agree less than half of the time (44% to be exact) when they are assigning codes to mission statements that they rate as falling into all categories other than the civic category.

To correct for the problem of inflation and to provide a more accurate estimate of rater agreement, we can calculate Cohen's kappa. To calculate kappa, we must begin by multiplying the marginal totals in order to arrive at an expected proportion for each cell (reported in parentheses in the table). Summing the product of the marginal values in the diagonal, we find that on the basis of chance alone, we expect an observed agreement value of .46:

$$P_c = .01 + 0 + .02 + .43 = .46.$$

Kappa provides an adjustment for this chance agreement factor. Thus, for the data in Table 1, kappa would be calculated as

$$\kappa = \frac{.71 - .46}{1.0 - .46} = .46.$$

In practice, kappa may be interpreted as the proportion of agreement between raters after accounting for chance. Consequently, a kappa value of zero suggests that the two raters agreed no more frequently than we would predict on the basis of chance alone. Furthermore, kappa can actually take on negative values if the raters were to agree less frequently than we would predict by chance alone, given the marginal values. Benchmarks for interpreting kappa are suggested in Table 2.

Three major assumptions underlie the use of Cohen's kappa:

1. Each of the units of analysis is independent.

2. Categories of the nominal scale must be mutually exclusive and exhaustive.

3. Raters must not work together to arrive at their final ratings.

Table 2 Benchmarks for Interpreting Kappa

Kappa Statistic	Strength of Agreement
<0.00	Poor
0.00 0.20	Slight
0.21 0.40	Fair
0.41 0.60	Moderate
0.61 0.80	Substantial
0.81 1.00	Almost perfect

Source: From Landis & Koch, 1977 (p. 165).

Using the Computer

Cohen's kappa may be calculated in SPSS by using the crosstabs procedure. The crosstabs procedure produces the output shown in Table 3.

Table 3 SPSS Crosstabs Output Calculating Cohen's Kappa

Symmetric Measure

	Value	Asymp. Std. Error[a]	Approx. T[b]	Approx. Sig.
Measure of Agreement Kappa	.458	.076	7.392	.000
N of Valid Cases	100			

a. Not assuming the null hypothesis.

b. Using the asymptotic standard error assuming the null hypothesis.

—*Steven E. Stemler*

See also Interrater Reliability

Further Reading

Cohen, J. (1960). A coefficient of agreement for nominal scales. *Educational and Psychological Measurement, 20,* 37–46.

Cohen, J. (1968). Weighted kappa: Nominal scale agreement with provision for scale disagreement or partial credit. *Psychological Bulletin, 70,* 213–220.

Kvalseth, T. O. (1989). Note on Cohen's kappa. *Psychological Reports, 65,* 223–226.

Stemler, S. E. (2004). A comparison of consensus, consistency, and measurement approaches to estimating interrater reliability. *Practical Assessment, Research & Evaluation*, 9(4). Retrieved May 10, 2006, from http://pareonline.net/getvn.asp?v=9&n=4

Uebersax, J. (2002). *Statistical methods for rater agreement.* Retrieved August 9, 2002, from http://ourworld.compuserve.com/homepages/jsuebersax/agree.htm

---

Applying Ideas on Statistics and Measurement

The following abstract is adapted from Hall, D. G., Veltkamp, B. C., & Turkel, W. J. (2004). Children's and adults' understanding of proper namable things. *First Language, 24*(1), 5–32.

D. Geoffrey Hall and his colleagues explored 5-year-olds' and adults' beliefs about entities that receive reference by proper names. In Study 1, two tasks were used. The first was a listing task, in which participants stated what things in the world can and cannot receive proper names. The second was an explanation task, in which they explained why some things merit proper names where two independent coders reached agreement which was verified by **Cohen's kappa**. Children's lists of proper namable things were more centered than adults' on living animate entities and their surrogates (e.g., dolls and stuffed animals). Both children's and adults' lists of nonnamable things contained a predominance of artifacts. Both age groups offered similar explanations for proper namability, the most common of which pertained to the desire or need to identify objects as individuals (or to distinguish them from other objects). In Study 2, the main results of the Study 1 listing task were replicated, using a modified set of instructions. The findings establish a set of norms about the scope and coherence of children's and adults' concept of a proper namable entity, and they place constraints on an account of how children learn proper names.

COMPLETE INDEPENDENCE HYPOTHESIS

Most studies involve multiple observations on multiple variables. With k variables, there are $k(k-1)/2$ bivariate correlations among the measures. Each of the individual correlations could be evaluated for statistical significance. Additionally, a multiple correlation could be obtained by regressing each of the k variables on the remaining $k-1$ variables. Due to the large number of parameters, trying to ascertain the joint significance of the entire set of correlations is complex. A more direct approach is to evaluate the k by k symmetric correlation matrix R for complete independence. A population in which the null hypothesis of complete independence is true is characterized by a population correlation matrix $P = I$, the identity matrix, in which all correlations are equal to 0. If this null hypothesis can be rejected, it may be concluded that the variables in the data set are significantly related. Two common statistical tests for assessing complete independence are denoted L_1 and L_2. L_1 is based on Fisher's Z or $\tanh^{-1}$ transformation of r_{ij}, the bivariate correlation between variables i and j. Because $\tanh^{-1}(r) = \{\log(1 + r) - \log(1 - r)\}/2$, where log is the natural or Naperian log, has variance of $1/(N-3)$, the statistic L_1 is distributed as a chi-square with $k(k-1)/2$ degrees of freedom where k is the number of variables:

$$L_1 = (N - 3)\Sigma_{i=1}^{k} \Sigma_{j=1}^{k} \tanh^{-1}(r_{ij})^2$$
$$i < j.$$

L_2 is based on the distribution of the determinant of R, denoted |R|, which ranges between 0 and 1. Values closer to 0 indicate greater dependence among the measures, and values closer to 1 indicate greater independence. The statistic L_2 is also distributed as a chi-square with $k(k-1)/2$ degrees of freedom for k variables, where the multiplier $\rho = -(N - 1 - (2k + 5)/6)$ and N is the sample size:

$$L_2 = -\rho \log |R|.$$

L_1 and L_2 have both been subjected to Monte Carlo sampling studies to evaluate Type I error rates (i.e., incorrectly rejecting the null hypothesis when it is true). A hypothesis test is considered to be biased if the estimated Type I error rate exceeds the test size α. When N is small relative to the number of variables, L_2 does not perform well. L_2 is biased when N is less than 4 times the number of variables. Even by employing finite sample correction terms, L_2 is biased when N is less than twice the number of variables. In contrast, L_1 is an unbiased hypothesis test, even for small N.

Power comparisons between L_1 and L_2 indicate that L_1 is a more powerful test of $P = I$ than is L_2. In small samples, relative to the number of variables, L_1 should be preferred in terms of both Type I and Type II error rates.

—*John R. Reddon and James S. Ho*

See also Correlation Coefficient; Type I Error; Type II Error

Further Reading

Reddon, J. R. (1990). The rejection of the hypothesis of complete independence prior to conducting a factor analysis. *Multivariate Experimental Clinical Research, 9,* 123–129.

COMPLETION ITEMS

Educational and psychological tests are composed of test items (questions or statements requiring a response) in many formats. One common format is the completion item. In this context, completion items come in several forms with several names.

Most commonly, completion items include some form of constructed response and are frequently called constructed-response items. The item does not contain options from which a person could select a response but requires the individual to construct a response. This may be accomplished by asking a complete question or providing a statement that must be completed, as the following examples demonstrate.

Item 1: What type of reliability can be estimated from one form of a test administered on a single occasion? Answer: Coefficient alpha, split-half reliability.

Item 2: Describe one advantage of true-false items compared with multiple-choice items. Answer: Less testing time per item, easier to construct.

Item 3: To be most useful, norms should be representative, relevant, and _____. Answer: recent.

Some people distinguish between constructed-response items and completion items. Many people consider completion items to be primarily of the short-answer type. Constructed-response items, on the other hand, may also include extended response and essay items (requiring extensive responses, potentially several paragraphs long), configural response items (such as items requiring manipulation of schematic diagrams), or computation problems (commonly found in mathematics, where the individual must compute the answer).

The use of completion items, including constructed-response items, has advantages and disadvantages. Among the advantages, completion items are appropriate when the objective being measured requires a written response; they are relatively easy to construct and, when responses are short or composed of a single word, easy to score; short-answer items can assess higher-order thinking skills; and completion items allow for novel responses or solutions. Disadvantages include scoring difficulty because of the many possible correct responses, which may reduce reliability of scores; need for longer testing time, compared with multiple-choice testing, to achieve adequate reliability; low likelihood of assessing higher-order thinking skills with single-word answer formats; and because constructed-response items take more time to complete, limitation of the content that can be covered in a single test period.

Although it is possible to construct multiple-choice items to measure higher-order thinking skills, it appears that the range of cognitive skills addressed by completion items is larger than the range addressed by multiple-choice testing. Empirical evidence suggests that when written to tap the same content and cognitive skill, completion items and multiple-choice items measure the same construct; when written to tap different cognitive skills, the two formats appear to measure substantially different constructs. So it is not the format that determines what is being measured, but the nature and quality of the problem presented by the item, whatever its format.

—*Michael C. Rodriguez*

See also Essay Items; Multiple Choice Items

Further Reading

Haladyna, T. M. (1997). *Writing test items to evaluate higher order thinking.* Boston: Allyn & Bacon.

Rodriguez, M. C. (2002). Choosing an item format. In G. Tindal & T. M. Haladyna (Eds.), *Large-scale assessment programs for all students: Validity, technical adequacy, and implementation* (pp. 213–231). Mahwah, NJ: Erlbaum.

Applying Ideas on Statistics and Measurement

The following abstract is adapted from Bornstein, M. H., Hahn, C.-S., & Haynes, O. M. (2004). Specific and general language performance across early childhood: Stability and gender considerations. *First Language, 24*(3), 267–304.

Children participated in four longitudinal studies of specific and general language performance cumulatively from age 1 year and 1 month to age 6 years and 10 months. Data were drawn from age-appropriate maternal questionnaires, maternal interviews, teacher reports, **completion items**, experimenter assessments, and transcripts of children's own spontaneous speech. Language performance at each age and stability of individual differences across age in girls and boys were assessed separately and together. Across age, including the important transition from preschool to school, across multiple tests at each age, and across multiple reporters, children showed moderate to strong stability of individual differences; girls and boys alike were stable. In the second through fifth years, but not before or after, girls consistently outperformed boys in multiple specific and general measures of language.

COMPUTATIONAL STATISTICS

The term *computational statistics* has two distinct but related meanings. An older meaning is synonymous with the term *statistical computing*, or simply computations for use in statistics. The more recent meaning emphasizes the *extensive* use made of computations in statistical analysis.

Statistical Computing: Numerical Analysis for Applications in Statistics

Statistical analysis requires computing, and applications in statistics have motivated many of the advances in numerical analysis. Particularly noteworthy among the subareas of numerical analysis are numerical linear algebra, numerical optimization, and the evaluation of special functions. Regression analysis, which is one of the most common statistical methods, as well as other methods involving linear models and multivariate analysis, requires fast and accurate algorithms for linear algebra. Linear regression analysis involves analysis of a linear model of the form $y = Xb + e$, where y is a vector of observed data, X is a matrix of observed data, b is a vector of unknown constants, and e is an unobservable vector of random variables with zero mean. Estimation of the unknown b is often performed by minimizing some function of the residuals $r(b) = y - Xb$ with respect to b. Depending on the function, this problem may be a very difficult optimization problem.

Numerical Linear Algebra

A very common approach to linear regression analysis is to minimize the sum of the squares of the residuals. In this case, the optimization problem reduces to a linear problem: Solve $X^{T}Xb = X^{T}y$. (Here, the superscript T means transpose.) This problem and other similar ones in the analysis of linear models are often best solved by decomposing X into the product of an orthogonal matrix and an upper triangular matrix without ever forming $X^{T}X$. Methods for doing this have motivated much research in numerical linear algebra.

Other important applications of numerical linear algebra arise in such areas as principal components analysis, where the primary numerical method is the extraction of eigenvalues and eigenvectors.

Numerical Optimization

Many statistical methods, such as regression analysis mentioned above, are optimization problems. Some problems, such as linear least squares, can be formulated as solutions to linear systems, and then the problems fall into the domain of numerical linear algebra. Others, such as nonlinear least squares and many maximum likelihood estimation problems, do not have closed-form solutions and must be solved by iterative methods, such as Newton's method, quasi-Netwon methods, general descent methods such as Nelder-Mead, or stochastic methods such as simulated annealing.

Another class of optimization problems includes those with constraints. Restricted maximum likelihood and constrained least squares are examples of statistical methods that require constrained optimization.

Evaluation of Special Functions

Methods for evaluation of cumulative distribution functions (probabilities) and inverse cumulative distribution functions (quantiles) are important in all areas of applied statistics. Some evaluations are straightforward, such as for z scores or for p values of common distributions such as t or F, but others are much more complicated. Computations involving posterior distributions in Bayesian analyses are often particularly difficult. Most of these computations are performed using Markov chain Monte Carlo methods.

Random Number Generation

Monte Carlo methods are widely used in statistics, both in development of statistical methodology and in applications of statistical methods. Monte Carlo methods require good programs for generating random numbers, firstly from a uniform distribution and secondly from various other distributions. (Standard methods for generating random variates from any given distribution utilize transformations of random variates from a uniform distribution.)

Most random number generators are cyclic; that is, they repeat after some fixed period. If the period is long enough, this repetition is not a problem, but many of the widely used random number generators have a period of approximately 2^{31}. This is much too small for serious work in Monte Carlo simulation. There are several good generators with periods greater than 2^{100}, and this should be a minimal standard for important Monte Carlo work.

In addition to problems with the period of generators, many generators have serious deficiencies in regard to the "randomness" of their output. Testing random number generators is a difficult task because of the nature of the problem: There is no standard "answer" with which to compare the output of the generator. The ways in which a generator can produce unacceptable results are many and varied. Some generators are thought to be good until someone discovers a systematic departure from randomness, sometimes several years after the generator entered service. Anyone using Monte Carlo methods should be very careful to use random number generators with long periods and with no known departures from randomness. Likewise, statistical software developers should remain abreast of current research in the area so as to be able to provide high-quality random number generators.

Computational Statistics: Computationally Intensive Statistical Methods

Many statistical methods require extensive computations, not just because the data set is large, but because the method itself involves simulation of a statistical distribution or because the method requires multiple analyses.

Resampling and Data-Partitioning Methods

An effective approach to data analysis is to use the empirical cumulative distribution function to make inferences about the distribution of the observed data. In this approach, the underlying, unknown distribution is approximated by a discrete uniform distribution with mass points at the values of the observed data. This empirical distribution of the sample is then used to make statistical inferences about the unknown distribution of the population. This is called a *bootstrap method*. Often in a bootstrap method, the sample is resampled randomly. This approach can be useful in reducing bias of statistical procedures or for estimating variances or setting confidence intervals.

Related methods involve partitioning the sample, or analyzing subsets of the sample and then combining the results. This kind of data partitioning includes so-called *jackknife methods*, which can be used to reduce bias or to estimate variance, and *cross-validation methods*, which can be used to choose between statistical models and parameter estimates.

Statistical Inference Based on Monte Carlo Methods

Many statistical methods require simulation, either by randomly resampling the given data as mentioned above or by generating random data under the assumptions of a hypothesis to be studied. In a Monte Carlo statistical test using a given sample, multiple data sets are generated according to the null hypothesis, a test statistic is computed from each, and then the test statistic from the given sample is compared to the set of test statistics from the simulated data sets. If the observed test statistic is extreme within this set, the hypothesis is rejected.

Discovery of Structure in Data and Statistical Learning

In many cases, there is no obvious model for analysis of a given set of data. The data may have been collected for one purpose, possibly just business record-keeping, and then it may be used as a source of information about any number of new questions, some of which are not even enunciated clearly. This kind of exploratory analysis is sometimes called *data mining* or *knowledge discovery*. The main objective is to discover relationships or structure in the data that was perhaps not anticipated and then to interpret these relationships in meaningful ways.

Graphical displays from multiple perspectives are important in these exploratory analyses.

Software

Good and easy-to-use software is very important, both in statistical analysis of given data and in development of new statistical methodology.

A wide range of software is available for different purposes. Many simple analyses can be performed using a spreadsheet program, such as Excel or Lotus. Other analyses require more powerful software that provides a wider array of analyses. Software packages such as SAS, SPSS, and Minitab implement the standard statistical analyses as well as many more-specialized analyses, all in an integrated environment that provides extensive abilities for data management and for graphical display of the data.

Some specialized analyses have a limited range of applications. Often the natural data structures for these applications are different from the more standard data structures for other statistical data. For such analyses and applications, stand-alone statistical software packages are available.

For implementing new research methods and for many exploratory analyses, an integrated programming environment is useful. Software packages such as SAS/IML and S-Plus provide flexible program-control structures, as well as a large library of standard functions.

The open source movement is important in the development of statistical software. Statisticians have traditionally shared programs with one another, but now there is a large, integrated statistical software system, called R, that benefits from input from statisticians around the world. The package is freely distributed (with restrictions on redistribution), and the source code is available for anyone to inspect and modify.

—James E. Gentle

See also Data Analysis Toolpak; Eigenvalues; Markov Chain Monte Carlo Methods; Monte Carlo Methods

Further Reading

Gentle, J. E. (2002). *Elements of computational statistics*. New York: Springer.

Gentle, J. E., Härdle, W., & Mori, Y. (Eds.). (2004). *Handbook of computational statistics: Concepts and methods*. New York: Springer.

Lange, K. (1999). *Numerical analysis for statisticians*. New York: Springer.

Thisted, R. A. (1988). *Elements of statistical computing*. New York: Chapman & Hall.

COMPUTERIZED ADAPTIVE TESTING

Computerized adaptive testing (CAT) is a method of administering tests that adapts to the examinee's trait level. A CAT test differs profoundly from a paper-and-pencil test. In the former, different examinees are tested with different sets of items. In the latter, all examinees are tested with an identical set of items. The major goal of CAT is to fit each examinee's trait level precisely by selecting test items sequentially from an item pool according to the current performance of an examinee. In other words, the test is tailored to each examinee's θ level, so that able examinees can avoid responding to too many easy items, and less able examinees can avoid being exposed to too many difficult items. The major advantage of CAT is that it provides more-efficient latent trait estimates (θ) with fewer items than would be required in conventional tests.

The earliest large-scale application of CAT is the computerized version of the Armed Services Vocational Aptitude Battery (ASVAB), now administered to more than half a million applicants each year. The paper-and-pencil version of the ASVAB takes 3 hours to complete, and the CAT version takes about 90 minutes. With the CAT version, an examinee's qualifying scores can be matched immediately with requirements for all available positions. CAT has become a popular mode of assessment in the United States. In addition to the ASVAB, examples of large-scale CATs include the Graduate Record Examinations (GRE), the Graduate Management Admission Test, and the National Council of State Boards of Nursing. The implementation of CAT has led to many advantages, such as new question formats, new types of skills that can be measured, easier and faster data analysis, and faster score reporting. Today the CAT GRE is administered year-round, which allows examinees to choose their own date and time for taking it, whereas the paper-and-pencil version is administered only 3 times per year.

Item Selection in CAT

The most important ingredient in CAT is the item selection procedure, which selects items during the course of the test. According to M. F. Lord, an examinee is measured most effectively when test items are neither too difficult nor too easy. Heuristically, if the examinee answers an item correctly, the next item selected should be more difficult; if the answer is

incorrect, the next item should be easier. Because different examinees receive different tests, in order to equate scores across different sets of items, it is necessary to use a convenient probability model for item responses, and this can be achieved by item response theory (IRT). According to IRT modeling, a difficult item will have large b-value, and an easy item will have small b-value. Knowing the difficulty levels of all the items in the pool, one can possibly develop an item selection algorithm based on branching. For instance, if an examinee answers an item incorrectly, the next item to be selected should have a lower b-value; if the examinee answers correctly, the next item should have a higher b-value.

In 1970, Lord proposed an item selection algorithm as an extension of the Robbins-Monro process, which has been widely used in many other areas, including engineering control and biomedical science. The Robbins-Monro process has been proved a method in minimizing the number of animals required to estimate the acute toxicity of a chemical. In order to use the method in CAT, item difficulty levels for all the items in the item pool must be calibrated before testing. Let $b_1, b_2, \ldots, b_n$ be a sequence of the difficulty parameters after administering n items to the examinee. The new items should be selected such that b_n approaches a constant b_0 (as n are indefinitely large), where b_0 represents the difficulty level of an item that the examinee has about a 50% chance of answering correctly, or $P\{X_n = 1 \mid \theta = b_0\} \approx 1/2$. Because our goal is to estimate θ, knowing b_0, we can use b_0 as a reasonable guess for θ. Notice that b_0 can be linearly transformed to any meaningful score scale, which makes it convenient for us to score the examinee's test responses by a function of b_0. Lord, writing in 1970, proposed several rules based on the Robbins-Monro process and envisioned that such testing could be implemented when computers became sufficiently powerful. A specific example of the item selection rule can be described by the following equation:

$$b_{n+1} = b_n + \frac{d_1}{n}(x_n - 0.5),$$

where x_n is the item response on the nth item ($x_n = 1$ if the answer is correct, $x_n = 0$ if the answer is incorrect), and d_1 is a positive number chosen before the testing. Clearly, the motivation for the adaptive design is to tailor the difficulty levels of the items administered to the latent trait of the examinee being tested.

In 1980, Lord proposed the maximum information (MI) approach, which has become a standard item selection procedure. Let $\hat{\theta}_n$ be an estimator of θ based on n responses. The MI method selects the item with the maximum Fisher item information evaluated at $\hat{\theta}_n$ as the next item. Under IRT, maximizing Fisher information means intuitively matching item difficulty parameter values with the latent trait level of an examinee. In addition, items with high discrimination, or equivalently, high a-parameter value, will be preferentially selected by the algorithm. Maximizing the Fisher information will lead to minimizing the sample variance of $\hat{\theta}_n$, and that makes $\hat{\theta}_n$ the most efficient. For this reason, the MI method has become the most popular item selection method. Though CAT was originally developed in educational assessments, it should be effective in many other areas, such as cognitive diagnosis and quality of life assessment.

Nonstatistical Constraints in CAT Design

In order to design an operational CAT test, the set of items selected for each examinee must satisfy certain nonstatistical constraints, such as item exposure control and content balance. The more constraints one has to impose, the fewer degrees of freedom one can include in a design. To design a good CAT algorithm, many complex controls are needed.

The item exposure rate for each item is defined as the ratio of the number of times the item is administered to the total number of examinees. Since CAT is designed to select the best items for each examinee, certain types of items tend to be always selected by the computers, and many items are not selected at all, thereby making item exposure rates quite uneven. Because CAT tests are usually administered to small groups of examinees at frequent time intervals, examinees who take tests earlier may share information with those who will take tests later,

escalating the risk that many items may become known. Therefore, item exposure rates must be controlled. A number of methods have been developed to control item exposure rate. The most common method of controlling exposure rate was developed by Sympson and Hetter, whose general idea is to put a "filter" between selection and administration such that an item that is selected by the MI criterion is evaluated to determine whether it will be administered. In this way, the exposure rate can be kept within a certain prescribed value. The Sympson and Hetter approach suppresses the use of the most over-exposed items, usually items with high a-parameters, and spreads their use over the next tier of over-exposed items. Chang and Ying proposed the a-stratified method with the objective of limiting the exposure of any given item by using that item at the most advantageous point in testing. It attempts to control item exposure by using less-discriminating items early in the test, when θ estimation is least precise, and saving highly discriminating items until later stages, when finer gradations of θ estimation are required. One of the advantages of the a-stratified method is that it tends to equalize the item exposure rates for all the items in the pool.

Methods have been developed to handle various types of content-balancing constraints. In particular, linear programming (LP) has been used to handle flexible content balancing, which selects items using LP based on numerous simultaneous constraints involving statistical and content considerations. One constraint is to maximize item information. Other constraints can be mathematical representations of the test specifications or a model to control for item overlap. A weighted deviations model has been proposed that includes LP as one component and also incorporates some heuristic steps when LP's solution may not be suitable. Actually, both the weighted deviations model and LP methods are capable of dealing with multiple constraints, among them content balancing constraints, exposure control, statistical optimization, and others. They are in general very powerful, with relatively more intensive computation than other methods. Recently, such content balancing constraints as item pool stratification have been proposed, and this method has been generalized for flexible content balancing.

Issues to Be Addressed

Although CAT has many advantages, issues regarding large-scale applications need to be addressed. One of them is the compatibility between CAT and paper-and-pencil tests. It has been speculated that some examinees may get much lower scores on a CAT test than they would on a paper-and-pencil version. As evidence of this, the Educational Testing Service (ETS) found that the GRE CAT system did not produce reliable scores for a few thousand examinees in 2000. ETS offered them a chance to retake the test at no charge. Another vital issue is test security and large-scale item theft. In August 2002, ETS suspended the CAT GRE and reintroduced paper-and-pencil-based versions in China, Hong Kong, Taiwan, and Korea (www.ets.org, August 20, 2002) following an investigation that uncovered a number of Web sites offering questions from live versions of the CAT GRE. Another issue is item pool usage. An examination of item usage within the GRE CAT pools found that as few as 12% of the available items can account for as many as 50% of the items actually administered. Without effective remedial measures, this state of affairs could significantly undermine the future of CAT.

In response to the problems that emerged from the initial large-scale applications, researchers proposed corrective procedures. They focused principally on refinement of item selection methods and also on how to assess the severity of organized item theft activities. The underestimation-of-performance problem of the GRE is very likely caused by the item selection strategy, which heavily relies on the items with the highest discrimination at the beginning of the test. A reasonable solution is to use a weighting mechanism to estimate the weights of the likelihood function during the early-stage estimation. To stabilize the initial estimation of the examinee's latent trait, items with low discrimination, instead of those with high discrimination, may be used at the beginning of the test.

To improve test security, several theorems have been derived on the basis of the hypergeometric distribution family for addressing questions such as "in order to compromise 200 items from a given item pool, how many thieves, at the most, would need to take the test?" The results may shed light on the relationship between optimal item pool size and test security.

It is important to be aware that test security can be enhanced by evenly using all the items in a pool. A computer using the constrained MI item selection method will not select many items in the pool, so the actual pool size becomes much smaller than the original pool, which makes item theft much easier. On the other hand, if the computer algorithm selects only high-a items, we may have to force item writers to generate only high-a items. Item writers may control such characteristics as item content and item difficulty level, but it is extremely challenging to produce only highly discriminating items. The common practice for generating more relatively high-a items is to discard items whose a-parameter values are lower than a given threshold. Once items are included in the pool, they have already undergone rigorous review processes and shown no problems. Items with relatively lower discrimination parameters are still of good quality and should be used. Obviously, test security can be greatly enhanced by increasing the use of lower-a items.

This research indicates that structuring an operational CAT exam with only several hundred items should be considered a design flaw. A high-stakes CAT exam must have a large item pool. This can be accomplished partly by including many items that have never been selected by the current item selection algorithms. Therefore, test security can be significantly improved by increasing the pool size and by evenly selecting all the items in the pool. If the item pool is sufficiently large, an examinee who has studied compromised items has relatively little advantage. But if the pool is small, the advantage can be huge.

Despite its limitations, CAT undoubtedly has a great future because cutting-edge developments in technology will enable us to solve the problems encountered in current large-scale applications.

—*Hua-Hua Chang and Zhiliang Ying*

See also Armed Services Vocational Aptitude Battery; Graduate Record Examinations

Further Reading

Chang, H., & Ying, Z. (1999). a-Stratified computerized adaptive testing. *Applied Psychological Measurement, 23,* 211–222.

Chang, H., & Zhang, J. (2002). Hypergeometric family and item overlap rates in computerized adaptive testing. *Psychometrika, 67,* 387–398.

Lord, M. F. (1970). Some test theory for tailored testing. In W. H. Holzman (Ed.), *Computer assisted instruction, testing, and guidance* (pp. 139–183). New York: Harper & Row.

Lord, M. F. (1980). *Applications of item response theory to practical testing problems.* Hillsdale, NJ: Erlbaum.

Robbins, H., & Monro, S. (1951). A stochastic approximation method. *Annals of Mathematical Statistics, 22,* 400–407.

Van der Linden, W. J., & Reese, L. M. (1998). A model for optimal constrained adaptive testing. *Applied Psychological Measurement, 22,* 259–270.

Yi, Q., & Chang, H. (2003). a-Stratified CAT design with content blocking. *British Journal of Mathematical and Statistical Psychology, 56,* 359–378.

COMREY, ANDREW L. (1923–)

Andrew L. Comrey was born in Charleston, West Virginia, on April 14, 1923. His childhood was marred by the Great Depression of the 1930s; however, he was a brilliant student and entered Union College with a full scholarship. While he was at Union College, his psychology teacher, Ernest M. Ligon, introduced him to psychological testing. Comrey worked in Ligon's laboratory giving Stanford-Binet IQ tests to young people in the Character Research Project. During this time, he read Louis Thurstone's *Vectors of Mind* and planned to attend the University of Chicago to study with Thurstone. However, World War II changed his plans. Andrew completed his BS degree in science and entered the U.S. Navy. During his service, he met and married Barbara Sherman, who was also serving in the military. They have two daughters, Cynthia and Corinne.

After the war, Comrey attended the University of Southern California. He studied measurement, psychometrics, and statistics with J. P. Guilford and earned his PhD in 1949. His dissertation on fundamental measurement included a treatise on a method of absolute ratio scaling. This method, published in *Psychometrika*, was among the most cited studies on scaling at that time.

Comrey's first academic appointment was at the University of Illinois. In 1951, he accepted a faculty position at the University of California, Los Angeles (UCLA). He has been at UCLA since 1951. During his time at UCLA, he was a Fulbright Research Fellow and held a National Science Foundation senior postdoctoral research fellowship. He has served as president of the Society for Multivariate Experimental Psychology. His major research contributions included the development of his own complete system of factor analysis. He invented the minimum residual method of factor extraction and the tandem criteria of rotation.

The minimum residual method of factor extraction is a controversial method that avoided the problem associated with communality estimates. The tandem criteria involved a two-phase procedure to obtain a simple structure solution. The first of the two criteria is very useful in finding general factors.

Comrey was the first researcher to write a fully integrated computer program that would process raw data through correlations, factor extraction, and rotation. He later used this process to develop the Comrey Personality Scales (CPS). The CPS was the result of his research on the Minnesota Multiphasic Personality Inventory and other personality tests. During the development of the CPS, he created the factored homogeneous item dimension as a basic unit of analysis in factor analysis.

Comrey has published more than 150 articles, chapters, and books. His textbook *A First Course in Factor Analysis* remains a popular and highly regarded work. It has been translated into Japanese and Italian.

—*Howard B. Lee*

Further Reading

Comrey, A. L. (1976). Mental testing and the logic of measurement. In W. L. Barnette (Ed.), *Readings in psychological tests and measurement.* Baltimore: Williams & Wilkins.

Comrey, A. L., & Lee, H. B. (1992). *A first course in factor analysis* (2nd ed.). Hillsdale, NJ: Erlbaum.

Andrew L. Comrey: http://www.today.ucla.edu/2002/020312 comrey.html

COMREY PERSONALITY SCALES

The Comrey Personality Scales (CPS), developed by factor analysis, is a personality inventory of 180 multiple-choice items. Each item uses one of two possible 7-choice answer scales. Scale X has the following possible answers: 7 (*always*), 6 (*very frequently*), 5 (*frequently*), 4 (*occasionally*), 3 (*rarely*), 2 (*very rarely*), and 1 (*never*). Scale Y has the following possible answers: 7 (*definitely*), 6 (*very probably*), 5 (*probably*), 4 (*possibly*), 3 (*probably not*), 2 (*very probably not*), and 1 (*definitely not*). A sample item using the X scale is "I love to work long hours." The CPS is published by the Educational and Industrial Testing Service (www.edits.net).

The CPS measures eight major factors of personality that were identified through a unique set of factor analytic methods and procedures. First, a collection of factored homogeneous item dimensions (FHIDs) was developed by culling ideas for important personality variables from many existing personality inventories and other sources. Then, each personality concept was defined in clear terms. Next, multiple-choice items were written that were deemed possible measures of each construct. Seven-choice items were chosen because seven proved to be optimal for giving good item response distributions and reliable items while not demanding too much from a respondent. Each FHID consisted of two items that were positively stated and two items that were negatively stated with respect to the construct dimension. This process was carried out for a large number of potentially useful constructs.

Next, item factor analyses were conducted in which the variables were items from six or more possibly useful constructs. If a factor was identified by the items measuring a given hypothesized construct, and no other, the items identifying that factor were

considered an FHID and a way of measuring that dimension. Many factor analyses were conducted, and items and dimensions were refined, culled, discarded, and replaced until a substantial number of FHIDs were selected. In these analyses, great care was exercised to make sure that each FHID was conceptually distinct from each other FHID in the analysis.

The number of factors that emerged in analyses of conceptually distinct FHIDs was found to be strictly limited. In fact, the author's extensive empirical investigations succeeded in turning up only eight major factors. These eight factors constitute the personality taxonomy on which the CPS is based. They are as follows: trust versus defensiveness (T), orderliness versus lack of compulsion (O), social conformity versus rebelliousness (C), activity versus lack of energy (A), emotional stability versus neuroticism (S), extraversion versus introversion (E), mental toughness versus sensitivity (M), and empathy versus egocentrism (P). Each of these major personality factors has been identified in previous studies under one name or another. CPS is unique because of the particular combination of factors that makes up its taxonomy and because each factor has been identified by a compelling rationale.

The CPS taxonomy has been validated with various kinds of samples in many different cultural settings. Factorial validity has been extensively documented for the eight CPS factors. These factors have been shown to be useful for predicting outcomes with respect to a number of different practical criteria. The clinical significance of CPS scores, particularly extreme scores, high and low, has been well documented. Brief descriptions and summaries of relevant published articles are given in the *Manual and Handbook of Interpretations* referenced below. A description of the factor analytic procedures used in developing the CPS is given in *A First Course in Factor Analysis*.

—Andrew L. Comrey

See also Minnesota Multiphasic Personality Inventory; NEO Personality Inventory; Personality Tests

Further Reading

Comrey, A. L. (1970). *Manual for the Comrey Personality Scales.* San Diego, CA: Educational and Industrial Testing Service.

Comrey, A. L. (1995). *Manual and handbook of interpretations for the Comrey Personality Scales.* San Diego, CA: EDITS Publishers.

Comrey, A. L., & Lee, H. B. (1992). *A first course in factor analysis* (2nd ed.). Hillsdale, NJ: Erlbaum.

Conditional Probability

Conditional probability is a mathematical description of the likelihood that a particular event will take place given the occurrence of a particular precursor event. Thus the probability of occurrence of event A is *conditional* on the probability of the prior occurrence of event B. Conditional probability is expressed as P (A\B), which is read as "the probability of A given B." In order to calculate the conditional probability of an event, there must be a priori knowledge of both the probability that the first of the events will occur and the probability that both events will occur together. The basic probabilities of the events involved can be expressed by a Venn diagram, as shown in Figure 1.

In Figure 1, the expressions used are defined as follows:

P (A) is the probability of event A occurring alone

P (B) is the probability of event B occurring alone

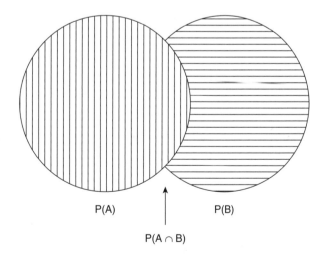

Figure 1   Venn Diagram Illustrating the Probabilities of Event A, Event B, and Events A and B Together

P (A∩B) is the probability of both events A and B occurring together, or the joint probability (∩ is the mathematical symbol used to represent the intersection of two sets)

The conditional probability of an event can be calculated by dividing the probability of the occurrence of the first event into the joint probability. The mathematical formula for this calculation is

$$P(A \backslash B) = \frac{P(A \cap B)}{P(B)} \text{ or, similarly,}$$

$$P(B \backslash A) = \frac{P(A \cap B)}{P(A)}.$$

It follows that the probability of occurrence of the primary event (the denominator of the equation) cannot be equal to zero. Without this condition, the equation would be mathematically impossible, as well as illogical (one cannot estimate the probability of a particular outcome without the occurrence of the outcome's predecessor).

Conditional probability can be applied to many situations in a variety of fields. For example, it could be used to determine a person's chance of developing a particular disease given the disease's presence or absence in the person's familial background or the probability of a person using the word *cabbage* in a sentence, given that the word directly preceding it was *eggplant*. For gamblers, conditional probability could be used to compare the odds of winning a game; the chances of having a winning poker hand in five-card draw are significantly greater if a player is dealt three queens than if the player gets a pair of twos. In everyday life, your chances of being mugged in a city might be dependent on how often you walk alone at night, or your chances of heartburn might be conditional on your eating spicy foods.

As an example, suppose there is a 3% chance that a girl in a senior high school class is both a cheerleader and class president. Additionally, suppose that the chance of a girl in the senior class being a cheerleader is 8%. What are the chances of a girl being elected senior class president given that she is a cheerleader?

$$P(A\backslash B) = \frac{P(A \cap B)}{P(B)}$$

$$P(A\backslash B) = \frac{.03}{.08} = .375 = 38\%$$

There is a 38% chance that a girl will be elected president of her senior class given that she is a cheerleader.

—*Allison B. Kaufman*

Further Reading

Glass, G. V., & Hopkins, K. D. (1995). *Statistical methods in education and psychology*. Boston: Allyn & Bacon.

Hays, W. L. (1994). *Statistics*. Belmont, CA: Wadsworth.

Conditional probability: http://en.wikipedia.org/wiki/Conditional_probability

---

CONFIDENCE INTERVALS

Confidence intervals (CIs) are common tools of inference, measuring how sure we are of our results. Confidence intervals do the following:

- Across studies, they tell us how accurately and consistently data operate over time.
- They invoke two primary concepts, intervals and confidence levels:
  Intervals are determined by the standard errors of statistics.
  Levels are chosen by the researcher and are given as percentages.

Simply put, a 95% confidence level says the method used by the researcher gives an interval that covers the true population parameter for 95% of the samples. For example, by calculating a confidence interval for your cholesterol level taken 20 times ($n = 20$), you can state how confident you are that the CI accurately contains your true cholesterol level. A range null hypothesis, say 160–200, is tested rather than a point null hypothesis (e.g., 180).

There exists a seesaw relationship between confidence levels and CIs: the higher the confidence level, the wider the interval or the larger the margin of error. The lower the confidence level, the narrower the interval or the smaller the margin of error. For the CI for the mean, the standard deviation also affects the margin of error, and there is more variance in the population if the interval is wider, as shown in Figures 1a and 1b. Figure 1c suggests that to make the margin of error smaller, the researcher must collect more data, which shrinks the margin of error because of the formula

$$\bar{X} \pm z^* \left(\frac{\sigma}{\sqrt{n}} \right),$$

where z^* is a z score related to the p value and is a measure of distance from the mean measured in standard deviations. The z^* for .05 is 1.96, equaling a 95% confidence level; z^* for .01 is 2.576, equaling a 99% confidence level.

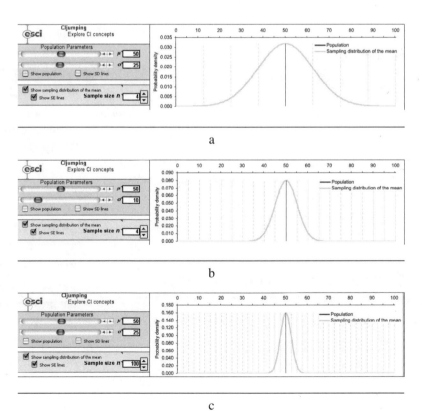

a

b

c

Figure 1   Effect of Changing Confidence Intervals

CIs should be used when reporting results for the following reasons:

- Graphical display of CI lends itself to enhanced understanding by readers.
- CIs are fairly easily obtained using common packages such as SPSS or the Exploratory Software for Confidence Intervals software developed by Cumming and Finch.
- CIs are helpful in compiling studies supporting meta-analytic thinking.

The American Psychological Association (APA) Task Force suggested that CIs should always be reported, and the APA *Publication Manual* said CIs were "the best" reporting device. One advantage of thoughtful use of CIs is that they provide a *graphical* tool to integrate or synthesize results across studies, thereby enhancing replicability. Researchers should present effect sizes as CIs because CIs contain much more information than significance tests.

—Mary Margaret Capraro

See also Hypothesis Testing; Significance Level

Further Reading

Cumming, G., & Finch, S. (2001). A primer on the understanding, use and calculation of confidence intervals that are based on central and noncentral distributions. *Educational and Psychological Measurement, 61*, 532–575.

Confidence intervals, Rice Virtual Lab in Statistics page: http://davidmlane.com/hyperstat/confidence_intervals.html
Exploratory Software for Confidence Intervals: http://www.latrobe.edu.au/psy/esci/

CONSTRUCT VALIDITY

Validity refers to the degree that a test measures what it purports to measure. In terms of classical measurement theory, it is inappropriate to refer to the validity of a test. Instead, the *use* of the test is validated for a specific measurement purpose.

Instrument reliability, the consistency with which a test measures whatever it measures, is a necessary but insufficient condition in determining whether a test is valid for a specific use. A test may be reliable but not valid for a particular purpose. However, a test that is not reliable cannot be valid for any meaningful measurement purpose.

In 1986, Crocker and Algina defined a construct as "informed scientific imagination." A construct is a fiction that is used to explain reality. For example, intelligence, reading readiness, and self-determination are constructs used to study and communicate inferable educational and psychological phenomena.

There are a variety of ways to collect evidence of the validity of a test to measure a construct. Frequently, test publishers rely on the Pearson product-moment correlation as evidence of construct validity. A random sample of examinees may be given two different intelligence tests. The presence of a high correlation of a newly constructed intelligence test with an established intelligence test is cited as evidence of construct validity. However, this technique is no stronger than the external evidence that supports the established intelligence test as a measure of intelligence, which is oftentimes historically problematic.

Another technique is to postulate differential effects among groups. An experimental design is carried out on a known intervention to determine whether the outcome is aligned with the a priori differentiation. This method is also problematic for a variety of reasons, such as limitations on the reliability of the data-gathering instruments and the unexpected failure of the intervention.

An enigmatic method that is nevertheless frequently used is factor analysis. In exploratory factor analysis, a reduced set of underlying variables is discovered that purports to account for the variation of the test items. This reduced set is known as the factor solution, which constitutes the construct being measured. Nevertheless, a plethora of choices make this approach untenable. They include the choice of eigenvalue minimum to extract (e.g., 1.0), a priori number of factors to extract, method of extraction (e.g., principal components, principal axis, maximum likelihood), and rotation method (e. g., varimax, equamax).

Confirmatory factor analysis, and structural equation modeling in general, presents an improvement on exploratory factor analysis in that the former provides a method for testing a theoretic measurement model and the goodness of fit of the data to

Table 1   Multitrait-Multimethod Matrix Data

	Trait:	Method 1			Method 2			Method 3		
		A	*B*	*C*	*A*	*B*	*C*	*A*	*B*	*C*
Method 1										
A		(.95)								
B		*.28*	(.86)							
C		*.58*	*.39*	(.92)						
Method 2										
A		<u>.86</u>	.32	.57	(.95)					
B		.30	<u>.90</u>	.40	*.39*	(.76)				
C		.52	.31	<u>.86</u>	*.55*	*.26*	(.84)			
Method 3										
A		<u>.74</u>	.10	.43	<u>.64</u>	.17	.37	(.48)		
B		.10	<u>.63</u>	.17	.22	<u>.67</u>	.19	*.15*	(.41)	
C		.35	.16	<u>.52</u>	.31	.17	<u>.56</u>	*.41*	*.30*	(.58)

Source: Adapted from Mosher, 1968.

Note: Correlations in parentheses are reliability coefficients, bold italics indicate validity coefficients, underscore indicates heterotrait monomethod coefficients, and regular type indicates heterotrait heteromethod coefficients.

that model. Despite its promise, however, Pedhazur and Schmelkin noted the "large and potentially bewildering number of models" (p. 670) that arise in confirmatory factor analysis, in addition to the many and stringent underlying assumptions that must be met.

In 1959, Campbell and Fiske provided a rigorous design for determining construct validity called the multitrait-multimethod matrix. The construct is partialed into constituent traits, which are then measured in a variety of ways. In 1995, for example, Field, Hoffman, & Sawilowsky defined the construct *self-determination* for students as consisting of the constituent traits of (1) knowing yourself, (2) valuing yourself, (3) being able to plan, (4) being able to act, and (5) being able to learn from outcomes. A battery of five instruments was developed to measure these traits via differing methodologies: (1) assessment of knowledge or skills, (2) behavioral observation checklist, (3) assessment of affect and belief, (4) teacher perception, and (5) parent perception.

The multitrait-multimethod matrix consists of four levels of data. They are, hierarchically from the highest to the lowest, reliability coefficients (usually placed in parentheses), validity coefficients (in bold italics), heterotrait monomethod coefficients (underscored), and heterotrait heteromethod coefficients. As an illustration, consider the multitrait-multimethod matrix data in Table 1.

Since the multitrait-multimethod matrix was developed in 1959, there have been many unsuccessful attempts to determine the appropriate method of statistical analysis for the data in the matrix. The reason for the lack of success is that the data in the diagonals and triangles often conflict. These methods are based on heuristic argument, analysis of variance models, nonparametric analogs to the analysis of variance models, and confirmatory factor analysis.

Campbell and Fiske stated that evidence of construct validity requires the data for the coefficients at the top level (i.e., reliability) to be as high as possible and somewhat higher than those at the second level (validity), which in turn should be higher than those on the third level (heterotrait monomethod), and so forth.

A quick, distribution-free method with easily remembered critical values was provided for this analysis by Sawilowsky in 2002:

Table 2   Obtaining Minimum, Median, and Maximum
            Values for the I Test for Construct Validity

Reliability coefficients
Original data:
.95, .86, .92, .95, .76, .84, .48, .41, .58
Ranked data:
.41, .48, .58, .76, .84, .86, .92, .95, .95
Minimum, median, maximum
.41, .84, .95

Validity coefficients
Original data:
.86, .90, .86, .64, .67, .56
Ranked data:
.56, .64, .67, .86, .86, .90
Minimum, median, maximum
.56, .765, .90

Heterotrait monomethod coefficients
Original data:
.28, .58, .39, .39, .55, .26, .15, .41, .30
Ranked data:
.15, .26, .28, .30, .39, .39, .41, .55, .58
Minimum, median, maximum:
.15, .39, .58

Heterotrait heteromethod coefficients
Original data:
.32, .57, .30, .40, .52, .31, .10, .43,
    .10, .17, .35, .16, .17, .37, .22, .19, .31, .17
Ranked data:
.10, .10, .16, .17, .17, .17, .19, .22, .30, .31, .31,
    .32, .35, .37, .40, .43, .52, .57
Minimum, median, maximum:
.10, .305, .57

Note: I = number of inversions.

Table 3   Test for Trend (Construct Validity)

Level	Minimum Value	I	Median Value	I	Maximum Value	I
Reliability	.41	0	.84	0	.95	0
Validity	.56	1	.765	0	.90	2
H-M	.15	0	.39	0	.58	3
H-H	.10	0	.305	1	.57	3

Notes: Total Inversions = 10. Probability [I$\leq$ = 10] = 0.00796807.
H-M = heterotrait monomethod, H-H = heterotrait heteromethod.

$$I = \sum_{i=1}^{k}\sum_{j=1}^{N-k}(x_i > x_{j+3}) + \sum_{i=4}^{2k}\sum_{j=4}^{N-k}(x_i > x_{j+3})$$

$$+ \sum_{i=7}^{3k}\sum_{j=7}^{N-k}(x_i > x_{j+3})$$

$$\begin{cases} 1 \ if \ (x_i > x_{j+3}) \\ 0 \ if \ (x_i \leq x_{j+3}) \end{cases}.$$

The null hypothesis is that the coefficients in the matrix are unordered. This is tested against the alternative hypothesis of an increasing trend from the lowest level (heterotrait heteromethod) to the highest level (reliability coefficients).

The test statistic, I, is the number of inversions (also known as U statistics). Consider the coefficients in Table 1. The data are ranked. Next, the minimum, median, and maximum values are determined, as indicated in Table 2. Then, count the number of inversions, beginning with the minimum value of the lowest level of the heterotrait heteromethod coefficients, as indicated in Table 3. For example, there are no inversions from the initial value of .10. The second value, .305, has one inversion (.15, which is the minimum value on the heterotrait monomethod level). The third value, .57, has three inversions (.15, .39, and .56).

In this example, I = 10. The critical values for $\alpha = 0.05$ and 0.01 are 10 and 14, respectively. Thus, in this example, the null hypothesis that the values are unordered is rejected in favor of the alternative hypothesis of an upward trend. This constitutes evidence of construct validity. A complete table of critical values, and the associated *p* values, may be found in Sawilowsky (2002).

—*Shlomo S. Sawilowsky*

See also Content Validity; Criterion Validity; Face Validity; Predictive Validity; Reliability Theory; Validity Theory

Further Reading

Field, S., Hoffman, A., & Sawilowsky, S. (1995). *Self-Determination Knowledge Scale, Form A and Form B.* Austin, TX: Pro-Ed.

Mosher, D. L. (1968). Measurement of guilt by self-report inventories. *Journal of Consulting and Clinical Psychology, 32,* 690–695.

Pedhazur, E. J., & Schmelkin, L. P. (1991). *Measurement, design, and analysis: An integrated approach.* Hillsdale, NJ: Erlbaum.

Sawilowsky, S. (2000). Psychometrics versus datametrics. *Educational and Psychological Measurement, 60,* 157–173.

Sawilowsky, S. (2000). Reliability. *Educational and Psychological Measurement, 60,* 196–200.

Sawilowsky, S. (2002). A quick distribution-free test for trend that contributes evidence of construct validity. *Measurement and Evaluation in Counseling and Development, 35,* 78–88.

CONTENT VALIDITY

In educational and psychological testing, the term *validity* refers to "the degree to which evidence and theory support the interpretations of test scores entailed by proposed uses of tests" (American Educational Research Association, 1999, p. 9). From this definition, it can be deduced that (a) tests can be evaluated only with respect to one or more specific testing purposes, (b) validation involves confirming the inferences derived from test scores, not confirming the test itself, and (c) evaluating inferences derived from test scores involves gathering and analyzing several different types of evidence. In many cases, the evidence most critical to evaluating the usefulness and appropriateness of a test for a specific purpose is based on *content validity.*

Content validity refers to the degree to which a test appropriately represents the content domain it is intended to measure. When a test is judged to have high content validity, its content is considered to be congruent with the testing purpose and with prevailing notions of the subject matter tested. For many testing purposes, such as determining whether students have mastered specific course material or determining whether licensure candidates have sufficient knowledge of the relevant profession, evidence of content validity provides the most compelling argument that the test scores are appropriate for inferring conclusions about examinees' knowledge, skills, and abilities. For this reason, content validity evidence is critically important in supporting the use of a test for a particular purpose. Thus, content validation is an important activity for test developers, and research on improved methods for evaluating test content continues to this day.

Characteristics of Content Validity

As the American Educational Research Association definition of validity implies, empirical evidence and cogent theory are needed to support the validity of inferences derived from test scores. Investigations of content validity involve both evaluating the theory underlying the test and gathering empirical evidence of how well the test represents the content domain it targets.

Content validity has at least four aspects: domain definition, domain representation, domain relevance, and appropriateness of the test construction process. *Domain definition* refers to the process used to operationally define the content domain tested. Defining the domain is typically accomplished by providing (a) detailed descriptions of the content areas and cognitive abilities the test is designed to measure, (b) test specifications that list the specific content "strands" (subareas), as well as the cognitive levels measured, and (c) specific content standards, curricular objectives, or abilities that are contained within the various content strands and cognitive levels. Evaluating domain definition involves acquiring external consensus that the operational definition underlying the test is commensurate with prevailing notions of the domain held by experts in the field (e.g., certified public accountants' verifying that the test specifications for the Uniform CPA Exam reflect the major knowledge and skill domains necessary for safe and effective practice in the profession).

The next aspect of content validity is *domain representation*, which refers to the degree to which a test represents and adequately measures all facets of the intended content domain. To evaluate domain representation, inspection of all the items and tasks on a test must be undertaken. The critical task is to determine whether the items fully and sufficiently represent the targeted domain. Studies of domain representation typically use subject matter experts to scrutinize test items and judge the degree to which they are congruent with the test specifications. Sometimes, as in the case of state-mandated testing in public schools, subject matter experts judge the extent to which test items are congruent with curriculum framework. These studies of domain representation have recently been classified within the realm of test *alignment* research.

Related to domain representation is *domain relevance*, which addresses the extent to which each item on a test is relevant to the domain tested. An item may be considered to measure an important aspect of a content domain, and so it would receive high ratings with respect to domain representation. However, if it were only tangentially related to the domain, it would receive low ratings with respect to relevance. For this reason, studies of content validity may ask subject matter experts to rate the degree to which each test item is relevant to specific aspects of the test specifications. The studies then aggregate those ratings within each content strand to determine domain representation. Taken together, study of domain representation and relevance can help evaluate (a) whether all important aspects of the content domain are measured by the test and (b) whether the test contains trivial or irrelevant content. As Messick described in 1989 in his seminal treatise on validity, "Tests are imperfect measures of constructs because they either leave out something that should be included . . . or else include something that should be left out, or both" (p. 34). A thorough study of content validity, prior to assembling tests, protects against these potential imperfections.

The fourth aspect of content validity, *appropriateness of the test development process*, refers to all processes used when constructing a test to ensure that test content faithfully and fully represents the construct intended to be measured and does not measure irrelevant material. The content validity of a test can be supported if strong quality control procedures are in place during test development and if there is a strong rationale for the specific item formats used on the test. Examples of quality control procedures that support content validity include (a) reviews of test items by content experts to ensure their technical accuracy; (b) reviews of items by measurement experts to determine how well the items conform to standard principles of quality item writing; (c) sensitivity review of items and intact test forms to ensure the test is free of construct-irrelevant material that may offend, advantage, or disadvantage members of particular subgroups of examinees; (d) pilot-testing of items, followed by statistical item analyses to select the most appropriate items for operational use; and (e) analysis of differential item functioning, to flag items that may be disproportionately harder for some groups of examinees than for others.

Conducting a Content Validity Study

As briefly mentioned earlier, many studies of content validity require subject matter experts to review test specifications and items according to specific evaluation criteria. Thus, a content validity study typically involves gathering data on test quality from professionals with expertise in the content domain tested. Content validity studies differ according to the specific tasks presented to the experts and the types of data gathered. One example of a content validity study is to give content experts the test specifications and the test items and ask them to match each item to the content area, educational objective, or cognitive level that it measures. In another type of study, the experts are asked to rate the relevance of each test item to each of the areas, objectives, or levels measured by the test.

The data gathered from these studies can be summarized using simple descriptive statistics, such as the proportion of experts who classified an item as it was listed in the test specifications or the mean relevance ratings for an item across all areas tested. A "content validity index" can be computed for a test by averaging these statistics over all test items. More-sophisticated procedures for analyzing these data have also been proposed, including a newer procedure based on experts' judgments regarding the similarity of skills being measured by pairs of test items. Other studies that provide evidence of content validity include job analyses (referred to as practice analyses for licensure testing). Job analyses are often conducted to operationally define the content domain to be tested. Data gathered from such analyses can be used to derive weights (e.g., proportions of test items) for specific content areas as well as to defend the specific areas tested.

Content Validity: Past, Present, and Future

The origins of contemporary, large-scale educational and psychological tests can be traced to the early 20th century. As the stakes associated with these tests increased, the methods used to evaluate tests also increased. The concept of content validity and the process of content validation emerged to address the limitations of purely statistical (correlational) approaches to test validation that were common in the early part of the 20th century. Content validity quickly became a popular term endorsed by validity theorists and by the Joint Committee on Testing Standards of the American Educational Research Association, the American Psychological Association, and the National Council on Measurement in Education. That popularity waned in the middle 1970s, when a unitary conceptualization of validity centered on construct validity was proposed. Proponents of this unitary conceptualization suggest using terms such as *content representativeness* in place of content validity because content validity focuses on the test itself rather than on inferences derived from test scores. This perspective was incorporated into the current version of the American Educational Research Association's *Standards for Educational and Psychological Testing*, which uses the phrase "evidence based on test content" in place of content validity. However, not all test specialists agree, and in educational testing, the attention paid to content validation is increasing at a staggering pace.

Regardless of debates over terminology, the fundamental characteristics of test quality encompassed by content validity (i.e., domain definition, domain representation, domain relevance, and appropriate test construction process) will remain important criteria for evaluating tests for as long as tests are used to make inferences regarding individuals' knowledge, skills, and abilities. Clearly, for interpretations of test results to be valid, (a) the content of a test needs to be congruent with the testing purpose, and (b) the content areas to which an assessment is targeted need to be adequately represented. Thus, for many educational and psychological tests, content validity is prerequisite for valid score interpretation.

—*Stephen G. Sireci*

See also Criterion Validity; Face Validity; Predictive Validity; Reliability Theory; Validity Theory

Further Reading

American Educational Research Association. (1999). *Standards for educational and psychological testing.* Washington, DC: Author.

Crocker, L. (2003). Teaching for the test: Validity, fairness, and moral action. *Educational Measurement: Issues and Practice, 22*(3), 5–11.

Ebel, R. L. (1956). Obtaining and reporting evidence for content validity. *Educational and Psychological Measurement, 16,* 269–282.

Messick, S. (1975). The standard problem: Meaning and values in measurement and evaluation. *American Psychologist, 30,* 955–966.

Ramsey, P. A. (1993). Sensitivity review: The ETS experience as a case study. In P. W. Holland & H. Wainer (Eds.), *Differential item functioning* (pp. 367–388). Hillsdale, NJ: Erlbaum.

Sireci, S. G. (1998). The construct of content validity. *Social Indicators Research, 45,* 83–117.

Sireci, S. G. (1998). Gathering and analyzing content validity data. *Educational Assessment, 5,* 299–321.

Sireci, S. G., & Geisinger, K. F. (1992). Analyzing test content using cluster analysis and multidimensional scaling. *Applied Psychological Measurement, 16,* 17–31.

CONTINUOUS VARIABLE

If members of a group of people (or animals or things) are the same in terms of a particular characteristic of interest, there is no variability in the group. Usually, however, there is at least some degree of heterogeneity among the group's members. In this second, more typical situation, the characteristic being focused on is said to be a variable.

A variable is said to be a *continuous variable* if it is theoretically possible for the group members to lie anywhere along an imaginary line segment with ends that represent small and large amounts of the characteristic. The litmus test for determining whether a particular variable is or is not a continuous variable is this pair of questions: (a) If a small difference exists between two of the people (or animals or things) in the group, is it possible for a third member of the group to be positioned between the first two? (b) If so, could the third member of the group be positioned between the first two no matter how small the difference between the first two?

To illustrate how this two-question test allows us to determine whether a variable is a continuous variable, imagine a group of people who are not all equally tall. Height, therefore, is a variable. To determine whether height is a continuous variable, first imagine two people in the group, A and B, who are nearly the same height; then, ask whether a third person, C, could be taller than A but shorter than B. Now comes the critical second question. Could C be between A and B in terms of height no matter how small the difference between A and B? The answer is "yes" so long as A and B are not the same height. Therefore, height is a continuous variable.

Other examples of continuous variables include measurements of many physical traits, such as weight, length, speed, and temperature. Many psychological traits, such as intelligence, paranoia, extroversion, and creativity, are also continuous variables. No matter how similar two rocks are in weight or how similar two people are in creativity, it is theoretically possible for a third rock to have a weight between the other two rocks or for a third person to have a level of creativity between the creativity levels of the other two people.

Continuous Versus Discrete Variables

For a variable to be a continuous variable, the characteristic being focused on must be quantitative in nature. The examples used in the previous paragraphs are quantitative in nature and also are continuous. Many other quantitative variables, however, are not continuous. Consider these two: the number of siblings a person has or the number of working televisions inside a house. If someone has one sibling whereas someone else has two siblings, it is not logically possible for someone else to be "in between" the first two people. Likewise, if one house had three working televisions while another house had four working televisions, it is impossible for another house to have between three and four working televisions. Quantitative variables such as these are called *discrete variables*.

Data Can Make a Continuous Variable Look Like a Discrete Variable

When visiting a doctor's office, people are typically measured in terms of their weight and their temperature. The weight data usually are whole numbers (e.g., 157 pounds) while the temperature data almost always are numbers containing one decimal place (e.g., 99.7° Fahrenheit). When such measurements are collected from groups of individuals, the data make it look as if weight and temperature are discrete rather than continuous variables.

This potential confusion as to whether a variable is continuous or discrete melts away if we think about the variable *without* focusing on the data created by attempting to measure the characteristic of interest. Thus, the fact that people's weights are typically reported in whole numbers or that their temperatures are normally reported with numbers containing just one decimal place does not alter the fact that both weight and temperature are continuous variables. It is the characteristic being focused on—rather than any data made available by trying to measure that characteristic—that determines whether a given variable is continuous.

The Distinction Between Continuous and Discrete Variables: Does It Matter?

When statistical techniques are used to summarize or analyze data, it often makes little difference whether the variable on which measurements have been taken is continuous or discrete. For example, the correlation between scores on two variables has the same meaning (and is arrived at using the same formula) regardless of whether the variables are continuous or discrete. Similarly, it doesn't matter whether the variable beneath one's data is continuous or discrete when a standard deviation is computed or interpreted.

Yet in certain situations, it does matter whether data are tied to a continuous variable or to a discrete variable. For example, discrete and continuous variables are treated differently in probability theory. With discrete variables, probabilities can be determined for particular *points* along the score continuum. In contrast, probabilities deal only with *intervals* along the score continuum if the variable is continuous.

—Young-Hoon Ham

See also Categorical Variable; Continuous Variable; Dependent Variable; Independent Variable

Further Reading

Cohen, B. H., & Lea, R. B. (2004). *Essentials of statistics for the social and behavioral sciences.* Hoboken, NJ: Wiley.

Huck, S. W. (2004). *Reading statistics and research* (4th ed.). Boston: Allyn & Bacon.

Ott, R. L., & Longnecker, M. (2001). *An introduction to statistical methods and data analysis* (5th ed.). Pacific Grove, CA: Duxbury.

Vogt, W. P. (1999). *Dictionary of statistics and methodology: A nontechnical guide for the social sciences* (2nd ed.). Thousand Oaks, CA: Sage.

CONTOUR PLOT

A contour plot (or diagram) is a two-dimensional representation of a three-dimensional surface. It consists of a set of curves called contours formed by projecting

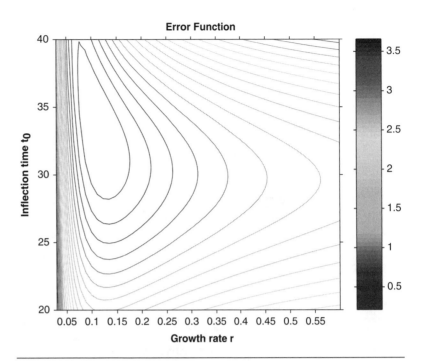

Figure 1 Contour Plot of U.S. Cumulative Underground Gas Storage Capacity

Source: Data from International Gas Consulting, Inc.

the curves of intersection of the surface with planes parallel to one of the coordinate planes. Typically, the surface is the graph of a function, which may be given as a formula or as output of measured data. The contours share the property that on any particular curve, the value of the dependent variable is constant. Normally, the diagram is such that the values between contours vary by a constant amount.

Figure 1 is an example of a contour plot. It was used to fit a logistic curve, that is, a curve of the form

$$y(t) = \frac{K}{1 + C\exp(-rt)},$$

in the least-squares sense to a set of data for the U.S. cumulative underground gas storage capacity from 1932 to 2000 (C is an arbitrary constant of integration). By manipulating the expression for a logistic function, it is possible to write a formula in terms of only two parameters: its growth rate and its inflection point. In order to minimize the corresponding least-square error function, one needs an accurate estimate of those parameters. This usually requires a

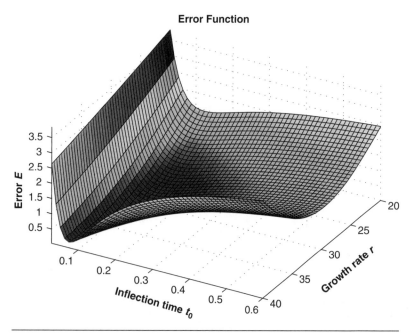

Error Function

Figure 2 Surface Plot of U.S. Cumulative Underground Gas Storage Capacity

first estimate, which in this example can be obtained more easily from the contour plot of the error function than from the three-dimensional graph (see Figure 2).

As with all contour plots, the contour plot illustrated above reflects the intersection of planes parallel to the inflection time-growth rate plane (t_0, r – plane) and the surface of the error function displayed in Figure 2. Each contour depicts a curve of constant error; that is, the value of the error function remains the same along a curve.

Graphing contour lines by hand is generally impractical. Instead, one uses either graphics software or a mathematical or statistical software package. The plots shown were created in Matlab; instead of labeling values of the error at some curves, values are indicated by a scale given by a color bar.

Contour plots are used in very diverse fields; in particular, they are widely used in the earth sciences. A common application is topographic maps, which display elevation in terms of longitude and latitude. Since the elevation between any two consecutive contours varies by the same amount, proximity of contour lines indicates the rate of change of elevation.

—*Silvia A. Madrid*

See also Dependent Variable; Logistic Regression Analysis

Further Reading

Mooney, D., & Swift, R. (1999). *A course in mathematical modeling.* Washington, DC: MAA.

Bermuda Atlantic Time Series Study: http://coexploration.org/bbsr/classroombats/html/visualization.html (illustrates use of contour plots in oceanography)

Reliability Hot Wire: http://www.weibull.com/hotwire/issue18/relbasics18.htm (discusses contour bounds and confidence bounds on parameters)

CONVENIENCE SAMPLING

Convenience sampling is a type of survey sampling in which interviewers are allowed to choose convenient members of the population to interview. The goal of a survey is to gather data in order to describe the characteristics of a population. A population consists of units, or elements, which, depending on the application, can be individuals, households, land areas, bank accounts, or hospital records at a specific time and location. A survey collects information on a sample, or subset, of the population. In some surveys, specific units or elements are chosen by the survey designers to be in the sample. Interviewers are assigned to interview the members of the selected sample. Sometimes multiple attempts at contacting and collecting data from the selected sample members are made. In convenience samples, on the other hand, interviewers themselves are given some latitude in selecting the population members to interview. That is, the survey designers and planners do not strictly control the selection of the sample.

Convenience samples occur in many forms. If an interviewer is told to stand on a corner or at the exit of a shopping mall and find adults to complete a survey about local schools, then this is a convenience sample because the instructions of whom to interview are not explicit. If customer satisfaction forms are distributed to certain customers in a restaurant, then this is a convenience sample if the waiters are allowed to choose which customers to give comment forms. Internet and call-in opinion polls also could be considered convenience samples in which the sample essentially selects itself by choosing to participate. A subtler example of convenience sampling occurs when a telephone interviewer dials the telephone numbers that are randomly generated from a computer until a willing respondent is found. Although the telephone numbers are being provided to the interviewer, the interviewer is going to speak to the first available and willing people reached. This is a convenience sample because the survey planners are not picking specific numbers that should be called. In this scenario, the people called by the interviewer essentially decide themselves whether or not to be in the sample.

In the shopping mall example, it is likely that the interviewer will tend to approach people who look friendly and are walking at a casual pace rather than people who are rushing and in a visibly bad mood. Interviewers might tend to choose people of their own gender, age group, ethnicity, or race to interview slightly more often than they choose others. The interviewer also is likely to choose a desirable place to stand and to avoid loud places, such as by the door to a video arcade, and smelly locations, such as near a garbage or designated smoking area. As a result of the chosen location and tendencies to approach certain types of individuals and avoid others, it is possible that the convenience sample will not produce results that are truly representative of the entire population of interest. The convenience sample could be representative of certain subgroups in the population, but due to the lack of control by the survey planners, it is difficult to specify which population exactly is being represented.

Estimates of population characteristics based on convenience samples are affected by *selection bias*. Since the interviewers choose respondents that they want to interview or respondents decide whether or not to participate, there is a potential for selection bias. If the respondents in the survey are systematically different from the general population on the variables being measured, then estimates of characteristics will be different on average from what they would have been with a controlled probability-sampling scheme. *Probability sampling* refers to a collection of survey sample designs in which the survey planner or researcher controls which units are in the sample and selects the sample using known probabilities of selection. The probabilities of selection can be used to produce estimates of population characteristics without the problem of selection bias. Probability sampling is the standard methodology for large-scale surveys intended to support scientific studies and decision making for government policy. That is not to say that convenience sampling should never be done. Sometimes it is very helpful to get some feedback and suggestions from people especially concerned with a problem or issue. One should be careful, however, about the limitations of general statements about a large population based on convenience samples.

—*Michael D. Larsen*

See also Nonprobability Sampling; Quota Sample; Random Sampling

Further Reading

Kelly, H., Riddell, M. A., Gidding, H. F., Nolan, T., & Gilbert, G. L. (2002). A random cluster survey and a convenience sample give comparable estimates of immunity to vaccine preventable diseases in children of school age in Victoria, Australia. *Vaccine, 20*(25–26), 3130–3136.

Schonlau, M. (2004). Will web surveys ever become part of mainstream research? *Journal of Internet Medical Research, 6*(3) article e31. Retrieved May 14, 2006, from http://www.jmir.org/2004/3/e31/

Schonlau, M., Fricker, R. D., Jr., & Elliott, M. N. (2001). *Conducting research surveys via e-mail and the Web* (chapter 4). Santa Monica, CA: RAND. Retrieved May 14, 2006, from http://www.rand.org/publications/MR/MR1480/MR1480.ch4.pdf

Nonprobability sampling: http://www.statcan.ca/english/edu/power/ch13/non_probability/non_probability.htm

Applying Ideas on Statistics and Measurement

The following abstract is adapted from Zelinski, E. M., Burnight, K. P., & Lane, C. J. (2001). The relationship between subjective and objective memory in the oldest old: Comparisons of findings from a representative and a convenience sample. *Journal of Aging and Health, 13*(2), 248–266.

Convenience sampling is only one of many different techniques that scientists use to select participants in a study. Elizabeth Zelinski and her colleagues tested the hypothesis that subjective memory ratings are more accurate in the oldest old than in the young old and also tested whether a representative sample was more accurate than a convenience sample. The results of analysis of subjective ratings and participant characteristics on recall were compared between a nationally representative sample of 6,446 adults ages 70 to 103 and a convenience sample of 326 adults ages 70 to 97. Researchers found that education interacted with memory ratings in the prediction of performance in the representative sample, with better prediction for more highly educated participants than for participants with lower levels of education. Neither hypothesis was supported.

COPING RESOURCES INVENTORY FOR STRESS

Coping refers to conscious or unconscious efforts to manage internal and external demands or situations that are appraised as taxing one's personal resources. Instruments measuring coping usually fall into one of two categories: those measuring coping processes and those measuring coping resources.

While coping processes are thoughts or behaviors occurring after stressful events have occurred, coping resources are factors in place before such stressors occur. Coping resources may include psychological traits, cognitive skills, belief systems, social support, physical health and fitness, and financial resources.

The Coping Resources Inventory for Stress (CRIS) is a comprehensive measure of personal resources for coping with stress. The CRIS offers 15 resource measures, an overall coping effectiveness measure, five validity keys, and a computer-generated interpretative report that suggests ways of strengthening deficit resources. The resource scales are self-disclosure, self-direction, confidence, acceptance, social support, financial freedom, physical health, physical fitness, stress monitoring, tension control, structuring, problem solving, cognitive restructuring, functional beliefs, and social ease.

The 280 true-false items of the CRIS were distilled from more than 700 items responded to by more than 3,500 participants during a 12-year period. Contributing to the development of the inventory were disparate group studies, factor analyses, item analyses, item bias studies, reliability coefficients, and meta-analytic reviews. The normative sample ($n = 1,199$) was selected to be representative of the United States population in terms of race, gender, and age. The CRIS may be administered using test booklets or by computer.

The CRIS scales have relatively high internal consistency reliabilities (.84 to .97; Mdn = .88; $n = 814$), test-retest reliabilities (.76 to .95 over a 4-week period; Mdn = .87; $n = 34$ college students), and moderate to low intercorrelations (range .05 to .62; Mdn = .33). These features allow the CRIS to be used as an inventory offering stable measures of subconstructs that all contribute to one superordinate construct, coping resources. Some of the studies for establishing the validity of the inventory include measures of illness, emotional distress, personality type, drug dependency, occupational choice, acculturation, and life satisfaction. The CRIS is published by Datamax Corporation, Atlanta, Georgia.

—*Kenneth. B. Matheny and*
William L. Curlette

Further Reading

Matheny, K. B., Aycock, D., Curlette, W. L., & Junker, G. (1993 November). Coping Resources Inventory for Stress: A measure of perceived coping resources. *Journal of Clinical Psychology, 49*(6), 815–830.

Matheny, K. B., & Curlette, W. L. (1998). The Coping Resources Inventory for Stress: A comprehensive measure of stress-coping resources. In C. P. Zaraquett & R. J. Wood (Eds.), *Evaluating stress: A book of resources.* Lanham, MD: Scarecrow.

Matheny, K. B., Curlette, W. L., Aysan, F., Herrington, A., Gfroerer, C. A., Thompson, D., et al. (2002). Coping resources, perceived stress, and life satisfaction among Turkish and American university students. *International Journal of Stress Management, 9*(2), 81–97.

CORRELATION COEFFICIENT

Correlation coefficient is a measure of association between two variables, and it ranges between –1 and 1. If the two variables are in perfect linear relationship, the correlation coefficient will be either 1 or –1. The sign depends on whether the variables are positively or negatively related. The correlation coefficient is 0 if there is no linear relationship between the variables. Two different types of correlation coefficients are in use. One is called the Pearson product-moment correlation coefficient, and the other is called the Spearman rank correlation coefficient, which is based on the rank relationship between variables. The Pearson product-moment correlation coefficient is more widely used in measuring the association between two variables. Given paired measurements (X_1, Y_1), (X_2, Y_2), . . . , (X_n, Y_n), the Pearson product-moment correlation coefficient is a measure of association given by

$$r_P = \frac{\sum_{i=1}^{n} (X_i - \bar{X})(Y_i - \bar{Y})}{\sqrt{\sum_{i=1}^{n} (X_i - \bar{X})^2 \sum_{i=1}^{n} (Y_i - \bar{Y})^2}},$$

where $\bar{X}$ and $\bar{Y}$ are the sample mean of $X_1, X_2, \ldots, X_n$ and $Y_1, Y_2, \ldots, Y_n$, respectively.

Case Study and Data

The following 25 paired measurements can be found at http://lib.stat.cmu.edu/DASL/Datafiles/Smoking andCancer.html:

77	84
137	116
117	123
94	128
116	155
102	101
111	118
93	113
88	104
102	88
91	104
104	129
107	86
112	96
113	144
110	139
125	113
133	146
115	128
105	115
87	79
91	85
100	120
76	60
66	51

For a total of 25 occupational groups, the first variable is the smoking index (average 100), and the second variable is the lung cancer mortality index (average 100). Let us denote these paired indices as (X_i, Y_i). The Pearson product-moment correlation coefficient is computed to be $r_p = 0.69$. Figure 1 shows the scatter plot of the smoking index versus the lung

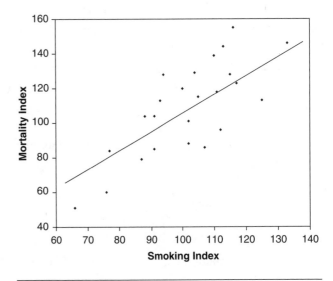

Figure 1   Scatter Plot of Smoking Index Versus Lung Cancer Mortality Index

Source: Based on data from Moore & McCabe, 1989.

Note: The straight line is the linear regression of mortality index on smoking index.

cancer mortality index. The straight line is the linear regression line given by $Y = \beta_0 + \beta_1 \times X$.

The parameters of the regression line are estimated using the least squares method, which is implemented in most statistical packages such as SAS and SPSS. The equation for the regression line is given by $Y = -2.89 + 1.09 \times X$. If (X_i, Y_i) are distributed as bivariate normal, a linear relationship exists between the regression slope and the Pearson product-moment correlation coefficient given by

$$\beta_1 \simeq \frac{\sigma_Y}{\sigma_X} r_P,$$

where σ_X and σ_Y are the sample standard deviations of the smoking index and the lung cancer mortality index, respectively ($\sigma_X = 17.2$ and $\sigma_Y = 26.11$). With the computed correlation coefficient value, we obtain

$$\beta_1 \simeq \frac{26.11}{17.20} \times 0.69 = 1.05,$$

which is close to the least squares estimation of 1.09.

Statistical Inference on Population Correlation

The Pearson product-moment correlation coefficient is the underlying population correlation ρ. In the smoking and lung cancer example above, we are interested in testing whether the correlation coefficient indicates the statistical significance of relationship between smoking and the lung cancer mortality rate. So we test. $H_0 : \rho = 0$ versus $H_1 : \rho \neq 0$.

Assuming the normality of the measurements, the test statistic

$$T = \frac{r_P \sqrt{n-2}}{\sqrt{1 - r_P^2}}$$

follows the t distribution with $n-2$ degrees of freedom. The case study gives

$$T = \frac{0.69 \sqrt{25 - 2}}{\sqrt{1 - 0.69^2}} = 4.54.$$

This t value is compared with the 95% quantile point of the t distribution with $n-2$ degrees of

freedom, which is 1.71. Since the t value is larger than the quantile point, we reject the null hypothesis and conclude that there is correlation between the smoking index and the lung cancer mortality index at significance level $\alpha = 0.1$. Although r_p itself can be used as a test statistic to test more general hypotheses about ρ, the exact distribution of ρ is difficult to obtain. One widely used technique is to use the Fisher transform, which transforms the correlation into

$$F(r_P) = \frac{1}{2} \ln \left(\frac{1 + r_P}{1 - r_P} \right).$$

Then for moderately large samples, the Fisher transform is normally distributed with mean $\frac{1}{2} \ln \left(\frac{1 + \rho}{1 - \rho} \right)$ and variance $\frac{1}{n-3}$. Then the test statistic is $Z = \sqrt{n-3} (F(r_P) - F(\rho))$, which is a standard normal distribution. For the case study example, under the null hypothesis, we have

$$Z = \sqrt{25 - 3} \left(\frac{1}{2} \ln \left(\frac{1 + 0.69}{1 - 0.69} \right) - \frac{1}{2} \ln \left(\frac{1 + 0}{1 - 0} \right) \right)$$

$$= 3.98.$$

The Z value is compared with the 95% quantile point of the standard normal, which is 1.64. Since the Z value is larger than the quantile point, we reject the null hypothesis and conclude that there is correlation between the smoking index and the lung cancer mortality index.

—*Moo K. Chung*

See also Coefficients of Correlation, Alienation, and Determination; Multiple Correlation Coefficient; Part and Partial Correlation

Further Reading

Fisher, R. A. (1915). Frequency distribution of the values of the correlation coefficient in samples of an indefinitely large population. *Biometrika, 10,* 507–521.

Moore, D. S., & McCabe, G. P. (1989). *Introduction to the practice of statistics.* New York: W. H. Freeman. (Original source: Occupational Mortality: The Registrar General's Decennial Supplement for England and Wales, 1970–1972, Her Majesty's Stationery Office, London, 1978)

Rummel, R. J. (n.d.). *Understanding correlation.* Retrieved from http://www.mega.nu:8080/ampp/rummel/uc.htm

Correlation coefficient page: http://mathworld.wolfram.com/CorrelationCoefficient.html

Spearman rank correlation coefficient: http://mathworld.wolfram.com/SpearmanRankCorrelationCoefficient.html

CORRESPONDENCE ANALYSIS

Correspondence analysis (CA) is an exploratory multivariate technique that converts data organized in a two-way table into graphical displays, with the categories of the two variables depicted as points. The objective is to construct a low-dimensional map that well summarizes the data, which in the case of CA are the associations between two categorical variables. Mathematically, the technique decomposes the χ^2 measure of association of the two-way table into components in a manner similar to that of principal component analysis for continuous data. In CA, no assumptions about the data-generating mechanism are made, a significant departure from log linear analysis. The primary objective of the technique is the representation of the underlying structure of the observed data.

CA can be traced back to the work of Hirschfeld (see de Leeuw). It has been rediscovered in various forms by Fisher, Guttman, Hayashi, and Benzécri, who emphasized the geometric aspects of the technique. Extensive expositions and a discussion of its similarities to and differences from other methods, such as dual scaling and canonical correlation, can be found in the books by Nishisato and Greenacre.

There are two variants of the technique: *simple* CA, which deals with two-way tables, and *multiple* CA, a generalization designed to handle more than two categorical variables.

Simple CA

Consider two categories variables V_1 and V_2, with I and J categories, respectively. Let α_2 denote the corresponding $I \times J$ two-way table, whose entries $x_{i,j}$ contain counts of the co-occurrences of categories i and j, and let N denote the grand total of $\mathbf{X}$ (i.e., $N = \sum_{i,j} x_{i,j}$). Let $\mathbf{Z}$ denote the probability matrix obtained as $N^{-1}\mathbf{X}$. Further, let $\mathbf{r} = \mathbf{Z}\mathbf{1}$ denote the vector of row marginals and $\mathbf{c} = \mathbf{Z}^T\mathbf{1}$ the vector of column marginals. Finally, define $\mathbf{D}_r = diag\{\mathbf{r}\}$ as the diagonal matrix containing the elements of vector $\mathbf{r}$, and similarly define $\mathbf{D}_c = diag\{\mathbf{c}\}$.

An example that illustrates the notation of a two-way table first used by Fisher is shown in Table 1. Data on 5,387 school children from Caithness, Scotland, were collected for two categorical variables, eye color and hair color.

The dependencies between the rows (columns) of $\mathbf{Z}$ can be captured by the so-called χ^2 distances defined (here between row i and i') as

$$d_\chi^2(i,i') = N \sum_{j=1}^{J} \frac{1}{c_j} \left(\frac{z_{i,j}}{r_i} - \frac{z_{i',j}}{r_{i'}} \right)^2. \quad (1)$$

Equation 1 shows that the χ^2 distance is a measure of the difference between the profiles of rows i and i'. It also shows that by correcting the entries in the table by the row marginals, proportional row profiles yield zero distances. Also note that squared differences between row categories i and i' are weighted heavily if the corresponding column marginal is small, while such differences contribute little to the distance measure if the column marginal is large.

The objective of CA is to approximate the χ^2 distances by Euclidean distances in some low-dimensional space. In order to derive the $I \times L$ coordinates $\mathbf{F}$ (with $L = 2$ or 3 for visualization purposes) in the new Euclidean space, we consider the singular value decomposition of the observed frequencies minus the expected frequencies, corrected for row and column marginals:

Table 1 Example of Two-Way Table

V_1 = eye color	V_2 = Hair color					
	Fair	Red	Medium	Dark	Black	Total (r)
Light	688	116	584	188	4	1,580
Blue	326	38	241	110	3	718
Medium	343	84	909	412	26	1,774
Dark	98	48	403	681	85	1,315
Total (c)	1,455	286	2,137	1,391	118	N = 5,387

$$D_r^{-\frac{1}{2}} \left(Z - rc^T \right) D_c^{-\frac{1}{2}} = P\Delta Q^T. \qquad (2)$$

The optimal coordinates of the row categories are given (after normalization) by

$$F = D_r^{-\frac{1}{2}} P, \qquad (3)$$

so that $F^T D_r F = I$ and $1^T D_r F = 0$ (i.e., in each dimension the row scores have a weighted variance of 1 and a weighted average of 0; note that several implementations of CA normalize the row factor scores such that their variance is equal to the corresponding eigenvalue; in this case the factor scores are computed as $F = D_r^{-\frac{1}{2}} P\Delta$).

Since Euclidean distances between the F coordinates of the row categories approximate the original χ^2 distances, it can be seen that when two categories are depicted close together, their profiles are similar, while they are different if their positions are far apart. Finally, when a row category is near the center of the F space, its profile is similar to that of the corresponding column marginal.

Given the above configuration for the row categories, we can compute the column category configuration as follows:

$$G = D_c^{-\frac{1}{2}} Q\Delta, \qquad (4)$$

which implies that the column points are in the center of gravity of the row points. Since the analysis is symmetric regarding rows and columns, one could have calculated χ^2 distances between the column categories and obtained the corresponding representation of row and column categories in L-dimensional Euclidean space. Some algebra shows that the Pearson's χ^2 statistic used for testing independence between two categorical variables is related to the formulas for CA by

$$\text{trace}\left\{ \Delta^2 \right\} = \frac{X^2}{N}, \qquad (5)$$

known as the *total inertia* in the literature.

An illustration of CA using Fisher's data from Table 1 is shown in Figure 1.

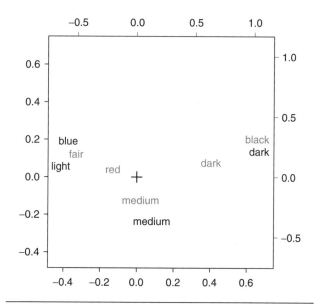

Figure 1   Correspondence Analysis Using Fisher's Data

It can be seen that there is high association between fair hair and light and blue eye color and similarly between black hair and dark eyes. On the other hand, dark hair is associated to a large extent with both dark and medium-colored eyes. Further, students with medium hair color have mostly medium eye color but can also have all three other eye colors.

Multiple Correspondence Analysis

In the presence of more than two categorical variables, there are two possible ways to proceed. We examine both of them next. Suppose that data have been collected on I objects and K categorical variables, with J_k categories per variable. Let X_k be a $I \times J_k$ indicator (binary) matrix with entries $x_{i,j} = 1$ if object i belongs to category j of variable k and 0 if not. Let $X = [X_1 | X_2 | \ldots | X_K]$ be the *superindicator* matrix obtained by concatenating the indicator matrices of all K variables. The symmetric matrix $B = X^T X$, known as the *Burt table*, contains the marginals for the categories of all variables along the main diagonal, together with all two-tables of the K variables in the off-diagonal.

Applying simple CA to the Burt table yields the following solution for the category points:

$$D_B^{-\frac{1}{2}}(B - M^{-1}D_B 11^T D_B)D_B^{-\frac{1}{2}} = P\Lambda P^T, \qquad (6)$$

where $\mathbf{D_B} = \text{diag}\{\mathbf{B}\}$ and $N = I \times K^2$ (i.e., N is the grand total of $\mathbf{B}$). The coordinates of the category points are given by

$$\mathbf{F} = \sqrt{N}\mathbf{D_B}^{-\frac{1}{2}}\mathbf{P\Lambda}. \qquad (7)$$

Multiple CA is the joint analysis of all the two-way tables of K categorical variables.

In many cases, one may want a joint representation of both objects and categories of variables they belong to. This objective can be achieved by applying simple correspondence analysis directly to the superindicator matrix $\mathbf{X}$. The coordinates $\mathbf{F}$ for the objects are given by the singular value decomposition of

$$\left(\mathbf{I} - I^{-1}\mathbf{11}^{T}\right)\mathbf{XD_B}^{-\frac{1}{2}} = \mathbf{P\Delta Q}^{T}, \qquad (8)$$

where the left-hand side corresponds to the superindicator matrix of the data expressed in deviations from the column means and weighted by the variables' marginal frequencies. Specifically, $\mathbf{F} = \sqrt{I}\mathbf{P}$ (i.e., the coordinates have unit variance). The coordinates of the categories can be obtained by $\mathbf{G} = K\mathbf{D_B}^{-1}\mathbf{X}^{T}\mathbf{F}$, which shows that a category point is located in the center of gravity of the objects that belong to it. An alternative derivation of the above solution as a graph-drawing technique is given in Michailidis and de Leeuw, and various extensions are discussed in Van Rijckevorsel and de Leeuw.

Multiple CA is illustrated in Figure 2 on a small data set of 21 objects (sleeping bags) and three categorical variables (price, comprised of three categories; fiber type, with two categories; and quality, with three categories).

From the joint map of objects and categories (connected by lines), it becomes apparent that there are good, expensive sleeping bags filled with down fibers and cheap, bad-quality ones filled with synthetic

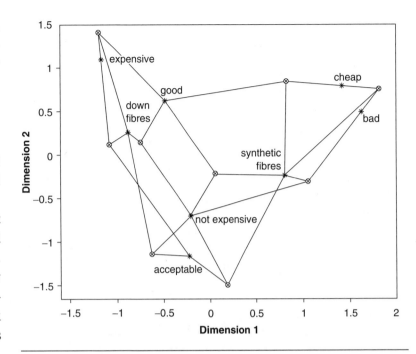

Figure 2   Multiple Correspondence Analysis

fibers. Further, there are some not particularly expensive sleeping bags of acceptable quality made of synthetic or down fibers.

—George Michailidis

See also Discriminant Analysis; Discriminant Correspondence Analysis; Distance; DISTATIS; Factor Analysis; Metric Multidimensional Scaling; Multiple Correspondence Analysis; Multiple Factor Analysis; STATIS

Further Reading

Benzécri, J. P. (1973). *L'analyse des données*. Paris: Dunod.

De Leeuw, J. (1983). On the prehistory of correspondence analysis. *Statistica Neerlandica, 37*, 161–164.

Gifi, A. (1990). *Nonlinear multivariate analysis*. Chichester, UK: Wiley.

Greenacre, M. J. (1984). *Theory and applications of correspondence analysis*. London: Academic Press.

Hayashi, C. (1952). On the prediction of phenomena from qualitative data and the quantification of qualitative data from the mathematico-statistical point of view. *Annals of the Institute of Statistical Mathematics, 5*, 121–143.

Michailidis, G., & de Leeuw, J. (2000). Multilevel homogeneity analysis with differential weighting. *Computational Statistics and Data Analysis, 32*, 411–442.

Nishisato, S. (1980). *Analysis of categorical data: Dual scaling and its applications.* Toronto, Canada: Toronto University Press.

Van Rijckevorsel, J., and de Leeuw, J. (Eds.). (1988). *Component and correspondence analysis.* Chichester, UK: Wiley.

COVARIANCE

Covariance is a measure of covariation, or linear relationship, between two variables that is expressed in the original units of measurement. Equation 1 formalizes this definition for the population covariance. Examination of the equation shows that covariance is a bivariate statistic that quantifies the joint dispersion of two variables from their respective means. Equation 1 also shows that covariance is the average of two sets of deviation scores:

$$E\left[(X - \mu_x)(Y - \mu_y)\right]$$
$$= \frac{\sum(X - \mu_x)(Y - \mu_y)}{N} = \sigma_{xy}. \quad (1)$$

The sample covariance is a statistic that estimates the degree to which two variables covary in the population. The sample covariance is an unbiased estimate of population covariance when observational pairs are sampled independently from the population. The sample covariance presumes that the functional relationship between the two variables is linear.

Equation 2 is the deviation score formula for the sample covariance for two variables X and Y:

$$COV_{XY} = s_{xy} = \frac{\sum_{i=1}^{n}(X_i - \bar{X})(Y_i - \bar{Y})}{n - 1}. \quad (2)$$

Steps to computing an unbiased estimate of the population covariance include (a) calculating the mean of the X scores and the mean of the Y scores, (b) calculating the deviation of the X and Y scores from their respective means, (c) calculating the product of the deviations for each pair of values (i.e., calculating the cross products), (d) summing these cross products, and (e) dividing the sum of the cross products by

$n - 1$ (degrees of freedom). Equation 3 shows that the covariance of a variable with itself is the variance:

$$s_{xx} = \frac{\sum_{i=1}^{n}(X_i - \bar{X})(X_i - \bar{X})}{n - 1}$$

$$= \frac{\sum_{i=1}^{n}(X_i - \bar{X})^2}{n - 1} = s^2. \quad (3)$$

The units of measurement of the covariance are not intuitive, because they are expressed in terms of the cross products of the scales of the X and Y scores. It is difficult to interpret covariance because it is very difficult to think in terms of a statistical value as summarizing how two different and frequently arbitrary metrics covary (e.g., IQ points and Graduate Record Examinations points).

Properties of the Covariance

Covariance has no limits and can take on any value between plus and minus infinity. Negative values indicate that high scores on one variable tend to be associated with low scores on the other variable. Positive values indicate that high scores on one variable tend to be associated with high scores on the other variable. A covariance of 0 indicates that there is no linear relationship between the two variables. Because covariance measures only linear dependence, covariance values of 0 do not indicate independence.

The sample covariances, along with sample sizes, sample means, and sample variances, form the building blocks of the general linear statistical model. Essentially, the covariance summarizes all the important information contained in a set of parameters of a linear model. Covariance becomes more positive for each pair of values that differ from their mean in the same direction, and it becomes more negative with each pair of values that differ from their mean in opposite directions. The more often the scores differ in the same direction, the more positive the covariance, and the more often they differ in opposite directions, the more negative the covariance.

Equation 4 shows that correlation is merely a scale-free measure of covariance or linear relationship; that is, correlation is merely a standardized covariance. When covariance is calculated, the sample means are subtracted from the scores, and when we calculate the correlation, we divide the covariance by the product of the standard deviations. This shows that the correlation is the covariance of the z_x and z_y scores,

$$r_{xy} = \frac{\sum_{i=1}^{n} z_X z_Y}{N}.$$

Clearly, the essence of correlation, that it measures both the strength and the direction of the linear relationship, is contained in the covariance:

$$\begin{aligned} correlation = r_{xy} &= \frac{COV_{XY}}{s_x s_y} = \frac{s_{xy}}{s_x s_y} \\ &= \frac{\sum_{i=1}^{n}(X_i - \bar{X})(Y_i - \bar{Y}) \big/ n - 1}{s_x s_y}. \end{aligned} \tag{4}$$

—*Ward Rodriguez*

See also Analysis of Covariance (ANCOVA); Linear Regression; Regression Analysis; Variance

Further Reading

Nunnally, J. C., & Bernstein, I. (1994). *Psychometric theory* (3rd ed.). New York: McGraw-Hill.

Stilson, D. W. (1966). *Probability and statistics in psychological research and theory* (pp. 251–255). San Francisco: Holden-Day.

Tamhane, A. C., & Dunlop, D. D. (2000). *Statistics and data analysis: From elementary to intermediate* (pp. 36–38). Upper Saddle River, NJ: Prentice Hall.

CRITERION-REFERENCED TESTS

Although criterion-referenced tests (CRTs) can be developed to measure performance at the domain level (e.g., mathematics, reading), they are much more commonly used to measure mastery of short-term objectives (e.g., a unit on the Civil War). As classroom tests, CRTs have existed for many decades, if not centuries. The work of Mager and Glaser in the early 1960s started an important and continuing movement to improve the way that educators estimate students' achievement. R. F. Mager wrote a popular book that motivated educators to be precise in explicating the skills they wanted their students to learn. Robert Glaser, who is generally credited with coining the term *criterion-referenced test*, initiated the movement to measure the mastery of instructional objectives with reliability and validity.

What Is a CRT?

A CRT is a measure designed to estimate mastery of an identified unit of a curriculum (e.g., battles of the Civil War, multidigit addition with regrouping, use of prepositions). CRTs are also referred to as *curriculum-based measures* and more broadly as *curriculum-based assessment*. CRTs are standardized instruments, which are constructed with sufficient precision that different examiners will administer, score, and interpret results in the same way. CRTs contain items designed to represent the unit of instruction adequately. Each item has a predetermined correct answer that can be scored objectively by the assessor. A CRT is used for two main purposes. First, it is used to determine whether a student is weak in a given skill and needs further instruction. Second, it is used to determine the effectiveness of instruction. Although CRTs are seldom normed nationally, it is beneficial to collect local norms for appropriate grade groups.

In contrast to norm-referenced tests, which use relative mastery criteria to interpret scores, CRTs use absolute mastery criteria. Therefore, the student's performance is not compared to that of other students but to a predetermined absolute standard of performance. Most commonly, CRTs measure performance as percentage correct. The particular measure used should be based on real-life demands. Because CRTs are usually used to measure short-term objectives, they tend to be formative rather than summative in nature. Thus, for skills at the lowest taxonomic levels (e.g., miniskills), educators may obtain mastery estimates on a weekly or even a daily basis.

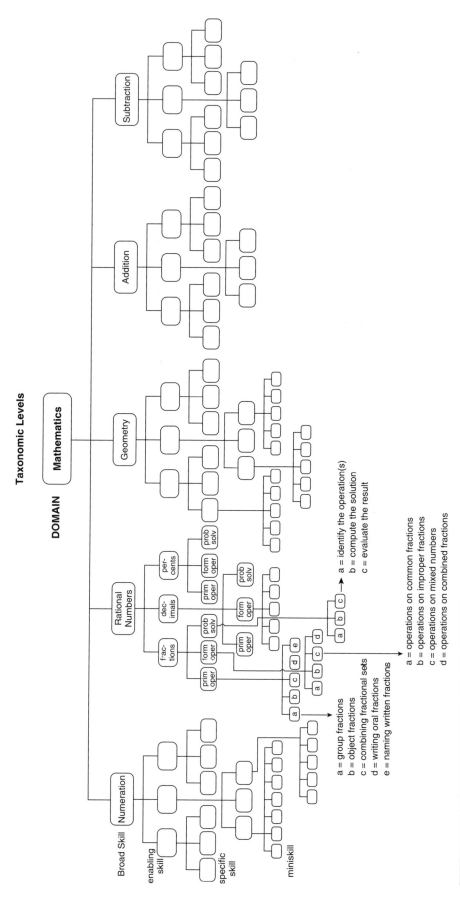

Figure 1   A Partial Taxonomy for Mathematics

Some writers distinguish between domain-referenced tests and objective-referenced tests. Domain-referenced tests provide a measure that is interpretable in the context of a clearly defined and delimited set of objectives that collectively constitute an entire domain (e.g., mathematics, reading). Objective-referenced tests provide a measure that is interpretable only for a particular instructional objective.

Selection of Taxonomies of Objectives

It is useful for practitioners to select taxonomies of objectives for domains relevant to their practice. For instance, a mathematics teacher would benefit from a complete specification of the broad, enabling, and specific math skills needed by American citizens. Such a taxonomy represents the results of a task analysis of a domain. Although there is no such thing as a perfect taxonomy, national organizations (e.g., the National Council of Teachers of Mathematics, National Council of Teachers of English, National Research Council-Science) often publish taxonomies. A layout of a partial math taxonomy might look like that displayed in Figure 1.

The layout should be accompanied by a document containing instructional objectives for each skill represented in the layout.

Here is a set of objectives for basic addition facts:

3.1.0   Given all possible permutations of the addition facts (addends 0–9) presented vertically and in random order, the child will write answers with at least 95% accuracy and at a rate of at least 20 correct per minute.

3.1.1   Given all possible permutations of the addition facts (addends 0–5) presented vertically and in random order, the child will write answers with at least 95% accuracy and at a rate of at least 25 correct per minute.

3.1.2   Given all possible permutations of the addition facts (addends 6–9) presented vertically and in random order, the child will write answers with at least 95% accuracy and at a rate of at least 20 correct per minute.

Objective 3.1.0 represents an enabling skill, enabling in the sense that mastery will enable the student to address higher-order skills in addition and in the domain of mathematics.

Notice that the objective contains the three critical features of a good objective:

1. A statement of the conditions under which the student will perform (i.e., "given all possible permutations of the addition facts [addends 0–9] presented vertically and in random order")

2. The behavior (i.e., "the child will write answers")

3. Criteria for minimally acceptable performance (i.e., "with at least 95% accuracy and at a rate of at least 20 correct per minute"; in this case, criteria for both accuracy and rate are specified)

When these three features are clearly explicated in the objective, it is easier for the test writer to construct items. For objective 3.1.0, there should be 100 items, exhausting every possible permutation of the addends 0 through 9. They should be randomly sequenced, and they should be presented vertically, not horizontally (e.g., 5 + 7 = ___). There can be little question of the content validity of the test because all 100 single-digit addition facts are represented, though some may argue that horizontally presented items should be included. The student will write answers, so it will be a paper-and-pencil test. Finally, the student must complete the test within 5 minutes and miss no more than five items.

Construction of CRTs

The construction of a CRT is a multistage process. Although it requires time and effort, the process is well worth the dividends it pays in accurate and valid decision making. The alternative, which is of little value, is to create hurriedly a weak instrument, which estimates mastery poorly and should never be used at all. A well-constructed CRT is worth filing for future use, though we recommend the creation of several alternate forms of tests that cover the same curriculum unit. Below is a presentation of each step in the development of a CRT.

Naming the Test

Although it seems trivial, it is important to give the test a name that accurately represents its content. Over the course of years, teachers construct many tests, and a filing system that allows efficient retrieval for future use demands that test names obviously reflect their content. For instance, the name *phonology* implies a lot: sounding out vowels, consonants, consonant blends, digraphs, and diphthongs in the initial, medial, and end positions in a word. In other words, the name implies that everything subsumed under the broad skill of phonology is measured by the test. If the test covers only consonant blends in the medial position, the name *phonology* misrepresents the test's content.

Objective(s) Represented by the Test

It is important that tests be created *after* objectives have been specified. The test items are then constructed to reflect mastery of the objectives, not the other way around. Ideally, the objectives will be drawn from a large taxonomy of objectives that covers the entire domain.

Conditions under which the behavior will occur include any condition that might influence the examinee's performance during testing. Many conditions are generic and cover nearly all testing situations: good lighting, comfortable temperature, seats and tables of the correct size, and so on. Other conditions are unique to a particular test: necessary materials, explicit instructions to the examinee, timing factors, and others. The statement of the behavior should ideally include an action verb (e.g., write, pronounce orally, walk). In other words, the behavior should be objectively defined such that two people would agree that the behavior has or has not occurred. Criteria should be in the form of one of a number of recognized scores: percentage correct, behavior rates, duration, response latency, intensity, standard score, percentile rank, and so on.

Instructions for Administration

This component tells the user how the test should be given. It elaborates the conditions element of the objective. The purpose of instructions for administration is to standardize data collection so that from occasion to occasion, from child to child, and from examiner to examiner, the test is administered in the same way. This makes the scores comparable. Typical elements included are (a) instructions to the child, (b) materials needed (e.g., two sharpened number 2 pencils, a watch for timing purposes), (c) ways to deal with interruptions, and (d) ways to deal with questions from the child. The test makers must ask themselves what elements impinge on the successful administration of the test.

Instructions for Scoring

This section tells the user how to transform the examinee's responses into item scores and total scores. This often means providing criteria for correct and incorrect responses to individual items in a scoring key. A formula may be required to obtain a total score (e.g., the formula for behavior rates), and it should be illustrated for the uninformed user.

Instructions for Interpretation

Here the user is told how to make decisions on the basis of the score(s) obtained from an administration of the instrument. Basically, the criteria for minimally acceptable performance laid out in the objective guide this process. If the criterion mentions 95% accuracy, then the user should compare the examinee's score with 95%. If the examinee's score equals or exceeds that value, the child has mastered the objective. If not, then the objective needs more instruction and practice.

Specific Items in the Instrument

The key here is for the test maker to ensure that the items in the test are representative of the skills specified in the objectives. First, there must be enough items to comprise a reliable sample of the skills in question. It is rarely possible to have a reliable measure of any objective with less than 25 items. Second, the items should adequately represent

Table 1 Estimated Standard Errors of Test Scores

Number of items	Standard error[a]	Exceptions: Regardless of the length of the test, the standard error is
< 24	2	0 when the score is zero or perfect
24–47	3	1 when 1 or 2 percentage points from 0 or 100%
48–89	4	2 when 3 to 7 percentage points from 0 or 100%
90–109	5	3 when 8 to 15 percentage points from 0 or 100%
110–129	6	
130–150	7	

Source: Used with permission ©1979 Ronald C. Eaves.

a. Standard errors are in raw score form. Items are assumed to be scored dichotomously (i.e., 0 or 1).

the various kinds of subskills contained within an objective. For instance, a test on addition facts is unrepresentative if it does not include items containing 6 or 8.

Standard Error of Measurement

The standard error of measurement (SEM) of a test can be estimated using the number of items contained in the test. This estimate should be included along with the other components of the test. As an example of the use of the SEM, consider the student who obtains a raw score of 7 on a test containing 11 items. The student's percentage correct is 64%. Because the percentage does not fall into one of the exceptions, the estimated SEM is 2 (for tests with less than 24 items). In order to construct a 95% confidence interval, the assessor should double the SEM (i.e., $2 \times 2 = 4$). Next, the product is subtracted from the student's raw score ($7 - 4 = 3$), and then the product is added to the student's raw score ($7 + 4 = 11$). These values represent the 95% confidence interval in raw-score form (i.e., 3–11). In percentage-correct form, the assessors can say, with the knowledge that they will be correct on 95 out of 100 such judgments, that the student's true score is contained within the interval of 27%–100%. Notice that such results on a test with few items provide virtually no useful information for decision making. The same relative performance on a

100-item test would result in a 95% confidence interval of 54%–74%.

—Ronald C. Eaves and Suzanne Woods-Groves

See also Computerized Adaptive Testing; Standards for Educational and Psychological Testing

Further Reading

Eaves, R. C., McLaughlin, P. J., & Foster, G. G. (1979). Some simple statistical procedures for classroom use. *Diagnostique, 4,* 3–12.

Glaser, R., & Klaus, D. J. (1962). Proficiency measurements: Assessing human performance. In R. M. Gagne (Ed.), *Psychological principles in systems development.* New York: Holt, Rinehart & Winston.

Gronlund, N. E. (1985). *Measurement and evaluation in teaching* (5th ed.). New York: Macmillan.

Mager, R. F. (1984). *Preparing instructional objectives* (2nd ed.). Belmont, CA: David S. Lake.

National Research Council. (1996). *National science education standards.* Washington, DC: National Academies Press.

National Council of Teachers of Mathematics standards for mathematics: http://standards.nctm.org/index.htm

---

Applying Ideas on Statistics and Measurement

The following abstract is adapted from Laugksch, R. C., & Spargo, P. E. (1996). Construction of a paper-and-pencil Test of Basic Scientific Literacy based on selected literacy goals recommended by the American Association for the Advancement of Science. *Public Understanding of Science, 5*(4), 331–359.

This study describes the construction and validation of a **criterion-referenced** paper-and-pencil Test of Basic Scientific Literacy (TBSL) specifically designed for high school students entering university-level education in South Africa. The scientific literacy test items, designed to be answered *true, false,* or *do not know,* are based on a pool of 472 items developed previously from selected literacy goals recommended by the AAAS in *Science for All Americans.* Test items were pilot tested on 625 students and were included in the 110-item TBSL on the basis of item discrimination, item difficulty, and student feedback. The TBSL consists of subtests on three constitutive dimensions of scientific literacy: the nature of science, science content knowledge, and the impact of science and technology on society. About 260 members of various South African professional science and engineering associations participated in setting a performance standard for each of the three dimensions of scientific literacy. The internal consistency of the individual TBSL subtests, and the reliability of mastery-nonmastery classification decisions based on the performance standard, was found to be about 0.80. The reliability of the overall 110-item TBSL was 0.95.

CRITERION VALIDITY

Criterion-related validity refers to the extent to which one measure estimates or predicts the values of another measure or quality. The first measure is often called the estimator or the predictor variable. The second measure is called the criterion variable in cases when a decision must be made or when the measure is regarded as valid. In some cases, neither measure has well-developed validity evidence, and there is no genuine criterion variable. There are two types of criterion-related validity: concurrent validity and predictive validity. The simple distinction between the two types concerns the time interval between obtaining the first and the second set of measurements. For concurrent validity, the data from both measures are collected at about the same time. For predictive validity, the data from the criterion measure are collected some period of time after the data of the predictor variable.

Concurrent Validity

When a developer designs an instrument intended to measure any particular construct (say, intelligence), one of the most straightforward ways to begin establishing its validity is to conduct a concurrent validity study. The basic task is to identify an available instrument (say, the Stanford-Binet Intelligence Scale), the

validity of which has already been established, that measures the same construct or set of constructs as the new instrument. The second job is for the developer to identify a large, ideally random sample of people who are appropriate for the purposes of the instrument. Next, data are collected for both instruments from every person in the sample, generally on the same day. In many circumstances, it is considered important to collect the data in a counterbalanced fashion in order to control for practice effects. Fourth, a correlational technique appropriate to the scale of measurement is applied to the pairs of scores (e.g., Pearson product-moment correlation, Spearman rank correlation). Finally, the developer compares the obtained correlation or correlations with those of the established instrument and other similar instruments collected under similar circumstances. To the extent that the results compare favorably with other available validity coefficients (as they are called), the developer has begun the lengthy process of establishing the validity of the new instrument.

In the case of norm-referenced instruments, a second analysis of the data is in order: the comparison of the mean scores for the two instruments. Although the validity coefficient, if sufficiently high, establishes the fact that the instruments measured similar constructs, at least in the current sample, it does not indicate that the new instrument is unbiased. If the standard score means are significantly different statistically, then the two instruments will lead to different decisions in practice. For instance, if the instruments both measure intelligence, and the IQ cutoff score for mental retardation is 70, a substantial number of individuals will be misdiagnosed by the new instrument. If the mean IQ is too high compared with the established intelligence test, then a considerable number of Type II errors will be made. If the opposite circumstance exists, then Type I errors are the problem. Commonly, the source of this problem is attributed to the unrepresentativeness of the new instrument's norm group.

Three additional circumstances exist in which concurrent validity studies are conducted. When an existing instrument is substantially revised, it is important for the developer to show that the new instrument measures the relevant construct in the same way as the old instrument. This was perhaps the most important question users asked when the Vineland Adaptive Behavior Scales replaced the Vineland Social Maturity Scale. When a new instrument attempts to measure a construct that has not previously been measured with a high degree of validity (i.e., there is no available valid criterion measure), the developer may embark on a series of concurrent validity studies to determine just what the new instrument actually measures. For example, a general measure of arousal might be compared with measures of attention, persistence, curiosity, preference for novelty, vigilance, and pupillary dilation. Finally, the developer of an instrument intended to predict some future performance may be unable or unwilling to wait for some lengthy period in order to obtain an appropriate criterion measure.

Predictive Validity

Predictive validity *must* be demonstrated when an instrument is specifically designed to estimate future performance. Although this need is obvious when applicants are selected for jobs or college enrollment, many instruments in fact serve a predictive function, particularly when the construct measured is known to be stable (e.g., intelligence, academic achievement, physical strength).

Consider a newly developed test (say, the Primary School Readiness Test), the purpose of which is to predict which kindergarten children will succeed and which will fail if allowed to move on to first grade. The primary and perhaps the only purpose of such a test is to make a simple prediction: who should be retained in kindergarten and who should move on to first grade. Whatever other evidence is available, the absence of predictive validity evidence for the Primary School Readiness Test would cause any potential users to look elsewhere for their instrument of choice.

The fundamental research design for predictive validity is the same as that described above for concurrent validity, but with one difference: a time interval between the collection of the predictor variable data and the collection of the criterion variable data. The length of the interval depends on the prediction to be made. For instance, the Primary School Readiness Test claims to predict success and failure in achieving first-grade curriculum objectives, which can best be determined at the end of first grade. Thus, a 1-year interval is called for. For tests designed to select high school students for college enrollment (e.g., the Scholastic Aptitude Test), the criterion measure is often final college grade point average. In this case, the time interval is 4 years or more. Because as time passes, performance levels can change, concurrent validity coefficients will almost always be higher than predictive validity coefficients, and shorter intervals will lead to higher predictive validity coefficients than longer intervals will.

An alternative to the conventional predictive validity study is the postdictive design. The test developer, who may be reluctant to wait a year or more to obtain predictive validity data, can sometimes use extant criterion data that were collected at some time in the past. For instance, to show that an intelligence test can effectively estimate academic achievement, the developer may correlate achievement data collected the previous year with currently obtained data from the intelligence test. Although the usual sequence of the data collection is reversed, Jensen argued that the resulting validity coefficients provide unbiased estimates of the criterion-related validity of the predictor.

Classification Accuracy

Classification accuracy studies provide another way of estimating the criterion-related validity of an instrument. Consider a test (the Always Accurate Autism Test, or AAAT) that claims to classify children with autistic disorder. If such a test were administered to 50 children previously classified as autistic (i.e., true positives) and 50 children previously classified as not autistic (i.e., true negatives), the test would ideally classify all 100 children accurately. That is seldom the case. Sensitivity is a term that refers to the percentage of true positives identified by the test, and specificity refers to the percentage of true negatives identified by the test. An inspection of Table 1 shows that the

Table 1   Classification Accuracy of the Always Accurate Autism Test

	Clinical Classification	
AAAT	*Autistic (n = 50)*	*Not Autistic (n = 50)*
Autistic	30 (60%)	22 (44%)
Not autistic	20 (40%)	28 (56%)
Overall classification accuracy	58 (58%)	

AAAT correctly identified 60% of the children with autism (i.e., sensitivity), and 56% of the children who did not have autism (specificity), and had an overall classification accuracy of 58%. Consequently, the classification accuracy of the AAAT was only a bit better than chance assignment.

The Problem With Criterion Measures

In many cases, the estimator or predictor variable (e.g., a newly developed test) may have good validity but suffer because the available criterion measures are not very valid. Although a record of performance (e.g., number of widgets made, rate of typing errors, number of tires changed) is appealing for many jobs, for many other situations (e.g., teachers, physicians, administrative assistants), no simple measure of production or performance is available. The criterion measures that are available (e.g., supervisor ratings) may be unreliable and consequently limited in their validity. For example, college grade point averages lack validity for a variety of reasons (e.g., restriction of range of college-student ability levels). This state of affairs guarantees a reduced validity coefficient between the estimator or predictor variable and the criterion variable even though the estimator or predictor variable is highly valid. In such instances, a commonly used technique is correction for attenuation. This procedure adjusts the reliability of the criterion measure so that it contains no error, providing a boost for the resulting validity coefficient and answering the question, What would the validity coefficient be if the criterion measure were perfectly reliable?

—*Ronald C. Eaves and Suzanne Woods-Groves*

See also Attenuation, Correction for; Predictive Validity; Validity Coefficient; Validity Theory

Further Reading

Jensen, A. R. (1980). *Bias in mental testing.* New York: Free Press.

Salvia, J., & Ysseldyke, J. E. (2004). *Assessment* (8th ed.). Boston: Houghton Mifflin.

Applying Ideas on Statistics and Measurement

The following abstract is adapted from Ice, G. H., & Yogo, J. (2005). Measuring stress among Luo elders: Development of the Luo Perceived Stress Scale. *Field Methods, 17*(4), 394–411.

This study describes the development of the Luo Perceived Stress Scale (LPSS) tested on 200 Luo elders. The LPSS consists of 23 emotions and uses alternating "local idioms of distress" and well-being. Due to the low level of education of the population, a yes-no format is used instead of a Likert-type scale. The scale was tested among 200 Luo elders and was found to be internally reliable. **Criterion validity** was examined through the associations between LPSS score and caregiving, social networks, depression, and cortisol. Known group validity was examined through comparisons of caregiving groups, genders, marital status, and participation in social groups. While these variables were generally associated with LPSS in the predicted direction, subsequent factor analysis suggested that the LPSS did not represent a single domain.

CRITICAL VALUE

The critical value is the value needed for rejection of the null hypothesis when it is true. For example, if the critical value for a particular type of statistic's distribution and the sample size at a particular level

Table 1   Critical Values

Degrees of freedom	Critical value for rejection of the null hypothesis at the .05 level of significance	Critical value for rejection of the null hypothesis at the .01 level of significance
40	2.021	2.704
60	2.000	2.660
120	1.980	2.617

of Type I error is 3.45, then the observed or computed value must exceed 3.455 for the outcome to be significant.

The following points about critical values should be remembered:

1. There is a different critical value depending on the size of the sample being evaluated (reflected in the degrees of freedom) and the Type I error set by the experimenter.

2. Critical values are usually shown in tables that accompany many statistical texts. A typical table, such as the one used for testing the difference between two independent means, would appear like Table 1. Note that the research hypothesis can be tested at both the .01 and .05 levels of significance.

3. Each test statistic (such as the t test or the F test) has its own distribution of critical values.

4. With the advent of computerized statistical analysis programs, critical values are no longer needed for comparison's sake. Rather, the exact probability of an outcome (the Type I error level) is printed out. For example, instead of the statement "The results were significant beyond the .05 level," a more accurate statement might be, "The probability of a Type I error was .043."

—*Neil J. Salkind*

Further Reading

Salkind, N. J. (2004). *Statistics for people who (think they) hate statistics*. Thousand Oaks, CA: Sage.

CRONBACH, LEE J. (1916–2001)

Lee J. Cronbach, known widely as the creator of Cronbach's alpha, was a man whose deep interests in psychological testing and educational psychology combined as the focus of more than 50 years of research into measurement theory, program evaluation, and instruction.

Cronbach was born in Fresno, California, and came to the attention of Blanche Cummings, a follower of Lewis Terman, when his precociousness at the age of 4 made itself known as she overheard him calculating the price of potatoes at a grocery store. Ms. Cummings gave the Stanford-Binet to Cronbach in 1921 and ensured wide publicity of his score of 200. According to Cronbach, this number was inflated; however, his future eminence was not, as evidenced by his many lifetime contributions.

Because of his mother and Ms. Cummings, Cronbach's education began, not with kindergarten, but with the second grade. He graduated from high school at 14 and immediately went to college, graduating at age 18. Interestingly, Cronbach's first higher educational interests lay in chemistry and mathematics; had not a lack of funds kept him at Fresno State, he may never have discovered his passion for educational research. He went on to Berkeley for a master's in education, gaining his teaching credentials at the same time. Cronbach then taught high school (math and chemistry) while he finished an education doctorate at the University of Chicago, graduating in 1940. He married Helen Claresta Bower while at Chicago, and their five children arrived between 1941 and 1956.

While at the University of Chicago, he became a research assistant for Ralph Tyler in the Eight-Year Study, which looked into how high school curriculum affected students' success in both admission to and graduation from colleges and universities. On graduation, Cronbach worked as an associate professor at Washington State University, where he taught myriad psychology courses. Toward the end of World War II, he worked as a military psychologist at the Naval

Sonar School in San Diego, California. Cronbach went back to the University of Chicago as an associate professor and then on to the University of Illinois as a full professor. In 1964, he landed in Palo Alto, California, where he taught, conducted research, and finally retired at Stanford University, gaining the prestigious Vida Jacks Professor of Education Emeritus honor (among many others) during his tenure.

Cronbach's most famous contributions to the area of tests and measurements were his efforts at strengthening tests and measures through a deeper understanding of what constituted measurement error; i.e., that error had many sources. This led to the 1951 paper "Coefficient Alpha and the Internal Structure of Tests." The subsequent results of this work led to further research and ultimately a rewriting of generalizability theory with Goldine Gleser. Referred to as G Theory, these results brought together mathematics and psychology as an aggregate structure within which error sources may be identified.

—*Suzanne M. Grundy*

See also Coefficient Alpha

Further Reading

Cronbach, L. J. (1951). Coefficient alpha and the internal structure of tests. *Psychometrika, 16*(3), 297–334.

Cronbach, L. J. (1989). Lee J. Cronbach. In G. Lindzey (Ed.), *A history of psychology in autobiography, Vol. 8* (pp. 62–93). Stanford, CA: Stanford University Press.

Lee Cronbach's two most influential papers: http://psychclassics.yorku.ca/Cronbach/construct.htm and http://psychclassics.yorku.ca/Cronbach/Disciplines

CULTURE FAIR INTELLIGENCE TEST

Fluid intelligence (Gf) taps "the level of complexity of relationships which an individual can perceive and act upon when he doesn't have recourse to answers to such complex issues already stored in memory" (Cattell, 1971, p. 99). It is "concerned with basic processes of reasoning and other mental activities that depend only minimally on learning and acculturation" (Carroll, 1993, p. 624). Therefore, tests of Gf have little informational content and require the ability to see complex relationships between simple elements like number and letter series, figure classification, figure analogies, spatial visualization, block designs, matrices, and so forth.

The Culture Fair Intelligence Test (CFIT) was designed by R. B. Cattell expressly as a nonverbal test to measure Gf. The CFIT comprises three scales: scale 1 for ages 4 to 8 as well as for mentally retarded adults, scale 2 for ages 8 to 13 as well as for average adults from the general population, and scale 3 for people of above-average intelligence. Scales 2 and 3 each have two parallel forms (A and B), which can be alternately used for retesting. The majority of these tests can be administered collectively, except some subtests from scale 1. The CFIT is highly speeded and requires detailed verbal instructions for administration.

Scale 1 includes eight subtests, but only half of them are really culturally fair. This scale cannot be recommended because some subtests must be administered individually, requiring complex instructions, and effects of familiarity with language and the habits of listening and attending are not minimized.

Scales 2 and 3 are quite similar, differing only in their difficulty level. They comprise four subtests: figure series (the individual is asked which figure logically continues a series of three model figures), figure classification (the individual is asked which two figures in each series go together), matrices (the individual must determine which of five alternatives most logically completes a given matrix pattern), and figure generalization (the individual must figure out the general rule for where a dot has to be placed by inferring the rule and picking the figure to which it applies). Each form of scales 2 and 3 takes about 30 minutes to administer.

Internal consistency and alternate-form reliability estimates generally range from .70 to more than .80. The lowest estimates are justified by Cattell on the scales' inclusion of several diverse formats to measure the same underlying construct. This is a main difference between the widely known Progressive Matrices Test and the CFIT. Cattell and Jensen discredited the former because of specific variance due to using only the matrix-problem format. These researchers agree that the CFIT does not contaminate the measurement of the construct of interest (Gf) with variance specific to item type. A fine-grained measure of Gf must employ several different subtests to wash out any contamination with test specificity.

Validity has been researched by means of factor analysis and correlations with other tests. CFIT correlates around .80 with a latent *g* factor, and correlations with other reasoning tests (i.e., Raven's Progressive Matrices, the Wechsler Intelligence Scale for Children, and the Wechsler Adult Intelligence Scale) are generally above .50. Predictive validity studies show moderate correlations with several scholastic and occupational criteria.

The CFIT is an excellent choice for assessing intelligence across cultures because of its fluid nature. It has been administered in several European countries and in North America, Africa, and Asia, and norms tend to remain unchanged in relatively close cultures.

—Roberto Colom and Francisco J. Abad

See also Fagan Test of Infant Intelligence; Gf-Gc Theory of Intelligence; Intelligence Quotient; Intelligence Tests

Further Reading

Buj, V. (1981). Average IQ values in various European countries. *Personality and Individual Differences, 2,* 169–170.

Cattell, R. B. (1971). *Abilities: Their structure, growth, and action.* Boston: Houghton-Mifflin.

Cattell, R. B. (1980). They talk of some strict testing of us—pish. *Behavioral and Brain Sciences, 3,* 336–337.

Cattell, R. B. (1987). *Intelligence: Its structure, growth, and action.* Amsterdam: North-Holland.

Colom, R., & García-López, O. (2003). Secular gains in fluid intelligence: Evidence from the Culture Fair Intelligence Test. *Journal of Biosocial Science, 35,* 33–39.

Jensen, A. R. (1980). *Bias in mental testing.* New York: Free Press.

Kline, P. (2000). *Handbook of psychological testing* (2nd ed.). London: Routledge.

Lynn, R., & Vanhanen, T. (2002). *IQ and the wealth of nations.* Westport, CT: Praeger.

CUMULATIVE FREQUENCY DISTRIBUTION

Once a frequency distribution has been created and the data are visually represented by means of a histogram or a frequency polygon, another option is to create a cumulative frequency distribution, or a visual representation of the cumulative frequency of occurrences by class intervals.

A cumulative frequency distribution is based on the same data as a frequency distribution, but with an added column (cumulative frequency), as shown in Table 1.

The cumulative frequency distribution begins by the creation of a new column labeled "Cumulative frequency." Then, the frequency in each class interval is added to all the frequencies below it. For example, for the class interval of 19–24, there are 3 occurrences and none below it, so its cumulative frequency is 3. For the class interval of 25–29, there are 4 occurrences and 3 below it, for a total of 7 (4 + 3) occurrences in that class interval or below it. The last class interval (65–69) contains 1 occurrence, and there is a total of 49 occurrences at or below that class interval.

Once the cumulative frequency distribution is created, the data can be plotted just as they were for a histogram or a frequency polygon. Another name for a cumulative frequency polygon is an *ogive*. And if

Table 1 Cumulative Frequency Distribution

Class Interval	Frequency	Cumulative Frequency
65–69	1	40
60–64	4	39
55–59	5	35
50–54	4	30
45–49	3	26
40–44	5	23
35–39	6	18
30–34	5	12
25–29	4	7
19–24	3	3

the distribution of the data is normal, then the ogive represents what is popularly known as a bell curve or a normal distribution.

—*Neil J. Salkind*

See also Frequency Distribution; Histogram; Ogive

CURRICULUM-BASED MEASUREMENT

Curriculum-based measurement (CBM) is a method for measuring student competency and progress in the basic skill areas of reading fluency (e.g., words read correctly per minute), math computation, written expression, and spelling. When using CBM, an examiner gives the student brief, timed samples or *probes* lasting from 1 to 5 minutes, depending on the skill being measured, and student performance is scored for speed and accuracy to determine proficiency. Although CBM has been used in educational settings for more than 20 years, it is probably more familiar to special education teachers and school psychologists than to general education teachers and other professionals.

History of CBM

CBM began with the work of Stanley Deno and a number of doctoral students at the University of Minnesota in the late 1970s. Borrowing from the field of applied behavioral analysis, Deno and his team developed a measurement system that could efficiently produce monitoring data, could be displayed in graphic form, and would permit students' academic progress to be evaluated in only a few minutes.

CBM was examined in the 1970s with school-aged children with and without disabilities to assess its technical quality (e.g., reliability, validity) and practical utility (e.g., ease of administration). Following this development and validation phase, interest in CBM expanded because it provided an efficient alternative to expensive and time-consuming norm-referenced tests and was closely aligned with the curriculum. CBM has had the support of the U.S. Department of Education since the 1980s.

Examples of CBM

Examples of the application of CBM to reading, mathematics, spelling, and writing follow.

1. In reading, students read aloud for 1 minute from reading probes taken from basal reading series or from other reading probes designed with some control for grade-based readability. The number of words read correctly per minute is the metric of interest for evaluating oral reading fluency. In practice, three reading probes are given, and the middle score is reported. Another reading measure commonly used is the maze-reading task, a multiple-choice *cloze* technique in which students read grade-level reading passages in which every seventh word has been deleted and replaced by a blank; students are asked to fill in the blank by selecting one of three alternatives that appear beneath the blank. The measure is scored by counting the number of correct word choices per 5 minutes.

2. In mathematics, students write answers to computational problems. The math probes last from 2 to 5 minutes, depending on the type of skill assessed. The number of digits correct and incorrect for each probe is counted.

3. In spelling, the examiner dictates words at specified intervals of time for 2 minutes, and the number of correct letter sequences and words spelled correctly is counted.

4. In writing, the student is given a "story starter" (e.g., "Jill got a surprise package in the mail") and is asked to write a story within 3 minutes. The number of words written, spelled correctly, correct word sequences, or both are counted.

CBM is designed to identify students whose level and rate (slope) of performance are below those of the reference group. Thus, equal weight is given to skill level (low achievement) and to progress (slope), regardless of the type of skill assessed.

Key Features of CBM

CBM has three key features. It is dynamic, it does not preclude the use of other measures, and it is designed to measure basic skills. As a dynamic measure, CBM is sensitive to the effects of instruction. When a student's learning improves as a result of a short-term intervention (i.e., 6 weeks), CBM is designed to detect this improvement whereas norm referenced tests may not be sensitive enough to do so. CBM has been described as an "academic thermometer." In the medical field, temperature is an efficient, important indicator of health. As an academic thermometer, CBM is an efficient, important indicator of academic health. For example, the number of words read correctly from text in 1 minute is an accurate yet efficient indicator of general reading achievement, including comprehension.

Although CBM assesses important skills, it does not measure all behaviors in an academic realm, and so it does not preclude the use of other specific measures. Finally, CBM is designed to assess basic skills necessary for success in later courses (e.g., social studies, science) that in turn are necessary for employment. Assessment of basic skills acquisition is particularly important for low-performing students through sixth grade and for the majority of special education students, who often continue to experience significant difficulty in basic skills throughout their schooling.

CBM and Its Use in a Problem-Solving Model

CBM is typically used in a problem-solving model that defines academic problems within a specific context and attempts to solve these problems. The problem-solving approach involves five steps: (a) problem identification, (b) problem certification, (c) exploration of solutions, (d) evaluation of solutions, and (e) problem solution. CBM is used in every step of this process to determine the severity of the problem, set goals, plan interventions, and evaluate the efficacy of these interventions. Within this framework, problems are defined as *situational*. A problem is conceived as a discrepancy between what is expected and what is occurring in a specific context. For instance, for a student experiencing reading difficulty, the problem would be defined in terms of how the student reads compared with a particular local standard (e.g., a community) rather than a national standard. In this approach, the need to assess situations or the effects of

interventions in addition to assessing the student is stressed.

An assessment approach like CBM often challenges researchers and clinicians to reconsider how children are assessed. Instead of measuring a student's skills at a single point in time, the child is assessed on an ongoing basis to evaluate the effect of instructional interventions. In this way, CBM takes into account the instructional context, something often overlooked in traditional assessment approaches. CBM shifts the focus from a summative evaluation perspective (e.g., determining what a student has learned) to a formative evaluation perspective (e.g., determining what the student is learning) that is continuous during instruction. CBM data is collected on a repeated, frequent basis, rather than in simple pre- or posttest fashion, to help determine the conditions under which student progress is facilitated. If student response to an academic intervention is unsatisfactory, the intervention is changed in some meaningful way with the aim of improving learning.

Figure 1 illustrates how CBM data are graphed to reflect learning level and slope. Each data point in Figure 1 represents the number of words a

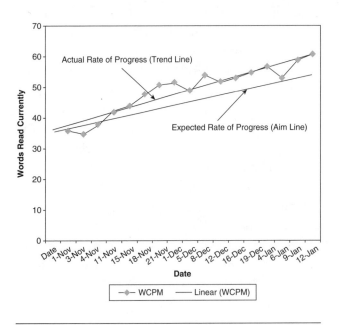

Figure 1 CBM Progress Monitoring Graph

Note: For example, the effects of an academic intervention on the reading achievement of a particular student over an 8-week period.

student read correctly per minute on a given day while exposed to a reading intervention. The heavy line indicates the trend, or the actual rate of progress under the academic intervention. The fine line is the aim line, or the expected level of performance for this child. The expected level of performance is an informed guess based on how typical students are expected to progress on a weekly basis. This information is used as a frame of reference for determining whether the referred student is performing at the same rate of improvement (i.e., slope) as classroom peers are. For example, there is some evidence to suggest that third-grade students typically improve about one word read correctly per week on a CBM oral reading measure. CBM practitioners call this learning trajectory the *average learning rate*. The average learning rate can help us make important comparisons among individuals (e.g., typical general education students and English language learners).

Advantages of CBM

Several advantages of CBM are evident. Stecker and Fuchs, for example, demonstrated improvements in academic growth among students with and without disabilities when teachers employed CBM, suggesting that CBM may be both an effective assessment tool and a powerful intervention technique to improve student performance. Because CBM takes only minutes to administer, it is possible to collect data on a large number of students and make local normative data available quickly to schools and districts. For certain populations, local norms may be preferred over national norms to identify which students are falling behind the general education curriculum. Local norms enable comparisons with students from similar geographic locations, who have similar curricular experiences and who share the same language or cultural background. CBM measures specific skills that are being taught in the classroom, ensuring content validity, whereas traditional norm-referenced tests often measure broad curriculum areas that may not be as well aligned with the curriculum. The alignment of test content and the curriculum plus the administration of multiple brief probes helps ensure valid, continuous

data about progress. Finally, recognition of CBM as a viable instrument to assess student performance can be found in a variety of task force documents on assessment and special education reform. CBM is also an integral part of the new, alternative approach to the identification of learning disabilities called Response to Intervention, which is part of the 2004 reauthorization of Individuals with Disabilities in Education Improvement Act.

Limitations of CBM

Despite the general acceptance of CBM as a measurement instrument, it has been subjected to criticism. Critics point out that CBM cannot assess the breadth and depth of the elementary, middle, and high school curriculum (e.g., content knowledge in various subjects). Advocates counter that CBM is intended to have an exclusive focus on basic skills assessment, not the assessment of broader skills or abilities. Critics also argue that a reliance on local norms would lead to variability between schools in the identification of students who are eligible for special education services under the Response to Intervention model, resulting in classification inconsistency from school to school. Proponents of CBM acknowledge this criticism but point out that classification variability already exists. Despite the criticisms, many followers of CBM would say that this measuring tool has earned a place among other measurement techniques that seek to assess academic difficulties and improve instruction within schools and districts.

—*Romilia Domínguez de Ramírez
and Thomas Kubiszyn*

Further Reading

Shapiro, E. S. (2004). *Academic skills problems: Direct assessment and intervention* (3rd ed.). New York: Guilford.

Shinn, M. R. (Ed.). (1998). *Advanced applications of curriculum-based measurement.* New York: Guilford.

Stecker, P., & Fuchs, L. (2000). Effecting superior achievement using curriculum-based measurement: The importance of individual progress monitoring. *Learning Disabilities Research & Practice, 15,* 128–135.

CBM testing materials page: http://aimsweb.com
Intervention Central: http://www.interventioncentral.org

CURSE OF DIMENSIONALITY

Curse of dimensionality refers to the rapid increase in volume associated with adding extra dimensions to a mathematical space. In the behavioral and social sciences, the mathematical space in question refers to the multidimensional space spanned by the set of V variables collected by the researcher. Simply put, the ability to simultaneously analyze large sets of variables requires large numbers of observations due to the fact that, as the number of variables increases, the multidimensional space becomes more and more sparse. This problem manifests itself in several analytical techniques (such as multiple regression and finite mixture modeling) in which difficulties arise because the variance-covariance matrix becomes singular (i.e., noninvertible) when the number of observations, N, exceeds the number of variables, V. Additionally, as N approaches V, the parameter estimates of the aforementioned models become increasingly unstable, causing statistical inference to become less precise.

For a mathematical example, consider multiple regression in which we are predicting y from a matrix of explanatory variables, $\mathbf{X}$. For ease of presentation, assume that the data are mean centered; then the unbiased estimate of the covariance matrix of $\mathbf{X}$ is given by

$$\Sigma = \mathbf{X}'\mathbf{X}\frac{1}{n-1}.$$

Furthermore, the general equation for multiple regression is

$$y = \mathbf{X}\beta + \varepsilon,$$

where

y is the $N \times 1$ vector of responses,

$\mathbf{X}$ is the $N \times V$ matrix of predictor variables,

β is the $V \times 1$ vector of parameter estimates corresponding to the predictor variables, and

ε is the $N \times 1$ vector of residuals.

It is well known that the estimate of β is given by

$$\beta = (\mathbf{X}'\mathbf{X})^{-1}\mathbf{X}'\gamma.$$

It is easily seen that the $(\mathbf{X}'\mathbf{X})^{-1}$ is proportional to the inverse of Σ. Thus, if there are any redundancies (i.e., Σ is not of full rank, or in regression terms, multicollinearity exists) in Σ, it will not be possible to take the inverse of Σ and, consequently, it will not be possible to estimate β. One possible introduction of multicollinearity into Σ is when V exceeds N.

Related to this general problem is the fact that, as V increases, the multidimensional space becomes more and more sparse. To illustrate, consider the Euclidean distance between any two points x and y,

$$d(x, y) = \sqrt{\sum_{i=1}^{v}(x_i - y_i)^2},$$

the square root of the sum of squared differences across all V dimensions. To begin, consider the two points $x = (1, 3)$ and $y = (4, 7)$, which results in the Euclidean distance of $d(x,y) = [(1-4)^2 + (3-7)^2]^{1/2} = [9 + 16]^{1/2} = 5$. Now assume that K additional, albeit meaningless, dimensions are added to each observation by sampling from a uniform distribution with lower bound of 0 and upper bound of 1 (denoted by $U(0,1)$). The new Euclidean distance, $d(x,y)^*$, is given by

$$d(x, y)^* = 5 + \sqrt{\sum_{k=1}^{K}(U(0,1)_k - U(0,1)_k)^2},$$

where the 5 represents the original Euclidean distance and the remainder of $d(x,y)^*$ represents the additional distance that is due to random noise alone. Clearly, as $K \to \infty$, then $d(x,y)^* \to \infty$, indicating that as more dimensions are added, the two points become farther and farther apart. In the extreme, an infinite amount of random noise results in the two points being infinitely far apart.

The problem is amplified when considering the computation of multivariate distance, D (also known as the Mahalonobis distance), between two $V \times 1$ vectors, $\mathbf{a}$ and $\mathbf{b}$:

$$D(\mathbf{a},\mathbf{b}) = (\mathbf{a} - \mathbf{b})'\Sigma^{-1}(\mathbf{a} - \mathbf{b}).$$

If Σ equals the $V \times V$ identity matrix, then D($\mathbf{a},\mathbf{b}$) reduces to $d(\mathbf{a},\mathbf{b})$, and the aforementioned problem exists when dimensions are added; however, when Σ does not equal the identity matrix, the aforementioned problems are accompanied by the fact that N must exceed V so that the inverse of Σ may be computed. Thus, any multivariate statistical technique (for example, multiple discriminant analysis) that relies on the inverse of the covariance matrix is subject to the curse of dimensionality.

To make the example more salient, consider the following visual demonstration. First, we generate 100 observations from a $U(0,1)$ distribution in one dimension (see upper left panel of Figure 1). Here the average distance between all points is .3415. The upper right panel of Figure 1 depicts the addition of an additional dimension, in which 100 more observations were generated from a $U(0,1)$ distribution, causing the average distance between all pairs of points to increase to .5436. The lower left panel of Figure 1 depicts the addition of yet another dimension generated from a $U(0,1)$ distribution, causing the average distance between all points to increase to .6818. The lower right panel indicates the distance of all points to the mean in each of the scenarios. It is easily seen that as the number of dimensions increases, so do the distances to the mean.

This depiction illustrates how quickly point clouds can become sparse, wreaking havoc on data analysis that takes advantage of the full amount of information available to the researcher. In fact, infinitely increasing the number of dimensions also produces a multidimensional space with an infinite amount of variance. Instead of the traditional formula computing the covariance between two variables, x and y,

$$\text{Cov}(x, y) = \sum_{i=1}^{N}(x_i - \bar{x})(y_i - \bar{y})/(N - 1),$$

which is represented by the distance of observations from the mean, the covariance matrix can be represented as a set of pairwise distances,

$$\text{Cov}(x, y) = \sum_{i=1}^{N}\sum_{j=1}^{N}(x_i - x_j)(y_i - y_j)/(2N).$$

Given the result discussed above, that an infinite number of dimensions results in an infinite distance between any pair of points, it is clear that the variances or covariances will also approach infinity as the number of dimensions approaches infinity. This increase in variance leads to the unstable estimation of parameters and joint distributions in high-dimensional spaces.

In response to sparse high-dimensional spaces, social science researchers often attempt to reduce the dimensionality of the data in such a manner as to retain the relevant information in the full dimensionality in substantially fewer dimensions. The two most popular techniques of data reduction are principal components

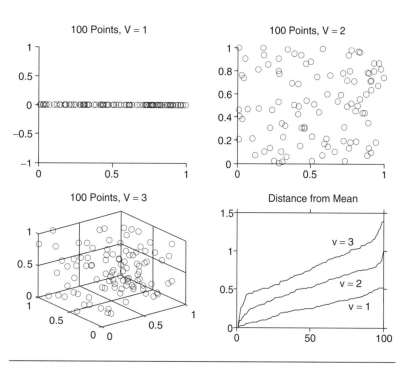

Figure 1   Interpoint Distance as a Function of Dimensionality

analysis and factor analysis. Principal components analysis attempts to extract a set of K new variables—called components—(where K is less than V) from the original data such that the K components are linear combinations of the original V variables. Thus, each of the new variables contains some information from each of the original variables. Furthermore, the K components are mutually orthogonal (i.e., uncorrelated). Usually, K is chosen such that an adequate amount of the variance originally present in V is still explained in the reduced dimensionality. In general, principal components analysis is a pure data reduction technique. On the other hand, factor analysis is the more popular method employed in the social sciences. Similar to the components in principal components analysis, the factors derived from factor analysis are linear combinations of the original V variables. However, unlike principal components analysis, factor analysis assumes that an underlying model consisting of a small number of factors (in comparison with the original number of variables) gives rise to the observed set of V variables, where the goal is to recreate the original $V \times V$ covariance matrix with a substantially smaller number of factors. After conducting a principal components analysis/factor analysis, the researcher often uses the components or factors in subsequent analyses (such as regression, MANOVA, or cluster analysis). Although this is a reasonable approach to dealing with the curse of dimensionality, the researcher should always remember that some information is necessarily lost when the data are reduced to a lower-dimensional space and that appropriate cautions should be taken when making subsequent inferences and interpretations.

—*Douglas Steinley*

Further Reading

Bellman, R. E. (1961). *Adaptive control processes*. Princeton, NJ: Princeton University Press.

Bishop, C. M. (1995). *Neural networks for pattern recognition*. Oxford, UK: Oxford University Press.

Scott, D. W. (1992). *Multivariate density estimation*. New York: Wiley.

CURVILINEAR REGRESSION

Researchers often use regression techniques to describe the relationship between two (or more) variables. In the simplest case (bivariate linear regression), it is assumed that the relationship can be described well by a straight line, $Y = a + bX$. One can use Student t to test hypotheses about or construct confidence intervals around the regression coefficients a (intercept or constant) and b (slope, number of units Y changes for each one-point change in X).

Often the relationship between variables can be better described with a line that is not straight. Curvilinear regression can be employed to describe some such relationships. In some cases, the researcher has good reason to expect a particular curvilinear relationship even before the data are collected. For example, an microbiologist may expect that the relationship between elapsed time and the number of bacteria in a rich medium is exponential. A psychophysicist may expect that the perceived intensity of a visual stimulus is a function of the logarithm of the physical intensity of the stimulus. A psychologist may expect that the relationship between the amount eaten by an individual and the number of persons present at the meal is a power function.

In other cases, the researcher does not expect any particular curvilinear relationship but discovers during data screening that the variables are not related in a linear fashion. One should always inspect a scatter plot of the data before conducting a regression analysis. All too often, researchers employ linear regression analysis when a much better fit would be obtained with a curvilinear analysis. Most researchers are familiar with linear regression and wish to stay within that framework when dealing with curvilinear relationships. This can be accomplished by applying a nonlinear transformation to one or both variables and then conducting linear regression analysis with the transformed data. Alternatively, one can conduct a polynomial regression (also known as a trend analysis), which is a multiple linear regression in which powers of the predictor variable(s) are included in the

Table 1   Simulated Data to Illustrate Curvilinear Regression

Number of Persons at Meal	Calories Consumed by Individual
1	413
1	332
1	391
1	392
1	436
2	457
2	534
2	457
2	514
2	537
3	551
3	605
3	601
3	598
3	577
4	701
4	671
4	617
4	590
4	592
5	587
5	596
5	611
5	552
5	679
6	745
6	692
6	666
6	716
6	815
13	762
13	631
13	670
13	720
13	685

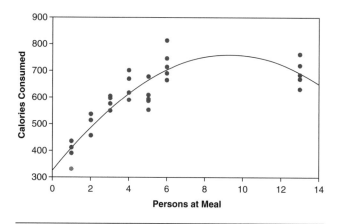

Figure 1   Scatter Plot With Quadratic Regression Line

to minimize the squared residuals for a linear regression on transformed data.

The Case Study and the Data

J. M. de Castro and E. M. Brewer investigated the relationship between the amount eaten by individuals and the number of persons at the meal. Table 1 presents data produced by a simulator that was designed to produce data similar to those obtained by de Castro and Brewer.

Plotting the Data

SPSS was employed to create a scatter plot with a quadratic regression line (Figure 1). Clearly, the relationship between number of persons and amount eaten can be described with a curved line better than with a straight line.

Polynomial Regression

For a linear regression, we would find a and b such that the errors in prediction would be minimized for the model $C = a + b_1P$, where C is calories consumed by the individual, and P is the number of persons at the meal. For a quadratic regression, we would add persons squared to the linear model, that is, $C = a + b_1P + b_2P^2$. Adding P^2 to the model allows the curve to have one bend in it. For a cubic regression, we would add

model. Less commonly, the researcher may choose to conduct a true nonlinear analysis. In such an analysis, the researcher estimates the values of the model parameters by attempting to minimize the squared residuals (differences between observed Y and predicted Y) for the actual nonlinear model rather than attempting persons cubed to the quadratic model, that is, $C = a + b_1P + b_2P^2 + b_3P^3$. Adding P^3 to the model allows a second bend in the regression line. For each additional power of the predictor variable added to the model, an additional bend is allowed in the regression line.

While it is not impossible to fit the model to the data with hand computations, it is extremely laborious and shall not be done here. Any of the major statistical programs can do the analysis with the same routine that is used to conduct multiple linear regression. Here is an SAS program that will conduct the polynomial regression:

```
data eat; infile 'C:\CurviData-Sage.txt';

input persons calories; pers2 =
persons*persons; pers3 = persons**3;

proc reg; LINEAR: model calories =
persons;

QUADRATIC: model calories = persons pers2;

CUBIC: model calories = persons pers2 pers3; run;
```

The statistical output for the linear model shows that there is a significant linear relationship between calories consumed and the number of people at the meal, $C = 489.4 + 20.97*P$, $r^2 = .464$, $p < .001$. If we had not produced and inspected a scatter plot, we might be tempted to report this linear analysis. Look at the statistical output for the quadratic model (Figure 2).

The relationship is now estimated as $C = 322.6 + 93.63*P - 5.012*P^2$. Notice that the proportion of variance explained by the model has increased from .464 to .812. This increase in R^2 is statistically significant, $t(32) = 7.69$, $p < .001$. Allowing one bend in the regression line produced significantly better fit to the data.

The R^2 for the cubic model (.816) is only slightly greater than that for the quadratic model, and the increase in R^2 falls well short of statistical

The REG Procedure Model: QUADRATIC Dependent Variable: Calories

Analysis of Variance

Source	DF	Sum of Squares	Mean Square	F Value	Pr > F
Model	2	364763	182382	69.02	<.0001
Error	32	84559	2642.46099		
Corrected Total	34	449322			

Root MSE	51.40487	R-Square	0.8118
Dependent Mean	591.22857	Adj R-Sq	0.8000
Coeff Var	8.69459		

Parameter Estimates

Variable	DF	Parameter Estimate	Standard Error	t Value	Pr > |t|
Intercept	1	322.61068	26.02751	12.39	<.0001
persons	1	93.63192	9.74149	9.61	<.0001
pers2	1	−5.01215	0.65194	−7.69	<.0001

Figure 2   SAS Output for Quadratic Model

significance, $t(31) = 0.86$, $p = .40$. Accordingly, the quadratic model is adopted.

Evaluating a Power Function

De Castro and Brewer tested the hypothesis that amount eaten (C, kilocalories) by individuals is a power function of the number of persons (P) at the meal. That is, $C = k*\log(P)$. Such a model can be estimated by applying a log transformation to both variables and then using a simple linear model to predict one transformed variable from the other transformed variable. Here is the SAS code to conduct such an analysis for our simulated data:

```
data power; set eat; logpers = log10(persons); logcal =
log10(calories);

proc reg; POWER: model logcal = logpers; run;
```

The resulting model is statistically significant, $r^2 = .748$, $t(33) = 9.91$, $p < .001$. The prediction equation, in log terms, is $\log(C) = 2.629 + .237*\log(P)$. Exponentiating both sides of this expression transforms

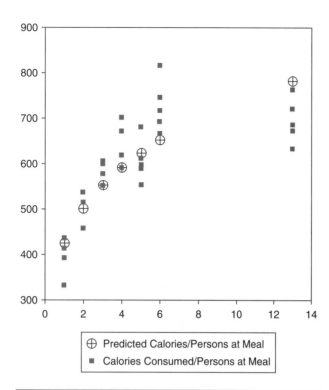

Figure 3   Scatter Plot With Values Predicted by the Power Function

the prediction equation to $C = 425.6*P^{.237}$. Figure 3 shows the data with the values predicted by the power function overlaid.

Confidence Interval on R²

It is desirable to report effect size estimates and to place confidence intervals around those estimates. In regression analysis, the squared correlation coefficient is commonly used as an effect size estimate. Constructing a confidence interval around r^2 requires an iterative procedure, but there are scripts and programs that make this easy. If the predictor variable(s) can be considered to be fixed rather than random, use the SAS program at http://core.ecu.edu/psyc/wuenschk/SAS/Conf-Interval-R2-Regr.sas or the SPSS script at http://core.ecu.edu/psyc/wuenschk/SPSS/CI-R2-SPSS.zip. For our sample data, the predictor is most reasonably considered random. Jim Steiger's R2 program (which can be downloaded at www.inter chg.ubc.ca/steiger/r2.zip, manual at http://www.inter chg.ubc.ca/steiger/r2.pdf) will construct such a

confidence interval. For our data, a 95% confidence interval for the power model r^2 extends from .55 to .86.

Assumptions of the Analysis

There are no assumptions for estimating the slope, the intercept, and the r^2, but one need keep in mind that the fit of the model to the data will be poor if one has chosen an inappropriate model, such as a linear model when a quadratic model would fit the data much better. When one is testing hypotheses about or creating confidence intervals around these estimates, there are three basic assumptions, each involving the error term (the residuals, the difference between actual values of Y and predicted values of Y):

1. Independence: The amount of error for each observation is assumed to be independent of the amount of error for any other observation.

2. Homoscedasticity (also known as homogeneity of variance): It is assumed that the error variance is constant across all values of the X variable(s).

3. Normality: It is assumed that the error term is normally distributed at each level of the X variable(s).

These assumptions are most commonly checked by inspecting residual plots—that is, plots with error on the ordinate and X (or predicted Y) on the abscissa. If the assumptions have been seriously violated, then one cannot trust the p values and confidence intervals.

Nonlinear Regression

In curvilinear regression, one obtains a curved line by applying nonlinear transformations to one or more of the variables and then employing a linear model. Truly nonlinear regression involves no transformations. The analyst provides a nonlinear model and starting values for each parameter in the specified model. The statistical software then uses an iterative process to fit the model to the data. Here is an SAS program used to fit a power function to our sample data:

proc nlin; parameters alpha=0 beta=1; model calories = alpha*persons**beta; run;

The nonlinear analysis converged on the model $C = 448.3*P^{.204}$. The relationship was statistically significant, $\eta^2 = .694$, $F(2, 33) = 1503$, $p < .001$.

—*Karl L. Wuensch*

See also Linear Regression; Logistic Regression Analysis; Regression Analysis

Further Reading

de Castro, J. M., & Brewer, E. M. (1991). The amount eaten in meals by humans is a power function of the number of people present. *Physiology & Behavior*, *51*, 121–125.

Luo, S., & Klohnen, E. C. (2005). Assortative mating and marital quality in newlyweds: A couple-centered approach. *Journal of Personality & Social Psychology*, *88*, 304–326.

Rotton, J., & Cohn, E. G. (2000). Violence is a curvilinear function of temperature in Dallas: A replication. *Journal of Personality & Social Psychology*, *78*, 1074–1081.

Curvilinear bivariate regression: http://core.ecu.edu/psyc/wuenschk/MV/multReg/Curvi.doc

Curvilinear regression: http://www.vias.org/tmdatanaleng/cc_regress_curvilin.html

Nonlinear regression in SAS: http://www.ats.ucla.edu/stat/sas/library/SASNLin_os.htm

Polynomial regression with Stata: http://web.archive.org/web/20000310035117/http://www.gseis.ucla.edu/courses/ed230bc1/notes3/curve.html

Applied research or basic research: Research is what I'm doing when I don't know what I'm doing.

—Werner Von Braun

DARWIN, CHARLES (1809–1882)

Charles R. Darwin was born on February 12, 1809. He first studied medicine at Edinburgh, and then ministry at Cambridge. His primary interests were, however, in natural history. Ironically, Darwin found his early academic experiences in natural history "incredibly dull. The sole effect . . . was the determination never as long as I lived to read a book on geology, or in any way study the science." Clearly, later academic and field experience reversed Darwin's early views. After graduating, Darwin became the naturalist on the HMS *Beagle* in 1831. It was on the ship's 5-year voyage that he gathered much of the evidence that later formed the basis for his ideas on evolution.

Darwin's most important intellectual contribution was his theory of evolution by natural selection, published in *On the Origin of Species by Means of Natural Selection* (1859). Darwin later published *The Descent of Man, and Selection in Relation to Sex* (1871), which focused on human evolution, sexual selection, and cognitive/behavioral characteristics in humans and other species. In *The Expression of the Emotions in Man and Animals* (1872), Darwin focused on patterns and mechanisms of emotional expression in humans and other animals. Darwin died on April 19, 1882, and was buried in Westminster Abbey.

Darwin's ideas about evolution, natural and sexual selection, and work on emotional expression emphasized the adaptive and functional aspects of structure, behavior, and even cognition. This generated developments in measurement in areas ranging from comparative psychology to later work on human emotional expression (e.g., Ekman's coding system of facial displays). Because Darwin's theory emphasized individual variations, it helped to generate work in measurement of human individual differences. This influence was most clearly expressed through the work of Darwin's cousin Francis Galton. As Galton himself notes in an 1869 letter to Darwin, "I always think of you . . . as converts from barbarism think of the teacher who first relieved them from . . . superstition. . . . Your book . . . was the first to give me freedom of thought." Galton referred to his own work as the "natural history of human faculty." Galton's work on testing led to a number of developments in statistics, and measures of human abilities, physical characteristics, and sensory acuities. Through Galton, Darwin indirectly affected many important figures in the history of measurement and testing, including Cattell, Pearson, and Spearman. Darwin's work thus had important direct and indirect influences on the fields of measurement and statistics.

—*Matthew J. Hertenstein and Kevin E. Moore*

See also Galton, Sir Francis

Further Reading

Simpson, G. G. (1995). *The book of Darwin*. New York: Washington State Press.

Darwin: http://pages.britishlibrary.net/charles.darwin/
Galton: http://www.mugu.com/galton/index.html

Applying Ideas on Statistics and Measurement

The following abstract is adapted from Shermer, M. B. (2002). This view of science: Stephen Jay Gould as historian of science and scientific historian, popular scientist and scientific popularizer. *Social Studies of Science, 32*(4), 489–524.

This paper pays needed attention to the depth, scope, and importance of Stephen Jay Gould's role as historian and philosopher of science, and his use of popular science exposition to reinforce old knowledge and generate new. It presents the results of an extensive quantitative content analysis of Gould's 22 books, 101 book reviews, 479 scientific papers, and 300 natural history essays in terms of their subject matter and places special emphasis on the interaction between the subjects and themes, how Gould has used the history of science to reinforce his evolutionary theory, and how his philosophy of science has influenced both his evolutionary theory and his historiography. **Darwin** said (and Gould cites) that, "All observation must be for or against some view if it is to be of any service." Gould followed Darwin's advice throughout his career, including his extensive writings on the history and philosophy of science.

DATA ANALYSIS TOOLPAK

The Analysis ToolPak is an Excel add-in that offers a special set of tools for completing a wide range of statistical analysis. If the Data Analysis item doesn't appear on the Tools menu, it needs to be installed.

The Data Analysis ToolPak offers tools in the following general categories:

ANOVA

Correlation

Covariance

Descriptive Statistics

Exponential Smoothing

F Test Two Sample for Variances

Fourier Analysis

Histogram

Moving Average

Random Number Generation

Rank and Percentile

Regression

Sampling

t Test

z Test

Using the Data Analysis Tool

As an example, examine the use of the ToolPak for completing a *t* test between two paired samples of observations, pre- and postintervention. In Figure 1, you see the scores for the 10 cases' data in column A (the Pre condition) and the scores for the same 10 cases in column B (the Post condition). Finally, you can also see the t-Test: Paired Two Sample for Means dialog box output of the Data Analysis ToolPak showing the following:

- Mean and Variance—the means and variances for each group
- Observations—the number of observations
- Pearson Correlation—the Pearson correlation coefficient
- The Hypothesized Mean Difference
- df—the degrees of freedom (*df*) associated with the *t* value
- t Stat—the *t* statistic

	A	B	C	D	E	F
1	Pre	Post		t-Test: Paired Two Sample for Means		
2	9	5				
3	7	6			Pre	Post
4	8	7		Mean	7.500	5.200
5	6	6		Variance	1.167	2.178
6	7	2		Observations	10.000	10.000
7	8	5		Pearson Correlation	-0.279	
8	9	4		Hypothesized Mean Difference	0.000	
9	8	5		df	9.000	
10	7	5		t Stat	3.535	
11	6	7		P(T<=t) one-tail	0.003	
12				t Critical one-tail	1.833	
13				P(T<=t) two-tail	0.006	
14				t Critical two-tail	2.262	
15						

Figure 1   Using the Data Analysis ToolPak for Analyzing Dependent Means

- P(T<=t) one-tail—the probability that a value of t would be different from chance for a one-tailed test
- t Critical one-tail – the critical value for rejection of the null hypothesis for a one-tailed test
- P(T<=t) two-tail—the probability that a value of t would be different from chance for a two-tailed test
- t Critical two-tail—The critical value for rejection of the null hypothesis for a two-tailed test

—*Neil J. Salkind*

See also Excel Spreadsheet Functions; Spreadsheet Functions

Further Reading

Salkind, N. J. (2007). *Statistics for people who (think they) hate statistics: The Excel edition.* Thousand Oaks, CA: Sage.

DATA COLLECTION

The word *data* is the Latin plural of the word *datum*, which itself is the past participle of the verb *dare* (DAH-reh), meaning "to give." So, it literally means "things given." *Data* is often used as a singular noun in English—what we call an "uncountable," or a "mass term," like "water," "energy," "information," and so on, although the *Oxford Advanced Learner's Dictionary* states that there is uncertainty with "data" as to whether it is singular or plural, and both are acceptable. But careful writers only ever use it as plural. Although data are useful to generate information, knowledge, and wisdom, they in themselves are not treated as information or knowledge. What, then, are data? Although the lexicon meaning of data is facts or information, data need not be facts or information. Data are subjective and objective human experiences, feelings, attitudes, beliefs, values, perceptions, views, opinions, judgments, and so on. They are also objective facts in the universe, interactions between human beings and objective facts, and human subjective construction of objects and facts, irrespective of their object and factual reality. Thus, some data are readily available as "things given," whereas some data need to be diligently discovered and collected with ethical considerations, depending upon the research problem, need, and the researcher.

Many of us naturally and generally collect data, make sense of them, and use the same for better living. In the research world, purposeful and systematic data collection is an important and essential activity. It is one of the significant elements or phases within the research design that is followed by the research problem formulation (objectives, hypotheses, research questions, concepts, and variables); the selection of research; and sampling methods. It is preceded by data analysis and interpretation, and report reporting phases. Because data collection occupies a crucial phase in the research design, no research can be conducted without data. To a significant extent, the quality and impact of research depends upon high-quality, accurate, and uncontaminated data. In view of the significance and relevance of the data collection process for researchers, it may be delineated and discussed by addressing the following questions: Why do researchers collect data? What are the types of data? What are the data collection methods? When should data be collected? What are the ethical issues in collecting data, and how should researchers deal with them? What factors are likely to affect the quality of data? How can researchers minimize the factors that are likely to negatively affect the quality of data?

The Necessity of Data

Because social needs, problems, and causes keep constantly changing, new data need to be collected to understand and address these emerging changes. Toward this, some researchers collect data to explore and gain an in-depth understanding of the phenomenon, whereas others do so to answer their bold research questions, to test or formulate new hypotheses, or to validate or falsify existing theories by refining casual relationships or discovering new ones. At the extreme, new data are also useful to destroy existing paradigms and erect new ones. Data are also needed to formulate, implement, and evaluate appropriate policies, programs, and products of government and nongovernmental organizations and corporations. They also can be used effectively to inform or educate people and organizations about new trends that are relevant to them. From the postmodern perspective, data also play an important role in demonstrating multiple realities.

Types of Data

The universe is filled with a huge amount of data, so it needs to be categorized broadly for the systematic conduct of research and synthesis of research outcomes. All of the available data may be classified broadly into primary and secondary data, and each of these in turn may be categorized into quantitative and qualitative data. Primary data are collected directly from the field by observing, interviewing, or administering a questionnaire. Secondary data are collected from already available sources (see examples in Table 1). Data that cannot be measured by assigning a value or by ordering them in ascending or descending order are generally considered qualitative data, and data that can be subjected to some kind of quantification or measurement are generally considered quantitative data. Furthermore, data may also be categorized as tangible and intangible (e.g., smell, air, unexpressed feelings or emotions). However, it may be noted that these categorizations or dichotomies are researchers' creations. In reality, these exist together, and thus in research, all types of data need to be collected and diligently integrated, if they enhance the understanding of reality.

Table 1 Types of Data

Data	Qualitative	Quantitative
Primary	Field observations, narratives	Age, income, educational level
Secondary	Letters, diaries	Census, annual reports

Data Collection Methods

Researchers often employ a specific method or several data collection methods to collect data, such as observation, case study, questionnaire, interview, focus groups, rapid rural appraisal, and secondary data. Some of these methods overlap with others, and some are more popular than the others. Many of these data collection methods have different variations within them; for example, the observation method has been further delineated into structured, unstructured, participant, and nonparticipant observation, and the case study method into intrinsic, instrumental, and collective case studies. There are different types of questionnaires and ways of administering them (one to one, in groups, or through mail, including e-mail). Interviews have been classified into structured, semistructured, and unstructured, which may be organized through face-to-face, by telephone, or by any other electronic mode. The focus group also has several types, including group interviews, group discussion, nominal group, and so on. These methods are very important because it is through these methods that data are collected.

Generally, research methodology books discuss details on these methods. Nonetheless, it is crucial to note a few points on them. First, researchers need to carefully select a method or a combination of data collection methods in such a way that they capture reality appropriately and accurately in order to answer the research questions and achieve the research objectives. Inappropriate or incorrect selection of data collection methods results in incorrect and misleading outcomes that distort the reality. Second, after having selected the most appropriate data collection method(s), researchers need to develop adequate knowledge and skills through training, practice, or some other relevant means to use the data collection methods effectively. These may include sharpening observation skills, memorizing, taking notes, constructing a questionnaire or an interview schedule, asking questions, listening, moderating, dealing with diversions and interruptions, and respecting respondents' privacy and self-determination. Third, it is important to be aware of the strengths and limitations of various data collection methods and where and when they can be best used. Fourth, we should be aware of and effectively use in moderation data collection means with which we are all gifted. These are our five sense perceptions: eyes (seeing/observing), ears (hearing/listening), nose (smell), tongue (taste), and skin (touch). Just as some data collection methods are more often used than others (e.g., questionnaire or interview schedule), we might have gotten accustomed to using some sense perceptions more intensively than the others (e.g., too much speaking, not enough listening; observing but not noting; or too much listening/carried away with the field or respondent without observing and speaking). These sensory perceptions need to be employed effectively to collect data rather than relying only on the data collection instruments. Finally, while collecting data through the chosen method(s), researchers should ponder the following questions to keep the data collection process on track.

- What am I trying to discover?
- Why have I chosen the methods (research, sampling, data collecting) I have chosen?
- Do these methods help or hinder my efforts toward understanding reality?
- Are there any alternative methods to understand the phenomenon I am trying to understand?
- Do these categories of methods make any sense in understanding the reality?

Resources for and Timeliness in Data Collection

Data collection is a resource-intense activity in terms of time, money, and other resources, more so in the case of primary data collection. Researchers need to liberally estimate time, budget, personnel, and other resources, and make arrangements for the same in

advance to ensure a smooth data collection process. Most important, timeliness is very important in data collection. Researchers need to approach respondents, whether individuals, families, groups, communities, or organizations, at a time that is convenient to them and they are available and willing to provide data. Another important aspect of timeliness is that researchers need to be in the field when the events occur so as to collect data in the natural setting, if the research issue/design requires such an approach. For example, field data on mass protests, mob behavior, village fares, or indigenous methods of harvesting cannot be collected whenever researchers desire to collect. They have to be timely in collecting these types of data, just like a natural scientist can collect data on an eclipse only when it occurs.

Ethical Considerations

Researchers need to collect data according to the set ethical standards, which are often based on certain values and principles: honesty, truthfulness, privacy and confidentiality, self-determination and voluntary involvement, zero physical and psychological harm, dignity and worth of human beings, accountability, right to know on the part of respondents, fairness and impartiality on the part of researchers, and informed consent. On the other hand, researchers should avoid breach of confidence and agreements, absence of informed consent or self-determination/autonomy of respondents, deception, risk of harm or offense, acts involving conflict of interest, and any unethical act.

Many government and nongovernment organizations, universities, and research firms have well-developed research ethics committees and ethics clearance application forms. Before beginning the data collection process, researchers should adhere to these ethical requirements and collect data accordingly. Those researchers who do not belong to any organizations or whose organizations have not developed such ethical standards and requirements should also collect data by setting their own ethical standards based on the above stated values and principles. They should explain the nature and purpose of research, provide satisfactory answers to all questions, inure that respondents are involved voluntarily and that no force is used, and allow the respondent to withdraw from the research at any time if he or she wishes to do so.

Impediments in Data Collection

Data collection is a planned, purposeful, and systematic activity. Despite choosing appropriate data collection methods; meticulously developing data collection instruments; planning adequate resources, including time; and meeting ethical standards, researchers may encounter several impediments in the data collection process. One probable reason for these impediments is that the nature of the setting, the research problem, the researcher, the researched, the time of research, and the prevailing social conditions vary every time. Thus, the data collection impediments may be analyzed by looking at three "R" factors: the researcher; the research problem; and the researched, or a combination of these factors.

Because the researcher is the main actor in the data collection process, he or she can contribute significantly to reducing or increasing field difficulties. Data collection experiences suggest that there are three main issues related to the researcher. First, researchers' state of mind affects the data collection process because they may sometimes feel nervous, anxious, incapacitated, irritated, uncomfortable, overwhelmed, frightened, frustrated, tired, and at times less confident. Several factors within and outside the researcher may contribute to such a state that might affect researchers' observation, interviewing, responding, and note-taking abilities. Second, researchers' negative attitudes, prejudices, and preconceived notions toward the research problem, the field, respondents, and communities may interfere with the data collection process and reduce the quality of data. Finally, researchers' action (i.e., how they actually behave in the field and with respondents) is also important and may obstruct the data collection process if not appropriate.

The second factor is the research problem. Some data collection difficulties are related to the nature of the research problem and the decision researchers

make to enter particular settings. If research problems deal with sensitive issues such as drug addiction, bankruptcy, the accused awaiting trial in the criminal justice system, ethnicity, development of toddlers and children, and so on, researchers often experience several challenges while collecting data. Data collection experiences have demonstrated that some respondents or communities may feel threatened and insecure because of the sensitivity of the issue. In some cases, data are simply not available, accessible, or discloseable. For example, while tracing genealogies of families, information on women may not be available in some cultures. In some regions and towns, it may not be possible to locate the universe of the community. Census reports may not have a particular type of information. A complete, up-to-date, and accessible list of agencies, organizations, and companies may not be available. At times, researchers may not have access to needed data or organizations. Information may not be well recorded and kept. These are real problems in the field that are beyond the control of researchers, and they can affect the quality of the data collection process. The difficult nature of the setting and lack of information about the setting (e.g., widely dispersed respondents or communities in rural, remote, and hilly areas; unclear addresses and road maps, etc.) may also lead to exhaustion and thereby weaken the data collection process, including its pace.

The third source of data collection impediments is the researched (i.e., respondents and communities). Data collection experiences suggest that researchers have faced the most common problem of making an entry (into the community) and gaining acceptance. Every means or way of approaching the respondent and the community (e.g., through written letters; health officials; government officials; local leaders, political or otherwise; friends/relatives; or independently without anybody's introduction) has pros and cons and may affect the accuracy of data being collected. Equally important is gaining acceptance. If the respondent's suspicions and doubts are not cleared, and acceptance is not gained, the data collection process will be hampered significantly, and that, in turn, may lead to inconsistent and incomplete data.

Experiences of interviewing respondents have revealed that an unsuitable location for the interview, lack of functional trust, refusal to give an interview, difficulty in convincing the respondents, interference by friends or members of the family, respondents' keenness to complete the interview quickly, more talkative respondents, and not knowing the local language can pose several impediments to the data collection process. In terms of the questionnaire, faulty design of the questionnaire, low return rates, difficulties in collecting a group of respondents at one place, lack of organizations' support to employees in completing the questionnaire, and approaching busy professionals at their workplace have hampered the data collection process. Ethical issues in observation studies, planned or arranged observations, and lack of prompt recording of observations appear to affect the quality of collected data. Delays in obtaining permissions to collect data from organizations, particularly from the government, and lack of cooperation of staff members to give access to the available data also create problems in data collection. Other factors such as adverse weather conditions, high sample mortality rates, lack of adequate resources, isolation, and health issues of the researcher also may get in the way of data collection.

Strategies to Ensure High-Quality Data Collection

Although the above presented impediments can affect the data collection process and reduce the quality of data, researchers can consciously employ some systematic strategies to ensure the collection of accurate data. In regard to the impediments stemming from the researcher, first, researchers need to be aware of their state of mind and reflect on it by raising the following questions: Why do I feel this way? What am I doing here? What are my attitudes toward respondents and communities? How am I behaving with people in the field? To what extent does my state of mind affect my data collection process? Is it blocking my efforts to understand field realities? How can I overcome these contextual feelings (state of mind) and change my attitude and behavior, if necessary? Second, these reflections should result in enhancing the competence

of researchers by acquiring needed knowledge, by developing practice skills and appropriate attitudes, and by taking right actions. It is important for researchers to feel comfortable and confident in the field, and enhanced competence will help achieve it. Finally, researchers' experiences suggest that additional reading, better information about the issue, adequate practice, acquaintance with the field, use of professional skills, anticipation of problems, and preparation of possible remedies will help. Regardless of respondents' background, status, communities and conditions, and cooperation or noncooperation, researchers should respect them. They also should be free from their own prejudices and preconceived notions about the field so as to develop conducive attitudes and behave appropriately in the field. In addition, researchers need to be assertive and flexible.

Several creative strategies need to be explored to prevent and to deal with data collection difficulties emanating from the research problem and setting. When the research issue is sensitive and respondents feel insecure and threatened, it is less likely that a good data collection process will begin. Strategies toward this issue will be discussed shortly. If the research problem and setting-related data collection difficulties are beyond the control of researchers, first, they should not get perturbed; second, they should study the problem; and third, they should look at possible alternatives. Once they analyze the possible alternatives, the most appropriate alternative can be chosen and changes can be introduced in the data collection strategies. Thorough pilot study should certainly signal such potential problems. Researchers need to anticipate and plan well, including logistics to cope with some of the realistic difficulties in the field. Careful use of local guides/volunteers and resources may reduce some of the problems. When research is undertaken in rural and remote communities and tribal areas, researchers must learn to live happily with limited facilities and without the luxuries of urban life. The pace of research work needs to be organized in such a way that it takes care of physical exhaustion. If it is not possible to collect data on some issues and from some settings, it may be necessary to alter the whole research design.

With regard to respondent-based data collection difficulties, a few strategies may be recommended. Because making an appropriate entry is a critical issue and there is no foolproof strategy to address it, researchers need to be conscious of how they are going to make an entry and how they will access respondents, and they need to make an assessment about likely implications on the quality of data. An analysis of the consequences of each entry option on data to be collected may be undertaken, and an entry approach that has minimum consequences on the data may be followed. It is also important to develop systematic plans to overcome those consequences. Another approach is that when the researcher feels confident that initial data were inconsistent and unreliable, such data may be excluded once the reliable data pattern is established. To gain acceptance and to deal with sensitive issues, researchers need to build functional trust and rapport, and establish credibility. Toward this, researchers need to provide simple, straight, and honest information to respondents, communities, and organizations, and answer all questions so as to overcome their suspicions and doubts. Efforts to overcome this problem might include ensuring direct contact with the respondent, rather than using a second person or intermediary to approach the respondent; maintaining strict confidentiality; suppressing actual names; exploring the respondent's version of the events, opinions, and so on; and avoiding using anything (e.g., tape recorder) that the respondent particularly finds threatening. Researchers should avoid defensive arguments with the respondents. They also must follow ethical guidelines that are appropriate to respondents' cultural practices. Most important, researchers should demonstrate warmth, empathy, friendliness, and pleasantness; show interest in what respondents say; and allow additional questions and discussion that may not be related to instruments and the research problem. These strategies are likely to facilitate a better data collection process to obtain rich, reliable, and valid data.

A mutually convenient location should be chosen for the data collection, whether it is an interview, administration of a questionnaire, or a focus group discussion. In the case of the respondent's refusal to provide data, researchers should politely thank him or her and withdraw from the process. It is also important to anticipate a range of interruptions from people other than respondents (e.g., relatives, friends, etc.) and prepare well to minimize them. Researchers need to prepare and plan well to work with the language difficulty, if they do not know the local language. They need to learn and develop local basic vocabulary. Most important, they need to identify, train, and employ neutral interpreters (who do not take the side of the researcher or the researched) who do not affect respondents and their responses. Long and exhausting data collection instruments should be avoided. By pretesting, the optimum length should be estimated. If an instrument takes a long time, breaks should be planned at appropriate stages of the data collection. In-depth or long interviews may be conducted in two to three separate sessions. If particular items of the interview/questionnaire do not work, the researcher should be flexible enough to consistently drop them from the schedule.

Recording of data, whether through handwritten notes or electronic devices, should be avoided if it is implicitly or explicitly resisted by respondents. An overreliance on electronic gadgets is not recommended because they may not work when researchers need them the most. If the data collection is based on the researcher's memory, the researcher must expand his or her notes and then write down his or her memories immediately after interviews. Delay would cause memories to fade and thus the collected data as well.

If questionnaire respondents are located in government, nongovernment, or business organizations, researchers may ask the organization head to issue a cover letter advising the respective employees to cooperate with the survey. This approach may facilitate the data collection process in organizations. Avoid contacting professionals during their busy hours, and approach them according to their availability and convenience.

In the case of a questionnaire, administering, completing, and collecting it in one session will yield better return rates than giving a questionnaire to respondents and asking them to return it later. Researchers must have some autonomy in observing so that they can get an adequate picture of the phenomenon being observed. Research experiences show that sometimes meaningful data may be collected through casual experiences, observations, and conversations. Researchers may not be able to capture such meaningful data when they approach respondents with a questionnaire/interview schedule in a formal way. If permission is required, it should be obtained well in advance. If the research topic is sensitive and securing permission is doubtful, the researcher may start work on the topic only after obtaining the permission. If high sample mortality is expected, researchers should plan for a larger sample size. They should also consciously plan opportunities to overcome the problem of isolation in the field. Modern communication technologies (e-mail, Internet chat, etc.) may also be used to achieve this purpose, if they are accessible. Finally, researchers need to take necessary steps to take care of themselves and to maintain good health.

Conclusion

As stated in the introduction, it may be reiterated that data collection activity is a crucial aspect of the research design. This entry has discussed the necessity of data collection, types of data, several data collection methods, resources required for and timeliness in data collection, ethical considerations, impediments, and strategies to ensure the collection of high-quality and accurate data. It may be noted that this discussion is neither comprehensive nor conclusive. The suggested strategies may work for some and not for others. However, this entry may provide important leads to researchers to further explore data collection methods, impediments, and strategies.

—*Manohar Pawar*

See also Descriptive Research; Variable

Further Reading

Briggs, C. L. (1986). *Learning how to ask: A sociolinguistic appraisal of the role of the interview in social science research.* Cambridge, UK: Cambridge University Press.

Cowie, A. P. (1989). *Oxford advanced learner's dictionary.* Oxford, UK: Oxford University Press.

Kuhn, T. (1962). *The structure of scientific revolution.* Chicago: University of Chicago Press.

Kuhn, T. (1974). *The structure of scientific revolution* (2nd ed.). Chicago: University of Chicago Press.

Lee, R. M., & Renzetti, C. M. (1993). The problem of researching sensitive topics: An overview and introduction. In C. M. Renzetti & R. M. Lee (Eds.), *Researching sensitive topics.* Newbury Park, CA: Sage.

Pawar, M. (2004). *Data collecting methods and experiences: A guide for social researchers.* Chicago: New Dawn Press.

Pawar, M. (2004). Learning from data collecting methods and experiences: Moving closer to reality. In M. Pawar, *Data collecting methods and experiences: A guide to social researchers.* Chicago: New Dawn Press.

Popper, K. (1965). *The logic of scientific discovery.* New York: Harper & Row.

Smith, C. D., & Carolyn, D. (1996). *In the field: Readings on the field research experience* (2nd ed.). Westport, CT: Praeger.

Applying Ideas on Statistics and Measurement

The following abstract is adapted from Shields, C. M. (2003). Giving voice to students: Using the Internet for data collection. *Qualitative Research, 3*(3), 397–414.

Good data collection techniques are essential for a research project to run smoothly and for the data to be trusted. This article explores the use of a Web-based survey as a means of **data collection** with more than 450 adolescents in an American school district with approximately 50 percent visible ethnic minority students. After describing the context of the study, the author explores issues related to the ease of data collection, the potential challenges and promise of the Web-based format, and the quantity and quality of data collected. Carolyn Shields demonstrates that the data collected were extremely rich, and that students appeared to be more comfortable with the electronic data collection than with an in-person interview. Moreover, the inherent issues of power differential related to race, class, and position may be overcome using this strategy for data collection.

DATA COMPRESSION

Data compression is the process by which statistical structure in data is used to obtain a compact representation for the data. Structure can exist in data in various ways. If there is a correlation between neighboring symbols, this correlation can be used to remove the predictable portion of the data and encode only what remains. If patterns exist in the data, they can be replaced by indices to a dictionary of patterns. Even when samples of a data sequence are independent of each other, they might show bias, with some symbols occurring more often than other symbols. This bias can also be used to provide compression. Sometimes, it is easier to focus on what is not present rather than what is present in the data. For example, the low pass nature of particular data can be taken advantage of by processing the data in the spectral domain and discarding the higher frequency coefficients. In brief, the characteristics of the data guide the compression process.

Depending on the requirements of the user, data compression techniques can be classified as lossless or lossy. Lossless data compression techniques allow the exact recovery of the original. Lossy data compression permits the introduction of distortion in a controlled fashion to provide greater compression. Lossy techniques are used only in situations where the user can tolerate distortion. We will discuss some commonly used data compression techniques in the following sections.

Application Areas

Data compression is used in a wide variety of applications. WinZip and Gzip are commonly used file compression utilities on computers. Images on the Internet and in many cameras are compressed using the JPEG algorithm. Video conferencing is conducted using compressed video. Cell phones use compression techniques to provide service under limitation of bandwidth. Digital television broadcasts would not be feasible without compression. In fact, compression is the enabling technology for the multimedia revolution.

Compression Approaches

Compression can be viewed, and compression techniques classified, in terms of the models used in the compression process and how those models are obtained. We can focus on the data, examining the different kinds of structures that exist in the data without reference to the source of the data. We will call these approaches data modeling approaches. We can try to understand how the data are generated and exploit the source model for the development of data compression algorithms. Finally, we can examine the properties of the data user because these properties will impose certain constraints on the data. We begin by looking at techniques based on properties gleaned from the data.

Data Modeling Approaches

With different applications, we get different kinds of structure in the data that can be used by the compression algorithm. The simplest form of structure occurs when there is no symbol-to-symbol dependence; however, the data symbols take on different values with differing probabilities. Compression schemes that make use of this statistical skew include Huffman coding and arithmetic coding.

Huffman coding, developed as a class project by David Huffman, assigns short codewords to symbols occurring more often and long codewords to symbols that occur less often. Let's look at the example in Table 1. There are five symbols in the original file. If we were to represent them using a fixed-length code, we would need three binary digits to represent each symbol. However, if we assign codewords of different lengths to each symbol according to their probability, as shown in Table 1, the average length (l) of binary bits needed to represent a symbol will be

$$l = 0.5 \times 1 + 0.2 \times 2 + 0.15 \times 3 + 0.1$$
$$\times 4 + 0.05 \times 4 = 1.95 bits/symbol.$$

Table 1   Huffman Coding

Symbols	Probability	Binary Representation	Codeword
A	0.5	000	1
B	0.2	001	01
C	0.15	010	000
D	0.1	011	0010
E	0.05	100	0011

Thus, on average, we save 1.05 bits (3 − 1.95) per symbol using Huffman coding to represent the original symbols. This might not seem like much until we consider the possibility that the source may be generating many millions of symbols per second, in which case the savings is on the order of millions of bits per second. The encoded sequence is uniquely decodable. By this we mean that a sequence of codewords corresponds to one and only one sequence of letters. This is because in a Huffman code, no codeword is a prefix of another. For example, if we see the bits 01, we have to decode it as B because no other codeword begins with 01. Thus, the "10100000100011," will be parsed into "1 01 000 0010 0011" and will be decoded into "ABCDE."

Another method for coding sequences in which some symbols occur with higher probability than others is arithmetic coding. In arithmetic coding, every sequence is assigned a subinterval in the unit interval [0,1) where the size of the subinterval is proportional to the probability of occurrence of the symbol. The binary representation of a "tag" in this subinterval is truncated to the ceiling function of $\lceil \log_2 (1/p) \rceil$ bits, where p is the probability of the sequence. Clearly, sequences that are more probable will have a shorter codeword than sequences that are less probable.

The reasoning behind using shorter codewords for more probable symbols can be extended to collection of symbols or phrases. Commonly occurring phrases in a text can be collected in a dictionary and encoded with an index into the dictionary. The problem then becomes one of constructing the dictionary. In two landmark papers in 1977 and 1978, Jacob Ziv and Abraham Lempel provided two different approaches to forming a dictionary. In their 1977 approach, the dictionary was simply a portion of the previously encoded text. A repeat of a phrase or pattern was encoded by sending the offset from the current text and the length of the text to be copied. This compression approach, known as LZ77, has been incorporated in such popular packages as gzip and PNG.

The second approach, proposed in their 1978 paper, built an explicit dictionary based on the past. Terry Welch popularized a variation of this approach, known as LZW, in a 1982 paper. Suppose we have the following input sequence: "HO_HO_HO_OPS_OPS_OPS." Assuming that the alphabet for the input file is {H, O, _, P, S}, the LZW dictionary initially looks like Table 2. The LZW algorithm finds the longest match in the dictionary to the sequence being encoded, encodes the index of this match, and concatenates the match with the next symbol to form a new entry in the dictionary. For the example sequence, initially, the beginning pattern "H" is the longest pattern in the dictionary, which is encoded as 1. At this time, "HO" is added as the sixth entry in the dictionary. Now, the uncoded sequence starts from "O" and the longest pattern in the dictionary will be "O," which is encoded as 2. "O_" will be the seventh entry in the dictionary.

Table 2   Initial LZW Dictionary

Index	Entry
1	H
2	O
3	_
4	P
5	S

Continuing in this manner, we build the two-letter patterns in the dictionary. When we reach the letter "H" in the second "HO_," we have eight entries in Table 3. The output sequence is 123. Now we can find matches of two letters in the dictionary and begin to construct patterns of three letters. The next match is "HO," which is encoded as 6. The ninth entry "HO_" is added to the dictionary. Continuing in this manner, we will have the dictionary shown in Table 3 and the output sequence is 1 2 3 6 8 7 2 4 5 3 12 14 16.

Table 3   The LZW Dictionary for the Above Sequence

Index	Entry	Index	Entry
1	H	10	_HO
2	O	11	O_O
3	_	12	OP
4	P	13	PS
5	S	14	S_
6	HO	15	_OP
7	O_	16	OPS
8	_H	17	S_O
9	HO_		

Note that when the encoder first meets the "OPS" pattern, it begins to build the two-letter entries in the dictionary again in Table 3 (Index 12). The dictionary is built dynamically according to the content in the data file. The decoding is similar to the encoding process. Because the decoder does not know the symbol right after the decoded symbol, it begins to build the dictionary entry only after decoding the second symbol. So the dictionary build-up in the decoder is one step behind the encoder. As long as the encoder does not encode the pattern using the entry just put in, there will not be a problem. The LZW algorithm has the special handling procedure for using the most recent entry in the encoder, which we will not discuss here.

Modeling the Source of Information

The use of models of the source of information represented by the data is a successful approach to compression. In particular, this approach is used for the compression of speech signals before they are transmitted over the digital cellular network. The approach used in cell phones essentially involves generating a model for the speech to be compressed and transmitting the parameters of the model to the receiver along with some information about aspects of the speech not incorporated in the model. The receiver then regenerates the speech. Speech is produced by forcing air first through the vocal cords, then through the laryngeal, oral, nasal, and pharyngeal passages, and finally through the mouth and the nasal cavity. Everything past the vocal cords is referred to as the vocal tract. The vocal tract can be modeled by a filter. The vibration of the vocal cords can be simulated by pulse sequences, which are called excitation signals. The Code Excited Linear Predictive (CELP) algorithm, which is widely used in the cellular system, is based on this model of human speech production to produce high-quality speech at low bit rates.

A diagram of a CELP encoder and decoder is shown in Figure 1. The input speech is divided into frames. For each frame, the parameters of the vocal tract filter are obtained from the original speech. An excitation signal is chosen from a stored excitation codebook. Because the human ear is very sensitive to pitch errors, a pitch filter is added between the excitation and the vocal tract filter, as shown in Figure 1. The index of the excitation signal, the gain of the excitation signal, and the parameters of the pitch filter are selected to reduce the perceptual difference between the original speech and the synthesized speech. After finding the best parameters, the encoder sends these parameters to the decoder instead of the original speech signal. At the decoder, the speech is synthesized based on these parameters.

Modeling the Users of Information

Examining the users of a class of information can tell us a lot about the characteristics of the information. The limitations of the users can provide opportunities for discarding information not perceptible to the user, thus leading to compression. Schemes that use this

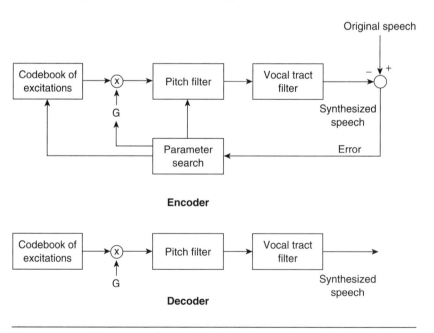

Figure 1   Diagram of CELP Encoder and Decoder

approach are particularly useful for classes of data that are not generated by a single type of source. For example, unlike human speech, music signals are generated by a variety of sources. Wonderful sounds can come from musical instruments, such as violins, pianos, and flutes, and can also be recorded from natural sources, such as birds, wind, or running water. It would be almost impossible to find a source model for these very different sources. However, although the sources are different, the user (of interest to us) is the human auditory system. Therefore, compression techniques can take advantage of the characteristic of the human auditory system.

The human ear can hear sounds from approximately 20 Hz to 20 kHz. However, even in this range, sounds below an audibility threshold cannot be heard. Furthermore, this audibility threshold can be raised locally through a phenomenon called *masking*. Spectral masking results in the raising of the audibility threshold in the spectral vicinity of a tone. Temporal masking results in the temporary raising of the threshold for a short period prior to and after a sound. Many audio compression algorithms are based on the masking effect. A block diagram of the popular MP3 algorithm is shown in Figure 2.

There are two important parts in the MP3 encoder— the filter bank and the psychoacoustic model. The psychoacoustic model finds the major components in the audio signal and calculates the masking curve imposed by these major components. The filter bank converts the audio input samples into samples of different frequency bands. The encoder then determines the active frequency bands and the quantization level needed for that band according to the given output bit rate and masking curve. For example, if the sound pressure level of the samples in a certain band is below the masking curve, the samples in this band are not needed because they are not audible to humans. If the sound pressure level in a band is much higher than the masking curve, more quantization levels are needed for this band. In the final step, the encoder packs all this information into an MP3 bitstream.

The structure of the decoder is rather simple, as shown in Figure 3. The input stream is first unpacked; then the samples in each band are reconstructed; and the samples in all the bands are remapped into audio samples, which sound the same as the input audio samples.

As in the case of music, images and video are also generated by a variety of sources. Again, as in the case of music, although the sources are diverse, there is only a single user of interest to us, namely, the human visual system. The images of interest to humans consist of regions of constant or stationary pixel values. In other words, most of the image consists of regions of low spatial frequency. Therefore, we can design compression schemes that take advantage of this fact. An example of a scheme that does that is the popular JPEG algorithm. A block diagram of the JPEG compression algorithm is shown in Figure 4.

The input image is divided into 8×8 blocks. The Discrete Cosine Transform (DCT) transform is then applied to each block. This results in a spatial frequency representation of the block. The basis functions of the

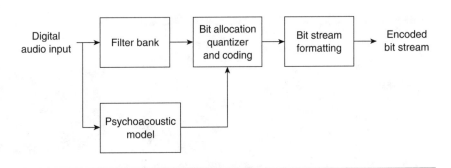

Figure 2   Block Diagram for the MP3 Encoder

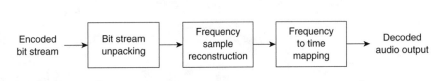

Figure 3   An MP3 Decoder

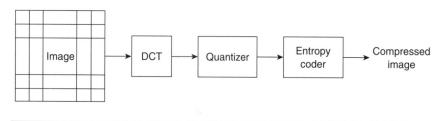

Figure 4   System Diagram of Baseline JPEG

DCT transform are shown in Figure 5. The low-frequency components are more important than the high-frequency components to characterize the images. This allows us to drop high-frequency components without degrading the perceptual quality of the reconstructed image. For example, Figure 6 shows the original image and reconstructed images obtained when some of the coefficients are discarded. The reconstructed images are based on only the first, second, and sixty-fourth DCT coefficients. It can be seen that the first few DCT coefficients contain most of the information about the image, whereas the sixty-fourth DCT coefficient has little visible information.

After the transform, the JPEG encoder quantizes these DCT coefficients. Because the coefficients with lower indices are more important, they are represented at a high resolution, whereas the coefficients with

higher indices are represented more crudely. The quantized coefficients are further encoded using a variation of the Huffman coder described earlier.

Video is a series of images that is presented in order and at a certain rate. Because the images are updated very quickly, the contents of images usually do not change much from one frame to the next. Most video compression algorithms use this temporal correlation between the frames by only transmitting the difference between the current frame and the previous frame after taking into account the motion of objects within a frame.

There are many video compression standards. The most popular video compression standard is known as MPEG2. MPEG stands for Moving Pictures Experts Group, which is the group responsible for this standard. The MPEG2 standard is used in digital cable TV and with DVDs. One of the important properties of the MPEG2 algorithm is its random access capability. This is necessary because the audience may switch the TV at any moment, or may forward or rewind the DVD to any location in the video stream. For random access capability, some frames need to be compressed

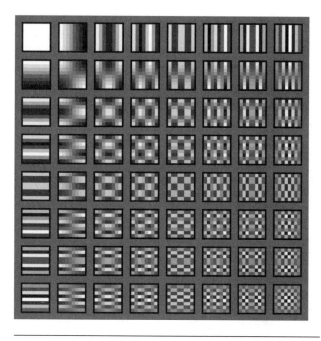

Figure 5   Sixty-Four DCT Basis Functions

Original image

Reconstructed image (DCT1)

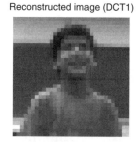

Reconstructed image (DCT2)

Reconstructed image (DCT64)

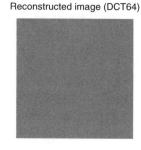

Figure 6   Images Based on DCT Coefficients

periodically without any reference to past frames. These frames are referred to as *I* frames. In order to improve compression efficiency, the MPEG algorithm contains two other kinds of frames, the predictive coded (*P*) frames and the bidirectional predictive coded (*B*) frames. The *P* frames are compressed using motion-compensated prediction from the last *I* or *P* frame, whichever happens to be closest. *I* and *P* frames are called anchor frames. The *B* frames are coded using motion-compensated prediction from the most recent anchor frames and the closest future anchor frames, as shown in Figure 7. *I* frames achieve the least compression efficiency because they do not use the information from neighboring frames. *B* frames achieve the highest compression efficiency because they use information from the two neighboring frames.

The different frames are organized together to form a group of pictures (GOP), as shown in Figure 7. A GOP is the smallest random access unit in the video sequence. There are many possible structures of a GOP. The GOP structure in Figure 7 is a common one, with 15 frames, and it has the sequence *IBBPBBPBBPBBPBB*. The ratio of *I*, *P*, and *B* pictures in the GOP structure is determined by the nature of the video stream, the bit rate constraints on the output stream, and the required encoding and decoding time.

Because of the reliance of the *B* frame on the future anchor frame, there are two different sequence orders. The display order is the sequence in which the video is displayed to the user as labeled in Figure 7. The other order is the bitstream order in which the frame is processed and transmitted. For the above example, the first frame is an *I* frame, which can be compressed by itself. The next frame to be compressed is the fourth frame, which is compressed based on the prediction from the first frame. Then the second and the third frames are compressed based on the prediction from the first and fourth frames. Hence, the bitstream order of the above example is *IPBBPBBPBBPBB*, and the corresponding display order is 1̲ 4̲ 2̲ 3̲ 7̲ 5̲ 6̲ 10̲ 8̲ 9̲ 13̲ 11̲ 12̲.

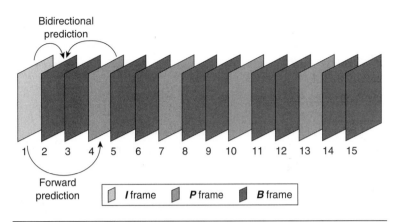

Figure 7   A Possible Arrangement for a Group of Pictures

Summary

This entry presented an overview of compression. We have motivated our discussion by looking at different ways in which structure in a particular source output can be modeled. We have also briefly described some popular compression techniques used for the compression of text, computer files, speech, music, images, and video.

—*Dongsheng Bi and Khalid Sayood*

See also Data Mining; Variable

Further Reading

Huffman, D. A. (1952). A method for the construction of minimum redundancy codes. *Proceedings of the IRE, 40*(9), 1098–1101.

Nelson, M., & Gailly, J.-L. (1996). *The data compression book* (2nd ed.). New York: M&T Books.

Salomon, D. (2004). *Data compression: The complete reference.* New York: Springer.

Sayood, K. (2000). *Introduction to data compression* (2nd ed.). San Francisco: Morgan Kaufmann.

Welch, T. A. (1984, June). A technique for high-performance data compression. *IEEE Computer, 17*(6), 8–19.

Ziv, J., & Lempel, A. (1977, May). A universal algorithm for data compression. *IEEE Transactions on Information Theory, 23*(3), 227–343.

Ziv, J., & Lempel, A. (1978, September). Compression of individual sequences via variable-rate coding. *IEEE Transactions on Information Theory, IT-24*(5), 530–536.

Data compression information: http://datacompression.info

Data compression principles and practices: http://www.data-compression.com

Data Mining

Data mining refers to the process of discovering useful patterns in very large databases. It uses methods from statistics, machine learning, and database management to restructure and analyze data to extract knowledge or information from the data. Data mining is also known as *knowledge discovery in databases* (KDD).

Data mining is used in a wide range of enterprises. Examples include fraud detection in banking, market segmentation, campaign optimization, genetics research, telecommunications customer turnover ("churn") prevention, Web site optimization, and crime prevention.

How Data Mining Differs From Traditional Statistical Analysis

Data mining differs from traditional statistical analysis in a number of ways, including amount and type of data used and the goals of the analysis.

Amount of Data

In traditional statistical analysis, the data set being analyzed tends to be small, with tens or hundreds of observations, and rarely more than 10 or 20 variables. For this reason, statistical methods often place a good deal of importance on *statistical efficiency*, or the method's ability to generate precise estimates with small data sets, in order to minimize the expense of data collection.

In contrast, data mining problems typically use very large databases, with thousands, millions, or even more observations and possibly hundreds or thousands of variables. Because of this, many analysis methods used in data mining focus on computational efficiency, or the ability of the algorithm to process a large number of cases and/or variables in a reasonable amount of time. In some data mining settings, sampling is used to reduce the data set to a manageable size.

Type of Data

In research studies of the type statisticians typically encounter, the data have been specifically planned and carefully collected for the express purpose of the study. The researcher has a good deal of control over the coding of variables, which variables are included in the data, and the format of the resulting data set.

In most data mining settings, the only data available are existing data warehouses or other operational data stores. Formatting and coding of the data have been predetermined by business or organizational needs, usually completely independent of the current analysis. Some fields that the analyst might wish for may be unavailable, and there is usually a lot of irrelevant information in the database that must be sifted through and removed. Because of this, a considerable proportion of effort in a data mining project is devoted to data management, cleaning, and conversion.

Goal of the Analysis

Traditional statistical models are usually used in confirmatory analyses, where the goal of the analysis is to test and confirm or reject specific hypotheses about the process under study. This leads to a strong emphasis on hypothesis testing.

In data mining, however, the goal is usually one of two things: exploratory modeling or practical modeling. *Exploratory modeling* is used to find previously unknown patterns in the data and to generate new hypotheses about the process described by the data. It typically emphasizes models with *transparency*, that is, models that are easy for an analyst to understand and integrate with a theoretical framework.

Practical modeling is used to find ways to optimize a particular process. Here, optimization is loosely defined as improving a business or organizational process in some important way, such as increasing profits for a marketing campaign or adapting a manufacturing process to react more quickly to changes in the economic climate. This kind of modeling is marked by an emphasis on predictive accuracy; for such projects, getting the right answer is generally more important than understanding *how* you got the right answer.

Of course, many data mining projects include both exploration and practical prediction as goals, and so have to balance one against the other to a certain extent.

Origins of Data Mining

Data mining grew largely out of the interaction of the machine learning and database management fields. It wasn't until large databases became widespread that a need was perceived for fast methods of analyzing data and finding patterns. Traditional statistical methods were good at finding structure in data but were not very good at handling the large data sets that enterprises were amassing, so were somewhat limited in their utility. Machine learning researchers developed methods for doing exactly that, and eventually software suites such as SPSS Clementine, IBM Intelligent Miner, and SAS Enterprise Miner were developed to make these machine learning techniques available to data analysts. As computing power became cheap and ubiquitous, and improved mathematical algorithms were discovered, it became more practical to apply some of the more computationally intensive statistical methods to large data sets as well, so they were adopted into the data mining toolbox.

Data Mining Terminology

Because of data mining's diverse ancestry, there is some inconsistency in the terminology to describe various aspects of data mining. Statisticians often have one name for a concept and machine learning theorists a different name, and database modelers a third. Table 1 shows several statistical concepts, along with other names by which the concepts are known to data miners.

The Data Mining Process

As indicated above, data mining is a complex process, of which model building is only a part. The process

Table 1   Data Mining Terminology

Statistical Concept	Synonymous Data Mining Terms
Variable	Field, Attribute, Feature, Column, Dimension
Case	Record, Row, Example, Instance
Dependent variable	Target (field), Output (field), Outcome (field)
Independent variable	Predictor (field), Input (field), Attribute
Nominal	Categorical, Set, Discrete
Continuous	Numeric, Real
Model estimation	Model building, Training, Teaching, Learning
Predictive modeling	Supervised learning
Clustering, exploratory factor analysis, other nonpredictive model building	Unsupervised learning
Outlier	Anomaly
Loss	Cost, Utility

includes understanding the problem and the data to be mined, preparing the data for mining, building models, evaluating the results of modeling, and deploying final models to directly address the original problem. The Cross Industry Standard Process for Data Mining (CRISP-DM) consortium has developed a detailed model for the complete data mining process. You can find out more about the model in the Further Reading at the end of this entry.

Modeling Procedures Used in Data Mining

Data miners use a wide variety of modeling methods borrowed from machine learning and statistics, as well as methods developed specifically for data mining. Some of the more popular methods are briefly described as follows.

Decision Trees

This family of algorithms uses recursive partitioning to split the data into subgroups, based on values of the predictor variables, such that each subgroup tends to have similar values for the target variable. The effect of the recursive partitioning is to build a "tree" of nodes, each representing a subgroup. The various methods differ primarily in the loss function used to decide each split, typically a statistical, entropy, or information criterion. Examples include CHAID, CART, C5.0, and QUEST.

Rule Induction

This family of algorithms derives rules of the form *IF x THEN y* from the data, where *x* is a set of *antecedent* conditions (values for predictor fields) and *y* is a *consequent* condition [value(s) for the target field(s)]. Such a rule can also be written as $x \rightarrow y$. For example, in a market basket analysis analyzing items purchased together at a store, you may get rules of the form *BREAD* $\rightarrow$ *BUTTER* (0.60), meaning that 60% of the customers who buy bread also buy butter. In this example, 60% is called the *confidence* for the rule *BREAD* $\rightarrow$ *BUTTER*. Examples of rule induction algorithms include Apriori and Carma.

Neural Networks

This family of algorithms attempts to simulate, in an abstract fashion, the way nerve cells process information in the brain. A neural network model consists of a set of interconnected nodes, each of which processes information in a simple way and then passes it on to other nodes to which it is connected, something like a (simplified) biological neuron. A neural network learns by adjusting the strengths of the connections between nodes (the weights), either to improve predictive performance or based on an internal loss function. The most common types of neural networks are backpropagation networks (also called *multilayer perceptrons*), radial basis function networks, and Kohonen networks (also called *self-organizing maps*).

Genetic Algorithms

Genetic algorithms work using evolutionary principles to select good models from a population of candidate models. An initial set of models is generated, usually randomly, and each model is tested for accuracy and/or other goodness criteria. Some number of models, those that give the best performance, are

saved, and the rest are discarded or *culled*. New models are created by randomly combining characteristics of the models saved from the previous round, analogous to sexual reproduction, and the models are evaluated again. In some cases, *mutations* are also added to each successive generation, where model parameters are changed randomly, independent of any other observed values in the saved candidate models from the previous iteration. The process then repeats, with the candidate models being culled, recombined, and tested again. This process, analogous to natural selection, will tend to produce better and better models with each successive generation. Iterations stop when one or more of the candidate models satisfies some criterion for judging the model(s) as adequate.

Note that genetic algorithms are a basic optimization method and can be used with a variety of model types.

Support Vector Machines

A support vector machine (SVM) is a method of constructing models based on kernel methods. An SVM works by projecting the input space (the space defined by the input fields or dimensions) into a very high-dimensional feature space, in which a linear discriminator or hyperplane (or a set of hyperplanes) can be used to separate target subgroups from one another. The use of kernel functions saves SVMs from having to represent the full high-dimensional feature space. SVMs use the maximum margin hyperplane in the feature space, which generally controls overfitting, in spite of the high dimensionality of the feature space.

Various kernels have been used with SVMs, including radial basis function, linear, polynomial, and Gaussian.

Nearest Neighbor Methods

This family of methods, also known as memory-based reasoning, uses examples from the training data to classify or make predictions for new data. A new record is compared to a table of exemplars from the training data, and the target value of the stored record most similar to the new record is used as the predicted value (or classification). In some cases, the k most similar records are identified, and the prediction is some combination of the target values for those records.

Clustering

Clustering methods attempt to identify homogeneous groups in the data set, usually without respect to known categories or any particular target field. Because there is no known correct answer, clustering is often referred to as unsupervised learning. (Predictive models are supervised because they usually involve comparing a predicted value to an observed target value and adjusting the model to reduce the distance between the two.) Clustering is often used to define group membership, which is then used to predict some other characteristic in a subsequent model. It can also be used to detect outliers or anomalies by highlighting records that don't fit well with any identifiable subgroup. The two most common types of clustering are *hierarchical clustering* and k-*means clustering.*

Hierarchical clustering works by starting with each record defining a separate cluster. The two most similar clusters are merged into a compound cluster. Then, the next two most similar clusters are merged, and so on until all records have been merged into one giant cluster. By selecting a cut-point in minimum intercluster distance, you can define a cluster solution with any number of clusters you want.

K-means clustering starts by defining the number of clusters a priori. A set of k randomly selected records defines the initial cluster centers. All of the other records in the data set are assigned to one of the k clusters: The assigned cluster is the closest cluster based on the Euclidean distance between the record and the cluster center. After the records have been assigned, a new cluster center is calculated for each cluster as the mean of the input fields for all records assigned to the cluster. Records are then reassigned to their closest clusters, and cluster centers are recalculated. Iterations continue until the clusters stabilize, that is, until no records need to be reassigned to a different cluster after cluster centers are updated.

Text Mining

Text mining refers to methods that attempt to find relationships and patterns in unstructured text, such as newspaper articles, Web sites, and academic papers. Text mining usually includes categorization of words or phrases and identification of related words and concepts. It is a fairly low-level kind of analysis and does not purport to automatically "understand" the texts being analyzed. However, by modeling relationships between word categories, often new information or hypotheses can be generated.

Statistical Methods

Several statistical methods have become widely used in data mining, including linear regression, logistic regression, and discriminant analysis.

—*Clay Helberg*

See also Artificial Neural Network; Cluster Analysis; Discriminant Analysis; Linear Regression; Logistic Regression Analysis; Support Vector Machines

Further Reading

Berry, M., & Linoff, G. (2004). *Data mining techniques: For marketing, sales, and customer relationship management* (2nd ed.). New York: Wiley.

Hastie, T., Tibshirani, R., & Friedman, J. (2001). *The elements of statistical learning.* New York: Springer.

Pyle, D. (1999). *Data preparation for data mining.* San Francisco: Morgan Kaufmann.

Ripley, B. (1996). *Pattern recognition and neural networks.* Cambridge, UK: Cambridge University Press.

The CRISP-DM consortium: http://www.crisp-dm.org/

The Data Mine, a data mining-oriented Web site: http://www.the-data-mine.com/

KD Nuggets, a clearinghouse for data mining information: http://www.kdnuggets.com/

Kurt Thearling's data mining page: http://www.thearling.com/

Two Crows: http://www.twocrows.com/

DECISION BOUNDARY

A decision boundary is a partition in n-dimensional space that divides the space into two or more response regions. A decision boundary can take any functional form, but it is often useful to derive the optimal decision boundary that maximizes long-run accuracy.

The use of decision boundaries is widespread and forms the basis of a branch of statistics known as discriminant analysis. Usually, discriminant analysis assumes a *linear* decision bound and has been applied in many settings. For example, the clinical psychiatrist might be interested in identifying the set of factors that best predicts whether an individual is likely to evidence some clinical disorder. To achieve this goal, the researcher identifies a set of predictor variables taken at Time 1 (e.g., symptoms, neuropsychological test scores, etc.) and then constructs a linear function of these predictors that best separates depressed from nondepressed or schizophrenic from nonschizophrenic patients diagnosed at Time 2. The resulting decision bound then can be applied to symptom and neuropsychological test data collected on new patients to determine whether they are at risk for that clinical disorder later in life. Similar applications can be found in machine learning (e.g., automated speech recognition) and several other domains.

To make this definition more rigorous, suppose we have two categories of clinical disorders, such as depressed and nondepressed individuals with predictor variables in *n*-dimensional space. Denote the two multivariate probability density functions $f_D(x)$ and $f_{ND}(x)$ and the two diagnoses R_D and R_{ND}. To maximize accuracy, it is optimal to use the following decision rule:

$$\text{If } f_D(x)/f_{ND}(x) > 1, \text{ then } R_D, \text{ else } R_{ND}. \quad (1)$$

Notice that the optimal decision bound is the set of points that satisfies

$$F_D(x)/f_{ND}(x) = 1.$$

It is common to assume that $f_D(x)$ and $f_{ND}(x)$ are multivariate normal. Suppose that μ_D and μ_{ND} denote the depressed and nondepressed means, respectively, and that Σ_D and Σ_{ND} denote the multivariate normal covariance matrices. In addition, suppose that $\Sigma_D = \Sigma_{ND} = \Sigma$. Under the latter condition, the optimal decision bound is linear.

Expanding Equation 1 yields

$$f_D(x)/f_{ND}(x) = 1$$

$$= \frac{(2\pi)^{-\frac{n}{2}}|\Sigma|^{-\frac{1}{2}} exp\left[-\frac{1}{2}(x - \mu_D)'\Sigma^{-1}(x - \mu_D)\right]}{(2\pi)^{-\frac{n}{2}}|\Sigma|^{-\frac{1}{2}} exp\left[-\frac{1}{2}(x - \mu_{ND})'\Sigma^{-1}(x - \mu_{ND})\right]} \quad (2)$$

$$= exp\left[-\frac{1}{2}(x - \mu_D)'\Sigma^{-1}(x - \mu_D) + \frac{1}{2}(x - \mu_{ND})'\Sigma^{-1}(x - \mu_{ND})\right]$$

Taking the natural log of both sides of Equation 2 yields

$$h(x) = \ln\left[f_D(x)/f_{ND}(x)\right] = (\mu_{ND} - \mu_D)'\Sigma^{-1}x + \frac{1}{2}(\mu_D'\Sigma^{-1}\mu_D - \mu_{ND}'\Sigma^{-1}\mu_{ND}), \quad (3)$$

which is linear in **x**.

As a concrete example, suppose that the objects are two-dimensional with $\mu_D = [100\ 200]'$, $\mu_{ND} = [200\ 100]$, $\Sigma_D = \Sigma_{ND} = \Sigma\ 50I$ (where I is the identify matrix). Applying Equation 3 yields

$$.04x_1 - .04x_2 = 0.$$

—*W. Todd Maddox*

See also Discriminant Analysis; Discriminant Correspondence Analysis

Further Reading

Ashby, F. G., & Maddox, W. T. (1993). Relations between prototype, exemplar, and decision bound models of categorization. *Journal of Mathematical Psychology, 37,* 372–400.

Fukunaga, K. (1972). *Introduction to statistical pattern recognition.* New York: Academic Press.

Morrison, D. F. (1967). *Multivariate statistical methods.* New York: McGraw-Hill.

Decision Theory

Every day, a multitude of decisions are made that affect not only a small number of individuals, but also potentially millions of people. These decisions, which take place in hospitals, pharmaceutical companies, government offices, investing companies, and so on, are made based on incomplete information and under various conditions of uncertainty as to the ability of the decision maker(s) to follow through with the commitments made. Thus, nations declare wars with incomplete information as to the capabilities of the others involved in the war, and with uncertainty as to what the impact of these actions might be on their own economies and citizens. A pharmaceutical company must decide whether to market a new drug based on limited information resulting from the clinical trials and economic uncertainty as to whether the drug can compete in the market with other drugs.

Decision theory consists of techniques, ideas, and methodologies that are appropriate for helping the decision maker to reach a decision in an optimal fashion in the face of uncertainty. Given the universality of decision theory in corporate life, government action, and everyday life, it is not surprising to find that decision theory has been embraced by almost every scientific discipline. Thus, game theory permeates the theory and applications in economics. Psychologists know game theory as the theory of social interactions, and political scientists study rational choice theory.

All of these approaches to decision making have several essential elements in common that will be discussed below in the context of statistical decision theory. Game theory served as the precursor to most of the ideas in decision theory, and its place in modern decision making was cemented by John von Neumann and Oskar Morgenstern's fundamental work on the *Theory of Games and Economic Behavior* (1944). Although decision theory developed from game theory, there is a fundamental difference between the two. Informally, whereas in game theory, players make decisions based on their beliefs of what other players—whose interests may be diametrically opposed to theirs—will do, decision theory concerns itself with the study of decisions of individuals unconcerned with the plans of others—their "opponent" being nature.

Wald unified at once ideas from game theory and Neyman's and Pearson's mathematical developments in the theory of statistics in his elegant work *Statistical Decision Functions*. It is this approach on which the rest of the discussion focuses.

Statistical Decision Theory

There are at least three common elements to all introductory courses of statistical theory and methodology: estimation, hypothesis testing, and confidence intervals. As taught in an introductory course, these three topics may appear as being unrelated. Toward the end of the course, however, the student learns to "invert" acceptance regions to obtain confidence intervals, and also learns to use confidence intervals to carry out tests of hypothesis. In addition, confidence intervals are introduced as point estimates together with a measure of precision of the estimates, typically 2 or 3 standard errors of the point estimate. Statistical decision theory unifies these ideas, and others, into one paradigm.

Let $X_1, \ldots, X_n$ represent the data observed as the outcome of an experiment E and let F represent the distribution of $(X_1, \ldots, X_n)$, which we assume to be parametrized by θ, where θ may be a vector of parameters, and the set of all possible values of θ, called the *parameter space,* is denoted by Θ. This dependence of F on θ will be denoted as F_θ. The objective is to use $(X_1, \ldots, X_n)$ to make inferences about θ. Faced with this problem, the statistician considers all the possible actions A (A is called the *action space*) that can be taken and makes a decision based on a criterion that involves minimizing the expected loss. This requires the statistician to define a function, the *loss function,* which represents the loss when the true state of nature is θ and the statistician decides for action a. This *loss function* is denoted as $L(\theta,a)$, and L is usually selected to be of the form

$$L(\theta,a) = v(a - \theta),$$

$$v(0) = 0,$$

$v(x)$ is increasing in $|x|$.

Examples of loss functions include the following:

Squared error loss: $L(\theta,a) = (a - \theta)^2$,

Absolute error loss: $L(\theta,a) = |a - \theta|$, and

Linex error loss: $L(\theta,a) = b(e^{c(a - \theta)} - c(a - \theta) - 1)$.

Historically, squared error loss has been used mostly because of the relative ease with which properties of the resulting procedures can be analyzed. It is common to assume symmetry of the loss function. This implies implicitly that overestimating by an amount d has the same consequences as underestimating by the same amount. Varian, in the context of real estate assessment, argued the need for the Linex loss as more representative of losses accrued when assessing the value of real estate.

Once the probability model for $(X_1, \ldots, X_n)$ and the action space A have been defined, and the loss function has been selected, the statistician attempts to make a decision $a(X_1, \ldots, X_n)$ that minimizes the risk function

$$R(\theta, a(X_1, \ldots, X_n)) = E_\theta(L(\theta, a(X_1, \ldots, X_n))),$$

for all θ and for all $a^* \neq a$. Of course, this is not possible because if $\theta^* \in \Theta$, then no other $a(X_1, \ldots, X_n)$ can be better than the action $a^*(X_1, \ldots, X_n) = \theta^*$, which disregards the data and always "guesses" θ^*. Thus, a need arises for eliminating procedures that "pay too much attention" to certain models and completely disregard others. Moreover, even when these "partial" estimators are eliminated, it usually happens that risk functions for different decision rules will, as functions of θ, crisscross, and then it is not clear which decision to use. Before discussing other ideas in decision theory, let us consider the following example.

Example

Consider the normal model with mean $\theta \in R$, and known variance s^2, and consider the three following problems:

1. Point estimation of θ: Here, $\Theta = A = R$. Choosing squared error as the loss function, the risk function is given by

$$R(\theta, a(X_1, \ldots, X_n)) = \text{Variance } (a(X_1, \ldots, X_n)) + \text{Bias } (a(X_1, \ldots, X_n))^2,$$

where Bias $(a(X_1, \ldots, X_n)) = E_\theta(a(X_1, \ldots, X_n)) - \theta$. This risk function is also known as the *mean squared error* of the estimator. In this case, for example, the

sample mean $a(X_1, \ldots, X_n) = \overline{X}_n$, being *unbiased*, has a risk function equal to $\frac{\sigma^2}{n}$.

2. Hypothesis testing: Consider testing the simple hypothesis $H_0 : \theta = \theta_0$ versus the simple hypothesis $H_1 : \theta = \theta_1$. In this setup, there are only two possible actions:

$$A = \{\text{Do not reject } H_0, \text{Reject } H_0\}$$

Let a *loss function* be defined as follows:

$$L(\theta, \text{Do not reject } H_0) = 0 \text{ when } \theta = \theta_0,$$

$$L(\theta, \text{Do not reject } H_0) = k_0 \text{ when } \theta = \theta_1,$$

$$L(\theta, \text{Reject } H_0) = k_1 \text{ when } \theta = \theta_0,$$

$$L(\theta, \text{Reject } H_0) = 0 \text{ when } \theta = \theta_1.$$

Note that the loss function is zero when the correct decision is made, the loss is k_0 if H_0 is not rejected when it should be rejected (an error of Type II), and the loss is k_1 if H_0 is rejected when it should not be rejected (an error of Type I), where the decisions of Rejecting H_0 and Not rejecting H_0 are defined in terms of the value of $a(X_1, \ldots, X_n) = \overline{X}_n$. The problem of selecting the test function based on $a(X_1, \ldots, X_n)$, that minimizes $P\{Type\ II\ error\} = P_{\theta_1}\{Do\ not\ Reject\ H_0\}$, subject to the condition that $P\{Type\ I\ error\} = P_{\theta_0}\{Reject\ H_0\} \leq \alpha$, for some preselected α, was addressed by Neyman and Pearson, and the solution is their fundamental Neyman-Pearson lemma (1938).

3. Confidence intervals for θ: Let A consist of all intervals $(\underline{a}(X_1, \ldots, X_n), \bar{a}(X_1, \ldots, X_n))$ with $\underline{a} < \bar{a}$. Let the loss function be of the form

$$L(\theta; \underline{a}, \bar{a}) = L_1(\theta, \underline{a}) + L_2(\theta, \bar{a})$$

where L_1 is nonincreasing in $\underline{a}$ for $\underline{a} < \theta$ and 0 for $\underline{a} \geq \theta$ and L_2 is nondecreasing in $\bar{a}$ for $\bar{a} > \theta$ and 0 for $\bar{a} \leq \theta$. The goal is then to find the interval $(\underline{a}^*, \bar{a}^*)$ that minimizes the risk function $E_\theta(L(\theta; \underline{a}, \bar{a}))$ subject to

$$P_\theta\{\underline{a} > \theta\} \leq \alpha_1 \text{ and } P_\theta\{\bar{a} < \theta\} \leq \alpha_2.$$

One example of a loss function of the type $L_1 + L_2$ is the function that takes the length $\bar{a} - \underline{a}$ of the interval as the loss. Taking, for example, $a_1 = a_2 = .025$, it is well-known that the usual 95% confidence interval

$$\left(\bar{X}_n - 1.96 \frac{\sigma}{\sqrt{n}}, \ \bar{X}_n + 1.96 \frac{\sigma}{\sqrt{n}} \right)$$

for θ in the normal case is optimal in the sense of minimizing the expected length subject to the constraint that

$$P_\theta\{\underline{a} > \theta\} \leq .025 \text{ and } P_\theta\{\bar{a} < \theta\} \leq .025.$$

In what follows, we will restrict attention to the case of point estimation, although most remarks to be made also apply more generally. As previously discussed, once the elements (action space, probability model, and loss functions) of the statistical decision theoretic problem have been selected, the statistician would like to choose a decision rule $a(X_1, \ldots, X_n)$ that, uniformly, in θ and in $a^* \in A$, minimizes the risk $E_q(L(\theta, a))$. That is, the goal is to find the decision rule $a(X_1, \ldots, X_n)$ such that

$$E_\theta(L(\theta, a(X_1, \ldots, X_n))) \leq E_\theta(L(\theta, a^*(X_1, \ldots, X_n))).$$

for all $\theta \in \Theta$ and all $a^* \in A$. There is, however, the difficulty alluded to earlier. It is not possible to carry out this program because there are decision rules that pay too much attention to some values of θ while disregarding most other values of θ. At this juncture, there are two possible ways to proceed. First, one may restrict the class of decision rules under consideration, for example, by eliminating those that only pay attention to a few points in parameter space. Thus, for example, restricting attention to decision rules that are unbiased eliminates many estimators, and the hope is that in this smaller class of decision rules, one may find one that is uniformly best. There is an extensive literature on finding the uniformly minimum variance unbiased estimators (UMVUE). When the problem satisfies certain symmetry properties, another way of restricting the class of estimators to a more manageable size with the hope of finding an estimator that is uniformly best in the reduced class is to consider only those estimators that are *equivariant*.

The second approach defines preference orders for the risk functions. One possible way of doing this is to integrate $R(\theta, a(X_1, \ldots, X_n))$ with respect to a probability distribution $\Pi(\theta)$ on Θ. This approach gives rise to Bayes estimators, and more generally to the Bayesian approach that interprets the distribution $\Pi(\theta)$ as representing the statistician's "prior" knowledge about Θ. Thus, informally, a Bayes estimator for θ with respect to a loss function $L(\theta, a)$ achieves the smallest area under the weighted risk function where the weight is provided by the specific prior distribution Π on Θ. That is, a Bayes estimator $\delta_\pi(x)$, with respect to the prior distribution $\Pi(\theta)$ and the loss function $L(\theta, a)$, minimizes the Bayes risk and therefore,

$$\int_\Theta R(\theta, \delta_\pi(x)) d\Pi(\theta) = \inf_{\delta \in A} \int_\Theta R(\theta, \delta(x)) d\Pi(\theta).$$

Alternatively, one may order risk functions, and hence decision rules, by preferring decision rule a_1 to decision rule a_2 if

$$\sup_{\theta \in \Theta} R(\theta, a_1) \leq \sup_{\theta \in \Theta} R(\theta, a_2).$$

A decision rule $a^* \in A$ is then said to be *minimax* if

$$\sup_{\theta \in \Theta} R(\theta, a^*) = \inf_{a \in A} \{ \sup_{\theta \in \Theta} R(\theta, a) \}.$$

Thus, a minimax estimator minimizes, among all estimators, the maximum risk.

Let the loss function be squared error. Consider the estimator $\bar{X}_n$. Its risk is constant and given by $\frac{\sigma^2}{\sqrt{n}}$. Because $\bar{X}_n$ is unbiased, it is of interest to determine if it is also best in the class of unbiased estimators. That is, is it UMVUE? It turns out that the estimator is UMVUE, and also minimax. However, it is not Bayes with respect to any prior distribution on Θ. In fact, except for very few cases, an unbiased estimator cannot be Bayes.

However, $\bar{X}_n$ is the limit of a sequence of Bayes estimators. More precisely, consider as a prior distribution on Θ the normal distribution with mean m and variance d^2. That is, the prior density is given as follows:

$$\lambda(\theta) = \frac{1}{\sqrt{2\pi}} \exp\left\{ -\frac{1}{2d^2}(\theta - \mu)^2 \right\}.$$

The Bayes estimator with respect to this prior and squared error loss is

$$a(X_1, \ldots, X_n) = \left\{ \frac{(n/\sigma^2)}{n/\sigma^2 + 1/d^2} \right\} \bar{X}_n$$

$$+ \left\{ \frac{(1/d^2)}{n/\sigma^2 + 1/d^2} \right\} \mu.$$

Thus, the Bayes estimator is a convex combination of the sample mean $\bar{X}_n$ and m, the mean of the prior distribution. Letting $b \to \infty$, it is seen that $\bar{X}_n$ arises as a limit of Bayes estimators.

—*Javier Rojo*

See also Bayesian Statistics; Evidence-Based Practice

Further Reading

Bergus, G. R., & Hamm, R. (1995). Clinical practice: How physicians make medical decisions and why medical decision making can help. *Primary Care, 22*(2), 167–180.

Braddock, C. H., III, Edwards, K. A., Hasenberg, N. M., Laidley, T. L., & Levinson, W. (1999). Informed decision making in outpatient practice: Time to get back to basics. *Journal of the American Medical Association, 282*(24), 2313–2320.

Green, D., & Shapiro, I. (1994). *Pathologies of rational choice theory: A critique of applications in political science.* New Haven, CT: Yale University Press.

Lehmann, E. L. (1983). *Theory of point estimation.* New York: Wiley.

Lehmann, E. L. (1991). *Testing statistical hypotheses.* Belmont, CA: Brooks/Cole.

Lehmann, E. L. (2004). Optimality and symposia: Some history. In J. Rojo & V. Perez-Abreu (Eds.), *The First Erich L. Lehmann Symposium: Optimality.* IMS Lecture Notes and Monograph Series, Vol. 44.

Neyman, J., & Pearson, E. S. (1933). On the problem of the most efficient tests of statistical hypotheses.

Philosophical Transactions of the Royal Society, Series A, 231, 289–337.

Rojo, J. (1987). On the admissibility of c $\bar{X}$ + d with respect to the linex loss function. *Commun. Statist. Theory and Meth.,* 16, 3745–3748.

Slovic, P., Fischhoff, B., & Lichtenstein, S. (1977). Behavioral decision theory. *Annual Review of Psychology, 28,* 1–39.

Varian, H. R. (1975). A Bayesian approach to real estate assessment. In S. E. Fienberg & A. Zellner (Eds.), *Studies in Bayesian econometrics and statistics in honor of Leonard J. Savage* (pp. 195–208). Amsterdam: Elsevier North-Holland.

Wald, A. (1950). *Statistical decision functions.* New York: Wiley.

Zellner, A. (1986). Bayesian estimation and prediction using asymmetric loss functions. *Journal of the American Statistical Association, 81,* 446–451.

DELPHI TECHNIQUE

The Delphi technique is a means of collecting data from a diverse group of people for the purpose of reaching a consensus. This entry presents the basic process of the Delphi technique as well as some variations on the process that can be used to meet specific needs. Although the Delphi technique allows for refinement of original ideas and therefore promotes high-quality decisions, it can be time consuming and subject to bias. Examples of how the process can be used in research are provided. From this entry, readers can determine if the Delphi technique is appropriate for their particular situations.

According to S. J. Adams, the Delphi technique provides a representation of varied backgrounds, and it prevents individuals with strong personalities from dominating a group. The purpose is to obtain information from participants to help in the areas of problem solving, planning, and decision making. The Delphi technique is a way to reach a consensus among a group of experts.

The RAND Corporation developed the technique during the 1950s as an approach to forecasting the likelihood and the potential impact of Russian bombing attacks on the United States. The approach was named for the Oracle of Delphi of Greek mythology. It was soon adopted by technological forecasting experts and eventually found its way into other types of research.

Theoretical Basis for the Delphi Technique

Consensus Theory

According to a variety of researchers, the objective of users of the Delphi technique is to achieve consensus. Some proponents of consensus theory believe that building consensus offers opportunity for communal renewal and for achieving group commitment to common goals.

Anonymity

Some researchers and theorists believe that anonymity is helpful for generating quality ideas. Others expect that using the Delphi process discourages individual dominance and simultaneously encourages each person to share his or her ideas without fear of intimidation.

Divergent Thought

Some researchers observe that divergent thinking occurs when individuals or groups are introduced to minority opinions. Anonymity and exposure to a variety of viewpoints contributes to improved creativity and decision making.

Purpose and Uses in Research

Researchers have used the Delphi technique for gathering broad-based opinions from experts, refining their views, and reaching consensus on predictions and plans for dealing with complex issues. The data generated have been used in forecasting, public budgeting, and goal setting. Decision makers in such diverse disciplines as education, safety management, family therapy research, environmental studies, government, medicine, and community health have relied on Delphi for all or portions of their research data.

Delphi Technique Process

Delphi technique involved several carefully structured steps. It bore some resemblance to Nominal Group Technique (NGT) in that with both processes,

individual contributions were made anonymously. However, the standard format for Delphi did not require participants to meet. Thus, not only were responses anonymous, but even the identity of other participants might be unknown to the group. The procedure involved two to four rounds of responses. However, prior to the first round, primary stakeholders had to do the following:

1. *Select a monitor or monitor group.* This person or persons should be experts both on the topic and on written communication skills.

2. *Select participants.* Participants usually were stakeholders as well. However, they could be noninvolved experts.

3. *Invite participants.* Selected participants were invited by telephone, mail, or e-mail to take part in the process.

4. *Develop a broad question or statement for consideration.* The monitor developed the initial question or statement, perhaps in conjunction with other stakeholders.

To begin the rounds, the monitor was responsible for (a) identifying and orienting participants; (b) getting the question to each participant; (c) receiving input from each participant; (d) summarizing the information; (e) sending the summary and a new, more focused question to the participants; and (f) determining that no more rounds were needed. The process concluded with a resolution. When consensus was reached, the resolution was announced to participants. Panel participants committed to the decision (see Figure 1).

It was recommended that 12 to 15 panel members were an appropriate size. Panel sizes ranged from a few to hundreds of members, depending on the research topic. A response rate of 70% or greater was typically acceptable. It was common for the iteration process to last only two or three rounds before consensus was reached.

Statistical Measures of Agreement

Panels commonly have used Likert scales to assess the rating of items. The Delphi monitor calculated

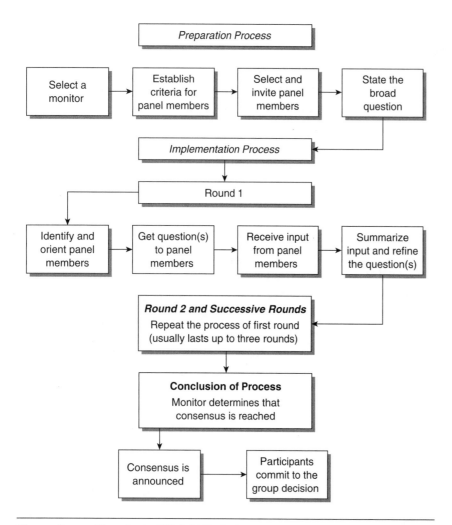

Figure 1   Flowchart of Delphi Technique

summary statistics, such as the median, following each round and reported them to the panel members for consideration during the next round. Researchers found the median to represent the most common value provided by a panel member and cited the interquartile range (the middle half of the scores) as a measure of consensus. The smaller the interquartile range, the greater the consensus. Several studies supported using the median and the interquartile range as measures of agreement and consensus.

Delphi scholars reported means to panel members in successive rounds and standard deviations as measures of consensus. However, other researchers suggested that providing standard deviations to expert panels was misleading because they were not applicable to ordinal data.

Variations of the Delphi Technique

Real-Time and Policy Delphi

Clayton identified three types of Delphi: (a) conventional, (b) real time, and (c) policy. The conventional process was presented earlier. Real-time Delphi differed in that it occurred face-to-face, within the context of a meeting or conference. Policy Delphi asked participants for information on which a decision was to be made. Policy Delphi and real-time Delphi could be combined. Consensus was not an objective in either case.

Combinations of Delphi With Nominal Group Technique

The possibility of voting when consensus could not be reached could be considered a variation on Delphi. It was a compromise of the ideal Delphi and borrowed the last phase from NGT.

Mixed Methods Studies

Some researchers have used mixed methodologies to complement one another. For example, one might use Delphi to determine items for a questionnaire that would be used in a mail survey regarding environmental policy.

Historic Delphi

In this variation, Strauss and Zeigler found that participants attempted to apply systematically the writings of classical political philosophers to current issues. That interesting study is presented in the *Historic Delphi Approach* section of this entry.

Reactive Delphi

A popular variation of Delphi was the reactive method, in which panel members reacted to pregenerated items or questions in Round 1, rather than producing a list of ideas. In this variation, the researcher prepared a list of items from a review of related literature, and the subject matter experts were asked to rate the importance of each item on some scale. The researchers found that such structured first rounds diminished the assessment properties found in the classic Delphi technique.

Advantages and Disadvantages of the Delphi Technique

Advantages of Delphi Technique

Effective structure. The process allowed participants to refine their original ideas. That resulted in high-quality decisions on complex issues. These results came from professionals who gained insights from one another's input during the successive rounds.

Fiscal economy. Little financial cost was involved in using the conventional Delphi technique. There are no travel costs, no need for accommodations, and usually no stipends for participants.

Collaboration. Several researchers noted that in reaching consensus, the Delphi technique fostered collaboration among parties who would be needed to carry out the group's decisions.

Disadvantages and Limitations of the Delphi Technique

Time requirements. Two aspects of time apply to Delphi. First, there is the requirement of the monitor(s) and of each participant. Also, the transmission of ideas could result in an overall time frame of several weeks. Difficulty in retaining participants throughout the process may be a problem. Sometimes, the latter could be lessened by using e-mail. However, that would require special care to maintain anonymity.

Inadequacy as sole method. According to several studies, when used alone, the Delphi technique was inadequate for forecasting. Also in this regard, one must consider the built-in dangers of bias. A discussion of such dangers follows.

Central tendency. Michigan State University Extension found that consensus building generally has involved finding a middle-of-the-road position, eliminating the extreme ends of the spectrum. This feature has caused some groups to feel that their views were rejected and that the process was rigged.

Bias. It is important to ensure that experts are not influenced by the researcher's objective. To guard against this, Delphi experiments usually use two or more separate groups of experts. There are numerous opportunities for introducing bias into the Delphi process, including (a) setting eligibility standards and soliciting participants, (b) formulating the questions, (c) summarizing participants' contributions, (d) rephrasing questions for successive rounds, (e) determining the number of rounds, (f) phrasing consensus statements, and (g) fostering commitment to decisions. For each step in the process, moderators must be accountable for keeping the process bias free.

Communication difficulties. Strauss and Zeigler discussed the possibility of misunderstandings, noting that the respondents may misunderstand the brief written inputs of the panelists. Others noted that Delphi relied heavily on the written communication skills of experts. This made the selection of participants especially difficult, because expertise in the field did not necessarily include communication expertise.

Ethical standards and need for trust. Conflict could arise from the many opportunities for bias using Delphi. Root causes could be intended or unintended bias or lack of group trust in the process. Without mutual trust, it would be impossible to reach consensus. Three types of disagreement involving ethics and trust are especially noteworthy:

1. *Forecast versus foresight.* Forecasting with the Delphi technique is used to predict what is likely to occur, whereas foresight implies that the process is guided toward a predetermined outcome. As mentioned elsewhere, the Delphi process cuts off extreme views and seeks a middle ground. Unfortunately, those whose opinions have been sacrificed may feel disenfranchised. Thus, when a facilitator records a

group's comments, the final outcome can be highly questionable.

2. *Consensus versus coalition.* The same principle applies here as to the forecasting versus foresight outcomes.

3. *Consensus and morality.* Among populations that must interrelate, pluralism was the only viable option. However, if Delphi technique participants represented a full spectrum of ethical values, absolutism, pluralism, and relativism, some participants might be open, some might be reluctantly persuaded, and some might feel excluded. If so, consensus could not be reached. However, the Delphi technique was designed especially to reach consensus on complex issues, and complex questions almost always involve moral values.

In a discussion of moral consensus, the following questions should be considered: Does consensus carry any moral authority? and Can groups ever achieve a valid consensus on issues of bioethics? Their considerations have raised questions about both the practicality and the propriety of using the Delphi technique to address the very issues for which the technique was designed. Perhaps one should consider the words of Mohandas Gandhi, "In matters of conscience, the law of majority has no place."

Research Applications

In this section is a brief overview of some of the institutional research applications using Delphi. They range from employee issues, such as selecting job candidates and handling occupational stress, to forecasting training needs and needed changes in human resource practices, to needs assessment.

Frazer and Sechrist examined the effects of occupational stress on employees in nuclear medicine, radiologic technology, and medical technology. They used the Delphi technique to determine 35 job stressors for each discipline. Improved communication strategies and managerial development were noted as solutions to occupational stress.

Olmstead-Schafer, Story, and Haughton used the Delphi method to forecast training needs of public health nutritionists. It was the consensus of their panel that communication, policy development, and managerial skills be included in the curriculum for training nutrition professionals.

Japanese firms used the Delphi method in forecasting needed changes in human resource practices. The panel made predictions regarding the year in which strongly held Japanese institutions of lifelong employment, seniority-focused compensation, and promotion from within at the exclusion of external recruiting would transition to practices consistent with Western cultures. The overall consensus was that it would take two decades to see significant changes.

Tavana, Kennedy, and Joglekar studied the effectiveness of the Delphi approach for ranking job candidates for a nursing management position. After two rounds, the experts reached consensus on the top applicant from a field of seven. Schuler found that the Delphi approach was beneficial in emergent and less structured subject areas such as human resource planning.

Finally, program evaluation was noted as another area for using Delphi. The Delphi technique is particularly useful for studies requiring a needs assessment.

Historic Delphi Application

Strauss and Zeigler conducted an interesting historic Delphi study. Their objective was to systematically scrutinize the great political philosophers of the past and to apply their wisdom to contemporary problems. Plato, Aristotle, Hobbes, Machiavelli, Swift, Burke, Rousseau, Locke, Marx, and Freud were the philosophers. Ten panels of six experts each (mostly university professors) represented the philosophers. The questionnaire contained 42 problem statements regarding serious issues in Western society, and each statement had a three-part question:

1. In general, what was political philosopher X's view on problem statement Y?

2. Based on your knowledge of political philosopher X, how would he have reacted to the problem statement in his own time?

3. If alive today, how would political philosopher X resolve the problem?

The second round consisted of multiple-choice options. The experts responded on a 5-point Likert scale that asked to what extent they agreed or disagreed with each item. The items in the second round were taken from each group's first-round responses.

The product of this academic exercise was a series of options for handling a variety of social problems based on Western philosophical thought. Strauss and Zeigler hoped that, in addition to accomplishing this pragmatic objective, their development of the historic Delphi approach would be a meaningful way for students to study philosophy.

Comparison of Delphi, Nominal Group, and Q-Sort Techniques

Delphi and NGT have many similarities. Each encourages divergent thought, preserves anonymity of participants' contributions, and is aimed at consensus. Each can be a powerful research technique for solving complex problems, and each has been adapted to a variety of needs through variants on the classical processes. Both processes require significant time commitments, and both are subject to bias. Both tend to discredit extreme positions and could alienate those stakeholders.

Q-Sort, on the other hand, is used primarily as an individual technique for developing theory related to human behavior and for identifying and describing human phenomena. The Q-Sort is a time-consuming process, as are Delphi and NGT. In contrast to those methods, Q-Sort researchers develop an instrument first, through literature review. The instrument is designed to measure using forced-choice options. Data collection is usually accomplished one-on-one. Table 1 depicts similarities and differences between these three research methods.

Summary

The Delphi technique was designed to identify the best solutions to complex organizational and other social problems; and researchers in diverse fields have used it in its conventional form and with several variants. However, the process is fraught with opportunities for contamination through bias, either actual or perceived. Necessary as it is in a pluralistic society, both the possibility and the propriety of reaching consensus remains illusive.

—*Ernest W. Brewer*

See also Decision Theory

Further Reading

Adams, S. J. (2001, October). Projecting the next decade in safety management: A Delphi technique study. *American Society of Safety Engineers, 32,* 26–29.

Table 1 Comparisons and Contrasts: Q-Sort, Delphi, and Nominal Group Technique

Name	Purpose	Data Collection	Primary Uses	Advantage	Disadvantage
Delphi	Consensus building	Group; anonymous	Medicine; social sciences	Divergent thinking; does not require panel participants to meet	Possible manipulation
NGT	Decision making	Group; anonymous	Social sciences	Divergent thinking	Possible manipulation; requires participants to meet
Q-Sort	Theory building; description	Individual; forced choice	Psychology; social sciences	Quantified subjective data	Generalizability difficult

Clayton, M. J. (1997). Delphi: A technique to harness expert opinion for critical decision-making tasks in education. *Educational Psychology, 17*(4), 373–386.

Frazer, G. H., & Sechrist, S. R. (1994). A comparison of occupational stressors in selected allied health disciplines. *Health Care Supervisor, 13*(1), 53–65.

Olmstead-Schafer, M., Story, M., & Haughton, B. (1996). Future training needs in public health nutrition: Results of a national Delphi survey. *Journal of the American Dietetic Association, 96,* 282–283.

Schuler, R. (1995). *Managing human resources* (5th ed.). New York: West.

Strauss, H. J., & Zeigler, L. H. (1975). The Delphi technique and its uses in social science research. *Journal of Creative Behavior, 9,* 253–259.

Tavana, M., Kennedy, D. T., & Joglekar, P. (1996). A group decision support framework for consensus ranking of technical manager candidates. *Omega, International Journal of Management Science, 24,* 523–538.

Ludwig, B. (1997). Predicting the future: Have you considered using the Delphi methodology? *Journal of Extension, 35*(5). Retrieved December 13, 2001, from http://www.joe.org/joe/1997october/tt2.html

Michigan State University Extension. (1994, October). *Delphi technique.* Issue Identification Information – III00006. Retrieved November 28, 2001, from http://www.msue.msu.edu/msue/imp/modii/iii00006.htm

Applying Ideas in Statistics and Measurement

The following abstract is adapted from Kelly, K. P. (2005). A survey of pediatric oncology nurses' perceptions of parent educational needs. *Journal of Pediatric Oncology Nursing, 22*(1), 58–66.

Educating parents of children with cancer is a primary nursing responsibility in pediatric oncology. Katherine Kelly used **Delphi techniques** with nurses attending a Children's Oncology Group Nursing Workshop to identify priority educational topics from pediatric oncology nurses' perspective. Nurses were asked to identify five priority educational topics and five topics on which they spend the most time teaching parents. Twenty-four educational categories were identified by 199 nurses, and responses were sorted by category and frequencies tabulated. Information about treatment was the most frequently cited priority. Bone marrow suppression was the second most important priority and was the topic on which nurses spent the most time. In Round 2 of data collection, 132 consenting participants from Round 1 were asked to rate the importance of the categories from Round 1 (presented in random order) during four time periods (diagnosis, initial treatment, maintenance, and off therapy). Nurses reported different teaching priorities across the continuum of treatment. Interestingly, teaching about end-of-life issues and alternative therapy were ranked as low in importance across all time points.

DELTA METHOD

The Delta method allows one to find the approximate distribution of a function of a random variable. Often, we are interested in the variability or asymptotic distribution not of the random variable X directly, but rather of a function of that random variable, call it $f(X)$. It is usually not easy to calculate characteristics of $f(X)$ exactly; indeed, in many cases, it is impossible or nearly so, hence the appeal to approximations. The Delta method is one of the standard approaches.

The Delta method is based on Taylor series expansions from standard calculus, which we now briefly review. Suppose we have a function $g(y)$ for which derivatives exist up to order k. The Taylor series expansion of $g(y)$ about the point a is

$$g(y) = g(a) + \frac{g'(a)}{1!}(y - a) + \frac{g''(a)}{2!}(y - a)^2 + \ldots + \frac{g^{(n-1)}(a)}{(n-1)!}(y - a)^{n-1} + \ldots,$$

where we can continue taking derivatives of $g(y)$ as long as they exist. In practice, of course, it will always be necessary to stop the expansion after a finite number of terms, which leads to Taylor's formula with remainder. The remainder converges to zero rapidly enough that it is negligible compared to the rest of the series expansion and can be ignored.

For statistical purposes, we usually need for only the first derivative to exist, giving the approximation $g(y) = g(a) + g'(a)(y - a) +$ remainder. Casting this in a more statistical light, suppose that y is a random variable with expected value θ and variance σ^2. We expand $g(y)$ in a first-order Taylor series around θ, ignoring the remainder term, to obtain $g(y) \approx g(\theta) + g'(\theta)(y - \theta)$. If we take expectations on both sides of this last equality, we have

$$E[g(y)] \approx g(\theta) + g'(\theta)E(y - \theta).$$

Because the expected value of y is θ, the second summand drops out and we are left with $E[g(y)] \approx g(\theta)$.

Approximating the variance is equally easy, because

$$Var[g(y)] = E[(g(y)] - g(\theta))^2]$$

$$\approx E[(g'(\theta)(y - \theta))^2]$$

$$= [g'(\theta)]^2 Var(y)$$

$$= \sigma^2 [g'(\theta)]^2.$$

With these in hand, we can derive a Central Limit Theorem for the function $g(y)$. This extension of the basic Central Limit Theorem is the Delta method. Suppose $X_1, X_2, \ldots, X_n$ is a sequence of random variables, and let T_n be a statistic based on the data such that $\sqrt{n}[T_n - \theta]$ converges in distribution to a normal with mean 0 and variance σ^2. Then $\sqrt{n}[g(T_n) - g(\theta)]$ converges in distribution to a normal with mean 0 and variance $\sigma^2[g'(\theta)]^2$, if $g'(\theta)$ exists and is not zero.

The result is best demonstrated via examples. In the first, let $X_1, X_2, \ldots, X_n$ be independent, identically distributed $N(\theta, \sigma^2)$ and the parameter of interest is θ^2. A reasonable estimator of θ is the sample average, $\overline{X}$, and a reasonable estimator of θ^2 is therefore the sample average squared, or $\overline{X}^2$. Here, $g(y) = y^2$, which yields $g'(y) = 2y$, so that $\sqrt{n}[\overline{X}^2 - \theta^2]$ converges in distribution to a normal with mean 0 and variance $4\theta^2\sigma^2$.

As a second example, let $X_1, X_2, \ldots, X_n$ be independent, identically distributed Bernoulli (zero–one) trials, with probability p of success. Instead of p itself, we are interested in the odds of success, given by

$p/(1 - p)$. We will typically estimate p by $\hat{p} = \overline{X}$, the sample average, which in this case is the proportion of successes in the sample. Now, $g(y) = y/(1 - y)$ and $g'(y) = 1/(1 - y)]^2$. Hence, our estimator $\hat{p}/(1 - \hat{p})$ is asymptotically normal, with mean $p/(1 - p)$ and variance $[g'(p)]^2 Var(\hat{p}) = p/n(1 - p)^3$.

The statement of the Delta method specifies that $g'(\theta)$ is not zero. If $g'(\theta)$ happens to equal zero, a modification of the result is necessary. This modification is simple: instead of taking a first-order Taylor expansion, we include the second-order term, that is $g(y) = g(a) + g'(a)(y - a) + g''(a)(y - a)^2 / 2 +$ remainder. Because the term involving the first derivative vanishes, we now have, again expanding around θ, that $g(y) \approx g(\theta) + g'(\theta)(y - \theta)^2 / 2$. Moving $g(\theta)$ to the left-hand side of the equation yields $g(y) - g(\theta) \approx g''(\theta)(y - \theta)^2 / 2$. The square of a standard normal distribution is χ^2 with 1 degree of freedom, leading to the modification of the basic Delta method: Suppose $X_1, X_2, \ldots, X_n$ are independent, identically distributed random variables, and T_n is a function of the data such that $\sqrt{n}[T_n - \theta]$ converges in distribution to a normal with mean 0 and variance σ^2. Then $n[g(T_n) - g(\theta)]$ converges in distribution to $\sigma^2 \frac{g''(\theta)}{2} \chi_1^2$, provided that $g''(\theta) \neq 0$.

Returning to the first example, suppose that $\theta = 0$. Then $g(\theta) = \theta^2 = 0$, and the standard Delta method cannot be applied. We can use the modification to study the distribution of $\overline{X}^2$ in this instance, because $g'(\theta) = 2\theta = 0$ when $\theta = 0$, but $g''(\theta) = 2$ no matter what the value of θ. We can then conclude that when $\theta = 0$, $n[\overline{X}^2 - \theta^2]$ converges in distribution to $\sigma^2 \frac{2}{2} \chi_1^2 = \sigma^2 \chi_1^2$.

A second modification of the basic method involves a function of multiple parameters that is estimated by a function of more than one random variable. The underlying theory stems from multivariate calculus and a multivariate version of the Taylor series expansion, but the essence of the technique is the same, namely, expand around the parameters to terms up to first order (i.e., partial first derivatives of the function with respect to each of the parameters). From this expression, we can derive the approximate mean and variance of the function for use in an asymptotic normal distribution. It is possible to extend the result even further by considering more than one function of the parameters simultaneously, leading to a multi-variate normal distribution in the Delta method approximation.

The modification to allow for functions of random variables is particularly useful for ratio estimators, which arise frequently in practice but can be difficult to handle theoretically. Again, a simple example is instructive. Suppose $X_1, X_2, \ldots, X_n$ and $Y_1, Y_2, \ldots, Y_n$ are samples of independent, identically distributed random variables, where $E(X) = \theta_X$, $E(Y) = \theta_Y$, $Var(X) = \sigma^2_X$, $Var(Y) = \sigma^2_Y$, and $Cov(X,Y) = \sigma_{XY}$. θ_X and θ_Y are both nonzero. The function of interest is $g(\theta_X, \theta_Y) = \theta_X/\theta_Y$. To proceed, first take the partial first derivatives of $g(\theta_X, \theta_Y)$ with respect to θ_X and θ_Y:

$$\frac{\partial}{\partial \theta_X} \frac{\theta_X}{\theta_Y} = \frac{1}{\theta_Y}$$

and

$$\frac{\partial}{\partial \theta_Y} \frac{\theta_X}{\theta_Y} = \frac{-\theta_X}{\theta_Y^2}$$

A natural estimator for $g(\theta_X, \theta_Y)$ is $\bar{X}/\bar{Y}$, the ratio of the sample averages. Then, by the same reasoning as in the univariate case,

$$E\left(\frac{\bar{X}}{\bar{Y}}\right) \approx \frac{\theta_X}{\theta_Y}$$

and

$$Var\left(\frac{\bar{X}}{\bar{Y}}\right) \approx \frac{1}{\theta_X^2} Var(\bar{X}) + \frac{\theta_X^2}{\theta_Y^4} Var(\bar{Y}) - 2\frac{\theta_X}{\theta_Y^3} Cov(\bar{X}, \bar{Y}).$$

These can then be used to obtain the approximate normal distribution of $\bar{X}/\bar{Y}$.

When competing estimators of the same parameter or function of the parameter are available, the Delta method provides a convenient way of comparing them, because one of its by-products is an estimate of variability.

—*Nicole Lazar*

See also Normal Curve; Random Sampling

Further Reading

Casella, G., & Berger, R. L. (2002). *Statistical inference* (2nd ed.). Pacific Grove, CA: Duxbury.

Lehmann, E. L. (1991). *Theory of point estimation*. Pacific Grove, CA: Wadsworth & Brooks/Cole.

DEMING, WILLIAM EDWARDS (1900–1993)

At the time of his death in 1993, Ed Deming was regarded as a world leader in quality management; he had been voted by the business staff of the *Los Angeles Times* as being one of the 50 most influential businesspeople of the century. His obituary in the *American Statistician* was headed "The Statistician Who Changed the World." However, Deming simply described himself as a "consultant in statistical studies."

Deming was born to a poor family in Sioux City, Iowa, on October 14, 1900. His mother was a music teacher, and Deming had a lifelong interest in music (he played the flute). He studied electrical engineering at the University of Wyoming, graduating in 1921. He followed this with an MS in mathematics and physics at the University of Colorado in 1925. As a summer job, he worked for the Western Electric Company in Chicago, where he first encountered Shewart's work on quality control. He obtained his doctorate in physics from Yale University in 1928.

Deming began working first for the U.S. Department of Agriculture and then for the U.S. Bureau of the Census, being responsible for the sampling methods used for the first time in the 1940 U.S. Census. Between 1930 and 1946, Deming was a special lecturer on mathematics and statistics in the graduate school of the National Bureau of Standards, giving lectures from 8 a.m. to 9 a.m. These led, in 1947, to the establishment of the Statistical Engineering Laboratory within the Bureau of Standards.

In 1946, Deming began his practice as a statistical consultant. In 1947, he spent three months in Japan helping with the Japanese census. On his return to Japan in 1950, he gave an extended course in quality control. The course was so successful and influential that he was invited back on many occasions and received by Emperor Hirohito. In 1960, Deming was awarded the Second Order of the Sacred Treasure. At that time, he was much better known in Japan than in his home country.

Deming's 14 key principles for transforming business effectiveness are summarized thus:

1. Create constancy of purpose.
2. Take the lead in adopting the new philosophy.
3. Cease dependence on mass inspection to achieve quality.
4. End the practice of awarding business on the basis of cheapness.
5. Improve constantly.
6. Institute training on the job.
7. Institute leadership.
8. Drive out fear and build trust.
9. Break down barriers between departments.
10. Eliminate slogans, exhortations, and targets.
11. Eliminate numerical goals, and management by objective. Substitute leadership.
12. Remove barriers to pride in workmanship.
13. Institute a program of education and self-improvement.
14. Put everybody to work to accomplish the transformation.

Deming was President of the Institute of Mathematical Statistics in 1945. In 1983, he was awarded the Wilks medal, the highest honor of the American Statistical Association. In 1987, he was awarded the National Medal for Technology. Deming died in Washington, DC, on December 20, 1993.

—*Graham Upton*

Further Reading

Walton, M. (1986). *The Deming management method.* New York: Perigee.

W. Edwards Deming Institute: http://www.deming.org/

Dependent Variable

The term *dependent variable* is derived from mathematics and is basic to understanding results in scientific research. The dependent variable, sometimes referred to as the *dependent measure, criterion variable,* or Y *variable,* is the experimental variable that is measured to determine the effects of an independent variable (e.g., experimental treatment) on selected subjects during a research experiment. Using the subjects' performance on the dependent variable, the researcher attempts to determine a relationship between the independent variable that is manipulated and outcomes on one or more dependent measures. For example, in a study of how the implementation of a newly designed reading program is related to improved scores on reading comprehension of fourth-grade students, the students' performance on the reading comprehension test after they were taught using the new reading program is the dependent variable, whereas the independent variable, the manipulated variable, is the reading program. *Dependent variable* is a generic term that can encompass many different types of measurements. Examples of dependent variables often seen in the research literature are posttest, transfer test, generalization test, probes, unit tests, and so on. The researcher typically reports the results of the study in table or graphic form. Regardless of the type of research design, the dependent variable is a necessary feature of the research.

Characteristics

A dependent variable, one in which both the researcher and consumer can have confidence, should have certain characteristics. Thus, in any well-designed research study, the dependent variable should be (a) clearly defined; (b) closely linked to the independent variable; (c) reliable and valid; (d) sensitive to treatment effects; and (e) administered by the researcher under prescribed, carefully monitored procedures.

Research Examples

Although the number and types of dependent variables are innumerable, several examples are presented across five specific, frequently used research methodologies.

Survey

Research question: What is the average income of physicians in the United States?

Dependent variable: Income of all physicians in the United States.

Independent variable: None.

Correlation

Research question: Are years of education related to income?

Dependent variable: Income of workers across all education levels.

Independent variable: Years of education of the research sample.

Experimental

Research question: Does a certain assertiveness training program help salespersons earn more money?

Dependent variable: Income of selected salespersons.

Independent variable: Assertiveness training program.

Naturalistic-Observational

Research question: What is the frequency of the use of punishment procedures by ninth-grade resource room, special education teachers during class?

Dependent variable: The frequency of punishment used by ninth-grade resource room teachers during class.

Independent variable: None.

Single-Subject Reversal Design

Research question: Does teacher reinforcement during instruction increase the attending behavior of a child with mild mental retardation?

Dependent variable: Percentage of instructional time the student is attending during reinforcement and teaching condition.

Independent variable: Use of teacher reinforcement during instruction.

—*Craig Darch and Ronald C. Eaves*

See also Independent Variable

Further Reading

Keppel, G., Saufley, W., & Tokunaga, H. (1992). *Introduction to design and analysis: A student's handbook.* New York: W. H. Freeman.

Research methods in the social and natural sciences: http://www.mcli.dist.maricopa.edu/proj/res_meth/

DESCRIPTIVE RESEARCH

Descriptive research provides a detailed account of a social setting, a group of people, a community, a situation, or some other phenomenon. This kind of research strives to paint a complete and accurate picture of the world by focusing on the factual details that best describe a current or past event. Researchers engaged in descriptive studies set out to identify who participates in an event, where and when it occurs, and what happens, without exploring the causal relationships involved in that event. For example, a descriptive study may examine the types of services offered by a government agency, the living conditions of a homeless population in a large urban center, the experiences of teachers in elementary school classrooms, or the daily needs of individuals living with breast cancer. One common example of a descriptive study is a census, which sets out to document demographic (e.g., age, gender) and other details (e.g., housing costs) about individuals living in a particular community. Census data are often collected over many years, allowing researchers to examine changes in demographic and social patterns within a particular nation, city, neighborhood, or other identified social grouping.

In compiling descriptive facts about various phenomena, descriptive research is allied most closely with quantitative approaches (including the use of descriptive statistics), although descriptive approaches may also be used in qualitative research to provide valuable background information for analyses of individuals' attitudes, opinions, and personal experiences of particular phenomena. Descriptive research is the most commonly used approach in the human (behavioral) sciences because it allows researchers to examine conditions that occur naturally in the home, hospitals, classrooms, offices, libraries, sports fields, and other locales where human activities can be systematically explored, documented, and analyzed.

Descriptive Research Methods

In quantitative research, descriptive studies are concerned with the functional relationships between variables, hypothesis testing, and the development of generalizations across populations. The findings of descriptive studies are valuable in that they provide information that enables researchers and practitioners to define specific variables clearly, to determine their current situations, and to see how these variables may relate to other variables. In qualitative approaches, descriptive research is often referred to as a form of naturalistic inquiry; this type of research allows the researcher to observe, document, and detail specific activities within a defined social setting in order to point to transferable findings. In both quantitative and qualitative approaches, descriptive research is marked by its exploration of existing events and conditions that would have happened even if the researcher was not there to observe and document the details. A number of different research methods are commonly used in quantitative and qualitative descriptive studies; the sections that follow will briefly examine the goals of some of these approaches.

Questionnaires and Structured Interviews

Methods designed to survey individuals about their experiences, habits, likes and dislikes, or even the number of televisions in their homes are commonly used to gather data from a large sample of a given population at a particular point in time. These methods are designed to generalize to the larger population in order to document the current or past activities and experiences that surround a particular phenomenon. For example, a questionnaire may be designed to identify young people's familiarity with different media outlets, to explore parents' knowledge about treatments for the common cold, or to document the demographic characteristics of new immigrants in rural communities. Large-scale questionnaires and structured interviews typically use some form of probability sampling to select a representative sample of a particular population. These methods take many different forms and can be used across topic areas, including telephone polls (e.g., to solicit voting patterns), mail-in or Web-based questionnaires (e.g., personal shopping habits), and in-person surveys (e.g., in-store product assessments). Researchers must take care to ensure high response rates that will represent the population, as participation rates as low as 15% can be common, especially in e-mail or Web-based surveys.

One of the most common examples of this type of research is an opinion poll, which is typically designed to document demographic details about individuals (e.g., their highest level of education) as well as their opinions on such topics as children being required to wear uniforms in schools, Internet use in the home, mass media as a source of health information, or other issues of social relevance. Question response types may include yes/no, multiple choice, Likert scale, open-ended (short answer) questions, or other appropriate designs. The results of such polls are typically analyzed with fairly simple techniques designed to organize and summarize the findings, such as the calculation of the mean number of women versus men in favor of capital punishment.

Observation

Observing human behavior in natural settings (such as watching shoppers as they stand in line at the grocery store, or patients as they sit in an emergency waiting room) can elicit insightful data that could not be captured using other data collection methods. The data gathered using observational approaches consist of detailed descriptions of people's activities and behaviors, as well as physical details about the social settings that surround and inform those activities. Observational techniques may be covert or overt, and may even result from a researcher's involvement in the particular social scene being investigated (e.g., librarian researchers who work at the public library's reference desk); this latter technique is known as participant observation. Researchers employing observational methods not only document details about the individuals within the setting under study (say, in an emergency room), but also examine the physical (e.g., location of triage facilities) and organizational (e.g., management hierarchies) structures within that setting. Data collection may be restricted to a single site (e.g., one classroom) or may involve multiple sites (e.g., all classrooms within all schools in a district), but typically extends over a long period of time in order to gather valid and complete data.

One example of an observational technique used for gathering information about individuals in a particular social context is the "seating sweeps" method that was developed for use in a public library context. This method involved the use of checklists to document basic demographic information about library patrons (e.g., gender); the activities in which they were engaged (e.g., computer use, reading); where they engaged in those activities (e.g., private study carrels, computer lab); and the materials that these patrons carried with them (e.g., briefcases, writing materials). A number of general patterns emerged about human behavior in the library using this observational technique, including the number of men who used the library at various times of the day and week, and the prevalence of personal entertainment devices used by library patrons.

In-Depth Interviews

In-depth interviews allow researchers to examine issues at length from the interview respondent's personal perspective, and they are commonly used in qualitative research approaches. The data gathered during interviews typically consist of verbatim responses to the interviewer's questions, which are designed to elicit descriptions of personal behaviors, and the opinions, feelings, and attitudes that inform those behaviors. Interviews typically last from 60 to 90 minutes, although the length varies depending on the scope of the project and the availability of participants. Common themes and patterns that emerge from the data derived from these interviews can guide researchers in the assessment of existing programs

and services and in the exploration of various social issues. Transferable findings generally occur at the point of saturation of themes in the data, which typically arise with a minimum of 15 to 18 participants. Increasing the number of interviewees is one way to enhance rigor in data collection and to speak more authoritatively about the findings under study. However, it is also worth noting here that anomalies in the data (such as the experiences of a single individual who provides details about an experience that is unlike that of other interviewees) can also be extremely valuable to qualitative researchers. These singular experiences can highlight individuals' particular needs, especially in settings where policies and practices have been designed for majority populations, and often point to areas that require additional research. In-depth interviews can also be combined with other methods (e.g., structured computer tasks used to assess Web site usability, quantitative questionnaires designed to elicit factual data) to provide a more complete picture of the phenomena under study.

Focus Groups

Focus groups also fall into the interview category and may be either highly structured (i.e., quantitative) in nature, or designed to be more of a personal dialogue between participants (i.e., qualitative). In either case, the defining feature of these interviews is that they occur with groups of individuals (typically five to eight people, with one or more groups in total) whose comments are focused on a particular issue of interest to the researcher. Participants are typically fairly homogeneous group members (e.g., new immigrants living in a particular city, undergraduate students using campus recreational facilities) who are asked to reflect on a series of questions or to react to new products or policies. These interviews can be more challenging to conduct than individual interviews because of the need to manage group dynamics (e.g., ensuring that all group members are able to speak their minds without feeling silenced by other group members). These interviews are best run by a trained facilitator, often require a more formal setting (such as a boardroom), and may take more time to coordinate than other survey methods.

Personal Journals and Diaries

Asking individuals to document their daily activities (such as when or how often they have used an organization's Web site) can be an effective way to document human behavior. One benefit of this approach is that data are collected as they happen, so that researchers need not rely on the accuracy of individuals' memories of events (as in interviews, questionnaires, or other methods where individuals are asked to discuss their behaviors). For example, this method can be used by physicians to track patients' meals and other activities related to personal health, or by education researchers to track students' study habits. Personal journals and diaries allow individuals to document quantitative elements of their activities (such as how often they go to the grocery store and how much money they spend per trip), as well as their thoughts, feelings, and experiences of shopping in particular stores or for particular items. Participants typically need some instruction in the researcher's expectations (e.g., how much detail to provide, how often to write an entry, what topics to include), but can often provide much more detail than is possible to gather using an interview or other research method. Individuals may keep diaries for a period of a week or more, and may write on a variety of topics, which can then be examined further with other, follow-up methods (e.g., personal interviews).

Whether used on their own or in conjunction with one another, all of these methods are useful tools for gathering data on various elements of human behavior. Descriptive research provides valuable insight into the social scenes that surround and inform our lives. The knowledge that we gain about social settings, people, specific experiences and activities, and other elements of social behavior are useful to practitioners (such as hospital and school administrators, or government officials), but also inform other research approaches. Descriptive research can act, for example, as a first step in a more detailed and complex study of social behavior, providing valuable background details about individuals or information on variables that require more advanced study. However, descriptive studies also stand in their own right as a means to examine, document, and reflect on the world and illuminate the social phenomena that inform individuals' personal and work-related lives.

—*Lisa M. Given*

See also Inferential Statistics

Further Reading

Given, L. M., & Leckie, G. J. (2003). "Sweeping" the library: Mapping the social activity space of the public library. *Library & Information Science Research, 25*(4), 365–385.

Ruane, J. M. (2005). *Essentials of research methods: A guide to social science research.* Malden, MA: Blackwell.

Sarafino, E. P. (2005). *Research methods: Using processes and procedures of science to understand behavior.* Upper Saddle River, NJ: Pearson-Prentice Hall.

DEVIATION SCORE

The deviation score is the difference between a score in a distribution and the mean score of that distribution. The formula for calculating the deviation score is as follows:

$$X - \overline{X}$$

where

$\overline{X}$ (called "X bar") is the mean value of the group of scores, or the mean; and

the X is each individual score in the group of scores.

Deviation scores are computed most often for the entire distribution. For example, for the following data set (see Table 1), there are columns representing scores on the variables X and Y for 10 observations. The deviation scores for X and Y have also been calculated. Notice that the means of the deviation score distributions are zero.

Thus, the deviation scores are simply a linear transformation of a variable. This can be demonstrated by calculating the Pearson correlations between X and Y and then between the deviation-X and deviation-Y scores. In both instances, the correlations are 0.866.

Table 1   Raw and Deviation Scores on Two Variables, X and Y

Observation	X	Y	X – 4.8	Y – 4.2
1	2	1	–2.8	–3.2
2	3	4	–1.8	–0.2
3	4	3	–0.8	–1.2
4	7	5	2.2	0.8
5	8	6	3.2	1.8
6	9	8	4.2	3.8
7	2	3	–2.8	–1.2
8	3	3	–1.8	–1.2
9	4	2	–0.8	–2.2
10	6	7	1.2	2.8
	$\bar{X} = 4.8$	$\bar{X} = 4.2$	$\bar{X} = 0.0$	$\bar{X} = 0.0$

The next question one might want to ask is, Why would one want to calculate such scores? The most frequent use of deviation scores is in conducting simultaneous solution regression analyses when there is an interest in the effects of interaction terms.

For example, assume one wants to predict a criterion (Z) with two main effects, X and Y, as well as their interaction. The interaction term is generated by multiplying X and Y, but this interaction term exhibits multicollinearity with each of the main effects, X and Y. However, if the interaction term is created from the deviation scores of X and Y, the multicollinearity no longer is a problem.

Table 2   Raw Scores and Interaction Terms for Nondeviation and Deviation Scores

Observation	X	Y	(X)(Y)	X – 4.8	Y – 4.2	(X – 4.8)(Y– 4.2)
1	2	1	2	–2.8	–3.2	8.96
2	3	4	12	–1.8	–0.2	0.36
3	4	3	12	–0.8	–1.2	0.96
4	7	5	35	2.2	0.8	1.76
5	8	6	48	3.2	1.8	5.76
6	9	8	72	4.2	3.8	15.96
7	2	3	6	–2.8	–1.2	3.36
8	3	3	9	–1.8	–1.2	2.16
9	4	2	8	–0.8	–2.2	1.76
10	6	7	42	1.2	2.8	3.36

To demonstrate this, the data set shown earlier is used (see Table 2). The interaction terms have been generated for each score. The correlations between the nondeviation interaction, (X)(Y), and the main effects are .955 with X and .945 with Y. The correlations between the deviation interaction (X – 4.8)(Y – 4.2) and the main effects are .479 with X and .428 with Y. This feature of deviation scores is of immense utility when conducting simultaneous linear regression-based analyses (such as multiple regression, discriminant function analysis, logistic regression, and structural equation modeling).

—*Theresa Kline*

See also Standard Deviation; Standard Scores; Variance

Further Reading

Aiken, L. S., & West, S. G. (1991). *Multiple regression: Testing and interpreting interactions.* Newbury Park, CA: Sage.

Kline, T. J. B., & Dunn, B. (2000). Analysis of interaction terms in structural equation models: A non-technical demonstration using the deviation score approach. *Canadian Journal of Behavioural Science, 32,* 127–132.

DIAGNOSTIC VALIDITY

Diagnostic validity applies to any test, measurement, or decision-making strategy that categorizes people. Also referred to as *categorical validity* or, more pragmatically, as the 2 × 2 table, diagnostic validity examines the relationship between how a test categorizes a subject and in which category the subject actually is. Relevant categories might include, among others, HIV-positive individuals, top employment prospects, violent recidivists, child molesters, fit parents, suitable graduate students, or incompetent defendants. Validity information answers questions regarding the probability that a classification is correct, the utility of the test or strategy for different purposes, and how to interpret the classification. This information also solves Bayes' theorem: We often know the percentage of paranoids, say, who score positively on a test of paranoia (by administering the test to a large group of paranoids); Bayes' theorem computes the reasonableness of inferring paranoia from a positive test score. The answer requires knowledge about the incidence of paranoia and about how nonparanoids do on the test.

In this entry, *test* is used specially to mean any score, sign, symptom, or series of these used to categorize people. The *Diagnostic and Statistical Manual of Mental Disorders, 4th edition (DSM-IV)* is a manual of tests. Each diagnosis is accompanied by a test to determine if a particular subject has the diagnosis in question. For example, the test for paranoid personality is (a) the presence of a personality disorder, plus (b) the presence of at least four of seven behaviors, plus (c) the exclusion of some other diagnoses. The fact that this is a test for paranoid personality is disguised by the failure of the publishers to include the 2 × 2 table that would answer questions about diagnostic validity. The test is made to look like the *definition* of the disorder instead of a method of detecting who has the disorder and who does not. Before the test was codified, there must have been some other way to determine who had paranoid personality disorder and who did not, and that method was extremely unlikely to be a perfect fit with the current criteria, even if that other way was only in the imagination of the test writers.

As an example, let's assume that the *DSM-IV* test for paranoid personality was a very good test. (We can only assume because the actual data have not been published.) Assume that some expert clinicians carefully identified 100 people as having this disorder. Further assume that the test published in *DSM-IV* gave a positive result for all 100 individuals, and that of 100 randomly selected psychiatric admissions without paranoid personality disorder, only 5 tested positive with the *DSM-IV* criteria. That would certainly be impressive, 100 out of 100 correctly identified with the disorder, and 95 out of 100 correctly identified without the disorder.

Now for some terminology. In this case, the expert clinicians' original diagnoses constitute the *gold standard,* which is the method by which subjects were placed in their actual categories. The gold standard is crucial for interpreting test results, because even the best test predicts only the categories assigned by the gold standard. Thus, for example, a test of violent recidivism usually has a gold standard of rearrest as the indicator of recidivism, so the test can never be better at identifying recidivists than rearrest is, and it is obvious that there are some people who recidivate but are not caught. Furthermore, there are some people who *are* arrested, but incorrectly, and not because they recidivated. Understanding the gold standard is crucial to understanding what a test that categorizes people is able to achieve.

Sensitivity is the accuracy of the test among people who have the condition (who are actually in the category). In our paranoid personality example, the sensitivity is 100/100, or 1.00. *Specificity* is the accuracy of the test among people who do not have the condition (who are not actually in the category). In this case, the specificity is 95/100. *True positives* (TP) are those subjects who are in the category and who are identified as such by the test. *True negatives* (TN) are correctly identified by the test as not being in the category. *False positives* (FP) are not actually in the category but the test says they are; *false negatives* (FN) are actually in the category, but the test says they are not. Sensitivity = TP/(TP + FN). Specificity = TN/(TN + FP).

The *cutoff score* is the decision point at which test results are considered positive or negative for being in the category. In the *DSM-IV,* the cutoff score for paranoid personality is a combination of meeting the first and third criteria, plus four of the behaviors listed in the second criterion. On a typing test to determine good employees, the cutoff score might be 60 words per minute; for graduate students administered the Graduate Record Exam, it might be 1200. Each cutoff score produces a different 2 × 2 table for the analysis of diagnostic validity. A statistic called the area under the curve (AUC) of the receiving operator characteristic curve (ROC) can be computed that evaluates the test as a whole, independent of the cutoff score. The AUC expresses the probability that a person in the category will score higher on the test than a person not in the category. For categorization, though, a cutoff score must be selected and analyzed in the 2 × 2 table (see Table 1).

Positive predictive value (PPV) is the accuracy of the test among people who test positive. It tells us how seriously to take a positive result. PPV = TP/(TP + FP). *Negative predictive value* (NPV) is the accuracy of the test among people who test negative. It tells us how seriously to take a negative result. NPV = TN/(TN + FN).

The *hit rate* of a test is the overall percentage of accurate classifications, or (TP + TN)/(TP + FP + FN + TN). The value of a test is, generally, in the improvement it produces over and above the hit rate that would be obtained from assigning everyone to the more populous category. An exception would be a test used for screening rather than for categorization. If a cheap, harmless medication were available for a serious disease, a desirable test would have perfect sensitivity, so that everyone with the disease got the treatment. But if the specificity were mediocre, that would be fine, because there would be little downside to overadministering the medication.

Before judging a test's validity, we need to know or estimate the *base rate* of the condition or category. The base rate is the incidence of the category among relevant subjects. If the *DSM-IV* test for paranoid personality were being used in employment screening, then the relevant base rate would be the incidence of

this disorder in the general population. If used to diagnose psychiatric patients, then the base rate would be the incidence among hospital admissions. For the sake of this discussion, assume that the incidence of paranoid personality is 0.5% in the general population, and 2% in psychiatric admissions. Because the specificity data (95/100) were obtained from 100 randomly selected psychiatric admissions, we have the data needed to analyze this as a test only in that context. Therefore, in filling in the 2 × 2 table, we need to adjust the column of persons without the condition so that they are represented according to their base rate (98%), while maintaining the test's specificity of 95%.

Notice that the numbers in Table 2 preserve the sensitivity of the test (100% of persons with the disorder are correctly classified); its specificity (95% of persons without the disorder are correctly classified); and the base rate (the table reflects a population in which 2% of persons, or 100 out of 5,000, have the disorder). The PPV is 100/345, meaning that there is only a 29% chance (given our assumptions) that a person diagnosed with paranoid personality disorder using the *DSM-IV* actually has the disorder. Such is the fate of trying to classify people into categories with low base rates. Because the base rate is, under our assumptions, only 2%, we could correctly classify 4,900 out of 5,000 admissions by simply claiming that none of them has the disorder. Even this excellent test, with its 100% sensitivity and 95% specificity,

Table 1   The Basic 2 × 2 Table

	G O L D	S T D	Actually in the category	Actually not in the category
Test says in the category			TP	FP
CUTOFF SCORE				
Test says not in the category			FN	TN

Table 2   Hypothetical Example: A Test of Paranoid Personality Disorder

	G O L D	S T D	Actually in the category	Actually not in the category
Test says in the category			TP = 100	FP = 245
CUTOFF SCORE				
Test says not in the category			FN = 0	TN = 4,655

Table 3 Hypothetical Example: A Racial Test of Violence Risk

	G O L D	S T D
	Actually in the category (violent intent)	*Actually not in the category (no violent intent)*
Test (black) says in the category	TP = 26	FP = 10,924
CUTOFF SCORE		
Test (not black) says not in the category	FN = 26	TN = 10,939,024

correctly classifies only 4,755 out of 5,000 admissions. In terms of Bayes' theorem, we have calculated the probability of A given B (the probability of having the disorder given a positive test score) from the probability of B given A (the probability of a positive test score given the disorder).

To demonstrate the breadth of the applicability of the 2 × 2 table, consider the case of *racial profiling*. Racial profiling is the statistical justification of police suspicion derived from an increased likelihood of criminal activity based on a suspect's race. In this hypothetical example, imagine a wealthy community whose police routinely stop black motorists. The police justify this conduct by noting that in this all-white community, 50% of all non-domestic violent crimes are committed by black people, while only 0.1% of cars observed in the town have black drivers. The category is *motorist intent on violent crime,* and the test is whether or not the motorist is perceived as black by the police. The probability of B (testing positive for looking black) given A (being a violent criminal) is 50%. What is required to justify stopping black motorists, though, is the probability that a black driver is a violent criminal, not the probability that a violent criminal is black. In other words, how good a test of criminality is being black under these circumstances?

To fill in the 2 × 2 table, we need to know or estimate the base rate of non-domestic violence perpetration among car drivers. Suppose this community's streets convey 30,000 motorists a day, and there is one violent crime a week. In the course of the year, the community sees 52 crimes and 10,950,000 car trips. (See Table 3.)

Even though half of all non-domestic violent crimes are committed by black people and black people account for only 0.1% of car trips, the probability of a black driver being a violent criminal in this scenario is only 26/10950. Two chances in a thousand does not justify a police stop. The low base rate of violent crime in this community makes the test of race a useless one, regardless of its consequences for social justice.

Special Problems With the Gold Standard

Data regarding test validity depend on the original sample that was separated into groups by the gold standard. Any sample may have idiosyncratic or unexpected features. For example, the *DSM-IV* test for paranoid personality includes an item about bearing grudges for insults, but it is conceivable that such grudges are a feature of paranoia only in some subcultures. For this reason, every test that categorizes people should be cross-validated on a separate sample. Cross-validation does not guarantee elimination of idiosyncrasies in the sample (or in the employment of the gold standard), because two samples may have the same idiosyncrasy, but lack of cross-validation makes the presence of an idiosyncrasy too likely for an uncrossed test to be trusted.

Care must be taken not to conflate the gold standard with test items, so as to avoid the creation of a pseudo-test. In the example above that deals with racial profiling, it is unclear what the gold standard was for determining which crimes were violent and which were not. Conceivably, the perceived race of the defendant might have influenced this determination. Then, to include race of the defendant as a test item for predicting violence conflates the test and the gold standard, and is bound to make the test look better than it is. This is a form of the logical error, begging the question, or assuming the conclusion.

Certain gold standards are so subjective that tests validated against them cannot be separated from the people on whose subjectivity they depend. In certain contexts, this is not a problem, because the desired use of the test is to please the original judges. For example, employers may choose which are the good current employees and which are the undesirable ones, as long as it is understood that the resulting test is designed to select employees with whom the employer will be pleased, and not employees who meet some other criterion. Tests of good parenting, competency to stand trial (CST), and mental retardation (MR), on the contrary, cannot escape the arbitrariness of the gold standard used to categorize the original sample. Good parenting is obviously subjective. CST is a category that does not occur in nature, but only in the minds of judges. For a test to be useful, the test must be cheaper or more convenient than the gold standard it tries to approximate. Any test of CST is an attempt to improve on a classification that is simple and, by definition, nearly perfect (judges' classifications of CST are rarely overturned by appellate courts). MR also does not occur in nature, but instead represents the arbitrary and politically determined percentage of people whom the society thinks is too limited to be held accountable for self-care. There are too few real differences between subjects who score 69 on an IQ test (MR) and those who score 75 (not MR) to employ an objective gold standard for the validation of, say, a test of adaptive functioning that purports to distinguish people with and without MR.

—*Michael Karson*

See also Validity Theory

Further Reading

Mart, E. G. (1999). Problems with the diagnosis of factitious disorder by proxy in forensic settings. *American Journal of Forensic Psychology, 17*(1), 69–82.

Wood, J. M. (1996). Weighing evidence in sexual abuse evaluations: An introduction to Bayes' theorem. *Child Maltreatment, 1*(1), 25–36.

Area under the curve and receiving operator characteristic curve description: http://www.anaesthetist.com/mnm/stats/roc/

Applying Ideas on Statistics and Measurement

The following abstract is adapted from Miller, J. D., Bagby, R. M., Pilkonis, P. A., Reynolds, S. K., & Lynam, D. R. (2005). A simplified technique for scoring *DSM-IV* personality disorders with the five-factor model. *Assessment, 12*(4), 404–415.

There are many different types of validity, with **diagnostic validity** being the one that examines how "true" or valid a set of diagnostic criteria is for a certain condition. The current study compares the use of two alternative methodologies for using the Five-Factor Model (FFM) to assess personality disorders (PDs). Across two clinical samples, a technique using the simple sum of selected FFM facets is compared with a previously used prototype matching technique. The results demonstrate that the more easily calculated counts perform as well as the similarity scores that are generated by the prototype matching technique. Optimal diagnostic thresholds for the FFM PD counts are computed for identifying patients who meet diagnostic criteria (used to help establish diagnostic validity) for a specific PD. These threshold scores demonstrate good sensitivity in receiver operating characteristics analyses, suggesting their usefulness for screening purposes. Given the ease of this scoring procedure, the FFM count technique has obvious clinical utility.

DIFFERENCE SCORE

The difference score indicates the amount of change between two testings. It is computed by subtracting the score on the first testing from the score on the second

$$d = Y - X,$$

where

d is the difference score (sometimes called *change score* or *gain score*),

X is the first test score (sometimes called the *baseline* or *pretest score*), and

Y is the second test score (sometimes called the *posttest score*).

In SPSS, difference scores are created by computing a new variable. This is done using the Compute function found under the Transform window. The syntax for computing a new variable called "change" to indicate the change from anxiety1 to anxiety2 would be as follows:

```
COMPUTE change = anxiety2 - anxiety1.
EXECUTE.
```

See the example in Table 1.

Table 1   Example of Difference Scores

ANXIETY1	ANXIETY2	CHANGE
23	20	−3.00
45	40	−5.00
26	23	−3.00
34	35	1.00
52	44	−8.00

In Table 1, four of the five participants showed a decrease in anxiety as indicated by the negative difference scores.

Difference scores can be treated like any other variable. The mean of difference scores equals the difference between the means from the two testings. In the above example, the mean of anxiety1 is 36.0, the mean of anxiety2 is 32.4, and the mean of the difference scores is −3.6. This shows that the average change from the first to the second testing was a *decrease* in anxiety of 3.6.

Advantages

Difference scores generally have much less variation than the scores from which they were created. This is because the subtraction operation removes any variation due to individual characteristics that is constant between the two testings. Thus, analyses using difference scores offer more statistical power than analyses conducted on posttest scores.

Difference scores allow a simpler design to be used. A one-way ANOVA comparing the means of difference scores yields a main effect that is identical in both value and meaning to the interaction term in a two-way ANOVA that used the pretest and posttest scores as a second, repeated measures variable. Post hoc comparisons of the mean changes are easier to conduct and interpret in the one-way design.

Disadvantages

Difference scores contain measurement error from both the pretest and posttest scores, and are also negatively correlated with baseline because of measurement error. However, neither of these factors prohibits their use as valid measures of change.

On the other hand, when data are skewed—for example, by a floor or ceiling effect—difference scores may not reflect the true amount of change.

Appropriateness for Comparing Changes in Means

In a randomized experiment, where the goal is to compare the mean changes of groups that receive different treatments, analysis of covariance (ANCOVA), with pretest as the covariate and posttest as the dependent variable, should be used instead of difference scores. ANCOVA provides a better adjustment for minor differences in the pretest means because these differences are entirely due to chance and will regress on the second testing.

However, with naturally occurring groups, where the goal is to compare the changes of different groups to the same treatment, difference scores should be used instead of ANCOVA because the pretest differences between groups are not entirely due to chance and will not regress. ANCOVA would yield incorrect and directionally biased conclusions; for example, when scores are increasing from pretest to posttest, greater increases would generally appear for the group with the higher baseline.

Appropriateness for Examining Predictors of Change

Difference scores should be used instead of residual scores to study predictors (correlates) of change, because correlations between predictors and residual scores are confounded by correlations between predictors and baseline. This is analogous to avoiding ANCOVA with naturally occurring groups. There is also an analogous directional bias; for example, residual scores are biased toward finding positive correlations with change for predictors that have positive correlations with baseline.

—*John Jamieson*

See also Dependent Variable

Further Reading

Salkind, N. J. (2007). *Statistics for people who (think they) hate statistics: The Excel edition.* Thousand Oaks, CA: Sage.

Applying Ideas on Statistics and Measurement

The following abstract is adapted from Edwards, J. R. (2001). Ten difference score myths. *Organizational Research Methods, 4*(3), 265–287.

Difference scores are used in all kinds of studies, and even though their use is widespread, they suffer from numerous methodological problems. Jeffrey Edwards discusses how these problems can be avoided with polynomial regression analysis, a method that has become increasingly prevalent during the past decade. However, a number of potentially damaging myths have begun to spread regarding the drawbacks of difference scores and the advantages of polynomial regression, and if unchecked, difference scores and the problems they create are likely to persist. This article reviews 10 myths about difference scores and attempts to dispel these myths.

DIFFERENTIAL APTITUDE TEST

The Differential Aptitude Test (DAT), first published in 1947 by The Psychological Corporation, is a battery of tests whose goal is to assess multiple separate aptitudes of students and adults. The latest (fifth) version of the DAT, published in 1990, assesses verbal and numerical reasoning, mechanical reasoning, perceptual ability, spatial relations, abstract reasoning,

spelling, and language usage. Separate scoring norms are available for individual tests in the battery. The DAT is available in two levels: Level 1 of the DAT was designed for students in Grades 7 to 9 and adults who have completed these grades, and Level 2 was designed for students in Grades 10 to 12 and adults who have completed more than 9 years of schooling, but have not graduated from high school. The tests were designed primarily for educational and career counseling of students in Grades 7 to 12, but can also be used to assess abilities of less educated adults. The test also includes a Career Interest Inventory that can be used in conjunction with the aptitude tests, and a shortened version called the Differential Aptitude Tests for Personnel and Career Assessment (DAT for PCA) is packaged as a selection tool. The total time to administer the complete version of the DAT is slightly under 4 hours. The readability of the tests was assessed by The Psychological Corporation, and all vocabulary used in directions and content is at the fifth-grade reading level. The Psychological Corporation conducted a careful study of the tryout form of the test to make sure there was no racial test bias in items or scoring. Scoring of the test can be done by hand or computer, and there is a computerized version of the test.

The following separate tests are included:

Career Interest Inventory (30 minutes): Students indicate their level of interest in performing activities related to work and school.

Verbal Reasoning (40 items, 25 minutes): Items include analogies.

Numerical Reasoning (40 items, 30 minutes): Items include addition, subtraction, numeric sequences, fractions, multiplication, division, computing percentages, and basic algebra.

Abstract Reasoning (40 items, 20 minutes): Items assess logic, pattern or rule recognition, attention to detail, and abstract reasoning skills.

Perceptual Speed and Accuracy (2 parts, 100 items each part, 3 minutes each part): Test takers are asked to choose the letter/number combinations that are the same as the underlined combinations.

Mechanical Reasoning (60 items, 25 minutes): Test takers are presented with a picture of some mechanical principle and presented with a question.

Space Relations (50 items, 25 minutes): Items assess perceptual abilities, attention to detail, pattern recognition, and spatial relationships.

Spelling (40 items, 10 minutes): Test takers must determine which word is spelled incorrectly.

Language Usage (40 items, 15 minutes): Items include sentences with errors of grammar, capitalization, or punctuation that test takers are asked to identify.

—*Jennifer Bragger*

See also Aptitude Tests

Further Reading

Henly, S. J., Klebe, K. J., McBride, J. R., & Cudek, R. (1989). Adaptive and conventional versions of the DAT: The first complete test battery comparison. *Applied Psychological Measurement, 13,* 363–371.

Wang, L. (1995). Differential aptitude tests (DAT). *Measurement and Evaluation in Counseling and Development, 28,* 168–170.

Differential Aptitude Tests for Personnel and Career Assessment: http://www.pantesting.com/products/Psych Corp/DAT.asp

DIGGLE-KENWARD MODEL FOR DROPOUT

In medical research, studies are often designed in which specific parameters are measured repeatedly over time in the participating subjects. This allows for modeling the process of change within each subject separately, based on both subject-specific factors (such as gender) and experiment-specific factors (such as treatment). The analysis of such longitudinal data requires statistical models that take into account the association between the measurements within subjects. During the past decade, a lot of effort has been put into the search for flexible longitudinal models.

In practice, longitudinal studies often suffer from attrition (i.e., subjects dropping out earlier than scheduled) for reasons outside the control of the investigator. The resulting data are then unbalanced with unequal numbers of measures for each participant. Nowadays, several statistical packages can handle unbalanced longitudinal data. However, they yield valid inferences only under specific assumptions for the dropout process.

Generally, valid inferences can be obtained only by modeling the response measurements and the dropout process simultaneously. Making various assumptions about the dropout mechanism, a large variety of models for continuous as well as categorical outcomes have been proposed in the statistical literature. With the volume of literature on models for incomplete data increasing, there has been growing concern about the critical dependence of many of these models on the validity of the underlying assumptions. To compound the issue, the data often have very little to say about the correctness of such assumptions.

When referring to the missing-value, or nonresponse, process we will use the terminology of Little and Rubin. A nonresponse process is said to be *missing completely at random* (MCAR) if the missingness is independent of both unobserved and observed data, and *missing at random* (MAR) if, conditional on the observed data, the missingness is independent of the unobserved measurements. A process that is neither MCAR nor MAR is termed *nonrandom* (MNAR). In the context of likelihood inference, and when the parameters describing the measurement process are functionally independent of the parameters describing the missingness process, MCAR and MAR are ignorable, whereas a nonrandom process is nonignorable. Ignorability implies that valid inferences about the measurement model parameters can be obtained by analyzing the observed data alone, obviating the need for formulation of a dropout model.

We will present one modeling framework that has been developed for incomplete longitudinal data of a continuous nature, proposed by Diggle and Kenward.

The model has been subject to criticism because it is rather vulnerable to the modeling assumptions made. These concerns will be discussed and a number of ways for dealing with it explored, with a prominent place given to sensitivity analysis.

The Diggle-Kenward Model for Dropout

We assume that for subject i in the study, $i = 1, \ldots,$ N, a sequence of measurements Y_{ij} is designed to be measured at time points t_{ij}, $j = 1, \ldots, n_i$, resulting in a vector $Y_i = (Y_{i1}, \ldots, Y_{in_i})'$ of measurements for each participant. If dropout occurs, Y_i is only partially observed. We denote the occasion at which dropout occurs by $D_i > 1$, and Y_i is split into the $(D_i - 1)$-dimensional observed component Y_i^{obs} and the $(n_i - D_i + 1)$-dimensional missing component Y_i^{mis}. In case of no dropout, we let $D_i = n_i + 1$, and Y_i equals Y_i^{obs}. The likelihood contribution of the ith subject, based on the observed data (y_i^{obs}, d_i), is proportional to the marginal density function

$$
\begin{aligned}
f(y_i^{obs}, d_i | \theta, \psi) &= \int f(y_i, d_i | \theta, \psi) dy_i^{mis} \\
&= \int f(y_i | \theta) f(d_i | y_i, \psi) dy_i^{mis}
\end{aligned}
\tag{1}
$$

in which a marginal model for Y_i is combined with a model for the dropout process, conditional on the response, and where θ and ψ are vectors of unknown parameters in the measurement model and dropout model, respectively.

Let $h_{ij} = (y_{i1}, \ldots, y_{i;j-1})$ denote the observed history of subject i up to time $t_{i, j-1}$. The Diggle-Kenward model for the dropout process allows the conditional probability for dropout at occasion j, given that the subject was still observed at the previous occasion, to depend on the history h_{ij} and the possibly unobserved current outcome y_{ij}, but not on future outcomes y_{ik}, $k > j$. These conditional probabilities $P(D_i = j \mid D_i = j,$ $h_{ij}, y_{ij}, \psi)$ can now be used to calculate the probability of dropout at each occasion:

$P(D_i = j | y_i, \psi) = P(D_i = j | h_{ij}, y_{ij}, \psi)$

$$
= \begin{cases}
P(D_i = j | D_i \geq j, h_{ij}, y_{ij}, \psi) & j = 2, \\
P(D_i = j | D_i \geq j, h_{ij}, y_{ij}, \psi) \\
\quad \times \prod_{k=2}^{j-1}[1 - P(D_i = k | D_i \geq k, h_{ik}, y_{ik}, \psi)] & j = 3, \ldots, n_i, \\
\prod_{k=2}^{n_i}[1 - P(D_i = k | D_i \geq k, h_{ik}, y_{ik}, \psi)] & j = n_i + 1.
\end{cases}
$$

Diggle and Kenward combine a multivariate normal model for the measurement process with a logistic regression model for the dropout process. More specifically, the measurement model assumes that the vector Y_i of repeated measurements for the ith subject satisfies the linear regression model $Y_i \sim N(X_i\beta, V_i)$, $(i = 1, \ldots, N)$. The matrix V_i can be left unstructured or is assumed to be of a specific form (e.g., resulting from a linear mixed model, a factor-analytic structure, or spatial covariance structure). The logistic dropout model is typically of the form

$$
\begin{aligned}
\text{logit }&[P(D_i = j \mid D_i \geq j, h_{ij}, y_{ij}, \psi)] \\
&= \psi_0 + \psi_1 y_{ij} + \psi_2 y_{i, j-1}.
\end{aligned}
\tag{2}
$$

More general models can be constructed easily by including the complete history $h_{ij} = (y_{i1}, \ldots, y_{i;j-1})$, as well as external covariates, in the above conditional dropout model. Note also that, strictly speaking, one could allow dropout at a specific occasion to be related to all future responses as well. However, this is rather counterintuitive in many cases. Moreover, including future outcomes seriously complicates the calculations because computation of the likelihood (Equation 1) then requires evaluation of a possibly high-dimensional integral. Note also that special cases of a model (Equation 2) are obtained from setting $\psi_1 = 0$ or $\psi_1 = \psi_2 = 0$, respectively. In the first case, dropout is no longer allowed to depend on the current measurement, implying random dropout (MAR). In the second case, dropout is independent of the outcome, which corresponds to completely random dropout (MCAR).

Diggle and Kenward obtained parameter and precision estimates by means of maximum likelihood. The likelihood involves marginalization over the unobserved outcomes Y_i^{mis}. Practically, this involves relatively tedious and computationally demanding forms of numerical integration. This, combined with likelihood surfaces tending to be rather flat, makes the model difficult to use. These issues are related to the problems to be discussed next.

Remarks on Sensitivity Analysis and Other Models

Apart from the technical difficulties encountered during parameter estimation, there are further important issues surrounding MNAR based models. Even when the measurement model (e.g., the multivariate normal model) would be the choice of preference beyond any doubt to describe the measurement process *should the data be complete,* then the analysis of the actually observed, incomplete version is, in addition, subject to further untestable modeling assumptions.

When missingness is MAR, the problems are less complex because it has been shown that, in a likelihood or Bayesian framework, it is sufficient to analyze the observed data without explicitly modeling the dropout process. However, the very assumption of MAR is itself untestable. Therefore, ignoring MNAR models is as little an option as blindly shifting to one particular MNAR model. A sensible compromise between, on one hand, considering a single MNAR model or, on the other hand, excluding such models from consideration is to study the nature of such sensitivities and, building on this knowledge, formulate ways for conducting sensitivity analyses. Indeed, a strong conclusion, arising from most sensitivity analysis work, is that MNAR models have to be approached cautiously. This was made clear by several discussants to the original paper by Diggle and Kenward, particularly Laird, Little, and Rubin, respectively. An implication is that, for example, formal tests for the null hypothesis of MAR versus the alternative of MNAR should be approached with the utmost caution.

Verbeke, Lesaffre, and Spiessens have shown, in the context of an onychomycosis study, that excluding a small amount of measurement error drastically changes the likelihood ratio test statistics for the MAR null hypothesis. Kenward revisited the analysis of the mastitis data performed by Diggle and Kenward. In this study, the milk yields of 107 cows were to be recorded during two consecutive years. Whereas data were complete in the first year, 27 animals were missing in the second year because they developed mastitis and their milk yield was no longer of use. In Diggle and Kenward's paper, there was strong evidence for MNAR, but Kenward showed that removing 2 out of 107 anomalous profiles completely removed this evidence. In addition, he showed that changing the conditional distribution of the Year 2 yield, given the Year 1 yield, from a normal distribution to a heavy-tailed *t* also led to the same result of no residual evidence for MNAR. This particular conditional distribution is of great importance, because a subject with missing data does not contribute to it and hence is a source of sensitivity issues. Once more, the conclusion is that fitting a MNAR model should be subject to careful scrutiny.

In addition to the instances described above, sensitivity to model assumptions has been reported for about two decades. In an attempt to formulate an answer to these concerns, a number of authors have proposed strategies to study sensitivity. We broadly distinguish between two types. A first family of approaches can be termed *substantive driven* in the sense that the approaches start from particularities of the problem at hand. Kenward's approach falls within this category. Arguably, such approaches are extremely useful, both in their own right and as a preamble to using the second family, where what could be termed *general purpose* tools are used.

Broadly, we could define a sensitivity analysis as one in which several statistical models are considered simultaneously and/or where a statistical model is further scrutinized using specialized tools (such as diagnostic measures). This rather loose and very general definition encompasses a wide variety of useful approaches. The simplest procedure is to fit a selected number of (MNAR) models that are all deemed plausible or one in which a preferred (primary) analysis is supplemented with a number of variations. The extent to which conclusions (inferences) are stable across such ranges provides an indication about the belief that can be put into them. Variations to a basic model can be constructed in different ways. The most obvious strategy is to consider various dependencies of the missing data process on the outcomes and/or on covariates. Alternatively, the distributional assumptions of the models can be changed.

Several authors have proposed the use of global and local influence tools. Molenberghs, Verbeke, Thijs, Lesaffre, and Kenward revisited the mastitis example. They were able to identify the same two cows found by Kenward, in addition to another one. Thus, an important question is, What exactly are the sources causing an MNAR model to provide evidence for MNAR against MAR? There is evidence to believe that a multitude of outlying aspects, but not necessarily the (outlying) nature of the missingness mechanism in one or a few subjects, is responsible for an apparent MNAR mechanism. The consequence of this is that local influence should be applied and interpreted with due caution.

Of course, the above discussion is not limited to the Diggle-Kenward model. A variety of other models have been proposed for incomplete longitudinal data. First, the model has been formulated within the selection model framework, in which the joint distribution of the outcome and dropout processes is factorized as the marginal distribution of the outcomes $f(y_i \mid \theta)$ and the conditional distribution of the dropout process, given the outcomes $f(d_i \mid y_i, \psi)$. Within this framework, models have been proposed for nonmonotone missingness as well, and furthermore, a number of proposals have been made for non-Gaussian outcomes. Apart from the selection model framework, so-called pattern-mixture models have gained popularity, where the reverse factorization is applied with factors $f(y_i \mid d_i, \theta)$ and $f(d_i \mid \psi)$. Also within this framework, both models and sensitivity analysis tools for them have been formulated. A third framework consists of so-called shared parameter models, where random effects are employed to describe the relationship between the measurement and dropout processes.

—*Geert Verbeke and Geert Molenberghs*

See also Longitudinal/Repeated Measures Data; Missing Data Method; Mixed Models; Repeated Measures Analysis of Variance

Further Reading

De Gruttola, V., & Tu, X. M. (1994). Modelling progression of CD4-lymphocyte count and its relationship to survival time. *Biometrics, 50,* 1003–1014.

Diggle, P., & Kenward, M. G. (1994). Informative drop-out in longitudinal data analysis (with discussion). *Applied Statistics, 43,* 49–93.

Diggle, P. J., Heagerty, P. J., Liang, K.-Y., & Zeger, S. L. (2002). *Analysis of longitudinal data* (2nd ed.). Oxford, UK: Clarendon.

Kenward, M. G. (1998). Selection models for repeated measurements with nonrandom dropout: An illustration of sensitivity. *Statistics in Medicine, 17,* 2723–2732.

Little, R. J. A., & Rubin, D. B. (2002). *Statistical analysis with missing data* (2nd ed.). New York: Wiley.

Molenberghs, G., & Verbeke, G. (2005). *Discrete longitudinal data.* New York: Springer.

Molenberghs, G., Verbeke, G., Thijs, H., Lesaffre, E., & Kenward, M. G. (2001). Mastitis in dairy cattle: Local influence to assess sensitivity of the dropout process. *Computational Statistics and Data Analysis, 37,* 93–113.

Verbeke, G., Lesaffre, E., & Spiessens, B. (2001). The practical use of different strategies to handle dropout in longitudinal studies. *Drug Information Journal, 35,* 419–434.

DIMENSION REDUCTION

Dimension reduction is a collection of statistical methodologies that reduces the dimension of the data while still preserving relevant information. High-dimensional data are very common in government agencies, academia, and industrials. However, the high dimension and large volume of data bring up at least two issues, among many others. One is to overcome the curse of dimensionality, which states that high-dimensional spaces are inherently sparse even with large number of observations. The other is how to present the information within data parsimoniously. Dimension reduction techniques address these issues to varying extents by reducing the set of variables to a smaller set of either the original variables or new variables, where the new variables are linear combinations or even nonlinear functions of the original ones. When the new dimension is relatively small, data visualization becomes possible, which often assists data modeling substantially.

Dimension Reduction Methodologies

Based on whether a response is specified or not, dimension reduction techniques generally can be divided into two major categories: supervised dimension reduction and unsupervised dimension reduction.

Unsupervised Dimension Reduction

Unsupervised dimension reduction treats all variables equally without specifying a response. The analysis usually has a natural definition about the information of interest. Unsupervised dimension reduction methods find a new set of a smaller number of variables that either provides a simpler presentation or discovers intrinsic structure in the data while retaining most of the important information. Listed below are only a few of the most widely used techniques.

Principal component analysis (PCA) finds a few orthogonal linear combinations of the original variables with the largest variances; these linear combinations are the principal components that would be retained for subsequent analyses. In PCA, the information is the variation within the data. Usually, principal components are sorted in descending order according to their variations. The number of principal components that should be included in the analysis depends on how much variation should be preserved.

Factor analysis assumes that a set of variables establishes the relationships among themselves through a smaller set of common factors. It estimates the common factors with assumptions about the variance-covariance structure.

Canonical correlation analysis identifies and measures the association between two sets of random variables. Often, it finds one linear combination of variables for each set, where these two new variables have the largest correlation.

Correspondence analysis is a graphical tool for an exploratory data analysis of a contingency table. It projects the rows and columns as points into a plot, where rows (columns) have a similar profile if their corresponding points are close together.

Projection pursuit defines a projection index that measures the "interestingness" of a direction. Then, it searches for the direction maximizing the index.

Multidimensional scaling finds a projection of the data into a smaller dimensional space so that the distances among the points in the new space reflect the proximities in the original data.

Supervised Dimension Reduction

Supervised dimension reduction techniques generally are applied in regression. A response Y is specified that can be one random variable, one random vector, or even a curve. The predictor vector X is p-dimensional. The object of interest is the relation between the response and the predictors, which is often summarized as $Y = f(X, \varepsilon)$, where ε denotes the error term. Some specific structures are imposed to facilitate the estimation of the function. Dimension reduction is a crucial part of the modeling process. For example, ordinary least squares regression can be considered as a special case of dimension reduction in regression.

To reduce the dimension in the predictor space, variable selection techniques select a small set of variables that is necessary instead of the whole p predictors. Single-index and multi-index models focus on only one or a small number of linear combinations of predictors. For example, a multi-index model assumes $Y = f(\beta_1^T X, \beta_2^T X, \ldots, \beta_k^T X, \varepsilon)$, where $\beta_i^T X, i = 1, 2, \ldots, k$ are linear combinations of X and ε is an error term.

In addition to reducing the dimension of the predictor space, we also can apply dimension reduction in the functional space. For example, a generalized additive model assumes $Y = \sum_{i=1}^{p} f_i(x_i) + \varepsilon$, where the additive nature of predictors' contributions to the model dramatically reduces the functional space considered for the regression.

Sufficient dimension reduction (SDR) in regression has generated considerable interest in the past decade. The basic idea is to replace the predictor vector with its projection onto a subspace of the predictor space without loss of information on the conditional distribution of $Y | X$. Specifically, suppose the response Y is independent of X given the values of d linear combinations of predictors ($\beta_1^T X, \beta_2^T X, \ldots, \beta_d^T X$). Thus, these d new variables carry all the information that X has about Y. The subspace spanned by the β_i s is called the SDR subspace. One advantage of working in SDR is that no prespecified model for $Y \mid X$ is required. Many methods have been proposed to estimate the SDR subspace.

Sliced inverse regression (SIR) is one of the most widely used methods. Without loss of generality, we assume X is a standardized predictor vector with a mean of zero and a covariance matrix as an identity matrix. Under mild conditions, the inverse conditional means of X given the response Y belong to the SDR subspace. When Y is discrete, it is easy to calculate the sample version of inverse conditional means. If Y is continuous, we only need to discretize Y by slicing on the range of the response. Suppose we have h slices. Let $\bar{X}_s$ denote the sample average of X within the sth slice, $s = 1, 2, \ldots, h$. Construct a SIR kernel matrix $M_{SIR} = \sum_{s=1}^{h} f_s \bar{X}_s \bar{X}_s^T$, where f_s is the proportion of the observations falling in the sth slice. If we determine that the dimension of the SDR subspace is d, then the d eigenvectors of M_{SIR} that correspond to the d largest eigenvalues constitute a basis for the SDR subspace.

Sliced average variance estimation (SAVE) is another important SDR method. Under the same setting as SIR, SAVE constructs a kernel matrix using the inverse conditional variance of X given Y: $M_{SAVE} = \sum_{s=1}^{h} f_s (I - \Omega_s)^2$, where Ω_s is the sample covariance matrix of X within the sth slice. As with SIR, the first few eigenvectors of M_{SAVE} serve as an estimated basis of the SDR subspace.

Principal Hessian directions (pHd) is an SDR method that does not require slicing. Its kernel matrix is constructed as $M_{pHd} = 1/n \sum_{i=1}^{n} (y_i - \bar{y}) X_i X_i^T$, where $\bar{y}$ is the sample average of the response and n is the number of observations. The estimated basis of the SDR subspace is the eigenvectors of M_{pHd} that correspond to eigenvalues with the largest absolute values.

Minimum average variance estimation (MAVE), which is one of the more recent developments, has virtually no assumptions on X but is computationally more intensive than SIR or SAVE. MAVE essentially is a local linear smoother with weights determined by some kernel functions.

Case Study

We consider a data set of 200 Swiss banknotes, among which half are genuine. The predictors are six

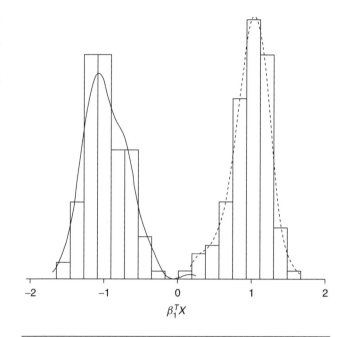

Figure 1   SIR Result of Swiss Banknotes Data

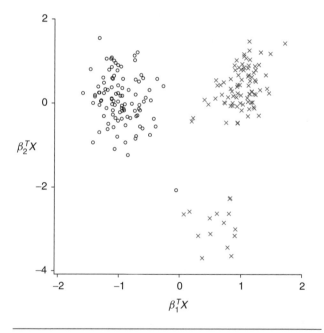

Figure 2   SAVE Result for Swiss Banknotes Data

measurements: the widths of the top margin, the bottom margin, the left edge, the right edge, the length of the bill, and the length of the image diagonal. The response is the status of the bill, which equals 1 if the bill is counterfeit and 0 otherwise. In this case, the response is discrete with two slices.

SIR can detect only one direction β_1 in the SDR subspace because there are only two slices. Figure 1 plots the histogram of the linear combination of the predictors $\beta_1^T X$, where smoothing density curves for both groups have been superimposed for visual enhancement. The left solid curve is for genuine banknotes. The direction that SIR detected separates these two groups very well.

For the same data, SAVE can detect more than one direction. Figure 2 plots the first two directions from SAVE, where circles denote genuine notes and crosses denote counterfeit notes. The first SAVE direction is almost identical to the SIR direction. The second SAVE direction brought up an interesting pattern in the data, which may suggest that there are two sources of counterfeit notes. It is also possible that this pattern is just a result of measurement errors.

—*Liqiang Ni*

Further Reading

Cook, R. D. (2000, June). *Using Arc for dimension reduction and graphical exploration in regression*. Retrieved from http://www.stat.umn.edu/arc/InvReg/DimRed.pdf

Cook, R. D., & Ni, L. (2005). Sufficient dimension reduction via inverse regression: A minimum discrepancy approach. *Journal of the American Statistical Society, 100,* 410–428.

Johnson, R. A., & Wichern, D. W. (2002). *Applied multivariate statistical analysis.* Englewood Cliffs, NJ: Prentice Hall.

Li, K.-C. (1991). Sliced inverse regression for dimension reduction. *Journal of the American Statistical Society, 86,* 316–342.

DISCRIMINANT ANALYSIS

The need for classification arises in most scientific pursuits. Typically, there is interest in classifying an entity, say, an individual or object, on the basis of some characteristics (feature variables) measured on the entity. This classification is usually undertaken in the context where there is a finite number, say, g, of predefined distinct populations, categories, classes, or groups, and the entity to be classified is assumed to belong to one (and only one) of these g possible groups. In order to assist with the construction of a classification rule or classifier for this purpose, there are usually available so-called training data from each group; that is, these training data comprise the features measured on some entities that are classified with respect to the g underlying groups. In statistical terminology, this classification process is referred to as *discriminant analysis*, whereas in pattern recognition and machine learning, it is referred to as *supervised learning* or *learning with a teacher.*

We let $G_1, \ldots, G_g$ denote the g possible groups, and we suppose that a (feature) vector x containing p variables can be measured on the entity. The group membership of the entity is denoted by the categorical variable z, where $z = i$ implies that the entity belongs to G_i ($i = 1, \ldots, g$). The problem is to estimate or predict z solely on the basis of x and the associated training data. An example in which an outright assignment is required concerns the rejection or acceptance of loan applicants by a financial institution. For this decision problem, there are two groups: G_1 refers to applicants who will service their loans satisfactorily, and G_2 refers to those who will not. The feature vector x for an applicant contains information such as age, income, and marital status. A rule based on x for allocating an applicant to either G_1 or G_2 (that is, either accepting or rejecting the loan application) can be formed from an analysis of the feature vectors of past applicants from each of the two groups. In some applications, no assignment of the entity to one of the possible groups is intended. Rather, the problem is to draw inferences about the relationship between z and the feature variables in x. An experiment might be designed with the specific aim to provide insight into the predictive structure of the feature variables. For example, a political scientist may wish to determine the socioeconomic factors that have the most influence on the voting patterns of a population of voters.

Allocation Rules

Let $r(x)$ denote an allocation or discriminant rule, where $r(x) = i$ implies that an entity with feature vector x is to be assigned to the ith group G_i. The allocation rates associated with this rule $r(x)$ are denoted by $e_{ij}(r)$, where $e_{ij}(r)$ is the probability that a randomly chosen entity from G_i is allocated to G_j ($i, j = 1, \ldots, g$).

For a diagnostic test using the rule $r(x)$ in the context where G_1 denotes the absence of a disease or condition and G_2 its presence, the error rate $e_{12}(r)$ corresponds to the probability of a false positive, whereas $e_{21}(r)$ is the probability of a false negative. The correct allocation rates $e_{22}(r)$ and $e_{11}(r)$ are known as the sensitivity and specificity, respectively, of the diagnostic test.

Decision theory provides a convenient framework for the construction of discriminant rules. More specifically, let π_i denote the prior probability that the entity comes from the ith group G_i, and let $f_i(x)$ denote the probability density function of the feature vector X in G_i. This is assuming that the variables in the feature vector x are of the continuous type. The unconditional density of X, $f(x)$, is therefore given by the mixture density, which is the sum of the group-conditional densities $f_i(x)$ weighted by their prior probabilities π_i. If they are discrete variables, then $f_i(x)$ can be viewed as the probability function. With this notation, the posterior probability that an entity belongs to G_i can be expressed via Bayes' theorem as

$$\tau_i(x) = \pi_i f_i(x)/f(x) \ (i=1, \ldots, g) \tag{1}$$

An optimal rule of allocation can be formed by assigning an entity with feature vector x to that group to which the entity has the greatest posterior probability of belonging. This rule is optimal in the sense of minimizing the overall correct allocation rate. It can be viewed also as optimal in a decision-theoretic framework of minimizing the so-called risk of allocation under certain assumptions on the loss function.

Sample-Based Allocation Rules

In practice, the group-conditional densities $f_i(x)$ are usually unknown. A basic assumption in discriminant analysis is that in order to estimate the unknown group-conditional densities, there are entities of known origin on which the feature vector X has been recorded for each. These data are referred to in the literature as *initial, reference, design, training,* or *learning data.*

The initial approach to the problem of forming a sample discriminant rule, and indeed to discriminant analysis in its modern guise, was developed by Fisher. In the context of $g = 2$ groups, he proposed that an entity with feature vector x be assigned on the basis of the linear discriminant function $a^T x$, where a maximizes an index of separation between the two groups. The index was defined to be the magnitude of the difference between the group sample means of $a^T x$ normalized by the pooled sample estimate of its assumed common variance within a group.

We let $r(x;t)$ denote a sample-based allocation rule formed from the training data t. An obvious way of forming $r(x;t)$ is to take it to be an estimated version of Bayes' rule, where the posterior probabilities of group membership $\tau_i(x)$ are replaced by some estimates $\hat{\tau}_i(x,t)$ formed from the training data t. A common approach, referred to as the sampling approach, is to formulate the $\tau_i(x)$ through the group-conditional densities $f_i(x)$. With the fully parametric approach to this problem, the group-conditional densities $f_i(x)$ are assumed to have specified functional forms except for a finite number of parameters to be estimated. A commonly used parametric family for the $f_i(x)$ for continuous feature data is the normal with either a linear or quadratic rule in x being obtained depending on whether the group covariance matrices are taken to be equal or unequal.

There is also the direct approach (the diagnostic paradigm) to the estimation of the $\tau_i(x)$, using either nonparametric estimates, as with nearest neighbor methods, or parametric estimates via the logistic model. With the latter approach, it is the ratios of the group-conditional densities that are being modeled. The fundamental assumption of the logistic approach is that these ratios are linear, which is equivalent to taking the log (posterior) odds to be linear. The linearity here is not necessarily in the basic variables; transforms of these may be taken. Another method for the direct modeling of the group posterior probabilities is to use neural networks, which have been coming under increasing attention by statisticians.

To illustrate the construction of sample-based allocation rules, we consider the construction of a discriminant rule for the problem of assessing loan applications, as mentioned earlier. Here, the applicant for a loan is a company, and the feature vector contains information on its key financial characteristics. For the purposes of our illustration, we consider the case where there are $p = 2$ feature variables, which are the first two principal components of three financial ratios concerning the debt, liquid assets, and working capital of a company. In Figure 1, we have plotted the boundary

$$\hat{\tau}_1 (x_j, t) = \hat{\tau}_2 (x_j, t)$$

for the sample version of the Bayes' rule (the sample linear discriminant rule) formed under the assumption that the feature vector has a bivariate normal distribution with a common group covariance matrix in each of the two groups G_1 and G_2, corresponding to good (satisfactorily serviced) and bad (unsatisfactorily serviced) loans. It can be seen that the overall error rate of this rule reapplied to the training data (its apparent error rate) is not as low as that of the quadratic rule formed without the restriction of a common group-conditional covariance matrix for the feature vector X. With its curved boundary, the quadratic rule misallocates only four (all bad) loans. One should be mindful, however, that the apparent error rate provides an optimistic assessment of the accuracy of a discriminant rule when it is applied to data not in the training set. We have also plotted in Figure 1 the boundary of the rule obtained by modeling the distribution of the feature vector X by a two-component normal mixture, which results in the misallocation of one bad loan at the expense of misallocating two good loans. The latter rule is an example of a more flexible approach to classification than that based on the assumption of normality for each of the group-conditional distributions, as to be considered now.

Flexible Discriminant Rules

A common nonparametric approach to discriminant analysis uses the kernel method to estimate the group-conditional densities $f_i(x)$ in forming an estimate of the Bayes' rule. More recently, use has been made of finite mixture models, mainly normal mixtures, to provide flexible rules of discrimination. Mixture models, which provide an extremely flexible way

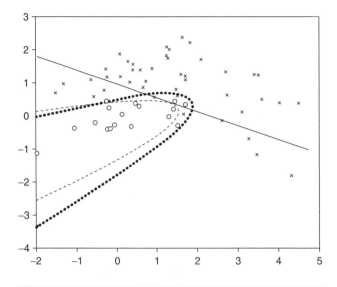

Figure 1   Boundaries of Linear Rule (solid line), Quadratic Rule (dashed line), and Mixture Model-Based Rule (dotted line)

Note: Crosses and circles denote good and bad loans, respectively.

of modeling a density function, can be fitted in a straightforward manner via the Expectation-Maximization algorithm. Among other work on flexible discrimination, there is the flexible discriminant analysis (FDA) approach based on nonparametric regression. The generic version of FDA based on smoothing splines proceeds by expanding the predictors in a large (adaptively selected) basis set, and then performing a penalized discriminant analysis in the enlarged space using a linear discriminant or a normal mixture model-based rule. The class of nonlinear regression methods that can be used includes additive models, the multivariate adaptive regression spline (MARS) model, projection pursuit regression, and neural networks. In machine learning, there has been increasing attention in the case of two groups given to nonlinear rules based on the foundations of support vector machines. With this approach, the initial feature space is mapped into a higher dimensional space by choosing a nonlinear mapping and then choosing an optimal separating hyperplane in the enlarged feature space.

A rather different approach to the allocation problem as considered up to now, is to portray the rule in terms of a binary tree. The tree provides a hierarchical representation of the feature space. An allocation is effected by proceeding down the appropriate branches of the tree. The Classification and Regression Tree (CART) methodology of Breiman et al. has contributed significantly to the growing popularity of tree classifiers. In the context of tree classifiers in particular, there has been growing interest in the use of boosting, which is one of the most important recent developments in classification methodology. Algorithms such as the Adaboost algorithm of Freund and Schapire and the bagging algorithm often can improve performance of unstable classifiers like trees or neural nets by applying them sequentially to reweighted versions of the training data and taking a weighted majority vote of the sequence of classifiers so formed. The test error of the weighted classifier usually does not increase as its size increases, and often is observed to decrease even after the training error reaches zero.

—*Geoffrey McLachlan*

See also Discriminant Correspondence Analysis

Further Reading

Bishop, C. M. (1995). *Neural networks for pattern recognition*. Oxford, UK: Oxford University Press.

Breiman, L., Friedman, J. H., Olshen, R. A., & Stone, C. J. (1984). *Classification and regression trees*. Belmont, CA: Wadsworth.

Fisher, R. A. (1936). The use of multiple measurements in taxonomic problems. *Annals of Eugenics, 7,* 179–188.

Freund, Y., & Schapire, R. (1996). Experiments with a new boosting algorithm. In *Machine learning: Proceedings of the Thirteenth International Conference* (L. Saitta, ed., pp. 148–156). San Francisco: Morgan Kaufmann.

Hand, D. J. (1997). *Construction and assessment of classification rules*. New York: Wiley.

Hastie, T., Tibshirani, R., & Friedman, J. (2001). *The elements of statistical learning: Data mining, inference, and prediction*. New York: Springer.

McLachlan, G. J. (1992). *Discriminant analysis and statistical pattern recognition*. New York: Wiley.

McLachlan, G. J., & Peel, D. (2000). *Finite mixture models*. New York: Wiley.

Ripley, B. D. (1996). *Pattern recognition and neural networks*. Cambridge, UK: Cambridge University Press.

DISCRIMINANT CORRESPONDENCE ANALYSIS

As the name indicates, discriminant correspondence analysis (DCA) is an extension of discriminant analysis (DA) and correspondence analysis (CA). Like discriminant analysis, the goal of DCA is to categorize observations in predefined groups, and like correspondence analysis, it is used with nominal variables.

The main idea behind DCA is to represent each group by the sum of its observations and to perform a simple CA on the groups by variables matrix. The original observations are then projected as supplementary elements, and each observation is assigned to the closest group. The comparison between the a priori and a posteriori classifications can be used to assess the quality of the discrimination. A similar procedure can be used to assign new observations to categories. The stability of the analysis can be evaluated using cross-validation techniques such as jackknifing or bootstrapping.

An Example

It is commonly thought that the taste of wines depends upon their origin. As an illustration, we have sampled 12 wines coming from three different origins (four wines per origin) and asked a professional taster (unaware of the origin of the wines) to rate these wines on five scales. The scores of the taster were then transformed into binary codes to form an indicator matrix (as in multiple correspondence analysis). For example, a score of 2 on the "Fruity" scale would be coded by the following pattern of three binary values: 010. An additional unknown wine was also evaluated by the taster with the goal of predicting its origin from the ratings. The data are given in Table 1.

Notations

There are K groups, with each group comprising I_k observations, and the sum of the I_ks is equal to I, which is the total number of observations. For convenience, we assume that the observations constitute the rows of the data matrix, and that the variables are the

Table 1 Data for the Three Region Wines Example

Wine	Region	Woody 1	2	3	Fruity 1	2	3	Sweet 1	2	3	Alcohol 1	2	3	Hedonic 1	2	3	4
1	1 Loire	1	0	0	0	0	1	0	1	0	1	0	0	1	0	0	0
2	1 Loire	0	1	0	0	0	1	0	0	1	0	1	0	0	0	1	0
3	1 Loire	1	0	0	0	1	0	0	1	0	1	0	0	0	1	0	0
4	1 Loire	1	0	0	0	0	1	0	0	1	0	1	0	0	0	0	1
Σ	1 Loire	3	1	0	0	1	3	0	2	2	2	2	0	1	1	1	1
5	2 Rhône	1	0	0	0	1	0	1	0	0	0	0	1	0	0	1	0
6	2 Rhône	0	1	0	1	0	0	1	0	0	0	0	1	0	1	0	0
7	2 Rhône	0	0	1	0	1	0	0	1	0	0	1	0	1	0	0	0
8	2 Rhône	0	1	0	0	0	1	0	0	1	0	0	1	0	0	0	1
Σ	2 Rhône	1	2	1	1	2	1	2	1	1	0	1	3	1	1	1	1
9	3 Beaujolais	0	0	1	1	0	0	0	0	1	1	0	0	1	0	0	0
10	3 Beaujolais	0	1	0	1	0	0	0	0	1	1	0	0	0	1	0	0
11	3 Beaujolais	0	0	1	0	1	0	0	1	0	0	1	0	0	0	0	1
12	3 Beaujolais	0	0	1	1	0	0	1	0	0	1	0	0	0	0	1	0
Σ	3 Beaujolais	0	1	3	3	1	0	1	1	2	3	1	0	1	1	1	1
W?	?	1	0	0	0	0	1	0	1	0	0	1	0	1	0	0	0

Notes: Twelve wines from three different regions are rated on five descriptors. A value of 1 indicates that the wine possesses the given value of the variable. The wine *W?* is an unknown wine treated as a supplementary observation.

columns. There are *J* variables. The *I* × *J* data matrix is denoted **X**. The *indicator* matrix is an *I* × *K* matrix denoted **Y** in which a value of 1 indicates that the row belongs to the group represented by the column, and a value of 0 indicates that it does not. The *K* × *J* matrix, denoted **N**, is called the "group matrix," and it stores the total of the variables for each category. For our example, we find that

$$\mathbf{N} = \mathbf{Y}^{\mathrm{T}}\mathbf{X}$$

$$= \begin{bmatrix} 3 & 1 & 0 & 0 & 1 & 3 & 0 & 2 & 2 & 2 & 2 & 0 & 1 & 1 & 1 & 1 \\ 1 & 2 & 1 & 1 & 2 & 1 & 2 & 1 & 1 & 0 & 1 & 3 & 1 & 1 & 1 & 1 \\ 0 & 1 & 3 & 3 & 1 & 0 & 1 & 1 & 2 & 3 & 1 & 0 & 1 & 1 & 1 & 1 \end{bmatrix} . \quad (1)$$

Performing CA on the group matrix **N** provides two sets of factor scores—one for the groups (denoted **F**) and one for the variables (denoted **G**). These factor scores are, in general, scaled such that their variance is equal to the eigenvalue associated with the factor.

The grand total of the table is noted *N*, and the first step of the analysis is to compute the probability matrix $\mathbf{Z} = N^{-1}\mathbf{N}$. We denote **r** the vector of the row totals of **Z** (i.e., $\mathbf{r} = \mathbf{Z1}$, with **1** being a conformable vector of **1**s); **c** the vector of the column totals; and $\mathbf{D}_{\mathrm{c}} = \mathrm{diag}\ \{\mathbf{c}\}$, $\mathbf{D}_{\mathrm{r}} = \mathrm{diag}\ \{\mathbf{r}\}$. The factor scores are obtained from the following singular value decomposition:

$$\mathbf{D}_{\mathrm{r}}^{-\frac{1}{2}}(\mathbf{Z} - \mathbf{rc}^{\mathrm{T}})\mathbf{D}_{\mathrm{c}}^{-\frac{1}{2}} = \mathbf{P\Delta Q}^{\mathrm{T}}. \quad (2)$$

(Δ is the diagonal matrix of the *singular* values, and $\Lambda = \Delta^2$ is the matrix of the *eigenvalues*.) The row and (respectively) column factor scores are obtained as

$$\mathbf{F} = \mathbf{D}_{\mathrm{r}}^{-\frac{1}{2}}\mathbf{P\Delta} \quad \text{and} \quad \mathbf{G} = \mathbf{D}_{\mathrm{c}}^{-\frac{1}{2}}\mathbf{Q\Delta}. \quad (3)$$

The squared (χ^2) distances from the rows and columns to their respective barycenters are obtained as

$$\mathbf{d}_{\mathrm{r}} = \mathrm{diag}\{\mathbf{FF}^{\mathrm{T}}\} \quad \text{and} \quad \mathbf{d}_{\mathrm{c}} = \mathrm{diag}\{\mathbf{GG}^{\mathrm{T}}\}. \quad (4)$$

The squared cosines between row i and factor ℓ and column j and factor ℓ are obtained respectively as

$$o_{i,\ell} = \frac{f_{i,\ell}^2}{d_{r,i}^2} \quad \text{and} \quad o_{j,\ell} = \frac{g_{j,\ell}^2}{d_{c,j}^2} \qquad (5)$$

(with $d_{r,i}^2$ and $d_{c,j}^2$ being respectively the ith element of $\mathbf{d}_r$ and the jth element of $\mathbf{d}_c$). Squared cosines help locate the factors important for a given observation. The contributions of row i to factor ℓ and of column j to factor ℓ are obtained respectively as

$$t_{i,\ell} = \frac{f_{i,\ell}^2}{\lambda_\ell} \quad \text{and} \quad t_{j,\ell} = \frac{g_{j,\ell}^2}{\lambda_\ell}. \qquad (6)$$

Contributions help locate the observations important for a given factor.

Supplementary or illustrative elements can be projected onto the factors using the so-called transition formula. Specifically, let $\mathbf{i}_{sup}^T$ be an illustrative row and $\mathbf{j}_{sup}$ be an illustrative column to be projected. Their coordinates $\mathbf{f}_{sup}$ and $\mathbf{g}_{sup}$ are obtained as

$$\mathbf{f}_{sup} = \left(\mathbf{i}_{sup}^T \mathbf{1}\right) \mathbf{i}_{sup}^T \mathbf{G} \boldsymbol{\Delta}^{-1} \text{ and } \mathbf{g}_{sup} = \left(\mathbf{j}_{sup}^T \mathbf{1}\right) \mathbf{j}_{sup}^T \mathbf{F} \boldsymbol{\Delta}^{-1}. \quad (7)$$

After the analysis has been performed on the groups, the original observations are projected as supplementary elements and their factor scores are stored in a matrix denoted $\mathbf{F}_{sup}$. To compute these scores, first compute the matrix of row profiles $\mathbf{R} = (\text{diag}\{\mathbf{X1}\})^{-1}\mathbf{X}$ and then apply Equation 7 to obtain

$$\mathbf{F}_{sup} = \mathbf{RG}\boldsymbol{\Delta}^{-1}. \qquad (8)$$

The Euclidean distance between the observations and the groups computed from the factor scores is equal to the χ^2-distance between their row profiles. The $I \times K$ distance matrix between observations and groups is computed as

$$\mathbf{D} = \mathbf{s}_{sup}\mathbf{1}^T + \mathbf{1s}^T - 2\mathbf{F}_{sup}\mathbf{F}^T \text{ with}$$
$$\mathbf{s}_{sup} = \text{diag}\{\mathbf{F}_{sup}\mathbf{F}_{sup}^T\} \text{ and } \mathbf{s} = \text{diag}\{\mathbf{FF}^T\}. \qquad (9)$$

Each observation is then assigned to the closest group.

Model Evaluation

The quality of the discrimination can be evaluated as a fixed-effect model or as a random-effect model. For the fixed-effect model, the correct classifications are compared to the assignments obtained from Equation 9. The fixed-effect model evaluates the quality of the classification on the sample used to build the model.

The random-effect model evaluates the quality of the classification on new observations. Typically, this step is performed using cross-validation techniques such as jackknifing or bootstrapping.

Results

Tables 2 and 3 give the results of the analysis and Figure 1 displays them. The fixed-effect quality of the model is evaluated by the following confusion matrix:

$$\begin{bmatrix} 4 & 0 & 0 \\ 0 & 3 & 0 \\ 0 & 1 & 4 \end{bmatrix}. \qquad (10)$$

In this matrix, the rows are the assigned groups and the columns are the real groups. For example, out of five wines assigned to the wine region Beaujolais (Group 3), one wine was, in fact, from the Rhône region (Group 2), and four wines were from Beaujolais. The overall quality can be computed from the diagonal of the matrix. Here, we find that 11 (4 + 3 + 4) wines out of 12 were classified correctly.

A jackknife procedure was used in order to evaluate the generalization capacity of the analysis to new wines (i.e., this corresponds to a random-effect analysis). Each wine was, in turn, taken out of the sample, a DCA was performed on the remaining sample of 11 wines, and the wine taken out was assigned to the closest group. This gave the following confusion matrix:

$$\begin{bmatrix} 2 & 1 & 1 \\ 1 & 2 & 1 \\ 1 & 1 & 2 \end{bmatrix}. \qquad (11)$$

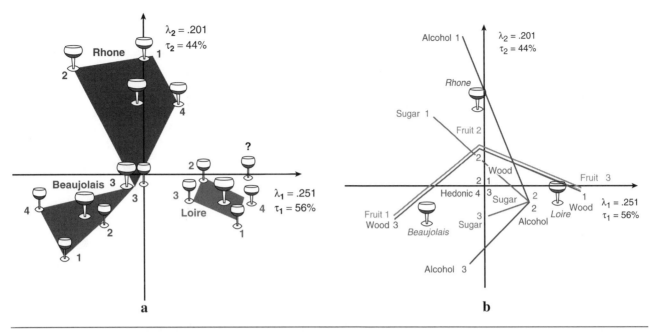

Figure 1   Discriminant Correspondence Analysis

Notes: Projections on the first 2 dimensions. (a) The *I* set: rows (i.e., wines). The wines are projected as supplementary elements, and *Wine?* is an unknown wine. (b) The *J* set: columns (i.e., descriptors). The wine categories have also been projected for ease of interpretation. Both figures have the same scale (some projection points have been slightly moved to increase readability). (Projections from Tables 2 and 3).

As expected, the performance of the model as a random effect is less impressive than as a fixed-effect model. Now, only 6 (2 + 2 + 2) wines out of 12 are classified correctly.

The differences between the fixed- and the random-effect models are illustrated in Figure 2, where the jackknifed wines have been projected onto the fixed-effect solution (using metric multidimensional

Table 2   Factor Scores, Squared Cosines, and Contributions for the Variables (*J* set)

			Woody			Fruity			Sweet			Alcohol			Hedonic			
			1	2	3	1	2	3	1	2	3	1	2	3	1	2	3	4
Axis	λ	%							Factor Scores									
1	.251	55	.93	−.05	−.88	−.88	−.05	.93	−.51	.33	.04	−.14	.33	−.20	0	0	0	0
2	.201	44	−.04	.35	−.31	−.31	.35	−.04	.64	−.13	−.28	−.74	−.13	1.40	0	0	0	0
Axis									Squared Cosines									
1			.998	.021	.892	.892	.021	.998	.384	.864	.021	.035	.864	.021	0	0	0	0
2			.002	.979	.108	.108	.979	.002	.616	.137	.979	.965	.137	.979	0	0	0	0
Axis									Contributions									
1			.231	*.001*	.207	.207	*.001*	.231	*.051*	.029	.001	*.007*	.029	*.008*	0	0	0	0
2			*.0006*	.0405	*.0313*	*.0313*	.0405	*.0006*	.1019	*.0056*	*.0324*	*.2235*	*.0056*	.4860	0	0	0	0

Note: Contributions corresponding to negative scores are in italic.

Table 3 Factor Scores, Squared Cosines, and Contributions for the Regions

Axis	λ	%	Region Loire	Loire Wines				Region Rhône	Rhône Wines				Region Beaujolais	Beaujolais Wines				W?
				1	2	3	4		1	2	3	4		1	2	3	4	
								Factor Scores										
1	251	55	0.66	0.82	0.50	0.43	0.89	−0.10	0.07	−0.66	−0.11	0.29	−0.56	−0.74	−0.41	−0.11	−0.96	1.01
2	201	44	−0.23	−0.42	−0.05	−0.25	−0.22	0.63	1.05	0.93	−0.10	0.64	−0.39	−0.73	−0.43	−0.10	−0.32	−0.15
								Squared Cosines										
1			.89	.79	.99	.75	.94	.03	.00	.33	.56	.17	.67	.51	.47	.56	.90	.98
2			.11	.21	.01	.25	.06	.97	1.00	.67	.44	.83	.33	.49	.53	.44	.10	.02
								Contributions										
1			*.58*	.	.	.	.	*.01*	.	.	.	.	*.41*	.	.	.	.	.
2			*.09*	.	.	.	.	.65	.	.	.	.	.26	.	.	.	.	.

Note: The supplementary rows are the wines from the region and the mysterious wine (W?). Contributions corresponding to negative scores are in italic.

274

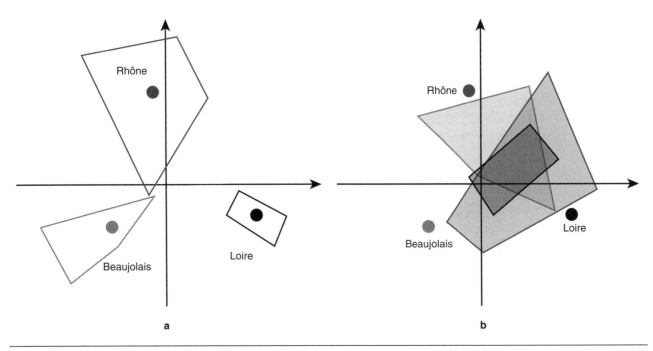

Figure 2 Discriminant Correspondence Analysis

Note: Projections on the first 2 dimensions. (a) Fixed effect model. The three regions and the convex envelop for the wines (b) Random effect model. The jackknifed wines have been projected back onto the fixed effect solution. The convex envelop shows that the random effect categories have a larger variability and have moved.

scaling). The quality of the model can be evaluated by drawing the convex envelop of each category. For the fixed-effect model, the centers of gravity of the convex envelops are the categories, and this illustrates that DCA is a least square estimation technique. For the random-effect model, the degradation of performance is due to a larger variance (the areas of the convex envelops are larger) and to a rotation of the envelops (the convex envelops are no longer centered on the category centers of gravity).

—Hervé Abdi

See also Centroid; Correspondence Analysis; Discriminant Analysis; Distance; Metric Multidimensional Scaling; Multiple Correspondence Analysis

Further Reading

Abdi, H. (2004). Multivariate analysis. In M. Lewis-Beck, A. Bryman, & T. F. Liao (Eds.), *The SAGE encyclopedia of social science research methods.* Thousand Oaks, CA: Sage.

Clausen, S. E. (1998). *Applied correspondence analysis.* Thousand Oaks, CA: Sage.

Greenacre, M. J. (1984). *Theory and applications of correspondence analysis.* London: Academic Press.

Greenacre, M. J. (1993). *Correspondence analysis in practice.* London: Academic Press.

Weller, S. C., & Romney, A. K. (1990). *Metric scaling: Correspondence analysis.* Newbury Park, CA: Sage.

DISSIMILARITY COEFFICIENT

A dissimilarity coefficient is a function that measures the difference between two objects. It is defined from a set $E \times E$ (e.g., $\mathbb{R} \times \mathbb{R}$, $\mathbb{R}^2 \times \mathbb{R}^2$, $\mathbb{R}^n \times \mathbb{R}^n$) to the nonnegative real numbers $\mathbb{R}^+$. Let g be a dissimilarity coefficient. Let x and y be two elements from E, and g verifies the following properties:

$$g(x,x) = 0 \ \ (C1),$$

$$g(x,y) = g(y,x) \ \ (C2: \text{symmetry}),$$

$$g(x,y) \geq 0 \ \ (C3: \text{positivity}).$$

The function g is said to be a pseudo-metric if and only if g verifies C1, C2, C3, and the following property. Let z be another element from E,

$$g(x,y) + g(y,z) \geq g(x,z) \ \ (C4: \text{triangle inequality}).$$

Furthermore, the function g is said to be a metric if and only if g verifies C1, C2, C3, C4, and the following additional property:

$$g(x, y) = 0 \rightarrow x = y \quad \text{(C5)}.$$

The value taken by g for two elements x and y is called "dissimilarity" if g is simply a dissimilarity coefficient; "semi-distance" if g is, in addition, a pseudo-metric; and "distance" if g is a metric.

The application of the function g to a finite set of S elements $\{x_1, \ldots, x_k, \ldots, x_S\}$ leads to a matrix of dissimilarities (or semi-distances, or distances) between pairs of the elements. This matrix is said to be Euclidean if and only if one can find S points M_k ($k = 1, \ldots, S$) that can be embedded in a Euclidean space so that the Euclidean distance between M_k and M_l is

$$g(x_k, x_l) = \| M_k M_l \|$$
$$= \sqrt{(c_k - c_l)^t \, (c_k - c_l)},$$

where c_k and c_l are the vectors of coordinates for M_k and M_l, respectively, in the Euclidean space. These vectors of coordinates can be obtained by a principal coordinate analysis. Consequently, the interest of this Euclidean property is the direct association between the dissimilarities and the obtention of a typology, a graphical representation of the dissimilarities among elements. Other types of graphical displays can be obtained with any dissimilarity coefficient by hierarchical cluster analysis and nonmetric multidimensional scaling.

Examples

Example 1

Let E be the Euclidean space $\mathbb{R}^n$, vector space of all n-tuples of real numbers $(x_1, \ldots, x_i, \ldots, x_n)$. An element of this space is noted x_k. In that case, each element may be characterized by n quantitative variables $X_1, \ldots, X_i, \ldots, X_n$. Let $\mathbf{x}_k = (x_{1k}, \ldots, x_{ik}, \ldots, x_{nk})^t$ and $\mathbf{x}_l = (x_{1l}, \ldots, x_{il}, \ldots, x_{nl})^t$ be two vectors containing the values taken by the objects k and l, respectively,

for each of the variables considered; $\mathbf{x}_k, \mathbf{x}_l \in \mathbb{R}^n$. The following dissimilarity coefficients can be used to measure the difference between the objects k and l:

- the Euclidean metric

$$g_1(\mathbf{x}_k, \mathbf{x}_l) = \sqrt{(\mathbf{x}_k - \mathbf{x}_l)^t \, (\mathbf{x}_k - \mathbf{x}_l)};$$

- the Jöreskog distance

$$g_2(\mathbf{x}_k, \mathbf{x}_l) = \sqrt{(\mathbf{x}_k - \mathbf{x}_l)^t \, \mathbf{V}^{-1} \, (\mathbf{x}_k - \mathbf{x}_l)},$$

where $\mathbf{V} = diag \, (V(Y_1), \ldots, V(Y_i), \ldots, V(Y_n))$ is the diagonal matrix containing the variances of the n variables

- the Mahalanobis distance

$$g_3(\mathbf{x}_k, \mathbf{x}_l) = \sqrt{(\mathbf{x}_k - \mathbf{x}_l)^t \, \mathbf{W}^{-1} \, (\mathbf{x}_k - \mathbf{x}_l)},$$

where $\mathbf{W}$ is the variance-covariance matrix for the n variables.

All of these dissimilarity coefficients are metrics and provide Euclidean dissimilarity matrices.

Example 2

Let E be the set of frequency vectors

$$E = \left\{ \mathbf{p} = (p_1, \ldots, p_k, \ldots, p_S) | p_k \geq 0, \right.$$
$$\left. \sum_{k=1}^{S} p_k = 1 \right\}.$$

In that case, let $\mathbf{p}$ and $\mathbf{q}$ be two vectors from E. Several functions can be used to measure the dissimilarity between the two frequency vectors:

- the Euclidean metric $g_1(\mathbf{p}, \mathbf{q})$
- the taxicab metric, also called Manhattan distance

$$g_4(\mathbf{p}, \mathbf{q}) = \sum_{k=1}^{S} |p_k - q_k|$$

Modifications of these functions have been proposed in genetics and ecology so that their values lie between 0 and 1:

- the Rogers distance

$$g_5(\mathbf{p}, \mathbf{q}) = \sqrt{\frac{1}{2}(\mathbf{p} - \mathbf{q})^t (\mathbf{p} - \mathbf{q})}$$

- the minimal distance from Nei

$$g_6(\mathbf{p}, \mathbf{q}) = \frac{1}{2}(\mathbf{p} - \mathbf{q})^t (\mathbf{p} - \mathbf{q})$$

- the absolute genetic distance from Gregorius

$$g_7(\mathbf{p}, \mathbf{q}) = \frac{1}{2}\sum_{k=1}^{S} |p_k - q_k|.$$

The dissimilarity coefficients g_4, g_5, and g_7 are metrics, but g_6 is not because it does not verify the triangle inequality (Property C4).

Other dissimilarity coefficients have been developed exclusively for frequency vectors. In 1946, Bhattacharyya introduced the notion of angular distance, considering two multinomial sets characterized by two frequency vectors $\mathbf{p}$ and $\mathbf{q}$. The two vectors $(\sqrt{p_1}, \ldots, \sqrt{p_s})$ and $(\sqrt{q_1}, \ldots, \sqrt{q_s})$ can be considered as the directions of two lines starting from the origin of a multidimensional space and separated by an angle θ whose cosine is

$$\cos \theta = \sum_{k=1}^{S} \sqrt{p_k q_k}.$$

The coefficient of dissimilarity proposed by Bhattacharyya is the squared value of this angle:

$$g_8(\mathbf{p}, \mathbf{q}) = \theta^2 = \left[\cos^{-1}\left(\sum_{k=1}^{S} \sqrt{p_k q_k}\right)\right]^2.$$

Another series of dissimilarity coefficients stems from the probability of drawing two similar objects from two populations with respective frequency vectors $\mathbf{p}$ and $\mathbf{q}$:

$$\sum_{k=1}^{S} p_k q_k.$$

Among the dissimilarity coefficients developed from this probability are Nei dissimilarity index in genetics

$$g_9(\mathbf{p}, \mathbf{q}) = -\ln\left(\frac{\displaystyle\sum_{k=1}^{S} p_k q_k}{\sqrt{\displaystyle\sum_{k=1}^{S} p_k^2}\sqrt{\displaystyle\sum_{k=1}^{S} q_k^2}}\right),$$

and Manly overlap index in ecology

$$g_{10}(\mathbf{p}, \mathbf{q}) = 1 - \frac{\displaystyle\sum_{k=1}^{S} p_k q_k}{\sqrt{\displaystyle\sum_{k=1}^{S} p_k^2}\sqrt{\displaystyle\sum_{k=1}^{S} q_k^2}}.$$

Example 3

Let E be the set of binary vectors

$$E = \{\mathbf{u} = (u_1, \ldots, u_k, \ldots, u_s) \mid u_k \in \{0,1\}\}.$$

In that case, many dissimilarity coefficients, whose values lie between 0 and 1, have been developed in ecology where a vector u gives the presence/absence of species in a community. They have been defined from similarity coefficients. Let $\mathbf{u}$ and $\mathbf{v}$ be two vectors from E. For each position in the vectors—that is to say, for $k = 1, \ldots, S$—the coefficients look at the similarity of the values taken by $\mathbf{u}$ and $\mathbf{v}$: u_k and v_k. Let a be the number of positions, for $k = 1, \ldots, S$, where $u_k = 1$ and $v_k = 1$, b the number of positions where $u_k = 1$ and $v_k = 0$, c the number of positions where $u_k = 0$ and $v_k = 1$, and d the number of positions where $u_k = 0$ and $v_k = 0$. The most used similarity coefficient is Jaccard similarity coefficient

$$s_{11}(\mathbf{u}, \mathbf{v}) = \frac{a}{a + b + c}.$$

A modification of s_{11}, the Sokal and Michener similarity coefficient

$$s_{18}(\mathbf{u}, \mathbf{v}) = \frac{a+d}{a+b+c+d},$$

takes into account the number of species absent from the two communities compared but present in other, comparable communities.

Two modifications of coefficients s_{11} and s_{12}, the Sokal and Sneath similarity coefficient

$$s_{13}(\mathbf{u}, \mathbf{v}) = \frac{a}{a+2(b+c)}$$

and the Rogers and Tanimoto similarity coefficient

$$s_{14}(\mathbf{u}, \mathbf{v}) = \frac{a+d}{a+2(b+c)+d},$$

give to the difference (measures b and c) twice as much weight as to the similitude (measures a and d) between the two communities compared. The most common dissimilarity coefficient associated to each similarity coefficient is equal to $g = 1 - s$. It is metric for $g_{11} = 1 - s_{11}$, $g_{12} = 1 - s_{12}$, $g_{13} = 1 - s_{13}$, and $g_{14} = 1 - s_{14}$. For all of these coefficients, a matrix of dissimilarities calculated by $g^* = \sqrt{1-s}$ is Euclidean.

Dissimilarity and Diversity Coefficients: Rao's Unified Approach

The concepts of dissimilarity and diversity have been linked together by C. R. Rao in a unified theoretical framework. The diversity is the character of objects that exhibit variety. A population in which the objects are numerous and different possesses variety. This variety depends on the relative abundance of the objects and the dissimilarity among these objects. This assertion is at the root of Rao's unified approach.

Consider a population i of S elements $\{x_1, \ldots, x_k, \ldots, x_S\}$ from any set E. Suppose that these elements are distributed in the population i according to the frequency vector $\mathbf{p}_i = (p_{1i}, \ldots, p_{ki}, \ldots, p_{Si})^t$. One can calculate $\Delta = [\delta_{kl}]$, $1 \le k \le S$, $1 \le l \le S$, a matrix of dissimilarities among the elements, by g, a chosen dissimilarity coefficient: $\delta_{kl} = g(x_k, x_l)$. The diversity in the population i depends on the frequency vector $\mathbf{p}_i$ and the dissimilarity matrix Δ. Rao defined a *diversity coefficient*, also called *quadratic entropy*, as

$$H(\mathbf{p}_i) = \sum_{k=1}^{S} \sum_{l=1}^{S} p_{ki} p_{li} \frac{\left[g(x_k, x_l)\right]^2}{2}.$$

Consider the matrix $\mathbf{D} = [\delta_{kl}^2/2]$, that is, $\mathbf{D} = [g(x_k, x_l)^2/2]$. Changing for $\mathbf{D}$ in the notations leads to

$$H(\mathbf{p}_i) = \mathbf{p}_i^t \mathbf{D} \mathbf{p}_i.$$

This coefficient has the special feature of being associated with the Jensen difference, a dissimilarity coefficient that calculates dissimilarities among two populations:

$$J(\mathbf{p}_i, \mathbf{p}_j) = 2H\left(\frac{\mathbf{p}_i + \mathbf{p}_j}{2}\right) - H(\mathbf{p}_i) - H(\mathbf{p}_j)$$

$$= -\frac{1}{2}(\mathbf{p}_i - \mathbf{p}_j)^t \mathbf{D} (\mathbf{p}_i - \mathbf{p}_j).$$

The sign of J depends on g via $\mathbf{D}$. It is positive if g is a metric leading to Euclidean matrices. In addition, where g is a metric leading to Euclidean matrices, the dissimilarity coefficient is

$$f(\mathbf{p}_i, \mathbf{p}_j) = \sqrt{2J(\mathbf{p}_i, \mathbf{p}_j)}.$$

Interestingly, f, as with g, is in that case a metric leading to Euclidean matrices. Consequently, the coefficients g and f are measures of inertia (dispersion of points) in a Euclidean space. This result is the heart of the new ordination method called double principal coordinate analysis. It allows a graphical representation of the dissimilarities among populations (coefficient f), together with a projection of the constituting elements.

Thus, the coefficients g and f are connected in a framework of diversity decomposition. The total diversity over several populations is equal to the sum of the average diversity within populations and the diversity among populations. Each component of the decomposition is measured by the quadratic entropy, but its formula depends either on g when it represents diversity among elements (total and intradiversity) or on f when it represents diversity among populations (interdiversity).

Consider r populations. A weight μ_i is attributed to population i so that $\sum_{i=1}^{r} \mu_i = 1$. The diversity and dissimilarity coefficients are connected in the following diversity decomposition:

$$H\left(\sum_{i=1}^{r} \mu_i \mathbf{p}_i\right) = \sum_{i=1}^{r} \mu_i H(\mathbf{p}_i)$$
$$+ \sum_{i=1}^{r} \sum_{j=1}^{r} \mu_i \mu_j \frac{f(\mathbf{p}_i, \mathbf{p}_j)^2}{2}.$$

The component

$$H\left(\sum_{i=1}^{r} \mu_i \mathbf{p}_i\right) = \sum_{k=1}^{s} \sum_{l=1}^{s} \left(\sum_{i=1}^{r} \mu_i p_{ki}\right)$$
$$\left(\sum_{i=1}^{r} \mu_i p_{li}\right) \frac{\left[g(x_k, x_l)\right]^2}{2}$$

stems from the total diversity irrespective of populations. It is measured by the quadratic entropy from g and the global frequencies of the S objects. The mean

$$\sum_{i=1}^{r} \mu_i H(\mathbf{p}_i) = \sum_{i=1}^{r} \mu_i \left[\sum_{k=1}^{s} \sum_{l=1}^{s} p_{ki} p_{li} \frac{g(x_k, x_l)^2}{2}\right]$$

is the average diversity within populations, also measured by the quadratic entropy from the dissimilarity coefficient g and from the frequencies of the objects within populations. Finally, the last term

$$\sum_{i=1}^{r} \sum_{j=1}^{r} \mu_i \mu_j \frac{f(\mathbf{p}_i, \mathbf{p}_j)^2}{2}$$

denotes the diversity among populations and is measured by the quadratic entropy from the dissimilarity coefficient f and the relative weights attributed to populations.

This general framework has two interesting specific cases.

1. Where E is the set of values taken by a qualitative variable X, and

$$\frac{g(x_k, x_l)^2}{2} = \begin{cases} 1 & \text{if } x_k \neq x_l \\ 0 & \text{if } x_k = x_l \end{cases},$$

then

$$H(\mathbf{p}_i) = 1 - \sum_{k=1}^{s} p_{ki}^2,$$

which is known as the Gini-Simpson diversity index, and

$$f(\mathbf{p}_i, \mathbf{p}_j) = \sqrt{(\mathbf{p}_i - \mathbf{p}_j)^t (\mathbf{p}_i - \mathbf{p}_j)}$$

is the Euclidean distance between $\mathbf{p}_i$ and $\mathbf{p}_j$.

2. Where E is the set of values taken by a quantitative variable X, and

$$g(x_k, x_l) = |x_k - x_l|, \tag{1}$$

then

$$H(\mathbf{p}_i) = \sum_{k=1}^{s} p_{ki} \left(x_k - \sum_{k=1}^{s} p_{ki} x_k\right)^2,$$

which is the variance of the quantitative variable X. Let $\mathbf{x}$ be the vector $(x_1, \ldots, x_k, \ldots, x_S)^t$,

$$f(\mathbf{p}_i, \mathbf{p}_j) = \sqrt{(\mathbf{p}_i^t \mathbf{x} - \mathbf{p}_j^t \mathbf{x})^t (\mathbf{p}_i^t \mathbf{x} - \mathbf{p}_j^t \mathbf{x})},$$

which can be written simply as the absolute difference between two means

$$f(\mathbf{p}_i, \mathbf{p}_j) = \left|\sum_{k=1}^{s} p_{ki} x_k - \sum_{k=1}^{s} p_{kj} x_k\right|. \tag{2}$$

This second writing highlights the consistency between coefficient g (Equation 1), measuring distances between elements, and coefficient f (Equation 2), measuring distances between populations.

In conclusion, the dissimilarity coefficients are functions that may correspond to inertia in Euclidean spaces provided that they verify additional properties. They are used in many disciplines and fit in perfectly with any diversity studies.

—*Sandrine Pavoine*

See also Distance

Further Reading

Chessel, D., Dufour, A.-B., & Thioulouse, J. (2004). The ade4 package-I: One-table methods. *R News, 4,* 5–10.

Gower, J. C. (1966). Some distance properties of latent root and vector methods used in multivariate analysis. *Biometrika, 53,* 325–338.

Legendre, P., & Legendre, L. (1998). *Numerical ecology* (2nd English ed.). Amsterdam: Elsevier Science.

Nei, M. (1987). *Molecular evolutionary genetics.* New York: Columbia University Press.

Pavoine, S., Dufour, A. B., & Chessel, D. (2004). From dissimilarities among species to dissimilarities among communities: A double principal coordinate analysis. *Journal of Theoretical Biology, 228,* 523–537.

Rao, C. R. (1982). Diversity and dissimilarity coefficients: A unified approach. *Theoretical Population Biology, 21,* 24–43.

ade4 package for R: http://pbil.univ-lyon1.fr/R/rplus/ade 4dsR.html (enables you to enter data and compute dissimilarity coefficients, diversity coefficients, the Principal Coordinates Analysis and the double Principal Coordinates Analysis)

DISTANCE

The notion of distance is essential because many statistical techniques are equivalent to the analysis of a specific distance table. For example, principal component analysis and metric multidimensional scaling analyze Euclidean distances, correspondence analysis deals with a χ^2 distance matrix, and discriminant analysis is equivalent to using a Mahalanobis distance. To define a distance is equivalent to defining rules to assign positive numbers between *pairs* of objects. The most important distances for statistics are Euclidean, generalized Euclidean (which include χ^2 and Mahalanobis), Minkowsky (which include the sorting and the symmetric difference distances), and the Hellinger distances.

Notation and Definition

For convenience, we restrict our discussion to distance between vectors because they are the objects mostly used in statistics. Let **a**, **b**, and **c** be three vectors with J elements each. A distance is a function that associates to any pair of vectors a real positive number, denoted $d(\mathbf{a},\mathbf{b})$, which has the following properties:

$$d(\mathbf{a}, \mathbf{a}) = 0 \qquad (1)$$

$$d(\mathbf{a},\mathbf{b}) = d(\mathbf{b},\mathbf{a}) \text{ [symmetry]} \qquad (2)$$

$$d(\mathbf{a},\mathbf{b}) = d(\mathbf{a},\mathbf{c}) + d(\mathbf{c},\mathbf{b}) \text{ [triangular inequality]} \qquad (3)$$

A Minimalist Example: The Sorting Distance

The axioms defining a distance are very easily met. For example, suppose that we consider two objects and assign the number 1 if we find them different and 0 if we find them alike. This procedure defines a distance called the *sorting* distance because the number assigned to a pair of same objects will be equal to 0 (this satisfies Axiom 1). Axiom 2 is also satisfied because the order of the objects is irrelevant. For the third axiom, we need to consider two cases, if $d(\mathbf{a},\mathbf{b})$ is equal to 0, the sum $d(\mathbf{a},\mathbf{c}) + d(\mathbf{c},\mathbf{b})$ can take only the values 0, 1, or 2, which will all satisfy Axiom 3. If **a** and **b** are different, $d(\mathbf{a},\mathbf{b})$ is equal to 1 and c cannot be identical to *both* of them, and therefore the sum $d(\mathbf{a},\mathbf{c}) + d(\mathbf{c},\mathbf{b})$ can take only the values 1 or 2, which will both satisfy Axiom 3.

With the same argument, we can see that if we ask a set of respondents to sort objects into piles, the number of participants who do not sort two objects together defines a distance between the sorted objects.

The Euclidean Distance

The most well-known distance is the *Euclidean distance,* which is defined as

$$d(\mathbf{a}, \mathbf{b}) = \|\mathbf{a} - \mathbf{b}\| = \sqrt{(\mathbf{a} - \mathbf{b})^T(\mathbf{a} - \mathbf{b})}$$
$$= \sqrt{\sum_j (a_j - b_j)^2} \quad (4)$$

(with $\|\mathbf{a}\|$ being the norm of $\mathbf{a}$, and a_j and b_j being the jth element of $\mathbf{a}$ and $\mathbf{b}$). Expressed as a squared distance (in a Euclidean world, it is always more practical to work with squared quantities because of the Pythagorean theorem), it is computed as

$$d^2(\mathbf{a}, \mathbf{b}) = (\mathbf{a} - \mathbf{b})^T(\mathbf{a} - \mathbf{b}). \quad (5)$$

For example, with

$$\mathbf{a} = \begin{bmatrix} 2 \\ 5 \\ 10 \\ 20 \end{bmatrix}, \text{ and } \mathbf{b} = \begin{bmatrix} 1 \\ 2 \\ 3 \\ 4 \end{bmatrix}, \quad (6)$$

the vector $\mathbf{a} - \mathbf{b}$ gives

$$\mathbf{a} - \mathbf{b} = \begin{bmatrix} 2 - 1 \\ 5 - 2 \\ 10 - 3 \\ 20 - 4 \end{bmatrix} = \begin{bmatrix} 1 \\ 3 \\ 7 \\ 16 \end{bmatrix}, \quad (7)$$

and

$$d^2(\mathbf{a},\mathbf{b}) = (\mathbf{a} - \mathbf{b})^T(\mathbf{a} - \mathbf{b})$$
$$= \sum_{j=1}^{4} (a_j - b_j)^2$$
$$= 1^2 + 3^2 + 7^2 + 16^2 \quad (8)$$
$$= 315.$$

The Euclidean distance between two vectors can also be expressed via the notion of scalar product and cosine between vectors. By developing Equation 5 for the distance between vectors, we find that

$$d^2(\mathbf{a},\mathbf{b}) = (\mathbf{a} - \mathbf{b})^T(\mathbf{a} - \mathbf{b})$$
$$= \mathbf{a}^T\mathbf{a} + \mathbf{b}^T\mathbf{b} - 2\mathbf{a}^T\mathbf{b} \quad (9)$$
$$= \|\mathbf{a}\|^2 + \|\mathbf{b}\|^2 - 2\|\mathbf{a}\| \times \|\mathbf{b}\| \times \cos(\mathbf{a},\mathbf{b}).$$

In the particular case of vectors with a unit norm, the distance between $\mathbf{a}$ and $\mathbf{b}$ simplifies to

$$d^2(\mathbf{a}, \mathbf{b}) = 2[1 - \cos(\mathbf{a}, \mathbf{b})]. \quad (10)$$

When two vectors are centered (i.e., when their mean is equal to 0), their cosine is equal to the coefficient of correlation. This shows that we can define a (Euclidean) distance between two series of numbers as 1 minus their correlation.

Generalized Euclidean

The Euclidean distance can be generalized by taking into account constraints expressed by a matrix conformable with the vectors. Specifically, let $\mathbf{W}$ denote a $J \times J$ *positive definite* matrix, the generalized Euclidean distance between $\mathbf{a}$ and $\mathbf{b}$ becomes

$$d_{\mathbf{W}}^2(\mathbf{a}, \mathbf{b}) = (\mathbf{a} - \mathbf{b})^T \mathbf{W}(\mathbf{a} - \mathbf{b}). \quad (11)$$

The most well-known generalized Euclidean distances are the χ^2 and the Mahalanobis distances.

χ^2 Distance

The χ^2 distance is associated with correspondence analysis. It is a distance between profiles. Recall that a vector is called a *profile* when it is composed of numbers greater than or equal to zero whose sum is equal to 1 (such a vector is sometimes called a *stochastic* vector). The χ^2 distance is defined for the rows (or the columns after transposition of the data table) of a contingency table such as the one shown in Table 1. The first step of the computation of the distance is to transform the rows into row profiles, which is done by dividing each row by its total. There are I rows and J columns in a contingency table. The *mass* of each row is denoted r_i, and the mass vector $\mathbf{r}$. The barycenter of the rows, denoted $\mathbf{c}$ is computed by transforming the total of the columns into a row profile. It can also be computed as the weighted average of the row profiles (with the weights being given by the mass vector $\mathbf{r}$). For the χ^2 distance, the $\mathbf{W}$ matrix is diagonal, which is equivalent to assigning a weight to each column.

This weight is equal to the inverse of the relative frequency of the column. This is expressed formally by expressing $\mathbf{W}$ as

$$\mathbf{W} = (\text{diag}\{\mathbf{c}\})^{-1}. \quad (12)$$

With this coding schema, variables that are used often contribute less to the distance between rows than variables that are used rarely. For example, from Table 1, we find that the weight matrix is equal to

$$\mathbf{W} = \mathbf{D_w} = \text{diag}\{\mathbf{w}\}$$

$$= \begin{bmatrix} .2973^{-1} & 0 & 0 \\ 0 & .5642^{-1} & 0 \\ 0 & 0 & .1385^{-1} \end{bmatrix}$$

$$= \begin{bmatrix} 3.3641 & 0 & 0 \\ 0 & 1.7724 & 0 \\ 0 & 0 & 7.2190 \end{bmatrix}. \quad (13)$$

For example, the χ^2 distance between Rousseau and Chateaubriand is equal to

$$d^2(\text{Rousseau, Chateaubriand})$$
$$= 3.364 \times (.291 - .270)^2 + 1.772$$
$$\times (.486 - .526)^2 + 7.219 \times (.223 - .214)^2 \quad (14)$$
$$= .0036.$$

This distance is called the χ^2 distance because the sum of the weighted distances from the rows to their barycenter is proportional to the χ^2 computed to test the independence of the rows and the columns of the table. Formally, if we denoted by N the grand total of the contingency table, by $d^2(i, g)$ the distance from row i to the barycenter of the table, and by $d^2(i,i')$ the distance from row i to row i', we obtain the following equality:

$$\sum_i^I r_i d^2(i, g) = \sum_{i>i'} r_i r_{i'} d^2(i, i') = \frac{1}{N}\chi^2. \quad (15)$$

The metric multidimensional scaling analysis of a χ^2 distance matrix (with masses given by $\mathbf{r}$) is equivalent to correspondence analysis.

Mahalanobis Distance

The Mahalanobis distance is defined between rows of a table. The weight matrix is obtained as the inverse of the columns variance/covariance matrix. Formally, if we denoted by $\mathbf{S}$ the variance/covariance matrix between the columns of a data table, the weight matrix of the Mahalanobis distance is defined as $\mathbf{W} = \mathbf{S}^{-1}$.

Table 1   Data for the Computation of the χ^2, Mahalanobis, and Hellinger Distances

| Author's name | Raw Data | | | $N \times \mathbf{r}$ | $\mathbf{r}$ | Row Profiles | | |
	Period	Comma	Other			Period	Comma	Other
Rousseau	7836	13112	6026	**26974**	**.0189**	.2905	.4861	.2234
Chateaubriand	53655	102383	42413	**198451**	**.1393**	.2704	.5159	.2137
Hugo	115615	184541	59226	**359382**	**.2522**	.3217	.5135	.1648
Zola	161926	340479	62754	**565159**	**.3966**	.2865	.6024	.1110
Proust	38177	105101	12670	**155948**	**.1094**	.2448	.6739	.0812
Giraudoux	46371	58367	14299	**119037**	**.0835**	.3896	.4903	.1201
$\sum N\mathbf{c}^{\mathrm{T}}$	**423580**	**803983**	**197388**	**1424951**	1.0000			
$\mathbf{c}^{\mathrm{T}}$	**.2973**	**.5642**	**.1385**					
$\mathbf{w}^{\mathrm{T}}$	**3.3641**	**1.7724**	**7.2190**					

Notes: The punctuation marks of six French writers (from Abdi & Valentin, 2006). The column labeled $N \times \mathbf{r}$ gives the total number of punctuation marks used by each author. The mass of each row is the proportion of punctuation marks used by this author. The row labeled $N \times \mathbf{c}^{\mathrm{T}}$ gives the total of each column. This is the total number of times this punctuation mark was used. The centroid row (or barycenter, or center of gravity), gives the proportion of each punctuation mark in the sample. The weight of each column is the inverse of the centroid.

Using, again, the data from Table 1, we obtain

$$\mathbf{S} = 10^{10} \times \begin{bmatrix} 0.325 & 0.641 & 0.131 \\ 0.641 & 1.347 & 0.249 \\ 0.131 & 0.249 & 0.063 \end{bmatrix} \text{ and } \mathbf{S}^{-1} = 10^{-7} \times \begin{bmatrix} 0.927 & -0.314 & -0.683 \\ -0.314 & 0.134 & 0.124 \\ -0.683 & 0.124 & 1.087 \end{bmatrix}. \tag{16}$$

With these values, we find that the Mahalanobis distance between Rousseau and Chateaubriand is equal to

$$d^2(\text{Rousseau, Chateaubriand}) = 10^{-7} \times \left(\begin{bmatrix} -45819 \\ -89271 \\ -36387 \end{bmatrix}^{\mathrm{T}} \times \begin{bmatrix} 0.927 & -0.314 & -0.683 \\ -0.314 & 0.134 & 0.124 \\ -0.683 & 0.124 & 1.087 \end{bmatrix} \times \begin{bmatrix} -45819 \\ -89271 \\ -36387 \end{bmatrix} \right) \tag{17}$$

$$\approx 4.0878.$$

The Mahalanobis distance can be seen as a multivariate equivalent of the z-score transformation. The metric multidimensional scaling analysis of a Mahalanobis distance matrix is equivalent to discriminant analysis.

Minkowski's Distance

The Euclidean distance is a particular case of the more general family of Minkowski's distances. The p distance (or a Minkowski's distance of degree p), between two vectors is defined as

$$\mathbf{a} = [a_1, \ldots, a_j, \ldots, a_J]^T \text{ and } \\ \mathbf{b} = [b_1, \ldots, b_j, \ldots, b_J]^T \tag{18}$$

as

$$d_p(\mathbf{a}, \mathbf{b}) = \|\mathbf{a} - \mathbf{b}\|_p = \left[\sum_j^J |a_j - b_j|^p \right]^{\frac{1}{p}}. \tag{19}$$

The most frequently used Minkowski's distances are the distances of degree 1, 2, and ∞. A distance of degree 1 is also called the *city-block* or *taxicab* distance. When the vectors are binary numbers (i.e., 1 and 0), the elements of the vector code for membership to a set (i.e., 1 means the element belongs to the set, 0 means it does not). In this case, the degree 1 distance is commonly referred to as the *Hamming distance* or the *symmetric difference distance*. (The symmetric difference distance is a set operation that associates to two sets a new set made of the elements

of these sets that belong to only one of them—i.e., elements that belong to both sets are excluded. The symmetric difference distance gives the number of the elements of the symmetric difference set.)

When p is equal to 2, we obtain the usual Euclidean distance. With $p = \infty$, we take the largest absolute value of the difference between the vectors as defining the distance between vectors.

For example, with the vectors

$$\mathbf{a} = \begin{bmatrix} 2 \\ 5 \\ 10 \\ 20 \end{bmatrix} \text{ and } \mathbf{b} = \begin{bmatrix} 1 \\ 2 \\ 3 \\ 4 \end{bmatrix}, \tag{20}$$

the Minkowski distance of degree 1 is

$$d_1(\mathbf{a}, \mathbf{b}) = \sum_{j=1}^{4} |a_j - b_j| = 1 + 3 + 7 + 16 = 27, \tag{21}$$

and the Minkowski distance of degree ∞ is

$$d_\infty(\mathbf{a}, \mathbf{b}) = \max_j |a_j - b_j| = \max\{1,3,7,16\} = 16. \tag{22}$$

Hellinger

The Hellinger distance is defined between vectors having only positive or zero elements. In general (like the χ^2 distance), it is used for row profiles. The Hellinger distance between vectors $\mathbf{a}$ and $\mathbf{b}$ is defined as

$$d(\mathbf{a}, \mathbf{b}) = \left[\sum_{j}^{J} \left(\sqrt{a_j} - \sqrt{b_j} \right)^2 \right]^{\frac{1}{2}}. \qquad (23)$$

Because the Hellinger distance is not sensitive to discrepancies between columns, it is sometimes used as an alternative to the χ^2 distance. An interesting property of the Hellinger distance when applied to row profiles is that the vectors representing these profiles can be represented as points on a sphere (or hypersphere when the number of elements of the vector is larger than 3).

For our example, we find that the Hellinger distance between the row profiles of Rousseau and Chateaubriand is equal to

$$d^2(\text{Rousseau, Chateaubriand})$$
$$= \left[\left(\sqrt{2905} - \sqrt{.2704} \right)^2 \right.$$
$$+ \left(\sqrt{.4861} - \sqrt{.5259} \right)^2 \qquad (24)$$
$$+ \left. \left(\sqrt{.2234} - \sqrt{.2137} \right)^2 \right]^{\frac{1}{2}}$$
$$= .0302.$$

How to Analyze Distance Matrices

Distance matrices are often computed as the first step of data analysis. In general, distance matrices are analyzed by finding a convenient graphic representation for their elements. These representations approximate the original distance by another distance such as (a) a low-dimensionality Euclidean distance (e.g., multidimensional scaling, DISTATIS); or (b) a graph (e.g., cluster analysis, additive tree representations).

—Hervé Abdi

See also Correspondence Analysis; Discriminant Analysis; Discriminant Correspondence Analysis; Dissimilarity Coefficient; DISTATIS; Metric Multidimensional Scaling

Further Reading

Abdi, H. (1990). Additive-tree representations. *Lecture Notes in Biomathematics, 84,* 43–59.

Abdi, H. (2004). Multivariate analysis. In M. Lewis-Beck, A. Bryman, & T. F. Liao (Eds.), *The SAGE encyclopedia of social science research methods.* Thousand Oaks, CA: Sage.

Abdi, H., & Valentin, D. (2006). *Mathématiques pour les sciences cognitives* (Mathematics for cognitive sciences). Grenoble, France: Presses Universitaires de Grenoble.

Escofier, B. (1978). Analyse factorielle et distances répondant au principe d'équivalence distributionnelle. *Revue de Statistiques Appliquées, 26,* 29–37.

Greenacre, M. J. (1984). *Theory and applications of correspondence analysis.* London: Academic Press.

Rao, C. R. (1995). Use of Hellinger distance in graphical displays. In E.-M. Tiit, T. Kollo, & H. Niemi (Eds.), *Multivariate statistics and matrices in statistics* (pp. 143–161). Leiden, Netherlands: Brill.

DISTATIS

DISTATIS is a generalization of classical multidimensional scaling (MDS) proposed by Abdi, Valentin, O'Toole, and Edelman. Its goal is to analyze several distance matrices computed on the same set of objects. The name DISTATIS is derived from a technique called STATIS, whose goal is to analyze multiple data sets. DISTATIS first evaluates the similarity between distance matrices. From this analysis, a compromise matrix is computed that represents the best aggregate of the original matrices. The original distance matrices are then projected onto the compromise.

The data sets to analyze are distance matrices obtained on the same set of objects. These distance matrices may correspond to measurements taken at different times. In this case, the first matrix corresponds to the distances collected at time $t = 1$, the second one to the distances collected at time $t = 2$, and so on. The goal of the analysis is to evaluate if the relative positions of the objects are stable over time. The different matrices, however, do not need to represent time. For example, the distance matrices can be derived from different methods. The goal of the analysis, then, is to evaluate if there is an agreement between the methods.

The general idea behind DISTATIS is first to transform each distance matrix into a cross-product matrix as it is done for a standard MDS. Then, these cross-product matrices are aggregated to create a compromise cross-product matrix that represents their consensus. The compromise matrix is obtained as a weighted average of individual cross-product matrices. The principal component analysis (PCA) of the compromise gives the position of the objects in the compromise space. The position of the object for each study can be represented in the compromise space as supplementary points. Finally, as a by-product of the weight computation, the studies can be represented as points in a multidimensional space.

An Example

To illustrate DISTATIS, we will use the set of faces displayed in Figure 1. Four different "systems" or algorithms are compared, each of them computing a distance matrix between the faces. The first system corresponds to PCA and computes the squared Euclidean distance between faces directly from the pixel values of the images. The second system starts by taking measurements on the faces (see Figure 2) and computes the squared Euclidean distance between faces from these measures. The third distance matrix is obtained by first asking human observers to rate the faces on several dimensions (e.g., beauty, honesty,

Figure 1   Six Faces to Be Analyzed by Different "Algorithms"

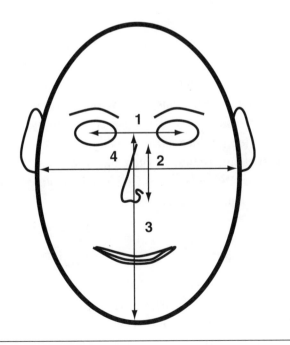

Figure 2   The Measures Taken on a Face

empathy, and intelligence) and then computing the squared Euclidean distance from these measures. The fourth distance matrix is obtained from pairwise similarity ratings (on a scale from 1 to 7) collected from human observers. The average similarity rating s was transformed into a distance using Shepard's transformation: $d = \exp\{-s^2\}$.

Notations

The raw data consist of T data sets and we will refer to each data set as a *study*. Each study is an $I \times I$ distance matrix denoted $\mathbf{D}_{[t]}$, where I is the number of objects and t denotes the study.

Here, we have $T = 4$ studies. Each study corresponds to a 6×6 distance matrix as shown below.

Study 1 (Pixels):

$$\mathbf{D}_{[1]} = \begin{bmatrix} 0 & .112 & .148 & .083 & .186 & .110 \\ .112 & 0 & .152 & .098 & .158 & .134 \\ .146 & .152 & 0 & .202 & .285 & .249 \\ .083 & .098 & .202 & 0 & .131 & .110 \\ .186 & .158 & .285 & .131 & 0 & .155 \\ .110 & .134 & .249 & .110 & .155 & 0 \end{bmatrix}.$$

Study 2 (Measures):

$$\mathbf{D}_{[2]} = \begin{bmatrix} 0 & 0.60 & 1.98 & 0.42 & 0.14 & 0.58 \\ 0.60 & 0 & 2.10 & 0.78 & 0.42 & 1.34 \\ 1.98 & 2.10 & 0 & 2.02 & 1.72 & 2.06 \\ 0.42 & 0.78 & 2.02 & 0 & 0.50 & 0.88 \\ 0.14 & 0.42 & 1.72 & 0.50 & 0 & 0.30 \\ 0.58 & 1.34 & 2.06 & 0.88 & 0.30 & 0 \end{bmatrix}.$$

Study 3 (Ratings):

$$\mathbf{D}_{[3]} = \begin{bmatrix} 0 & 0.54 & 1.39 & 5.78 & 10.28 & 6.77 \\ 0.54 & 0 & 1.06 & 3.80 & 6.83 & 4.71 \\ 1.39 & 1.06 & 0 & 8.01 & 11.03 & 5.72 \\ 5.78 & 3.80 & 8.01 & 0 & 2.58 & 6.09 \\ 10.28 & 6.83 & 11.03 & 2.58 & 0 & 3.53 \\ 6.77 & 4.71 & 5.72 & 6.09 & 3.53 & 0 \end{bmatrix}.$$

Study 4 (Pairwise):

$$\mathbf{D}_{[4]} = \begin{bmatrix} 0 & .014 & .159 & .004 & .001 & .002 \\ .014 & 0 & .018 & .053 & .024 & .004 \\ .159 & .018 & 0 & .271 & .067 & .053 \\ .004 & .053 & .271 & 0 & .001 & .008 \\ .001 & .024 & .067 & .001 & 0 & .007 \\ .002 & .004 & .053 & .008 & .007 & 0 \end{bmatrix}.$$

Distance matrices cannot be analyzed directly and need to be transformed. This step corresponds to MDS and transforms a distance matrix into a cross-product matrix.

We start with an $I \times I$ distance matrix $\mathbf{D}$, with an $I \times 1$ vector of mass (whose elements are all positive or zero and whose sum is equal to 1) denoted $\mathbf{m}$, such that

$$\underset{1 \times I \times 1}{\mathbf{m}^T \mathbf{1}} = 1. \tag{1}$$

If all observations have the same mass (as in here) $m_i = \frac{1}{I}$. We then define the centering matrix, which is equal to

$$\underset{I \times I}{\mathbf{\Xi}} = \underset{I \times I}{\mathbf{I}} - \underset{I \times I \times 1}{\mathbf{1} \ \mathbf{m}^T} \tag{2}$$

and the cross-product matrix denoted by $\tilde{\mathbf{S}}$ is obtained as

$$\tilde{\mathbf{S}} = -\frac{1}{2}\mathbf{\Xi}\mathbf{D}\mathbf{\Xi}^T. \tag{3}$$

For example, the first distance matrix is transformed into the following cross-product matrix:

$$\tilde{\mathbf{S}}_{[1]} = -\frac{1}{2}\mathbf{\Xi}\mathbf{D}_{[1]}\mathbf{\Xi}^T$$

$$= \begin{bmatrix} 0.042 & -0.013 & 0.002 & -0.001 & -0.028 & -0.003 \\ -0.013 & 0.045 & 0.000 & -0.007 & -0.012 & -0.013 \\ 0.002 & 0.000 & 0.108 & -0.027 & -0.044 & -0.039 \\ -0.001 & -0.007 & -0.027 & 0.040 & -0.001 & -0.004 \\ -0.028 & -0.012 & -0.044 & -0.001 & 0.088 & -0.002 \\ -0.003 & -0.013 & -0.039 & -0.004 & -0.002 & 0.062 \end{bmatrix}.$$

In order to compare the studies, we need to normalize the cross-product matrices. There are several possible normalizations; here we normalize the cross-product matrices by dividing each matrix by its first eigenvalue (an idea akin to multiple factor analysis). The first eigenvalue of matrix $\tilde{\mathbf{S}}_{[1]}$ is equal to $\lambda_1 = .16$, and matrix $\tilde{\mathbf{S}}_{[1]}$ is transformed into a normalized cross-product matrix denoted $\mathbf{S}_{[1]}$ as

$$\mathbf{S}_{[1]} = \lambda_1^{-1} \times \tilde{\mathbf{S}}_{[1]}$$

$$= \begin{bmatrix} .261 & -.079 & .013 & -.003 & -.174 & -.018 \\ -.079 & .280 & .002 & -.042 & -.077 & -.084 \\ .013 & .002 & .675 & -.168 & -.276 & -.246 \\ -.003 & -.042 & -.168 & .249 & -.009 & -.026 \\ -.174 & -.077 & -.276 & -.009 & .552 & -.015 \\ -.017 & -.084 & -.246 & -.026 & -.015 & .388 \end{bmatrix}. \tag{4}$$

Computing the Compromise Matrix

The *compromise matrix* is a cross-product matrix that gives the best compromise of the studies. It is obtained as a weighted average of the study cross-product matrices. The weights are chosen so that studies agreeing the most with other studies will have the larger weights. To find these weights, we need to analyze the relationships between the studies.

The *compromise matrix* is a cross-product matrix that gives the best compromise of the cross-product matrices representing each study. It is obtained as a weighted average of these matrices. The first step is to derive an optimal set of weights. The principle to find this set of weights is similar to that described for STATIS and involves the following steps.

Comparing the Studies

To analyze the similarity structure of the studies we start by creating a *between-study cosine matrix* denoted **C**. This is a $T \times T$ matrix whose generic term $c_{t,t'}$ gives the cosine between studies t and t'. This cosine, also known as the R_V coefficient, is defined as

$$R_V = [c_{t,t'}] = \frac{\text{trace}\left\{\mathbf{S}_{[t]}^T \mathbf{S}_{[t']}\right\}}{\sqrt{\text{trace}\left\{\mathbf{S}_{[t]}^T \mathbf{S}_{[t]}\right\} \times \text{trace}\left\{\mathbf{S}_{[t']}^T \mathbf{S}_{[t']}\right\}}}. \quad (5)$$

Using this formula, we get the following matrix **C**:

$$\mathbf{C} = \begin{bmatrix} 1.00 & .77 & .76 & .40 \\ .77 & 1.00 & .41 & .53 \\ .76 & .41 & 1.00 & .30 \\ .40 & .53 & .30 & 1.00 \end{bmatrix}. \quad (6)$$

PCA of the Cosine Matrix

The cosine matrix has the following eigen-decomposition

$$\mathbf{C} = \mathbf{P}\Theta\mathbf{P}^T \text{ with } \mathbf{P}^T\mathbf{P} = \mathbf{I}, \quad (7)$$

where **P** is the matrix of eigenvectors and Θ is the diagonal matrix of the eigenvalues of **C**. For our example, the eigenvectors and eigenvalues of **C** are

$$\mathbf{P} = \begin{bmatrix} .58 & .28 & -.21 & .74 \\ .53 & -.24 & -.64 & -.50 \\ .48 & .56 & .51 & -.44 \\ .40 & -.74 & .53 & .11 \end{bmatrix} \text{ and diag}\{\Theta\} = \begin{bmatrix} 2.62 \\ 0.80 \\ 0.49 \\ 0.09 \end{bmatrix}.$$

An element of a given eigenvector represents the projection of one study on this eigenvector. Thus, the T studies can be represented as points in the eigenspace and their similarities analyzed visually. This step corresponds to a PCA of the between-studies space. In general, when we plot the studies in their factor space, we want to give to each component the length corresponding to its eigenvalue (i.e., the inertia of the coordinates of a dimension is equal to the eigenvalue of this dimension, which is the standard procedure in PCA and MDS). For our example, we obtain the following coordinates:

$$\mathbf{G} = \mathbf{P} \times \Theta^{\frac{1}{2}} = \begin{bmatrix} .93 & .25 & -.14 & .23 \\ .85 & -.22 & -.45 & -.15 \\ .78 & .50 & .36 & -.13 \\ .65 & -.66 & .37 & .03 \end{bmatrix}.$$

As an illustration, Figure 3 displays the projections of the four algorithms onto the first and second eigenvectors of the cosine matrix.

Because the matrix is not centered, the first eigenvector represents what is common to the different studies. The more similar a study is to the other studies, the more it will contribute to this eigenvector. Or, in other words, studies with larger projections on the first eigenvector are more similar to the other studies than studies with smaller projections. Thus, the elements of the first eigenvector give the optimal weights to compute the compromise matrix.

Computing the Compromise

As for STATIS, the weights are obtained by dividing each element of $\mathbf{p}_1$ by their sum. The vector containing these weights is denoted α. For our example, we obtain

$$\alpha = [.29 \quad .27 \quad .24 \quad .20]^T. \quad (8)$$

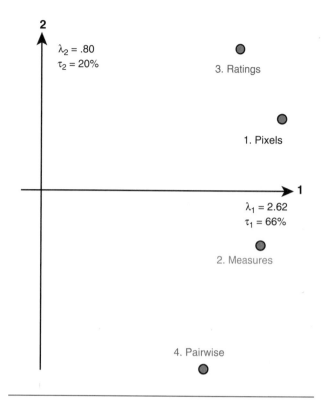

Figure 3   Plot of the Between-Studies Space (i.e., eigenanalysis of the matrix **C**)

With α_t denoting the weight for the tth study, the compromise matrix, denoted $\mathbf{S}_{[+]}$, is computed as

$$\mathbf{S}_{[+]} = \sum_t^T \alpha_t \mathbf{S}_{[t]}. \tag{9}$$

In our example, this gives

$$\mathbf{S}_{[+]} = \begin{bmatrix} .176 & .004 & -.058 & .014 & -.100 & -.036 \\ .004 & .178 & .022 & -.038 & -.068 & -.010 \\ -.058 & .022 & .579 & -.243 & -.186 & -.115 \\ .014 & -.038 & -.243 & .240 & .054 & -.027 \\ -.100 & -.068 & -.186 & .054 & .266 & .034 \\ -.036 & -.010 & -.115 & -.027 & .034 & .243 \end{bmatrix}.$$

How Representative Is the Compromise?

To evaluate the quality of the compromise, we need an index of quality. This is given by the first eigenvalue of matrix **C**, which is denoted ϑ_1. An alternative index of quality (easier to interpret) is the ratio of the first eigenvalue of **C** to the sum of its eigenvalues:

$$\text{Quality of compromise} = \frac{\vartheta_1}{\sum_\ell \vartheta_\ell} = \frac{\vartheta_1}{\text{trace}\{\Theta\}}. \tag{10}$$

Here, the quality of the compromise is evaluated as

$$\text{Quality of compromise} = \frac{\vartheta_1}{\text{trace}\{\Theta\}} = \frac{2.62}{4} \approx .66. \tag{11}$$

So, we can say that the compromise "explains" 66% of the inertia of the original set of data tables. This is a relatively small value, and this indicates that the algorithms differ substantially on the information they capture about the faces.

Analyzing the Compromise

The eigendecomposition of the compromise is

$$\mathbf{S}_{[+]} = \mathbf{Q\Lambda Q}^T \tag{12}$$

with, in our example,

$$\mathbf{Q} = \begin{bmatrix} .017 & .474 & -.451 & -.107 & -.627 \\ .121 & .400 & .256 & .726 & .258 \\ .823 & -.213 & .114 & -.308 & .053 \\ -.388 & .309 & .159 & -.566 & .492 \\ -.348 & -.443 & .549 & .043 & -.462 \\ -.192 & -.527 & -.626 & .211 & .287 \end{bmatrix} \tag{13}$$

and

$$\text{diag }\{\mathbf{\Lambda}\} = [.80 \;\; .35 \;\; .26 \;\; .16 \;\; .11]^T. \tag{14}$$

From Equations 13 and 14, we can compute the compromise factor scores for the faces as

$$\mathbf{F} = \mathbf{Q\Lambda}^{\frac{1}{2}}$$

$$= \begin{bmatrix} -.015 & .280 & -.228 & -.043 & -.209 \\ .108 & .236 & .129 & .294 & .086 \\ .738 & -.126 & .058 & -.125 & .018 \\ -.348 & .182 & .080 & -.229 & .164 \\ -.312 & -.262 & .277 & .018 & -.155 \\ -.172 & -.311 & -.316 & .086 & .096 \end{bmatrix}. \tag{15}$$

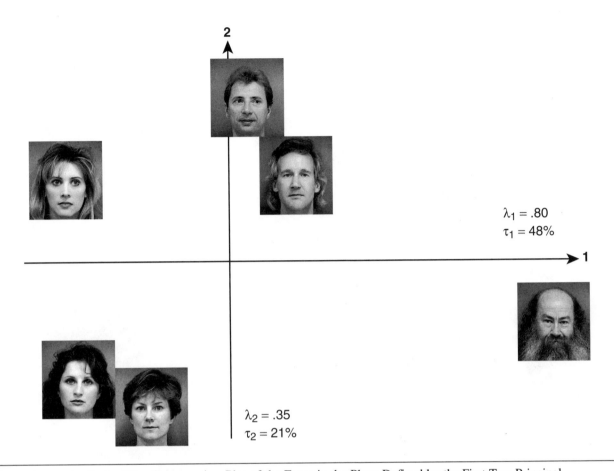

$\lambda_1 = .80$
$\tau_1 = 48\%$

$\lambda_2 = .35$
$\tau_2 = 21\%$

Figure 4   Analysis of the Compromise: Plot of the Faces in the Plane Defined by the First Two Principal Components of the Compromise Matrix

In the **F** matrix, each row represents an object (i.e., a face) and each column a component. Figure 4 displays the faces in the space defined by the first two principal components. The first component has an eigenvalue equal to $\lambda_1 = .80$; such a value explains 48% of the inertia. The second component, with an eigenvalue of .35, explains 21% of the inertia. The first component is easily interpreted as the opposition of the male to the female faces (with Face #3 appearing extremely masculine). The second dimension is more difficult to interpret and seems linked to hair color (i.e., light hair vs. dark or no hair).

Projecting the Studies Into the Compromise Space

Each algorithm provided a cross-product matrix, which was used to create the compromise cross-product matrix. The analysis of the compromise reveals the structure of the face space common to the algorithms. In addition to this common space, we want also to see how each algorithm "interprets" or distorts this space. This can be achieved by projecting the cross-product matrix of each algorithm onto the common space. This operation is performed by computing a projection matrix that transforms the scalar product matrix into loadings. The projection matrix is deduced from the combination of Equations 12 and 15, which gives

$$\mathbf{F} = \mathbf{S}_{[+]}\mathbf{Q}\boldsymbol{\Lambda}^{-\frac{1}{2}}. \tag{16}$$

This shows that the projection matrix is equal to $(\mathbf{Q}\boldsymbol{\Lambda}^{-\frac{1}{2}})$. It is used to project the scalar product matrix of each study onto the common space. For example, the coordinates of the projections for the first study are obtained by first computing the matrix

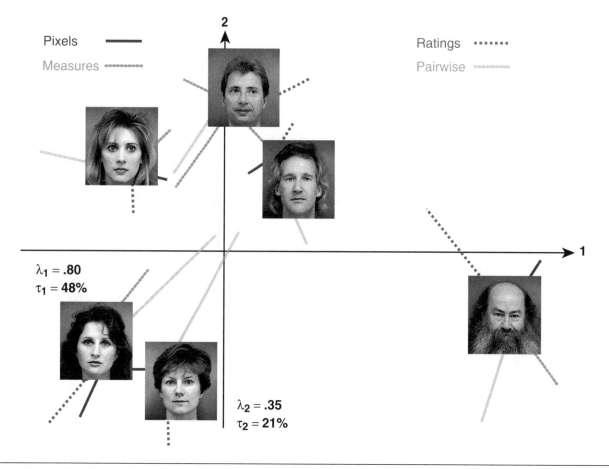

Pixels ——

Measures ··········

Ratings ·······

Pairwise ▨▨▨▨▨▨▨▨▨

$\lambda_1 = .80$
$\tau_1 = 48\%$

$\lambda_2 = .35$
$\tau_2 = 21\%$

Figure 5   The Compromise: Projection of the Algorithm Matrices Onto the Compromise Space

$$\mathbf{Q}\boldsymbol{\Lambda}^{-\frac{1}{2}} = \begin{bmatrix} -0.02 & 0.80 & -0.89 & -0.26 & -1.88 \\ 0.13 & 0.68 & 0.51 & 1.79 & 0.77 \\ 0.92 & -0.36 & 0.23 & -0.76 & 0.16 \\ -0.43 & 0.52 & 0.31 & -1.40 & 1.48 \\ -0.39 & -0.75 & 1.09 & 0.11 & -1.39 \\ -0.21 & -0.89 & -1.24 & 0.52 & 0.86 \end{bmatrix}, \quad (17)$$

and then using this matrix to obtain the coordinates of the projection as

$$\mathbf{F}_{[1]} = \mathbf{S}_{[1]}\left(\mathbf{Q}\boldsymbol{\Lambda}^{-\frac{1}{2}}\right)$$

$$= \begin{bmatrix} .07 & .30 & -.44 & -.24 & -.33 \\ .11 & .24 & .22 & .53 & .34 \\ .85 & .11 & .09 & -.44 & .01 \\ -.26 & .19 & .04 & -.31 & .30 \\ -.47 & -.50 & .67 & .18 & -.57 \\ -.30 & -.33 & -.59 & .28 & .25 \end{bmatrix}. \quad (18)$$

The same procedure is used to compute the matrices of the projections onto the compromise space for the other algorithms.

Figure 5 shows the first two principal components of the compromise space along with the projections of each of the algorithms. The position of a face in the compromise is the barycenter of its positions for the four algorithms. In order to facilitate the interpretation, we have drawn lines linking the position of each face for each of the four algorithms to its compromise position. This picture confirms that the algorithms differ substantially. It shows also that some faces are more sensitive to the differences between algorithms (e.g., compare Faces 3 and 4).

*—Hervé Abdi and
Dominique Valentin*

See also Distance; Metric Multidimensional Scaling; Multiple Correspondence Analysis; Multiple Factor Analysis, R_V and Congruence Coefficients; STATIS

Further Reading

Abdi, H. (2004). Multivariate analysis. In M. Lewis-Beck, A. Bryman, & T. F. Liao (Eds.), *The SAGE encyclopedia of social science research methods.* Thousand Oaks, CA: Sage.

Abdi, H., Valentin, D., O'Toole, A. J., & Edelman, B. (2005). DISTATIS: The analysis of multiple distance matrices. *Proceedings of the IEEE Computer Society: International Conference on Computer Vision and Pattern Recognition,* pp. 42–47.

Escofier, B., & Pagès, J. (1998). *Analyses factorielles simples et multiples.* Paris: Dunod.

DIXON TEST FOR OUTLIERS

In statistics, we assume that our data come from some probability model, a hypothetical or ideal model for doing statistical analysis mathematically. In the real-life world, unfortunately, the data in our hands usually have some outliers: outlying observations discordant from the hypothesized model. It is well known that outliers in the data set can severely distort the result of statistical inference.

Generally speaking, there are two strategies to deal with outliers. One way is to use some robust methods to accommodate outliers in the data, such as using the sample median (instead of the sample mean) to estimate a population mean. The other way is to try to identify outliers in the sample and then modify or simply delete them for further data analysis. Our topic here is the identification of outliers in the sample data.

Suppose that our sample data $x_1, x_2, \ldots, x_n$ come from an interesting population or distribution. Arrange the sample observations $x_1, x_2, \ldots, x_n$ in ascending order: $x_{(1)} \leq x_{(2)} \leq \ldots \leq x_{(n)}$, which are called order statistics. Suppose that we have k suspicious lower outliers $x_{(1)}, x_{(2)}, \ldots, x_{(k)}$ or upper outliers $x_{(n-k+1)}, \ldots, x_{(n-1)}, x_{(n)}$ in the sample (the case of having both lower and upper outliers is too complicated to be considered here), where k (the number of suspicious outliers) is much smaller than the sample size n. We want to test if they are significantly discordant from the rest of sample observations.

Hypothesis Test for Outliers

To test the discordancy of suspicious outliers, we need to propose statistical hypotheses. For example, to test the discordancy of k suspicious upper outliers $x_{(n-k+1)}, \ldots, x_{(n-1)}, x_{(n)}$ in a normal sample, suppose that the underlying distribution of the sample is a normal distribution $N(\mu, \sigma^2)$ with mean μ and variance σ^2, where μ and variance σ^2 are unknown.

Under a *null hypothesis*, the sample data $x_1, x_2, \ldots, x_n$ are a random sample from $N(\mu, \sigma^2)$. Under an *alternative hypothesis*, unsuspicious observations $x_1, x_2, \ldots, x_{(n-k)}$ belong to $N(\mu, \sigma^2)$, but the suspicious upper outliers $x_{(n-k+1)}, \ldots, x_{(n-1)}, x_{(n)}$ belonging to $N(\mu + a, \sigma^2)$ $(a > 0)$, which has a larger mean $\mu + a$ shifted right from the original mean μ.

In other words, we need to test the null hypothesis

$$H_0: a = 0$$

against the mean-shifted alternative hypothesis

$$H_1: a > 0.$$

The likelihood-ratio statistic for testing $H_0: a = 0$ against $H_1: a > 0$ is

$$[x_{(n-k+1)} + \ldots + x_{(n-1)} + x_{(n)} - k \cdot \bar{x}]/s,$$

where $\bar{x}$ and s stand for the sample mean and sample standard deviation, and large values of the test statistic reject the null hypothesis H_0, identifying $x_{(n-k+1)}, \ldots, x_{(n-1)}, x_{(n)}$ as outliers or discordant observations.

If the underlying distribution of the sample is a nonnormal distribution, say, a gamma distribution (which includes exponential distribution as a special case), then the likelihood-ratio test statistic will be

$$[x_{(n-k+1)} + \ldots + x_{(n-1)} + x_n]/\textstyle\sum x_i.$$

Dixon Test

There are many varieties of statistical tests for detecting outliers in the sample. Generally speaking, powerful tests are based on sophisticated test statistics, such as the likelihood-ratio test statistics discussed before.

Dixon test is a very simple test that is often used to test outliers in a small sample. The general form of Dixon statistic in the literature is defined by

$$T = \frac{x_{(s)} - x_{(r)}}{x_{(q)} - x_{(p)}}, \quad p \le r < s \le q,$$

in terms of the ratio of intervals of ordered values.

The advantage of Dixon test is the simplicity of its test statistic for hand calculation. Because Dixon statistic simply uses the sample information from four observations $x_{(p)}, x_{(r)}, x_{(s)}, x_{(q)}$, the power of Dixon test is relatively low unless the sample size is very small.

There are many different versions of Dixon tests. In the simplest case,

$$T_1 = \frac{x_{(n)} - x_{(n-1)}}{x_{(n)} - x_{(1)}} \text{ or } \frac{x_{(2)} - x_{(1)}}{x_{(n)} - x_{(1)}}$$

can be used to test a single suspicious upper outlier $x_{(n)}$ or lower outlier $x_{(1)}$.

Large values of T_1 will reject the null hypothesis, identifying $x_{(n)}$ or $x_{(1)}$ as outlier. Similarly, we can use

$$T_2 = \frac{x_{(n)} - x_{(n-2)}}{x_{(n)} - x_{(1)}} \text{ or } \frac{x_{(3)} - x_{(1)}}{x_{(n)} - x_{(1)}}$$

to simultaneously test a pair of upper outliers $x_{(n-1)}, x_{(n)}$ or lower outliers $x_{(1)}, x_{(2)}$.

statistics T_1 and T_2, assuming that the underlying distribution of the sample is normal. More detailed tables can be found in the references listed in the Further Reading section at the end of this entry.

When T_1 is larger than its critical value t_α, we will reject the null hypothesis at significance level α, identifying $x_{(n)}$ or $x_{(1)}$ as outlier.

Similarly, if T_2 is larger than its critical value t_α, we will reject the null hypothesis at significance level α, simultaneously identifying $x_{(n-1)}, x_{(n)}$ or $x_{(1)}, x_{(2)}$ as outliers.

A simple way to test multiple outliers is to apply sequential or consecutive tests. That is, sequentially apply a test for a single outlier. Nevertheless, sequential tests are generally less powerful.

For example, to test the discordancy of three suspicious upper outliers $x_{(n)}, x_{(n-1)}, x_{(n-2)}$ in the sample data, we can use an inward or outward method to test them sequentially. The inward method tests $x_{(n)}$ first. If it is accordant, stop the procedure and declare $x_{(n-1)}$ and $x_{(n-2)}$ accordant as well. Otherwise, delete $x_{(n)}$ from the sample and then repeat the same procedure to test $x_{(n-1)}$ and $x_{(n-2)}$. On the other hand, the outward method tests $x_{(n-2)}$ first by deleting $x_{(n-1)}$ and $x_{(n)}$. If $x_{(n-2)}$ is discordant, stop the procedure and declare $x_{(n-1)}$ and $x_{(n)}$

Applying Dixon Test

To apply Dixon test for outliers at a given significance level $\alpha (0 < \alpha < 1)$, we need to know the critical value or percentage point of the test statistic. If the Dixon statistic T is larger than its critical value t_α, reject the null hypothesis at level α, identifying the suspicious observations as outliers.

The critical value of a test statistic is determined by the sampling distribution of the statistic under the null hypothesis, which in turn depends on the underlying distribution of the sample. For example, Table 1 gives some of the critical values of Dixon

Table 1 Critical Values t_α of Dixon Statistics for Normal Samples

	$T_1 = \frac{x_{(n)} - x_{(n-1)}}{x_{(n)} - x_{(1)}}$ or $\frac{x_{(2)} - x_{(1)}}{x_{(n)} - x_{(1)}}$		$T_2 = \frac{x_{(n)} - x_{(n-2)}}{x_{(n)} - x_{(1)}}$ or $\frac{x_{(3)} - x_{(1)}}{x_{(n)} - x_{(1)}}$	
n	$\alpha = 5\%$	$\alpha = 1\%$	$\alpha = 5\%$	$\alpha = 1\%$
5	0.642	0.780	0.845	0.929
6	0.560	0.698	0.736	0.836
7	0.507	0.637	0.661	0.778
8	0.468	0.590	0.607	0.710
9	0.437	0.555	0.565	0.667
10	0.412	0.527	0.531	0.632
12	0.376	0.482	0.481	0.579
14	0.349	0.450	0.445	0.538
16	0.329	0.426	0.418	0.508
18	0.313	0.407	0.397	0.484
20	0.300	0.391	0.372	0.464
25	0.277	0.362	0.343	0.428
30	0.260	0.341	0.322	0.402

discordant as well. Otherwise, add $x_{(n-1)}$ into the sample and then test $x_{(n-1)}$, and so on.

Both inward and outward methods have advantages and disadvantages. They may suffer from masking or swamping effect, which is the inability to correctly identify an outlier in the presence of other outliers. This is always a tough issue in multiple-outlier situations.

Example

In a comparison of strength of various plastic materials, one important characteristic is the percent elongation at break. The following data are 10 measurements of percent elongation at break made on certain material:

$x_{(1)}$	$x_{(2)}$	$x_{(3)}$	$x_{(4)}$	$x_{(5)}$	$x_{(6)}$	$x_{(7)}$	$x_{(8)}$	$x_{(9)}$	$x_{(10)}$
2.02	2.22	3.04	3.23	3.59	3.73	3.94	4.05	4.11	4.13

where $x_{(1)}$ and $x_{(2)}$ appear to be lower outliers in the sample data.

Because Dixon statistic

$$T_2 = \frac{x_{(3)} - x_{(1)}}{x_{(n)} - x_{(1)}} = \frac{3.04 - 2.02}{4.13 - 2.02} = 0.4834,$$

which is smaller than its 5% critical value 0.531 in Table 1 with $n = 10$, we fail to identify $x_{(1)}$ and $x_{(2)}$ as outliers at the 5% significance level.

Similarly, we will get the same result if sequential tests are used. In fact,

$$T_1 = \frac{x_{(2)} - x_{(1)}}{x_{(n)} - x_{(1)}}$$

$$= \frac{2.22 - 2.02}{4.13 - 2.02} = 0.0948 \qquad (n = 10)$$

$$T_1 = \frac{x_{(3)} - x_{(2)}}{x_{(n)} - x_{(2)}}$$

$$= \frac{3.04 - 2.22}{4.13 - 2.22} = 0.4293 \qquad (n = 9, \text{ deleting } x_{(1)})$$

which are respectively smaller than the 5% critical values 0.412 and 0.437. Therefore, both inward and outward methods will fail to identify $x_{(1)}$ and $x_{(2)}$ as outliers at the 5% significance level. However, it should be pointed out that the likelihood-ratio test $[\bar{x} - x_{(1)} - x_{(2)}]/s$ will detect $x_{(1)}$ and $x_{(2)}$ as outliers at the 5% significance level.

—Jin Zhang

See also Normal Curve

Further Reading

Barnett, V., & Lewis, T. (1994). *Outliers in statistical data* (3rd ed.). Chichester, UK: Wiley.

Dixon, W. J. (1951). Ratios involving extreme values. *Annals of Mathematical Statistics, 22*(1), 68–78.

Likes, J. (1966). Distribution of Dixon's statistics in the case of an exponential population. *Metrika, 11,* 46–54.

Zhang, J. (1998). Tests for multiple upper or lower outliers in an exponential sample. *Journal of Applied Statistics, 25,* 245–255.

Zhang, J., & Yu, K. (2004). The null distribution of the likelihood-ratio test for two upper outliers in a gamma sample. *Journal of Statistical Computation and Simulation, 74,* 461–467.

Zhang, J., & Yu, K. (2006). The null distribution of the likelihood-ratio test for one or two outliers in a normal sample. *Test, 15,* 141–150.

Dixon test for outliers has been implemented in the R project, a free software environment for statistical computing and graphics: http://finzi.psych.upenn.edu/R/library/outliers/html/dixon.test.html

DUNN'S MULTIPLE COMPARISON TEST

Olive Jean Dunn's work was one of the earliest attempts to provide researchers with a way to select, in advance, and test a number of contrasts from among a set of mean scores. Fisher, Scheffé, and Tukey had already provided techniques for testing comparisons between all possible linear contrasts among a set of normally distributed variables. Dunn's contribution meant that researchers no longer needed to test all possible comparisons when they were interested in only a few such comparisons, yet they maintained control over an inflated Type I error rate.

Although the groundwork for Dunn's multiple comparison tests is usually attributed to Carlos Emilio Bonferroni, it actually originated with George Boole, who worked in the middle of the 19th century. Boole's inequality (also known as the union bound) states that for any finite set of events, the probability that at least one of the events will occur is no greater than the sum of the probabilities of the individual events. Bonferroni expanded Boole's inequality by demonstrating how upper and lower bounds (i.e., a confidence interval) could be calculated for the probability of the finite union of events. These are called Bonferroni's inequalities.

Dunn, and later, Dunn and Massey, used a Bonferroni inequality to construct simultaneous confidence intervals for k means, m comparisons, and v degrees of freedom based on the Student's t statistic. She demonstrated the differences in confidence intervals obtained when the variances of the means were unknown, and when the variances were unknown but equal; she also showed how her confidence intervals could be used in fitting data to locate regression curves (e.g., growth in height or weight). As such, no comprehensive table for different numbers of means, comparisons, and degrees of freedom was produced until B. J. R. Bailey did so in 1977. Bailey noted that Dunn's tables were incomplete, were rounded to two decimal places, and contained errors in the tabled values. Although Dunn conducted the initial work showing how complete tables might be constructed, Bailey honored the forerunner by titling his paper "Tables of the Bonferroni t Statistic"; nevertheless, the overlapping t values are, except for rounding errors, identical. To date, there remains confusion about the attribution of this multiple comparison method, no doubt partly because Bonferroni's publications were written in Italian.

Perhaps adding to the confusion, Zbynek Sidák constructed a partial set of tables using the multiplicative inequality to control family-wise Type I error, whereas Dunn had employed the additive inequality for the same purpose. Sidák showed that using the multiplicative inequality produced slightly smaller confidence intervals than using the additive inequality.

This increases the probability of finding statistically significant differences between pairs of means, making the test more powerful. Ten years later, Paul Games published a more complete set of tables using Sidák's method. Nowadays, one often sees references to the Dunn-Sidák multiple comparison test, but, as noted above, the two methods are not identical and produce somewhat different results.

Why the Dunn Multiple Comparison Test Is Used

Dunn's multiple comparison test is an adjustment used when several comparisons are performed simultaneously. Although a value of alpha may be appropriate for one individual comparison, it is not appropriate for the set of all comparisons. In order to avoid a surfeit of Type I errors, alpha should be lowered to account for the number of comparisons tested.

Suppose a researcher has collected data on 20 independent variables (e.g., gender, intact vs. divorced parents, age, family income, etc.) that might (or might not) be related to some dependent variable of interest (e.g., level of physical violence displayed). The researcher might be tempted to go on a fishing expedition, making comparisons between all possible means produced by each independent variable (e.g., boys vs. girls, rich vs. poor families, etc.) In all, 20 comparisons could be made. If the alpha level was set at .05, the researcher has a pretty good chance of finding at least one statistically significant difference even if all of the independent variables are completely unrelated to displays of physical violence. That is because when the alpha level is set at .05, we know that the odds of obtaining a difference deemed statistically significant would happen by chance on only 1 out of 20 occasions on repeated sampling. In this example, the researcher has given him- or herself 20 chances of finding a statistically significant difference, so it is not surprising that one of them met the critical value for significance. The Dunn adjustment effectively raises the standard of evidence needed when researchers are comparing a large number of means simultaneously.

How to Use the Dunn Multiple Comparison Test

The simplest way to understand the Dunn procedure is to understand that, if we are making n comparisons instead of just one, we must divide the selected alpha by n. For example, if we were testing the effect of social praise on the math achievement of elementary, middle school, and high school students, we should not set alpha at the traditional .05 level, but at the alpha = .05/3, or .0167 level. This ensures that across all three comparisons, the chance of making a Type I error remains at .05.

Dunn's approach in creating confidence intervals is simply a different way of accomplishing the same outcome. Table 1 represents Dunn's multiple comparisons for the effect of three levels of curiosity on externalizing affect scores. To obtain the confidence interval for the comparison of high versus medium curiosity, simply multiply the standard error of the difference (SE_{diff}) for the contrast by Dunn's tabled t value: $1.52 \times 2.40 = 3.648$, or 3.65. This is the value that must be subtracted from and added to the mean difference (Ψ) to obtain the lower and upper limit for the 95% confidence interval: $\Psi \pm 3.65$. Therefore, $10.41 - 3.65 = 6.76$, and $10.41 + 3.65 = 14.06$. The odds are 95 out of 100 that the true difference between the means for high curiosity and medium curiosity is contained within the confidence interval from 6.76 to 14.06 (i.e., $6.76 \leq \Psi \leq 14.06$). Ninety-five percent confidence intervals that do not contain the value zero are considered statistically significant. Because none of the three confidence intervals contains zero, the researcher would have a high degree of confidence in saying that each level of curiosity produced a mean that was significantly different from every other level, with high curiosity leading to the highest level of externalizing affect, and low curiosity leading to the lowest level of externalizing affect. The probabilities in Table 1 were adjusted for the fact that multiple comparisons were made.

Table 1 Dunn Multiple Comparisons for the Effect of Three Levels of Curiosity on Externalizing Affect Scores

Comparison	df	Mean Difference	SE_{diff}	t	p	95% Confidence Interval
Curiosity						
High vs. Medium	703	10.41	1.52	2.40	.000	6.76 to 14.06
High vs. Low	456	14.34	1.77	2.40	.000	10.09 to 18.59
Medium vs. Low	702	3.92	1.52	2.40	.003	0.27 to 7.57

Final Considerations

When the variables in a comparison are correlated, the normal Dunn correction is more conservative, causing less power, so further adjustment should be used. In this case, the corrected alpha falls between the usual Dunn correction and no correction at all.

The decision to use (or not use) a multiple comparison test like Dunn's hinges not on the fact that several comparisons are to be made, but on an understanding of the theory and logic of the research design. For instance, an investigator may collect data to test three independently derived hypotheses, say, the relationship between gender and anxiety, the influence of three kinds of primary reinforcer on reading achievement, and the impact of physical size (small and large) on the extent of physical violence displayed. Although five comparisons can be made with these data, only the three hypotheses associated with the primary reinforcer data should be corrected with Dunn's multiple comparison test.

—Ronald C. Eaves and Anthony J. Guarino

See also Bonferroni Test; Post Hoc Comparisons; Tukey-Kramer Procedure

Further Reading

Bailey, B. J. R. (1977). Tables of the Bonferroni *t* statistic. *Journal of the American Statistical Association, 72,* 469–478.

Dunn, O. L. (1961). Multiple comparisons of means. *Journal of the American Statistical Association, 56,* 52–64.

Dunn, O. L., & Massey, F. J., Jr. (1965). Estimation of multiple contrasts using *t*-distributions. *Journal of the American Statistical Association, 60,* 573–583.

Games, P. A. (1977). An improved *t* table for simultaneous control on *g* contrasts. *Journal of the American Statistical Association, 72,* 531–534.

Hsu, J. C. (1996). *Multiple comparisons: Theory and methods.* London: Chapman & Hall.

Sidák, Z. (1967). Rectangular confidence regions for the means of multivariate normal distributions. *Journal of the American Statistical Association, 62,* 626–633.

Bonferroni correction: http://www.cmh.edu/stats/ask/bonferroni.asp

Bonferroni correction/adjustment: http://home.clara.net/sisa/bonhlp.htm

Boole's inequality and Bonferroni's inequalities description: http://www.absoluteastronomy.com/encyclopedia/b/bo/booles_inequality.htm

E

Behavioral psychology is the science of pulling habits out of rats.

—Dr. Douglas Busch

ECOLOGICAL MOMENTARY ASSESSMENT

Ecological momentary assessment (EMA) allows the study of behavior, psychological states, and physiological functions in their natural contexts. EMA and its predecessors (e.g., the experience sampling method) were developed with several purposes in mind. First, there was concern that retrospective autobiographical memory was fallible, due primarily to the use of cognitive heuristics during recall. EMA reduces these biases by generally limiting the period over which information is recalled. Second, although laboratory research offers the benefit of experimental control, it is not clear if processes observed in the laboratory are similar to what occurs in the "real" world. EMA often has greater ecological validity and generalizability because assessments can be collected in everyday settings. Third, EMA enables a closer examination of dynamic and temporal processes. EMA designs usually incorporate a large number of repeated measures, which provide a movielike view of processes over time. Such data not only allow examination of temporal patterns but also provide considerable information about (although not confirming) causal associations among variables.

EMA involves participants reporting on current or recent psychological states, behaviors, and/or environmental conditions, typically multiple times each day, for days or even weeks. Responses are collected in several ways, of which some are self-initiated by research participants and others request responses after some signal (e.g., a pager, a handheld computer alarm). The three most commonly used approaches are interval-contingent, event-contingent, and signal-contingent responding. *Interval-contingent recording* involves completing assessments at regular times (e.g., every hour on the hour, before bed). *Event-contingent schedules* entail completing assessments in response to specific events (e.g., smoking a cigarette, argument with a spouse). *Signal-contingent schedules* require individuals to report on experiences in response to random or semirandom signals across the day. Recent technological advances, most notably palmtop computers, provide a number of advantages to EMA data capture over paper-and-pencil approaches. As participants can respond directly on a handheld computer, portability is optimized, compliance can be automatically tracked (reports are date- and time-stamped), data can be transferred directly to statistical software, and researchers have greater control over the format and order of assessment items.

Despite the advantages of EMA approaches, they are not without limitations. First, implementation of EMA designs requires considerable time and expertise. There are many logistical issues: the design of the sampling scheme, thoughtful consideration of questionnaire design, training and motivating participants to follow the protocol, and dealing with the technical difficulties inherent in the use of technological devices (e.g., programming the devices). Second, momentary data collection techniques yield masses of complex, time-dependent data. Although such data are a strength of the approach, considerable statistical and data management acumen are necessary to manipulate and appropriately analyze these data sets. Third, given the intensive nature of data collection (e.g., five times each day for 2 weeks), the majority of participants are likely to have some missing data. This presents a problem for EMA research and must be accounted for in the statistical/analytic approach and interpretation of the data (e.g., are missing data random or reflective of an altered environmental state?).

Conclusion

EMA and other strategies for capturing momentary data provide researchers with a new assessment technique for studying behavior, psychological states, and physiological functions as they occur in individuals' natural environments. This method can reduce retrospective recall biases, provides a dynamic picture of people's daily lives, and may reveal potential causal relationships among variables of interest. New technological advances, such as palmtop computers and interactive voice recognition systems, are opening up exciting new avenues for real-time data capture in naturalistic settings.

—*Joshua Smyth and Kristin Heron*

See also Data Mining

Further Reading

Stone, A., & Shiffman, S. (1994). Ecological Momentary Assessment (EMA) in behavioral medicine. *Annals of Behavioral Medicine, 16,* 199–202.

Experience sampling method: http://seattleweb.intel-research .net/projects/ESM/index.html

EDUCATIONAL TESTING SERVICE

Educational Testing Service (ETS) is the world's largest private educational testing and measurement organization. With an annual budget approaching $1 billion, it develops, administers, or scores more than 24 million tests annually (as of 2005) in more than 180 countries at more than 9,000 locations internationally. With locations worldwide, its operations are headquartered in Princeton, New Jersey.

ETS was founded by Henry Chauncey in 1947, with key support from the American Council on Education, The Carnegie Foundation for the Advancement of Teaching, and the College Entrance Examination Board. The core ideas behind ETS were put forth by former Harvard president James Conant. Its mission is to "advance quality and equity in education for all people worldwide."

ETS encompasses five areas—research, assessment development, test administration, test scoring, and instructional products and services—but it is best known for assessment development. Perhaps its most well-known test, the SAT®, is actually published by the College Board, although ETS develops and administers the test as a work-for-hire (a procedure it also does for the Advanced Placement Exams). The SAT I measures Mathematics, Critical Reading, and Writing. The SAT IIs are subject-based tests that assess particular areas of learning.

Major ETS assessments include the GRE® (Graduate Record Examinations), TOEFL® (Test of English as a Foreign Language), and the Praxis tests for teacher certification. The GRE has three subtests: Verbal, Quantitative, and Analytical Writing. The latter subtest replaced an Analytic Reasoning subtest on October 1, 2002. The TOEFL exam is currently paper based, although there is a shift toward an Internet-based measure. The paper-based measure assesses Listening Comprehension, Structure and Written Expression, and Reading Comprehension. The new Internet-based measure assesses along the four dimensions of Listening, Structure, Reading, and Writing. The Praxis is a series of three different tests: the first measures basic academic skills; the second measures general and subject-specific knowledge and teaching skills; and the third measures classroom performance. These three assessments represent only a hint of the many different ones offered by ETS.

ETS has many critics, perhaps most notably FairTest (although such critics tend to be against all methods of standardized testing, not solely ETS). FairTest and other critics argue that ETS tests are biased, overly coachable, and prone to misuse. One example of such criticisms is that men outperform women on the GRE Quantitative test by nearly a standard deviation despite the fact that women often outperform men in advanced mathematics in the classroom. The performance-based assessments that FairTest advocates, however, would likely create similar confounding issues.

Perhaps the primary competitor of ETS is the ACT, formerly the American College Testing Program, which produces the ACT tests. The ACT test is usually accepted in lieu of the SATs by most universities. In addition, ACT recently took over the development of the GMAT (Graduate Management Admissions Test) from ETS.

—*James C. Kaufman*

See also Ethical Issues in Testing; Standards for Educational and Psychological Testing

Further Reading

Educational Testing Service: http://www.ets.org
FairTest: http://www.fairtest.org

EDWARDS PERSONAL PREFERENCE SCHEDULE

The *Edwards Personal Preference Schedule* (EPPS) (publisher: The Psychological Corporation) is a scale designed to measure 15 personal needs, originally proposed by H. A. Murray. The scale, authored by Allen Edwards, was constructed to provide ipsative information on how people rank one need relative to their other needs, as well as normative information on their needs compared with other people's. Edwards discussed needs as nonclinical personality variables and considers the EPPS foremost a personality measure. The EPPS has been used in vocational counseling to encourage discussion about how individuals want to relate to coworkers and their desired levels of responsibility on the job.

The EPPS includes 15 personality scales and two scales for assessing the validity of an individual's results. The personality dimensions include needs for Achievement (succeeding and fulfilling high standards), Deference (concern for the opinions of or approval from others), Order (organization and fastidiousness), Exhibition (social attention), Autonomy (freedom to self-determine), Affiliation (attachment to friends), Intraception (psychological-mindedness and introspection), Succorance (sympathy and affection from others), Dominance (leading and decision making), Abasement (feeling guilt for wrongdoings), Nurturance (helping others), Change (variety and novelty of activity), Endurance (task focus and forbearance), Heterosexuality (engaging the opposite sex romantically or sexually), and Aggression (being derisive, critical, and vengeful toward others).

The items on the EPPS pair two statements, each reflecting 1 of the 15 dimensions, and require test takers to identify which is more typical of themselves. Statements reflecting each of the personality variables are paired two times with statements reflecting each of the others. Overall, the test requires approximately 45 minutes to administer. Raw scores from the test can be used to identify the relative importance of a need to an individual, whereas normative data, collected in the late 1950s from a college sample and a survey of U.S. households, supplies information on how test takers' personal needs compare with others'.

The test and its norms were most recently updated in 1959; consequently, the instrument has been criticized for having normative data that are too old to serve as a meaningful index. However, the EPPS has been praised for the degree to which its item structure reduces the influence of social desirability, and overall evidence suggests that the individual scales show moderate-to-favorable internal consistency and satisfactory stability over a week. In addition, the evidence of convergent validity for the scale scores, most of which was collected in the 1950s, shows that the EPPS scale scores relate modestly, though as predicted, to other personality measures. For example, measures of agreeableness showed small positive correlations with deference and nurturance scales and small-to-medium negative correlations with aggression and dominance scales.

—*Matthew E. Kaler and Jo-Ida C. Hansen*

See also Jackson Personality Inventory–Revised; Personality Tests

Further Reading

Edwards, A. L. (1959). *Manual: Edwards Personal Preference Schedule.* Washington, DC: The Psychological Corporation.

Helms, J. E. (1983). *Practitioner's guide to the Edwards Personal Preference Schedule.* Springfield, IL: Charles C Thomas.

Thorson, J. A., & Powell, F. C. (1992). Vagaries of college norms for the Edwards Personal Preference Schedule. *Psychological Reports, 70,* 943–946.

EFFECT SIZE

Effect size is a term used to describe the magnitude of a treatment effect. More formally, it can be defined as the degree to which the null hypothesis is false, versus a true alternative hypothesis. Measuring effect size has taken on increasing study and importance during the last 30 years. Effect size is important in three phases of the research process. First, it is important prior to collecting data, as it is required for estimating sample sizes that are necessary to ensure statistical power. Second, reporting effect size is important for interpreting statistical tests of significance. Reporting effect size is fundamental to any good statistical report of results, since statistical tests and their associated *p* values are functions of both effect size and sample size. Finally, effect size measures are the raw scores of a meta-analysis.

Effect size measures attempt to strip away the effects of sample size and produce a simple and easily interpretable measure of the size of the effect. To achieve this goal, effect size indices have the following three properties: (1) standardization to allow cross-study comparison and to enhance interpretability of unfamiliar scales, (2) preservation of the direction of the effect, and (3) independence from sample size. Three common classes of effect size measures are standardized mean differences, correlation coefficients or their squared values, and odds ratios (common in medical but not educational and behavioral research). For many common statistical tests (e.g., *t* tests), the raw or unstandardized effect size is the numerator of the test statistic. The use of the "unstandardized" mean difference along with a confidence interval may be preferable to reporting effect size statistics when the dependent variable is measured on a familiar scale or is readily understood in the field of study.

Why It Is Important to Report Effect Size

Statistical tests combine in various ways effect size and sample size. Equation 1 summarizes the general relationship between tests of statistical significance and effect size. Clearly, the value of the statistical test and its corresponding *p* value depend on both effect size and sample size. Reexpressing the equation shows that by dividing a statistical test by its sample size, it is possible to get a measure of the effect that is independent of sample size:

$$\text{Significance test} = \text{Effect size} \times \text{Sample size or}$$
$$\text{Effect size} = \frac{\text{Significance test}}{\text{Sample size}}. \qquad (1)$$

In 1991, Rosenthal provided a comprehensive set of formulas that describe the specific relationship between tests of significance, effect size, and study sample size. Table 1 shows this relationship for a few important statistical tests.

Reporting effect size helps avoid the misleading decision dichotomy ($p \leq .05$ versus $p > .05$) inherent in classical null hypothesis statistical testing by "stripping away" the effect of sample size from the test statistic. With the sample size factored out, measures of effect size help researchers answer the

Table 1   Selected Statistics: Statistic[1] = Effect Size × Study Size

Chi-Square Test for Contingency Table	Independent Sample t Test	Two Independent Sample F Test
$\chi^2 = \phi^2 \times N$	$t = [(\bar{X}_1 - \bar{X}_2)/S_{(\text{pooled})}] \times \sqrt{\dfrac{n_1 n_2}{n_1 + n_2}} = d \times \sqrt{\dfrac{n_1 n_2}{n_1 + n_2}}$	$F = [(\bar{X}_1 - \bar{X}_2)/S^2] \times \dfrac{n_1 n_2}{n_1 + n_2}$

1. Note that because a *p* value is determined by the value of the test statistic, it is also a function of the effect size and study size.

important clinical or practical question: What is the size of the treatment or intervention effect? The publication style manuals for both the American Psychological Association (2001) and the American Medical Association, among others, require that measures of effect size be reported with statistical tests.

Measuring Effect Size: Two Types of Effect Size Indices

There are basically two types of effect size measures: measures of standardized or relative mean differences and measures of relationship or correlation, including measures of relationship for nonquantitative variables. Most measures of effect size overestimate the population effect size. However, because overestimation is small except when sample size is extremely small, adjustments for bias are seldom used. Table 2 shows these two types of effect size measures for a few common statistics. Because statistical significance is monotonically related to sample size, it is important to report effect size for both statistically significant and nonsignificant results. Presently, there is little consensus regarding which of the various effect size measures to report. Wolf, in 1986, gave available formulas for converting various test statistics *(X², t, F)* to an effect size measure, and computer programs for these calculations are also readily available (see Computer Programs for Calculating Effect Size). A comprehensive list of effect size measures, their formulas, and calculation examples is found in Rosenthal (for a focus on control versus treatment effect size measures); Grissom and Kim (for a

comprehensive review of effect size measures, especially when violations to the normal model are suspected); and Olejnik and Algina (for an overview of measures of effect size for multigroup comparative studies).

Standardized Mean Difference

Cohen's *d* is a measure of effect size in standard deviation units that is very commonly used as a basis to estimate the sample sizes required to ensure statistical power for a two-sample problem and as the data for conducting a meta-analysis. To calculate *d,* positive values are assigned to mean differences favoring the treatment, and negative values are assigned to differences unfavorable to the treatment. The scale used to standardize the mean difference is, alternatively, the control group alone (Glass's *g'* index, preferred when the treatment affects the variance) or for two repeated measures, the pretest (using the pretest ensures that the treatment does not affect the variance); the pooled standard deviation of the groups that are compared (Cohen's *d*, preferred when the treatment does not affect the variance in important ways); or the pooled standard deviation for all of the treatments in multigroup designs (Hedges's *g*).

Correlation and Proportion of Variance Measures

The point-biserial correlation coefficient (r_{pb}), for *t* tests for two independent samples; the phi coefficient (ϕ), for chi-square tests for contingency tables

Table 2   Effect Size Measures for Selected Test Statistics

Effect Measure

Test Statistic	Raw Unstandardized Effect[2] (Mean Difference)	Relative Effect[1]/ RawEffect/Standard Error or *t*/Sample Size Ratio	Correlation or Correlation Squared
One-Sample *t*	$(\bar{X}_1 - \mu)$	$d = [(\bar{X}_1 - \mu)/S_x]$ $d = \dfrac{t}{\sqrt{df}}$	$r = \sqrt{\dfrac{t^2}{t^2 + df}}$
Two-Sample *t*	$(\bar{X}_1 - \bar{X}_2)$	$d = [(\bar{X}_1 - \bar{X}_2)/S_{(pooled)}]$ $d = t\sqrt{\dfrac{n_1 + n_2}{n_1 n_2}}$	$r^2 = \eta^2 = \dfrac{t^2}{t^2 + df}$ or $\omega^2 = \dfrac{t^2 - 1}{t^2 + df + 1}$
Dependent Sample *t*	$(\bar{D} - \mu)$	$d = [(\bar{D} - \mu)/S_D]$ $d = \dfrac{2t}{\sqrt{df}}$	
One-Way ANOVA[3]	$(\bar{X}_{largest} - \bar{X}_{smallest})$ or MS_A	$f_{effect} = \dfrac{S_A}{S_e} = \dfrac{\sqrt{MS_A}}{\sqrt{MS_e}}$	$\omega_A^2 = \dfrac{(k-1)(F-1)}{(k-1)(F-1) + kn}$ $r^2 = \eta^2 = \dfrac{F}{F + df_{error}} = \dfrac{SS_A}{SS_{TO}}$

1. Cohen's *d* expresses the raw effect size relative to the standard deviation.

2. The raw effect serves as the numerator for many standard tests for mean differences.

3. *f* is an extension of *d* to ANOVA and multigroup designs and is used to calculate sample size estimates (Cohen, 1988, effect size interpretive guidelines: small = .10; medium = .25; large = .40).

when both variables are dichotomous; and Spearman's rank order correlation coefficient, when both variables are rank ordered, are all common measures of effect size.

Measures of the proportion of variance in the dependent variable that is associated with the independent variable, such as the point-biserial correlation coefficient squared (r^2, n^2, and ω^2), are all used to report effect size. Eta squared and partial eta squared are estimates of the degree of association for the sample. Omega squared, virtually almost always smaller than

eta squared, estimates the degree of association in the population. SPSS displays eta or partial eta squared when the "display effect size" option is selected in the program GLM. A limitation of squared values is that they can obscure the direction of the effect.

Interpreting Effect Size Measures

Table 3 summarizes widely used guidelines proposed by Cohen for the interpretation of effect size in the behavioral and social sciences. Although widely used, these guidelines suffer from a number of limitations. Interpretation of an effect size depends on a number of factors, including the specific research design used, knowledge of the substantive area of study, an appreciation of real-world consequences, and the theoretical importance of the effect. For example, effect sizes for independent and dependent group designs may be difficult to compare, as they control for different sources of bias. A small effect that is easy to implement, does not have adverse consequences or side effects, and requires few resources may provide small but important benefits. Small effects may be important for serious and difficult-to-treat problems. Small effects when applied to an individual may be important when applied to the entire population. For example, following these guidelines, many biomedically useful treatments have very small effects (cf. Salk vaccine and paralytic polio, $r = .01$; and psychotherapy and improvement, $r = .39$). Ultimately, interpretation of the effect size is extrastatistical and based on the knowledge of the field of study. Some argue that because importance is ultimately not a statistical issue, reporting effect size measures serves only to obfuscate further understanding of the results.

Rosnow and Rosenthal have argued that proportion-of-variance measures are prone to misinterpretation and encourage an overly pessimistic interpretation of many "small" but important effects. Instead, they have suggested that researchers report measures of correlation. For example, some suggest that r be interpreted in terms of success rates (e.g., Rosenthal & Rubin's binomial effect size display [BESD]) in the treatment and comparison groups, assuming an overall success rate of 50%. Mathematically, the BESD is a transformation of r to X^2, where success rate = $0.50 \pm {}^r/_2$. For example, the medium effect size $r = .30$ [$r^2 = .09$] converts to a BESD comparison group success rate of .35 and to a treatment group success rate of .65. For an alternative intuitive measure, see Cohen's $U3$, which describes the percentage of scores in the comparison group that was exceeded by the mean score in the treatment group.

Other factors that influence the effect size include the range of treatments studied (increasing the range of treatments generally increases effect size). Almost any violation of the normal model may cloud interpretation. Nonnormality, heterogeneity of variance, low measurement reliability, and the presence of outliers all influence effect size estimation. In short, interpreting effect size and comparing effect sizes across studies requires attention to the specific design features of the various studies and the assumptions underlying the statistical tests. In light of these limitations, Table 4 summarizes perspectives for interpreting effect size measures.

Computer Programs for Calculating Effect Size

Effect Size Calculator is an especially user-friendly shareware program. Effect Size Determination Program is somewhat more comprehensive and designed to facilitate coding for a meta-analysis. Most meta-analysis computer programs calculate one or more effect size measures (e.g., MetaWin).

—*Ward Rodriguez*

See also Significance Level; Type I Error; Type II Error

Table 3 Cohen's Guidelines for Interpreting Effect Size Measures

Effect Size Measure	*Small*	*Medium*	*Large*
Standardized Mean Difference	0.20	0.50	0.80
Correlation Coefficient	0.10	0.30	0.50
Correlation Squared	0.01	0.06	0.14

Further Reading

Anderson, N. H. (2001). *Empirical direction in design and analysis.* Mahwah, NJ: Erlbaum.

Cohen, J. (1988). *Statistical power analysis for the behavioral sciences* (2nd ed.). Hillsdale, NJ: Erlbaum.

Glass, G. V., McGraw, B., & Smith, M. L. (1981). *Meta-analysis in social research.* Beverly Hills, CA: Sage.

Table 4 Perspectives for Interpreting Effect Size Measures

Cohen's Guidelines	d	r	r²	Percentile Standing	Percent Nonoverlap Control vs. Treatment
	2	0.707	0.5	97.7	81.10%
	1.9	0.689	0.474	97.1	79.40%
	1.8	0.669	0.448	96.4	77.40%
	1.7	0.648	0.419	95.5	75.40%
	1.6	0.625	0.39	94.5	73.10%
	1.5	0.6	0.36	93.3	70.70%
	1.4	0.573	0.329	91.9	68.10%
	1.3	0.545	0.297	90	65.30%
	1.2	0.514	0.265	88	62.20%
	1.1	0.482	0.232	86	58.90%
	1	0.447	0.2	84	55.40%
	0.9	0.401	0.168	82	51.60%
Large	0.8	0.371	0.138	79	47.40%
	0.7	0.33	0.109	76	43.00%
	0.6	0.287	0.083	73	38.20%
Medium	0.5	0.243	0.059	69	33.00%
	0.4	0.196	0.038	66	27.40%
	0.3	0.148	0.022	62	21.30%
Small	0.2	0.1	0.01	58	14.70%
	0.1	0.05	0.002	54	7.70%
	0	0	0	50	0%

Grissom, R. J., & Kim, J. J. (2005). *Effect sizes for research: A broad practical approach.* Hillsdale, NJ: Erlbaum.

Olejnik, S., & Algina, J. (2000). Measures of effect size for comparative studies: Applications, interpretations, and limitations. *Contemporary Educational Psychology, 25,* 241–286.

Rosenthal, R. (1991). *Meta-analytic procedures for social research.* Newbury Park, CA: Sage.

Rosenthal, R. (1994). Parametric measures of effect size. In H. Cooper & L. V. Hedges (Eds.), *The handbook of research synthesis* (pp. 231–244). New York: Russell Sage Foundation.

Wolf, F. M. (1986). Meta-analysis: *Quantitative methods for research synthesis.* Beverly Hills, CA: Sage.

EIGENDECOMPOSITION

Eigenvectors and *eigenvalues* are numbers and vectors associated with square matrices, and together they provide the *eigendecomposition* of a matrix, which analyzes the structure of this matrix. Even though the eigendecomposition does not exist for all square matrices, it has a particularly simple expression for a class of matrices often used in multivariate analysis, such as correlation, covariance, or cross-product matrices. The eigendecomposition of this type of matrices is important in statistics because it is used to find the maximum (or minimum) of functions involving these matrices. For example, principal component analysis is obtained from the eigendecomposition of a covariance matrix and gives the least square estimate of the original data matrix.

Eigenvectors and eigenvalues are also referred to as *characteristic vectors and latent roots* or *characteristic equation* (in German, *eigen* means "specific to" or "characteristic of"). The set of eigenvalues of a matrix is also called its *spectrum.*

Notations and Definition

There are several ways to define eigenvectors and eigenvalues. The most common approach defines an eigenvector of the matrix **A** as a vector **u** that satisfies the following equation:

$$\mathbf{Au} = \lambda\mathbf{u}. \tag{1}$$

When rewritten, the equation becomes

$$(\mathbf{A} - \lambda\mathbf{I})\mathbf{u} = \mathbf{0}, \tag{2}$$

where λ is a scalar called the eigenvalue associated to the eigenvector.

In a similar manner, a vector **u** is an eigenvector of a matrix **A** if the length of the vector (but not its direction) is changed when it is multiplied by **A**. For example, the matrix

$$\mathbf{A} = \begin{bmatrix} 2 & 3 \\ 2 & 1 \end{bmatrix} \tag{3}$$

has the eigenvectors

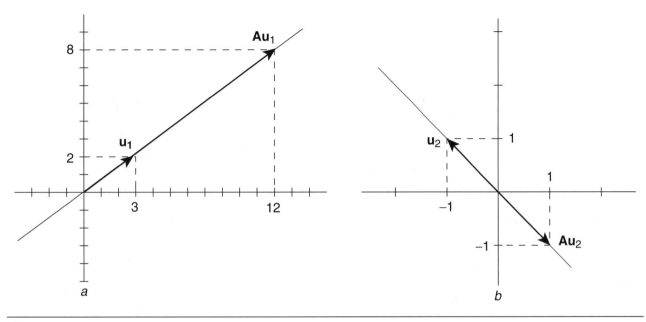

Figure 1   Two Eigenvectors of a Matrix

$$\mathbf{u}_1 = \begin{bmatrix} 3 \\ 2 \end{bmatrix} \qquad \text{with eigenvalue } \lambda_1 = 4 \qquad (4)$$

and

$$\mathbf{u}_2 = \begin{bmatrix} -1 \\ 1 \end{bmatrix} \qquad \text{with eigenvalue } \lambda_2 = -1. \qquad (5)$$

We can verify (as illustrated in Figure 1) that only the lengths of $\mathbf{u}_1$ and $\mathbf{u}_2$ are changed when one of these two vectors is multiplied by the matrix $\mathbf{A}$:

$$\begin{bmatrix} 2 & 3 \\ 2 & 1 \end{bmatrix} \begin{bmatrix} 3 \\ 2 \end{bmatrix} = 4 \begin{bmatrix} 3 \\ 2 \end{bmatrix} = \begin{bmatrix} 12 \\ 8 \end{bmatrix} \qquad (6)$$

and

$$\begin{bmatrix} 2 & 3 \\ 2 & 1 \end{bmatrix} \begin{bmatrix} -1 \\ 1 \end{bmatrix} = -1 \begin{bmatrix} -1 \\ 1 \end{bmatrix} = \begin{bmatrix} 1 \\ -1 \end{bmatrix}. \qquad (7)$$

For most applications, we normalize the eigenvectors (i.e., transform them so that their length is equal to one):

$$\mathbf{u}^{\mathrm{T}}\mathbf{u} = 1. \qquad (8)$$

For the previous example, we obtain

$$\mathbf{u}_1 = \begin{bmatrix} .8331 \\ .5547 \end{bmatrix}. \qquad (9)$$

We can check that

$$\begin{bmatrix} 2 & 3 \\ 2 & 1 \end{bmatrix} \begin{bmatrix} .8331 \\ .5547 \end{bmatrix} = \begin{bmatrix} 3.3284 \\ 2.2188 \end{bmatrix} = 4 \begin{bmatrix} .8331 \\ .5547 \end{bmatrix} \qquad (10)$$

and

$$\begin{bmatrix} 2 & 3 \\ 2 & 1 \end{bmatrix} \begin{bmatrix} -.7071 \\ .7071 \end{bmatrix} = \begin{bmatrix} .7071 \\ -.7071 \end{bmatrix} = -1 \begin{bmatrix} -.7071 \\ .7071 \end{bmatrix}. \qquad (11)$$

Traditionally, we put together the set of eigenvectors of $\mathbf{A}$ in a matrix denoted $\mathbf{U}$. Each column of $\mathbf{U}$ is an eigenvector of $\mathbf{A}$. The eigenvalues are stored in a diagonal matrix (denoted $\mathbf{\Lambda}$), where the diagonal elements give the eigenvalues (and all the other values are zeros). The first equation can be rewritten as follows:

$$\mathbf{AU} = \mathbf{\Lambda U}; \qquad (12)$$

or also as

$$\mathbf{A} = \mathbf{U\Lambda U}^{-1}. \qquad (13)$$

For the previous example, we obtain

$$\mathbf{A} = \mathbf{U \Lambda U}^{-1}$$

$$= \begin{bmatrix} 3 & -1 \\ 2 & 1 \end{bmatrix} \begin{bmatrix} 4 & 0 \\ 0 & -1 \end{bmatrix} \begin{bmatrix} 2 & 2 \\ -4 & 6 \end{bmatrix} \qquad (14)$$

$$= \begin{bmatrix} 2 & 3 \\ 2 & 1 \end{bmatrix}.$$

It is important to note that not all matrices have eigenvalues. For example, the matrix $\begin{bmatrix} 0 & 1 \\ 0 & 0 \end{bmatrix}$ does not have eigenvalues. Even when a matrix has eigenvalues and eigenvectors, the computation of the eigenvectors and eigenvalues of a matrix requires a large number of computations and is therefore better performed by computers.

Digression: An Infinity of Eigenvectors for One Eigenvalue

It is only through a slight abuse of language that we can talk about *the* eigenvector associated with *one* given eigenvalue. Strictly speaking, there is an *infinity* of eigenvectors associated with each eigenvalue of a matrix. Because any scalar multiple of an eigenvector is still an eigenvector, there is, in fact, an (infinite) family of eigenvectors for each eigenvalue, but they are all proportional to each other. For example,

$$\begin{bmatrix} 1 \\ -1 \end{bmatrix} \qquad (15)$$

is an eigenvector of the matrix $\mathbf{A}$

$$\begin{bmatrix} 2 & 3 \\ 2 & 1 \end{bmatrix}. \qquad (16)$$

Therefore,

$$2 \times \begin{bmatrix} 1 \\ -1 \end{bmatrix} = \begin{bmatrix} 2 \\ -2 \end{bmatrix} \qquad (17)$$

is also an eigenvector of $\mathbf{A}$:

$$\begin{bmatrix} 2 & 3 \\ 2 & 1 \end{bmatrix} \begin{bmatrix} 2 \\ -2 \end{bmatrix} = \begin{bmatrix} -2 \\ 2 \end{bmatrix} = -1 \times 2 \begin{bmatrix} 1 \\ -1 \end{bmatrix}. \qquad (18)$$

Positive (Semi-) Definite Matrices

A type of matrices used very often in statistics is called *positive semi-definite*. The eigendecomposition of these matrices always exists and has a particularly convenient form. A matrix is said to be positive semi-definite when it can be obtained as the product of a matrix by its transpose. This implies that a positive semi-definite matrix is always symmetric. So, formally, the matrix $\mathbf{A}$ is positive semi-definite if it can be obtained as

$$\mathbf{A} = \mathbf{X X}^{\mathrm{T}} \qquad (19)$$

for a certain matrix $\mathbf{X}$ (containing real numbers). Positive semi-definite matrices of special relevance for multivariate analysis include correlation matrices, covariance matrices, and cross-product matrices.

The important properties of a positive semi-definite matrix are that its eigenvalues are always positive or null and that its eigenvectors are pairwise orthogonal when their eigenvalues are different. The eigenvectors are also composed of real values (these last two properties are a consequence of the symmetry of the matrix). Because eigenvectors corresponding to different eigenvalues are orthogonal, it is possible to store all the eigenvectors in an *orthogonal matrix* (recall that a matrix is orthogonal when the product of this matrix by its transpose is a diagonal matrix).

This implies the following equality:

$$\mathbf{U}^{-1} = \mathbf{U}^{\mathrm{T}}. \qquad (20)$$

We can, therefore, express the positive semi-definite matrix $\mathbf{A}$ as

$$\mathbf{A} = \mathbf{U \Lambda U}^{\mathrm{T}}, \qquad (21)$$

where $\mathbf{U}^{\mathrm{T}} \mathbf{U} = \mathbf{I}$ are the normalized eigenvectors; if they are not normalized, then $\mathbf{U}^{\mathrm{T}} \mathbf{U}$ is a diagonal matrix.

For example, the matrix

$$\mathbf{A} = \begin{bmatrix} 3 & 1 \\ 1 & 3 \end{bmatrix} \qquad (22)$$

can be decomposed as

$$\mathbf{A} = \mathbf{U}\boldsymbol{\Lambda}\mathbf{U}^{\mathrm{T}}$$

$$= \begin{bmatrix} \sqrt{\frac{1}{2}} & \sqrt{\frac{1}{2}} \\ \sqrt{\frac{1}{2}} & -\sqrt{\frac{1}{2}} \end{bmatrix} \begin{bmatrix} 4 & 0 \\ 0 & 2 \end{bmatrix} \begin{bmatrix} \sqrt{\frac{1}{2}} & \sqrt{\frac{1}{2}} \\ \sqrt{\frac{1}{2}} & -\sqrt{\frac{1}{2}} \end{bmatrix} \qquad (23)$$

$$= \begin{bmatrix} 3 & 1 \\ 1 & 3 \end{bmatrix},$$

with

$$\begin{bmatrix} \sqrt{\frac{1}{2}} & \sqrt{\frac{1}{2}} \\ \sqrt{\frac{1}{2}} & -\sqrt{\frac{1}{2}} \end{bmatrix} \begin{bmatrix} \sqrt{\frac{1}{2}} & \sqrt{\frac{1}{2}} \\ \sqrt{\frac{1}{2}} & -\sqrt{\frac{1}{2}} \end{bmatrix} = \begin{bmatrix} 1 & 0 \\ 0 & 1 \end{bmatrix}. \qquad (24)$$

Diagonalization

When a matrix is positive semi-definite, Equation 21 can be rewritten as follows:

$$\mathbf{A} = \mathbf{U}\boldsymbol{\Lambda}\mathbf{U}^{\mathrm{T}} \iff \boldsymbol{\Lambda} = \mathbf{U}^{\mathrm{T}}\mathbf{A}\mathbf{U}. \qquad (25)$$

This shows that we can transform the matrix $\mathbf{A}$ into an equivalent *diagonal matrix*. As a consequence, the eigendecomposition of a positive semi-definite matrix is often referred to as its *diagonalization*.

Another Definition for Positive Semi-Definite Matrices

A matrix $\mathbf{A}$ is said to be positive semi-definite if we observe the following relationship for any nonzero vector $\mathbf{x}$:

$$\mathbf{x}^{\mathrm{T}}\mathbf{A}\mathbf{x} \geq 0 \quad \forall \mathbf{x} \qquad (26)$$

(when the relationship is ≤ 0, the matrix is *negative semi-definite*).

When all the eigenvalues of a symmetric matrix are positive, the matrix is *positive definite*. In that case, Equation 26 becomes

$$\mathbf{x}^{\mathrm{T}}\mathbf{A}\mathbf{x} > 0 \quad \forall \mathbf{x}. \qquad (27)$$

Trace, Determinant, and Rank

The eigenvalues of a matrix are closely related to three important numbers associated to a square matrix, namely its trace, determinant, and rank.

Trace

The *trace* of a matrix $\mathbf{A}$ is denoted trace$\{\mathbf{A}\}$ and is equal to the sum of its diagonal elements. For example, with the matrix

$$\mathbf{A} = \begin{bmatrix} 1 & 2 & 3 \\ 4 & 5 & 6 \\ 7 & 8 & 9 \end{bmatrix}, \qquad (28)$$

we obtain

$$\text{trace}\{\mathbf{A}\} = 1 + 5 + 9 = 5. \qquad (29)$$

The trace of a matrix is also equal to the sum of its eigenvalues,

$$\text{trace}\{\mathbf{A}\} = \sum_{\ell} \lambda_{\ell} = \text{trace}\{\boldsymbol{\Lambda}\}, \qquad (30)$$

with $\boldsymbol{\Lambda}$ being the matrix of the eigenvalues of $\mathbf{A}$. For the previous example,

$$\boldsymbol{\Lambda} = \text{diag}\{16.1168, -1.1168, 0\}. \qquad (31)$$

We can verify that

$$\text{trace}\{\mathbf{A}\} = \sum_{\ell} \lambda_{\ell} = 16.1168 + (-1.1168) = 15. \qquad (32)$$

Determinant and Rank

Another classic quantity associated to a square matrix is its *determinant*. This concept of determinant, which was originally defined as a combinatoric notion, plays an important role in computing the inverse of a matrix and in finding the solution of systems of linear equations (the term *determinant* is used because this quantity determines the existence of a solution in systems of linear equations). The determinant of a matrix is also equal to the product of its eigenvalues. Formally, if |**A**| is the determinant of **A**,

$$|\mathbf{A}| = \prod_\ell \lambda_\ell \text{ with } \lambda_\ell \text{ being the } \ell\text{-th eigenvalue of } \mathbf{A}. \tag{33}$$

For example, the determinant of matrix **A** (from the previous section) is equal to

$$|\mathbf{A}| = 16.1168 \times -1.1168 \times 0 = 0. \tag{34}$$

Finally, the *rank* of a matrix can be defined as being the number of nonzero eigenvalues of the matrix. In this example,

$$\text{rank}\{\mathbf{A}\} = 2. \tag{35}$$

For a positive semi-definite matrix, the rank corresponds to the dimensionality of the Euclidean space, which can be used to represent the matrix. A matrix whose rank is equal to its dimensions is called *full rank*. When the rank of a matrix is smaller than its dimensions, the matrix is called *rank-deficient, singular,* or *multicollinear.* Only full-rank matrices have an inverse.

Statistical Properties of the Eigendecomposition

The eigendecomposition is important because it is involved in problems of optimization. For example, in principal component analysis, we want to analyze an $I \times J$ matrix **X**, where the rows are observations and the columns are variables describing these observations. The goal of the analysis is to find row *factor scores,* such that these factor scores "explain" as much of the variance of **X** as possible and the sets of factor scores are pairwise orthogonal. This amounts to defining the factor score matrix as

$$\mathbf{F} = \mathbf{XP}, \tag{36}$$

under the constraints that

$$\mathbf{F}^{\mathrm{T}}\mathbf{F} = \mathbf{P}^{\mathrm{T}}\mathbf{X}^{\mathrm{T}}\mathbf{XP} \tag{37}$$

is a diagonal matrix (i.e., **F** is an orthogonal matrix) and that

$$\mathbf{P}^{\mathrm{T}}\mathbf{P} = \mathbf{I} \tag{38}$$

(i.e., **P** is an orthonormal matrix). There are several ways of obtaining the solution to this problem. One possible approach is to use the technique of Lagrangian multipliers, where the constraint from Equation 38 is expressed as multiplication by a diagonal matrix of Lagrangian multipliers, denoted **Λ**, in order to give the following expression:

$$\mathbf{\Lambda}(\mathbf{P}^{\mathrm{T}}\mathbf{P} - \mathbf{I}). \tag{39}$$

This amounts to defining the following equation:

$$\mathcal{L} = \mathbf{F}^{\mathrm{T}}\mathbf{F} - \mathbf{\Lambda}(\mathbf{P}^{\mathrm{T}}\mathbf{P} - \mathbf{I}) = \mathbf{P}^{\mathrm{T}}\mathbf{X}^{\mathrm{T}}\mathbf{XP} - \mathbf{\Lambda}(\mathbf{P}^{\mathrm{T}}\mathbf{P} - \mathbf{I}). \tag{40}$$

To find the values of **P** that give the maximum values of $\mathcal{L}$, we first compute the derivative of $\mathcal{L}$ relative to **P**,

$$\frac{\partial \mathcal{L}}{\partial \mathbf{P}} = 2\mathbf{X}^{\mathrm{T}}\mathbf{XP} - 2\mathbf{\Lambda P}, \tag{41}$$

and then set this derivative to zero:

$$\mathbf{X}^{\mathrm{T}}\mathbf{XP} - \mathbf{\Lambda P} = 0 \iff \mathbf{X}^{\mathrm{T}}\mathbf{XP} = \mathbf{\Lambda P}. \tag{42}$$

Because **Λ** is diagonal, this is clearly an eigendecomposition problem, and this indicates that **Λ** is the matrix of eigenvalues of the positive semi-definite matrix $\mathbf{X}^{\mathrm{T}}\mathbf{X}$ ordered from the largest to the smallest and that **P** is the matrix of eigenvectors of $\mathbf{X}^{\mathrm{T}}\mathbf{X}$ associated to **Λ**. Finally, we find that the factor matrix has the form

$$\mathbf{F} = \mathbf{P\Lambda}^{\frac{1}{2}}. \tag{43}$$

The variance of the factor scores is equal to the eigenvalues

$$\mathbf{F}^{\mathrm{T}}\mathbf{F} = \mathbf{\Lambda}^{\frac{1}{2}}\mathbf{P}^{\mathrm{T}}\mathbf{P}\mathbf{\Lambda}^{\frac{1}{2}} = \mathbf{\Lambda}. \tag{44}$$

Taking into account that the sum of the eigenvalues is equal to the trace of $\mathbf{X}^{\mathrm{T}}\mathbf{X}$, this shows that the first factor scores "extract" as much of the variance of the original data as possible, that the second factor scores extract as much of the variance left unexplained by the first factor, and so on for the remaining factors. Incidentally, the diagonal elements of the matrix $\mathbf{\Lambda}^{\frac{1}{2}}$ that are the standard deviations of the factor scores are called the *singular values* of matrix $\mathbf{X}$.

—Hervé Abdi

See also Correspondence Analysis; Discriminant Analysis; DISTATIS; Eigenvalues; Exploratory Factor Analysis; Factor Analysis; Metric Multidimensional Scaling; Multiple Correspondence Analysis; Multiple Factor Analysis; Multivariate Analysis of Variance (MANOVA); Partial Least Square Regression; Principal Component Analysis; Singular and Generalized Singular Value Decomposition; STATIS

Further Reading

Abdi, H. (2004). Multivariate analysis. In M. Lewis-Beck, A. Bryman, & T. F. Liao (Eds.), *The SAGE encyclopedia of social science research methods*. Thousand Oaks, CA: Sage.

Abdi, H., & Valentin, D. (2006). *Mathématiques pour les sciences cognitives* [Mathematics for cognitive sciences]. Grenoble, France: Presses Universitaires de Grenoble.

Harris, R. (2001). *A primer of multivariate statistics*. Mahwah, NJ: Erlbaum.

Strang, G. (2003). *Introduction to linear algebra*. Wellesley, MA: Wellesley-Cambridge Press.

EIGENVALUES

Given a real (or complex) $p \times p$ matrix, $\mathbf{A}$, for what vectors, $\mathbf{x}_{p \times 1} \neq \mathbf{0}_{p \times 1}$, and for what scalars, λ, is it true that

$$\mathbf{A}\mathbf{x} = \lambda\mathbf{x} ? \tag{1}$$

A nonzero vector satisfying the above equality is called an *eigenvector* (also characteristic vector or latent root) of $\mathbf{A}$, and the associated value, λ, is called an *eigenvalue* (also characteristic root or latent root) of $\mathbf{A}$. Equation 1 holds if and only if

$$(\mathbf{A} - \lambda\mathbf{I})\mathbf{x} = \mathbf{0}, \tag{2}$$

where $\mathbf{I}$ is the $p \times p$ identity matrix. This equation represents a system of p equations in p unknowns, which has a unique solution if and only if

$$\det(\mathbf{A} - \lambda\mathbf{I}) = \mathbf{0}, \tag{3}$$

where Equation 3 is called the *characteristic equation*. Thus, a square matrix of full rank will have p-unique (i.e., different) eigenvalues λ_i, with associated eigenvectors (normalized to have unit length) $\mathbf{e}_i$. Furthermore, the set of p eigenvectors of order $p \times 1$ are all mutually orthogonal. If $\mathbf{A}$ is not of full rank, then some of the eigenvalues will be redundant and equal zero.

In the social and behavioral sciences, the eigenvalues that researchers are usually most interested in are those of the variance-covariance matrix, $\mathbf{\Sigma}$. Although, in the absence of redundant variables, it is uncommon to observe eigenvalues equal to zero, it is often the case that some of the eigenvalues of $\mathbf{\Sigma}$ will be close to zero. Ordering the eigenvalues from largest to smallest,

$$\lambda_1 \geq \lambda_2 \geq \ldots \geq \lambda_p,$$

a primary interest is reducing the variable space from p dimensions to k dimensions, where k is some dimensionality that retains an adequate amount of the variability present in the original dimensionality. Furthermore, the original $n \times p$ data matrix, $\mathbf{X}$, is reduced to k-dimensional space by the operation $\mathbf{X}_{n \times p} \mathbf{e}^{\mathrm{T}}_{p \times k} = \mathbf{X}^*_{n \times k}$. Thus, the k-transformed variables in $\mathbf{X}^*$ are each a linear combination of the original p variables. Finally, since all eigenvectors are orthogonal, the transformed variables in $\mathbf{X}^*$ are uncorrelated.

To understand the relevance of the data reduction process, it is important to realize the following two results:

$$tr(\mathbf{\Sigma}) = \sum_{i=1}^{p} \Sigma_{ii} = \sum_{i=1}^{p} \lambda_i$$

and

$$\mathbf{\Sigma} = \lambda_1 \mathbf{e}_1 \mathbf{e}_1' + \lambda_2 \mathbf{e}_2 \mathbf{e}_2' + \ldots + \lambda_p \mathbf{e}_p \mathbf{e}_p'.$$

The first result indicates that the larger eigenvalues account for more of the variance in the p-dimensional space, while the second result indicates that the original variance-covariance matrix, $\mathbf{\Sigma}$, can be represented as a sum of p matrices all of size $p \times p$ (this decomposition is known as the *spectral decomposition*). Popular techniques such as principal components analysis and some types of factor analysis (which often include rotation of the eigenvectors to introduce interpretability and/or correlation into the reduced dimensionality) reduce the number of dimensions from p to k such that an adequate percentage of variance,

$$\frac{\sum_{i=1}^{k}\lambda_i}{tr(\Sigma)},$$

is explained. Some other multivariate techniques relying on eigenvalues and eigenvectors are canonical correlation, cluster analysis (some types), correspondence analysis, multiple discriminant analysis, and multivariate analysis of variance.

—*Douglas Steinley*

See also Factor Analysis; Multiple Factor Analysis

Further Reading

Carroll, J. D., & Green, P. E. (1997). *Mathematical tools for applied multivariate analysis.* San Diego, CA: Academic Press.

Johnson, R. A., & Wichern, D. W. (2002). *Applied multivariate statistical analysis* (5th ed.). Upper Saddle River, NJ: Prentice Hall.

Leon, S. J. (1998). *Linear algebra with applications* (5th ed.). Upper Saddle River, NJ: Prentice Hall.

EM ALGORITHM

One central goal of statistical inference is to estimate parameters of a model. In a typical statistical analysis, a likelihood function, $L(\text{data};\theta)$, is used to describe the relationship between the data and some unknown parameters θ that control the behavior of the data. A good estimate of θ is a value that maximizes the likelihood function, for example, the "most likely" value supported by the data. This estimate is called the *maximum likelihood estimate* (MLE). In some cases, we can find the MLEs analytically. But more often, we need to use numerical methods. The EM algorithm is one of the numerical techniques for this purpose.

The *EM algorithm* is an iterative algorithm for finding the MLEs of the parameters when the data are incomplete. The term *incomplete* refers to two situations: The first occurs when some of the data are *missing,* due to difficulties in data collection process for example. The second situation occurs when the direct optimization of the likelihood function is difficult but when *latent* parameters are added, the problem becomes more tractable.

Although the two situations might sound different in description, from a statistical point of view, they are similar and share the same features. First, a complete data set is divided into an "observed" part and an "unobserved" part. The unobserved part can be either missing or latent. Second, direct optimization of the likelihood function based on the observed data might be difficult, but it becomes manageable with the likelihood function based on the complete data. The EM algorithm provides a bridge to find the MLEs of the observed data using the complete data likelihood.

EM stands for *expectation* and *maximization.* They are the two essential steps in the algorithm: the expectation step (E-step) and the maximization step (M-step). The intuition of the EM algorithm is simple: We first guess the unobserved values using their expected values (E-step) and then pretend the guessed values were observed a priori and proceed to estimate the parameters based on the complete data (M-step). Because the M-step provides us with new estimates of the parameters, we again guess the unobserved values based on these new estimates. This iterative process is repeated until convergence; for example, two consecutive estimates of the parameters yield very close values.

This idea had been widely adapted in various disciplines for a long period of time, although the most frequent citation of the EM algorithm was made by Dempster, Laird, and Rubin in 1977. They provided a rigorous framework to implement this idea: That is, the correct procedure is not to impute the individual unobserved observations, but instead the complete data sufficient statistics, or more generally the (log) likelihood function itself, by the conditional expectation given the observed data. There had also been many similar formulations of the same idea prior to this paper.

The formulation of the EM algorithm is as follows. Let Y_{obs} and Y_{unobs} be the observed and unobserved data, respectively. The observed data likelihood is $L(Y_{obs};\theta)$, and the complete data likelihood is

$L(Y_{\text{obs}}, Y_{\text{unobs}}; \theta)$. The EM algorithm obtains $\hat{\theta}$ for $L(Y_{\text{obs}}; \theta)$ via the following steps:

1. Take an initial guess of the parameter values $\theta^{(t)}$, with $t = 0$.

2. E-step: Compute the conditional expected value of the log of the complete data likelihood, log $L(Y_{\text{obs}}, Y_{\text{unobs}}; \theta)$, given the observed data Y_{obs}, assuming $\theta = \theta^{(t)}$:

$$Q\left(\theta; \theta^{(t)}\right) = E[\log L(Y_{\text{obs}}, Y_{\text{unobs}}; \theta) | Y_{\text{obs}}; \quad (1)$$
$$\theta = \theta^{(t)}].$$

The expectation is calculated based on the density

$$f\left(Y_{\text{unobs}} | Y_{\text{obs}}, \theta = \theta^{(t)}\right).$$

3. M-step: Determine a new value $\theta^{(t+1)}$ that maximizes $Q(\theta; \theta^{(t)})$.

Repeat Steps 1 and 2 until $\|\theta^{(t+1)} - \theta^{(t)}\| \leq \varepsilon$, where ε is a certain predetermined precision value and $\|\cdot\|$ represents a certain distance measure (for example, it can be the Euclidean distance, or maximum absolute difference between two vectors, if θ is high dimensional). Once this criterion is satisfied, the EM algorithm has converged.

The EM algorithm results in a sequence of $\theta^{(t)}$ that always increases the values of the likelihood function, $L\left(Y_{\text{obs}}; \theta^{(t+1)}\right) \geq L\left(Y_{\text{obs}}; \theta^{(t)}\right)$. Verification of this is beyond the scope of this entry. References can be found in many standard textbooks.

In practice, this monotonicity property implies that an EM algorithm can converge only to a local maximum of the observed likelihood function. Therefore, it is essential to either choose a good starting value for $\theta^{(0)}$ or, if that is not possible, repeat the algorithm a number of times with starting points that are far apart. This would safeguard against the possibility of reaching only a local maximum estimate.

We illustrate the algorithm using a simple example adopted from Rao, from 1973. Suppose that the complete data have five data points, y_1, y_2, y_3, y_4, y_5, and the data have a multivariate distribution with probabilities

$$\left(\frac{1}{2}, \frac{\theta}{4}, \frac{1-\theta}{4}, \frac{1-\theta}{4}, \frac{\theta}{4}\right),$$

where $0 \leq \theta \leq 1$. The complete data likelihood function is

$$L\left(Y_{\text{obs}}, Y_{\text{unobs}}; \theta\right)$$
$$= \frac{N!}{\prod_{i=1}^{5} y_i!} \left(\frac{1}{2}\right)^{y_1} \left(\frac{\theta}{4}\right)^{y_2} \quad (2)$$
$$\left(\frac{1-\theta}{4}\right)^{y_3} \left(\frac{1-\theta}{4}\right)^{y_4} \left(\frac{\theta}{4}\right)^{y_5},$$

where

$$N = \sum_{i=1}^{5} y_i.$$

This is a straightforward estimation problem if all the data points are available. We can obtain the MLE of θ using Equation 2 by first taking the derivative with respect to θ:

$$\frac{\partial L(Y_{\text{obs}}, Y_{\text{unobs}}; \theta)}{\partial \theta} = \frac{(y_2 + y_5)}{\theta} - \frac{(y_3 + y_4)}{1 - \theta}. \quad (3)$$

Setting Equation 3 to zero, we obtain a solution for θ:

$$\frac{y_2 + y_5}{y_2 + y_3 + y_4 + y_5}. \quad (4)$$

However, suppose that instead of five data points, we observe only four counts: $Y_{\text{obs}} = (y_1 + y_2, y_3, y_4, y_5,) = (125, 18, 20, 34)$. The data point y_1 (or y_2) is not observed directly. Based on these four data points, we have an observed data likelihood function $L(Y_{\text{obs}}; \theta)$:

$$L(Y_{\text{obs}}; \theta) \propto \left(\frac{1}{2} + \frac{\theta}{4}\right)^{y_1 + y_2} \left(\frac{1-\theta}{4}\right)^{y_3}$$
$$\left(\frac{1-\theta}{4}\right)^{y_4} \left(\frac{\theta}{4}\right)^{y_5}. \quad (5)$$

We can still obtain the MLE of θ using Equation 5 by taking the derivative

$$\frac{\partial L(Y_{obs}; \theta)}{\partial \theta} = \frac{y_1 + y_2}{2 + \theta} + \frac{y_5}{\theta} - \frac{y_3 + y_4}{1 - \theta}, \quad (6)$$

setting it to zero, and solving for θ. However, instead of working with a linear function based on Equation 3, we now have a quadratic function in θ that is more difficult to obtain an answer to:

$$(y_1 + y_2)\theta(1 - \theta) + y_5(2 + \theta)(1 - \theta) - (y_3 + y_4)\,\theta(2 + \theta) = 0. \quad (7)$$

Here is a situation where it is easier to optimize $L(Y_{obs}, Y_{unobs}; \theta)$, Equation 2, than $L(Y_{obs}; \theta)$, Equation 5. And this calls for the use of the EM algorithm.

The E-step works as follows. By Equation 1, given the observed $Y_{obs} = \{y_1 + y_2 = 125, y_3 = 18, y_4 = 20, y_5 = 34\}$ and $\theta^{(t)}$, we have

$$Q(\theta; \theta^{(t)})$$

$$= E\left(\log L(Y_{obs}, Y_{unobs}; \theta)|Y_{obs}; \theta = \theta^{(t)}\right)$$

$$= E\left\{C + y_2 \log\left(\frac{\theta}{4}\right) + (y_3 + y_4) \log\left(\frac{1 - \theta}{4}\right)\right.$$

$$\left. + y_5 \log\left(\frac{\theta}{4}\right) |Y_{obs}; \theta = \theta^{(t)}\right\}$$

$$= C + E\left(y_2|y_1 + y_2 = 125; \theta = \theta^{(t)}\right) \log\left(\frac{\theta}{4}\right)$$

$$+ E\left(y_3 + y_4|y_3 = 18, y_4 = 20\right) \log\left(\frac{1 - \theta}{4}\right) \quad (8)$$

$$+ E\left(y_5|y_5 = 34\right) \log\left(\frac{\theta}{4}\right)$$

$$= C + 125 \times \frac{\theta^{(t)}/4}{1/2 + \theta^{(t)}/4} \log\left(\frac{\theta}{4}\right)$$

$$+ 38 \times \log\left(\frac{1 - \theta}{4}\right) + 34 \times \log\left(\frac{\theta}{4}\right).$$

C represents a constant term in $Q(\theta; \theta^{(t)})$ that is independent of the parameter. Note the distribution of y_2 given that $y_1 + y_2 = 125$ follows a binomial $(125, \frac{\theta/4}{1/2 + \theta/4})$. (That is, a binomial distribution with 125 number of trials and the "success" probability being $\frac{\theta/4}{1/2 + \theta/4}$). Hence,

$$E\left(y_2|y_1 + y_2 = 125; \theta = \theta^{(t)}\right)$$

$$= 125 \times \frac{\theta^{(t)}/4}{1/2 + \theta^{(t)}/4}.$$

The M-step is also easy. Using the same technique as we used to find the MLE based on the complete data likelihood (Equations 3 and 4), the maximum of Equation 8 can be found at

$$\theta^{(t+1)} = \frac{125 \times \dfrac{\theta^{(t)}/4}{1/2 + \theta^{(t)}/4} + 34}{125 \times \dfrac{\theta^{(t)}/4}{1/2 + \theta^{(t)}/4} + 72}.$$

We initialized the EM algorithm with a starting value of $\theta^{(0)} = 0.5$ and used a stopping criterion of $|\theta^{(t+1)} - \theta^{(t)}| < 10^{-8}$. Table 1 lists iteration numbers, estimated values of $\theta^{(t)}$, and stepwise differences. The stopping criterion is satisfied after 10 iterations, with $\hat{\theta} = 0.62682150$. Different starting values of $\theta^{(0)}$ do not change the result.

Analytical solution of Equation 7 yields an MLE of θ that is very close to the EM estimate:

$$\hat{\theta} = \frac{15 + \sqrt{15^2 + 4 \times 197 \times 68}}{2 \times 197} \approx 0.6268215.$$

Currently, there is no software that implements the EM algorithm for a general problem, and almost

Table 1   Estimated Values of θ in the EM Iterations

t	$\theta^{(t)}$	$|\theta^{(t)} - \theta^{(t-1)}|$
0	0.50000000	—
1	0.60824742	0.1082474
2	0.62432105	0.01607363
3	0.62648888	0.002167829
4	0.62677732	0.0002884433
5	0.62681563	3.830976e-05
6	0.62682072	5.086909e-06
7	0.62682140	6.754367e-07
8	0.62682142	8.968368e-08
9	0.62682149	1.190809e-08
10	0.62682150	1.581141e-09

every problem requires both tailored implementations and careful personal monitoring (e.g., starting values and convergence). Although some problems can be solved efficiently using high-level but relatively slow statistical languages, such as R or Splus, more complicated problems can potentially take a long time to complete, both in human effort and in computational resources. Various attempts have been proposed to improve the speed of the EM algorithm. One direction involves the direct extension of the original EM algorithm. These approaches include the expectation-conditional maximization (ECM), the expectation-conditional maximization either (ECME), the space-alternating generalized EM algorithm (SAGE), the alternating expectation-conditional maximization (AECM), and the parameter-expanded EM algorithm (PX-EM). Another school of thought for speeding up convergence is to combine EM with various numerical acceleration techniques. These approaches include combining EM with (a) Aitken's acceleration method, (b) Newton-type method, and (c) conjugate-gradient acceleration method.

Finally, the EM algorithm presented in this entry provides us with only an MLE of the parameter. There exist modifications that augment the EM algorithm with some computations to produce the standard errors of the MLEs. The standard errors of the estimates are often estimated via asymptotic theory.

—Jung-Ying Tzeng

See also Inferential Statistics

Further Reading

Dempster, A., Laird, N., & Rubin, D. (1977). Maximum likelihood from incomplete data via the EM algorithm. *Journal of the Royal Statistical Society, Series B, 39,* 1–38.

Fessler, J. A., & Hero, A. O. (1994). Space-alternating generalized expectation-maximization algorithm. *IEEE Transactions on Signal Processing, 4,* 2664–2677.

Jamshidian, M., & Jennrich, R. I. (2000). Standard errors for EM estimation. *Journal of the Royal Statistical Society, Series B, 62,* 257–270.

Lange, K. (1995). A quasi-Newton acceleration of the EM algorithm. *Statistica Sinica, 5,* 1–18.

Liu, C., & Rubin, D. B. (1994). The ECME algorithm: A simple extension of EM and ECM with faster monotone convergence. *Biometrika, 81,* 633–648.

Liu, C., Rubin, D. B., & Wu, Y. (1998). Parameter expansion to accelerate EM: The PX-EM algorithm. *Biometrika 85,* 755–770.

Louis, T. A. (1982). Finding the observed information matrix when using the EM algorithm. *Journal of the Royal Statistical Society, Series B, 44,* 226–233.

McLachlan, G., & Krishnan, T. (1997). *The EM algorithm and extensions* (Wiley Series in Probability and Statistics). New York: Wiley.

Meilijson, I. (1989). A fast improvement of the EM algorithm in its own terms. *Journal of the Royal Statistical Society, Series B, 51,* 127–138.

Meng, X. L., & Rubin, D. B. (1993). Maximum likelihood estimation via the ECM algorithm: A general framework. *Biometrika, 80,* 267–278.

Meng, X. L. & van Dyk, D. (1997). The EM algorithm—An old folk-song sung to a fast new tune. *Journal of the Royal Statistical Society, Series B, 59,* 511–567

Neal, R. M., & Hinton, G. E. (1998). A view of the EM algorithm that justifies incremental, sparse, and other variants. In M. I. Jordan (Ed.), *Learning in graphical models* (pp. 355–368). Cambridge: MIT Press.

Rao, C. R. (1973). *Linear statistical inference and applications.* New York: Wiley.

Tanner, M. (1996). *Tools for statistical inference.* New York: Springer-Verlag.

EMBEDDED FIGURES TEST

The Embedded Figures Test (EFT) is a measure of individual differences in how surrounding fields influence a person's perception (i.e., the ability to avoid the confusion of conflicting perceptual cues). Although the EFT is a cognitive task, its relation to personality is the primary interest. During his research on perception, Witkin noticed that people varied markedly in their abilities to perform on the Rod and Frame Test and in a task judging body orientation in a tilted room. To demonstrate these same perceptual differences in a paper-and-pencil format, Witkin chose materials Gottschaldt used in his studies of the role of past experiences in perception. For these materials, one identifies a simple figure, previously seen, within a larger, more complex figure. Witkin chose 8 of Gottschaldt's simple figures and 24 of his complex figures. Preliminary experiments demonstrated an insufficient number of difficult examples using this material. Using the same principles of patterning to create new figures proved ineffective, so Witkin used coloring to reinforce patterns. This obscured the simple patterns and increased difficulty. The primary goals in the final selection of materials for the EFT were achieving a graded difficulty and containing sufficient variety of simple figures to reduce the potential for practice effects.

The EFT is administered individually and consists of 24 trials, each using different complex figures and never using the same simple figures in 2 successive trials. During each trial, the figures are presented separately in the sequence of complex figure, simple figure, then complex figure. This pattern is used to impress upon the participant the complex figure and discourage the participant from concentrating on the simple figure at its expense, thereby increasing difficulty. The administrator notes the time at which the participant verbally indicates he or she has identified the simple figure and continues timing until the participant successfully traces it within the complex figure. The score is the time at which the participant verbally indicates he or she has identified the simple figure, provided it is confirmed correct. The total score is the summation of the time to complete all trials. Lower scores are considered field independent, and higher scores are considered field dependent.

It has been shown that people are consistent across trials in their abilities to locate simple figures, indicating that personal factors, not the structure of the field alone, are responsible for the individual differences observed. Also, Witkin noted a sex difference, with men outperforming women. There are relationships to other tests, including concept formation tests and intelligence tests, which have generated debate as to whether the EFT is a measure of cognitive ability or cognitive style. Relationships to measures of general intelligence support the ability thesis. Supporting the style thesis, comparisons with the Vigotsky Test show that field dependents are related to those who use the perceptual approach and field independents are related to those who use the conceptual approach.

—*John R. Reddon and Shane M. Whippler*

See also Personality Tests

Further Reading

Witkin, H. A. (1950). Individual differences in ease of perception of embedded figures. *Journal of Personality, 19,* 1–15.

EQUIVALENCE TESTING

An *equivalence test* is a method of hypothesis testing that is a variation of the more commonly used method of significance testing. In *significance testing,* the idea is to test a null hypothesis that two means are equal. Rejecting the null hypothesis leads to the conclusion that the population means are significantly different from each other. *Equivalence testing,* on the other hand, is used to test a null hypothesis that two means are not equal. Rejection of the null hypothesis in an equivalence test leads to the conclusion that the population means are equivalent. The approach of equivalence testing differs from the more familiar hypothesis tests, such as the two-sample *t* test, where rejection of the null is used to infer that the population means are significantly different.

Equivalence testing originated in the fields of biostatistics and pharmacology, where one often wishes to show that two means are "equivalent" within a certain bound. Many researchers often incorrectly conclude that the failure to reject the null hypothesis in a standard hypothesis test (such as a *t* test) is "proof" that the null hypothesis is true and hence that the populations are "equivalent." This erroneous inference neglects the possibility that the failure to reject the null is often merely indicative of a Type II error, particularly when the sample sizes being used are small and the power is low.

We will consider a common equivalence test known as the *two one-sided tests* procedure, or TOST. It is a variation of the standard independent-samples *t* test. With a TOST, the researcher will conclude that the two population means are equivalent if it can be shown that they differ by less than some constant τ, the equivalence bound, in both directions. This bound is often chosen to be the smallest difference between the means that is practically significant. Biostatisticians often have the choice for τ made for them by government regulation.

The null hypothesis for a TOST is H_0:$|\mu_1 - \mu_2| \geq \tau$. The alternative hypothesis is H_1:$|\mu_1 - \mu_2| < \tau$.

The first one-sided test seeks to show that the difference between the two means is less than or equal to $-\tau$. To do so, compute the test statistic

$$t_1 = \frac{\overline{x}_1 - \overline{x}_2 + \tau \overline{x}_2}{s_p \sqrt{1/n_1 + 1/n_2}}$$

where s_p is the pooled standard deviation of the two samples. Then, compute the p value as $p_1 = P(t_1 < t_v)$, where t_v has a t-distribution with $\eta = n_1 + n_2 - 2$ degrees of freedom.

Similarly, the second one-sided test seeks to show that the difference between the two means is greater than or equal to $+\tau$. To do so, compute the test statistic

$$t_2 = \frac{\overline{x}_1 - \overline{x}_2 - \tau \overline{x}_2}{s_p \sqrt{1/n_1 + 1/n_2}} .$$

Compute the p value as $p_2 = P(t_2 > t_v)$. Then let $p = \max(p_1, p_2)$ and reject the null hypothesis of nonequivalence if $p < \alpha$.

Establishing equivalence between two treatments or groups has applications not just in biostatistical and pharmacological settings but also in many situations in the social sciences. Many hypotheses currently tested and interpreted with standard significance testing should be approached with equivalence testing.

—*Christopher J. Mecklin and Nathaniel R. Hirtz*

See also Hypothesis and Hypothesis Testing; Null Hypothesis Significance Testing

Further Reading

Berger, R., & Hsu, J. (1996). Bioequivalence trials, intersection-union tests and equivalence confidence sets. *Statistical Science, 11*, 283–319.

Blair, R. C., & Cole, S. R. (2002). Two-sided equivalence testing of the difference between two means. *Journal of Modern Applied Statistics, 1*, 139–142.

Rogers, J., Howard, K., & Vessey, J. (1993). Using significance tests to evaluate equivalence between two experimental groups. *Psychological Bulletin, 113*, 553–565.

Schuirmann, D. (1981). On hypothesis testing to determine if the mean of the normal distribution is contained in a known interval. *Biometrics, 37*, 617.

Westlake, W. (1979). Statistical aspects of comparative bioequivalence trials. *Biometrics, 35*, 273–280.

Essay Items

Essay items require the test taker to write a coherent and informative response to a question, with the purpose of assessing how well the test taker can organize information and express his or her ideas in writing.

Essay questions can be open-ended (also called unrestricted or extended) questions or closed-ended (also called restricted) questions. An *open-ended essay question* is one in which there are no restrictions on the response, including the amount of time allowed to finish, the number of pages written, or material included. A *closed-ended question* is one in which there are restrictions on a response.

Guidelines for writing an essay question are as follows:

1. Adequate time should be allowed to answer the question. By their very design, essay questions can take a considerable amount of time to answer. Regardless of whether an essay question is closed- or open-ended, the test preparer must know how much time will be allowed, as must the test taker.

2. The essay question needs to be complete and clear.

3. The same essay question should be administered to all test takers. This reduces the burden placed on the developer of the test questions in terms of time needed to create more than one item but also reduces the likelihood that questions on the same topic are of different levels of difficulty.

Advantages and Disadvantages of Using Essay Items

Essay items have several advantages. First, they are the best way of finding out what the test taker knows and also how well the test taker can relate ideas to one another. Second, security is increased, since it is very difficult to plagiarize during an essay item examination. Finally, and this is very important, if the test constructor knows the material well, essay questions can effectively tap higher-order learning.

However, there are disadvantages to essay items as well. First, they emphasize writing and do not necessarily tap the test taker who is knowledgeable about ideas and their relationships to one another but just cannot express this in words. Second, it is difficult for essay questions to adequately sample the entire universe of what the test taker might have learned. Third, essay questions are not easy to score, with even a small number of items and a small number of test takers resulting in a large number of essays to read and grade.

Scoring Essay Items

Scorers should provide plenty of time to score an essay item. Each item has to be read and then scored, and often the scorer reads the items more than once, the first time for a general overview of the content and the second time for a more detailed analysis, including an assessment of content (again) and writing skills (such as grammar, transitions, and sentence usage).

A model of a correct answer should also be used to serve as a basis for comparison. Having a model greatly increases the likelihood that the scorer will evaluate each answer fairly and have as objective a standard as is possible, since the scorer can compare what is there (the test taker's response) to what should be there (the model response).

All items should also be scored across all test takers. The model answer for Question #1, for example, should be used to score Item #1 for all test takers. This allows the scorer not only to make absolute judgments in comparison to the model answer but also to make relative judgments (if necessary) within any one item.

Finally, responses should be graded without knowing the test taker's identity. Since there is a subjective element that can enter into the grading of essay questions, not knowing who the test taker is (and avoiding that possible bias) can be a great help.

— *Neil J. Salkind*

See also Multiple-Choice Items; Standards for Educational and Psychological Testing

Further Reading

Salkind, N. J. (2006). *Tests and measurement for people who (think they) hate tests and measurements.* Thousand Oaks, CA: Sage.

Computer grading of essays: http://www.salon.com/tech/feature/1999/05/25/computer_grading/

Applying Ideas on Statistics and Measurement

The following abstract is adapted from Curren, R. R. (2004). Educational measurement and knowledge of other minds. *Theory and Research in Education, 2*(3), 235–253.

This article addresses the capacity of high-stakes tests to measure the most significant kinds of learning and discusses the value of several different test items, such as multiple choice and essay. It begins by examining a set of philosophical arguments pertaining to construct validity and alleged conceptual obstacles to attributing specific knowledge and skills to learners, and it continues to examine the difficulties involved in combining adequate validity and reliability in one test. The literature on test item formats is discussed as it relates to the potential validity of multiple-choice items, and the rater reliability of constructed-response items (such as **essay items**) is addressed through discussion of the methods used by the Educational Testing Service and a summary report of alternative methods developed by the author.

ESTIMATES OF THE POPULATION MEDIAN

The median (θ), the point on a scale below which 50% of the observations fall, is an ancient but commonly used measure of central tendency or location parameter of a population. The sample median can be written as

$$M_S = (1 - k)X_{(i)} + kX_{(i+1)}, \tag{1}$$

where $i = [(n+1)/2]$ and $k = \{(n + 1)/2\}$ are the whole and decimal portions of the $(n + 1)/2$, respectively.

The sample median, however, suffers from several limitations. First, its sampling distribution is intractable, which precludes straightforward development of an inferential statistic based on a sample median.

Second, the sample median lacks one of the fundamental niceties of any sample statistic. It is not the best unbiased estimate of the population median. Indeed, a potentially infinite number of sample statistics may more closely estimate the population median.

One of the most commonly used competitors of the sample median is the Harrell-Davis estimator, from 1982, which is based on Maritz and Jarrett, from 1978. Let $X = (X_1, \ldots, X_n)$ be a random sample of size n and $\tilde{X} = (X_{(1)}, \ldots, X_{(n)})$ be its order statistics ($X_{(1)} \le \ldots \le X_{(n)}$). The estimator for pth population quantile takes the form of a weighted sum of order statistics with the weights based on incomplete beta function:

$$M_{HD} = \sum_{i=1}^{n} W_{n,i}^{HD} X_{(i)}, \quad (2)$$

where the weights $W_{n,i}^{HD}$ can be expressed as

$$W_{n,i}^{HD} = I_{i/n}((n+1)/2, (n+1)/2) - I_{(i-1)/n} \\ ((n+1)/2, (n+1)/2), \quad (3)$$

where $i = 1, \ldots, n$.

An interesting property of Equation 3 is that the resulting beta deviates represent the approximation of the probability that the ith-order statistic is the value of the population median. However, that observation is irrelevant to the task of finding the best estimate of the population median (or any specific quantile). In other words, this observation neither proves that the Harrell-Davis is the best estimator nor precludes the possibility that other multipliers may be substituted for Equation 3 in Equation 2 that produce a closer estimate of the population median.

A new competitor was recently proposed by Shulkin and Sawilowsky, in 2006, which is based on a modified double-exponential distribution. Calculate the weights $W_{n,i}^{AltExp}$ in the following form:

$$W_{n,i}^{AltExp} = \int_{-\infty}^{-n/3+2i/3} \frac{1}{2}(1 + \mathrm{sgn}(x)(1 - e^{-8|x|/n}))dx \\ - \int_{-\infty}^{-n/3+2(i-1)/3} \frac{1}{2}(1 + \mathrm{sgn}(x)(1 - e^{-8|x|/n}))dx, \quad (4)$$

where $i = 1, \ldots, n$.

The weights in Equation 4 can be interpreted as the probability that a random variable falls between $-n/3 + 2(i-1)/3$ and $-n/3 + 2i/3$. The modified form of the Laplace distribution used here was obtained through a series of Monte Carlo minimization studies. The estimate is calculated as a weighted sum,

$$M_{AltExp} = \sum_{i=1}^{n} W_{n,i}^{AltExp} X_{(i)}. \quad (5)$$

There are two ways to judge which competitor is superior in estimating the population median regardless of distribution or sample size. One benchmark is the smallest root mean square error from the population median. Another is the closeness to the population median.

Let M^P be the population median. Let N_R be a number of Monte-Carlo repetitions and M_i^j be the median estimate by the jth method in i^{th} repetition, $j = 1, \ldots, N_M$. Here N_M is the number of methods. Then, mean square error (MSE) can be defined as follows:

$$\varepsilon_{MSE}^j = \frac{\sqrt{\sum_{i=1}^{N_R} (M^P - M_i^j)^2}}{N_R}. \quad (6)$$

Further, calculate deviation of each estimate from the population median:

$$\Delta M_i^j = \left| M^P - M_i^j \right|, j = 1, \ldots, N_M, i = 1, \ldots N_R. \quad (7)$$

For each $i = 1, \ldots, N_R$. find a set of indexes $I(j)$, $j = 1, \ldots, N_M$, such that

$$\Delta M_i^{I(1)} \le \Delta M_i^{I(2)} \le \ldots \le \Delta M_i^{I(N_M)}. \quad (8)$$

The rank-based error (RBE) can now be defined as follows:

$$\varepsilon_{RBE}^j = \frac{\sum_{i=1}^{N_R} (I(j) - 1)/N_M}{N_R}. \quad (9)$$

A Monte Carlo study was conducted to compare these three sample statistics. The distributions that were sampled included the standard normal (De Moivre or Gauss), uniform, exponential ($\mu = \sigma = 1$), chi-squared ($df = 2$), and Student's t ($df = 3$). The sample sizes were $n = 5, 10, 15, 20, 25, 30,$ and 50. Results showed that the modified double exponential minimizes the mean square error from the population median, followed by the Harrell-Davis estimator, and, finally, the sample median. The modified double exponential had the largest frequency of occurrences of being the closest to the population median, with the Harrell-Davis and the sample median obtaining fewer occurrences of being the closest, respectively.

Example

Let $X = (10, 12, 13, 15, 20)$ be a random sample of size $n = 5$, drawn from an unknown population. The task is to estimate the population median based on these data points. $\tilde{X} = (10, 12, 13, 15, 20)$ is its order statistic.

Sample Median

The sample median is M = 13. This result is available in most computer statistics packages. For example, in SPSS, the commands are Analyze | Descriptive Statistics | Explore.

Harrell-Davis

The weights are available by taking expected values for size n from the beta distribution. In this example, the weights are $W_{n,1}^{HD} = .0579$, $W_{n,2}^{HD} = .2595$, $W_{n,3}^{HD} = .3651$, $W_{n,4}^{HD} = .2595$, and $W_{n,5}^{HD} = .0579$. Thus,

$$M_{HD} = .0579 \times 10 + .2595 \times 12 + .3651 \times 13 + .2595 \times 15 + .0579 \times 20 = 13.4912.$$

Modified Double Exponential

The weights are available in Shulkin, from 2006. In this example, they are calculated as $W_{n,1}^{AltExp} = .0662$, $W_{n,2}^{AltExp} = .1923$, $W_{n,3}^{AltExp} = .4133$, $W_{n,4}^{AltExp} = .1923$, and $W_{n,5}^{AltExp} = .0662$. Thus,

$$M_{AltExp} = .0662 \times 10 + .1923 \times 12 + .4133 \times 13 + .1923 \times 15 + .0662 \times 20 = 12.5539.$$

—*Boris Shulkin and Shlomo S. Sawilowsky*

See also Measures of Central Tendency; Median

Further Reading

Harrell, F. E., & Davis, C. E. (1982). A new distribution-free quantile estimator. *Biometrika, 69,* 635–640.

Maritz, J. S., & Jarrett, R. G. (1978). A note on estimating the variance of the sample median. *Journal of the American Statistical Association, 73*(361), 194–196.

Shulkin, B. (2006). *Estimating a population median with a small sample.* Unpublished doctoral dissertation, Wayne State University, Detroit, MI.

ETHICAL ISSUES IN TESTING

All professional activities of psychologists, including psychological testing, are governed by ethical standards and principles, such as the ethics code of the American Psychological Association (APA). In this entry, the discussion focuses on the ethical practice of formal testing activities as outlined in the APA ethics code.

Selection and Use of Tests

Before the first test item is administered, the evaluator makes important decisions regarding the specific tests to be employed with a particular client. When evaluators select tests, they are ethically obligated to ensure that the tests fall within their areas of competence. For example, a psychologist trained exclusively to work with children will probably be adequately trained to administer children's IQ tests but may need additional training to reach a level of competence with adult IQ tests. Also, tests should be selected for a particular evaluation only if they are appropriate for the purpose of that evaluation. Similarly, evaluators should select tests that are suitable for the client being evaluated, especially considering the client's age, cultural background, and linguistic abilities. Thus, if a psychologist's task is to conduct a personality evaluation for which a popular test, such as the Minnesota Multiphasic Personality Inventory-Second Edition (MMPI-2), might be appropriate, the psychologist should be familiar with the age range restrictions of the various versions of the adolescent and adult forms of the test, as well as the languages in which it is available.

Evaluators should select tests that have established reliability and validity. If no such test is available and the evaluator chooses to use a test with questionable or unknown reliability and validity, this fact should be noted in the report of the results. Likewise, evaluators should use tests in accordance with the purpose and administration procedure outlined in the tests' manuals. This is particularly important with standardized face-to-face tests, such as the Wechsler IQ tests, where uniform administration and scoring are essential to the validity of the test results.

Informed Consent Regarding Testing

Also, before the first test item is administered, the evaluator is ethically obligated to obtain informed consent from the client or from his or her legal guardian, when appropriate. This obligation stands unless the testing is mandated by law or governmental regulations or in other isolated cases, as explained in the APA ethics code. Even when it is not necessary to obtain informed consent, ethical evaluators still inform clients about the testing activities they are about to undergo. In practice, there is some variability among evaluators regarding the specific information they present to a client prior to testing, but in general, this process should include an explanation of the nature and purpose of the testing, any costs or fees, the involvement of third parties (such as third-party payers, legal authorities, or employers), and the limits of confidentiality. In testing situations, confidentiality may be limited by state laws involving a psychologist's "duty to warn" or mandated child abuse reporting. Typically in these cases, a psychologist who, during testing, discovers that a client intends to cause harm to himself or herself or another individual or that a child is being abused breaks confidentiality in order to protect the individual at risk. It is also important to discuss the limits of confidentiality with minors and

their parents or guardians, especially regarding the access to testing information that the parents or guardians may have.

Clients should be informed about testing in language they can understand, and their consent should be voluntary rather than coerced. Moreover, the evaluator is ethically obligated to give the client an opportunity to ask questions and receive answers about the testing process before it begins. Generally, it is important to ensure that the client is adequately informed and agreeable to the testing process before beginning.

The Test Itself

When the creators of psychological tests design, standardize, and validate their tests, they should use appropriate psychometric procedures and up-to-date scientific knowledge. Test developers should also aim to minimize test bias as much as possible and should create a test manual that adequately educates test administrators about when, how, and with whom the test should be used.

Evaluators are ethically obligated to avoid obsolete tests. A test may become obsolete when it is replaced by a revision that represents a significant improvement in terms of psychometrics, standardization, or applicability. For example, both the child and adult versions of the Wechsler intelligence tests have been repeatedly revised, with each new edition superseding the previous edition. Likewise, the original Beck Depression Inventory was made obsolete when a revised edition was created in the 1990s to better match depression symptoms as listed in the revised *Diagnostic and Statistical Manual of Mental Disorders (DSM-IV)*. In other cases, a test may be become obsolete without being replaced by a more current edition. Several projective tests created in the first half of the 20th century may fit this description, either because their standardization sample has become antiquated or because they no longer meet professional standards for reliable and valid tests.

Like tests themselves, the data obtained via tests can become outdated as well. For example, data collected during a child's learning disability evaluation via intelligence or achievement test remains applicable to the child for only a limited period of time. As time passes, the child's development and education warrant that similar tests be readministered. Likewise, data obtained via neuropsychological testing may remain accurate for only a limited period of time. After this period, its optimal use may be for comparison to data collected more recently via similar tests.

Qualifications of the Evaluator

Psychological testing should be conducted only by individuals with appropriate qualifications. The evaluator must have competencies specific to the test and the client in question; merely possessing a license to practice psychology does not support unlimited use of psychological tests. An important exception to this rule is the psychological trainee under supervision. Such individuals can conduct testing for training purposes but should do so with supervision suitable to their levels of training and should inform the people they evaluate (or their parents or guardians) of their status.

Scoring and Interpretation

When scoring or interpreting psychological test results, evaluators should consider client-specific variables, such as situational, linguistic, ethnic, and cultural factors. Notes regarding interpretations made in these contexts should be included in the report.

If a psychologist utilizes a scoring or interpretation service in the process of an evaluation, the psychologist should ensure that the procedure is valid for the purpose of the particular test or evaluation. Even if the scoring or interpretation was completed by another person (or computer service), the psychologist conducting the evaluation retains professional responsibility. Those offering scoring or interpretation services to other professionals should nonetheless create reliable and valid procedures and should accurately describe their purpose, method, and applications.

Use of Test Results

Although previous editions of the APA ethics code generally prohibited the release of raw test data to clients, the most recent edition obligates psychologists to release test data to clients (with a signed release from the client) unless substantial harm or misuse can be reasonably expected. In this context, test data include client responses to test items but not the stimuli, questions, or protocols that elicited the responses. This category also includes raw and scale scores as well as notes about the client's behavior during the testing. Without a release signed by the client, psychologists should maintain the confidentiality of test data unless required by law or court order to provide these data. It is important for those conducting testing to be familiar with state laws governing these issues, as well as relevant ethical standards.

In most cases, clients will not seek their own test data. Nonetheless, all clients are entitled to receive feedback regarding their test results. In general, ethical evaluators provide an intelligible explanation to clients (or their parents or guardians) regarding their test results, the meaning of these results, and their possible implications or consequences. In some circumstances (such as some forensic evaluations or organizational assessments), this feedback or explanation procedure may be precluded; in these cases, the evaluator should inform the client during the informed consent procedure that no explanation of results will be forthcoming.

Test Security

Psychologists and others who administer psychological tests are ethically bound to maintain the security of these tests. The APA ethics code requires that reasonable efforts should be taken to maintain the integrity and security of test materials. Individual test takers should not be able to access and review psychological tests before the test administration. When individuals have prior access to tests, test questions, or test answers, the psychometric integrity of the tests is compromised. For example, if a person were to have access to the questions contained in an IQ test beforehand, the individual's test scores could be artificially inflated. Such prior access to test materials would make the test administration invalid. This breach in test security could lead to a gradual weakening in the validity of the test in question if the test stimuli were shared with other potential test takers.

Professionals who are responsible for psychological tests should take reasonable steps to make sure that individuals are not able to review tests before administration, keep scoring keys and test materials secure, and not allow unqualified individuals access to test materials. Copyright law should also be considered before test materials are published or disclosed. Before any portion of a copyrighted test is reproduced, permission should be gained from the publisher or copyright holder.

The security of test materials may be compromised by publishing test materials in scholarly writing, including test materials in court records, maintaining poor control of test materials in academic settings, and the unauthorized distribution or publications of the test materials through Web sites and other means. Reproducing test materials in scholarly writing could compromise test security if test items or stimuli were included in the publication. Caution should be exercised in such cases to maintain test security and adhere to copyright laws. Controlling the security of tests in court settings may be obtained by asking the court to restrict the release of subpoenaed test materials to a psychologist or other individual bound by the applicable ethical standards. Tests can be kept secure in academic settings by keeping them in a secure area and by allowing only those individuals who have been deemed competent test users to have access to the tests. However, even highly trained individuals may at times be unaware of the guidelines promulgated by test publishers that identify the different levels of training necessary for competent test use. For example, some social science researchers may use psychological tests in research that were designed for use primarily in clinical settings. However, these researchers may be unaware of the ethical guidelines that control the security of these tests. Tests designed for clinical purposes that are used in research should be maintained at a high level of security.

The Internet provides an easy method for the unauthorized distribution of test materials by individuals who are not competent test users. Furthermore, nonprofessionals are not bound by the same ethical standards as psychologists and other test users. The unauthorized distribution or publication of test materials may not be under the control of test administrators, but test users are responsible for taking steps to avoid any opportunity for test materials and test scores to be obtained by fraudulent means.

—*Andrew M. Pomerantz and Bryce F. Sullivan*

See also Educational Testing Service; Ethical Principles in the Conduct of Research With Human Participants; Standards for Educational and Psychological Testing

Further Reading

American Educational Research Association, American Psychological Association, & National Council on Measurement in Education. (1999). *Standards for educational and psychological testing.* Washington, DC: American Educational Research Association.

American Psychological Association. (2002). Ethical principles of psychologists and code of conduct. *American Psychologist, 57,* 1060–1073.

Fisher, C. B. (2003). *Decoding the ethics code: A practical guide for psychologists.* Thousand Oaks, CA: Sage.

Koocher, G. P., & Rey-Casserly, C. M. (2002). Ethical issues in psychological assessment. In J. R. Graham & J. A. Naglieri (Eds.), *Handbook of assessment psychology.* New York: Wiley.

APA Ethics Code, including a section on assessment: http://www.apa.org/ethics/code2002.html

APA statement on test security in educational settings: http://www.apa.org/science/securetests.html

Test security: http://www.apa.org/journals/amp/testsecurity .html

ETHICAL PRINCIPLES IN THE CONDUCT OF RESEARCH WITH HUMAN PARTICIPANTS

Ethics is the study of assumptions believed to assist in distinguishing between right and wrong for the purpose of making sound moral judgments. *Ethical principles* are standards or rules that may serve as policy for determining modes of action in situations that involve or require moral judgment and decision making. The conduct of scientific research using human participants necessarily involves ethical decision making and is rife with potential for ethical conflict. Largely in response to flagrant occurrences of unethical research with human participants, professional organizations and government agencies began specifying ethical principles to guide researchers in the mid-20th century. These principles vary somewhat but typically emphasize beneficence and nonmaleficence; fidelity, responsibility, and trust; integrity; justice; and respect for the dignity and autonomy of persons. The complexities of many ethical decisions require more than the rigid application of rules; researchers are responsible for using sound, well-reasoned judgment in planning and implementing research in a way that maximizes benefits, minimizes harm, and promotes the dignity and worth of all human participants.

History

Although ethical considerations have influenced researchers on an informal and individual basis throughout history, the first formal recognition of the importance of ethical principles in research occurred in 1947, after the Nuremberg Trials of Nazi war criminals. These trials revealed to the public that during World War II, physicians and scientists had conducted biomedical experiments on involuntary participants drawn from Nazi concentration camps. Some of these experiments were designed to assess human responses to poisons, extreme temperatures, and infections, and they essentially resembled torture. Noting that there was at the time no international law or ethics code to refer to in addressing such egregious treatment of human participants, Leo Alexander, an American physician and consultant to the prosecution during the trials, submitted a report that presented standards for legitimate, ethical research. This report formed the basis of the subsequently developed Nuremberg Code, the first formal code of ethical principles addressing the conduct of research with human participants. The Nuremberg Code emphasized principles such as informed consent, avoidance of harm, the necessity of researchers having appropriate training, and freedom of participants to withdraw at any time.

The Nuremburg Code played a significant role in shaping the content of ethical guidelines published by professional organizations such as the American Psychological Association (APA). The APA first published a general ethics code for psychologists in 1953. In 1966, APA established an ad hoc committee to further examine research ethics. In 1973, the committee published a booklet titled "Ethical Principles in the Conduct of Research With Human Participants." This booklet, along with APA's general ethical guidelines, has subsequently undergone revision. The most recent APA ethics code, which includes guidelines for research, was published in 2002.

The Nuremberg Code also influenced federal regulations that were set forth by the U.S. Congress in the National Research Act of 1974. This legislation created a National Commission for the Protection of Human Subjects in Biomedical and Behavioral Research and required the formation of an institutional, or internal, review board (IRB) by every university or other organization that receives federal funds for research. The purpose of the IRB is to review proposals for research with the aim of preventing ethically questionable studies from being conducted with human participants. During the mid-1970s, the National Commission held hearings on a series of ethically problematic research efforts, including the Tuskegee Syphilis Study, which examined the degenerative course of syphilis in rural, underprivileged African American males by deliberately withholding treatment of the disease. These hearings led the National Commission to develop specific recommendations for research with human participants, published in "The Belmont Report," which set the framework for federal regulation of research. The U.S. Department of Health and Human Services issued a set of regulations in 1981, called "Protection of Human Subjects." This document and its subsequent revisions have continued to emphasize the principles of beneficence, justice, and respect for persons, as outlined in the Belmont Report.

Philosophical Approaches to Ethical Decisions

The ethical guidelines currently in use by biomedical and behavioral research communities have the

Western philosophical underpinnings of the deontological and utilitarian traditions. The deontological tradition, based on the assumption that ethics reflects a universal moral code, emphasizes respect for the autonomy of the individual. The utilitarian tradition, based on the assumption that moral judgments depend on the consequences of particular actions, emphasizes an optimal balance of the possible harms and potential benefits to people. The shared goal embedded in these approaches is to uphold the welfare and protection of individuals and groups by respecting the intrinsic worth and dignity of all persons and by carefully weighing the pros and cons of potential courses of action.

Cost-Benefit Considerations

Ethics codes such as those adopted by the APA generally emphasize utilitarian considerations guiding ethical decision making with respect to research. That is, instead of specifying a concrete set of rules, the guidelines require that researchers engage in a cost-benefit analysis before conducting a particular study. There are a number of possible costs of conducting research with human participants. Costs to participants may include their time, resources, and effort; possible injury, stress, anxiety, pain, social discomfort, and threats to self-esteem; and the risk of breached confidentiality. Other costs of research include the use of resources and monetary expenses required for salaries, equipment, and supplies, and possible detriment to the profession or to society, as in the case of an experimental treatment that unintentionally harms participants and causes distrust toward behavioral research.

These costs must be weighed against the possible benefits of the research. Such benefits include the advancement of basic scientific knowledge; the improvement of research or assessment methods; benefits for society, such as improved psychotherapy techniques or enhanced classroom teaching and learning processes; benefits for researchers and research trainees, such as increased knowledge and advancement toward professional and educational goals; and benefits for research participants, such as when a study testing an experimental treatment for depression

helps participants become less depressed. Researchers bear responsibility to society, science, students and trainees, and research participants. The main focus of the current ethical guidelines for research is on responsibility to participants, but this responsibility must always be held in balance with researchers' other three responsibilities.

Five Ethical Principles for Research With Human Participants

There are five general principles in the 2002 APA ethics code designed to "guide and inspire psychologists toward the very highest ethical ideals of the profession." These principles include beneficence and nonmaleficence (i.e., benefit people and do no harm); fidelity and responsibility; and integrity, justice, and respect for people's rights and dignity. The Belmont Report identified three basic ethical principles when conducting research: respect for persons, justice, and beneficence. The following are five basic ethical principles presented in the order of the general principles in the APA code that apply specifically to conducting biomedical and behavioral research with human participants.

Principle 1: Beneficence and Nonmaleficence

Representing the utilitarian tradition, this principle requires that researchers, using considerations such as those described above, strive to maximize potential benefits while minimizing risks of their research. Although the cost-benefit mandate seems straightforward, it is rarely unambiguous in practice because costs to participants and benefits to the profession and to society are difficult to accurately estimate in advance and no universally agreed-upon method or criteria exist for optimally balancing the two. Where questions arise related to the degree of risk, researchers are responsible for seeking ethical advice and implementing safeguards to protect participants. Risks that are identified in advance must be communicated to prospective research participants or their legal equivalent, and informed consent must be obtained (except in special cases approved by the

IRB, such as research involving a placebo control, in which fully informed consent compromises a scientifically required research design). Sometimes research presents risks to groups of people or social institutions. No consensus exists for whether a representative can provide consent on behalf of a collective entity, but full compliance to Principle 1 requires sensitivity to this issue.

Principle 2: Fidelity, Responsibility, and Trust

This principle requires researchers to establish and maintain a relationship of trust with research participants. For example, before individuals agree to participate in research, investigators must be clear and explicit in describing to prospective participants what they will experience and what consequences may result from participation. Researchers also are obligated to honor all promises and commitments that are made as part of the agreement to participate. When full disclosure is not made prior to obtaining informed consent (e.g., information germane to the purpose of the study would compromise its validity), safeguards must be implemented to protect the welfare and dignity of participants. In general, procedures that involve concealment or deception in a research design can be implemented only after rigorous criteria for the necessity of such procedures are met and the study is approved by the IRB. (Such instances also require a thorough debriefing of participants at the conclusion of their participation.) When children or adults with limited understanding serve as participants, researchers must implement special protective safeguards. When unintended negative consequences of research participation occur, researchers are obligated to detect, remove, and/or correct these consequences and ensure that they do not persist over time. Understandably, past ethical breaches have resulted in what some describe as widespread mistrust of biomedical and behavioral research in contemporary society. Principle 2 requires researchers to make every effort to foster trust and avoid causing further public mistrust.

Principle 3: Integrity

This principle requires researchers to "do good science," to truthfully report their results, to take reasonable steps to correct errors that are discovered, to present work that is their own (or to otherwise make appropriate citations), to take responsibility and credit only for work that is their own, to avoid "piecemeal publication" (i.e., submitting redundant analyses of a single data set for multiple publications), to share data on which results are published with other qualified professionals provided they seek only to verify substantive claims and do not use the data for other any other purpose, and to respect the proprietary rights of others engaged in the scientific enterprise.

Principle 4: Justice

In following this principle, researchers strive for two forms of justice. The first, *distributive justice,* requires psychologists to entitle all persons equal access to the benefits of research, as well as to ensure that the risks for harm from research are not disproportionately greater for a particular group or category of persons within society. The second, *procedural justice,* refers to the adequacy of research procedures to ensure fairness, such as when easily accessible mechanisms are made available to participants to address any concerns they may have related to their participation in research.

Researchers also are promoting Principle 3 when they attend to the special concerns of underrepresented groups in developing programs of research, so as to avoid continued underinclusion and lack of representation in the knowledge base.

Principle 5: Respect for the Dignity and Autonomy of Persons

Representing the deontological tradition, this principle asserts that researchers respect research participants as human beings with intrinsic worth, whose participation is a result of their autonomous choices. The implications of this principle are far-reaching and relate to matters of obtaining informed consent, avoiding coercive and deceptive practices, upholding confidentiality and privacy, and preserving the self-determination of participants. In abiding by this principle, psychologists are also aware of and respect individual differences, including those influenced by gender, age, culture, role, race, ethnicity, sexual orientation, religious identity, disability, linguistic background, economic status, or any other characteristic related to group membership.

Ethical Conflicts and Decision Making

The potential for ethical conflict is ubiquitous in biomedical and behavioral research. When making ethical decisions about research, it may be prudent to develop a systematic approach to reviewing all relevant sources of ethical responsibility, including one's own moral principles and personal values; cultural factors; professional ethics codes, such as the APA code; agency or employer policies; federal and state rules and regulations; and even case law or legal precedent. A process-oriented approach to ethical decision making may involve some variation of the following: (1) writing a description of the ethically relevant parameters of the situation; (2) defining the apparent dilemma; (3) progressing through the relevant sources of ethical responsibility; (4) generating alternative courses of action; (5) enumerating potential benefits and consequences of each alternative; (6) consulting with the IRB, relevant colleagues, and/or legal professionals; (7) documenting the previous six steps in the process; and (8) evaluating and taking responsibility for the results of the course of action selected. As previously mentioned, all research studies must be approved by the relevant IRB. However, approval of a research proposal by an IRB does not remove the mandate of ethical responsibility from the researcher. In making ethical decisions, researchers should consider the likelihood of self-serving bias that can lead to overestimation of the scientific value of a proposed study and underestimation of its risks.

Conclusion

Scientific research with human participants is an inherently ethical enterprise, and ethical conflicts in research are virtually inevitable. Researchers who exercise the privilege to conduct research with human participants bear the responsibility of being familiar with and abiding by the ethical principles and relevant rules and regulations established by their professional organizations and by federal and state governments. However, rigid application of rules is not a substitute for well-reasoned, responsible ethical decision making.

—*Bryan J. Dik*

See also Ethical Issues in Testing; Standards for Educational and Psychological Testing

Further Reading

American Psychological Association. (2002). Ethical principles of psychologists and code of conduct. *American Psychologist, 57,* 1060–1073.

Bersoff, D. N. (Ed.). (2003). *Ethical conflicts in psychology* (3rd ed.). Washington, DC: American Psychological Association.

Miller, C. (2003). Ethical guidelines in research. In J. C. Thomas & M. Herson (Eds.), *Understanding research in clinical and counseling psychology* (pp. 271–293). Mahwah, NJ: Erlbaum.

Office for Protection from Research Risks, Protection of Human Subjects. National Commission for the Protection of Human Subjects of Biomedical and Behavioral Research. (1979). *The Belmont Report: Ethical principles and guidelines for the protection of human subjects of research* (GPO 887-809). Washington, DC: U.S. Government Printing Office.

Sales, B. D., & Folkman, S. (Eds.). (2000). *Ethics in research with human participants.* Washington, DC: American Psychological Association.

Sieber, J. E. (2004). Empirical research on research ethics. *Ethics and Behavior, 14,* 397–412.

2002 APA Ethics Code: http://www.apa.org/ethics

The Belmont Report: http://www.hhs.gov/ohrp/humansubjects/guidance/belmont.htm

Federal regulations on the protection of human participants: http://www.hhs.gov/ohrp/humansubjects/guidance/45cfr46.htm

EVIDENCE-BASED PRACTICE

The quest to determine what works in psychotherapy is a critical one. Evidence for therapeutic interventions can be defined in many ways. Building consensus on the definition of evidence and ensuring that *evidence-based practice* (EBP) in psychology recognizes not only the research but also the clinician's expertise and the patient's preferences, values, and culture is important to providing quality patient care and to the future of the profession of psychology. Some psychologists believe that psychological interventions should be based solely on randomized clinical trials, while others claim that other forms of evidence have their value. Regardless of their positions, most psychologists recognize that the EBP movement in U.S. society is a juggernaut, racing to achieve accountability in medicine, psychology, education, public policy, and even architecture. The zeitgeist is to require professionals to base their practice on evidence to whatever extent possible.

The American Psychological Association (APA) developed and adopted a policy statement and received a longer report on EBP in psychology at the meeting of its Council of Representatives in August 2005. The policy statement was based on the three components of the Institute of Medicine definition of EBP in medicine. Thus, the APA statement on EBP in psychology aimed to affirm the importance of attending to multiple sources of research evidence and to assert that psychological practice based on evidence is also based on clinical expertise and patient values. The statement begins, "Evidence-Based Practice in Psychology . . . is the integration of the best available research with clinical expertise in the context of patient characteristics, culture and preferences."

1. The APA policy statement has a broad view of research evidence, including multiple research designs, research in public health, health services research, and health care economics, while recognizing that there is a progression of evidence.

2. The APA policy statement explicates the competencies that make up clinical expertise. It also defines the appropriate role of clinical expertise in treatment decision making, including attention to both the multiple streams of evidence that must be integrated by clinicians and to the heuristics and biases that can affect clinical judgment.

3. The APA policy statement articulated the role of patient values in treatment decision making, including the consideration of the role of ethnicity, race, culture, language, gender, sexual orientation, religion, age, and disability status and the issues of treatment acceptability and consumer choice.

The statement concludes,

Clinical decisions should be made in collaboration with the patient, based on the best clinically relevant evidence and with consideration of the probable costs, benefits, and available resources and options. It is the treating psychologist who makes the ultimate judgment regarding a particular intervention or treatment plan.

—*Ronald F. Levant*

See also Ethical Principles in the Conduct of Research With Human Participants

Further Reading

Institute of Medicine. (2001). *Crossing the quality chasm: A new health system for the 21st century.* Washington, DC: National Academy Press.

Norcross, J. C., Beutler, L. E., & Levant, R. F. (Eds.). (2005). *Evidence based practice in mental health: Debate and dialogue on the fundamental questions.* Washington, DC: American Psychological Association.

APA policy statement: http://www.apa.org/practice/ebpstatement.pdf

APA report: http://www.apa.org/practice/ebpreport.pdf

EXCEL SPREADSHEET FUNCTIONS

A spreadsheet function is a predefined formula. Excel, the most popular spreadsheet, has several categories of functions, including one labeled *statistical*.

One of the most simple of these functions is AVERAGE, which computes the average of a set of

Table 1   Excel Functions That Perform Statistical Operations

The Function Name	What It Does
AVERAGE	Returns the average of its arguments
CHIDIST	Returns the one-tailed probability of the chi-squared distribution
CHITEST	Returns the test for independence
CORREL	Returns the correlation coefficient between two data sets
FDIST	Returns the F probability distribution
FORECAST	Returns a value along a linear trend
FREQUENCY	Returns a frequency distribution as a vertical array
FTEST	Returns the result of an F test
GEOMEAN	Returns the geometric mean
KURT	Returns the kurtosis of a data set
LINEST	Returns the parameters of a linear trend
MEDIAN	Returns the median of the given numbers
MODE	Returns the most common value in a data set
NORMDIST	Returns the normal cumulative distribution
NORMSDIST	Returns the standard normal cumulative distribution
PEARSON	Returns the Pearson product moment correlation coefficient
QUARTILE	Returns the quartile of a data set
SKEW	Returns the skewness of a distribution
SLOPE	Returns the slope of the linear regression line
STANDARDIZE	Returns a normalized value
STDEV	Estimates standard deviation based on a sample
STDEVA	Estimates standard deviation based on a sample, including numbers, text, and logical values
STDEVP	Calculates standard deviation based on the entire population
STDEVPA	Calculates standard deviation based on the entire population, including numbers, text, and logical values
STEYX	Returns the standard error of the predicted y-value for each x in the regression
TDIST	Returns the student's t distribution
TREND	Returns values along a linear trend
TTEST	Returns the probability associated with a student's t test
VAR	Estimates variance based on a sample
VARA	Estimates variance based on a sample, including numbers, text, and logical values
VARP	Calculates variance based on the entire population
VARPA	Calculates variance based on the entire population, including numbers, text, and logical values

values. For example, the following statement averages the numbers in cells A1 through A3:

$$= \text{AVERAGE(A1:A3)}$$

The name of the function is AVERAGE, and the argument is A1:A3n.

A similar common function produces the sum of a set of cells as follows:

$$= \text{SUM(A1:A3)}$$

In both cases, the results of these calculations are placed in the cell that contains the statement of the

	A11	▼		*fx* =SUM(A1:A10)	
	A	**B**	**C**	**D**	
1	5				
2	6				
3	5				
4	6				
5	7				
6	8				
7	7				
8	6				
9	5				
10	6				
11	61				
12					

Figure 1   Using the SUM Function as an Example

function. For example, to use the SUM (or any other) function, follow these steps:

1. Enter the function in the cell where you want the results to appear.

2. Enter the range of cells you want the function to operate on.

3. Press the Enter key, and there you have it. Figure 1 shows the function, the argument, and the result.

Functions can be entered directly when the name of the function and its syntax are known or using the Insert command. Some selected Excel functions that perform statistical operations are shown in Table 1.

—*Neil J. Salkind*

See also Spreadsheet Functions

Further Reading

Instruction on using spreadsheet functions: http://spread sheets.about.com/od/excelfunctions/

EXPLORATORY DATA ANALYSIS

Exploratory data analysis (EDA) looks at data to see what they seem to say. The distribution of the observed data is examined without imposing an arbitrary probability model on it. We look for *trends,* such as patterns and linear or nonlinear relationships between variables, and *deviations* from the trends, such as local anomalies, outliers, or clusters. This facilitates discovering the unexpected as well as confirming suspicions, rather like detective work.

EDA is sometimes viewed as a grab bag of tools, but this is a misconception. It is more accurate to view EDA as a procedure for data analysis. We start from a set of expectations or specific questions arising from the data context and explore the data with these in mind, while remaining open to observing unexpected patterns. The approach involves making many plots and numerical models of the data. Plots allow us to examine the distribution of the data without an imposed probability model; thus, statistical graphics form the backbone of EDA. Plots provide simple, digestible summaries of complex information that enable discovering unexpected structure. With the assistance of techniques such as bootstrapping, permutation, and model selection methods, we can assess whether the observed patterns in the data are more than random noise.

EDA is different from confirmatory statistical analysis. In *confirmatory analysis,* we start from a hypothesis and work to confirm or reject the hypothesis. EDA is a hypothesis discovery process. EDA provides approximate answers to any question of interest, instead of an exact answer to the wrong question. In the process of exploration, the data may suggest hypotheses, leading to follow-up confirmatory analysis with new data.

Methods in common usage that have arisen from EDA include the boxplot, stem-and-leaf plot, median polish, and projection pursuit.

History

The term *exploratory data analysis* was coined by John W. Tukey, and it is the title of his landmark book, published in 1977. It is a very idiosyncratic book, jam-packed with ways to make calculations on and draw pictures of data with paper and pencil. It is full of opinions, such as the following:

Pictures based on the exploration of data should *force* their messages upon us. Pictures that emphasize what we already know—"security blankets" to reassure us—are frequently not worth the space they take. Pictures that have to be gone over with a reading glass to see the main point are wasteful of time and inadequate of effect. The greatest value of a picture is when it *forces* us to notice what we never expected to see.

Such opinions communicate a wisdom learned from experiences with data. The intensity of this written work, emphasized by bold and italic typeface, communicates practical advice on working with data. This integral component of Tukey's conceptualization of EDA is unfortunately missing from later treatments of EDA, which tend to make EDA look like a loose collection of ad hoc methods. In 2001, Salsburg published an easy-reading biography of Tukey's contributions on EDA in the context of other major statistical developments of the previous century.

Tukey places credit for the EDA ideas with Charles P. Winsor, who taught him "many things about data analysis that weren't in the books." Practical issues of data analysis traverse the history of statistics. Data analysts evince the value of exploring data to see what they seem to say. EDA both descends from these matters and transcends them. IDA is the necessary prior data inspection to check that the assumptions required for formal analysis are satisfied by the data. Checking the data quality early in the analysis may save some red faces later. EDA is about the data for its own sake. There may be no need or desire for further analysis. Tukey's book may drown the reader in the author's thrill of pushing methodology in intricate dimensions, but ultimately, EDA is about the data. The methods are the tools used to dissect the data, which EDA borrows from and lends to IDA.

The Evolution of EDA

Tukey produced all of his scratched-down numbers and pictures using pencil and paper, but today, as he predicted, the computer is invaluable for EDA. EDA has evolved from a pencil-and-paper activity on tiny data sets to highly sophisticated algorithms and interactive computer-generated graphics on any size of data and any complexity of data. *Software,* a word coined by Tukey, such as R enables rapid data

calculations and making pictures easy. Software such as GGobi and Mondrian supports the use of interactive and dynamic graphics for exploring data, and emerging packages for R, such as iPlots, iSPlot, and RGtk, are enabling the integration of dynamic graphics with numerical analyses. We might call this computer-dependent approach "the new EDA." It remains heavily dependent on statistical graphics.

EDA has expanded in many directions. For data with a spatial context, EDA has matured into exploratory spatial data analysis (ESDA). New diagnostic statistical quantities, such as local indicators for spatial dependence, and graphics, such as variocloud plots, help to find observations that are unusual in the context of their spatial neighbors. Robust methods for downweighting contamination have evolved from median polish to the expansive field of robust statistics. Quite ironically, robust approaches are sometimes described as relieving the data analyst from the task of inspecting the data. For large electronically stored databases, algorithms have emerged to mine the data for information. Examples of these algorithms are trees, forests, neural networks, and support vector machines. A statistical treatment of the area can be found in the publication by Hastie, Tibshirani, and Friedman, in 2001, including the application of bootstrapping methods to evaluate uncertainty.

EDA is permeating through statistics education. For example, introductory statistics courses, such as can be found in the publication by DeVeaux, Velleman, and Bock, in 2005, have been reframed to present statistics from an EDA perspective before introducing confirmatory methods.

An Example

This is an example derived from a case study, in 1995, by Bryant and Smith. The data on tips are collected by one waiter over a 2.5-month period at one restaurant. He recorded the tip, total bill, sex of the bill payer, smoking or nonsmoking section, size of the dining party, and the time of day. The question of interest is "What factors affect the tips?"

A basic analysis fits a multiple regression model using tip rate as the response variable to the remaining variables. It yields a model for the data with only one significant explanatory variable, $tip\hat{r}ate = 0.18 - 0.01 \times size$, which can be interpreted as follows: For each increase of one person in the size of the dining party, tip rate decreases by 1%, starting from a rate of 17% for a party size of one. The model explains very little of the variation in tip rate, as you can see from the plot of the data and the model in Figure 1. The EDA approach is different from this: First, make many plots of the data and then model them. It is surprising what these deceptively casual data reveal!

To examine the variable tips, the conventional plot to use is a histogram. Tukey might have scratched up a stem-and-leaf of tips, but using the computer, a histogram is simple to produce today. EDA would suggest that several histograms of tips are generated using a variety of bin widths. Because the units are dollars and cents, a commonsense scale utilizes these units. The histograms using a full-dollar bin width show a skewed distribution, with tips centered around $2 and few tips larger than $6. When a bin width of 10¢ is used, it reveals something unpredicted: There are peaks at full- and half-dollar amounts. This is interesting! Are people rounding their tips? Additional observations from this plot are as follows: There are three outlying tips larger than $7 and, surprisingly, no tips smaller than $1.

In examining the two variables together, tips and total bill, a linear association between the two would be expected. Tips are conventionally calculated as a percentage of the bill. Total bill should explain the amount of tip. This plot is shown in Figure 1 at lower left. A linear relationship can be seen between the two variables. It is not as strong as might be expected, and there is a surprising pattern: If the plot is divided on a diagonal running from low bill/low tip to high total/high tip, there are more points in the lower right triangle. This region corresponds to tips that are lower than expected. There are very few points in the upper left triangle, where tips are higher than expected. This is also interesting! It suggests a tendency toward cheap rather than generous tips.

The data shows more unanticipated patterns when subset by the categorical variables "sex" and "smoking party." The plots in Figure 1 (bottom right) show tip and total bill conditioned by sex and smoking party. There is a big difference in the relationship between tip and bill in the different subsets. There is more variation in tips when the dining party is in the smoking section. The linear association is much stronger for nonsmoking parties. In the plot of female nonsmokers, with the exception of three points, the association between tip and bill is nearly perfect. The few large bills are paid mostly by males, or when paid by a female, the tips are lower than expected. The largest relative tip was paid by a male nonsmoker. These are interesting observations!

What have the data revealed? This is a small data set, but it is rich on information. It is a bit shocking and pleasing to discover so many intricate details in the numbers. Here is a summary of the observations that were made:

- Many tips are rounded to the nearest-dollar and half-dollar value.
- There are no tips less than $1 reported.
- Tip and total bill are not as strongly associated as might be expected.
- There is more tendency toward cheap tips than generous tips.
- Smoking parties have more variation in tip and total bill.
- Males pay most of the largest bills, but when a female pays a large bill, the tip tends to be disproportionately low.
- Finally, the only factor in the data that affects tips is the size of the dining party. Tip rate has a weak negative dependence on the size of the party: The larger the party, the lower the tip rate, $tip\hat{r}ate = 0.18 - 0.01 \times size$.

What was accomplished in this example? A problem was posed for the collected data but was not constrained to it; many simple plots were used; and some calculations were made. The observations can be brought forward as hypotheses to be tested in confirmatory studies about tipping behavior. This is the process of exploring data.

—Dianne Cook

See also Data Mining; Graphical Statistical Methods

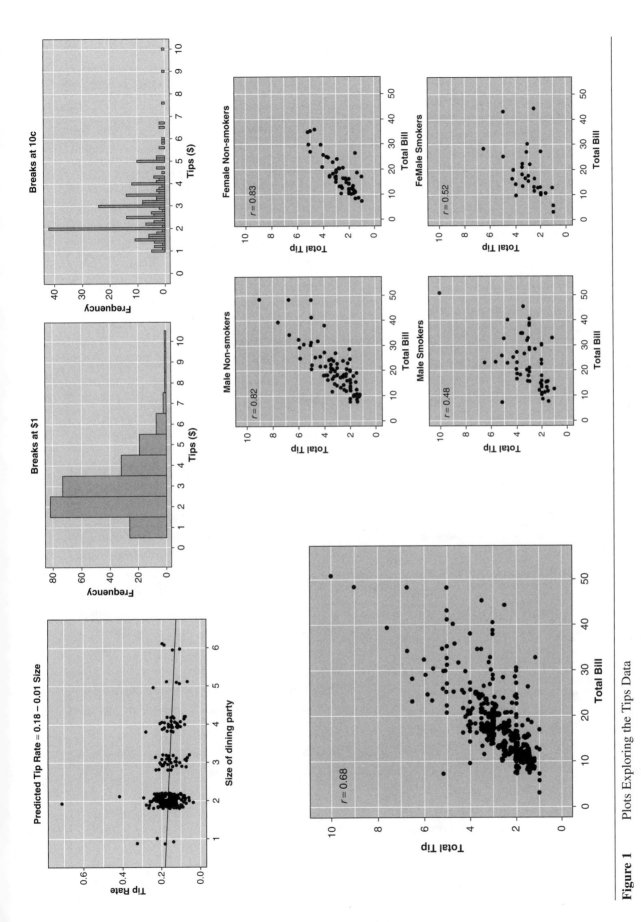

Figure 1 Plots Exploring the Tips Data

a. Tip rate *vs.* size (jittered), to support the linear model.
b. Histograms using different bin widths reveal different features of tips.
c. Scatterplot showing the relationship between tip and total bill.
d. The relationship between tip and total bill is much weaker for smoking parties than nonsmoking parties.
Note: These plots have been enhanced for presentation purposes. The discoveries made on the data occurred with much rougher, quickly generated graphics.

331

Further Reading

Breiman, L. (2001). Random forests. *Machine Learning, 45*(1), 5–32.

Bryant, P. G., & Smith, M. A. (1995). *Practical data analysis: Case studies in business statistics.* Homewood, IL: Richard D. Irwin.

Crowder, M. J., & Hand, D. J. (1990). *Analysis of repeated measures.* London: Chapman & Hall.

DeVeaux, R. D., Velleman, P. F., & Bock, D. E. (2005). *Intro stats* (2nd ed.). Boston: Addison-Wesley.

Hastie, T., Tibshirani, R., & Friedman, J. (2001). *The elements of statistical learning.* New York: Springer.

Hoaglin, D. C., Mosteller, F., & Tukey, J. W. (Eds.). (1983). *Understanding robust and exploratory data analysis.* New York: Wiley.

R Development Core Team. (2003). *R: A language and environment for statistical computing.* Vienna, Austria: R Foundation for Statistical Computing.

Salsburg, D. (2001). *The lady tasting tea: How statistics revolutionized science in the twentieth century.* New York: W. H. Freeman.

Tukey, J. (1977). *Exploratory data analysis.* Boston: Addison-Wesley.

Vapnik, V. (1999). *The nature of statistical theory.* New York: Springer-Verlag.

EXPLORATORY FACTOR ANALYSIS

Exploratory factor analysis (EFA) is a statistical method used to explore the underlying structure of correlations among observed variables. The goal of EFA is to describe this underlying structure in a parsimonious manner by specifying a small number of factors that can account for the correlations among a set of measured variables. EFA (as opposed to *confirmatory factor analysis*) is undertaken when the researcher has no strong a priori theories about the number and nature of the underlying factors.

The mathematical basis of EFA is the common factor model, which proposes that measured variables can be explained by *underlying factors* (also called latent variables) that cannot be directly measured, but influence the measured variables. There are two types of underlying factors. *Common factors* are those that influence more than one measured variable in a set, whereas *unique factors* are those that influence only one measured variable.

The common factor model is often expressed using the following equation:

$$P = \lambda \Phi \lambda^{T} + D_{\psi},$$

where P is the correlation matrix in the population, λ are the factor loadings (i.e., numerical values representing the strength and direction of influence of the common factors on the measured variables), Φ is the matrix of correlations among the common factors, and D_{ψ} is the matrix of unique factor variances (i.e., the proportion of variance in each measured variable that is explained by its unique factor).

Conducting an EFA essentially involves computing estimates for the elements in the above equation. Statistical software provides the results of such calculations, including a factor-loading matrix (λ) and a common factor correlation matrix (Φ). Programs customarily do not directly report the unique variances (D_{ψ}). Instead, they report the communalities (i.e., proportions of variance accounted for by the common factors), which are inversely related to the unique variances.

To illustrate the use of EFA, imagine that four ability tests (paragraph comprehension, vocabulary, arithmetic skills, and mathematical word problems) are administered. An EFA is then conducted on the correlations between these four variables. To identify and describe the underlying factors, researchers first examine the pattern of factor loadings. These values represent the magnitude and direction of influence of the common factors on the measured variables. As shown in Table 1, Paragraph Comprehension, Vocabulary, and Math Word Problems appear to load highly on Factor 1 (i.e., are strongly influenced by Factor 1), and

Table 1   Sample Factor Loading Matrix

	Factor 1	*Factor 2*
Paragraph Comprehension	.70	.10
Vocabulary	.70	.00
Arithmetic	.10	.70
Math Word Problems	.60	.60

Arithmetic Skills and Math Word Problems load highly on Factor 2 (i.e., are strongly influenced by Factor 2). Based on this pattern, Factor 1 might be interpreted as a verbal ability factor and Factor 2 as mathematical ability factor.

The common factor correlation matrix in Table 2 demonstrates that the verbal and mathematical ability factors are moderately correlated ($r = .41$), indicating that these factors are distinct but related constructs. The commonalities in Table 3 show that a moderate-to-large proportion of the variance in each measured variable is explained by the two common factors.

Table 2   Sample Phi Matrix

	Factor 1	Factor 2
Factor 1	—	.41
Factor 2	.70	—

Table 3   Sample Commonalities

Variable	Commonality
Paragraph Comprehension	.84
Vocabulary	.78
Arithmetic Skills	.42
Math Word Problems	.38

Decisions in Conducting EFA

Performing an EFA is a complex process that requires a researcher to make a number of decisions. For each step, researchers must choose from a variety of procedures.

The Number of Common Factors

The first decision that must be made in EFA is the appropriate number of common factors. Several statistical procedures exist to accomplish this task. These procedures are often used in combination with other considerations such as the interpretability and replicability of the factor analysis solutions.

The Kaiser Criterion

This commonly used procedure involves generating eigenvalues from the correlation matrix. *Eigenvalues* are numerical values that can be calculated from a correlation matrix and represent the variance in the measured variables accounted for by each common factor. The number of eigenvalues computed is equal to the number of measured variables. If a factor has a low eigenvalue, it does not account for much variance and can presumably be disregarded. The Kaiser criterion (also called the "eigenvalues-greater-than-1 rule") proposes that a researcher should retain as many factors as there are eigenvalues greater than 1. Unfortunately, although easy to use, this procedure has often been found to perform poorly.

Scree Plot

Another popular method for determining the number of common factors is the scree plot. The scree plot is a graph of the eigenvalues, plotted from largest to smallest. This graph is then examined to determine where the last major drop in eigenvalues occurs. The number of factors equivalent to the number of eigenvalues that precede the last major drop are retained. For example, in Figure 1, the scree plot would suggest retention of three common factors. Although somewhat subjective, this procedure has been found to function reasonably well when clear dominant factors are present.

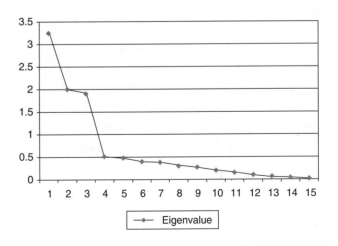

Figure 1   Scree Plot

Parallel Analysis

Parallel analysis involves comparing eigenvalues obtained from the data with eigenvalues that would be expected from random data with an equivalent number of variables and equivalent sample size. The number of factors retained is equivalent to the number of eigenvalues in the sample data set that are greater than the corresponding eigenvalues expected from the random data. Table 4 provides an example of a parallel analysis that suggests retaining three factors. Studies have suggested that parallel analysis functions well when strong factors are present in the data.

Table 4 Sample Parallel Analysis

	Observed Eigenvalues	Eigenvalues Expected From Random Data Set
1.	1.8934	1.3848
2.	1.7839	1.2390
3.	1.7738	1.1907
4.	1.0003	1.0332
5.	.6987	.7986
6.	.4205	.5334
7.	.4133	.4202
8.	.2454	.3454

Goodness of Fit

When conducting certain kinds of EFAs, goodness-of-fit indices can be computed. These are numerical indices that evaluate how well the model accounts for the data. These indices can be compared for a series of models with increasing numbers of common factors. The appropriate number of factors is determined by finding the model in which a model with one less factor demonstrates substantially poorer fit and a model with one more factor provides little improvement in fit.

Model Fitting

The goal of model fitting (also called factor extraction) is to obtain estimates for the model parameters. A variety of methods can be used to accomplish this goal.

Principal Axis Factors

For any EFA model, numerical values can be calculated for the model and used to generate a predicted correlation matrix (i.e., the model's predictions of how the measured variables should be correlated). The predicted matrix can then be compared with the observed correlation matrix to obtain a residual matrix (i.e., a matrix of the differences between the predicted and observed correlations). Noniterated principal axis factors (PAF) compute model parameters such that the sum of the squared residual matrix values is minimized. Iterated PAF uses the same mathematical procedure but with an additional series of steps to refine the estimates. At each step, the estimates from the prior step serve as the starting point for the next set of calculations. This process continues until the estimates at the start of the calculations are extremely similar to the estimates at the end of a step of calculations.

Maximum Likelihood

Maximum likelihood (ML) is a model-fitting procedure based on the likelihood function. The *likelihood function* refers to the relative likelihood that a given model with a set of estimates could have produced the observed data. ML seeks to find the set of estimates for a given model that is maximally likely to have produced the data. One strength of ML is that it provides indices of model fit and confidence intervals for estimates. A disadvantage of ML is that, unlike PAF, it assumes the data are multivariate normal.

Principal Components Analysis

A final model-fitting procedure that is sometimes used for EFA is principal components analysis (PCA). Although PCA is popular and computationally similar in some respects to PAF, this method is not a factor analysis in the strict sense of the term. Specifically, the method is not based on the common factor model. Most notably, this procedure does not distinguish between common and unique variance. Thus, PCA does not take into account the existence of random error.

Rotating a Solution

When examining EFA models with more than one factor, there will be a family of best-fitting solutions for the data. Thus, it is necessary to choose which of these equally fitting solutions is most readily interpretable. This process is accomplished using rotation. Most rotations seek the solution with the best "simple structure." According to Louis Thurstone, simple structure exists when each factor influences a distinct subset of measured variables, there is little overlap in the subsets of measured variables, and each measured variable is influenced only by a subset of the common factors.

Numerous rotations have been proposed. Some of these procedures are *orthogonal rotations* (i.e., rotations that assume factors are uncorrelated). The most widely used orthogonal rotation is Varimax rotation. Other rotations are *oblique rotations* (i.e., rotations that allow, but do not require, factors to be correlated). Popular oblique rotations include Direct Quartimin, Promax, and Harris-Kaiser Orthoblique rotation. Orthogonal and oblique rotations will lead to similar results if factors are relatively uncorrelated, but oblique rotations may produce better simple structure when factors are correlated.

—Naomi Grant and Leandre Fabrigar

See also Exploratory Data Analysis; Factor Analysis; Factor Scores; Multiple Factor Analysis

Further Reading

Browne, M. W., & Cudeck, R. (1992). Alternative ways of assessing model fit. *Sociological Methods and Research, 21*, 230–258.

Fabrigar, L. R., Wegener, D. T., MacCallum, R. C., & Strahan, E. J. (1999). Evaluating the use of exploratory factor analysis in psychological research. *Psychological Methods, 4*, 272–299.

Gorsuch, R. L. (1983). *Factor analysis* (2nd ed.). Hillsdale, NJ: Erlbaum.

Harman, H. H. (1976). *Modern factor analysis* (3rd ed.). Chicago: University of Chicago Press.

Thurstone, L. L. (1947). *Multiple factor analysis*. Chicago: University of Chicago Press.

SAS and SPSS syntax files to assist in exploratory factor analysis: http://flash.lakeheadu.ca/~boconno2/nfactors.html

---

Applying Ideas on Statistics and Measurement

The following abstract is adapted from Conway, J. M., & Huffcutt, A. I. (2003). A review and evaluation of exploratory factor analysis practices in organizational research. *Organizational Research Methods, 6*(2), 147–168.

When there are large data sets, factor analysis is often selected as the technique to help reduce the data set to a more manageable size (and to see how well this data reduction fits on the hypothesis that may have been proposed). In this study, the authors surveyed **exploratory factor analysis (EFA)** practices in three different organizational journals, published from 1985 through 1999, to investigate the use of EFA. The review of 371 studies shows reason for optimism, with the tendency to use multiple number-of-factors criteria and oblique rotations increasing. The authors also found that researchers tend to make better decisions when EFA plays a more consequential role in the research. They stress the importance of careful and thoughtful analysis, including decisions about whether and how EFA should be used.

EYEBALL ESTIMATION

Eyeball estimation refers to inspecting data and quickly making an educated guess about the approximate magnitude of relevant statistics without using a calculator or statistical tables.

Here are some examples:

• To eyeball estimate the mean from data presented as a histogram, imagine that the histogram is cut out of plywood. The mean of the distribution is the point where that piece of plywood would balance.

• To eyeball estimate the mean from data presented in a table, find the largest and the smallest values; the mean will be approximately halfway between those values. For example, if the values of X are 7, 8, 6, 7, 5, 6, 4, 7, 6, 8, 9, 7, 8, 9, 7, 6, 6, 7, 4, 5, 6, 5, 4, 8, 7, the largest value is 9 and the smallest value is 4; the mean will be approximately 6.5. (It is actually 6.48.)

- To eyeball estimate the standard deviation from data presented as a histogram, superimpose a sketch of a normal distribution over the histogram—make the normal distribution cut through the tops of some of the histogram's bars. The standard deviation will be approximately the distance from the mean to the inflection point of the normal distribution.

- To eyeball estimate the standard deviation from data presented in a table, find the range (the largest value minus the smallest value). The standard deviation is roughly a quarter of the range. For example, for the data above, the largest value is 9 and the smallest value is 4, so the range is $9 - 4 = 5$. The standard deviation will be approximately 5/4, or 1.25. (It is actually 1.45.)

The other commonly used descriptive statistics (correlation coefficients, regression constants, areas under normal distributions) can also be eyeball estimated, as can straightforward inferential statistics such as t tests and analyses of variance.

Eyeball estimation is not a substitute for accurate computation. Eyeball estimates are "in-the-ballpark" approximations that can be affected (sometimes dramatically) by such factors as skew. However, eyeball estimation is a valuable skill. It enables the observer to get a sense of the data and to spot mistakes in the computations.

Students benefit from eyeball estimation because it cultivates genuine understanding of statistical concepts. The ability to make an in-the-ballpark, educated guess is better evidence of comprehension than is the ability to compute an exact result from a formula. Furthermore, eyeball estimation is quick. A beginning student can eyeball estimate a standard deviation in about 15 seconds; computation would take the same student about 15 minutes. Furthermore, while students are eyeball estimating standard deviations, they are developing their comprehension of the standard deviation as a measure of the width of a distribution. By contrast, almost no time involved in the computation of a standard deviation is focused on that comprehension.

—*Russell T. Hurlburt*

See also Bar Chart; Line Chart; Pie Chart

Further Reading

Hurlburt, R. T. (2006). *Comprehending behavioral statistics.* Belmont, CA: Wadsworth.

There is a very easy way to return from a casino with a small fortune: go there with a large one.

—Jack Yelton

FACE VALIDITY

Face validity is most often understood as a subjective and cursory judgment of a concept, assessment instrument, or any other conceptualization to ascertain whether, on its face, it appears valid (i.e., that the concept being measured seems reasonable; that a test instrument appears to measure what it purports to measure; that the association between the concept and how it is measured seems appropriate and relevant at first glance), without further regard to the underlying legitimacy of the nomological network, concept, instrument and test items, or the construct it purports to measure.

Face validity is the least reliable validity judgment among validity measures and should serve only as a preliminary screening, given that it addresses appropriateness without empirical data. However, if the minimum requirement of face validity cannot be established, then it is highly unlikely that any of the more rigorous validity criteria will hold.

Face validity, therefore, may reflect reasonable, consistent, and understandable surface connections between the instrument and test items on the one hand and their underlying construct on the other. Conversely, face validity might fail to reveal such connections, irrespective of whether, on closer scrutiny, they actually exist. Therefore, there can be no claim of a logical relationship between face validity and true validity, although correlations between face validity and true validity are possible.

Judgments about face validity are closely connected to the knowledge and experience of the test user. For example, the more a test instrument and its items appear to test takers, on the basis of their experience, to be understandable, reasonable, and clearly related to the test criterion, the more likely it will be that the test takers will judge the test to have a high level of face validity. However, the face validity of a test instrument is more likely to be judged accurately by a psychometrician than by an individual without psychometric training.

Practical Aspects

Advantages

The notion of face validity embodies a number of advantages; for example, it may enable someone to narrow the number of instruments or reports under consideration. However, its most significant contribution is bringing the experience and contexts of test takers into consideration during test construction. For example, potential test items might be examined by representatives of potential test populations to determine whether the items are recognizable and appropriate for inclusion in the final version of a test. That is, the level of face validity is established by a test taker who rates a test, test item, or battery of tests as relevant or irrelevant. Face validity, therefore, is judged from the point of view of the user's knowledge, experience, and attention.

If test items appear to be related to appropriate and relevant content, test takers are more likely to be highly motivated to do their best, thereby making the instrument more valid and reliable. Equally, if the content of the test or items is perceived to be inappropriate or irrelevant, then the test takers' level of motivation for test performance may well be lower. Higher levels of test-taking motivation ensure that test takers are also likely to be more cooperative, more satisfied with their performance, and less likely to blame the test if they obtain low scores.

Relatedly, high levels of face validity are significant when selecting tests that rely heavily on test takers' cooperation. Finally, high levels of face validity may also be a potent factor in marketing the test commercially.

Disadvantages

Face validity also comprises a number of less positive attributes. For example, face validity may actually, in some instances, work against high levels of motivation to complete a test properly if test takers are coerced in some way to take the test and if they are not accustomed to test-taking behavior. In some test areas, such as tests that measure levels of performance rather than more abstract concepts, any distortion related to this motivational attribute may not be significant. However, among tests that attempt to measure more subjective areas (such as personality traits), a test with high face validity might well fail because respondents do not wish to answer the test items truthfully.

Other problems might occur. For example, while high levels of motivation on the part of test takers may be assumed and desirable, there is the possibility that even their most diligent attempts might not reflect what the test is actually measuring. Further, the only evidence of the test or test items' face validity is the judgment of the test taker.

In sum, face validity is considered the chief means of generating acceptance from the general public, from organizations that are considering using a test, and from test takers themselves.

Context

Historically, the exact nature of validity in general has undergone several changes and has assumed great significance in the area of psychometrics.

While commonly acknowledged, by implication, as tangential in test and test item construction for many decades, issues of face validity were largely ceded to the publishers and other vendors of psychometric tests by the early 1900s. Face validity emerged more prominently in the 1940s and 1950s, but dissension among scholars caused several leaders in the field to suggest that use of the term *face validity* be eliminated from psychometrics altogether.

This problem was largely put to rest by the publication of the first set of *Standards for Educational and Psychological Tests* by the American Psychological Association in 1954. The *Standards* largely reinforced the claims made for face validity by Lee Cronbach (1949) and colleagues, particularly Anne Anastasi (1954). Proponents of face validity claimed (a) that it was distinct in its own right, (b) that it was different from other forms of validity, (c) that face validity was not interchangeable with other forms of validity, and (d) perhaps most important, that it was a key practical aspect of test construction related to test acceptability in the eyes of consumers and test takers.

Subsequent American Psychological Association standards have, however, increasingly downplayed the worth of face validity. The 1966 and 1974 *Standards* specified only that face validity should, in psychometrics, be separated from more substantial forms of content validity in psychometrics. The 1985 *Standards* ignored the issue of face validity altogether. That same year, however, Baruch Nevo made the case that face validity should be considered and reported in test construction, although primarily to enhance acceptability rather than as a formal psychometric aspect of test construction.

Implied Meanings of Face Validity

Nevo argued that three and possibly four meanings of face validity have a bearing on judgments about instruments and their test items: validity by assumption, by definition, by appearance, and possibly by hypothesis.

Assumption

Face validity is established when the test user assumes the predictability of the tested criterion by identifying the degree of reasonableness of the test items as related to the objective of the test. The assumption thus made is so strong that recourse to further statistical evidence is unlikely or unwarranted. Establishing face validity in this way is problematic because whatever the level of the test's or test items' perceived practical value, more substantial statistical evidence, whether supportive or conflicting, may be disregarded.

Definition

Face validity by definition makes a judgment of tests or test items via a sample judged by an expert to thoroughly represent the universe of such questions. Historically, this meaning comes closest to what face validity was intended to explain. The better defined the test criterion and the closer it is related to the test items themselves, the more likely that face validity, by definition, can be established. Obviously, face validity assumptions can only be extrapolated to the larger population from which the sample items were drawn.

Appearance

Face validity by appearance makes judgments of a test instrument and its items without recourse to statistical tests to verify stability. Validity is established by those who judge the test and its items relevant, practical, and closely related to the purpose of the test and test performance criteria. Such tests, therefore, are likely to have a high degree of acceptance among those who use them as well as those who take the tests.

Hypothesis

Face validity by hypothesis is arguably a secondary consideration associated with assumption and definition. Face validity is judged in this case when it is necessary and practical to use a test in the real world before statistical information can validate the test. The test is hypothesized as having at least some degree of validity on the basis of other valid tests with the same or similar test criteria and objectives. This form of face validity differs from the first three, all of which judge face validity on easily identifiable and logical ties between the test items and the test criterion. With face validity by hypothesis, the level of confidence in the test's validity rests on the level of confidence in the hypothesis and the amount of research that supports it. Furthermore, the level of confidence in the hypothesis will determine the feasibility of when, how, or whether the testing should proceed.

Other Aspects

Since 1985, discussion of face validity has not been widespread, although some isolated pockets of interest seem to persist. For example, Mark Mostert constructed and applied face validity criteria to meta-analyses in special education, contending that meta-analysis is often assumed to derive definitive quantitative answers from an entire body of research. However, face validity of published meta-analyses (in special education, in this case) can be substantially affected by the information supplied to the user, an observation that has important implications for theory and practice.

This study noted that published meta-analytic results rely heavily on several essential interpretive aspects, including (a) the definition and relationships between the primary study independent variables, (b) the manner in which the independent variables are coded, and (c) how these key variables are interrelated and reported. Face validity is especially germane in view of meta-analyses that have been conducted on the same body of primary studies but that have yielded dissimilar findings.

To establish the exact nature of face validity in special education meta-analyses, the study developed a set of criteria to clarify mega-analytical study characteristics that needed to be available in order for a user to judge face validity. The criteria, which encompass six domains, are discussed in the following sections.

Locating Studies and Establishing Context

The first set of information to provide to users in order to establish face validity includes (a) a literature review (to briefly describe studies and to contextualize the meta-analysis), (b) search procedures used to obtain the primary studies, (c) the dates of the search, (d) the number of primary studies used in the meta-analysis (to establish whether they are a population or a sample of a known universe of studies), and (e) confirmation that the primary studies are clearly noted.

Specifying Inclusion Criteria

The primary study data set must also be justified by reporting the criteria used to select the primary studies and the criteria used to eliminate other primary studies.

Coding Independent Variables

In this step, the meta-analyst must provide (a) a general description of the primary studies around the central research question, (b) a description of the independent variables, (c) descriptions of relationships between variables to explain the conceptual and rational connections between variables (if more than one variable is to be entered into the meta-analysis), and (d) notes explaining any variation among the coded variables.

Calculating Individual Study Outcomes

The meta-analysis requires extensive reporting of the statistical calculations, including (a) the number of effects sizes (ESs) calculated; (b) ES range and standard deviation as general indicators of the scope of variability found in the primary studies, noting both n sizes (ESs for each primary study) and the overall N (used to calculate the ES for the meta-analysis) to measure the overall effect of the meta-analyzed intervention; (c) factors affecting ES (e.g., pooled ESs or the use of placebo groups); and (d) interrater reliability to demonstrate coding of the independent variables by more than one researcher in order to add credence to the analysis and the overall interpretation of the meta-analytical outcomes.

Analyzing Data

After executing and reporting the basic statistical calculations, the analyst should proceed to add interpretive aspects: (a) reporting fail-safe sample size (the number of nonsignificant studies needed outside of those in the meta-analysis to negate the meta-analytic results); (b) summarizing statistics for significant findings (e.g., F and t ratios or rs; useful for drawing generalized research conclusions); (c) reporting nonsignificant findings along with or instead of significant findings to establish the overall integrity of the analysis; (d) explaining the proportion of variance accounted for by the treatment effect after statistical artifacts and other moderators have been acknowledged; (e) providing a summation of research applications and important findings of the meta-analysis, adding analytical coherence to the research hypothesis; and (f) suggesting how findings may be practically and theoretically applied.

Documenting the Limits of the Meta-Analysis

Finally, the limits of the meta-analytic findings should be discussed in order to circumscribe the interpretation of the data.

On the basis of these face validity criteria, the study reported that of 44 special education meta-analyses, the mean proportion of face validity criteria evident from the publications was .60, with a range of .26–1.0.

—Mark Mostert

See also Psychometrics; Validity Theory

Further Reading

Adams, S. (1950). Does face validity exist? *Educational and Psychological Measurement, 10,* 320–328.

Cronbach, L. J. (1971). Test validation. In R. L. Thorndike (Ed.), *Educational measurement* (2nd ed., pp. 443–507). Washington, DC: American Council on Education.

Cronbach, L. J., & Meehl, P. E. (1955). Construct validity in psychological tests. *Psychological Bulletin, 52*(4), 281–302.

Gynther, M. D., Burkhart, B., & Hovanitz, C. (1979). Do face validity items have more predictive validity than subtle items? *Journal of Consulting and Clinical Psychology, 47,* 295–300.

Jenkins, J. G. (1946). Validity for what? *Journal of Consulting Psychology, 10,* 93–98.

Mostert, M. P. (2001). Characteristics of meta-analyses reported in mental retardation, learning disabilities, and emotional and behavioral disorders. *Exceptionality, 9*(4), 199–225.

Turner, S. P. (1979). The concept of face validity. *Quality and Quantity, 13,* 85–90.

FACTOR ANALYSIS

Factor analysis (FA) is a statistical technique used to examine the structure of correlations among a set of observed scores. Although initially developed as a method for studying intelligence, FA has become widely used in numerous areas of psychology was well as in other social sciences, business, economics, and biology.

The Common Factor Model

Although Charles Spearman is largely credited with development of the first formal FA model, Louis L. Thurstone is generally regarded as having provided the foundations of contemporary FA with his development of the common factor model (CFM). The goal of the CFM is to represent the structure of correlations among observed scores by estimating the pattern of relationships between the common factors and the measured variables (a set of observed scores). This relationship is represented numerically by a factor loading in the analysis. Thurstone posited that each measured variable in a set of measured variables is a linear function of two types of latent factors. Common factors, which are unobserved latent variables (constructs), influence more than one measured variable and thus account for the correlations among the measured variables. Unique factors, also latent variables, influence only one measured variable in a set and thus do not account for correlations among measured variables. Unique factors consist of two components (i.e., a specific factor and an error of measurement) although in practice these components are not separately estimated.

The CFM can be expressed in several forms. When expressed as a data model, its goal is to explain the structure of the raw data. Each participant's score on each of the measured variables is represented by a separate equation. The data model for the CFM is expressed by the equation

$$x_{ij} = \mu_j + \lambda_{j1}z_{i1} + \lambda_{j2}z_{i2} + \ldots + \lambda_{jm}z_{im} + \upsilon_{ij},$$

where

i is the individual,

j is the measured variable,

x_{ij} is the score of the individual on the measured variable,

μ_j is the mean of the measured variable,

z_{im} is the common factor (latent variable) score for individual i on factor m,

λ_{jm} is the factor loading on test j on factor m, and

υ_{ij} is the unique factor score for person i on the unique factor j.

The components of the unique factor are represented by the equation

$$\upsilon_{ij} = s_{ij} + e_{ij},$$

where

s_{ij} is the factor score of individual i on the specific factor j and

e_{ij} is the factor score of individual i on the unique factor j.

Although the data model is conceptually useful, in practice its values are impossible to estimate because individuals' scores on unobservable latent variables cannot be known.

The data model, however, does provide the theoretical basis for an alternative expression of the model that can be used. Specifically, given the data model and making certain distributional assumptions, it is possible to mathematically derive a version of the CFM designed not to explain the structure of raw data but instead to account for the structure of correlations among measured variables. The correlational structure version of the CFM is represented by the equation

$$P = \lambda \, \phi \, \lambda^{T} + D_{\psi},$$

where

P is the correlation matrix in the population,

λ is the factor loadings matrix,

ϕ is the matrix of correlations among common factors,

λ^{T} is transpose of the factor loadings matrix, and

D_{ψ} is the matrix of unique variances.

This equation states that a matrix of correlations among measured variables is a function of the common factor loadings (λ), the correlations among common factors (ϕ), and the unique variances (D_{ψ}).

Yet another way in which the CFM can be represented is in the form of a "path diagram" (see Figure 1). In these diagrams, circles or ovals represent latent variables and factors (both common and unique), and squares or rectangles represent measured variables. The other components of the diagram are directional arrows, which imply a linear causal influence, and bidirectional arrows, which represent an association with no assumption of causality. Figure 1 provides an example of how the CFM can be represented in a case where it is hypothesized that two common factors (F1 and F2) and four unique factors (U1–U4) can be used to explain correlations among four measured variables (X1–X4). Note that in the present example, the two common factors are assumed to each influence two measured variables, and each unique variable influences only one measured variable.

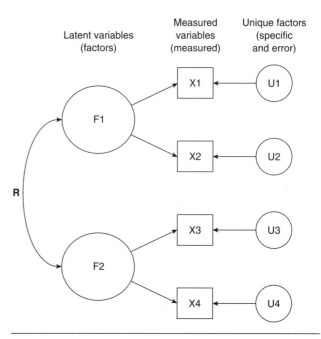

Figure 1   Path Diagram for a Common Factor Model With Two Common Factors and Four Measured Variables

Exploratory Factor Analysis

In practice, factor analysis involves a set of statistical procedures used to arrive at numerical values for the elements of the matrices expressed in the correlation structure version of the CFM. In some cases, this is accomplished in an exploratory fashion. Exploratory factor analysis (EFA) (also called unrestricted factor analysis) is used when there is little empirical or theoretical basis for specifying a precise a priori model. In brief, EFA is a collection of procedures for determining the precise model that is appropriate for the data and arriving at estimates of the numerical values for that model. Several steps must be undertaken to accomplish these objectives.

First, the correct number of common factors must be determined. Procedures for performing this step include the scree plot, parallel analysis, model fit, and Kaiser criterion (the "eigenvalue is greater than one" rule). Importantly, not all these procedures work well (e.g., the Kaiser criterion), and none are infallible. Thus, methodologists recommend using several of the best-performing procedures in conjunction with one another. Methodologists also recommend that researchers consider the interpretability and replicability of the solution in addition to these statistical procedures when determining the appropriate number of factors.

Second, given a model with a specific number of factors, the model must then be fit to the data (a process also called factor extraction). This process involves calculating the actual numerical values for the model. A number of model fitting procedures are available (e.g., noniterated principal axis factors, iterated principal axis factors, and maximum likelihood). Although the procedures use different mathematical approaches, all of them share a common goal of attempting to find the set of numerical values that will result in the best fit of the model to the data. One advantage of the principal axis factors methods is that they do not make strong distributional assumptions. In contrast, maximum likelihood does make assumptions of multivariate normality but provides more information (e.g., model fit indices, confidence intervals for parameter estimates).

Finally, because more than one best-fitting solution is possible for an EFA involving two or more factors, a single solution is arrived at through "rotation." The goal of the rotation process is to select that solution that is most readily interpretable. Various rotation procedures have been proposed. Some of these procedures (e.g., varimax rotation) are orthogonal rotations in that they assume common factors to be uncorrelated. Others (e.g., direct quartimin, Promax, and Harris-Kaiser orthoblique) are oblique rotations in that they permit (but do not require) common factors to be correlated. Given that in most cases it is difficult to know if factors will be correlated, oblique rotation is usually more conceptually sensible than orthogonal rotation.

Confirmatory Factor Analysis

In other cases, researchers may have a strong empirical or theoretical basis to make predictions regarding the number and nature of the common factors. In these contexts, confirmatory factor analysis (CFA) is used. CFA can be broken into several phases. First, the researcher must specify the model. This process involves specifying how many common factors exist and exactly where zero factor loadings will occur (i.e., which measured variables will not load on each common factor). Model specification also requires the researcher to specify which, if any, common factors are correlated with one another and which, if any, unique factors will correlate with one another.

Once the model is specified, it must be fit to the data. As in EFA, this involves finding the set of numerical values that provides the best fit of the model to the data. Various model fitting procedures are available (e.g., generalized least squares and asymptotic distribution-free estimation), but maximum likelihood is by far the most frequently used procedure. Because the specific pattern of zero and nonzero factor loadings is specified in CFA, rotation of solutions is not necessary.

The third phase of CFA is model evaluation. This step involves examining the results of the analysis and assessing the adequacy of the proposed model. Several types of information are considered. For example, most CFA model fitting procedures permit the computation of goodness-of-fit indices. Numerous fit indices have been proposed, but these indices are often categorized as falling into two groups. Absolute fit indices assess the absolute magnitude of the discrepancy between the model and the data. Popular indices of this type include root mean square error of approximation and standardized root mean square residual. Incremental fit indices evaluate the fit of the model to the data relative to some comparison model (usually the null model, which postulates no underlying structure in the data). Popular fit indices of this type include the nonnormed fit index (or Tucker-Lewis fit index) and the normed fit index.

The second category of information used in model evaluation is the parameter estimates of the model. Unlike EFA, CFA analyses not only report the estimates of the parameters but also routinely report confidence intervals and significance tests for all estimates. All of this information is examined to evaluate the theoretical plausibility of the estimates. Additionally, it is sometimes the case in CFA that a researcher has specific hypotheses to test regarding certain parameters in the model. For example, the researcher might postulate that a given factor is more highly correlated with one factor than another. Precise hypotheses involving comparisons of parameters can be tested by placing equality constraints on the model (e.g., constraining the two correlations being compared to be equal) and then comparing the constrained model to the original model. A formal statistical test comparing the fit between the two models (a chi-square difference test) can then be conducted. If significant, such a test indicates that the constraint is not appropriate and thus the constrained parameters are significantly different from one another.

The final step in CFA is model modification. When a proposed model is found to perform poorly (as a result of either poor model fit or implausible parameter estimates), researchers sometimes consider modifications to the model. Most structural equation modeling programs used to conduct CFA provide numerical indices that can be used as a guide to which parameters originally fixed in the model might be freed to improve model fit. Unfortunately, use of these indices has proven problematic because such changes often do not have a firm theoretical basis. Additionally, studies have suggested that these modification indices are not especially effective in identifying model misspecifications. Thus, most methodologists recommend that model modification be guided by theory rather than the use of these indices.

Conclusions

EFA and CFA can be thought of as complementary rather than opposing approaches to data analysis. Specifically, EFA may be the approach of choice during the early phases of a research program, when comparatively little is known about the underlying structure of correlations among a set of measured variables. Once EFA analyses have helped establish a firm theoretical and empirical basis for more precise predictions, later studies may make use of CFA to conduct more rigorous and focused tests of the researchers' theory.

—Ronald D. Porter and Leandre R. Fabrigar

See also Exploratory Factor Analysis; Factor Scores; Multiple Factor Analysis

Further Reading

Fabrigar, L. R., Wegener, D. T., MacCallum, R. C., & Strahan, E. J. (1999). Evaluating the use of exploratory factor analysis in psychological research. *Psychological Methods, 4,* 272–299.

Finch, J. F., & West, S. G. (1997). The investigation of personality structure: Statistical models. *Journal of Research in Personality, 31,* 439–485.

Gorsuch, R. L. (1983). *Factor analysis* (2nd ed.). Hillsdale NJ: Erlbaum.

Harman, H. H. (1976). *Modern factor analysis* (3rd ed.). Chicago: University of Chicago Press.

Thompson, B. (2004). *Exploratory and confirmatory factor analysis: Understanding concepts and applications.* Washington, DC: American Psychological Society.

Thurstone, L. L. (1947). *Multiple factor analysis.* Chicago: University of Chicago Press.

Wegener, D. T., & Fabrigar, L. R. (2000). Analysis and design for nonexperimental data: Addressing causal and noncausal hypotheses. In H. T. Reis & C. M. Judd (Eds.), *Handbook of research methods in social and personality psychology* (pp. 412–450). Cambridge, UK: Cambridge University Press.

Factor analysis: http://en.wikipedia.org/wiki/Factor_analysis

Factor analysis software sampling: http://quantrm2.psy.ohio-state.edu/browne/software.htm

Applying Ideas on Statistics and Measurement

The following abstract is adapted from Hogarty, K. Y., Hines, C. V., Kromrey, J. D., Ferron, J. M., & Mumford, K. R. (2005). The quality of factor solutions in exploratory factor analysis: The influence of sample size, communality, and overdetermination. *Educational and Psychological Measurement, 65*(2), 202–226.

Factor analysis is one of many techniques that allows us to better understand threads common to large sets for data. The purpose of this study was to investigate the relationship between sample size and the quality of factor solutions obtained from one type of factor analysis, exploratory factor analysis. This research expanded on the range of conditions previously examined, employing a broad selection of criteria for the evaluation of the quality of sample factor solutions. Results showed that when communalities are high, sample size tended to have less influence on the quality of factor solutions than when communalities are low. Overdetermination of factors was also shown to improve the factor analysis solution. Finally, decisions about the quality of the factor solution depended on which criteria were examined.

FACTOR SCORES

The purpose of conducting factor analysis is to explain the interrelationships between a set of measured variables and a reduced set of theoretically meaningful common factors. An attractive feature of this multivariate procedure is the capability to rank order the measured objects (usually people) on the common factors. These novel factor scores can be used in subsequent statistical analyses or employed in decision making processes. For instance, factor scores can be correlated with other variables, entered as predictor variables in regression analyses, or used as dependent measures in analyses of variance. They can also be employed in applied settings, such as when a clinical psychologist uses a client's factor scores on measures of psychological well-being to determine a treatment plan or when a school psychologist uses factor scores from an intelligence test to make judgments regarding a child's cognitive abilities. Given their utility, factor scores are widely employed in both research and practice.

Factor Scores Explained

As a contrived example study, consider 200 individuals who rate themselves on six questionnaire items written to measure personality traits. The individuals rate on a 5-point scale the extent to which each statement (e.g., "I have many close friends," "I do not get stressed-out easily") applies to themselves. A common factor analysis is subsequently conducted on the ratings, and two factors are extracted. After the factors are rotated with an oblique transformation, they are labeled Extroversion and Emotional Stability. Factor

scores for the 200 individuals can now be computed by regressing the six item scores onto the two factors. Common factors are often referred to as *latent* or *unobservable* because their scores must be derived through such a regression analysis based on the original items. The resulting regression weights are referred to as *factor score coefficients*, and they can be applied to the standardized item responses to compute the factor scores. For example, Extroversion factor scores may be computed as follows:

$$(\text{Item}1_z)(.45) + (\text{Item}2_z)(.32) + (\text{Item}3_z)(.72)$$
$$+ (\text{Item}4_z)(.02) + (\text{Item}5_z)(-.12) + (\text{Item}6_z)(.05).$$

The values .45, .32, .72, and the rest are the factor score coefficients, which are standardized regression weights. Coefficients are computed for all six items, and their relative absolute magnitudes indicate that the first three items contribute most to the prediction of scores on the Extroversion factor, while the remaining three items contribute less (their weights are near zero). Item 5 contributes negatively to the computation of Extroversion factor scores in this example.

Now consider two individuals, Joe and Mary. If their standardized responses (i.e., their z scores) on the rating scale are placed in the equation, their Extroversion factor scores are as follows:

$$\text{Joe's Extroversion} = (.90)(.45) + (1.02)(.32) + (1.10)$$
$$(.72) + (.25)(.02) + (.43)(-.12)$$
$$+ (.22)(.05) = 1.49$$

$$\text{Mary's Extroversion} = (-.68)(.45) + (.19)(.32)$$
$$+ (-1.29)(.72) + (.45)(.02)$$
$$+ (.77)(-.12) + (.15)(.05)$$
$$= -1.25$$

Since high scores on the rating scale indicate greater extroversion, Joe is found to be extroverted and Mary is introverted. The standardized Emotional Stability factor scores can be computed similarly:

$$\text{Joe's Emotional} = (.90)(.05) + (1.02)(.01) + (1.10)$$
$$\text{Stability} \qquad (-.03) + (.25)(.60) + (.43)(.70)$$
$$+ (.22)(.53) = .59$$

Mary's Emotional = (−.68)(.05) + (.19) (.01)
    Stability   + (−1.29)(−.03) + (.45)(.60)
                     + (.77) (.70) + (.15)(.53) = .90

The second numbers (e.g., .05, .01, −.03) in each product are the factor score coefficients for the Emotional Stability factor, and the first numbers are Joe's and Mary's z scores for the six items. The results indicate that Mary is slightly more emotionally stable than Joe. The same coefficients for both factors could similarly be used to compute factor scores for the remaining 198 individuals in the study.

Computing factor scores is thus a matter of regressing the items onto the factors to derive factor score coefficients. These standardized regression weights are then applied to the standardized scale responses to compute each individual's relative standing on the factors. How, exactly, are the factor score coefficients computed? Unfortunately, the answer to this question is not straightforward because of a historic intellectual puzzle referred to as *factor score indeterminacy.*

In the early days of factor analysis, a peculiar property of the common factor model was discovered; specifically, the algebra underlying the computation of factor scores involves solving a set of equations with more unknowns than equations. The implication is that a unique solution for the factor scores does not exist. Instead, an infinite number of sets of factor scores can be computed for any given analysis. The scores for Joe and Mary above on the Extroversion and Emotional Stability factors are thus one of an infinite number of sets of factor scores that can be computed! What would happen if in another solution, Joe was introverted and Mary was extraverted? There would be no way of choosing between the two different conclusions regarding Joe and Mary since both sets of factor scores represent valid solutions. Obviously, factor score indeterminacy is a serious issue. If the individuals (or measured objects) in the study cannot be unambiguously rank ordered along the Extroversion and Emotional Stability factors, one must wonder if the factors are of any scientific value.

Refined and Coarse Factor Scores

Since it was discovered in the early 1900s, psychometricians have attempted to understand the analytical, practical, and theoretical meaning of factor score indeterminacy. One implication is that computed factor scores are imperfect representations of the factors themselves. Consequently, the statistical properties of the factor scores may not always match those of the factors for which they are computed. For instance, while the common factors in a given analysis are uncorrelated (i.e., orthogonal), the factor scores may be slightly or moderately correlated. To adjust for these discrepancies, psychometricians have developed a number of methods for computing factor scores, and these methods can be divided into two groups: *refined* and *coarse.* The former produce multidecimal factor score coefficients like those in the examples above. They are often referred to by their distinct statistical properties or by the names of the scholars responsible for their derivation and are summarized in Table 1.

Table 1   Methods for Computing Refined Factor Scores

Author	Name	Desirable Property
Thurstone	Regression	Indeterminacy is minimized (i.e., determinacy is maximized).
Anderson-Rubin	Orthogonal	Factor scores for different factors are uncorrelated (i.e., perfectly orthogonal); only appropriate for orthogonal factors.
Bartlett	Univocal	Factor scores for a given factor are not correlated with other factors in the analysis; only appropriate for orthogonal factors.
McDonald	Correlation-preserving	Correlations between factor scores match the correlations between the factors; appropriate for orthogonal or correlated factors.

The most popular of the refined factor scoring methods can be found in many statistical programs, and their equations are readily available (see Further Reading at the end of this entry). None of these methods are clearly superior to the others, however, and the choice between the different refined factor scores rests entirely with the researcher, who alone can decide which property is most important for a particular investigation.

The coarse methods offer popular alternatives to the refined factor scores. With coarse methods the factor scores are computed as simple sums of the original or standardized item scores. For example, Joe's Extroversion factor score might be computed as follows:

$$\text{Joe's Extroversion} = \text{Item1}_z + \text{Item2}_z + \text{Item3}_z$$
$$= .90 + 1.02 + 1.10 = 3.02$$

Such scores are often referred to as scale scores, sum scores, or total scores, among other names. As long as they are based on the results of a factor analysis, they are also appropriately referred to as factor scores since they indicate the relative standings of the people (or objects) on the factors. This point can be understood by realizing that the simple summing process involves an implicit weighting scheme:

$$\begin{aligned}\text{Joe's Extroversion} = &(1)(\text{Item1}_z) + (1)(\text{Item2}_z)\\ &+ (1)(\text{Item3}_z) + (0)(\text{Item4}_z)\\ &+ (0)(\text{Item5}_z) + (0)(\text{Item6}_z)\end{aligned}$$

$$\begin{aligned}= &(1)(.90) + (1)(1.02) + (1)(1.10) + (0)(.25)\\ &+ (0)(.43) + (0)(.22) = 3.02\end{aligned}$$

It is easy to see that the coarse method of computing Joe's factor scores is a simplification of the refined method; the multidecimal factor score coefficients have been replaced with whole numbers. In this example, the fourth, fifth, and sixth items are given weights of zero, essentially dropping them from the computation of the coarse factor scores. Since the six items are all measured on the same scale, it should also be noted that Joe's coarse factor scores could be computed by summing his original responses instead of the z scores.

The coarse methods differ with regard to the processes used to determine the whole weights. The most common approach for determining the weights is to examine the structure coefficients (i.e., the correlations between the factors and the items) and choose the most salient items. A salience criterion is determined using some rule-of-thumb value such as |.30| or |.40|. Items with salient positive structure coefficients are given weights of 1, and items with salient negative coefficients are given weights of −1. Items with non-salient structure coefficients are given weights of zero. The pattern coefficients are sometimes used instead of the structure coefficients in this scheme. Either way, these particular coarse factor scores are problematic because they run the risk of being very poor representations of the factors themselves. In other words, coarse factor scores based on the structure or pattern coefficients may not be highly correlated with the very factors they are intended to quantify. Consequently, although they are popular in the scientific literature, they are not recommended. Instead, the coarse factor scores should be based on a process of simplifying the factor score coefficients. The process therefore begins by using one of the refined factor scoring methods to derive the factor score coefficients. The resulting coefficients are then simplified to whole numbers and used as weights to compute the coarse factor scores. This coarse method is superior because it is based on the factor score coefficients, which are specifically designed for computing factor scores. The relative magnitudes of the pattern and structure coefficients may be quite discrepant from the factor score coefficients, leading to an inaccurate weighting scheme and invalid factor scores.

Evaluating Factor Scores

Tools are available for assessing the amount of indeterminacy in any given common factor analysis as well as for evaluating the quality of the computed factor scores. Many statistical programs, for instance, report the squared multiple correlations for the common factors. These values indicate the proportion of determinacy in the common factors, and results near 1 are desirable (1 = no indeterminacy), whereas results equal to or less than .80 are generally considered to indicate too much indeterminacy. When a common factor is judged as highly indeterminate, factor scores should not be computed via any method above. If a factor is judged sufficiently determinate, and factor scores are computed, they should be evaluated for their validity, correlational accuracy, and univocality. Validity refers to the correlation between the factor scores and the factors themselves, and correlational accuracy refers to the correspondence between the factor score intercorrelations and the factor intercorrelations. Univocality refers to the degree of overlap between factor scores and noncorresponding factors in the analysis. Macros for SAS are readily available for assessing these different properties of refined and coarse factor scores (see Further Reading at the end of this entry).

Additional Issues

A number of additional issues regarding factor scores should be noted. First, principal component analysis (PCA) always produces refined component scores that are determinate. The four methods in Table 1 thus produce identical results for PCA. If coarse component scores are computed, however, they should be based on the component score coefficients and evaluated for their quality. Second, image analysis is the only common factor model that yields determinate factor scores. It is not as popular as other factor techniques (e.g., maximum likelihood or iterated principal axes), but it offers a viable alternative if one wishes to avoid indeterminacy and still use a common factor model. Last, other latent trait statistical methods such as structural equation modeling and item response theory are indeterminate. Although it has not been discussed at great length with these other methods, indeterminacy is an important concern that should not be overlooked indefinitely.

—*James W. Grice*

See also Exploratory Factor Analysis; Multiple Factor Analysis

Further Reading

Grice, J. W. (2001). Computing and evaluating factor scores. *Psychological Methods, 6,* 430–450.

Guttman, L. (1955). The determinacy of factor score matrices with applications for five other problems of common factor theory. *British Journal of Statistical Psychology, 8,* 65–82.

Steiger, J. H., & Schonemann, P. H. (1978). A history of factor indeterminacy. In S. Shye (Ed.), *Theory construction and data analysis* (pp. 136–178). Chicago: University of Chicago Press.

Factor scores computation and evaluation tools: http://psychology.okstate.edu/faculty/jgrice/factorscores/

FACTORIAL DESIGN

Factorial design is one of the most popular research tools in many areas, including psychology and education. Factorial design investigates two or more independent variables simultaneously, along with interactions between independent variables. Each independent variable can be either a treatment or a classification. Ideally, all possible combinations of each treatment (or classification) occur together in the design. The purpose is to investigate the effect of each independent variable and interaction on a dependent variable.

In a one-way design, a single independent variable is investigated for its effect on a dependent variable. For example, we might ask whether three therapies produce different recovery rates or whether two drugs lead to a significant difference in average adjustment scores. In a factorial design, we might ask whether the two drugs differ in effectiveness and whether the effectiveness of the drugs changes when they are applied at different dosage levels. The first independent variable is the type of drug (with two levels), and the second independent variable is the dosage (with two levels). This design would be a 2 × 2 factorial design. Each independent variable could have more than two levels.

An Example of a 2 × 2 Design

Table 1 presents hypothetical data and means in which the data are presented for scores under two drugs and two dosage levels. Each of the four cell means is based on three observations. That is, three different

Table 1 Summary Table for Two Factor Design

Drug/ Dosage	B_1 10 mg	B_2 20 mg	Overall
A_1	8.0	10.0	
Drug 1	7.0	9.0	
	6.0	8.0	
Means	7.0	9.0	$M_{A_1} = 8.0$
SS	2.0	2.0	$N_{A_1} = 6$
A_2	5.0	3.0	
Drug 2	4.0	2.0	
	3.0	1.0	
Means	4.0	2.0	$M_{A_2} = 3.0$
SS	2.0	2.0	$N_{A_2} = 6$
Overall	$M_{B_1} = 5.5$ $N_{B_1} = 6$	$M_{B_1} = 5.5$ $N_{B_2} = 6$	$M_T = 5.5$

Note: SS = sum of squares; *M* = mean.

individuals were given either Drug 1 or Drug 2 and either 10 mg or 20 mg of the drug. The 12 individuals were randomly assigned to one of the four combinations of drug and dosage level. Higher mean adjustment scores indicate better adjustment.

As in a simple, independent-sample *t* test or one-way analysis of variance (ANOVA), the variability within each treatment condition must be determined. The variability within the four groups is defined as SS_{WG} where

$$SS_{WG} = SS_1 + SS_2 + SS_3 + SS_4$$
$$SS_{WG} = 2.0 + 2.0 + 2.0 + 2.0$$
$$SS_{WG} = 8.0.$$

With three observations in each group, there are $3 - 1 = 2$ degrees of freedom (*df*) within each group. The degrees of freedom within all groups are

$$df_{WG} = 2 + 2 + 2 + 2 = 8.$$

The within-groups variability is known as the mean square (*MS*) within groups, defined as

$$MS_{WG} = \frac{SS_{WG}}{df_{WG}} = \frac{8.0}{8} = 1.0.$$

The overall difference between drugs is Factor A, Drug Type. The null and alternative hypotheses are

$$H_0: \mu_{A_1} = \mu_{A_2}$$
$$H_1: \mu_{A_1} \neq \mu_{A_2}.$$

The variability among the drug means is

$$SS_A = N_{A_1}(\bar{X}_{A_1} - \bar{X}_T)^2 + N_{A_2}(\bar{X}_{A_2} - \bar{X}_T)^2$$
$$SS_A = 6(8.0 - 5.5)^2 + 6(3.0 - 5.5)^2$$
$$SS_A = 6(2.5)^2 + 6(-2.5)^2$$
$$SS_A = 6(6.25) + 6(6.25)$$
$$SS_A = 75.$$

With *a* levels of Factor A, the degrees of freedom will be

$$df_A = a - 1 = 2 - 1 = 1.$$

The *MS* for Factor A is

$$MS_A = \frac{SS_A}{df_A} = \frac{75}{1} = 75.$$

The *F* test for Factor A is

$$F_A = = = 75.$$

To test the null hypothesis at $\alpha = .01$, we need the critical value CV $= F_{.99}(1,8) = 11.26$. The null hypothesis is rejected because $F_A = 75.0 > 11.26$. The overall mean, $M_{A_1} = 8.0$, for Drug 1 is significantly greater than the overall mean, $M_{A_2} = 3.0$, for Drug 2. Drug 1 produces significantly greater adjustment that does Drug 2.

Applying similar calculations to Factor B, Dosage Level, we have the hypotheses

$$H_0: \mu_{B_1} = \mu_{B_2}$$
$$H_1: \mu_{B_1} \neq \mu_{B_2}.$$

The variability among the drug means is

$$SS_B = N_{B_1}(\bar{X}_{B_1} - \bar{X}_T)^2 + N_{B_2}(\bar{X}_{B_2} - \bar{X}_T)^2$$
$$SS_B = 6(5.5 - 5.5)^2 + 6(5.5 - 5.5)^2$$
$$SS_A = 0.0.$$

With *b* levels of Factor B, the degrees of freedom will be

$$df_B = b - 1 = 2 - 1 = 1.$$

The MS for Factor B is

$$MS_B = \frac{SS_B}{df_B} = \frac{0.0}{1} = 0.0.$$

The F test for Factor B is

$$F_B = \frac{MS_A}{MS_{WG}} = \frac{0.0}{1} = 0.0.$$

To test the null hypothesis at $\alpha = .01$, we need the critical value (CV) = $F_{.99}(1,8) = 11.26$. The null hypothesis is not rejected because $F_B = 0.0 < 11.26$. The overall mean, $M_{B_1} = 5.5$, for 10 mg is not significantly different from the overall mean, $M_{B_2} = 5.5$, for 20 mg. There is no overall difference between the dosage levels.

To investigate the interaction effect, we define the following population means:

μ_{11} = Population mean for Drug 1 and Dosage 10 mg,

μ_{12} = Population mean for Drug 1 and Dosage 20 mg,

μ_{21} = Population mean for Drug 2 and Dosage 10 mg, and

μ_{22} = Population mean for Drug 2 and Dosage 20 mg.

The null and alternative hypotheses for the interaction are

H_0: $\mu_{11} - \mu_{21} = \mu_{12} - \mu_{22}$

H_1: $\mu_{11} - \mu_{21} \neq \mu_{12} - \mu_{22}$.

One way to evaluate the interaction variability is to first calculate the variability among the four cell means. We call this the cells SS, defined as

$$SS_{CELLS} = N_{11}(\overline{X}_{11} - \overline{X}_T)^2 + N_{12}(\overline{X}_{12} - \overline{X}_T)^2$$
$$+ N_{21}(\overline{X}_{21} - \overline{X}_T)^2 + N_{22}(\overline{X}_{22} - \overline{X}_T)^2$$
$$SS_{CELLS} = 3(7.0 - 5.5)^2 + 3(9.0 - 5.5)^2$$
$$+ 3(4.0 - 5.5)^2 + 3(2.0 - 5.5)^2$$
$$SS_{CELLS} = 3(1.5)^2 + 3(3.5)^2 + 3(-1.5)^2 + 3(-3.5)^2$$
$$SS_{CELLS} = 3[2.25 + 12.25\ 2.25 + 12.25]$$
$$SS_{CELLS} = 3[29]$$
$$SS_{CELLS} = 87.$$

There are four cell means or four different treatments among the two drugs and two dosage levels. In a larger factorial design, we might have more than two levels of Factor A, more than two levels of Factor B, or more than two levels of both. If the total number of cells or treatment combinations is k, then the value of CELLS degrees of freedom would be

$$df_{CELLS} = k - 1.$$

In the present case we have

$$df_{CELLS} = 4 - 1 = 3.$$

The interaction sum of squares, SS_{AB}, can be found from

$$SS_{AB} = SS_{CELLS} - SS_A - SS_B.$$
$$SS_{AB} = 87 - 75 - 0.0$$
$$SS_{AB} = 12.$$

$$df_{AB} = df_A \times df_B = 1 \times 1 = 1.$$

From the above we have

$$MS_{AB} = \frac{SS_{AB}}{df_{AB}} = \frac{12.0}{1} = 12.0.$$

We test the interaction null hypothesis with

$$F_{AB} = \frac{MS_{AB}}{MS_{WG}} = \frac{12.0}{1} = 12.0.$$

Testing at $\alpha = .01$, we reject H_0 because $12.0 > 11.26$. The greater adjustment for Drug 1 compared with Drug 2 is significantly greater for 20 mg $(7.0 = 9.0 - 2.0)$ than for 10 mg $(3.0 = 7.0 - 4.0)$.

Some researchers like to test simple main effects to aid in the interpretation of a significant interaction. For example, the difference between adjustment scores of the two drugs when both are administered at 20 mg is 7.0. It can be shown that the difference is significant at the .01 level. It can also be shown that the difference of 3.0 for 10 mg is also significant at the .01 level. Thus, these two simple main effects are not helpful for the data in Table 1 because the same pattern of significance is found for both simple main effects. The interpretation that the 7.0 difference is significantly greater than the 3.0 difference can be made without any additional testing.

There are three assumptions for each of the F tests in a factorial design. They are the same three assumptions as for the independent-samples t test and the one-way, independent-groups ANOVA. They are as follows:

1. Independent observations are assumed in each cell of the design. This includes random assignment to groups. Failure of this assumption can completely invalidate the results of the F tests.

2. The populations are normally distributed. The F tests are relatively robust to failure of the normality assumption. With markedly nonnormal populations, alternative tests, such as nonparametric procedures, must be considered.

3. Population variances are assumed to be equal. With equal sample sizes that are not too small, the F tests are relatively robust to failure of the equal variances assumption. Equal N of 7 to 15 may be needed, depending on the degree of inequality of variances.

Although equal Ns are not a requirement of factorial designs, they are highly recommended, even if the equal variances assumption is satisfied. Equal sizes are necessary to maintain independence of the three effects in factorial design. In fact, unequal cell sizes lead to a number of complications in the testing and interpretation of the effects of factorial design.

—*Philip H. Ramsey*

See also Analysis of Covariance (ANCOVA); Analysis of Variance (ANOVA); Multivariate Analysis of Variance (MANOVA)

Further Reading

Boik, R. J. (1979). Interactions, partial interactions, and interaction contrasts in the analysis of variance. *Psychological Bulletin, 86,* 1084–1089.

Kirk, R. E. (1995). *Experimental design: Procedures for the behavioral sciences.* Pacific Grove, CA: Brooks/Cole.

Maxwell, S. E., and Delaney, H. D. (1990). *Designing experiments and analyzing data.* Belmont, CA: Wadsworth.

Winer, B. J., Brown, D. R., and Michels, K. M. (1991). *Statistical principles in experimental designs.* New York: McGraw-Hill.

FAGAN TEST OF INFANT INTELLIGENCE

The Fagan Test of Infant Intelligence (FTII, published by Infantest Corporation) purports to index infant intelligence by assessing infants' information processing capacities. The degree to which continuity exists between infant cognitive capacities and later intelligence has interested researchers since the 1930s. Until the early 1980s, intelligence in infancy was thought to be unrelated to intellectual functioning in childhood and adulthood. This sentiment was based on the lack of association between researchers' indices of infant intelligence, which assessed sensory-motor functioning, and adult measures of intelligence.

The FTII was developed in the early 1980s by Joseph F. Fagan, III, to assess infant information processing capacities such as visual recognition memory, habituation, and discrimination and relate them to intellectual functioning later in life. The FTII and other tests tapping infant information processing have led researchers to believe today that there is a relation between infant intellectual capacities and later intellectual functioning.

The FTII procedure is conducted on infants between 3 and 12 months of age and rests on the well-known tendency of infants to gaze more at novel stimuli than at familiar stimuli. The standard procedure involves two phases; the timing of each phase varies according to the age of the infant. In the "familiarization phase," the infant sitting in the parent's lap is presented with two identical stimuli, such as faces or geometric patterns, until the infant gazes at them for a predetermined amount of time. In the "test phase," one of the familiar stimuli is then paired with a novel stimulus. This procedure is repeated approximately 10 times during one sitting. The proportion of total looking time during which the infant gazes at the novel stimulus is used to derive a novelty preference score thought to reflect some of the cognitive capacities of the infant.

There is mixed evidence as to whether the FTII predicts later intellectual functioning. A quantitative review of several empirical investigations suggests that the FTII and other similar measures of infant cognitive functioning positively correlate with later intellectual performance. There is also evidence that the FTII is a valid screening device in infancy that predicts mild to severe mental retardation with up to 80% accuracy. Nevertheless, the FTII has been criticized for its low predictive validity and lack of reliability. As a whole, the FTII assesses infant cognitive capacities, but some controversy surrounds the degree to which the procedure accurately predicts later intelligence.

—Matthew J. Hertenstein and Lauren E. Auld

See also Culture Fair Intelligence Test; Gf-Gc Theory of Intelligence; Intelligence Quotient; Intelligence Tests

Further Reading

Fagan, J. F., & Detterman, D. K. (1992). The Fagan Test of Infant Intelligence: A technical summary. *Journal of Applied Developmental Psychology, 13,* 173–193.

FTII description and other measures of infant cognitive assessment: http://ehp.niehs.nih.gov/members/2003/6205/6205 .html#comp

FAMILY ENVIRONMENT SCALE

The Family Environment Scale (FES; published by Mind Garden, www.mindgarden.com) is composed of 10 subscales that measure the actual, preferred, and expected social environments of all types of families. The 10 subscales assess three sets of dimensions: (a) relationship dimensions (cohesion, expressiveness, conflict); (b) personal growth or goal orientation dimensions (independence, achievement orientation, intellectual-cultural orientation, active-recreational orientation, moral-religious emphasis); and (c) system maintenance dimensions (organization, control). The relationship and system maintenance dimensions primarily reflect internal family functioning; the personal growth or goal orientation dimensions primarily reflect the linkages between the family and the larger social context.

The FES has three forms:

1. The Real Form (Form R) measures people's perceptions of their current family or their family of origin. This form is used to assess individuals' perceptions of their conjugal and nuclear families, formulate clinical case descriptions, monitor and promote improvement in families, focus on how families adapt to life transitions and crises, understand the impact of the family on children and adolescents, and predict and measure the outcome of treatment.

2. The Ideal Form (Form I) measures people's preferences about an ideal family environment. This form is used to measure family members' preferences about how a family should function; assess family members' value orientations and how they change over time, such as before and after family counseling; and identify areas in which people want to change their family.

3. The Expectations Form (Form E) measures people's expectations about family settings. This form is used in premarital counseling to clarify prospective partners' expectations of their family, help members of blended families describe how they expect their new family to function, and identify parents' expectations about their family after a major life transition, such as retirement or the youngest child's leaving home.

The FES manual presents normative data on 1,432 normal families and 788 distressed families, describes the derivation and application of a family incongruence score that assesses the extent of disagreement among family members, presents psychometric information on the reliability and stability of the subscales, and covers the research applications and validity of the subscales. The manual includes a conceptual model of the determinants and outcomes of the family environment and reviews studies focusing on families of youth with behavioral, emotional, or developmental disabilities; families with a physically ill child; families with a history of physical or sexual abuse; and families of patients with medical and psychiatric disorders. The FES has also been used to focus on the relationship between the family environment and child development and adult adaptation and on families coping with life transitions and crises, such as parent or child death, unemployment and economic deprivation, immigration and acculturation, and combat and war.

—*Rudolf H. Moos and Bernice S. Moos*

See also Social Climate Scale

Further Reading

Moos, R. (2001). *The Family Environment Scale: An annotated bibliography* (3rd ed.). Redwood City, CA: Mind Garden.

Moos, R., & Moos, B. (1994). *Family Environment Scale manual* (3rd ed.). Redwood City, CA: Mind Garden.

FILE DRAWER PROBLEM

A meta-analysis is a quantitative summary or synthesis of findings of studies that focus on a common question; one example is a quantitative synthesis of results of studies that focus on the efficacy of psychotherapy. Unfortunately, studies that are included in a meta-analysis can be unrepresentative of all the methodologically sound studies that address this common question, so the combined results of the studies in the meta-analysis can be misleading. Included studies may be unrepresentative because of the well-documented "publication bias," which refers to a bias against publication of results of studies that do not yield statistically significant results. Because of this bias, results of studies that are not statistically significant often (a) do not appear in print (either as journal articles or as published abstracts of presentations), (b) wind up tucked away in researchers' "file drawers," and (c) remain undetected or inaccessible to meta-analysts. In the most extreme case of the "file drawer problem," the collection of studies included in a meta-analysis consists exclusively of those that yielded results significant at the conventional .05 level.

The most popular method of dealing with the file drawer problem involves calculation of Robert Rosenthal's Fail-Safe-N (FSN). The FSN—which was derived under the (questionable) assumptions that (a) the studies targeted by meta-analyses use two-tailed (nondirectional) tests and (b) the studies in the file drawers average null results—is an estimate of the minimum number of unpublished studies (tucked away in file drawers) that would threaten the validity of significant combined results of a meta-analysis. For example, for a well-known 1982 meta-analysis (by Landman and Dawes) focusing on a set of 42 studies of efficacy of psychotherapy that were considered (by the meta-analysts) to be appropriately controlled, the FSN was 461. Since the combined results of this meta-analysis indicated statistically significant beneficial effects of psychotherapy, it was inferred (by FSN users) that there would have to exist at least 461 unpublished file drawer studies (averaging null results) to threaten the validity of this conclusion. Although there are no firm guidelines for interpretation of FSNs, Rosenthal suggested using $FSN_c = K(5) + 10$ as a critical value or rule of thumb (where $K =$ number of studies in the meta-analysis); thus only FSNs below FSN_c would be considered to threaten significant combined results of a meta-analysis. For the Landman and Dawes meta-analysis, the FSN of 461 is well above the FSN_c of 220 (i.e., 42(5) + 10 = 220), suggesting to users of the FSN that the file drawer problem was negligible in this meta-analysis.

—*Louis M. Hsu*

See also Meta-Analysis

Further Reading

Darlington, R. B., & Hayes, A. F. (2000). Combining independent p values: Extensions of the Stouffer and binomial methods. *Psychological Methods, 4*, 496–515.

Hsu, L. M. (2000). Effects of directionality of significance tests on the bias of accessible effect sizes. *Psychological Methods, 5*, 333–342.

Hsu, L. M. (2002). Fail-Safe Ns for one- and two-tailed tests lead to different conclusions about publication bias. *Understanding Statistics, 1*, 85–100.

Iyengar, S., & Greenhouse, J. B. (1988). Selection models and the file drawer problem. *Statistical Science, 3,* 109–135.

Light, R. J., & Pillemer, D. B. (1984). *Summing up: The science of reviewing research.* Cambridge, MA: Harvard University Press.

FISHER, RONALD AYLMER (1890–1962)

Ronald Aylmer Fisher was a statistician, eugenicist, evolutionary biologist, and geneticist who helped lay the foundations of modern statistical science. At an early age, Fisher's special abilities were apparent. Because of his poor eyesight—extreme myopia—he was forbidden to read with the aid of electric lights. In the evenings, his mother and teachers would read to him and provide instruction without visual aids. Fisher's exceptional ability to solve mathematical problems in his head and his geometrical approach to statistical problems are attributed to this early form of instruction.

Fisher obtained a bachelor's degree in mathematics from the University of Cambridge in 1912. The following year, he took a statistical job with the Mercantile and General Investment Company of London, a position he held for two years. Because of his poor eyesight, he was rejected for military service during World War I and spent the war years teaching mathematics and physics at various public schools. In 1917, he married Ruth Eileen Guinness. The marriage produced two sons and eight daughters.

In 1919, Fisher accepted the newly created position of statistician at Rothamsted Experimental Station, approximately 20 miles north of London. The career move proved to be a fortunate choice. It brought him into close contact with researchers who were concerned with the interpretation of agricultural field experiments and with laboratory and greenhouse experiments. Rothamsted provided an environment in which Fisher was free to pursue his interests in genetics and evolution; carry out breeding experiments on mice, snails, and poultry; and develop statistical methods for small samples.

While at Rothamsted, Fisher invented the analysis of variance and revolutionized the design of experiments. The publication of Fisher's books *Statistical Methods for Research Workers* in 1925 and *The Design of Experiments* in 1939 gradually led to the acceptance of what today are considered the cornerstones of good experimental design: randomization, replication, local control or blocking, confounding, randomized blocks, and factorial arrangements. Other notable contributions include the concept of likelihood and the maximum likelihood estimator, the development of methods suitable for small samples, the discovery of the exact distribution of numerous statistics derived from small samples, the Fisher information measure, and contributions to hypothesis testing. In 1933, Fisher succeeded Karl Pearson as the Galton Professor of Eugenics at University College, London. Ten years later, he accepted an appointment as the Arthur Balfour Chair of Genetics at Cambridge, a position he held until his retirement in 1957.

Friends described Fisher as charming and warm but possessing a quick temper and a devotion to scientific truth as he saw it. The latter traits help explain his long-running disputes with Karl Pearson and Pearson's son Egon. Fisher was the recipient of numerous honors and was created a Knight Bachelor by Queen Elizabeth in 1952.

—*Roger E. Kirk*

See also Analysis of Variance (ANOVA)

Further Reading

Box, J. F. (1978). *R. A. Fisher: The life of a scientist.* New York: Wiley.

Ronald A. Fisher biographical essay: http://en.wikipedia.org/wiki/Ronald_Fisher

FISHER EXACT PROBABILITY TEST

The Fisher exact probability test (also called the Fisher-Irwin test) is one of several tests that can be used to detect whether one dichotomous variable is related to another. The rationale of this test, as well as its principal advantages and limitations, can be presented in the context of the following hypothetical small randomized experiment designed to determine whether a dichotomous "treatment" variable (Drug vs. Placebo) is related to a dichotomous "outcome" variable (Survival vs. Death).

A physician believes that a new antiviral drug might be effective in the treatment of SARS (severe acute respiratory syndrome). Assume that the physician carries out a randomized double-blind drug efficacy study involving 6 SARS patients (designated A, B, C, D, E, and F), 3 of whom (say, A, B, and C) were randomly selected from this group and given the drug and the remaining 3 of whom (D, E, and F) were given a placebo. Four months later, the 3 patients who received the drug were still alive whereas the 3 patients who received the placebo were not.

Results of this study may be summarized in a 2 × 2 table (see Table 1, which has 2 rows and 2 columns, ignoring row and column totals). More generally, results of any randomized treatment efficacy study involving dichotomous treatment and outcome variables may be summarized using the notation shown in Table 2. Do the results in Table 1 support the belief that the new drug is effective (relative to the placebo)? Or, more generally, do results of a randomized study that can be summarized as in Table 2 support the belief that the two dichotomous variables are related—for example, that patient outcomes are related to the treatments to which they have been exposed?

The fact that, in the physician's study, all the drug patients survived and all the placebo patients died (Table 1) would seem consistent with the belief that the patient outcomes were related to treatments they received. But is there a nonnegligible probability that such a positive result could have occurred if the treatment had in fact been unrelated to the outcome? Consistent with absence of relation of outcomes to treatments, let us hypothesize (this will be called the null hypothesis, and designated H_0 hereafter) that patients A, B, and C, who actually survived, would have survived whether they received the drug or the

Table 1   Results of a 2 x 2 Design

	Drug	Placebo	Row Totals
Survived	$X = 3$	0	3
Died	0	3	3
Column total	3	3	6

Table 2   Summary of Study Results

	Treatment 1	Treatment 2	Row Totals
Success	$X = a$	b	N_s
Failure	c	d	N_f
	N_1	N_2	N

placebo, and that D, E, and F, who actually died, would have died whether they received the drug or the placebo. Now we ask, Would the positive results in Table 1 have been unlikely if this H_0 had been true?

This H_0 has two important implications that are relevant to answering the question: First, the total number of survivors and nonsurvivors would be 3 and 3, respectively, regardless of which 3 patients were selected to receive the drug (and which other 3 received the placebo), so that the marginal totals of Table 1 would be fixed regardless of results of the randomization. Second, the number of survivors among the drug patients (which will be designated X hereafter), as well as the other 3 entries in the 2 × 2 table, would be determined by which patients were selected to receive the drug. For example, with the selection A, B, and C, the number of drug patients who would survive (X) would be 3, and the results of the study would be as displayed in Table 1. But with the selection of A, B, and D, then X would be 2, and the four cells of the 2 × 2 table would then have entries of [2 1] for row 1 and [1 2] for row 2 (note that since marginal totals of Table 1 are fixed, irrespective of which 3 patients are selected to receive the drug, knowledge of X determines entries in the other three cells of the 2 × 2 table; these entries are therefore redundant with X). With fixed marginal totals, the variable X is clearly relevant to tenability of the H_0 relative to the hypothesis that

Table 3   Patient Selection Possibilities for Receiving Drug

ABC(3)								
ABD(2)	ABE(2)	ABF(2)	ACD(2)	ACE(2)	ACF(2)	BCD(2)	BCE(2)	BCF(2)
ADE(1)	ADF(1)	AEF(1)	BDE(1)	BDF(1)	BEF(1)	CDE(1)	CDF(1)	CEF(1)
DEF(0)								

the drug is effective. There were, in fact, 20 possible ways in which the 3 patients who were to receive the drug could have been selected; these 20 selections are listed in Table 3, together with values of X they would have determined under the H_0.

Since the selection was random (meaning that all 20 possible selections were equiprobable), it is apparent that the probabilities of $X = 0, 1, 2$, and 3 given H_0 (designated $P(X \mid H_0)$) can be determined by counting how many of the 20 assignments yield each value of X and dividing this count by 20. Table 4 lists the probabilities obtained by applying this enumeration method.

Table 4   Probabilities Obtained by Applying This Enumeration Method

X	0	1	2	3
$P(X \mid H_o)$	1/20 = .05	9/20 = .45	9/20 = .45	1/20 = .05

Table 4 shows that the very positive result of the physician's study (in particular, $X = 3$) is improbable under the H_0 that the outcome (survival, death) was unrelated to treatment assignment for each of the 6 patients (in particular, $P(X = 3 \mid H_0) = 0.05$). This result, however, would be consistent with the hypothesis that the new drug worked. Table 4 also implies that a researcher who decided to reject the H_0 (i.e., to conclude that outcomes were related to treatments) if $X = 3$ would be taking a risk of 0.05 of making a Type I error (defined as "rejection of a true null hypothesis"). Note also that if a researcher decided to reject the H_0 if $X \geq 2$, then the researcher would be taking a very large risk (viz., .45 + .05 = .50) of making a Type I error.

Determining Fisher Exact Probabilities From Hypergeometric Distributions

In general (see Table 2), given (a) random assignment of N_1 participants (drawn from a pool of N participants) to Treatment 1 and $N_2 = (N - N_1)$ participants to Treatment 2, (b) N_s were observed to "Succeed" (e.g., survive) and N_f were observed to "Fail" (e.g., die), and (c) the null hypothesis (H_0) that the outcome is unrelated to treatment assignment, the probability of $(X = a)$ successes among participants exposed to Treatment 1 can be obtained using the formula

$$P(X = a \mid H_0)$$

$$= \frac{\dfrac{N_s! N_f!}{a!(N_s - a)!(N_1 - a)!(N_f - N_1 + a)!}}{\dfrac{N!}{N_1!(N - N_1)!}},$$

where any number (say, M) followed by an exclamation point ($M!$) is defined as follows:

$$M! = M\,(M{-}1)\,(M{-}2) \ldots (3)\,(2)\,(1)$$
$$(\text{e.g., } 6! = (6)(5)(4)(3)(2)(1) = 720),$$

and where $0! = 1! = 1$. For example, the $P(X = 2 \mid H_0)$ for Table 1 would be

$$P(X = 2 \mid H_0) = \frac{\dfrac{3!}{2!\,(3-2)!}\,\dfrac{3!}{1!\,(3-1)!}}{\dfrac{6!}{3!\,(6-3)!}}$$

$$= \frac{\dfrac{(3)(2)(1)}{(2)(1)\,(1)}\,\dfrac{(3)(2)(1)}{(1)\,(2)(1)}}{\dfrac{(6)(5)(4)(3)(2)(1)}{(3)(2)(1)\,(3)(2)(1)}} = \frac{9}{20} = .45$$

Note that the numerator yields the number of equiprobable selections of N_1 from N participants that would result in $X = 2$ (cf. the second line in Table 3) and that the denominator (obtained from $N! / (N_1!(N - N_1))!)$ is a count of the total number of possible equiprobable selections of N_1 from N (cf. all four lines in Table 3). The above formula, which calculates $P(X \mid H_0)$ using efficient counting principles, is called the general term of the hypergeometric distribution, and the probability distribution of X that can be used to generate (e.g., Table 1) is called the hypergeometric distribution.

The Fisher exact test is therefore appropriate for randomized designs (with random selection of N_1 participants, drawn from a pool of N participants, for assignment to Treatment 1 and $N_2 = N - N_1$ participants for assignment to Treatment 2, and with N_s Successes and N_f Failures) to address questions about relations of dichotomous "treatment" and "outcome" variables (see Table 2). The null hypothesis (H_0) in these designs is that, for each of the N participants, the outcome is unrelated to the treatment assignment. This H_0 implies that the selection (treatment assignment) does not affect the total numbers of Successes or Failures observed in the study (i.e., fix the row totals, N_s and N_f) but determines a, the value of X (see Table 2), as well as values of b, c, and d (since the value of a determines the values of b, c, and d, given the fixed marginal totals). Given randomization, X will have the hypergeometric distribution under H_0. Evidence against H_0, in a given study, consists of obtained values of X (the number of Treatment 1 patients who Succeed) so extreme as to have been very unlikely to have occurred had H_0 been true (say $p \leq .05$, as determined from the hypergeometric distribution). When the researcher's prediction or experimental hypothesis implies high values of X, the expression "exact probability" in the Fisher "exact probability" test usually refers to $P(X \geq X_{obtained} \mid H_0)$, where $X_{obtained}$ is the value of X obtained in the study and where the probabilities that are cumulated to calculate $P(X \geq X_{obtained} \mid H_0)$ are determined by the right side or "right tail" of the hypergeometric distribution. For example (see Table 1), if in the physician's study, $X_{obtained} = 2$ (i.e., 2 of the 3 patients who were given the

drug survived), then $P(X \geq X_{obtained} \mid H_0)$ would be .45 + .05 = .50. This probability is called a one-tailed p value of the Fisher exact test. Similarly, when the experimental hypothesis implies low values of X, the "exact probability" of Fisher's test results in another one-tailed p value, defined as $P(X \leq X_{obtained} \mid H_0)$, the sum of probabilities of $X \leq X_{obtained}$, located on the left side or left tail of the hypergeometric distribution. A "two-tailed p value" for the Fisher test would be the sum of probabilities of X at least as extreme as $X_{obtained}$ in both tails of the hypergeometric distribution. For example, if $X_{obtained} = 3$, results at least as extreme in the hypergeometric distribution would be $X = 3$ and $X = 0$, and the two-tailed p value of the Fisher test would therefore be .05 + .05 = .10 (see Table 4).

Assumptions and Limitations

The above information draws attention to two important characteristics of the Fisher exact test. First, the exact probability generated for this test is based on two important assumptions: (a) that both column and row marginal totals of the 2 × 2 table are fixed under the H_0 and (b) that the $[N! / (N_1! (N - N_1)!)]$ possible results of the experiment are all equiprobable under the H_0. These assumptions are required for the derivation of the hypergeometric distribution that is used to calculate the "exact probabilities" of this test. In the randomized design illustrations (above), assumption (a) is satisfied by the researcher's decision to select N_1 (drawn from the pool of N) participants for assignment to Treatment 1 and $N_2 = N - N_1$ participants for assignment to Treatment 2 (this decision fixes the column totals) and by the definition of the H_0 (which fixes the row totals, as explained above). Assumption (b) is satisfied, in these illustrations, by the random assignment. Second, the exact probability associated with the Fisher test is relevant, in these illustrations, to inferences about the relation of the outcome to the treatment *only for the N participants included in the study.* For example, the p value of .05 corresponding to the results of the physician's study warrants the conclusion (assuming that a risk of .05 of a Type I error is acceptable) that the H_0 can be rejected *for the 6 patients included in the physician's study.* The *p* value of the Fisher test does not support statistical inferences about efficacy of the drug with patients other than the 6 who took part in the study (although nonstatistical inferences may be possible).

The Fisher exact probability test can be applied to 2×2 table data of studies that do not involve random assignment of participants to conditions, as long as the hypergeometric distribution assumptions (viz., fixed marginal totals for both rows and columns of the 2×2 table and equiprobability under H_0 of the $[N! / (N_1!(N - N_1)!)]$ are plausible under the researcher's H_0. It is noteworthy that the experiment R. A. Fisher originally chose to illustrate his exact test did not involve random assignment of *N* participants to treatments but instead involved a selection made by a single participant. Fisher's experiment was designed to test a tea-drinking lady's claim that she could taste the difference between two cups of tea with milk, one in which the milk was added prior to the tea, and the other in which the tea was added prior to the milk. Fisher's experiment consisted of presenting the lady with eight cups (in random order) after informing her that in half of the cups, milk had been added first and in the other half, tea had been added first, and asking her to select the four in which the milk had been added first. The H_0 was that her claim was false and that her selection of four from the eight cups could then in effect be viewed as a random selection of four from eight cups. The number of successes (X = number of cups in which milk was added first) for the four cups she selected, which could be 0, 1, 2, 3, or 4, is relevant to testing her claim and can be viewed as a hypergeometric random variable if the H_0 is true. Clearly, the larger the value of X, the stronger the evidence against the H_0 (and indirectly for the lady's claim). Assuming that the lady obtained $X = 4$ successes, the exact one-tailed *p* level of the Fisher exact probability test would be $1/70 = .014$ (which may be verified by enumeration or by applying the general term of the hypergeometric distribution); in other words, it is improbable that she could have had that many successes if her claim had been false (and if her selection had in effect been a random selection of four from the eight cups). (Historical note: R. A. Fisher, who designed this interesting little experiment, once told M. G. Kendall that he never actually carried it out.)

A researcher who considers a *p* level of .014 too large for rejection of the H_0 could easily modify the study by increasing the number of cups so that more convincing evidence against the H_0 could be obtained. Thus, for example, if from a set of 16 cups the lady correctly identified the 8 cups in which milk had been poured first, the one-tailed *p* level of the Fisher exact test would be $1/12,870 = .0000777$ (which can easily be determined from the general term of the hypergeometric distribution). This result would provide very convincing evidence against the hypothesis (H_0) that her selection had been a random selection. However, as in the physician's study (above), the Fisher test would not allow statistical inferences about persons not included in the study: In particular, a very small *p* value for the tea-tasting experiment would not allow statistical inferences about tea-tasting abilities of any person other than the lady who took part in the study.

Using the Computer

SYSTAT offers two-tailed *p* values for the Fisher exact probability test as an option in its "cross-tab" module when the cross-tabulation involves two dichotomous variables. The SYSTAT output for the 16-cup tea-tasting experiment in which the lady correctly selected all (i.e., $X = 8$) of the cups in which milk had been poured first includes the 2×2 table and the exact two-tailed *p* value of the Fisher test:

	Milk First	*Tea First*	*Total*
Selected	8	0	8
Not selected	0	8	8
Total	8	8	16

Fisher exact test (two-tailed) probability = .000155.

—Louis M. Hsu

Further Reading

Fisher, R. A. (1971). *The design of experiments*. New York: Hafner. (Original work published in 1935)

Hodges, J. L., Jr., & Lehmann, E. L. (1970). *Basic concepts of probability and statistics* (2nd ed.). San Francisco: Holden-Day.

Maxwell, S. E., & Delaney, H. D. (2004). *Designing experiments and analyzing data* (2nd ed.). Mahwah, NJ: Erlbaum.

Fisher's exact test calculation: http://www.unc.edu/~preacher/fisher/fisher.htm

FISHER-IRWIN TEST

See FISHER EXACT PROBABILITY TEST

FISHER'S LSD

The analysis of variance (ANOVA) can be used to test the significance of the difference between two or more means. A significant overall F test leads to the rejection of the full null hypothesis that all population means are identical. However, if there are more than two means, then some population means might be equal. R. A. Fisher proposed following a significant overall F test with the testing of each pair of means with a t test applied at the same level α as the overall F test. No additional testing is done following a nonsignificant F because the full null hypothesis is not rejected. This procedure was designated the least significant difference (LSD) procedure.

If there are exactly three means in the ANOVA, the probability of one or more Type I errors is limited to the level α of the test. However, with four or more means, that probability can exceed α. A. J. Hayter proposed a modification to LSD that limits the probability of a Type I error to α regardless of the number of means being tested.

If the number of means is k then Tukey's honestly significant difference (HSD) procedure can be used to test each pair of means in an ANOVA using critical values from the Studentized range distribution. Hayter proposed replacing Fisher's t tests with the HSD critical values that would be used with $k - 1$ means even though the number of means is k. That is, a significant F test is followed by testing all pairs of means from the k means with the HSD critical value for $k - 1$ means.

Illustrative Example

Table 1 presents a hypothetical data set in which four groups containing five observations each produce a within-groups MS of 2.0. An independent-groups ANOVA applied to such data would produce an overall $F = 22.62$, which would exceed the critical value, $F_{.95}(1,16) = 3.24$.

Table 1 A Hypothetical Data Set in Which Four Groups Contain Five Observations

Group 1	Group 2	Group 3	Group 4
2.00	4.31	6.61	9.00

Following the significant F test, the LSD procedure requires testing all pairs of means. In Hayter's modification, a critical difference for all pairs at the .05 level is obtained from the formula

$$CD = SR_{.95,k-1,v}\sqrt{\frac{MS_E}{N}},$$

where

$SR_{.95,k-1,v}$ is the Studentized range statistic,

k is the number of means,

v is the error degrees of freedom,

MS_E is the error term (in this case the Mean Square within groups), and

N is the common group size.

For the data in Table 1, we obtain the result

$$CD = 3.65\sqrt{\frac{2.0}{5}} = 3.65\sqrt{0.4}$$
$$= 3.65(.63245) = 2.31.$$

Table 2 presents the six pairwise differences and shows that all pairs are significantly different except for Group 2 and Group 3. That difference of 2.30 is less than the critical difference of 2.31.

Table 2   The Six Possible Pairwise Differences

	Group 1 2.0	Group 2 4.31	Group 3 6.61	Group 4 9.00	Critical Difference
2.0	–	2.31*	4.61*	7.00*	2.31
4.31		–	2.30	4.69*	
6.61			–	2.39*	

* = Significantly different at α = .05.

The Hayter-Fisher version of LSD will always be more powerful than Tukey's HSD for testing all pairwise differences following an ANOVA *F* test. In the case of testing exactly three means, the Hayter-Fisher version gives the same results as the original LSD.

Most computer packages apply the original version of LSD. In the case of testing exactly three means, those results will be accurate. However, when testing more than three means, such packages will risk excessively high Type I error rates.

Most computer packages also provide Tukey's HSD procedure. Following a significant overall *F* test, any pair of means found significantly different by HSD will also be significantly different by the Hayter-Fisher version of LSD. Also, any pair of means found not to be significantly different by the original LSD will also not be significantly different by the Hayter-Fisher version. Thus, in most cases the results of the Hayter-Fisher procedure can be found from a computer package that provides HSD and the original LSD. In cases where a pair of means is not significant by HSD but is significant by the original LSD, the final decision for the Hayter-Fisher can be determined quite easily as described above. Of course, computer packages could easily modify their procedures to offer the Hayter-Fisher method.

—*Philip H. Ramsey*

See also Bonferroni Test; Post Hoc Comparisons

Further Reading

Hayter, A. J. (1986). The maximum familywise error rate of Fisher's least significant difference test. *Journal of the American Statistical Association, 81,* 1000–1004.

Kirk, R. E. (1995). *Experimental design: Procedures for the behavioral sciences.* Pacific Grove, CA: Brooks/Cole.

Ramsey, P. H. (2002). Comparison of closed procedures for pairwise testing of means. *Psychological Methods, 7,* 504–523.

FISHER'S Z TRANSFORMATION

Fisher's Z transformation is a procedure that rescales the product-moment correlation coefficient into an interval scale that is not bounded by ± 1.00. It may be used to test a null hypothesis that an obtained correlation is significantly different from some hypothesized value (usually a nonzero value, because a *t* test is available to test whether $\rho = 0$), to test the significance of the difference between two independent correlations, to find the average of several correlations, or to form a confidence interval (CI) for a correlation coefficient.

Like all statistics, the correlation coefficient is subject to sampling variation. For a given population, the sample correlation coefficient (r) has a sampling distribution around its population parameter, ρ (Greek lowercase letter rho), and this distribution has a standard error, the standard error of the correlation coefficient, σ_r. However, the sampling distribution of r has a different shape, depending on the value of ρ. The possible values of r are limited to the range between +1.0 and −1.0. If the value of ρ is about zero, sample deviations can occur equally in either direction, and the distribution is symmetric. However, as ρ departs from zero, this symmetry is lost because one end of the sampling distribution is more restricted than the other due to the limiting values of ± 1.0. There is more space on one side of the parameter than on the other. For extreme values of ρ, the sampling distribution of r becomes markedly skewed. The skew becomes noticeable at about $\rho = .40$.

A solution to this problem was developed by R. A. Fisher, who proposed a transformation for r that would normalize the distribution. The resulting index is called Fisher's Z or Z_F. Note that this is not the same quantity as the standard score or the critical ratio, each of which is a deviation of an observed value from the distribution mean, divided by the standard deviation. The statistic Fisher developed,

$$Z_F = 1/2 \ln \left(\frac{1+r}{1-r} \right), \qquad (1)$$

has the advantage that its sampling distribution is almost exactly normal for any value of ρ and has a standard error of

$$\sigma_{Z_F} = \frac{1}{\sqrt{N-3}}. \qquad (2)$$

This standard error does not depend on the value of ρ, unlike the standard error used in the t test for testing the hypothesis that $\rho = 0$. Also, σ_{z_F} is calculated, not estimated, so the test statistic is a critical ratio Z and is more powerful than the t test.

Because r can have only a limited number of values (to 2 decimal places) and the distribution is symmetric around zero, some statistics books contain tables for transforming r to Z_F and Z_F back to r. However, the equations for transforming a correlation to the metric of Z_F and back again are so simple that they are easily entered into a cell of a spreadsheet or programmed as a macro. The equation for the reverse transformation is

$$r = (\exp(2 * Z) - 1)/(\exp(2 * Z) + 1)$$
$$= \frac{e^{2Z} - 1}{e^{2Z} + 1}, \qquad (3)$$

where the first form of the expression is in the notation used for computations by EXCEL and the second is in standard notation. However, many spreadsheets also include functions for converting to and from Z_F in their function libraries. For example, EXCEL has a function called FISHER for the r-to-Z_F transformation in Equation 1 and one called FISHERINV for the reverse transformation in Equation 3. Pasting FISHER into a cell produces the dialog box in Figure 1. Entering the observed r for X produces Z_F. In this example, $r = .80$ produces $Z_F = 1.0986$.

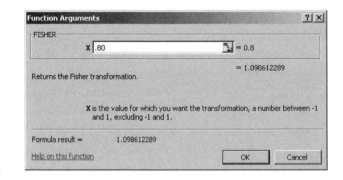

Figure 1 Excel Screen Image for Transforming r to Z_F

The process is reversed by pasting FISHERINV into a cell. In the example in Figure 2, we have reversed the transformation to recover our original correlation of .80.

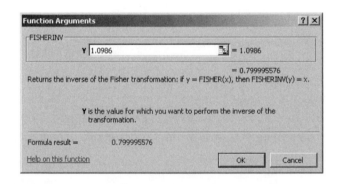

Figure 2 Excel Screen Image for Transforming Z_F to r

Applying Z_F to Hypothesis Testing

Sometimes we might wish to test a hypothesis that ρ is some value other than 0. Suppose we wish to test the null hypothesis that the correlation between scores on a reaction-time measure (RT) and scores on Thorndike's Precarious Prognosticator of Potential Proficiency (the TP[4]) is $-.75$. Because the sampling distribution of r around a population parameter as high as this is definitely not symmetric, we must use Fisher's Z transformation. We transform the r and the ρ to Z_Fs and carry out the test using the formula

$$Z = \frac{Z_{F_r} - Z_{F_\rho}}{\dfrac{1}{\sqrt{N-3}}}, \qquad (4)$$

where Z_{F_r} is the transformed value of the observed correlation and Z_{F_ρ} is the transformed value of the hypothesized population correlation. If Z from Equation 4 exceeds the usual critical value (1.96, 2.58, or another value we might choose), we would reject the null hypothesis that $\rho = 0.75$.

Suppose we have data from a sample of 68 participants, and the observed correlation between RT and the TP[4] is −.59. The transformed values are $Z_{F_r} = -.678$ and $Z_{F_\rho} = -.973$, so with this sample size, we obtain

$$Z = \frac{-.678 - (-.973)}{\sqrt{\dfrac{1}{65}}} = \frac{+.295}{.124} = +2.38.$$

Since a Z of 2.38 exceeds the critical value of 1.96, we would reject the hypothesis that $\rho = -.75$ in the population that produced this sample at the $p \leq .05$ level. That is, it is unlikely that this sample was drawn from a population in which $\rho = -.75$. The fact that the Z is positive suggests that the sample was probably drawn from a population in which ρ is less than −.75 (that is, not as large a negative correlation).

We can see how important Fisher's Z transformation is if we compare the result above with what we would get if we tested the same hypothesis without the transformation. The appropriate equation (see *t* test of a correlation coefficient) produces

$$t_{66} = \frac{-.59 - (-.75)}{\sqrt{\dfrac{(1 - .55^2)}{(68 - 2)}}} = \frac{.16}{.099} = 1.62.$$

A t of 1.62 with $df = 66$ is not significant, so we would not reject the hypothesis that $\rho = -.75$. Had we been testing the hypothesis that $\rho = 0$, either test would have been appropriate, and either would have led to the same conclusion. The difference is caused by the asymmetry of the sampling distribution of r for large values of ρ.

Confidence Intervals for Correlations

A second situation that we occasionally encounter and that calls for Z_F is the need to place a CI for ρ on an observed r. For example, in the section above, we were able to conclude that it is unlikely that the population from which we drew our sample is one in which the correlation is −.75, but what is a reasonable range for this correlation? A CI provides an answer.

The first step is to determine Z_F for the obtained r. Next, calculate σ_{Z_F} using Equation 2. Using the appropriate normal deviate Zs for our chosen confidence level (Z_α) (for example, ±1.96 for the 95% CI), we compute the upper and lower CI limits for Z_F using the usual linear transformations

$$CI_L = (-Z_\alpha)\sigma_{Z_F} + Z_{Fr}$$

and

$$CI_U = (+Z_\alpha)\sigma_{Z_F} + Z_{F_r}.$$

These limits, which are in the metric of Z_F, are then transformed into correlation values.

To find the 95% CI for the relationship between RT and the TP[4], we would proceed as follows: The obtained r was −.59 computed on 68 participants, the Z_F was .678, and $\sigma_{Z_F} = 0.124$.

The upper- and lower-limit values for the 95% CI in the metric of Z_F are

$$(-1.96)(0.124) + (-.678) = -.921$$

and

$$(+1.96)(0.124) + (-.678) = -.435.$$

This CI is symmetric in terms of probability and in terms of Z_F but not in terms of r. With FISHERINV, we can transform the values of Z_F into the metric of r. The CI in the scale of r goes from −.409 to −.726, with its center at −.59, reflecting the fact that the sampling distribution of r in this region is positively skewed. (The sampling distribution would be negatively skewed for positive correlations.)

Hypotheses About Two Correlations From Independent Samples

We occasionally encounter a situation where we want to test a null hypothesis that two correlations are equal or that they differ by a specified amount. If the two correlations involve the same variables in two different samples, such as testing whether a correlation is the same for men as it is for women, we can use Z_F. First, transform both rs to Z_Fs, then calculate the standard error of the difference between two Z_Fs:

$$\sigma_{(Z_{F_1}-Z_{F_2})} = \sqrt{\frac{1}{N_1-3} + \frac{1}{N_2-3}}. \quad (5)$$

A critical ratio Z of the usual form then provides the test statistic for the null hypothesis that $\rho_1 = \rho_2$ ($\rho_1 - \rho_2 = 0$):

$$Z = \frac{Z_{F_{r_1}} - Z_{F_{r_2}} - (Z_{F_{\rho_1}} - Z_{F_{\rho_2}})}{\sigma_{(Z_{F_1}-Z_{F_2})}}. \quad (6)$$

Suppose we found the correlations between midterm and final examination scores for students in a statistics class. For the 17 men in the class, the correlation is 0.78, and for the 24 women, r is 0.55. The null hypothesis that $\rho_M = \rho_F$ is tested by finding

$$\sigma_{(Z_{F_1}-Z_{F_2})} = \sqrt{\frac{1}{17-3} + \frac{1}{24-3}} = \sqrt{.119} = .345$$

and

$$Z = \frac{(1.045 - .618) - 0}{.345} = \frac{+.427}{.345} = 1.24.$$

Clearly, we cannot reject the null hypothesis of equal correlations on the basis of these data, but we also cannot reach the conclusion that they are equal.

Averaging Correlations

Another application is the problem of averaging the correlation between two variables across several groups of people. For example, research on the Wechsler Intelligence Scale for Children sometimes involves several groups of children who differ in age. For some research questions, it is desirable to collapse the results across ages to obtain larger samples. It is not appropriate simply to consider all children to be a single sample, because cognitive ability is related to age. Therefore, correlations are computed within each age group and then averaged across ages.

Because the sampling distribution of the correlation coefficient is highly skewed for large values of ρ, the meaning of differences between correlations changes depending on where we are in the range of possible values. For this reason, we cannot use simple averaging techniques with rs. We can, however, use Z_F because it represents a variable on an interval scale. Whenever it is necessary to find an average of several correlations, particularly when they differ by more than about .10, the appropriate procedure is as follows:

1. Transform all rs to Z_Fs.

2. Find $\bar{Z}_F$ (the mean of the Z_Fs).

3. Then reverse the transformation using $\bar{Z}_F$ to find the mean r, or $\bar{r}$.

When the correlations being averaged are based on samples of different sizes, it is necessary to compute a weighted average. Under these conditions, the proper weighting is given by the formula in Equation 7:

$$\bar{Z}_F = \frac{(N_1-3)Z_{F_1} + (N_2-3)Z_{F_2} + \cdots + (N_K-3)Z_{F_K}}{(N_1-3) + (N_2-3) + \cdots + (N_K-3)}. \quad (7)$$

The mean correlation, $\bar{r}$, is found by transforming $\bar{Z}_F$ back into the metric of r using Equation 3. Hypotheses concerning this mean correlation should be tested using $\bar{Z}_F$, which has a standard error of

$$\sigma_{\bar{Z}_F} = \frac{1}{\sqrt{(N_1 - 3) + (N_2 - 3) + \cdots + (N_K - 3)}}. \quad (8)$$

The critical ratio test statistic for testing null hypotheses concerning $\bar{r}$ is

$$Z = \frac{\bar{Z}_F - Z_{F_\rho}}{\sigma_{\bar{Z}_F}}. \quad (9)$$

As usual, Z_{F_ρ} is the Z_F of ρ, the correlation under the null hypothesis, which is usually zero but may take on any appropriate value.

Imagine that we have the correlation between the midterm exam scores and final exam scores for each of three classes in statistics. The data are

$$
\begin{array}{lll}
r_1 = 0.77 & N_1 = 12 & Z_{F_1} = 1.020 \\
r_2 = 0.47 & N_2 = 18 & Z_{F_2} = 0.510 \\
r_3 = 0.25 & N_3 = 57 & Z_{F_3} = 0.255.
\end{array}
$$

We may wish to find $\bar{r}$ and test the hypothesis that the mean correlation is zero. This is done by using Equations 7–9 to find

$$\bar{Z}_F = \frac{9(1.020) + 15(.510) + 54(.255)}{9 + 15 + 54}$$

$$= \frac{30.6}{78} = .392$$

$$\bar{r} = 0.373$$

$$\sigma_{\bar{Z}_F} = \frac{1}{\sqrt{78}} = .113$$

$$Z = .373/.113 = 3.30,$$

from which we can conclude that the mean correlation of 0.373 differs significantly from zero.

We can place a CI on this mean correlation in the usual way. For the 95% CI, we start with

$$\bar{Z}_F = .392 \qquad \sigma_{\bar{Z}} = .113 \qquad Z_{0.95} = \pm 1.96.$$

Finding the lower and upper limits of the CI for $\bar{Z}_F$ yields

$$CI_L = -1.96(.113) + .392 = .171$$
$$CI_U = +1.96(.0864) + .221 = .653.$$

Converting these Z_Fs back into correlations produces a CI centering on +.37 and running from +.17 to +.57.

—Robert M. Thorndike

See also Correlation Coefficient

Further Reading

Darlington, R. B. (1990). *Regression and linear models.* New York: McGraw-Hill.

Hays, W. L. (1994). *Statistics* (5th ed.). Orlando, FL: Harcourt Brace.

Marascuilo, L. A., & Serlin, R. C. (1988). *Statistical methods for the social and behavioral sciences.* New York: Freeman.

Thorndike, R. M. (1994). Correlational procedures in data analysis. In T. Husen & N. Postlethwaite (Eds.), *International encyclopedia of education* (2nd ed., pp. 1107–1117). New York: Pergamon.

Thorndike, R. M., & Dinnel, D. L. (2001) *Basic statistics for the behavioral sciences.* Upper Saddle River, NJ: Prentice Hall.

Fisher's Z description with formulas: http://davidmlane.com/hyperstat/A50760.html

Fisher's z'-Transformation, from *MathWorld*—a Wolfram Web resource, by E. W. Weisstein: http://mathworld.wolfram.com/Fishersz-Transformation.html

R reference: http://www.maths.lth.se/help/R/.R/library/SIN/html/fisherz.html

SAS reference: http://support.sas.com/ctx/samples/index.jsp?sid=494

FOURIER TRANSFORM

The Fourier transform takes a function (or sequence) defined in the time or spatial domain and transforms it to the frequency domain, which provides a natural environment for studying many problems. Fourier analysis (often referred to as spectral analysis) is usually associated with the study of periodic behavior (e.g., sunspots) but is also used to understand nonperiodic and stochastic behavior. Spectral analysis techniques are some of the most ubiquitous tools in modern science and are used in fields as diverse as signal processing, astronomy, geophysics, medical imaging, neurophysiology, speech analysis, and optics.

The Fourier transform can be applied to multidimensional processes; however, it has undoubtedly been applied most widely to one-dimensional processes. Hence, this discussion will refer only to functions (or sequences) defined in the time domain.

Historical Aspects

The Fourier transform is named after the French engineer Jean Baptiste (Joseph Baron) Fourier (1768–1830), who, motivated by his work modeling heat conduction, proposed that any function could be decomposed into a superposition of sinusoidal (sine and cosine) terms. It has since been found that the decomposition is valid only for functions that satisfy certain conditions, which are rather technical (the interested reader is referred to the references). However, almost all functions that arise in physical applications will satisfy the conditions or at least will be well approximated by a sum of sinusoidal terms.

Which Fourier Transform?

Without context, the term *Fourier transform* generally refers to the continuous Fourier transform, which is a linear mapping from a continuous time interval to the frequency domain. The discrete Fourier transform is then the equivalent form for discrete time.

The frequency domain representation allows analysis of a function's frequency characteristics, such as the contribution of the function to

sinusoids at different frequencies. The inverse Fourier transform reverses the transformation from the frequency domain back to the time domain. The mapping is unique, so the inverse Fourier transform will reproduce the original function exactly. The dual transforms are called the *Fourier transform pair*.

What Do We Mean by Frequency?

Frequency is the number of times a function repeats itself within a unit of time. If the time unit is a second, the frequency measure is hertz, the number of cycles per second. The period is the time taken for the function to repeat; in other words, period is the reciprocal of frequency: *Frequency = 1/Period*. Frequency can intuitively be considered in terms of sound waves: A bass note is a low-frequency sound, and a whistle is a high-frequency sound.

The period between successive peaks of the solid line in Figure 1 is 8 seconds, giving a frequency of $f = \frac{1}{8}$ Hz. The dotted line is of a higher frequency, $f = \frac{1}{4}$, shown by the period of 4 seconds. The amplitude of a

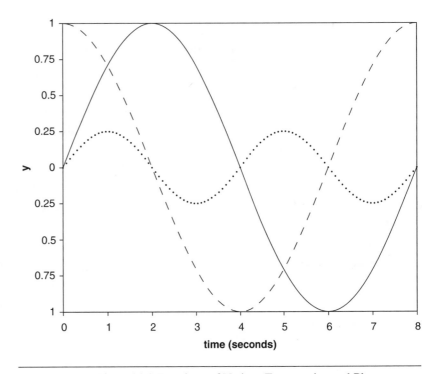

Figure 1   Sinusoidal Functions of Various Frequencies and Phases

Note: Solid line is $\sin(2\pi ft)$ with frequency $f = \frac{1}{8}$, dashed line is $\sin(2\pi t + \pi/2) = \cos(2\pi ft)$, and dotted line is $\sin(2\pi ft)/4$ with twice the frequency, or $f = \frac{1}{4}$.

sinusoid is the height of each peak or trough. The solid line has amplitude one, whereas the dotted line has amplitude $\frac{1}{4}$. The phase of a sinusoid indicates which part of the cycle the function commences at time zero. The solid line has phase 0 (a sine term), whereas the dashed line has the same frequency, but the phase is shifted by $\pi/2$ (equivalent to a cosine term). Hence, cosine functions are simply phase-shifted sine functions.

Continuous Fourier Transform

The continuous Fourier transform $X(f)$ of a function $x(t)$ at frequency f can be expressed as

$$X(f) = \int_{-\infty}^{\infty} x(t)e^{-i2\pi ft}dt,$$

with corresponding inverse Fourier transform

$$x(t) = \int_{-\infty}^{\infty} X(f)e^{i2\pi ft}df,$$

where i is the square root of -1. The integrals decompose the function into sinusoidal terms at an infinite division of frequencies. The Fourier transform can be used for complex-valued functions. However, in most applications, the functions are real-valued, which will be assumed in this discussion.

It is not possible to venture into the mathematical detail of the Fourier transform. The interested reader is referred to the references. However, it is useful to consider why the integrand involves complex exponentials rather than sinusoidal terms, as one might expect. Insight comes from Euler's formula:

$$e^{i\vartheta} = \cos(\vartheta) + i\sin(\vartheta).$$

Hence, the complex exponential gives a complex number whose real part is a cosine term and whose imaginary part is a sine term. We know that a sinusoid term with a particular phase angle can be written as a combination of simple sine and cosine terms. Hence, the complex exponential allows us to consider sinusoidal functions, but in a much more convenient functional form (integrals of exponential functions are easier than sinusoids).

The Fourier transform of a function carries information about the amplitude and phase of contributions at each frequency. The absolute value of the Fourier transform is related to the amplitude. The phase is given by the angle in complex space (called the *argument of the complex number*). A plot of the square of the absolute value of the Fourier transform against frequency is called the *power spectrum of the signal*. The corresponding plot of the phases is the *phase spectrum*. For real functions, the power spectrum is symmetric, and the phase spectrum is antisymmetric, so only the positive frequencies are usually shown.

The Fourier transform has many interesting properties. For example, the Fourier transform of an even function is entirely real and even, whereas for an odd function, it is entirely complex and odd. A time shift changes only the phase, not the amplitude, so the power spectrum is unchanged. The Fourier transform of the sum of two functions is simply the sum of their respective Fourier transforms (known as *linearity*). Examples of a few important functions and their Fourier transforms are shown in Figure 2. A delta function can be thought of as infinity at a single point. The sinc function is defined as $\sin(\pi f)/\pi f$.

One of the most useful properties of the Fourier transform is its behavior under convolution, which makes an efficient computational tool in many scientific problems. Convolution includes operations like smoothing and filtering of a function (signal). The result of the convolution of a function in the time domain is equivalent to multiplication of the Fourier transform of the signal with the transform of the convolution function. Similarly, convolution in the frequency domain is equivalent to multiplication in the time domain. Hence, a convolution (usually a computationally intensive operation) can efficiently be carried out by a simple multiplication in the alternate domain.

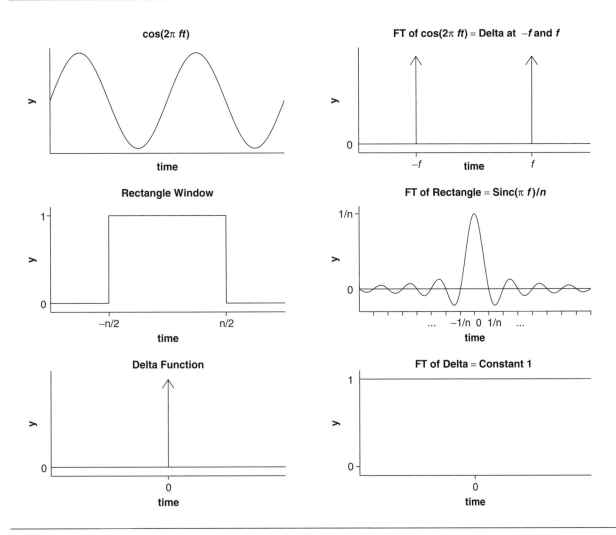

Figure 2   Plots of Various Functions and Their Fourier Transforms

Note: From top to bottom: cosine function, rectangular window, and delta function.

Discrete Fourier Transform

In most practical applications, to enable analysis using computers, a signal is regularly sampled (equally spaced) over a finite time interval. The details associated with irregular sampling are deferred to the interested reader. The sample period, often known as the *fundamental*, is the length of time between the regularly sampled points. The fundamental frequency is then $\frac{1}{Fundamental\ Period}$. Integer multiples of the fundamental frequency give the Fourier frequencies. The sampling frequency must be sufficiently small to provide an accurate approximation of the function, in particular to prevent aliasing, discussed further as follows.

Sinusoids at multiples of the fundamental frequency are called harmonics. A harmonic will complete a whole number of cycles within the time interval; for example, first harmonic completes one cycle, second harmonic two cycles, and so on. Consider the sound produced when a string is struck. The vibrations that produce the sound travel along the string and back again; in other words, the fundamental period is twice the string length. The initial burst of energy produces vibrations at many frequencies. Most frequencies will die away quickly, their energy being used in producing the sound and some heat. However, the harmonic frequencies will continue to resonate, as they simply bounce back and forth between the ends. The harmonics will slowly die away as energy is lost on producing the sound you hear.

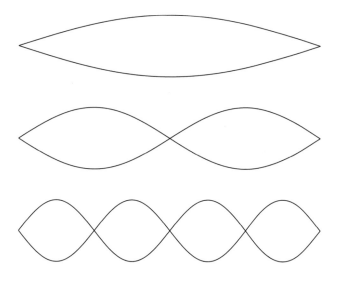

Figure 3   First Three Harmonic Vibrations Along a String, Showing Movement Back and Forth

The discrete Fourier transform takes a sampled signal x_t of finite length n and produces a frequency domain representation X_f,

$$X_f = \frac{1}{n} \sum_{t=0}^{n-1} x_t e^{-i2\pi ft},$$

with inverse discrete Fourier transform,

$$x_t = \sum_{f=0}^{n-1/n} X_f e^{i2\pi ft}.$$

Usually it is evaluated only at the Fourier frequencies

$$f = -\frac{1}{2}, \dots, -\frac{2}{n}, -\frac{1}{n}, 0, \frac{1}{n}, \frac{2}{n}, \dots, \frac{1}{2}.$$

Some textbooks present the discrete Fourier transform adjusting for different fundamental periods, but this detail is superfluous to this entry.

Essentially, the integral of the continuous Fourier transform is replaced with a summation, which is appropriately normalized. There is no strict convention on whether the normalization $(1/n)$ should apply to the discrete Fourier transform or its inverse $(1/\sqrt{n})$ or both. The different normalizations can have a physical meaning in certain contexts. In statistics, it is useful that the power spectrum of the autocovariance function has the same shape as the transform of the original series, but with different phases. This property can enable efficient calculation of the autocorrelation function, often the starting point in time series analysis.

The maximum absolute frequency the discrete Fourier transform can resolve is the Nyquist frequency 1/2. The signal should be bandlimited so that there is no periodic variation outside of the Nyquist frequency range $(-1/2, 1/2)$. Alternatively, a signal can be subject to an antialiasing filter (called a low-pass filter) prior to sampling, to remove variation outside this range. This is important because of an issue known as aliasing. If a signal has periodicities higher than the Nyquist frequency, then this high-frequency variation is not distinguishable at the sampled points from a signal at lower frequency. Power from all frequencies outside the Nyquist range is folded back into this range. Figure 4 provides an example of sampled sinusoidal signals above the Nyquist frequency indistinguishable from a signal below the Nyquist frequency. Aliasing is the reason stagecoach wheels seem to rotate backwards in some old "western" movies shot at a low frame rate.

As the discrete Fourier transform is usually calculated only at the Fourier frequencies, components between these frequencies are not shown. This problem is known as the *picket fence effect*. For evaluation of the discrete Fourier transform at a higher division of frequencies, the series can be zero-padded (zeros appended to end), which will not impact the power spectrum.

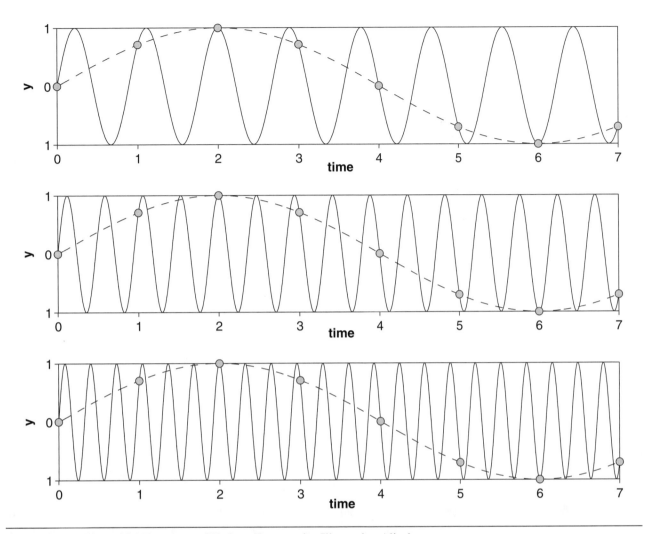

Figure 4   Sinusoidal Functions of Various Frequencies Illustrating Aliasing

Notes: Signal sampled at times $0, \ldots, 7$. Dashed line is $\sin(2\pi ft)$ at frequency. $f = \frac{1}{8}$. Solid lines (top to bottom) are $\sin[2\pi\,(f+1)t]$, $\sin[2\pi\,(f+2)t]$, and $\sin[2\pi\,(f+3)t]$.

Spectral leakage is caused by observation of a signal of infinite extent over a finite time interval. Observation over a finite interval is equivalent to multiplying the signal by a rectangular window, as in Figure 2. Hence, when the Fourier transform is applied, the resultant series is a convolution of the Fourier transform of the true signal and the transform of the rectangular window, or the sinc kernel shown in Figure 2. The power from each frequency will leak into the rest of the spectrum, a phenomenon known as *spectral leakage*, which can substantially distort the spectrum. It is possible to multiply a series by an alternative taper window to improve the leakage properties.

The fast Fourier transform is an extremely efficient algorithm for calculating the discrete Fourier transform. The algorithm reduces the number of computations involved from order n^2 to $n\log(n)$. The algorithm requires the length of the series to be a multiple of low-order primes, such as $n = 2^{10} = 1024$.

—Carl J. Scarrott

See also Autocorrelation; Smoothing; Time Series Analysis

Further Reading

Bloomfield, P. (2000). *Fourier analysis of time series: An introduction*. New York: Wiley.

Bracewell, R. (1999). *The Fourier transform and its applications* (3rd ed.). New York: McGraw-Hill.

Percival, D. B., and Walden, A. T. (1993). *Spectral analysis for physical applications: Multitaper and conventional univariate techniques*. Cambridge, UK: Cambridge University Press.

Shatkay, H. (1995). *The Fourier transform—A primer*. Brown University Technical Report CS-95–37. Retrieved from http://www.cs.brown.edu/publications/techreports/reports/CS-95-37.html

Thibos, L. N. (2003). *Fourier analysis for beginners*. Indiana University School of Optometry Research Library. Retrieved from http://research.opt.indiana.edu/Library/FourierBook/title.html

Fourier transform article: http://en.wikipedia.org/wiki/Fourier_transform

Fourier transformations information by Wolfram Research: http://mathworld.wolfram.com/FourierTransform.html

FRACTAL

There is no universally accepted definition of what constitutes a fractal. However, it is usually clear what one means by a fractal. Fractal objects are objects with strong scaling behavior. That is, there is some relation between the "behavior" of the object at some scale and at finer scales. Figure 1 illustrates some of the *self-similar* geometric fractals (self-similar means that they are similar to pieces of themselves).

IFS Fractals

A particularly nice class of fractal objects is those objects defined by *iterated function systems* (IFSs). An IFS is a formal way of saying that an object is self-similar (i.e., made up of smaller copies of itself). Consider the Sierpinski Gasket, S (shown in Figure 2). We can see that it is made up of three smaller copies of itself. If we think of S as living in $[0,1] \times [0,1]$ and we define the three maps

$$w_1(x,y) = (x/2, y/2), \ w_2(x,y) = (x/2 + 1/2, y/2), \ w_3(x,y) = (x/2, y/2 + 1/2),$$

then we see that $S = w_1(S) \cup w_2(S) \cup w_3(S)$. The collection of functions $\{w_1, w_2, w_3\}$ make up the IFS. We notice that each w_i is contractive in that for any two points x, y, we see that $d(f(x), f(y)) = (1/2)d(x,y)$, where d measures the usual distance in the plane. Because of this, the combined set mapping $W(B) = w_1(B) \cup w_2(B) \cup w_3(B)$ is also contractive (in the appropriate sense), so by the contraction mapping theorem there is a unique set A with $W(A) = A$. This set A is the *attractor* of the IFS (in this case, the Sierpinski Gasket).

One nice consequence of the contractivity of the IFS mapping W is that we can start with any set B, and the iterates $W^n(B)$ will converge to the attractor of the IFS. As illustrated in Figure 3, after one application of W, we have 3 smaller copies of our original set (a smile in this case), then 9 even smaller copies, then 27 still smaller copies, and on and on until, eventually, all the details of the original set are too small to see and all we see is the overall structure of the Sierpinski Gasket. A moment's thought will convince you that the same thing would happen with any other initial set.

Now we give a more formal definition of a (geometric) IFS. We start with a complete metric space (X,d) and a finite collection of self-maps $w_i \colon X \to X$, with $d(w_i(x), w_i(y)) \leq s_i d(x,y)$ for all x,y, where $0 \leq s_i < 1$ is the contraction factor for w_i. Let $H(X)$ denote the set of all nonempty compact subsets of X, and define the metric h (the Hausdorff metric) on $H(X)$ by

$$h(A,B) = \max\{\sup_{a \in A} \inf_{b \in B} d(a,b), \sup_{b \in B} \inf_{a \in A} d(a,b)\}.$$

It turns out that this is a metric on $H(X)$, which makes it into a complete metric space. Furthermore, under this metric, the set map $W \colon H(X) \to H(X)$ defined by

$$W(B) = \cup_i w_i(B)$$

is contractive with contractivity factor s.

Geometric fractals are interesting and useful in many applications as models of physical objects, but many times one needs a functional model. It is easy to extend the IFS framework to construct fractal functions.

a   b

c   d

Figure 1   Three Self-Similar Fractal Shapes

Fractal Functions

There are several different IFS frameworks for constructing fractal functions, but all of them have a common core, so we concentrate on this core. We illustrate the ideas by constructing fractal functions on the unit interval; that is, we construct functions $f : [0,1] \to IR$. Take the three mappings $w_1(x) = x/4$, $w_2(x) = x/2 + 1/4$, and $w_3(x) = x/4 + 3/4$ and notice that $[0,1] = w_1[0,1] \cup w_2[0,1] \cup w_3[0,1]$, so that the images of $[0,1]$ under each w_i tile $[0,1]$.

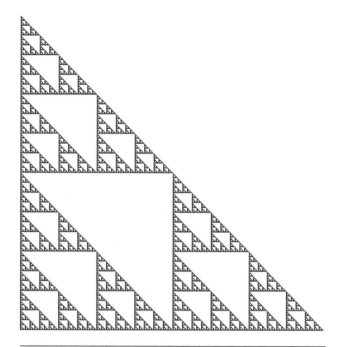

Figure 2   The Sierpinski Gasket

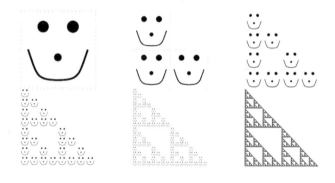

Figure 3   Smiles Converging to the Sierpinski Gasket

Choose three numbers α_1, α_2, α_3 and three other numbers β_1, β_2, β_3 and define the operator T by

$$T(f)(x) = \alpha_i f(w_i^{-1}(x)) + \beta_i \quad \text{if } x \, E \, w_i([0,1]),$$

where $f:[0,1] \rightarrow IR$ is a function. Then clearly $T(f)$: $[0,1] \rightarrow IR$ is also a function, so T takes functions to functions.

There are various conditions under which T is a contraction. For instance, if $|\alpha_i| < 1$ for each i, then T is contractive in the supremum norm given by

$$\|f\|_{\sup} = \sup_{x \in [0,1]} |f(x)|,$$

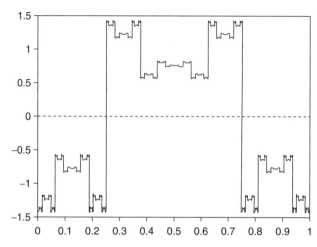

Figure 4   The Attractor of an IFS With Maps

so $T^n(f)$ converges uniformly to a unique fixed point $\bar{f}$ for any starting function f.

Figure 4 illustrates the limiting fractal functions in the case where $\alpha_1 = -\alpha_2 = \alpha_3 = 0.3$ and $\beta_1 = -\beta_2 = \beta_3 = -1$.

It is also possible to formulate contractivity conditions in other norms, such as the L^P norms. These tend to have weaker conditions, so they apply in more situations. However, the type of convergence is clearly different (the functions need not converge pointwise anywhere, for instance, and may be unbounded).

Statistically Self-Similar Fractals

Many times a fractal object is not self-similar in the IFS sense, but it is self-similar in a statistical sense. That is, either it is created by some random self-scaling process (so the steps from one scale to the next are random) or it exhibits similar statistics from one scale to another. The object in Figure 5 is an example of this type of fractal.

These types of fractals are well modeled by random IFS models, where there is some randomness in the choice of the maps at each stage.

Other Types of Fractals

IFS-type models are useful as approximations for self-similar or almost self-similar objects. However, often these models are too hard to fit to a given situation.

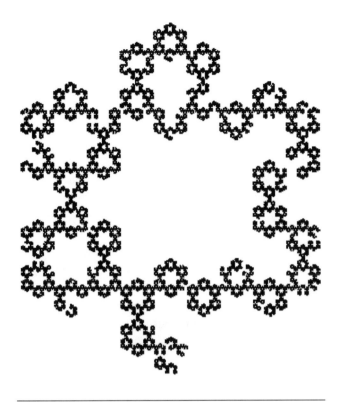

Figure 6   A DLA Fractal

Figure 5   A Statistically Self-Similar Fractal

For these cases, we have a choice—we can either build some other type of model governing the growth of the object, or we can give up on finding a model of the interscale behavior and just measure aspects of this behavior.

An example of the first instance is a simple model for diffusion limited aggregation (DLA), illustrated in Figure 6. In this growth model, we start with a seed and successively allow particles to drift around until they "stick" to the developing object. Clearly the resulting figure is fractal, but our model has no explicit interscale dependence. However, these models allow one to do simulation experiments to fit data observed in the laboratory. They also allow one to measure more global aspects of the model (like the fractal dimension).

Fractal objects also frequently arise as so-called *strange attractors* in chaotic dynamical systems. One particularly famous example is the butterfly-shaped attractor in the Lorentz system of differential equations. These differential equations are a toy model of a weather system and exhibit "chaotic" behavior. The attractor of this system is an incredibly intricate filigreed structure of curves. The fractal nature of this attractor is evident by the fact that, as you zoom in on the attractor, more and more detail appears in an approximately self-similar fashion.

Fractal Random Processes

Since the introduction of fractional Brownian motion (fBm) in 1968 by Benoit Mandelbrot and John van Ness, self-similar stochastic processes have been used to model a variety of physical phenomena (including computer network traffic and turbulence). These processes have power spectral densities that decay like $1/f^a$.

An fBm is a Gaussian process $x(t)$ with zero mean and covariance,

$$E[x(t)x(s)] = (\sigma^2/2)[|t|^{2H} + |s|^{2H} - |t - s|^{2H}],$$

and is completely characterized by the *Hurst exponent* H and the variance $E[x(1)^2] = \sigma^2$. An fBm is statistically self-similar in the sense that for any scaling $a > 0$, we have

$$x(at) = a^H x(t),$$

where by equality we mean equality in distribution. (As an aside and an indication of one meaning of H, the sample paths of an fBm with parameter H are almost surely Hölder continuous with parameter H, so the larger the value of H, the smoother the sample paths of the fBm). Because of this scaling behavior, an fBm exhibits very strong longtime dependence. It is also clearly not a stationary (time invariant) process. This causes many problems with traditional methods of signal synthesis, signal estimation, and parameter estimation. However, wavelet-based methods work rather well, as the scaling and finite time behavior of wavelets match the scaling and nonstationarity of the fBm. With an appropriately chosen (i.e., sufficiently smooth) wavelet, the wavelet coefficients of an fBm become a stationary sequence without the long-range dependence properties. This aids in the estimation of the Hurst parameter H.

Several generalizations of fBms have been defined, including a multifractal Brownian motion. This particular generalization allows the Hurst parameter to be a changing function of time, $H(t)$, in a continuous way. Since the sample paths of an fBm have Hölder continuity H (almost surely), this is particularly interesting for modeling situations in which one expects the smoothness of the sample paths to vary over time.

Fractal Dimension

There are several parameters associated with a fractal object. Of these, fractal dimension (of which there are several variants) is one of the most widely used. Roughly speaking, this "dimension" measures the scaling behavior of the object by comparing it to a power law.

An example will make it more clear. Clearly the line segment $L = [0,1]$ has dimension equal to one. One way to think about this is that if we scale L by a factor of s, the "size" of L changes by a factor of s^1. That is, if we reduce it by a factor of $1/2$, the new copy of L has $1/2$ the length of the original L.

Similarly the square $S = [0,1] \times [0,1]$ has dimension equal to two since if we scale it by a factor of s, the "size" (in this case, area) scales by a factor of s^2. How do we know that the "size" scales by a factor

of s^2? If $s = 1/3$, say, then we see that we can tile S by exactly $9 = 3^2$ reduced copies of S, which means that each copy has "size" $(1/3)^2$ times the size of the original.

Now take the Sierpinski Gasket S. We see that S is covered by three smaller copies of itself, each copy having been reduced in size by a factor of two. Thus, for $s = 1/2$, we need 3 reduced copies to tile S. This gives

$$\text{size of original} = 3 \times \text{ size of smaller copy}$$
$$\text{copy} \qquad = 3' \times (1/2)^D \text{ size of original copy,}$$

so $3(1/2)^D = 1$ or $D = \log(3)/\log(2)$. That is, for the Sierpinski Gasket, if we shrink it by a factor of $1/2$, then the "size" gets reduced by a factor of $(1/2)^{\log(3)/\log(2)} = 1/3$. In this sense, the Sierpinski Gasket has dimension $\log(3)/\log(2) \approx 1.5849$, so it has a dimension that is fractional, and so it is a fractal.

We need a different method or definition for the fractal dimension of objects that are not exactly self-similar. The DLA fractal in Figure 6 is a fractal but is not strictly self-similar.

One very common way to estimate the dimension of such an object is the *box counting method*. To do this, cover the image with a square grid (of side length ε) and count how many of these boxes are occupied by a point in the image. Let $N(\varepsilon)$ be this number. Now repeat this for a sequence of finer and finer grids (letting ε tend to 0). We want to fit the relation $N(\varepsilon) = a\varepsilon^{-D}$, so we take logarithms of both sides to get $\log(N) = \log(a - D\log(\varepsilon)$. To estimate D, we plot $\log(N(\varepsilon))$ versus $\log(\varepsilon)$ and find the slope of the least squares line.

For the object in Figure 6, we have the data in Table 1, which give a fractal dimension of 1.60.

Fractals and Wavelets

We briefly mentioned the connection between fractals and wavelets. Wavelet analysis has become a very useful part of any data analyst's tool kit. In many ways, wavelet analysis is a supplement (and, sometimes, replacement) for Fourier analysis; the wavelet functions replace the usual sine and cosine basis functions.

Table 1 A Fractal Dimension of 1.60

e	$N(\varepsilon)$
1/2	4
1/4	16
1/8	52
2^{-4}	174
2^{-5}	580
2^{-6}	1,893
2^{-7}	6,037
2^{-8}	17,556
2^{-9}	44,399
2^{-10}	95,432

The connection between wavelets and fractals comes because wavelet functions are nearly self-similar functions. The so-called scaling function is a fractal function, and the "mother wavelet" is simply a linear combination of copies of this scaling function. This scaling behavior of wavelets makes it particularly nice for examining fractal data, especially if the scaling in the data matches the scaling in the wavelet functions. The coefficients that come from a wavelet analysis are naturally organized in a hierarchy of information from different scales, and hence doing a wavelet analysis can help one find scaling relations in data, if such relations exist.

Of course, wavelet analysis is much more than just an analysis to find scaling relations. There are many different wavelet bases. This freedom in choice of basis gives greater flexibility than Fourier analysis.

—Franklin Mendivil

Further Reading

Barnsley, M. G. (1988). *Fractals everywhere*. New York: Academic Press.

Dekking, M., Lévy Véhel, J., Lutton, E., & Tricot, C. (Eds.). (1999). *Fractals: Theory and applications in engineering*. London: Springer.

Feder, J. (1988). *Fractals*. New York: Plenum.

Hutchinson, J. E. (1981). Fractals and self-similarity. *Indiana University Mathematics Journal, 30*, 713–747.

Lévy Véhel, J., & Lutton, E. (Eds.). (2005). *Fractals in engineering: New trends in theory and applications*. London: Springer.

Lévy Véhel, J., Lutton, E., & Tricot, C. (Eds.). (1997). *Fractals in engineering*. London: Springer.

Mallat, S. (1999). *A wavelet tour of signal processing*. San Diego, CA: Academic Press.

Mandelbrot, B. (1983). *The fractal geometry of nature*. San Francisco: W. H. Freeman.

Mandelbrot, B., & van Ness, J. (1968). Fractional Brownian motions, fractional noises and applications. *SIAM Review, 10*, 422–437.

Ruelle, D. (1988). *Chaotic evolution and strange attractors: The statistical analysis of time series for deterministic nonlinear systems*. Cambridge, UK: Cambridge University Press.

FRACTIONAL RANDOMIZED BLOCK DESIGN

A fractional randomized block design (also called a randomized block fractional factorial design) reduces the number of treatment combinations that must be included in a multitreatment experiment to some fraction ($\frac{1}{2}$, $\frac{1}{3}$, $\frac{1}{4}$, $\frac{1}{8}$, $\frac{1}{9}$, and so on) of the total number of treatment combinations. Consider an experiment with five treatments, denoted by the letters *A*, *B*, *C*, *D*, and *E*. If each treatment has two levels, the number of treatment combinations in the experiment is $2 \times 2 \times 2 \times 2 \times 2 = 32$. By using a $\frac{1}{2}$ or a $\frac{1}{4}$ fractional randomized block design, the number of treatment combinations can be reduced to 16 or 8, respectively. However, the reduction in the size of the experiment comes at a price: Considerable ambiguity may exist in interpreting the results of the experiment. Ambiguity occurs because in the case of a $\frac{1}{2}$ fractional design, two names, called *aliases*, can be given to each source of variation. For example, a sum of squares could be attributed to the effects of treatment *A* and the *BCDE* interaction. In a one-fourth fractional randomized block design, each source of variation has four aliases. Treatments are customarily aliased with higher-order interactions that are assumed to equal zero. This helps minimize but does not eliminate ambiguity in interpreting the outcome of an experiment. One can never be sure that the higher-order interaction is really equal to zero. Because the interpretation of fractional randomized block designs always involves some ambiguity, the designs are most useful for pilot experiments and for exploratory research situations that permit follow-up experiments to be performed. Thus, a large number of treatments, typically seven or more, can be investigated efficiently in an initial experiment, with subsequent smaller experiments designed to clarify the results or follow up on the most promising independent variables.

A $\frac{1}{2}$ fractional randomized block design in which each treatment has two levels is denoted by 2^{k-1}, where 2^k indicates that each of the k treatments has 2 levels. The -1 in 2^{k-1} indicates that the design is a one-half fraction of a complete 2^k factorial design. This follows because the designation for a one-half fraction of 2^k can be written as $\frac{1}{2}2^k = 2^{-1}2^k = 2^{k-1}$. A one-fourth fractional randomized block design is denoted by 2^{k-2} because $\frac{1}{4}2^k = \frac{1}{2^2}2^k = 2^{-2}2^k = 2^{k-2}$.

Procedures for Constructing a Fractional Randomized Block Design

A 2^{5-1} design reduces the number of treatment combinations in an experiment from 32 to 16. The highest-order interaction, $ABCDE$, is typically used to determine which treatment combinations are in the experiment. This interaction, which is called the *defining relation*, divides the treatment combinations into two sets, each containing 16 combinations.

Several schemes have been devised to partition the treatment combinations into orthogonal subsets. One scheme that uses modular arithmetic is applicable to designs of the form p^{k-i}, where i indicates that the design is a $\frac{1}{2}$, $\frac{1}{3}$, and so on, fractional replication and p is a prime number. Let a_j, b_k, c_l, d_m, e_o, z, and p correspond to properties of a design as follows:

$a_j, b_k, c_l, d_m,$ and e_o denote levels of treatments A through E, respectively, where the first level of a treatment is denoted by 0 and the second level is denoted by 1;

$z = 0$ or 1 identifies one of the defining relations: $(ABCDE)_z = (ABCDE)_0$ or $(ABCDE)_1$; and

p denotes the number of levels of each treatment.

The expression $a_j + b_k + c_l + d_m + e_o = z \pmod{p}$ says to add the treatment levels (0 or 1) represented by $a_j, b_k, c_l, d_m,$ and e_o and reduce the sum modulo p; that is, express the sum as a remainder equal to z with

respect to the modulus p. For example, to find a treatment combination in the subset of treatment combinations denoted by $(ABCDE)_0$, find a combination whose sum when divided by p leaves the remainder $z = 0$. Each of the following 16 treatment combinations is in this subset:

00000, 00011, 00101, 01001, 10001, 00110, 01010,
10010, 01100, 10100, 11000, 01111, 11011, 11101,
10111, 11110 $= a_j + b_k + c_l + d_m + e_o = 0 \pmod 2$.

For example, the sum of the treatment levels represented by $0 + 0 + 0 + 1 + 1 = 2$. When 2 is divided by $p = 2$, the remainder is 0. Hence, the treatment combination represented by 00011 satisfies the relation $(ABCDE)_0$. The treatment combinations that satisfy the relation $(ABCDE)_1$ are

00001, 00010, 00100, 01000, 00111, 01011, 01101,
01110, 10000, 11100, 11010, 11001, 10110, 10101,
10011, 11111 $= a_j + b_k + c_l + d_m + e_o = 1 \pmod 2$.

A researcher can flip a coin to decide which of the two sets of 16 treatment combinations to use in an experiment.

A *confounding contrast* is used to assign the 16 treatment combinations in the subset, say, $(ABCDE)_0$, to two groups of blocks. Suppose the researcher chooses CD as the confounding contrast. The following eight treatment combinations satisfy the two relations $(ABCDE)_0$ and $(CD)_0$:

00000, 00110, 01001, 01111, 10001, 10111, 11000,
11110 $= a_j + b_k + c_l + d_m + e_o = 0 \pmod 2$ and
$c_l + d_m = 0 \pmod 2$.

The remaining eight treatment combinations satisfy the relations $(ABCDE)_0$ and $(CD)_1$:

00011, 00101, 01010, 01100, 10010, 10100, 11101,
11011 $= a_j + b_k + c_l + d_m + e_o = 0 \pmod 2$ and
$c_l + d_m = 1 \pmod 2$.

This design has two blocks of size eight.

It is often difficult to obtain two blocks of eight experimental units such that the units in a block are

Table 1 Layout for Fractional Randomized Block Design With Five Treatments

	Treatment Combinations			
Block $(CD)_0$ (CE_0)	$a_0\,b_0\,c_0\,d_0\,e_0$ Y_{00000}	$a_0\,b_1\,c_1\,d_1\,e_1$ Y_{01111}	$a_1\,b_0\,c_1\,d_1\,e_1$ Y_{10111}	$a_1\,b_1\,c_0\,d_0\,e_0$ Y_{11000}
Block $(CD)_0$ $(CE)_1$	$a_0\,b_0\,c_1\,d_1\,e_0$ Y_{00110}	$a_0\,b_1\,c_0\,d_0\,e_1$ Y_{01001}	$a_1\,b_0\,c_0\,d_0\,e_1$ Y_{10001}	$a_1\,b_1\,c_1\,d_1\,e_0$ Y_{11110}
Block $(CD)_1$ $(CE)_0$	$a_0\,b_0\,c_1\,d_0\,e_1$ Y_{00101}	$a_0\,b_1\,c_0\,d_1\,e_0$ Y_{01010}	$a_1\,b_0\,c_0\,d_1\,e_0$ Y_{10010}	$a_1\,b_1\,c_1\,d_0\,e_1$ Y_{11101}
Block $(CD)_1$ $(CE)_1$	$a_0\,b_0\,c_0\,d_1\,e_1$ Y_{00011}	$a_0\,b_1\,c_1\,d_0\,e_0$ Y_{01100}	$a_1\,b_0\,c_1\,d_0\,e_0$ Y_{10100}	$a_1\,b_1\,c_0\,d_1\,e_1$ Y_{11011}

Note: Defining relation = $(ABCDE)_0$, confounding contrasts = $(CD)_z$ and $(CE)_z$, generalized interaction = $(DE)_z$.

relatively homogeneous. To reduce the block size from eight to four, two confounding interactions can be used. Suppose a researcher chooses CE as the second confounding contrast. The first block contains the treatment combinations that satisfy three relations, $(ABCDE)_0$, $(CD)_0$, and $(CE)_0$:

00000, 01111, 10111, 11000 = $a_j + b_k + c_l + d_m + e_o$ = 0(mod 2), $c_l + d_m$ = 0(mod 2), and c_l + e_o = 0(mod 2).

The second through the fourth blocks contain the combinations that satisfy the relations (a) $(ABCDE)_0$, $(CD)_0$, and $(CE)_1$, (b) $(ABCDE)_0$, $(CD)_1$, and $(CE)_0$, and (c) $(ABCDE)_0$, $(CD)_1$, and $(CE)_1$. The design is shown in Table 1.

When two confounding contrasts are used to reduce the block size, a third interaction or treatment, called the *generalized interaction* or *generalized treatment*, also is confounded with the between-block variation. For the design in Table 1, the generalized interaction is obtained by multiplying the confounding contrasts and reducing the sums of the exponents modulo p, that is, expressing the sums as a remainder with respect to the modulus p. For example,

$$CD \times CE = C^2 D^1 E^1 = 0(\text{mod } 2)$$
$$= C^0 D^1 E^1 = D^1 E^1 = DE.$$

Hence, the generalized interaction of the two confounding interactions is DE.

The alias for a source of variation is obtained by multiplying the label for the source of variation by the defining relation and reducing the sums of the exponents modulo p. For example, the alias for the source

Table 2 ANOVA Table for Fractional Randomized Block Design With Five Treatments

Source	Alias	df
Blocks (CD), (CE), (DE)	(ABE), (ABD), (ABC)	3
A	$(BCDE)$	1
B	$(ACDE)$	1
C	$(ABDE)$	1
D	$(ABCE)$	1
E	$(ABCD)$	1
AB	(CDE)	1
AC	(BDE)	1
AD	(BCE)	1
AE	(BCD)	1
BC	(ADE)	1
BD	(ACE)	1
BE	(ACD)	1
Error = pooled two- and three-treatment interactions		7
Total		15

Note: Defining relation = $(ABCDE)_0$, confounding contrasts = $(CD)_z$ and $(CE)_z$, generalized interaction = $(DE)_z$.

Table 3 Computational Procedures for Fractional Randomized Block Design With Four Treatments

	ABCD Summary Table, Entry is Y_{jklm}				
	$a_0 b_0 c_0 d_0$	$a_0 b_0 c_1 d_1$	$a_1 b_1 c_0 d_0$	$a_1 b_1 c_0 d_0$	
Block $(AB)_0$	11	14	12	18	55
	$a_0 b_1 c_0 d_1$	$a_0 b_1 c_1 d_0$	$a_1 b_0 c_0 d_1$	$a_1 b_0 c_1 d_0$	
Block $(AB)_1$	15	22	5	3	45

AB Summary Table			AC Summary Table			BC Summary Table		
Entry is $\Sigma_{l=1}^{r} Y_{jklm}$			Entry is $\Sigma_{k=1}^{q} Y_{jklm}$			Entry is $\Sigma_{j=1}^{p} Y_{jklm}$		
	b_0	b_1		c_0	c_1		c_0	c_1
a_0 25	37	62	a_0 26	36	62	b_0 16	17	33
a_1 8	30	38	a_1 17	21	38	b_1 27	40	67
33	67	100	43	57	100	43	57	100

Notes: Y_{jklm} = a score for the experimental unit in treatment combination $a_j b_k c_l d_m$; $j = 1, \ldots, p$ levels of treatment A (a_j); $k = 1, \ldots, q$ levels of treatment B (b_k); $l = 1, \ldots, r$ levels of treatment C (c_l); $m = 1, \ldots, t$ levels of treatment D (d_m).

Sums and Sums of Squares

$$\sum_{j=1}^{p} \sum_{k=1}^{q} \sum_{l=1}^{r} \sum_{m=1}^{t} Y_{jklm} = 11 + 14 + \cdots + 3 = 100.00$$

$$\sum_{j=1}^{p} \sum_{k=1}^{q} \sum_{l=1}^{r} \sum_{m=1}^{t} Y_{jklm}^2 = (11)^2 + (14)^2 + \cdots + (3)^2 = 1{,}528.00$$

$$SSBLOCKS = \frac{(55)^2}{4} + \frac{(45)^2}{4} - \frac{(100.00)^2}{(2)(2)(2)} = 12.50$$

$$SSA = \frac{(62)^2}{(2)(2)} + \frac{(38)^2}{(2)(2)} - \frac{(100.00)^2}{(2)(2)(2)} = 72.00$$

$$SSB = \frac{(33)^2}{(2)(2)} + \frac{(67)^2}{(2)(2)} - \frac{(100.00)^2}{(2)(2)(2)} = 144.50$$

$$SSC = \frac{(43)^2}{(2)(2)} + \frac{(57)^2}{(2)(2)} - \frac{(100.00)^2}{(2)(2)(2)} = 24.50$$

$$SSD = \left[(11)^2 + (14)^2 + \cdots + (3)^2 \right] - \left[\frac{(25)^2}{2} + \cdots + \frac{(30)^2}{2} \right] - \left[\frac{(26)^2}{2} + \cdots + \frac{(21)^2}{2} \right]$$

$$- \left[\frac{(16)^2}{2} + \cdots + \frac{(40)^2}{2} \right] + \left[\frac{(62)^2}{(2)(2)} + \frac{(38)^2}{(2)(2)} \right] + \left[\frac{(33)^2}{(2)(2)} + \frac{(67)^2}{(2)(2)} \right] + \left[\frac{(43)^2}{(2)(2)} + \frac{(57)^2}{(2)(2)} \right]$$

$$- \frac{(100.00)^2}{(2)(2)(2)} = 2.00$$

$$SSAC = \left[\frac{(26)^2}{2} + \cdots + \frac{(21)^2}{2} \right] - \left[\frac{(62)^2}{(2)(2)} + \frac{(38)^2}{(2)(2)} \right] - \left[\frac{(43)^2}{2} + \cdots + \frac{(57)^2}{2} \right] + \frac{(100.00)^2}{(2)(2)(2)} = 4.50$$

$$SSBC = \left[\frac{(16)^2}{2} + \cdots + \frac{(40)^2}{2} \right] - \left[\frac{(33)^2}{(2)(2)} + \frac{(67)^2}{(2)(2)} \right] - \left[\frac{(43)^2}{(2)(2)} + \frac{(57)^2}{(2)(2)} \right] + \frac{(100.00)^2}{(2)(2)(2)} = 18.00$$

$$SSERROR = SSAC + SSBC = 4.50 + 18.00 = 22.50$$
$$SSTOTAL = 1{,}528.00 - 1{,}250.00 = 278.00$$

Note: Defining relation = $(ABCD)_0$, confounding contrast = $(AB)_z$.

of variation labeled treatment *A,* where the defining relation is *ABCDE,* is

$$ABCDE \times A = A^2 B^1 C^1 D^1 E^1$$
$$= 0(\text{mod } 2) = A^0 B^1 C^1 D^1 E^1$$
$$= BCDE.$$

Hence, treatment *A* and the *BCDE* interaction are alternative names for the same source of variation. The source of variation represented by the blocks has seven aliases: blocks plus the two confounding contrasts and generalized interaction, plus their aliases. The sources of variation and aliases for the design are shown in Table 2.

Computational Example

The computational procedures for a 2^{4-1} design with $(ABCD)_0$ as the defining relation and *AB* as the confounding contrast will be illustrated. A fractional factorial design with only four treatments is unrealistically small, but the small size simplifies the presentation. The layout and computational procedures for the design are shown in Table 3.

The analysis is summarized in Table 4. An examination of the table reveals that the $\frac{1}{2}$ fractional design contains the treatment combinations of a complete factorial design with treatments *A, B,* and *C.* Treatment *D* and all interactions involving treatment *D* are aliased with the sources of variation for the three-treatment design.

Advantages of Fractional Randomized Block Designs

Each source of variation for the design in Table 4 has two labels. You may wonder why anyone would use such a design—after all, experiments are supposed to resolve ambiguity, not create it. Fractional factorial designs are usually used in exploratory research situations where a large number of treatments must be investigated. In such designs, it is customary to limit all treatments to either two or three levels, thereby increasing the likelihood that higher-order interactions are small relative to treatments and lower-order

Table 4 ANOVA Table for Fractional Randomized Block Design With Four Treatments

Source (Alias)	SS	df	MS	F
Blocks or (*AB*), (*CD*)	12.50	$n - 1 = 1$	12.50	1.11
A (*BCD*)	72.00	$p - 1 = 1$	72.00	6.40
B (*ACD*)	144.50	$q - 1 = 1$	144.50	12.84
C (*ABD*)	24.50	$r - 1 = 1$	24.50	2.18
D (*ABC*)	2.00	$t - 1 = 1$	2.00	0.18
ERROR	22.50		11.25	
AC (*BD*)		$(p-1)(r-1)$		
+ *BC* (*AD*)		$+ (q-1)(r-1) = 2$		
Total	278.00	$pqr - 1 = 7$		

Note: Defining relation = $(ABCD)_0$; confounding contrast = $(AB)_z$.

interactions. Under these conditions, if a source of variation labeled treatment *A* and its alias, say the *BCDEFG* interaction, is significant, it is likely that the significance is due to the treatment rather than the interaction. A fractional factorial design can dramatically decrease the number of treatment combinations that must be run in an experiment. An experiment with seven treatments, each having two levels, contains 128 treatment combinations. By the use of a one-fourth fractional factorial design, 2^{7-2} design, the number of treatment combinations in the experiment can be reduced from 128 to 32. If none of the seven-treatment *F* statistics are significant, the researcher has answered the research questions with one fourth the effort required for a complete factorial design. On the other hand, if several of the *F* statistics are significant, the researcher can follow up with several small experiments to determine which aliases are responsible for the significant *F* statistics. Many researchers would consider ambiguity in interpreting the outcome of the initial experiment a small price to pay for the reduction in experimental effort.

—*Roger E. Kirk*

See also Factorial Design; Multivariate Analysis of Variance (MANOVA)

Further Reading

Kirk, R. E. (1995). *Experimental design: Procedures for the behavioral sciences* (3rd ed.). Pacific Grove, CA: Brooks/Cole.

Frequency Distribution

Frequency distribution graphs present all the actual data for a single variable. Their purpose is to illustrate the shape and distribution of the data, making it easier to identify outliers, gaps, clusters, and the most common data points.

Stem-and-leaf plots are examples of frequency distributions. Each number in the data set is divided into a stem and a leaf. The stem consists of the first digit or digits, and the leaf consists of the last digit. The stem can have any number of digits, but the leaf will contain only one number. For example, the number 1004 would be broken down into 100 (stem) and 4 (leaf), and the number 1.9 would be broken down into 1 (stem) and 9 (leaf).

Table 1 is a stem-and-leaf plot of grades in a history course. The graph was created using Word (a vertical bar was typed on each line). The plot illustrates that there are 21 grades, one grade of 39, none in the 40s, one grade of 57, two of 63, one of 64, one of 65, one of 67, three of 70, and so on.

Table 1 Final Grades for Students in a History Course

3	9
4	
5	7
6	33457
7	0001122356
8	145
9	4

To create a stem-and-leaf plot, follow these steps:

1. Put all the raw data in numerical order.

2. Separate each number into a stem and a leaf.

—*Adelheid A. M. Nicol*

See also Cumulative Frequency Distribution; Histogram; Stem-and-Leaf Display

Further Reading

Friel, S. N, Curcio, F. R., & Bright, G. W. (2001). Making sense of graphs: Critical factors influencing comprehension and instructional implications. *Journal for Research in Mathematics Education, 32,* 124–158.

Friedman Test

The Friedman test is a rank-based, nonparametric test for several related samples. This test is named in honor of its developer, the Nobel laureate and American economist Milton Friedman, who first proposed the test in 1937 in the *Journal of the American Statistical Association.* A researcher may sometimes feel confused when reading about the Friedman test because the "related samples" may arise from a variety of research settings. A very common way to think of Friedman's test is that it is a test for treatment differences for a randomized complete block (RCB) design. The RCB design uses blocks of participants who are matched closely on some relevant characteristic. Once the blocks are formed, participants within each block are assigned randomly to the treatment conditions. In the behavioral and health sciences, a common procedure is to treat a participant as a "block," wherein the participant serves in all the treatment conditions of an independent variable—also commonly referred to as a repeated measures design or a within-subjects design.

Although it is seen relatively rarely in the research literature, there is another research situation in which the Friedman test can be applied. One can use it in the context in which one has measured two or more comparable (also referred to as "commensurable") dependent variables from the same sample, usually at the same time. In this context, the data are treated much like a repeated measures design wherein the commensurable measures are levels of the repeated measures factor.

There is an additional source of confusion when one thinks about the Friedman test for repeated measures designs because for the RCB design, the parametric method for testing the hypothesis of no differences between treatments is the two-way ANOVA, with treatment and block factors. The Friedman test, which depends on the ranks of the dependent variable within each block, may therefore be considered a two-way ANOVA on ranks.

It is known in theoretical statistics that the Friedman test is a generalization of the sign test and has similar modest statistical power for most distributions that are likely to be encountered in behavioral and health research. For normal distributions, the asymptotic relative efficiency (ARE) of the Friedman test with respect to the F test, its counterpart among parametric statistical tests, is $0.955k/(k+1)$, where k is the number of treatment groups. When $k = 4$, the ARE of the Friedman test relative to the F test is 0.764. There is evidence from computer simulation studies that the ARE results, which are for very large sample sizes, are close to the relative efficiency to be expected for small and moderate sample sizes.

It is useful to note that in our desire to select the statistical test with the greatest statistical power, we often select the test with the greatest ARE. Therefore, for a normal distribution, the parametric test is more statistically powerful, leading us to recommend the ANOVA F test over the Friedman test. However, in the case of nonnormal distributions of dependent variables, the recommendation favors the Friedman test. Given the frequency at which nonnormal distributions are encountered in research, it is remarkable that nonparametric tests, such as the Friedman test, or other more-powerful tests, such as (a) the Zimmerman-Zumbo repeated measures ANOVA on ranks, wherein the scores in all treatment groups are combined in a single group and ranked, or (b) the Quade test, which uses information about the range of scores in the blocks relative to each other, are not used more often.

The Case Study and the Data

In the field of art education, there is a great deal of interest in whether parents participate in art activities with their young children and whether this participation changes over the early school years. It is often noted in the educational literature that talking with children about book illustrations, providing writing materials at home, and having children try various forms of expression such as drawing and painting enable children to express their creativity and can lead to their using artwork as material for instruction, play, and creative display.

For the purposes of demonstrating the Friedman test, 20 children (11 boys, 9 girls), average age 67.6 months, were selected from the Early Childhood Longitudinal Study, Kindergarten (ECLS-K) class of 1998–99. The ECLS-K focuses on children's early school experiences, collecting information from children and their parents, teachers, and schools. The question "How often do you help your child do art?"—with four response options: (a) *not at all*, (b) *once or twice per week*, (c) *3 to 6 times per week*, and (d) *every day*—was asked of parents when their child was in kindergarten, Grade 1, and Grade 3. The statistical software package SPSS version 13 was used for the analyses. The data are listed in Table 1 by each child's gender, age in months at the kindergarten assessment, and three parent responses to the question "How often do you help your child do art?"

The Assumptions Underlying the Friedman Test

The two assumptions for the test are stated here in terms of the RBC design:

Table 1 Raw Data From the ECLS-K Study

Gender	Age in Months	Kindergarten	Grade 1	Grade 3
Male	67.40	3	2	3
Male	67.40	4	2	3
Female	64.33	2	2	2
Female	64.40	2	2	2
Female	75.20	3	2	2
Male	67.20	4	2	2
Male	70.47	3	3	3
Female	69.03	1	2	3
Male	67.30	3	3	2
Female	75.17	3	2	2
Male	68.47	2	2	1
Male	62.70	2	2	2
Male	65.80	4	3	3
Female	74.47	2	3	2
Female	66.10	3	2	2
Female	68.23	3	3	2
Female	69.17	3	4	4
Male	61.83	2	1	1
Male	62.77	2	2	1
Male	65.33	3	2	2

- The dependent variable is quantitative in nature (ordinal, interval, or ratio scale) so that the rank transformation can be applied.
- The scores within one block do not influence the scores within the other blocks. This is an assumption of statistical independence across blocks. Violation of this assumption will seriously inflate the Type I error rates of the hypothesis test.

The Research Hypothesis

For our example, the "treatment" condition, in RCB design notation, is the grade (i.e., kindergarten, Grade 1, and Grade 3). The most general statistical hypothesis is:

H_0: The treatment conditions have identical effects. That is, each ranking of the dependent variable within a block is equally likely.

H_a: At least one of the treatment conditions tends to yield larger or smaller observed values than at least one other treatment.

The Friedman test is both an unbiased and a consistent test when testing these hypotheses. If one is willing to make additional assumptions about the distributions of dependent variables, for example that they are symmetric, the Friedman test can also test the equality of mean ranks of the treatments.

To compute the Friedman test, the scores within each block are compared with each other, and the rank of 1 is assigned to the smallest value, the rank of 2 to the next smallest, and so on. Average ranks are used in the case of ties. The computations for the Friedman test are then based on the sum of ranks for each treatment. The resulting test statistic does not follow a regularly shaped (and known) probability diostribution, and so an approximation is usually used. The approximate distribution for the Friedman statistic is the chi-square distribution with $k - 1$ degrees of freedom. For this example, SPSS was used to compute the Friedman test of equal mean ranks. The SPSS output below shows that the mean ranks in kindergarten, Grade 1, and Grade 3 are not equal, $\chi^2 (2) = 8.32, p < .05$.

Although it is beyond the scope of this entry, a post hoc multiple comparison procedure is available. Also, although we demonstrated the Friedman test using the

Ranks

	Mean Rank
how often parent helps child with art - kindergarten	2.40
how often parent helps child with art - first grade	1.90
how often parent helps child with art - third grade	1.70

Test Statistics[a]

N	20
Chi - Square	8.320
df	2
Asymp. Sig.	.016

a. Friedman Test

Figure 1   SPSS Results Based on the ECLS-K Study Data

SPSS software, it is also available in other statistical packages, such as SAS, Minitab, and S-Plus.

—*Bruno D. Zumbo*

See also Inferential Statistics

Further Reading

Beasley, T. M., & Zumbo, B. D. (2003). Comparison of aligned Friedman rank and parametric methods for testing interactions in split-plot designs. *Computational Statistics and Data Analysis*, 42, 569–593.

Conover, W. J. (1999). *Practical nonparametric statistics* (3rd ed.). New York: Wiley.

Friedman, M. (1937). The use of ranks to avoid the assumption of normality implicit in the analysis of variance. *Journal of the American Statistical Association*, 32, 675–701.

Zimmerman, D. W., & Zumbo, B. D. (1993). Relative power of parametric and nonparametric statistical methods. In G. Keren & C. Lewis (Eds.), *A handbook for data analysis in the behavioral sciences: Vol. 1. Methodological issues* (pp. 481–517). Hillsdale, NJ: Erlbaum.

Zimmerman, D. W., & Zumbo, B. D. (1993). Relative power of the Wilcoxon test, the Friedman test, and repeated-measures ANOVA on ranks. *Journal of Experimental Education*, 62, 75–86.

Friedman's Test Applet (allows you to enter data and calculate the test statistic): http://www.fon.hum.uva.nl/Service/Statistics/Friedman.html

G

A mathematician is a device for turning coffee into theorems.

—Paul Erdös

GALTON, SIR FRANCIS (1822–1911)

A prodigy, Sir Francis Galton was born of two important families. His mother was Charles Darwin's aunt and the daughter of Erasmus Darwin. His father's line included wealthy bankers and gunsmiths. By age six, Galton was conversant with the *Iliad* and the *Odyssey*. At age seven, he read Marmion's, Cowper's, Pope's, and Shakespeare's works for pleasure. After reading a page twice, he could repeat the text verbatim.

After studying medicine and mathematics at Cambridge and failing to excel in either discipline, Galton took a poll degree in 1843. After his father died, Galton pursued his passion for exploration. In so doing, he became a published author, received gold medals from two geographic societies, and was elected to the Royal Society. Galton developed a method for mapping atmospheric circulation and was the first to recognize the effects of high-pressure systems on weather. Another of his achievements was research proving that one's fingerprints are unique.

In statistics, Galton showed that the law of error could be used not only to estimate true scores, but also to investigate populations in terms of individuals' deviations from the mean. He developed the concept of regression, which allowed for the first scientific attempts to study the relationship of heredity and human behavior. Galton measured the heights of children and their parents. He plotted the data in such a fashion that the initial regression line decreased the error in prediction. Using sweet pea samples selected on the basis of the weight of parent seeds, he discovered that the progeny seed weights reverted (i.e., regressed) toward the mean of the parent distribution. This discovery led to the development of the concept of correlation. The statistical concepts of regression toward the mean and correlation allowed the field of psychometrics to move forward significantly. Researchers were able to study the stability of human attributes. For instance, through the use of regression and correlation, the relationship between the intelligence scores of parents and their children could be examined.

In *Hereditary Genius* (1869), Galton contended that intellect is inherited. To collect evidence to test his theory, he founded an anthropometric laboratory through which he measured an array of physical attributes (e.g., height, reaction time, and head circumference). Although his notion was fatally flawed, throughout his life Galton argued that nature dominates nurture in the development of human mental ability.

Galton used Darwin's comments on the selective breeding of plants and animals to suggest that humans could be improved by similar methods. In 1883, he coined the term for such practices, *eugenics,* and a long and bitter controversy ensued. Although his name is often linked to negative eugenics (e.g., Hitler's attempts to exterminate "inferior races"), for the most part Galton favored positive approaches (e.g., "genetically superior" people should marry early and produce more children). Nevertheless, he urged that "undesirables" be restricted from free reproduction, even supporting their sterilization.

—Ronald C. Eaves

See also Correlation Coefficient; Intelligence Quotient; Intelligence Tests

Further Reading

Brookes, M. (2004). *Extreme measures: The dark visions and bright ideas of Francis Galton.* London: Bloomsbury.

Sir Francis Galton: http://www.mugu.com/galton/

Applying Ideas on Statistics and Measurement

The following abstract is adapted from Huberty, C. J. (2002). A history of effect size indices. *Educational and Psychological Measurement,* 62(2), 227–240.

Depending on how one interprets what an effect size index is, it may be claimed that its history started around 1940, or about 100 years prior to that with the ideas of **Sir Francis Galton**, Charles Darwin (Galton's cousin), and others. An attempt is made in this article to trace histories of a variety of effect size indices. Effect size bases discussed pertain to (a) relationship, (b) group differences, and (c) group overlap. Multivariate as well as univariate indices are considered in reviewing the histories.

GAMBLER'S FALLACY

The *gambler's fallacy* is a common invalid inductive inference. It involves the mistaken intuition or belief that the likelihood of a particular outcome of a process that generates independent random events increases as a function of the length of a run of consecutive nonoccurrences of that outcome.

For example, a person playing a casino roulette wheel would commit the gambler's fallacy if he or she had a greater tendency to gamble on red than on black after four consecutive black outcomes, than after a shorter run of black outcomes. Such a tendency, or belief that red is more likely to occur as a function of its nonoccurrence, is erroneous, because the outcomes of the spins of a properly calibrated roulette wheel are independent, and the probabilities of red and black are equal and remain constant from spin to spin of the wheel. Similarly, a flip of a fair coin is not more likely to produce tails after a run of heads; nor is a pregnant woman more likely to give birth to a girl if she has, in the past, given birth to three boys consecutively.

The most widely cited explanation of the gambler's fallacy effect involves the hypothesis that people judge the randomness of an observed series of outcomes in terms of the extent to which it represents the output that would be expected of a prototypical random process—one that contains few orderly sequences such as long runs, symmetries, or strict alternations of one outcome, and few over- or underrepresentations of possible outcomes. Perhaps the gambler's fallacy arises because the occurrence of a locally less frequent outcome would produce a sample that would better represent randomness than the alternative sample would. For example, given five flips of a fair coin, heads might seem more likely after a series such as *THTTT,* because *THTTTH* has a shorter run of tails, and overrepresents tails less, than *THTTTT* does. People may also believe that a random device is somehow capable of correcting for the local scarcity of one outcome by overproducing instances of that outcome. Such thinking is faulty. A random device has no memory or means by which to correct its output, or to prevent patterns from appearing in a sample of outcomes.

Generalization from frequently encountered cases involving finite populations sampled without replacement could also explain this fallacy. For example, a motorist who is stopped at a railroad crossing waiting for a freight train to pass would be using sound reasoning if he or she counted freight cars that have passed the crossing and compared this number to his or her knowledge of the finite distribution of train lengths to determine when the crossing will clear. However, such reasoning is invalid when applied to large populations sampled without replacement.

—*David M. Boynton*

See also Law of Large Numbers

Further Reading

Gold, E. (1997). *The gambler's fallacy.* Unpublished doctoral dissertation, Carnegie Mellon University.

Kahneman, D., & Tversky, A. (1972). Subjective probability: A judgment of representativeness. *Cognitive Psychology, 3,* 430–454.

Applying Ideas on Statistics and Measurement

The following abstract is adapted from Johnson, J., & Tellis, G. J. (2005). Blowing bubbles: Heuristics and biases in the run-up of stock prices. *Journal of the Academy of Marketing Science, 33*(4), 486–503.

Ads of stocks and mutual funds typically tout their past performance, despite a disclosure that past performance does not guarantee future returns. Are consumers motivated to buy or sell based on past performance of assets? More generally, do consumers (wrongly) use sequential information about past performance of assets to make suboptimal decisions? Use of this heuristic leads to two well-known biases: the hot hand and the **gambler's fallacy**. This study proposes a theory of hype that integrates these two biases—that a positive run could inflate prices, and a negative run could depress them, although the pattern could reverse on extended runs. Tests on two experiments and one event study of stock purchases strongly suggest that consumers dump "losers" and buy "winners." The latter phenomenon could lead to hyped-up prices on the stock market for winning stocks. The authors discuss the managerial, public policy, and research implications of the results.

GAUSS, CARL FRIEDRICH (1777–1855)

Gauss, who was born April 30, 1777, in Brunswick, Germany, the child of a poor family, was a prodigy who became famous for his advances in many branches of science, but he was, above all else, a mathematician.

Mathematics came naturally to Gauss, who is said to have corrected his father's wage calculations when he was aged three. Early evidence of his ability was provided by his speedy answer to the request by his schoolteacher to sum the numbers from 1 to 100. He saw immediately that each of $(1 + 100)$, $(2 + 99)$, . . . summed to 101 and thus the answer was 5050. He had invented the formula for himself, and this was typical of his early career—he was frequently inventing results and discovering later that these results had been found before. Gauss's ability came to the attention of the Duke of Brunswick, who became his patron and sent him, in 1795, to the University of Göttingen. It was only a matter of time before Gauss outdid his predecessors: In 1796, he showed that it would be possible, using ruler and compasses only, to construct a regular figure with

$$2^{2^n} + 1$$

sides for any integer n.

In 1801, Gauss summarized his discoveries of the previous 5 years in *Disquisitiones Arithmeticae*, a masterpiece that immediately established him as the foremost living mathematician. Turning to astronomy, Gauss next developed new methods for calculating the motions of planets. This was spectacularly confirmed by his ability to predict where astronomers should search for the minor planet Ceres. Gauss's achievement was based on his development of the method of least squares and the use of an error distribution now known variously as the normal or Gaussian distribution. The procedures were set out in his 1809 work *Theoria Motus Corporum Coelestium in sectionibus conicis solem ambientium*.

In 1805, Gauss was happily married to Johanna Ostoff, and he soon had a son and daughter. In 1807, the family moved to Göttingen, where Gauss was appointed director of the observatory. In 1809, Johanna died in childbirth, and the following year, Gauss married her best friend, Minna Waldeck, although it appears that this marriage was not a happy one.

Gauss's astronomical work resulted in inventions such as the heliotrope, an instrument for accurate direction-finding by means of reflected sunlight. Gauss also experimented with magnetometers; photometers; and, some 5 years before Samuel Morse, the telegraph. He died peacefully at Göttingen in the early morning of February 23, 1855.

—Graham Upton

See also Normal Curve

Further Reading

Dunnington, G. W. (2004). *Carl Friedrich Gauss: Titan of science.* Washington, DC: Mathematical Association of America.

Carl Friedrich Gauss article: http://en.wikipedia.org/wiki/Carl_Friedrich_Gauss

GENERALIZED ADDITIVE MODEL

Estimating the linear model $Y_i = \beta 0 + \beta 1 X1_i + \ldots + \beta k Xk_i + e_i$ is at the core of many of the statistics conducted today. If you allow the individual X variables to be products of themselves and other variables, the linear model is appropriate for factorial ANOVAs and polynomial regressions, as well as estimating the mean, t tests, and so on. The flexibility of the linear model has led authors of some textbooks and software to call this the *general linear model.* I try to avoid this phrase because it can be confused with the *generalized linear model,* or GLM. The GLM is an important extension that allows researchers to analyze efficiently models where the responses are proportions and counts, as well as other situations. More on this later.

The main focus of this entry is extending the linear model into an additive model. In the linear model, each X variable is multiplied by a scalar, the β value. This is what makes it a linear model, but this restricts

the relationship between X and Y (conditioned on all the other Xs). With additive models, the β values are replaced by usually fairly simple (in terms of degrees of freedom) functions of the X variables. The model can be rewritten as $Y_i = \alpha + f1(X1_i) + \ldots + fk(Xk_i) + e_i$. The functions are usually assumed to be splines with a small number of knots. More complex functions can be used, but this may cause the model to overfit the observed data and thus not generalize well to new data sets. The typical graphical output shows the functions and the numeric output shows the fit of the linear and nonlinear components. The choice of functions, which often comes down to the type and complexity of the splines, is critical.

To illustrate this procedure, Berndt's 1991 data from 534 respondents on hourly wages and several covariates (experience in years, gender, and education in years) are considered. One outlier with an hourly wage of \$44 ($z = 6.9$) is removed, but the data remain skewed (1.28, $se = 0.11$). Logging these data removes the skew (0.05, $se = 0.11$), so a fairly common approach is to use the logged values as the response variable and assume that the residuals are normally distributed. Suppose the researchers' main interests are in the experience variable, and whether income steadily increases with experience or whether it increases rapidly until some point and then increases but less rapidly. For argument's sake, let us assume that the increases are both linear with the logged wages. The researchers accept that wages increase with education and believe that the relationship is nonlinear, and so they allow this relationship to be modeled with a smoothing spline. Because the variable *female* is binary, only a single parameter is needed to measure the difference in earnings between males and females. Although categorical variables can be included within generalized additive models (GAMs), the purpose of GAMs is to examine the relationships between quantitative variables and the response variable. The first model is

$$\ln wages_i = \beta 0 + \beta 1 female_i + \beta 2 Exper_i + f1(Educ_i) + e_i.$$

This is like a normal multiple linear regression for the variables *female* and *Exper*; the model fits both as conditionally linear with the log of wages, but the relationship for education is allowed to be curved. This was fit with the gam package for S-Plus with the default spline (smoothing spline with *df* = 4). The residual deviance is 103.74. There is a positive linear relationship between experience and the log of wages and a positive curved relationship between education and the log of wages. The effect for *female* is negative, meaning that after controlling for experience and education, females earn less than their male counterparts. The top three plots in Figure 1 show this model. With GAMs, people usually rely on plots to interpret the models and compare the deviance values, or they use methods of cross-validation to decide how complex the model (including the complexities of the individual *f*ks) should be. Here, the deviance values will be compared.

The bottom three plots of Figure 1 show the model

$$\ln wages_i = \beta0 + \beta1 female_i + f1(Exper_i) + f2(Educ_i) + e_i.$$

*f*1 has been set to a piecewise linear model, so two lines are connected at a knot determined by the algorithm. The residual deviance drops to 97.55, which is statistically significant ($\chi^2(1) = 6.20$, $p = .01$). The package used (gam) allows different types of curves (including loess) to be included in the model, although the efficiency of the algorithm works best if the same type is used. What is clear from this model is that a single linear term of experience is not sufficient to account for these data. If we allow the relationship between experience and the log of wages to be a *df* = 4 spline, the

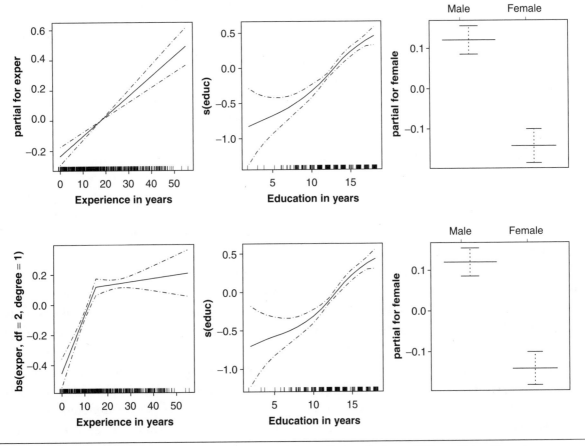

Figure 1   Plots for the Predictor Variables for Two Models Predicting the Log of Wages Using Experience, Education, and Gender

Notes: The top row shows the GAM where experience is a linear predictor. The bottom row has experience as a piecewise linear relationship with a single knot estimated at approximately 15 years' experience. The dashed lines are for standard errors and rugplots are used to show the univariate distributions of experience and education.

residual deviance drops only to 96.85. Although this is not an improvement in the fit of the model, the researcher might still opt for this unless he or she has a theoretical explanation for the sudden change in slope for the previous model.

Just as the generalized linear model allows researchers to model proportions and counts efficiently using the basic concepts of the linear model, the generalized additive model also allows this. The user chooses an error distribution from the exponential family and an associated link function, denoted $g()$. Popular distributions are the normal distribution (associated link is the identity function), the binomial distribution (associated link is the logit function), and the Poisson distribution (associated link is the natural log, or ln, function). In fact, the above example could have been modeled with the log link and assuming Poisson error, and this approach shows that a smooth spline does fit experience better than the piecewise linear model. Generalizing the additive model can be done in the same way as generalizing the linear model. If μ_i is the value of the response variable, then $E(g(\mu_i)) = \eta_i$, where η_i is an additive model of the form $\Sigma fk(Xk_i)$ where one of the X variables is a constant so that an intercept is included. Including the error term, this is $g(\mu_i) = \eta_i + e_i$, where the e_i are assumed to follow some distribution. The wages example could be fit with the following GAM:

$$1n(\mu_i) = \eta_i + e_i$$
$$\eta_i = \alpha + f1(Exper_i) + f2(Educ_i) + \beta1 female_i$$
$$e_i \sim Poisson(\mu_i).$$

To illustrate a logistic additive model, Vriji's 2005 data inspired by truth and lie detection using criteria-based content analysis (CBCA) will be used. This is a method used in several countries to try to determine whether a child is telling the truth or a lie when questioned, usually in connection with cases of child sexual abuse. There are 19 criteria, and each statement can be given a 0, 1, or 2. These are summed so that each person can get a score from 0 to 38, with high scores indicating more truthfulness. One problem with this procedure is that people with more linguistic skills tend to have higher scores than people with fewer linguistic

skills. Because of this, there is assumed to be a complex relationship between age, CBCA score, and truth.

Suppose there are 1,000 statements from people who are 3 to 22 years old. All of the statements have CBCA scores, and it is known whether or not they are truthful. For these data, age and truth were created independently, so age, on its own, does not predict truth ($t(998) = 1.04$, $p = .30$). Three GAMs were estimated. The first has just CBCA to predict truth. This uses the logit link function and assumes binomial variation. The default smoothing function for the gam package is used, and the result (in the upper left hand corner of Figure 2) shows that the probability of truth increases with CBCA scores. The deviation from linear is statistically insignificant ($\chi^2(3) = 44.18$, $p < .01$). The residual deviance of this model is 1251.65.

The next model has $\eta_i = \alpha_i + f1(CBCA_i) + f2(age_i)$, where both $f1$ and $f2$ are $df = 4$ smoothing splines, and the resulting curves are shown in the second row of Figure 2. CBCA is again positively related to truth. However, age is negatively related (because it is conditional on CBCA). Both curves show marked nonlinearity. The residual deviance is 1209.60, which is a large improvement in fit on the previous model ($\chi^2(3.82) = 42.05$, $p < .001$). The final row in Figure 2 shows the GAM, which includes an interaction term. The graph of the interaction effect (new residual deviance 1201.51, change $\chi^2(3.96) = 28.09$, $p = .09$) shows that the predictive value of the CBCA scores increases with age. To examine this interaction further, values of the age variable were placed into four approximately equal sized bins, and separate GAMs were run on each. The resulting ogives for these are shown in Figure 3. Simple monotonic curves appear to represent the relationship between CBCA and truthfulness for the older people, but not for the younger groups. It appears either that the relationship between CBCA and truthfulness is different for the age groups, or that the CBCA is only diagnostic of truthfulness above about 16 or 17 points (which the older people do not score below for either true or false statements). Given that these are data created for illustration, it is not appropriate to speculate further about either explanation.

GAMs are useful generalizations of the basic regression models. Like GLMs, they allow different link functions and distributions that are appropriate

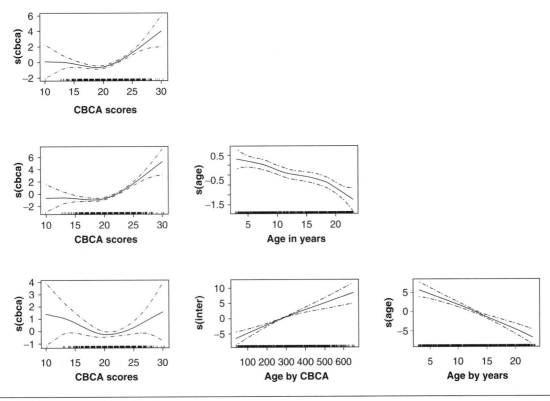

Figure 2 Plots for the Predictor Variables for Three Models Predicting the Probability of a Statement Being Truthful Based on CBCA Score and Age

Notes: The first (upper left hand corner) uses just CBCA score. The second model (row two) also uses age. The third model (row three) also includes the interaction. The dashed lines are for standard errors and rugplots are used to show the univariate distributions.

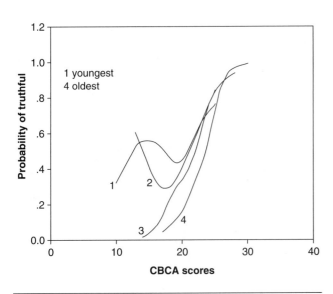

Figure 3 Individual GAMs for Four Different Age Groups

Notes: 1 = 3.0 to 7.9 years, 2 = 7.9 to 13.0 years, 3 = 13.0 years to 18.1 years, and 4 = 18.1 years and higher. There are relatively smooth monotonic curves for the two older age groups. However, the curves for the younger age groups appear more complex, particularly for low CBCA values.

for a large amount of data collected in science. Furthermore, the additive components allow an extremely flexible approach to data modeling. There are several extensions to GAMs not discussed here, such as model selection and regularization techniques, multilevel GAMs, and different types of estimation. Current software allows many different types of curves to be fit within GAMs. Two were illustrative, a theory-driven example where a linear model was compared with a piecewise linear model, and a data-driven example that included an interaction. As algorithms and software advance, these models should become more flexible and more widely used.

—*Daniel B. Wright*

See also Ogive; Smoothing

Further Reading

Berndt, E. R. (1991). *The practice of econometrics*. New York: Addison-Wesley.

Hastie, T., & Tibshirani, R. (1990). *Generalized additive models*. London: Chapman & Hall.

McCullagh, P., & Nelder, J. A. (1989). *Generalized linear models* (2nd ed.). London: Chapman & Hall.

Vrij, A. (2005). Criteria-based content analysis—A qualitative review of the first 37 studies. *Psychology, Public Policy, & Law, 11,* 3–41.

GENERALIZED METHOD OF MOMENTS

When information on a set of parameters is given in the form of moments (expectations), equations containing this information are called the *moment conditions*. For example, if $y_t = x_t'\theta + u_t$ is considered and the statistician knows a priori that x_t and u_t are uncorrelated, then the corresponding moment conditions are $Ex_t(y_t - x_t'\theta) = 0$. Alternatively, if it is believed that z_t and u_t are uncorrelated for some random variables z_t, then the moment conditions would be $Ez_t(y_t - x_t'\theta) = 0$. In the above examples, the functions $x_t(y_t - x_t'\theta)$ and $z_t(y_t - x_t'\theta)$, whose expectations are set to zero, are called the *moment functions*. In general, for some functions $g(X_t, \theta)$ of random variables X_t and unknown parameter vector θ, the moment conditions are expressed as $Eg(X_t, \theta) = 0$.

Identification and Overidentification

For a given set of moment functions $g(X_t, \theta)$, the true parameter sets the expected moment functions to zero by definition. When $Eg(X_t, \theta) = 0$ at only the true parameter, we say that the true parameter vector is *identified* by the moment conditions. A necessary condition for the identification of the true parameter is that the number of moment conditions should be at least as large as the number of parameters. When the number of moment conditions is exactly equal to the number of parameters (and when the true parameter is identified), we say that the true parameter is *exactly identified*. On the other hand, if there are more moment conditions than necessary, we say that the true parameter is *overidentified*.

Generalized Method of Moments

When there is a set of moment conditions that exactly identifies a parameter vector, *method of moments estimation* is widely used. As the true parameter sets the population moments to zero, the method of moments estimator sets the sample moments to zero. More precisely, when the true parameter is exactly identified by $Eg(X_t, \theta) = 0$, the method of moments estimator $\hat{\theta}$ satisfies $T^{-1}\sum_{t=1}^{T} g(X_t, \hat{\theta}) = 0$.

If the true parameter is overidentified, that is, if there are more moment conditions than are necessary to identify θ, then it is usually impossible to set the sample moment vector to zero (because there are more equations than parameters). The *generalized method of moments* (GMM) was introduced by Lars Peter Hansen in 1982 in order to handle this case. Let $\overline{g}(\theta) = T^{-1}\sum_{t=1}^{T} g(X_t, \theta)$ for notational simplicity. Instead of setting the sample moment functions simultaneously to zero (which is usually impossible), Hansen proposed to minimize the quadratic distance of the sample moment vector from zero, that is, to minimize $\overline{g}(\theta)'\overline{g}(\theta)$ with respect to θ over the parameter space. The minimizer is called the *generalized method of moments (GMM) estimator*.

The GMM estimator is consistent and asymptotically normal. In addition, the GMM procedure contains method of moments estimation as a special case. The method of moments estimator sets $\overline{g}(\hat{\theta}) = 0$, in which case the criterion function $\overline{g}(\theta)'\overline{g}(\theta)$ attains the minimal value zero at $\theta = \hat{\theta}$.

Weighted GMM and Optimal GMM

A symmetric and positive definite constant matrix W can be used in the criterion function to form a weighted criterion function $\overline{g}(\theta)'W\overline{g}(\theta)$, whose minimizer is called the *weighted GMM estimator* using the matrix W as weights. Because any symmetric and positive definite matrix can be decomposed into $A'A$ for some nonsingular matrix A (e.g., by a Cholesky decomposition), we observe that any weighted criterion function can be regarded as the (unweighted) quadratic distance of the transformed sample moment vector $A\overline{g}(\theta) = T^{-1}\sum_{t=1}^{T} Ag(X_t, \theta)$ from zero. Because W is a constant matrix, A is also a constant matrix, and therefore the transformed moment conditions are also valid, because $E[Ag(X_t,\theta)] = AEg(X_t,\theta) = 0$. This obvious fact shows that any weighted GMM estimator (using a symmetric and positive definite weight matrix) is also consistent and asymptotically normal.

When the moment conditions exactly identify a parameter, a weighted GMM can still be considered. But in that case, the resulting weighted GMM estimator is always equal to the method of moments estimator satisfying $\bar{g}(\hat{\theta}) = 0$. Therefore, weighted GMM needs to be used only in the case of overidentification.

The asymptotic variance of a weighted GMM estimator depends on the associated weight matrix. Optimal weights would correspond to the transformation of the moment conditions such that all the moment functions have identical variance and are pairwise uncorrelated. More specifically, the optimal weight, which yields the most efficient GMM estimator in the class of weighted GMM estimators, is Ω^{-1}, where $\Omega = E[g(X_t,\theta)g(X_t,\theta)']$. The weighted GMM estimator using this optimal weight is called the *optimal GMM estimator*. The optimal GMM estimator is again obviously consistent because $E[Ag(X_t,\theta)] = AEg(X_t,\theta)$, where $A'A = \Omega^{-1}$.

Under the assumption that the random variables X_t are *iid* for all t, and some other technical assumptions, the asymptotic distribution of the optimal GMM estimator is

$$\sqrt{T}(\hat{\theta} - \theta) \to_d N\left(0, (D'\Omega^{-1}D)^{-1}\right),$$

where $D = E\partial g(X_t,\theta)/\partial\theta'$, and both D and Ω are evaluated at the true parameter. This optimal GMM estimator is efficient in the class of consistent estimators based on a given set of moment conditions.

In practice, the optimal weight matrix Ω^{-1} is unknown, and as such, the estimator based on $\bar{g}(\theta)'\Omega^{-1}\bar{g}(\theta)$ is *infeasible*. We can make this procedure *feasible* using a consistent estimate of Ω. Usually, a two-step procedure is used by practitioners.

1. A consistent estimator of Ω is found. Often, this is done using an unweighted GMM, or method of moments estimation with an exactly identifying subset of the moment conditions. If $\tilde{\theta}$ is the resulting estimator, then Ω is estimated by

$$\tilde{\Omega} = T^{-1}\Sigma_{t=1}^{T} g(X_t,\tilde{\theta})\, g(X_t,\tilde{\theta})'.$$

2. We then minimize $\bar{g}(\theta)'\tilde{\Omega}^{-1}\bar{g}(\theta)$ to yield an efficient GMM estimator.

This estimator is called the *two-step efficient GMM estimator*. The asymptotic distribution of the two-step efficient GMM estimator is identical to that of the (infeasible) optimal GMM estimator using Ω^{-1} as weights.

Sometimes, estimation of Ω and the efficient GMM estimator are repeated until the first step estimator and the second step estimator coincide. This estimator, called the *continuous updating estimator*, also has the same asymptotic distribution as the optimal GMM estimator.

The continuous updating estimator is also obtained by minimizing

$$\bar{g}(\theta)'\left[\frac{1}{T}\sum_{t=1}^{T} g(X_t,\theta)g(X_t,\theta)'\right]^{-1}\bar{g}(\theta)$$

with respect to θ. The difference between this criterion function and the loss function for the two-step efficient GMM is that in the continuous updating estimation, the weighting matrix is a function of the parameter and is adjusted to attain the global minimum.

When $\hat{\theta}$ is the optimal GMM estimator (feasible or infeasible), the variance-covariance matrix $(D'\Omega^{-1}D)^{-1}$ is estimated by $(\hat{D}'\hat{\Omega}^{-1}\hat{D})^{-1}$, where

$$\hat{D} = \frac{1}{T}\sum_{t=1}^{T} \frac{\partial g(X_t,\hat{\theta})}{\partial\theta'} \text{ and}$$

$$\hat{\Omega} = \frac{1}{T}\sum_{t=1}^{T} g(X_t,\hat{\theta})g(X_t,\hat{\theta})'.$$

When computing $\hat{D}$, if the first derivative is not algebraically obtained, we may use a numerical procedure to differentiate the moment functions.

Inferences on the parameters may still be done using this numerical approximation.

When an overidentifying set of moment conditions is available, method of moments estimation using an exactly identifying subset of the moment conditions is always an available option that yields a consistent and asymptotically normal estimator. Moreover, this method of moments estimator based on a subset does not involved weighting and therefore is simpler computationally and conceptually. However, mathematical theorems show that the asymptotic variance of the optimal GMM estimator never increases as moment conditions are added to a given set of moment conditions, which is natural because a bigger set of moment conditions means more information, and an optimal utilization of more information should not yield a worse estimator. So, from the perspective of asymptotic efficiency, it is more desirable to make use of all the moment conditions available and consider optimal GMM. However, when the sample size is small, it is known that too many moment conditions are likely to lead to a poor (e.g., biased) estimator, and methods with which to choose an optimal number of moment conditions are being researched actively.

In order for the GMM estimators (unweighted, weighted, optimal, two-step, and continuous updating) to be consistent and asymptotically normal, the moment conditions must clearly identify the true parameter in the sense that the slope of the moment functions is steep enough to clearly separate the true parameter from its neighborhood. If the moment functions fail this condition, we say that the moment functions *weakly identify* the true parameter. In this case, the two-step efficient GMM estimator has severe bias in general. However, available evidence suggests that the continuous updating estimator has little or no bias. In the example of linear structural equations models, the two-stage least squares estimator with weak instruments is biased, and the estimator corresponds to the two-step efficient GMM estimator. In this same setting, the limited information maximum likelihood estimator corresponds to the continuous updating estimator, and these appear not to have any bias. Formalizing the properties of the GMM estimators in the case of weak identification is an active research area.

Overidentification Test

Now consider testing if the specification $Eg(X_t, \theta) = 0$ is correct. If the true parameter is exactly identified, then it is impossible to test this specification because GMM estimation is achieved by setting $\overline{g}(\hat{\theta}) = 0$. But if the moment conditions overidentify the true parameter, then a test is available based on $\overline{g}(\hat{\theta})$. This test is called the *overidentification test*.

If H_0: $Eg(X_t, \theta) = 0$ is true, then the sample moments $\overline{g}(\hat{\theta})$, evaluated at the GMM (consistent) estimator, will be close to zero, whereas if H_0 is incorrect, then the sample moments will be far from zero. When H_0 is correct, it can be shown that $T\overline{g}(\hat{\theta})'\hat{\Omega}^{-1}\overline{g}(\hat{\theta})$ is approximately χ^2 distributed with degrees of freedom equal to the degree of overidentification, that is, the number of moment conditions minus the number of parameters. If the test statistic is large, then this implies that there are some moment conditions that are not compatible with the others, and so some elements of $Eg(X_t, \theta)$ are not zero, leading us to reject H_0. Unfortunately, the test does not indicate which of the moment conditions are correctly specified and which are incorrectly specified.

Examples

Any estimator that uses information given in the form of moment conditions can be classified as a GMM estimator. For example, the ordinary least squares estimator is the GMM (or more exactly, the method of moments) estimator using the moment conditions that each regressor is uncorrelated with the error term. The two-stage least squares estimator is another example of GMM based on the moment conditions that the instruments and the error term are uncorrelated. The maximum likelihood estimator can also be regarded as a GMM estimator, because the estimator satisfying the first order condition $T^{-1}\sum_{t=1}^{T}\partial \log L_t(\hat{\theta})/\partial\theta = 0$ can be regarded as a method of moments estimator using $E\partial \log L_t(\theta)/\partial\theta = 0$ as moment conditions.

Application

Consider a random sample of T observations: $X_1, \ldots, X_T$. If we identify the true parameter θ as

$\theta = E(X_t)$, that is, $E(X_t - \theta) = 0$, then the method of moments estimator for θ is $\hat{\theta}_{mm} = T^{-1}\sum_{t=1}^{T}X_t$, whose variance may be estimated by $\hat{V}_{mm} = T^{-2}\sum_{t=1}^{T}(X_t - \hat{\theta}_{mm})^2$.

Now suppose that the statistician also knows a priori that the third central moment of X_t is zero, that is, that $E[(X_t - \theta)^3] = 0$. Then we have two moment functions

$$g(X_t, \theta) = \begin{bmatrix} X_t - \theta \\ (X_t - \theta)^3 \end{bmatrix}$$

for the θ parameter. For the two-step efficient GMM estimation, we first get a consistent estimate of θ to construct a consistent estimate for the optimal weighting matrix. We may use the above $\hat{\theta}_{mm}$ to get $\tilde{\Omega} = (1/T)\sum_{t=1}^{T}g(X_t, \tilde{\theta})g(X_t, \tilde{\theta})'$, and then the feasible optimal weight is $\tilde{\Omega}^{-1}$. Now the two-step efficient GMM estimator minimizes $\bar{g}(\theta)'\tilde{\Omega}^{-1}\bar{g}(\theta)$, where $\bar{g}(\theta) = (1/T)\sum_{t=1}^{T}g(X_t, \theta)$. Let $\hat{\theta}_{gmm}$ denote this two-step efficient GMM estimator. The variance of the asymptotic distribution of $\sqrt{T}(\hat{\theta}_{gmm} - \theta)$ is $(D'\Omega^{-1}D)^{-1}$, where

$$D = E\frac{\partial g(X_t, \theta)}{\partial \theta} = -\begin{bmatrix} 1 \\ 3E[(X_t - \theta)^2] \end{bmatrix}$$

and $\Omega = E[g(X_t, \theta)g(X_t, \theta)']$ as before. These D and Ω are estimated consistently by replacing θ with $\hat{\theta}_{gmm}$ and the expectation operator with the sample mean over the T observations. The continuous updating estimation is straightforward.

Table 1 contains a sample of 40 observations of X_t. The method of moments estimator $\hat{\theta}_{mm}$, which is the sample mean of $X_1, \ldots, X_{40}$, equals 1.0230 with standard error $\hat{V}^{1/2} = 0.1554$. The S-plus program for the two-step efficient GMM estimation is listed in Table 2, and that for the continuous updating estimation is in Table 3. The resulting two-step GMM estimate is

Table 1 Data: 40 Observations

−0.012	0.442	0.508	1.301	−0.462	0.214	1.693	−0.620
1.281	1.705	1.029	0.807	2.436	−0.349	2.275	2.449
1.593	−0.102	0.756	1.506	0.500	1.407	−0.193	1.095
2.219	1.547	−0.090	2.219	2.003	2.688	0.190	−0.269
1.677	0.576	1.842	−0.107	−0.736	2.318	1.704	1.881

Table 2 S–Plus and R Code for Two–Step Efficient GMM

```
x <- read.csv ("datafile.csv")
n <- NROW(x)
g.matrix <- function(p) {
        m1 <- x-p
        as.matrix(cbind(m1,m1^3))
}
gmm.func <- function(p) {
        gbar <- as.numeric(colMeans(g.matrix(p)))
        t(gbar)%*%W%*%gbar
}
std.error <- function(p) {
        Omega <- crossprod (g.matrix (p))/n
        D <- -c(1,3*mean((x-p)^2)) # algebraic differentiation
        1/(t(D)%*%solve(Omega)%*%D)/sqrt(n)
}
est1 <- mean(x) # First step MM
W <- solve(crossprod (g.matrix(est1))/n) # Weighting matrix
gmm2 <- nlm(gmm.func,est1) # Second step efficient GMM
est2 <- gmm2$estimate
## Overidentification test
overid <- n*gmm2$minimum
```

Table 3 S-Plus and R Code for Continuous Updating Estimation

```
code continued from Table 2
cue.func <- function(p) {
    gbar <-as.numeric(colMeans (g.matrix (p)))
    W <- solve(crossprod (g.matrix(p))/n)
    t(gbar)%*%W%*%gbar
}
est3 <- nlm(cue.func,est1)$estimate
se3 <- std.error(est3)
```

0.9518 with standard error 0.0456, and the continuous updating estimate is 0.9513 with standard error 0.0456. The sample mean is the method of moments estimator based on the first moment condition only, and the other GMM estimators make use of both moment conditions. As might be expected, the two GMM estimators are more efficient than the sample mean (because more information is used). The overidentification test statistic based on the two-step GMM is computed easily by multiplying the sample size by the minimized criterion function, which is approximately distributed χ^2_1. For the data set above, the test statistic is 0.3040 with a p value of 0.5814. So, the specification that $E(X_t - \theta) = 0$ and $E[(X_t - \theta)^3] = 0$ is regarded as correct.

—*Chirok Han and John Randal*

See also Instrumental Variables

Further Reading

Hansen, L. P. (1982). Large sample properties of generalized method of moments estimators. *Econometrica, 50,* 1029–1054.

Lee, M. (1996). *Methods of moments and semiparametric econometrics for limited dependent variable models.* New York: Springer.

GENERALIZED PROCRUSTES ANALYSIS

Generalized Procrustes Analysis (GPA) is a method for determining the degree of agreement, or consensus, among data matrices. For instance, consider 20 judges who rate four brands of coffee on 10 attributes (e.g., bitterness, richness, smoothness). The ratings for each judge can be recorded in a two-dimensional (10×4) matrix. GPA then can be used to determine the extent to which the judges agree in their views of the four brands of coffee. To the extent the 20 judges do not agree, individual differences in the patterns of ratings can also be examined with GPA. At the heart of the analysis is a *consensus configuration,* which is derived through a process of scaling, rotating, and averaging the original rating matrices. Each judge's ratings can be compared to this consensus configuration, and an overall *consensus proportion* can be computed that indicates the degree of similarity among the judge's views of the four coffees. GPA is also extremely flexible and can accommodate any number of matrices of varying dimensions. Qualitative judgments or quantitative data can be analyzed, and the matrices must be matched on only a single dimension. For instance, each of the 20 judges could rate the four brands of coffee using a different set of attributes as well as a different number of attributes. The flexibility of GPA can also be seen in the variety of studies in which it has been employed. Researchers have examined individuals' perceptions of food, products, medical treatments, genetic engineering, and personality traits using this technique.

Abbreviated Example

Four managers from a department store freely describe and then rate six of their employees on 5-point scales constructed from their individual descriptive adjectives. A high score on the rating scale indicates that a particular adjective is an accurate description of the employee. The data are reported in Table 1.

The goal of GPA is to assess the degree of similarity among the managers' views of the employees. More specifically, the goal is to determine if the patterns, or profiles, of the six employees are similar across the four managers. Because the focus is on the profiles of the employees, the analysis does not require a fixed set of attributes.

Table 1 Managers' Ratings of Six Employees

	Manager 1							*Manager 2*					
	John	Bob	Amy	Jan	Fred	Jill		John	Bob	Amy	Jan	Fred	Jill
Extraverted	1	1	5	4	5	3	Blunt	2	3	1	3	4	1
Sharing	5	5	2	1	2	3	Patient	5	1	4	2	2	3
Motivated	2	2	4	3	4	1	Creative	5	2	3	4	1	3
Funny	1	2	2	2	4	1	Outgoing	2	4	1	4	3	3
Loud	1	2	2	1	4	1							
	Manager 3							*Manager 4*					
Outgoing	2	4	2	4	5	3	Easygoing	2	3	1	3	4	3
Carefree	2	4	3	4	4	2	Outgoing	1	3	1	5	5	1
Generous	3	2	4	2	2	5	Nurturing	3	3	5	5	1	5
Trusting	3	2	4	3	2	4	Calm	5	2	4	1	2	5
Organized	4	3	3	2	3	3	Intelligent	5	3	5	2	3	3
Athletic	3	2	2	2	4	2							

A number of prescaling methods are typically recommended when conducting GPA. As with any scaling method, the investigator must consider the impact of controlling statistical differences in the data. It is well known, for example, that the mean and standard deviation of z scores are equal to zero and one, respectively. Converting any two variables to z scores will thus equate the two variables on their means and standard deviations. With GPA, three scaling methods are recommended: *centering, dimensional,* and *isotropic.*

Centering rescales each manager's ratings such that the mean of each attribute is equal to zero. Isotropic scaling "shrinks" or "expands" each manager's ratings to remove individual differences in scale usage. The ratings for those managers who use relatively few scale values will be expanded with a multiplicative constant greater than one, and the ratings for those managers who use relatively more extreme scale values will be shrunken with a multiplicative constant less than one. The isotropic scaling values for the four managers (.75, 1.01, 1.48, and .94, respectively) indicate that the overall range in the third manager's ratings was less than the range in the other managers' ratings. In fact, it can be seen in Table 1 that the third manager did not use the full range of scale values (1–5). Finally,

dimensional scaling adjusts for differences in the number of attributes in the managers' matrices. The magnitudes of the original values are uniformly increased or decreased depending on the size of the matrix. In this way, matrices with large numbers of attributes will not spuriously influence the results.

Once the original matrices have been rescaled, GPA works through an iterative algorithm in which the six rated employees are maximally aligned across managers. Space does not permit a complete explanation of this algorithm or the equations that underlie GPA, and the Further Reading list at the end of this entry should be consulted. Nonetheless, as the name of the technique implies, Procrustes transformations play an important role in the computations. In essence, the rescaled matrices are sequentially rotated (i.e., transformed) to maximal agreement with an average matrix that is continually updated throughout the process. This average matrix of rescaled ratings is referred to as the *consensus configuration.* At the end of each pass through the four managers' rotated matrices, the consensus configuration is computed and compared to the consensus from the previous iteration. After a number of iterations, changes in the consensus configuration will be negligible, indicating that the procedure has converged on a final solution.

The consensus configuration is therefore the average of rescaled (if scaling options are applied) and rotated ratings, and its dimensionality will equal the largest original matrix. A principal components analysis can be conducted on the consensus configuration, and the employees can be plotted in the space created from the first two components. Results shown in Figure 1 reveal that the managers view John and Amy as highly similar to one another and more similar to Jill than the other three employees.

The attributes generated by the four managers can also be plotted in the component space. It can be seen that Fred, Bob, and Jan are generally viewed as outgoing, easygoing, and carefree compared to Amy, Jill, and John, who are viewed as calm, generous, and patient.

The four managers' individual rating matrices can be compared to the consensus configuration using analysis of variance. The results from such an analysis are shown in Table 2.

As can be seen, an overall *consensus proportion* is produced from the analysis. A value of 1.0 would indicate perfect agreement among the four managers. In such an instance, the four managers' rescaled and rotated matrices would all match the consensus configuration perfectly. Here, the managers' consensus proportion is .79, and a randomization test indicates that this value is statistically significant ($p < .04$).

Table 2   Analysis of Variance Results

	Consensus	Residual	Total
Employee			
John	16.71	2.33	19.04
Bob	5.47	6.28	11.76
Amy	9.74	5.87	15.61
Jan	11.01	3.55	14.56
Fred	24.10	1.41	25.51
Jill	11.54	1.99	13.52
Grids			
Manager 1		9.87	16.09
Manager 2		5.42	24.61
Manager 3		2.64	29.94
Manager 4		3.51	29.36
Total SS	78.57	21.43	100.00

Consensus Proportion = .79

Table 2 also shows results for the individual managers and for the four employees. The residual values from these results can be examined to identify points of difference between the individual matrices and the consensus configuration. The residual for the first manager is substantially higher than the others, indicating that this manager is most deviant from the consensus. The residuals for the employees indicate that the ratings for Bob and Amy vary most across the four managers compared to the consensus configuration. The specific residuals shown in Table 3 indicate further that much of the disagreement regarding Bob and Amy is a result of the first manager's ratings. The second manager's ratings of Bob also show relatively high deviance from the consensus configuration.

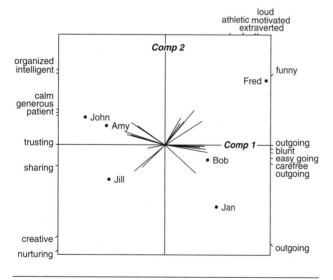

Figure 1   Plot of First and Second Principal Components of the Consensus Grid

Table 3   Specific Residuals From Analysis of Variance

	Manager 1	Manager 2	Manager 3	Manager 4
John	0.77	0.75	0.18	0.63
Bob	3.65	1.94	0.62	0.08
Amy	3.39	0.86	0.54	1.07
Jan	0.95	1.31	0.13	1.17
Fred	0.72	0.09	0.21	0.39
Jill	0.38	0.47	0.97	0.17

The first manager's ratings can be submitted to a principal components analysis to examine the nature of the disagreement. The employees and attributes can be plotted in the space created by the first two components, as shown in Figure 2. Comparing the patterns of employees in the consensus configuration in Figure 1 and the first manager's ratings in Figure 2 shows that the manager essentially swapped Bob and Amy. Whereas in the consensus configuration Amy is similar to Jill and John, from the first manager's point of view Bob is similar to Jill and John and Amy is similar to Fred and Jan.

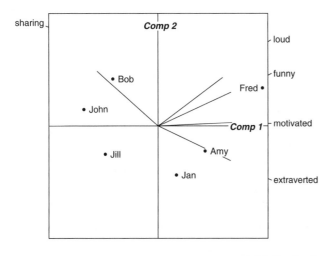

Figure 2   Plot of First and Second Principal Components of the First Manager's Ratings

Additional Issues

The heartbeat of GPA is the consensus configuration. Although its name implies that some sort of agreement has been reached through the analysis, the consensus configuration is essentially a matrix of aggregate values. It is perhaps thus best referred to as the *average configuration* or *centroid configuration*. Nonetheless, the degree of variation around the consensus configuration can be quantified and reported as the consensus proportion. A long-standing criticism of Procrustes transformations is their ability to generate high agreement among even matrices of random numbers. Therefore, the consensus proportion should be tested routinely for statistical significance using a randomization test, as was done above. The issue of prescaling

discussed above is also important. Although all three scaling methods are typically recommended, only the investigator can determine if variability in scale means, scale extremities, or matrix dimensionality represents spurious differences that must be removed from his or her data. Given the convenience of modern computers, conducting the GPA with and without the different scaling options is therefore recommended in order to assess their impact on the results.

—James W. Grice

Further Reading

Dijksterhuis, G. B., & Gower, J. C. (1991/2). The interpretation of generalized Procrustes analysis and allied methods. *Food Quality and Preference, 3,* 67–87.

Fewer, L. J., Howard, C., & Shepherd, R. (1997). Public concerns in the United Kingdom about general and specific applications of genetic engineering: Risk, benefit, and ethics. *Science, Technology, & Human Values, 22,* 98–124.

Gower, J. C. (1975). Generalized Procrustes analysis. *Psychometrika, 40,* 33–51.

Generalized Estimating Equations

Correlated data sets arise from repeated measures studies where multiple observations are collected from a specific sampling unit (a specific patient's status over time), or from grouped or clustered data where observations are grouped based on sharing some common characteristic (animals in a specific litter). When measurements are collected over time, the term *longitudinal* or *panel data* is preferred. Generalized estimating equations (GEEs) provide a framework for analyzing correlated data. This framework extends the generalized linear models methodology, which assumes independent data. We discuss the estimation of model parameters and associated variances via generalized estimating equation methodology.

The usual practice in model construction is the specification of the systematic and random components of variation. Classical maximum likelihood models then rely on the validity of the specified components. Model construction proceeds from the (components of variation) specification to a likelihood and, ultimately, an estimating equation. The estimating equation for maximum likelihood estimation is obtained by equating zero to the derivative of the log-likelihood with respect to the parameters of interest. Point estimates of unknown parameters are obtained by solving the estimating equation.

Generalized Linear Models

The theory and an algorithm appropriate for obtaining maximum likelihood estimates where the response follows a distribution in the exponential family was introduced in 1972 by Nelder and Wedderburn. They introduced the term *generalized linear model* (GLM) to refer to a class of models that could be analyzed by a single algorithm. The theoretical and practical application of GLMs has since received attention in many articles and books.

GLMs encompass a wide range of commonly used models such as linear regression, logistic regression for binary outcomes, and Poisson regression for count data outcomes. The specification of a particular GLM requires a link function that characterizes the relationship of the mean response to a vector of covariates. In addition, a GLM requires specification of a variance function that relates the variance of the outcomes as a function of the mean.

The derivation of the iteratively reweighted least squares (IRLS) algorithm appropriate for fitting GLMs begins with the likelihood specification for the exponential family. Within an iterative algorithm, an updated estimate of the coefficient vector may be obtained via weighted ordinary least squares where the weights are related to the link and variance specifications. The estimation is then iterated to convergence where convergence may be defined, for example, as the change in the estimated coefficient vector being smaller than some tolerance.

For any response that follows a member of the exponential family of distributions, $f(y) = \exp\{[y\,\theta - b(\theta)]/\phi + c(y, \phi)\}$, where θ is the canonical parameter and ϕ is a proportionality constant, we can obtain maximum likelihood estimates of the $p \times 1$ regression

coefficient vector β by solving the estimating equation given by

$$\Psi(\beta) = \sum_{i=1}^{n} \Psi_i = \sum_{i=1}^{n} X_i^{\mathrm{T}}(y_i - \mu_i)/[\phi V(\mu_i)]\,[\partial\mu_i/\partial\eta_i]$$
$$= 0_{(p\times1)}.$$

In the estimation equation, X_i is the ith row of an $n \times p$ matrix of covariates X, $\mu_i = g(x_i\beta)$ represents the expected outcome $E(y) = b'(\theta)$ in terms of a transformation of the linear predictor $\eta_i = x_i\beta$ via a monotonic (invertible) link function $g()$, and the variance $V(\mu_i)$ is a function of the expected value proportional to the variance of the outcome $V(y_i) = \phi\,V(\mu_i)$. The estimating equation is also known as the score equation because it equates the score vector $\Psi(\beta)$ to zero.

Modelers are free to choose a link function as well as a variance function. If the link-variance pair of functions is chosen from a common member of the exponential family of distributions, the resulting estimates are equivalent to maximum likelihood estimates. However, modelers are not limited to these choices. When one selects variance and link functions that do not coincide to a particular exponential family member distribution, the estimating equation is said to imply existence of a quasi-likelihood, and the resulting estimates are referred to as maximum quasi-likelihood estimates.

The link function that equates the canonical parameter θ with the linear predictor $\eta_i = x_i\beta$ is called the canonical link. If this link is selected, an advantage to interpretation of results is that the estimating equation simplifies to

$$\Psi(\beta) = \sum_{i=1}^{n} \Psi_i = \sum_{i=1}^{n} X_i^{\mathrm{T}}(y_i - \mu_i)/\phi = 0_{(p\times1)}.$$

A second advantage of the canonical link over other link functions is that the expected Hessian matrix is equal to the observed Hessian matrix.

The Independence Model

A basic individual-level model is written in terms of the n individual observations y_i for $i = 1, \ldots, n$. When observations may be clustered, due to repeated observations on the sampling unit or because the observations are related to some cluster identifier variable, the model may be written in terms of the observations y_{it} for the clusters $i = 1, \ldots, n$ and the within-cluster repeated, or related, observations $t = 1, \ldots, n_i$. The total number of observations is then $N = \sum_i n_i$. The clusters may also be referred to as panels, subjects, or groups. In this presentation, the clusters i are independent, but the within-clusters observations it may be correlated. An independence model, however, assumes that the within-cluster observations are not correlated.

The independence model is a special case of more sophisticated correlated data approaches (such as GEE). This model assumes that there is no correlation within clusters. Therefore, the model specification is in terms of the individual observations y_{it}. Although the independence model assumes that the repeated measures are independent, the model still provides consistent estimators in the presence of correlated data. Of course, this approach is paid for through inefficiency, although the efficiency loss is not always large. As such, this model remains an attractive alternative because of its computational simplicity. The independence model also serves as a reference model in the derivation of diagnostics for more sophisticated models for clustered data (such as GEE models).

Analysts can use the independence model to obtain point estimates along with standard errors based on the modified sandwich variance estimator to ensure that inference is robust to any type of within-cluster correlation. Although the inference regarding marginal effects is valid (assuming that the model for the mean is correctly specified), the estimator from the independence model is not efficient when the data are correlated.

The validity of the (naive) model-based variance estimators depends on the correct specification of the variance; in turn, this depends on the correct specification of the working correlation model. A formal justification for an alternative estimator known as the *sandwich variance estimator* is given in Huber.

It should be noted that assuming independence is not always conservative; the model-based (naive) variance estimates based on the observed or expected Hessian matrix are not always smaller than those of the modified sandwich variance estimator. Because the sandwich variance estimator is sometimes called the *robust variance estimator*, this result may seem counterintuitive. However, it is easily seen by assuming negative within-cluster correlation leading to clusters with both positive and negative residuals. The clusterwise sums of those residuals will be small, and the resulting modified sandwich variance estimator will yield smaller standard errors than the model-based Hessian variance estimators.

Other obvious approaches to the nested structure assumed for the data include fixed effects and random effects models. Fixed effects models incorporate a fixed increment to the model for each group, whereas random effects models assume that the incremental effects from the groups are from a common random distribution; in such a model, the parameters of the assumed random effects distribution are estimated rather than the effects. In the example at the end of this entry, we consider two different distributions for random effects in a Poisson model.

Subject-Specific Versus Population-Averaged Models

There are two main approaches to dealing with correlation in repeated or longitudinal data. One approach focuses on the marginal effects averaged across the individuals (population-averaged approach), and the second approach focuses on the effects for given values of the random effects by fitting parameters of the assumed random effects distribution (subject-specific approach).

The population-averaged approach models the average response for observations sharing the same covariates (across all of the clusters or subjects), whereas the subject-specific approach explicitly models the source of heterogeneity so that the fitted regression coefficients have an interpretation in terms of the individuals.

The most commonly described GEE model is a population-averaged approach. Although it is possible to derive subject-specific GEE models, such models are not currently supported in commercial software packages and so do not appear nearly as often in the literature.

The basic idea behind this approach is illustrated as follows. We consider the estimating equation for GLMs; that estimating equation, in matrix form, is for the exponential family of distributions

$$\Psi(\beta) = \sum_{i=1}^{n} \Psi_i$$

$$= \sum_{i=1}^{n} X_i^T D[\partial\mu_i/\partial\eta_i] V^{-1}(\mu_i)(y_i - \mu_i)/\phi$$

$$= \sum_{i=1}^{n} X_i^T D[\partial\mu_i/\partial\eta_i] V^{-1/2}(\mu_i)$$

$$I_{(n \times n)} V^{-1/2}(\mu_i)(y_i - \mu_i)/\phi = 0_{(p \times 1)}.$$

Assuming independence, $V^{-1}(\mu_i)$ is clearly an $n_i \times n_i$ diagonal matrix that can be factored with an identity matrix in the center playing the role of the correlation of observations within a given group or cluster. This corresponds to the independence model already mentioned.

The genesis of the original population-averaged generalized estimating equations is to replace the identity matrix with a parameterized working correlation matrix $R(\alpha)$. To address correlated data, the working correlation matrix imposes structural constraints. In this way, the independence model is a special case of the GEE specifications where $R(\alpha)$ is an identity matrix.

Formally, Liang and Zeger introduce a second estimating equation for the structural parameters of the working correlation matrix. The authors then establish the properties of the estimators resulting from the solution of these estimating equations. The GEE moniker was applied because the model is derived through a generalization of the GLM estimating equation; the second-order variance components are introduced directly into the estimating equation rather than appearing in consideration of a multivariate likelihood.

Several software packages support estimation of these models. These packages include R, SAS, S-PLUS, Stata, and SUDAAN. R and S-PLUS users can easily find user-written software tools for fitting GEE models, whereas such support is included in the other packages.

Estimating the Working Correlation Matrix

One should consider carefully the parameterization of the working correlation matrix, because including the correct parameterization leads to more efficient estimates. We want to consider this choice carefully even if we employ the modified sandwich variance estimator in the calculation of standard errors and confidence intervals for the regression parameters. Although the use of the modified sandwich variance estimator ensures robustness in the case of misspecification of the working correlation matrix, the advantage of more efficient point estimates is still worth this effort. There is no controversy as to the fact that the GEE estimates are consistent, but there is some controversy as to how efficient they are. This controversy centers on how well the correlation parameters can be estimated.

Typically, a careful analyst chooses some small number of candidate parameterizations. Pan also discusses the quasi-likelihood information criterion (QIC) measures for choosing between candidate parameterizations. This criterion measure is similar to the well-known Akaike information criterion (AIC).

The most common choices for the working correlation R matrix are given by parameterizing the elements of the matrix, as shown in Table 1.

The independence model admits no extra parameters, and the resulting model is equivalent to a generalized linear model specification, and the

Table 1   Common Correlation Structures

Independent	$R_{uv} = 0$
Exchangeable	$R_{uv} = \alpha$
Autocorrelated – AR(1)	$R_{uv} = \alpha^{|u-v|}$
Stationary (k)	$R_{uv} \alpha_{|u-v|}$ if $|u - v| \leq k$
	0 otherwise
Nonstationary (k)	$R_{uv} \alpha_{(u,v)}$ if $|u - v| \leq k$
	0 otherwise
Unstructured	$R_{uv} = \alpha_{(u,v)}$

Note: Values are given for $u \neq v$; $R_{uu} = 1$.

exchangeable correlation parameterization admits one extra parameter. The most general approach is to consider the unstructured (only imposing symmetry) working correlation parameterization, which admits $M(M-1)/2 - M$ extra parameters, where $M = \max_i \{n_i\}$. The *exchangeable* correlation specification is also known as *equal correlation, common correlation,* and *compound symmetry*.

The elements of the working correlation matrix are estimated using the Pearson. Estimation alternates between estimating the regression parameters β, assuming the current estimates of α are true, and then assuming β estimates are true to obtain residuals to update the estimate of α.

Example

To highlight the interpretation of GEE analyses and point out the alternate models, we focus on a simple example (Table 2).

These data have been analyzed in many forums and are from a panel study on Progabide treatment of epilepsy. Baseline measures of the number of seizures in an 8-week period were collected and recorded as

Table 2 Data From Progabide Study on Epilepsy (59 Patients Over 5 Weeks)

id	age	trt	base	s1	s2	s3	s4
1	31	0	11	5	3	3	3
2	30	0	11	3	5	3	3
3	25	0	6	2	4	0	5
4	36	0	8	4	4	1	4
5	22	0	66	7	18	9	21
6	29	0	27	5	2	8	7
7	31	0	12	6	4	0	2
8	42	0	52	40	20	23	12
9	37	0	23	5	6	6	5
10	28	0	10	14	13	6	0
11	36	0	51	26	12	6	22
12	24	0	33	12	6	8	5
13	23	0	18	4	4	6	2
14	36	0	42	7	9	12	14
15	26	0	87	16	24	10	9
16	26	0	50	11	0	0	5
17	28	0	18	0	0	3	3
18	31	0	111	37	29	28	29
19	32	0	18	3	5	2	5
20	21	0	20	3	0	6	7
21	29	0	12	3	4	3	4
22	21	0	9	3	4	3	4
23	32	0	17	2	3	3	5
24	25	0	28	8	12	2	8
25	30	0	55	18	24	76	25
26	40	0	9	2	1	2	1
27	19	0	1-	3	1	4	2
28	22	0	47	13	15	13	12
29	18	1	76	11	14	9	8
30	32	1	38	8	7	9	4
31	20	1	19	0	4	3	0
32	20	1	10	3	6	1	3
33	18	1	19	2	6	7	4
34	24	1	24	4	3	1	3
35	30	1	31	22	17	19	16
36	35	1	14	5	4	7	4
37	57	1	11	2	4	0	4
38	20	1	67	3	7	7	7
39	22	1	41	4	18	2	5
40	28	1	7	2	1	1	0
41	23	1	22	0	2	4	0
42	40	1	13	5	4	0	3
43	43	1	46	11	14	25	15
44	21	1	36	10	5	3	8
45	35	1	38	19	7	6	7
46	25	1	7	1	1	2	4
47	26	1	36	6	10	8	8
48	25	1	11	2	1	0	0
49	22	1	151	102	65	72	63
50	32	1	22	4	3	2	4
51	25	1	42	8	6	5	7
52	35	1	32	1	3	1	5
53	21	1	56	18	11	28	13
54	41	1	24	6	3	4	0
55	32	1	16	3	5	4	3
56	26	1	22	1	23	19	8
57	21	1	25	2	3	0	1
58	36	1	13	0	0	0	0
59	37	1	12	1	4	3	2

Table 3   Estimated Incidence Rate Ratios and Standard Errors for Various Poisson Models

Model	time	trt	age	baseline
Independence	0.944 (0.019, 0.033)	0.832 (0.039, 0.143)	1.019 (0.003, 0.010)	1.095 (0.002, 0.006)
Gamma RE	0.944 (0.019)	0.810 (0.124)	1.013 (0.011)	1.116 (0.015)
Gaussian RE	0.944 (0.019, 0.033)	0.760 (0.117, 0.117)	1.011 (0.011, 0.009)	1.115 (0.012, 0.011)
GEE(exch)	0.939 (0.019, 0.019)	0.834 (0.058, 0.141)	1.019 (0.005, 0.010)	1.095 (0.003, 0.006)
GEE(ar 1)	0.939 (0.019, 0.019)	0.818 (0.054, 0.054)	1.021 (0.005, 0.003)	1.097 (0.003, 0.003)
GEE(unst)	0.951 (0.017, 0.041)	0.832 (0.055, 0.108)	1.019 (0.005, 0.009)	1.095 (0.003, 0.005)

base for 59 patients. Four follow-up 2-week periods also counted the number of seizures; these were recorded as *s1*, *s2*, *s3*, and *s4*. The *base* variable was divided by four in our analyses to put it on the same scale as the follow-up counts. The *age* variable records the patient's age in years, and the *trt* variable indicates whether the patient received the Progabide treatment (value recorded as one) or was part of the control group (value recorded as zero).

An obvious approach to analyzing the data is to hypothesize a Poisson model for the number of seizures. Because we have repeated measures, we can choose a number of alternative approaches. In our illustrations of these alternative models, we use the baseline measure as a covariate along with the *time* and *age* variables.

Table 3 contains the results of several analyses. For each covariate, we list the estimated incidence rate ratio (exponentiated coefficient). Following the incidence rate ratio estimates, we list the classical and sandwich-based estimated standard errors. We did not calculate sandwich-based standard errors for the gamma distributed random effects model.

We emphasize again that the independence model coupled with standard errors based on the modified sandwich variance estimator is a valid approach to modeling data of this type. The weakness of the approach is that the estimators will not be as efficient as a model including the true underlying within-cluster correlation structure. Another standard approach to modeling this type of repeated measures is to hypothesize that the correlations are due to individual-specific random intercepts. These random effects (one could also hypothesize fixed effects) will lead to alternate models for the data.

Results from two different random effects models are included in the table. The gamma-distributed random effects model is rather easy to program and fit to data because the log-likelihood of the model is in analytic form. On the other hand, the normally distributed random effects model has a log-likelihood specification that includes an integral. Sophisticated numeric techniques are required for the calculation of such a model.

We could hypothesize that the correlation follows an autoregressive process because the data are collected over time. However, this is not always the best choice in an experiment because we must believe that the hypothesized correlation structure applies to both the treated and untreated groups.

The QIC values for the independence, exchangeable, ar1, and unstructured correlation structures are respectively given by −5826.23, −5826.25, −5832.20, and −5847.91. This criterion measure indicates a

Table 4   Fitted Correlation Matrices

1.00					1.00			
0.51	1.00				0.25	1.00		
0.26	0.51	1.00			0.42	0.68	1.00	
0.13	0.26	0.51	1.00		0.22	0.28	0.58	1.00

preference for the unstructured model over the autoregressive model. The fitted correlation matrices for these models (printing only the bottom half of the symmetric matrices) are given by Table 4.

—*James W. Hardin*

Further Reading

Glonek, G. F. V., & McCullagh, R. (1995). Multivariate logistic models. *Journal of the Royal Statistical Society–Series B, 57,* 533–546.

Huber, P. J. (1967). The behavior of maximum likelihood estimates under nonstandard conditions. In *Proceedings for the Fifth Berkeley Symposium on Mathematical Statistics and Probability* (Vol. 1, pp. 221–223). Berkeley: University of California Press.

Liang, K.-Y., & Zeger, S. L. (1986). Longitudinal data analysis using generalized linear models. *Biometrika, 73,* 13–22.

McCullagh, P., & Nelder, J. A. (1989). *Generalized linear models* (2nd ed.). London: Chapman & Hall.

Nelder, J. A., & Wedderburn, R. W. M. (1972). Generalized linear models. *Journal of the Royal Statistical Society–Series A, 135*(3), 370–384.

Pan, W. (2001). Akaike's information criterion in generalized estimating equations. *Biometrics, 57,* 120–125.

GERONTOLOGICAL APPERCEPTION TEST

The Gerontological Apperception Test, developed by Wolk and Wolk in 1971, is a projective test published by Behavioral Publications that is designed to compensate for the reputed weakness of many apperceptive tests in the assessment of older adults. Because at least one older adult is depicted in a situation frequently encountered by the aged, identification with the test stimuli is assumed to be evocative of responses. This enhances an understanding of the aged personality and his or her reactions to common situations.

Specifically, the Gerontological Apperception Test consists of a set of 14 achromatic cards, each card reflecting a situation with which older adults could identify. The pictures are designed to elicit more relevant themes such as isolation, loss of physical mobility/sexuality, dependency, and ageism. There is no standard set of cards to be administered. Cards are selected for administration based on suspected personal issues and concerns of each individual subject. At the time of the initial publication of the Gerontological Apperception Test, there was not a standard scoring procedure. Protocols were typically analyzed for the presence of themes.

The Gerontological Apperception Test has been criticized on the bases of (a) the negative tone of the pictures (all achromatic), (b) the stereotypic presentation of older people on the cards, and (c) no accepted scoring system that would permit the development of norms to guide clinical use. However, a revised and more differentiated scoring system for the Gerontological Apperception Test was developed by Hayslip and his colleagues.

The literature on the Gerontological Apperception Test is not extensive, nor does the literature demonstrate that the test is more successful than the Thematic Apperception Test in eliciting relevant themes from older adults. Therefore, although the test shows promise for clinical use with older adults, more research is required before the clinical utility of the Gerontological Apperception Test has been demonstrated effectively.

—*Paul E. Panek*

See also Thematic Apperception Test

Further Reading

Hayslip, B., Jr., Francis, J., Radika, L. M., Panek, P. E., & Bosmajian, L. (2002). The development of a scoring system for the Gerontological Apperception Test. *Journal of Clinical Psychology, 58,* 471–478.

Wolk, R. L., & Wolk, R. B. (1971). *The Gerontological Apperception Test.* New York: Behavioral Publications.

GF-GC THEORY OF INTELLIGENCE

There are a number of widely known and respected theories of human intelligence (e.g., Howard Gardner's

Theory of Multiple Intelligences, Robert Sternberg's Tir-archic Theory of Intelligence), but in recent years, the Gf-Gc theory has become increasingly important in the field of intellectual assessment. This is at least partially due to the fact that the Gf-Gc theory is based on factor analytical studies of the results from IQ tests. Many of the other theories, although intriguing, do not have a means of actually measuring their constructs in an individual.

In the early 1900s, Charles Spearman applied statistical analyses to the concept of mental ability and arrived at the conclusion that there is one general factor (g) that is related to all aspects of intelligence. Although this is expressed in many different ways, underlying it all is one thing that we think of as intelligence. This concept took root and is the basis for the single IQ score that was generated with early measures of intelligence and, although controversial, continues to be reflected in the Full Scale IQ or similar score found on most measures of cognitive ability today.

It was not until the 1940s that Raymond Cattell, building on Spearman's work, proposed the existence of two general types of intelligence: fluid intelligence (Gf) and crystallized intelligence (Gc). Fluid intelligence was related to biological and neurological factors and is exemplified by inductive and deductive reasoning. Although experience may influence it indirectly (e.g., introduction of new paradigms allows for different ways of organizing problems), it is not dependent upon learned information. Conversely, crystallized intelligence was seen as being the direct result of experience, learning, and education, and was relatively free from the influence of biological and neurological factors. This dichotomy was frequently thought of loosely as innate and learned abilities, right and left hemisphere abilities, or nonverbal and verbal abilities, respectively. Although useful conceptually, these alternative ways of thinking about the two types of intelligence were not fully supported by the research and remain controversial at best.

In the early 1980s, John Horn, using the decades of factor analytic research on human cognitive abilities since Cattell's original postulation, added to the original Gf-Gc theory to form what became known as the Cattell-Horn Gf-Gc theory of intelligence. This new theory contained 9 to 10 broad abilities by the mid-1990s and began to be used more and more as a basis for interpreting the results of intelligence tests.

At this same time, John Carroll conducted a meta-analysis of more than 400 different data sets that had been collected from 1925 on. He looked at the raw scores, conducted exploratory factor analyses, and concluded that the results fit a hierarchical three-stratum model: 69 narrow abilities at the first level; 8 broad abilities (that roughly corresponded to the broad abilities articulated by Horn-Cattell) at the second level; and a general factor, g, above them all at the third level. Subsequently, these two models were merged by Kevin McGrew and others to form the Cattell-Horn-Carroll (CHC) theory of cognitive abilities. CHC theory and Gf-Gc theory are now essentially analogous.

Current articulations of Gf-Gc theory typically include 10 different broad abilities. Two of these are usually found on measures of achievement and are considered basic academic skills. These two are Quantitative Knowledge (Gq), which represents an individual's store of acquired mathematical knowledge, and Reading/Writing Ability (Grw), which represents an individual's acquired store of knowledge related to the comprehension of written material and the expression of thoughts in writing. It is important to differentiate Gq from Quantitative Reasoning (RQ), which is a narrow ability that is part of Fluid Reasoning (Gf). Gq is evident in applying a mathematical formula to arrive at a solution, whereas RQ would be involved in finding the missing number in a number series. Grw is not clearly defined but appears to consist of reading decoding, reading comprehension, reading speed, spelling, grammar and punctuation, and written expression. Both Gq and Grw are generally found on measures of achievement and not on measures of intelligence.

The remaining eight abilities—Fluid Reasoning (Gf); Crystallized Intelligence (often referred to as Comprehension-Knowledge, or Gc); Short-Term Memory (Gsm); Visual Processing (Gv); Auditory Processing (Ga); Long-Term Storage and Retrieval (Glr); Processing Speed (Gs); and Decision/Reaction Time or Speed (Gt)—are typically found on intelligence tests. Depending upon the measure of intelligence, different abilities may be emphasized or absent. For example, the Wechsler Scales do not have measures of Auditory Processing (Ga) but have multiple measures of Comprehension-Knowledge (Gc), and the Woodcock Johnson-III (WJ-III) has multiple measures of all but Decision/Reaction Time (Gt).

Fluid Reasoning (Gf) is basically novel problem solving and reasoning. It subsumes the narrow abilities of General Sequential Reasoning, Induction, Quantitative Reasoning, Piagetian Reasoning, and Reasoning Speed. In everyday life, it is the ability to form concepts, apply logic, manipulate abstractions and relations, and solve problems that include novel information and procedures. It is particularly important in fields that require the logical application of creativity (e.g., engineering, research science).

Crystallized Intelligence, or Comprehension-Knowledge (Gc), is an individual's breadth and depth of knowledge, the ability to communicate (especially verbally) that knowledge, and the ability to apply that knowledge in reasoning. Under the broad Gc ability, we find the narrow abilities of Language Development; Lexical Knowledge; Listening Ability; Information (General, Cultural, Science, Geography); Communication Ability; Oral Production & Fluency; Grammatical Sensitivity; and Foreign Language (Proficiency and Aptitude). Of all the factors, Gc is the most heavily culturally loaded because it depends upon experience for development and is the most resistant to neurological damage, such as traumatic brain injury. It is also the single factor that is likely to increase as we age and gain additional experience and the factor mostly closely correlated to academic performance.

Short-Term Memory (Gsm) is the ability to apprehend and hold information in immediate awareness and to use it within a few seconds. It is composed of the narrow abilities of Memory Span, Working Memory, and Learning Abilities (also under Glr). Measurement of Gsm is highly sensitive to attentional problems (have to actually perceive it before you can remember it) and anxiety. It is a foundational ability that will influence many other abilities. For example, you cannot solve a multivariable problem if you can keep only one variable in awareness at a time.

Visual Processing (Gv) is the ability to perceive and manipulate visual shapes and to analyze and synthesize visual information. It includes the narrow abilities of Spatial Relations, Visual Memory, Closure Speed, Flexibility of Closure, Spatial Scanning, Serial Perceptual Integration, Length Estimation, Perceptual Illusions, Perceptual Alterations, Visualization, and Imagery. It is the ability to see things in your mind's eye; to manipulate those things mentally (rotate, rearrange, resize, assemble, take apart, etc.); and to use these skills to solve real-world problems. Typically, someone high in Gv will be considered a visual learner.

Auditory Processing (Ga) is the analog of Gv with auditory stimuli rather than visual. It is the ability to perceive, discriminate, analyze, and synthesize auditory information. The narrow abilities under Ga are Phonetic Coding (Analysis and Synthesis), Speech Sound Discrimination, Resistance to Auditory Distortion, Memory for Sound Patterns, General Sound Discrimination, Temporal Tracking, Musical Discrimination and Judgment, Sound-Intensity/Duration Discrimination, Sound-Frequency Discrimination, Hearing and Speech Threshold Factors, Absolute Pitch, and Sound Localization. Although understanding of a language is not necessary for measuring Ga, it is likely to be very important in the development of language and is related to musical ability.

Long-Term Storage and Retrieval (Glr) is the ability to store information in and then fluently retrieve that information from long-term memory through the use of association. It is the process of storage and retrieval, and not the information that is actually stored, that constitutes Glr. Under the umbrella of Glr are the following narrow abilities: Associative; Meaningful and Free Recall Memory; Fluency (Ideational, Associational, and Expressional) Naming Facility; Word and Figural Fluency; Figural Flexibility; Sensitivity to Problems; Originality/Creativity; and Learning Abilities. Clearly, Glr is of critical importance in everyday life to be able to not only acquire and store new information, but to be able to access that information when needed. One analogy that captures the essence of Glr is that of the fisherman's net. The knots or intersections represent the pieces of information and the strands that you must traverse in Glr.

Processing Speed (Gs) is the ability to perform cognitive tasks fluently and automatically, especially when under pressure to maintain focused attention and concentration. It is basically the ability to make routine things automatic so that each step of the task does not have to be processed (e.g., alphabetizing files or other clerical tasks). It consists of Perceptual Speed, Rate-of-Test Taking, Number Facility, and Semantic Processing Speed. Individuals low in processing speed not only may find themselves taking more time to perform tasks, but also may find those tasks more effortful and tiring because they cannot do them automatically.

—*Steve Saladin*

See also Intelligence Quotient; Intelligence Tests

Further Reading

Flanagan, D. P., McGrew, K. S., & Ortiz, S. O. (2000). *The Wechsler Intelligence Scales and Gf-Gc theory: A contemporary approach to interpretation.* Boston: Allyn & Bacon.

Kaufman, A. S., & Lichtenberger, E. O. (2006). *Assessing adolescent and adult intelligence* (3rd ed.). Hoboken, NJ: Wiley.

Sternberg, R. J. (2000). *Handbook of intelligence.* New York: Cambridge University Press.

GOODENOUGH HARRIS DRAWING TEST

The Goodenough Harris Drawing Test, published by Psychological Corporation, is a nonverbal test of mental ability that is appropriate as either a group or an individual test. The test takes 10 to 15 minutes to administer to children ages 3 to 15. The directions given to the children are simple: "Make a picture of a man; make the very best picture you can." The current version of the test is essentially the 1963 revision of the original Draw a Man Test.

The purpose of constructing the Goodenough Harris Drawing Test was to substitute the concept of intelligence with the notion of *intellectual maturity* or, more accurately, *conceptual maturity*. Thus, intellectual maturity means the ability to form concepts of an abstract character. This encompasses (a) the ability to perceive (i.e., to distinguish between likenesses and differences), (b) the ability to abstract (i.e., to put into groups objects according to likenesses and differences), and (c) the ability to generalize (i.e., to assign newly experienced objects to the correct class). Therefore, evaluation of children's drawings of the human figure helps to measure the complexity of the child's concept formation. The human figure is employed because it is the most familiar and significant figure for the children.

The evaluation of children's drawings is carried out by two different scoring procedures, the Point Scale and the 12-Point Quality Scale. According to the first procedure, each item is rated as pass or fail (1 point or 0), which is based on the presence or absence of a body part or a specific detail (e.g., eyes are present). The Draw a Man Test has 73 items and the Draw a Woman Test 71 items. The scorable items of both drawings are chosen on the basis of (a) age differentiation, (b) relationship to tests of general intelligence, and (c) diversification of children of lower to higher intellectual ability. The score (marking) on the Goodenough Harris Drawing Test is a single one. A detailed scoring guide is offered in the test manual. The second procedure relies on a 12-Point Quality Scale in which 1 indicates the lowest category and 12 the highest.

Norms for both the Point Scale and the 12-Point Quality Scale are provided. The psychometric properties are good, although the test is better employed for children ages 5–15. The test is simple to administer, is enjoyed by the children, and measures general intelligence. However, its cross-cultural use is questionable. The test works well with younger children, especially those of lower intellectual abilities, language handicapped, minority, and bilingual children.

—*Demetrios S. Alexopoulos*

See also Personality Tests

Further Reading

Harris, D. D. (1963). *Children's drawings as measures of intellectual maturity: A revision and extension of the Goodenough Harris Draw a Man Test.* New York: Harcourt, Brace & World.

Sattler, J. M. (1992). *Assessment of children: Revised and updated* (3rd ed.). San Diego, CA: Author.

Scott, L. D. (1981). Measuring intelligence with the Goodenough-Harris Drawing Test. *Psychological Bulletin, 89*, 483–505.

Goodenough-Harris drawing test: http://gri.gallaudet.edu/~catraxle/INTELLEC.html#goodenough

GOODNESS-OF-FIT TESTS

Most of the commonly used statistical methods are known to be parametric tests, which impose distributional assumptions on the data. For instance, the *t* test is popular in comparing the means of two independent samples. This test assumes that the underlying distribution from which each of the samples came is a normal distribution. This assumption is critical, especially in cases where the sample sizes are small. If this distributional assumption is not met, results may be invalid and misleading. Some statistical procedures based on the normal distribution are still approximately valid regardless of the distribution of the data as long as the sample size is large enough. The problem is that it is not clear what "large enough" means. In some cases, a sample size of 30 is large enough, whereas in other cases, a sample size of 30 is not sufficient. On the other hand, one may opt to use nonparametric statistical methods, which do not assume a specific form of the distribution of the samples. These procedures are valid regardless of the sample size. However, it is a well-known fact that nonparametric tests are not as powerful as parametric tests; that is, a nonparametric test requires a larger sample size than its corresponding parametric test to detect a difference, if one truly exists, as long as the distributional assumption of the parametric test is satisfied. Therefore, it is important, especially when sample sizes are small, that the distributional assumption of parametric tests be checked and validated before reporting the results of the statistical analyses are reported. Goodness-of-fit (GOF) tests provide methods to achieve this purpose.

The null and alternative hypotheses of the GOF tests are as follows:

Null hypothesis (H_0): assumed distribution has a good fit

Alternative hypothesis (H_a): assumed distribution is not a good fit

A GOF test does not try to prove that the underlying distribution is true. Instead, it starts by assuming that the data follow the underlying distribution. It rejects this assumption if there is strong evidence of violation of this assumption, and it does not suggest an alternative distribution to consider. A GOF test does not give any information on how the data deviate from the hypothesized distribution; for this reason, it is highly recommended that GOF tests be accompanied by graphical representation of the data distribution, such as a probability plot, if one exists for the distribution being tested, or a histogram. Moreover, it is possible that GOF tests will not reject a number of distributions, implying that these distributions are a good fit to the data. GOF tests are not designed to choose which among these distributions best fits the data.

Numerous goodness-of-fit tests exist, and they can range from simple to very complex depending on whether the underlying distribution is univariate or multivariate. The most popular and simplest univariate GOF tests are the chi-square goodness-of-fit test and the Kolmogorov-Smirnov test. The chi-square GOF test may be applied whether the underlying distribution is discrete and continuous. The Kolmogorov-Smirnov test applies only when the underlying distribution is continuous. Both of these tests are available in most statistical packages.

Chi-Square Goodness-of-Fit Test

The idea behind the chi-square GOF test is simple. It compares the observed proportion to the expected proportion based on the assumed distribution. Because distributions depend on parameters that are typically unknown, these parameters are first estimated from the data. These estimates will be plugged in to the distribution to compute the expected proportion.

Consider a data set with *n* observations. The following are steps in a chi-square GOF test.

1. Define K classes in which to assign each observation. If data are continuous (interval scale), the classes defined in constructing a histogram may be used. In this case, classes need not be of equal interval size.

2. Count the number of observations that fall on the ith class and denote this by O_i.

3. Compute the expected number of observations that will fall on the ith class based on the underlying distribution and denote this by E_i. In the continuous case, where the cumulative distribution function is denoted by $F(x)$, the expected number falling in the interval $[L_i, U_i]$ is

$$E_i = n*[\hat{F}(U_i) - \hat{F}(L_i)],$$

where $\hat{F}$ is the cumulative distribution function using the estimated values of any unknown parameters.

4. Compute the test statistic, χ^2, as

$$\chi^2 = \sum_{i=1}^{K} \frac{(O_i - E_i)^2}{E_i}.$$

5. Finally, reject the null hypothesis at an approximate level α if

$$\chi^2 > \chi^2_{\alpha, K-1-p},$$

where K is the number of classes, p is the number of estimated parameters in the underlying distribution, and α is the $(1 - \alpha)$th percentile of a chi-squared distribution with degrees of freedom $K - 1 - p$.

The chi-square GOF test requires adequate sample size to be valid. Furthermore, it requires all cells to be nonempty and have expected counts of at least 5. Collapsing cells is a common remedy to this problem. However, if cells represent categories that are not related, collapsing may not be a good idea.

Kolmogorov-Smirnov Test

The Kolmogorov-Smirnov (KS) goodness-of-fit test compares the theoretical cumulative distribution function, $F(x)$, with the empirical distribution function, which is an estimate of the cumulative distribution function based on the data. If the distribution being tested is a good fit, then the theoretical and empirical cumulative distribution functions should be close to each other. The KS statistic is based on the maximum distance between these two functions. As previously mentioned, a major limitation of the KS test is that it cannot be applied to discrete data.

The steps in the KS goodness-of-fit test are as follows.

1. Arrange the observations in increasing order and label them as $X_{(1)}, X_{(2)}, \ldots, X_{(n)}$, so that $X_{(1)}$ and $X_{(n)}$ are the smallest and largest observations, respectively.

2. Compute the KS test statistic based on the formula

$$D = \max_{1 < i < n} \left[F(X_{(i)}) - \frac{i-1}{n}, \frac{i}{n} - F(X_{(i)}) \right]$$

3. Finally, if the value of the D statistic is larger than the KS critical value at a given level of significance, then we reject the hypothesis that the assumed distribution is a good fit to the data. Tables of KS critical values are readily available in the literature. These critical values are applicable only when the parameters of the distribution are completely specified. Otherwise, the critical values are computed via simulation.

Other GOF Tests

Other GOF tests are available for continuous data, such as Anderson-Darling, empirical distribution function, and Cramer-von Mises tests, to name a few. GOF tests for discrete data are available for specific discrete distributions, such as the Poisson distribution.

GOF tests are also available in other commonly used statistical procedures. In ordinary regression analysis and analysis of variance, the distribution of the error term is assumed to follow a normal distribution, and hence, the response variable also has a normal distribution. GOF tests are not applied to the response variable because its distribution depends on the predictors or factors in the model. To test the distributional assumption of these procedures, univariate GOF tests are instead applied to residuals, whose distribution does not depend on the predictor variables or factors in the model.

A cautionary note: GOF tests, just like any statistical test of a hypothesis, will tend to reject the null hypothesis as the sample size increases. Therefore, one should be very careful in interpreting the results of GOF tests when the sample sizes are very large. Sometimes, performing a GOF test is no longer advisable. Instead, graphical techniques are better suited to assessing distributional assumptions.

An Illustration

One hundred observations (Y) were generated using SAS from a normal distribution with mean 3 and variance 0.5. A set of X observations was obtained from Y via the transformation $X = e^Y$. In this case, X is known to have a lognormal distribution. GOF tests were performed on X and Y observations testing the fit of the normal and lognormal distributions.

Figure 1 displays the SAS code used in this illustration, which provides results of Kolmogorov-Smirnov, Cramer-von Mises, Anderson-Darling, and chi-square goodness-of-fit tests. Figure 2 displays the histogram of the X observations with the best fit normal and lognormal densities showing that lognormal is a better fit than normal. Portions of the output from SAS displaying the results of the GOF tests on X observations are presented in Tables 1 and 2. Table 1 contains the result of fitting a normal distribution. The interval size used for the chi-square test is 30 units, with the midpoint starting at 0. Except for the chi-square test, all other tests are significant at the 5% level of significance, indicating that the normal distribution is not a good fit to the data. Table 2 contains the results of fitting a lognormal distribution. Again, except for the chi-square test, all other tests have the same conclusion, which is to not reject the lognormal distribution. It should be noted that because of the way the intervals were defined, the

```
data a;
do j = 1 to 100;
    y=3+sqrt (.5)*rannor (934410);
        x=expr(y);
        output;
end;
run;

proc means;
var x y ;
run;

/* goodness of fit test of X observations*/
proc capability data=a;
var x ;
histogram /
midpoints=0 30 60 90 120 150 180
lognormal (l=1  color=red)
        normal      (l=8  color=yellow)
        cframe  = ligr;

run;

/* goodness of fit test of Y observations*/
proc capability data=a;
var y;
histogram /
midpoints=1 2 3 4 5 6
        lognormal (l=1  color=red)
        normal      (l=8  color=yellow)
        cframe  = ligr;

run;
```

Figure 1   SAS Program

chi-square test will not be valid because intervals for larger values of X are mostly empty and have expected values less than 5. In fact, SAS sends out

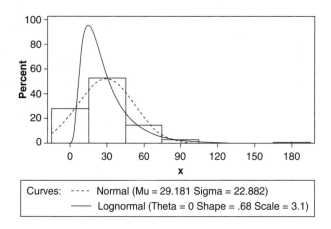

Curves: ---- Normal (Mu = 29.181 Sigma = 22.882)
        —— Lognormal (Theta = 0 Shape = .68 Scale = 3.1)

Figure 2   Histogram of Data With Fitted Normal and Lognormal Densities

Table 1 SAS Output: Goodness-of-Fit Tests on X

Test		Statistic	DF	p Value	
Kolmogorov-Smirnov	D	0.14540565		Pr > D	<0.010
Cramer-von Mises	W-Sq	0.74062491		Pr > W-Sq	<0.005
Anderson-Darling	A-Sq	4.51011616		Pr > A-Sq	<0.005
Chi-Square	Chi-Sq	3.66244120	4	Pr > Chi-Sq	0.454

Note: H_0: normal distribution is a good fit.

Table 2 SAS Output: Goodness-of-Fit Tests on X

Test		Statistic	DF	p Value	
Kolmogorov-Smirnov	D	0.05567901		Pr > D	> 0.150
Cramer-von Mises	W-Sq	0.05199648		Pr > W-Sq	0.486
Anderson-Darling	A-Sq	0.34639466		Pr > A-Sq	0.484
Chi-Square	Chi-Sq	9.54984429	4	Pr > Chi-Sq	0.049

Note: H_0: lognormal distribution is a good fit.

Table 3 SAS Output: Goodness-of-Fit Tests on Y

Test		Statistic	DF	p Value	
Kolmogorov-Smirnov	D	0.05567901		Pr > D	> 0.150
Cramer-von Mises	W-Sq	0.05199648		Pr > W-Sq	> 0.250
Anderson-Darling	A-Sq	0.34639466		Pr > A-Sq	> 0.250
Chi-Square	Chi-Sq	3.71521303	2	Pr > Chi-Sq	0.156

Note: H_0: normal distribution is a good fit.

the following message as a reminder: "The chi-square statistic has been computed using expected values less than 1. You can regroup the data using the MIDPOINTS= option." Because SAS does not allow unequal interval size, one has to use other programs to perform the chi-square test using carefully defined intervals so that there will be no intervals that are empty nor have expected values less than 5.

Table 3 displays the results of testing the normality assumption on Y. As expected, the normal fit was not rejected. Even the chi-square test, which is still not valid in this case because of some intervals with expected values less than 5, has the same conclusion as the other tests. Note that Y may be obtained from X via the transformation $Y = \log X$. This technique of transforming data is commonly used in applications as a remedy to get normal data from nonnormal data.

*—Inmaculada Aban
and Edsel Pena*

See also Chi-Square Test for Goodness of Fit; Chi-Square Test for Independence

Further Reading

D'Agostino, R. B., & Stephens, M. A. (Eds.). (1986). *Goodness-of-fit-techniques*. New York: Marcel Dekker.

Huber-Carol, C., Balakrishnan, N., Nikulin, M. S., & Mesbah, M. (Eds.). (2002). *Goodness of fit tests and model validity*. Papers from the International Conference held in Paris, May 29–31, 2000. Boston: Birkhäuser Boston.

NIST/SEMATECH e-Handbook of Statistical Methods: http://www.itl.nist.gov/div898/handbook/

GRADUATE RECORD EXAMINATIONS

The Graduate Record Examinations (GRE) test, published by Educational Testing Service, is a standardized test to be taken prior to applying for graduate education. The College Board was originally designed to develop and implement standardized tests for the admission and placement of undergraduate students. After the success of the Scholastic Aptitude Test (SAT) in determining a student's readiness for postsecondary education, the College Board went a step higher, developing a series of tests for graduate admission in 1936, which included the GRE.

Presently, the GRE is designed to supplement undergraduate achievements, including grade point average (GPA), providing graduate admission committees a common measure from which to compare the qualifications of applicants. Many graduate programs have an explicit cut-off for applicant GRE scores and rarely admit students scoring below these levels.

The GRE offers two different tests for students, a General Test and a Subject Test, both of which may be required for applying to an accredited graduate or professional program. The GRE General Test produces a different score for each of its three sections:

1. The analytic writing section measures the student's ability to articulate and evaluate meaningful, supported arguments. This section focuses more on critical thinking than on the basic mechanics of language.

2. The verbal reasoning section measures the student's ability to analyze written material. Test takers are expected to synthesize information and recognize relationships between words, sentences, and overarching concepts.

3. The quantitative reasoning section measures the student's ability to solve problems using the basic concepts of arithmetic, algebra, geometry, and data analysis.

The GRE Subject Test evaluates undergraduate achievement in eight specific areas of study: Biochemistry/Cell and Molecular Biology, Biology, Chemistry, Computer Science, Literature in English, Mathematics, Physics, and Psychology.

Sternberg and Williams evaluated the GRE's ability to predict graduate marks for psychology students at Yale University. The GRE General Test predicted graduate grades only modestly (correlation of .17), whereas the GRE Subject Test in psychology predicted marks more strongly (correlation of .37). The Graduate Record Examinations Board has reported that when combined, undergraduate GPA, the GRE General Test, and the GRE Subject Test strongly predicted (correlation of .50) first-year grades in graduate school for psychology students. Beyond predicting first-year graduate marks, however, GRE scores are not found to be useful for predicting other aspects of graduate performance, including the ratings of analytical, creative, research, and teaching abilities by primary advisers, and the ratings of dissertation quality by faculty members. Therefore, it appears that the GRE should be taken into consideration along with other indicators of qualification, including undergraduate GPA and past experience, when evaluating applicants to graduate studies.

—*John R. Reddon and Michelle D. Chudleigh*

See also Educational Testing Service

Further Reading

Graduate Record Examinations Board. (1997). *GRE 1997–98: Guide to the use of scores.* Princeton, NJ: Educational Testing Service.

Sternberg, R. J., & Williams, W. M. (1997). Does the Graduate Record Examination predict meaningful success in the graduate training of psychologists? *American Psychologist, 52,* 630–641.

Graduate Record Examinations Web site: http://www.gre.org

GRAND MEAN

The grand mean is most often used in the computation of the *F* value in analysis of variance, or ANOVA. It is the overall mean from which group means are subtracted when computing the between-group variance. The between-group variance and the within-group variance are the two variance estimates that are used to create the *F* ratio. The grand mean can also be used as an estimate of the average of all the scores in a group.

Table 1   Sample Data for Computing the Means and Grand Mean

	Group 1	Group 2	Group 3
	6	7	8
	4	6	7
	5	5	6
	6	3	5
	5	4	6
	4	5	5
	3	3	4
	4	2	4
	5	3	3
	6	3	3
Group Average	**4.8**	**4.1**	**5.1**
Grand Mean	**4.7**		

For example, Table 1 shows three sets of 10 scores along with the mean for each of the groups. The grand, or overall, mean is shown in this table as well.

—Neil J. Salkind

See also Analysis of Variance (ANOVA); Average; Mean

GRAPHICAL STATISTICAL METHODS

The use of diagrams as a means for summarizing and analyzing data has a long tradition in data exploration. Long before the discipline of statistics was established, people saw the need to summarize available data. Maps are probably the earliest diagrams used to depict and pass on information. The 19th century saw a surge in the creation of beautiful artistic charts with a more data-oriented background. Some of the most influential persons creating and establishing statistical graphics were Charles Joseph Minard, Dr. John Snow, Florence Nightingale, and William Playfair.

Charles Joseph Minard (1781–1870) was a French engineer. He is best known for his rich portfolio of intricate maps. His most famous piece of work is the chart of Napoleon's March to Moscow (see Figure 1), which, according to Tufte, is the best statistical graphic ever drawn. Minard manages to artistically incorporate complex data in a single chart: size of the army, marching direction, spatial location, temperature, and the dates of river crossings tell the sad story of the deaths of hundreds of thousands of French soldiers.

Dr. John Snow (1813–1858) is one of the founding fathers of modern epidemiology. During the 1854 cholera outbreak in central London, Dr. Snow used a map (see Figure 2) to mark all outbreaks and put them in geographical reference to the water pumps regularly used by the victims. In this way, he was able to identify the pump near Broad Street as the source of the epidemic.

William Playfair (1759–1823) was a Scottish inventor and writer. He introduced some of the chart types still in use today, such as the pie chart, the bar chart, and line diagrams to depict time series. In 1786, he published *The Commercial and Political Atlas,* which contained 43 time series plots and one bar chart. One of the most famous charts is shown in Figure 3, describing the relationship of food prices and wages throughout the reigns of Elizabeth I to George IV.

Florence Nightingale's (1820–1910) most famous diagram discusses insufficient sanitary conditions in military field hospitals during the Crimean War,

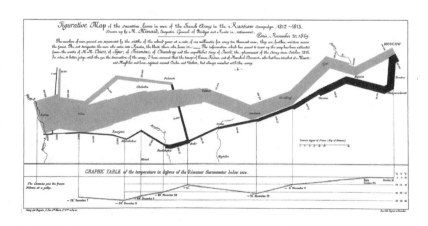

Figure 1   Minard's Chart of Napoleon's 1812 March on Moscow

Figure 2   Snow's Map of Central London Investigating the Cause for the Cholera Epidemic of 1854

which led to the (preventable) deaths of thousands of soldiers. She invented polar-area diagrams, where the statistic being represented is proportional to the area of a wedge in a circular diagram. In 1858, Florence Nightingale was elected the first female member of the Royal Statistical Society, and she became an honorary member of the American Statistical Association

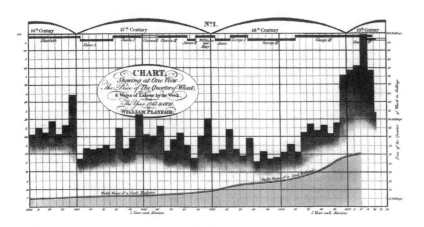

Figure 3   Playfair's "Prices, Wages, and Reigns"

in 1874. Karl Pearson acknowledged Nightingale as a "prophetess" in the development of applied statistics.

Birth of Modern Statistical Graphics

With the invention of computers, the time for hand-drawn maps and charts had run out. Much simpler and more abstract computer graphics are used now, for both presentation and exploration of data. The founder of this modern era of statistical graphics was John Wilder Tukey (1915–2000). He was one of the great statisticians of the 20th century, leaving his prints in many areas of statistics. Tukey was the first to emphasize the difference between exploratory data analysis and confirmatory analysis. For exploratory data analysis in particular, he suggested the use of graphics. In his monograph on exploratory data analysis, Tukey introduced a variety of now well-known and used diagram types, such as the box plot (box-and-whisker plot) and the (slightly outdated) stem-and-leaf plot (see Figure 5 for examples). The ground-breaking new features of Tukey's inventions are their abstractness. Data points are plotted along axes that do not have a direct relation to space or time. In this respect, Tukey is the founding father of statistical graphics as it is seen today. We use visualization methods to portray abstract relationships among variables. This is the essential difference between statistical graphics and other areas of information visualization, which are principally concerned with the rendering of objects and phenomena in physical 3-D space.

Today, the standard ensemble in the toolkit of a statistician consists of the following:

- one-dimensional plots: bar charts and pie charts for categorical variables, histograms, dot plots, and box plots for continuous variables
- two-dimensional plots, such as the scatter plot for continuous variables, and combination of one-dimensional plots for a mixture of one continuous variable and categorical variables
- mosaic plots for displaying multivariate categorical data
- rotating plots for three dimensions
- projection techniques for higher dimensional data
- interactive tools, such as selection and linked highlighting to gain insight in higher dimensional structures in the data

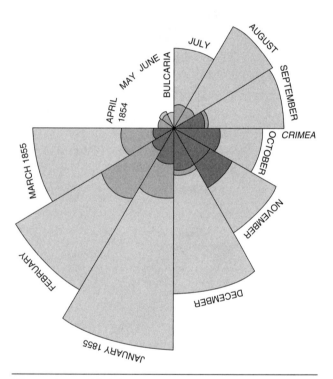

Figure 4   Nightingale's Polar-Area Diagram of the Causes of Mortality in the Army in the East

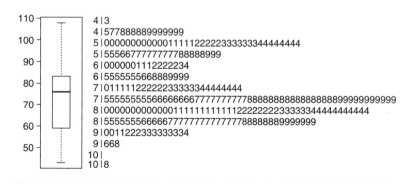

Figure 5   Box Plot (left) and Stem-and-Leaf Plot (right) of the Time Between Eruptions of Old Faithful

This list is certainly not complete—there are variations of each of these diagrams under various names; there are other types of diagrams; and there are new kinds of data, such as data streams or (Internet) network data, which cannot be displayed well by any of the diagrams mentioned above. Some of the ongoing research in graphics deals with the problem of how best to display new types of data. Other research deals with how best to present information and how to come up with "good" (i.e., faithful) graphics, because bad graphics seem to appear everywhere, particularly in nonstatistical environments. Ground-breaking work has been published by Edward R. Tufte in this area. In *The Visual Display of Quantitative Information,* Tufte describes a set of rules for preserving and checking graphical integrity in charts.

The *Semiology of Graphics* (first edition in French in 1967) by Jean-Jacques Bertin provides a summary of elements of graphics and conceptual principles. Leland Wilkinson's monograph *The Grammar of Graphics* can be seen as a logical successor to Bertin, even though the book is self-reliant. Wilkinson describes elements of graphics and presents an algebra for them that allows a flexible and consistent way of constructing and describing graphs.

Interactive Statistical Graphics

With the rise of computer technology and general availability of personal computers on almost everybody's desk, software for statistical graphics became widely accessible. This led statisticians to search for ways of "interacting" with their data. The collection of movies in the ASA Statistical Graphics Section Video Lending Library paint an impressive picture of the developments in statistical graphics since 1960. But what makes software interactive? There is an almost bewildering abundance of applications that go under the heading of interactive software, yet there seem to be quite different opinions of what interactivity means. The definition and use of this term is not quite clear, even among computational statisticians, as a survey on this topic by Swayne and Klinke made clear.

Here, we will refer to human-computer interaction based on the definition proposed by Unwin as the direct manipulation of plots and plotting elements in them. This goes back to one of the first definitionsof interactivity made by Becker and Cleveland and Becker et al.: "dynamic methods have two important properties: direct manipulation and instantaneous change." The data analyst takes an action of an input device and something happens, virtually instantaneously, on a computer graphics screen. Huber (1988) corrects the term of dynamic graphics to high-interaction graphics. "Virtually instantaneously" is often interpreted as real time changes, with the maximum response time set to 20 ms or, equivalently, an update speed of 20 frames per second. This, however, looks rather dangerous because it emphasizes the role of the underlying hardware and may even lead to different decisions about which methods can be classified as interactive. Therefore, it is probably better to speak of a potentially interactive method if it fulfills the proposition of being directly manipulative. Direct manipulation depends on two conditions:

1. Immediacy of place—by using a pointing device such as a mouse, the analyst can specify visually the areas of the plot, which are meant as a starting point of an action.

2. Immediacy of action—the action is triggered by using a clicking device such as a mouse, pressing keys on the keyboard (but not typing in commands), or via some other input device.

Interactive methods let graphics become real tools of data analysis. The most commonly used methods are linked highlighting, brushing, identifying, and zooming. Brushing was first introduced by Becker et al. as a tool for identifying and cross-linking points in scatterplot matrices. The idea of brushing is to mark all points inside the brushing area, usually a rectangle, and mark corresponding values in other graphs in the same way. Moving the brushing area to different positions leads to changes of marked points in all other graphs, revealing relationships between variables. The most commonly used brushing technique is highlighting. Figure 6 shows an example of linked highlighting in the iris data set: The brush is

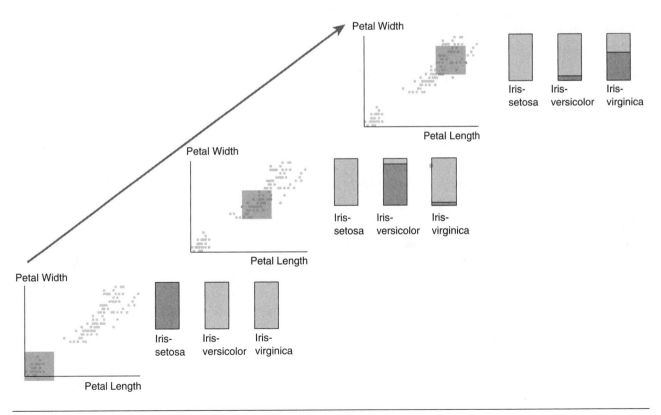

Figure 6   Example of Linked Highlighting in the Iris Data Set

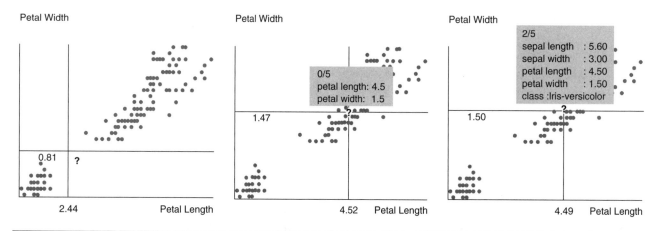

Figure 7   Examples of Identifying Objects in Scatterplots

moved along the diagonal of a scatterplot showing petal length versus petal width. Corresponding values are highlighted by color in a linked bar chart of iris type. As the brush moves from bottom left to top right, iris species are *setosa,* then predominantly *versicolor,* and finally *virginica.*

Being able to identify objects and individuals in graphs is crucial. Interactive querying allows the output of context-sensitive information. This operation is normally triggered by a movement of the mouse or by point and click of a graphical object such as an axis, a point, or a bar. Figure 7 shows examples of identifying objects in scatterplots. Query-clicking in empty space (left) gives the coordinates along the *x*- and *y*-axes. Query-clicking points triggers output of the number of observation (five, in the example) and their coordinates. More in-depth information is shown on the right: All available information for Observation #2 pops up.

Of course, all interactive methods depend highly on the specific implementation of a particular software. On the up side, though, basically all interactive systems now do have implementations of these crucial interactive methods even though names and functionality may vary slightly.

The final interactive, which seems to be common to all interactive systems for data exploration, is logical zooming. Whereas standard zooming enlarges the displayed graphical elements, logical zooming works on the underlying model and changes it to display

more details. Logical zooming is quite natural when working with maps. Starting with a country map, we zoom into a regional map, a city map, and finally a street map, which shows us the neighborhood in every detail. This gives us a tool for breaking down large data sets into smaller parts, which are easier to analyze.

—*Heike Hofmann*

See also Area Chart; Bar Chart; Line Chart; Pie Chart

Further Reading

Becker, R. A., & Cleveland, W. S. (1987). Brushing scatterplots. *Technometrics, 29,* 127–142.

Becker, R. A., Cleveland, W. S., & Weil, G. (1988). The use of brushing and rotation for data analysis. In W. S. Cleveland & M. E. McGill (Eds.), *Dynamic graphics for statistics* (pp. 247–275). Pacific Grove, CA: Wadsworth.

Friendly, M., & Denis, D. J. (2006). *Milestones in the history of thematic cartography, statistical graphics, and data visualization.* Retrieved from http://www.math.yorku.ca/SCS/Gallery/milestone/

Nightingale, F. (1858). *Notes on matters affecting the health, efficiency, and hospital administration of the British Army, founded chiefly on the experience of the late war.* London: Harrison and Sons.

Playfair, W. (1786). *The commerical and political atlas.* London: Debrett.

Swayne, D., & Klinke, S. (1999). Introduction to the special issue on interactive graphical data analysis: What is interaction? *Journal of Computational Statistics, 1,* 1–6.

Tufte, E. R. (1983). *The visual display of quantitative information.* Cheshire, CT: Graphics Press.

Tufte, E. R. (2001). *The visual display of quantitative information* (2nd ed.). Cheshire, CT: Graphics Press.

Tukey, J. W. (1977). *Exploratory data analysis.* Reading, MA: Addison-Wesley.

Unwin, A. R. (1999). Requirements for interactive graphics software for exploratory data analysis. *Journal of Computational Statistics, 1,* 7–22.

Statistical graphics video lending library: http://www.am stat-online.org/sections/graphics/library.php

GRESHAM, FRANK M. (1949–)

Frank Gresham was born in the small town of Greenville, South Carolina, in April 1949. As a young man growing up in Simpsonville, South Carolina, Frank was a good football player and was offered a scholarship to play football for a small local college. However, Frank had other plans and left home to pursue his college education.

He earned his Bachelor of Science degree in psychology from Georgia State University in 1973. He then went on to the University of South Carolina (USC), where he earned his M.Ed. in Rehabilitation Counseling. While working as a counseling coordinator for the South Carolina Department of Corrections, he went on to earn his PhD in psychology from USC.

After receiving his PhD, Dr. Gresham accepted a position at Iowa State University. Two years later, he was asked to become the director of the School Psychology Program at Louisiana State University. Dr. Gresham held this position for 8 years and published dozens of articles in the areas of applied behavior analysis, social skills, and behavioral consultation. As a result of his extraordinary research, he was given the Lightner Witmer Award in 1982. The highly coveted Lightner Witmer Award is given by the American Psychological Association (APA) for outstanding research contributions by a school psychologist. In 1985, he was recognized as a Fellow by both the APA and the APA's Division of School Psychology.

In 1989, Dr. Gresham accepted a position as the director of the Combined Clinical and School Psychology Program at Hofstra University. His most notable accomplishment during his 2 years at Hofstra University was to co-author the Social Skills Rating System (SSRS). The SSRS is used frequently by school psychologists throughout the United States and abroad for the assessment of children experiencing social, emotional, and behavioral difficulties. In 1991, Dr. Gresham accepted a position as the director of the School Psychology Program at the University of California, Riverside (UCR). During his 14 years at UCR, Dr. Gresham continued to publish research articles and chapters at an unparalleled rate. He was the recipient of eight federally funded grants for the study of learning disabilities, literacy, and emotional and behavioral disorders, and he received many honors for his scholarly work and research, including the Senior Scientist Award by the APA and the rank of Distinguished Professor.

Currently, the field of school psychology is undergoing a major paradigm shift in the identification of children with learning disabilities. The Response-to-Intervention model proposed by Dr. Gresham to the U.S. Office of Special Education Programs in 2001 was recently approved by the U.S. Congress to replace the traditional discrepancy model used for identifying learning disabilities for the past 30 years.

In addition to his work as a researcher, teacher, and mentor, Dr. Gresham was appointed as an expert witness to the President's Commission on Excellence in Special Education. Dr. Gresham is also a consultant to state psychological associations in more than 45 states, as well as Canada and Australia.

Dr. Frank Gresham continues to be one of the most respected and prolific scholars of our time in the field of school psychology.

—*Alberto Restori*

Further Reading

Frank Gresham home page: http://www.behavioralinstitute .org/Frank%20Gresham.htm

GROUNDED THEORY

Grounded theory is a broad perspective on how to conduct qualitative social science research. It comprises a distinctive methodology, a particular view of scientific method, and a set of procedures for analyzing data and constructing theories. The methodology provides a justification for undertaking qualitative research as a legitimate, indeed rigorous, form of inquiry. The conception of scientific method depicts research as a process of inductively generating theories from closely analyzed data. The specific procedures used in grounded theory comprise an array of coding and sampling procedures for data analysis, and a set of interpretative procedures that assist in the construction of theory that emerges from, and is grounded in, the data. In all of this, grounded theory researchers are expected to meet the canons of doing good scientific research, such as reproducibility and generalizability.

Grounded theory has been employed by researchers in a variety of disciplines, including sociology, nursing studies, education, management science, and psychology. It is probably the best known and widely used qualitative research methodology available today.

History

The grounded theory method was introduced in the 1960s by two American sociologists, Barney Glaser and Anselm Strauss, and has been further developed by them and others. Grounded theory was introduced to serve three purposes. First, it endeavored to close the gap between theory and empirical research by having theory emerge from the data. Second, it began to spell out the inductive logic involved in producing grounded theory. Finally, it provided a justification for the careful and rigorous use of qualitative research methods in sociology.

Deriving its theoretical underpinnings from the philosophy of American pragmatism and the related social theory, symbolic interactionism, grounded theory portrays research as a problem-solving endeavor concerned with understanding action from the perspective of the human agent. Strauss was heavily influenced by the University of Chicago tradition in qualitative social research, with its emphasis on the method of comparative analysis and the use of participant observation. Glaser was strongly influenced by the quantitative research tradition at Columbia University, and he brought to grounded theory important ideas from this tradition and translated them into qualitative terms.

Both Glaser and Strauss continued to develop the methodology of grounded theory, although in separate publications. From the 1980s onwards, their formulations of grounded theory diverged somewhat. Glaser sees himself as having remained true to the original conception of grounded theory, with its emphasis on studying basic social processes, the use of the constant comparison method, and the formulation of theories by letting abstract relationships between theoretical categories emerge from the data. Strauss, in association with Juliet Corbin, developed new methods of analysis in place of the strategy of constant comparative analysis, and they stressed the importance of verification of theory as well as its generation. Glaser has strongly objected that Strauss and Corbin's approach forces data and their analysis into preconceived categories instead of letting the categories emerge from the data. Although Strauss acknowledges that there are differences, he maintains that both he and Glaser advocate use of the same basic procedures for doing grounded theory research.

Philosophical Perspectives

Grounded theory has also been presented from a number of different philosophical positions. Glaser adopts a general empiricist outlook on inquiry. This has sometimes been described by commentators as "positivism." However, given the influence of pragmatism on his early formulations of grounded theory, this is an unfair characterization. Strauss's own characterization of grounded theory leans toward a social constructionist perspective. Kathy Charmaz has provided an explicitly constructivist depiction of grounded theory that breaks with the objectivism of Glaserian grounded theory. On a constructionist perspective, social reality is not revealed so much as socially constructed in the course of inquiry. David

Rennie offers a hermeneutic interpretation of the grounded theory method that is able to provide an understanding of the meaning of text and reconcile the tensions that exist between realism and relativism in orthodox accounts of the method. Finally, Brian Haig offers a reconstruction of grounded theory methodology from a broadly scientific realist perspective. On this interpretation, grounded theory method involves the inductive discovery of empirical phenomena followed by the abductive construction of theory to explain the phenomena.

Procedures

The variety of interpretations of grounded theory extend to characterizations of the method itself. In efforts to identify empirical social phenomena, and construct theories that explain those phenomena, almost all accounts of grounded theory adopt the three major research strategies of data coding, memo writing, and theoretical sampling. In grounded theory, data gathering and data analysis are interactive: From the time data collection begins, grounded theorists engage in data analysis, which leads to further data collection, subsequent data analysis, and so on.

The first data-analytic phase of grounded theory begins with the coding of data. This is undertaken to conceptualize the data by discovering categories into which they fit. The coding process has three phases: open coding, axial coding, and selective coding. In open coding, researchers describe the data by looking at them line by line. This strategy of focusing on small units of data, and their interpretation, encourages the development of a theoretical sensitivity to new ideas about the data and helps prevent the forcing of data into existing categories. Strauss and Corbin maintain that when a full array of categories has been identified, one should undertake axial coding, whereby one puts the data back together again in new ways by making connections between the numerous categories. After that, a selective coding step is implemented in which the researcher looks to systematically identify those categories that relate closely to the core category. The core category lies at the heart of the emerging theory and is central to the theory's integration.

Although memo writing can occur at any stage of the research process, it frequently takes place between the coding of data and the writing of the initial draft of the research report. Memos are written to identify, develop, and keep track of theoretical ideas. Where relevant, they are recorded, recalled, and reworked to produce new theoretical memos. Memo writing becomes more systematic, focused, and intense as theory of greater density and coherence is produced.

Memos written about data codes and theoretical ideas enable the researcher to identify gaps that require the collection of further data. For this, theoretical sampling is undertaken. With theoretical sampling, in contrast with traditional representative sampling, decisions about which data to collect, code, analyze, and interpret are directed by the emerging grounded theory. Theoretically relevant events, activities, and populations are all sampled, and the comparisons between these are aimed at increasing the conceptual density and integration of the emerging theory. Thinking effectively about data in theoretical terms requires an adequate degree of theoretical sensitivity. When the additional gathering and analysis of data no longer contribute to the understanding of a concept or category, a point of theoretical saturation is reached. At this point, one stops collecting data in respect of a category and moves to consider another category or concept.

Grounded theory considers writing to be an important part of the research process. This extends beyond the writing of memos to writing up the research report itself. One of the major goals in drafting the research report is to present a fully integrated account of the phenomena studied. This will involve highlighting areas that are insufficiently integrated and working to remedy these through multiple drafts if needs be. Grounded theory provides a number of rules of thumb, or heuristics, to improve the integrative value of the research report.

Criticisms

Despite its popularity, grounded theory has been subjected to a number of criticisms. One criticism asserts that grounded theory is a regression to a simple "Baconian" form of inductive science. In this interpretation, grounded theory is depicted as a tabula rasa view of inquiry, which maintains that data analysis and interpretation are not dependent on concepts or theories. However, this is an unwarranted criticism. In their first book on grounded theory, Glaser and Strauss explicitly stated that the researcher must have a perspective in order to discern relevant data and abstract relevant categories from them. In their view, the researcher seeks to obtain emergent diverse categories at different levels of abstraction by bracketing potentially relevant existing facts and theories for some time.

A further criticism of grounded theory is the claim that the reasoning involved in the generation of grounded theory is not inductive, as Glaser and Strauss claim, but abductive. Inductive reasoning is typically a generalizing inference, and it is difficult to see how such descriptive inferences could lead to the causes that explain generalizations. In contrast, abductive inference is explanatory inference, often from presumed effects to underlying causes. It is this type of reasoning process that leads from facts to explanatory theories. It is surprising that the originators of grounded theory have not appealed to abductive reasoning, given its prominence in the work of the pragmatist tradition from which they have drawn.

Yet another criticism of grounded theory points out that its methodology stresses the importance of theory generation at the expense of theory verification, or validation. However, whereas the first writings on grounded theory method deemphasized theory validation in favor of theory generation, this was in part due to Glaser and Strauss's desire to break from the hypothetico-deductive emphasis on theory testing that dominated 20th-century sociology. Glaser has continued to see grounded theory primarily as a theory generation method, but Strauss has come to emphasize the importance of theory verification in grounded theory research.

Although grounded theory does not articulate a precise account of the nature of theory testing, some writings on the method make it clear that there is more to theory appraisal than testing for empirical adequacy. Clarity, consistency, parsimony, density, scope, integration, fit to data, explanatory power, predictiveness, heuristic worth, and application are all mentioned by Glaser and Strauss as relevant evaluative criteria, although they do not elaborate on these, nor do they work them into an integrated view of theory appraisal.

Conclusion

Grounded theory methodology continues to be the subject of critical epistemological examination. Its methods continue to be employed widely, both in full and in part, in social science research, especially with the aid of computer programs for qualitative data analysis. Although initially developed as an approach to qualitative research, the use of grounded theory method in the future is likely to employ a mix of qualitative and quantitative research methods and to link with other methods that give explicit emphasis to the construction of theory that is undertaken to explain the data patterns obtained about empirical social phenomena.

—*Brian Haig*

See also Authenticity

Further Reading

Charmaz, K. (2000). Grounded theory: Constructivist and objectivist methods. In N. Denzin & Y. Lincoln (Eds.), *Handbook of qualitative research* (2nd ed., pp. 509–535). Thousand Oaks, CA: Sage.

Dey, I. (1999). *Grounding grounded theory.* San Diego, CA: Academic Press.

Glaser, B. G. (1992). *Emerging versus forcing: Basics of grounded theory analysis.* Mill Valley, CA: Sociology Press.

Glaser, B. G., & Strauss, A. L. (1967). *The discovery of grounded theory.* Chicago: Aldine.

Haig, B. D. (1995). *Grounded theory as scientific method* (Philosophy of Education Society Yearbook 1995, pp. 281–290). Urbana: University of Illinois Press.

Rennie, D. L. (2000). Grounded theory methodology as methodological hermeneutics: Reconciling realism and relativism. *Theory and Psychology, 10,* 481–502.

Strauss, A. L. (1987). *Qualitative analysis for social scientists.* Cambridge, UK: Cambridge University Press.

Strauss, A. L., & Corbin, J. (1998). *Basics of qualitative research: Grounded theory procedures and techniques* (2nd ed.). Thousand Oaks, CA: Sage.

Grounded theory resources: http://dmoz.org/Science/Social_Sciences/Methodology/Grounded_Theory/

Applying Ideas on Statistics and Measurement

The following abstract is adapted from Rennie, D. L. (2000). Grounded theory methodology as methodical hermeneutics: Reconciling realism and relativism. *Theory and Psychology, 10*(4), 481–502.

David Rennie argues that the realism-relativism duality addressed by the grounded theory approach to qualitative research is best accounted for when the method is understood to be an inductive approach to hermeneutics. Phenomenology, C. S. Peirce's theory of inference, philosophical hermeneutics, pragmatism, and the new rhetoric are drawn upon in support of this argument. It is also held that this formulation of the **grounded theory** method opens the possibility that the method improves on earlier approaches to methodical hermeneutics. As an outcome of this formulation, the debate on the validity and reliability of returns from the grounded theory approach is cast in a new light. The new methodical hermeneutics is discussed in terms of prior attempts to relate hermeneutics to method.

GUTTMAN SCALING

Guttman scaling (also called *scalogram analysis*) is a method of scaling involving items that reflect increasing levels of extremity on a single dimension of interest. This procedure was developed by Louis Guttman and was introduced in response to the concern that prior attitude measures might sometimes tap multiple constructs. For instance, a scale might include (among others) the statements presented in Table 1.

These statements both represent negative views toward obesity. Item 1 is the most extreme, and it seems reasonable to expect that individuals who endorse it might also endorse Item 2. However, it is

Table 1 Obesity Items Reflecting Two Dimensions

Items

Obesity is a serious health threat that leads to early death.

Obese individuals are less physically attractive than people who aren't overweight.

plausible that an individual might have an attitude toward obesity based solely on the associated health risks. This person might agree with the more extreme (health-related) item, but disagree with the less extreme attractiveness item. A scale containing these types of items would be assessing more than one construct. Therefore, it would be difficult to determine whether two people receiving the same score actually reported the same attitude, or whether their scores were driven by different dimensions. Guttman's approach was designed to correct this potential problem.

Guttman Scale Criteria

A Guttman scale is composed of a set of statements to which respondents indicate their level of agreement. Because these scales are meant to assess a single dimension, items are selected to vary on extremity alone. Therefore, statements chosen must be unipolar, reflecting gradations of either support or rejection. It is expected that individuals will agree with all items leading up to their most extreme endorsement and will disagree with items of higher extremity. With this goal in mind, researchers aim to select items that will fit a stepwise sequence of extremity. In fact, successful Guttman scales often consist of nested statements, such that agreeing with any one item almost necessitates agreement with items of lower extremity. This is a useful strategy because individuals with extreme attitudes might otherwise reject more moderate items on the basis that they denote too weak a stance. For example, the statements presented in Table 2 might be used to examine respondents' attitudes toward the film *Casablanca*.

Table 2 Sample Guttman Scaling Items

Items

Casablanca is the greatest movie ever made.	(most extreme)
Casablanca is one of the top 5 movies of all time.	
Casablanca is an exceptional film, one of the best.	
Casablanca is a great film, well above average.	
Casablanca is a good movie.	(least extreme)

To satisfy the requirements of a Guttman scale, individuals who agree with Item 1 should also agree with all other statements listed because they represent less extreme views. Likewise, respondents who disagree with Item 1 but agree with Item 2 should endorse all remaining items, and so on. This not only ensures that scores obtained are interpretable (because individuals with the same score will have endorsed the same statements), but it also introduces the possibility that knowledge of individuals' scores alone will allow exact replication of their responses. This "reproducibility" is a key element of Guttman scaling.

Evaluating Reproducibility

To assess the criterion of reproducibility, researchers first organize their data by creating a matrix in which columns represent scale items and rows represent respondents. If an individual agrees with a statement, a 1 is placed in the cell common to both the item and the respondent, and if a person disagrees with a statement, a 0 is placed in that cell. Individuals' scores are calculated by counting the number of 1s in each row. If this type of matrix were created for the *Casablanca* items mentioned earlier, it might look like Table 3. This table indicates, for example, that Persons 3 and 9 agreed with all items, whereas Person 6 agreed only with Item 1.

After creating this preliminary matrix, rows and columns must then be rearranged according to the number of 1s they contain. This is done such that the column with the most 1s is placed at the far right and the row with the most 1s is at the top (see Table 4). This matrix is used to identify items of equivalent extremity and to determine which items produce inconsistent response patterns.

In a perfect Guttman scale, respondents would agree with all statements leading up to their most extreme endorsement, overall response patterns would support the hypothesized extremity of each statement, and all individuals with a given score would agree and disagree with the same statements. Furthermore, because scores would be entirely dependent on the extremity of the statements endorsed, the data from such a scale would be completely reproducible from the scores alone. In practice, such a pattern is seldom achieved. For example, the data presented in Table 4 are not consistent with a perfect Guttman scale. In fact, both Person 4 and Person 6 endorse the most extreme statement (Item 1) and subsequently disagree with items deemed lower in extremity. Individuals who break the pattern by responding unexpectedly are said to have committed errors. Violations of this type serve to undermine reproducibility because response patterns can no

Table 3   Initial Response Matrix (Items by Respondents)

		Items				
Person #1	2	3	4	5	Total Score	
1	0	0	0	1	1	2
2	0	0	1	1	1	3
3	1	1	1	1	1	5
4	1	0	0	1	1	3
5	0	0	0	0	1	1
6	1	0	0	0	0	1
7	0	0	0	1	1	2
8	0	1	1	1	1	4
9	1	1	1	1	1	5
10	0	1	1	1	1	4

Table 4   Reordered Response Matrix, Including Errors

			Items				
Person #	1	2	3	4	5	Total Score	Errors
3	1	1	1	1	1	5	0
9	1	1	1	1	1	5	0
8	0	1	1	1	1	4	0
10	0	1	1	1	1	4	0
2	0	0	1	1	1	3	0
4	1	0	0	1	1	3	1
1	0	0	0	1	1	2	0
7	0	0	0	1	1	2	0
5	0	0	0	0	1	1	0
6	1	0	0	0	0	1	1

longer be determined from scores alone. Because reproducibility is a proxy for unidimensionality in Guttman scaling, procedures have been devised to assess the degree to which a set of responses violates the ideal pattern.

The coefficient of reproducibility (defined as [1 − total number of errors/total number of responses]) was suggested by Guttman in 1950 and is used to indicate the level of reproducibility. Guttman proposed a coefficient of .90 as the level needed to assume unidimensionality. The total number of responses for a scale is equal to the number of respondents multiplied by the number of items, but the number of errors is ambiguous initially, so determining the total error count is more complicated. A limited number of response sets fit the pattern required for Guttman scaling, and it is necessary to establish which of these a person "should" have given to determine a person's number of errors. Errors are thus conceptualized as the number of responses that need to be changed to create one of the acceptable patterns. This "intended" response pattern is selected to optimize reproducibility, so each individual is charged with the fewest errors possible.

For example, in Table 4, one break from the ideal pattern occurs with Person 6. This individual agreed with the most extreme item, but disagreed with all statements deemed lower in extremity. This response set can be explained in several ways. It could be assumed that because the individual endorsed the most extreme item, he or she should also have agreed with the remaining items (resulting in four errors). However, the pattern can also be explained with fewer errors if the endorsement of Item 1 is considered a mistake. This assumption charges only one error to Person 6 and so is the appropriate choice.

Researchers have questioned the merit of Guttman's reproducibility coefficient because large coefficients are not necessarily evidence for unidimensionality. For instance, the reproducibility of a statement with two response options (e.g., agree/disagree) cannot be less than the proportion of people who gave the most popular response for that item. That is, if 95 out of 100 respondents agree with a statement, the maximum number of errors for that item is 5, so the smallest possible reproducibility for

the statement would be .95. Therefore, if several items are selected to which a large percentage of respondents agree (or disagree), it is conceivable that a scale could be highly reproducible for reasons unrelated to content. To remedy this, a more precise alternative, the error ratio, has been proposed to assess reproducibility. This ratio is calculated by dividing the number of observed errors by the maximum number of errors possible, so that the ratio will range from 0.00 (no observed errors) to 1.00 (maximum error observed). This index is more sensitive to the absence of unidimensionality, with higher ratios indicating lower reproducibility.

Strengths and Weaknesses

The major asset of Guttman scaling is its focus on unidimensionality. Relative to other methods, Guttman scales are more likely to succeed in tapping only a single construct. Hence, scores often have more straightforward interpretations. However, several drawbacks are also evident. First, because increasing the number of items makes it more difficult to satisfy Guttman criteria, scales are necessarily short. Hence, variability among respondents' scores may be reduced, thereby making it difficult to discriminate among individuals. Additionally, the stringent standards of Guttman scaling can themselves be a disadvantage. In fact, some strategies used to overcome these difficulties can lead to additional problems. Researchers often start the development process with several items, generally selected using some rationale. Then, based on the observed results, items that weaken reproducibility are eliminated. Because these omissions often occur without theoretical backing, scale validity can be compromised.

Because of its challenges, Guttman's technique is rarely used. As a result, the reliability and validity of this approach relative to other methods have not been established definitively.

*—Leandre Fabrigar and
Karen MacGregor*

See also Attitude Tests; Likert Scaling; Thurstone Scales

Further Reading

Borgatta, E. F. (1955). An error ratio for scalogram analysis. *Public Opinion Quarterly, 19,* 96–100.

Dotson, L. E., & Summers, G. F. (1970). Elaboration of Guttman scaling techniques. In G. F. Summers (Ed.), *Attitude measurement* (pp. 203–213). Chicago: Rand McNally.

Edwards, A. L. (1957). *Techniques of attitude scale construction* (pp. 172–199). New York: Appleton-Century-Crofts.

Guttman, L. (1944). A basis for scaling qualitative data. *American Sociological Review, 9,* 139–150.

Guttman, L. (1970). The Cornell technique for scale and intensity analysis. In G. F. Summers (Ed.), *Attitude measurement* (pp. 187–203). Chicago: Rand McNally.

Mueller, D. J. (1986). *Measuring social attitudes: A handbook for researchers and practitioners* (pp. 47–51). New York: Teachers College Press.

Applying Ideas on Statistics and Measurement

The following abstract is adapted from Guest, G. (2000). Using Guttman scaling to rank wealth: Integrating quantitative and qualitative data. *Field Methods, 12*(4), 346–357.

Wealth ranking in given field sites can be problematic for a number of reasons. This article explores the usefulness of **Guttman scaling** and AnthroPac software in such contexts, using a small fishing community on the northern coast of Ecuador as an example. The author provides a step-by-step description of procedures for implementing and analyzing Guttman scale methodology and discusses the issue of construct validity. The complementary relationship between qualitative and quantitative data is highlighted throughout.

Index

Aalen-Breslow estimator, **3:**987
Abdi, H., **1:**284, **2:**540–542, 598
Abduction, grounded theory and, **1:**420
Ability
  achievement and, **1:**8
  approaches to understanding, **1:**2–3
  definition and dimensions of, **1:**2–3
  See also **Ability tests**
Ability tests, 1:1–5
  assumptions of, **1:**3
  examples of, **1:**3–4
  group differences and, **1:**4–5
  historical overview of, **1:**1–2
  purpose, **1:**2
  technology and, **1:**5
Absolute error loss, **1:**237
Absolute ratio scaling, **1:**174
Absolute zero, **3:**825
Abstracts, 1:5–6
  contents of, **1:**6
  descriptive versus informative, **1:**5
Accelerated failure time model, **1:**126
Acceptable quality level (AQL), **1:**6
Acceptance error, **3:**1021
Acceptance limit, **1:**7
Acceptance number, **1:**7
Acceptance phase, **3:**897
Acceptance sampling, 1:6–7
  consumer's risk, **1:**6–7
  hypergeometric distribution, **2:**444–445
  producer's risk, **1:**6
Accidental correlation, **3:**938
Achievement
  ability domain, **1:**8
  definition, **1:**2, 8–9
  intelligence versus, **1:**9
  knowledge/skill domain, **1:**8
Achievement tests, 1:7–11

aptitude tests versus, **1:**40, 42–43
assessments versus, **1:**8
classroom, **1:**9
formative versus summative, **1:**9
high-stakes, **1:**10
intelligence tests versus, **1:**9, **2:**478–479
Iowa Test of Basic Skills, **2:**487
Iowa Tests of Educational Development, **2:**488
length, **1:**8
purpose, **1:**2, 9
reference books for, **1:**8
reliability, **1:**8
scoring, **1:**7
selected versus constructed, **1:**7
standardized, **1:**10
validity, **1:**9
Wechsler Individual Achievement Test, **3:**1048
Acquiescence bias, **2:**539, **3:**843
Acta Eruditorum, **2:**500
Action space, **1:**237
Active life expectancy (ALE), **1:11**
Activities of daily living (ADLs), **1:**11
Activity dimension of connotative meaning, **3:**878, 881
ACT tests, **1:**299
Ada, Countess of Lovelace, **1:**70
Adams, S. J., **1:**240
Adaptive Behavior Inventory for Children, **3:**988
Adaptive behavior measures
  Adaptive Behavior Inventory for Children, **3:**988
  Vineland Adaptive Behavior Scales, **3:**1044
  Vineland Social Maturity Scale, **3:**1045
Adaptive sampling design, 1:12
Additive conjoint measurement, **2:**583–584
Adjective Checklist (ACL), **1:12–13**, **2:**767
Adjectives, measures using
  Adjective Checklist, **1:**12–13, **2:**767
  semantic differential method, **3:**878–882
Adjusted value, **1:**158, 161, **2:**649

Basic Personality Inventory, **1:**71–72, **2:**442
Basic research, **1:**72–73
  applied versus, **1:**39, 72–73
  hypothesis testing, **1:**72
  purpose, **1:**72
Bates, Marston, **3:**1057
Bayes, Thomas, **1:**79
Bayes factors, **1:**74–76
  alternatives, **1:**75
  Bayesian information criterion and, **1:**75, 76–77
  criticisms of, **1:**75
  utility of, **1:**74–75
Bayesian inferential procedures, **1:**75
Bayesian information criterion (BIC), **1:**17, 76–79
  alternative formulas, **1:**78–79
  Bayes factor and, **1:**75, 76–77
  definition, **1:**76
  example of, **1:**77–78
  model selection and, **1:**78
Bayesian statistics, **1:**79–81
  bivariate distributions, **1:**99
  decision theory and, **1:**239–249
  multiple imputation for missing data, **2:**664
  posterior distribution, **2:**781
  prior distribution, **2:**786–787
Bayes' theorem, **1:**79–80, 255
Bayley Scales of Infant and Toddler Development
    (Bayley-III), **1:**81
Bayley Scales of Infant Development (BSID-II),
    1:81–82
Beck, Aaron T., **1:**82
Beck Depression Inventory (BDI), **1:**82–83, 121, **2:**605,
    769, **3:**1050
Becker, R. A., **1:**415
Bedrick, Edward J., **1:**96, 97
Begg, Colin, **2:**597
Begging the question, **1:**257
Behavioral Publications, **1:**403
Behavior Assessment System for Children (BASC-2),
    1:83–84, **3:**846
Behrens-Fisher Test, **1:**84–85
Belanger, A., **3:**804
Bell, Alexander Graham, **1:**27
Bell curve, **1:**206, **2:**690–695
The Bell Curve (Herrnstein & Murray), **1:**45
Belmont Report, **1:**322, 323, **2:**466, 481
Bender, Lauretta, **1:**85
Bender Visual Motor Gestalt Test, **1:**85–86, **3:**988
Beneficence, in research, **1:**323–324
Bentler, Peter, **2:**501

Benzécri, J. P., **2:**653
Berger, A., **1:**154
Berger, Vance W., **2:**501
Berk, Richard, **3:**831
Bernoulli, Jakob, **1:**86–87, **2:**772
Bernoulli, Johann, **1:**86
Bernoulli distribution, **2:**619, 622
Bernoulli trials, **1:**87
Bertin, Jean-Jacques, **1:**414
Best Linear Unbiased Predictors (BLUPs), **2:**615
Beta error, **3:**1021
Beta weights, **2:**549–550
Between-groups ANOVA, **1:**33, **2:**713
Between-study cosine matrix, **1:**286, **3:**957–958
Bias
  acquiescence, **2:**539
  attrition, **1:**57–60
  Delphi technique and, **1:**243
  Hello-Goodbye Effect, **2:**429–430
  hidden, **2:**706
  item and test, **2:**489–493
  naive estimates and, **2:**705
  order effects, **3:**810
  overt, **2:**705–706
  prediction, **2:**492
  publication, **1:**353, **2:**596, 597
  selection, **2:**689
  systematic measurement error, **2:**585
Big Five personality domains, **2:**679, 769–770, **3:**918
Bihistogram, **2:**440
Bimodal data set, **2:**586
Bimodal distribution, **2:**623
Binet, Alfred, **1:**1, 39, **2:**473–474, 476–477, **3:**950
Binet-Simon Intelligence Scale, **1:**1, 39
**Binomial distribution/binomial and sign
    tests**, **1:**87–89
Binomial effect size display (BESD), **1:**303
Binomial test, **1:**88, 89–90
Binomial theorem, **1:**87
Bins, **2:**623, 651
  See also **Class interval**
Bioinformatics, **1:**90–94
  disciplines contributing to, **1:**90
  methodologies, **1:**91
  questions addressed by, **1:**91
  software programs, **1:**92–93
  subtopics, **1:**92
  utility of, **1:**91
Biometrics Bulletin, **1:**27
Biometrika, **2:**750**